AF752993

Beyond Treaties: Rethinking Legal Mechanisms for International Climate Governance

Türkan Gülce Budak

Beyond Treaties: Rethinking Legal Mechanisms for International Climate Governance

Springer

Türkan Gülce Budak
University of Zurich, Faculty of Law
Zurich, Switzerland

ISBN 978-3-031-86021-8 ISBN 978-3-031-86022-5 (eBook)
https://doi.org/10.1007/978-3-031-86022-5

Dissertation of the Faculty of Law of the University of Zurich to obtain the degree of Doktorin der Rechtswissenschaft (corresponds to Doctor of Law, PhD) submitted by Türkan Gülce Budak.

Approved at the request of Prof. Dr. Johannes Reich, LL.M. (Yale) and Prof. Dr. Rolf H. Weber, 2024.

The Faculty of Law hereby authorizes the printing of this dissertation, without indicating an opinion on the views expressed in the work.

Zurich, 2 October 2024
The Dean: Prof. Dr. Thomas Gächter.

This work was supported by Schweizerischer Nationalfonds zur Förderung der Wissenschaftlichen Forschung (10BP12_232571 / 1).

© The Editor(s) (if applicable) and The Author(s) 2025. This book is an open access publication.

Open Access This book is licensed under the terms of the Creative Commons Attribution 4.0 International License (http://creativecommons.org/licenses/by/4.0/), which permits use, sharing, adaptation, distribution and reproduction in any medium or format, as long as you give appropriate credit to the original author(s) and the source, provide a link to the Creative Commons license and indicate if changes were made.
The images or other third party material in this book are included in the book's Creative Commons license, unless indicated otherwise in a credit line to the material. If material is not included in the book's Creative Commons license and your intended use is not permitted by statutory regulation or exceeds the permitted use, you will need to obtain permission directly from the copyright holder.
The use of general descriptive names, registered names, trademarks, service marks, etc. in this publication does not imply, even in the absence of a specific statement, that such names are exempt from the relevant protective laws and regulations and therefore free for general use.
The publisher, the authors and the editors are safe to assume that the advice and information in this book are believed to be true and accurate at the date of publication. Neither the publisher nor the authors or the editors give a warranty, expressed or implied, with respect to the material contained herein or for any errors or omissions that may have been made. The publisher remains neutral with regard to jurisdictional claims in published maps and institutional affiliations.

This Springer imprint is published by the registered company Springer Nature Switzerland AG
The registered company address is: Gewerbestrasse 11, 6330 Cham, Switzerland

If disposing of this product, please recycle the paper.

Acknowledgements

I would like to express my deepest gratitude to my supervisor, Prof. Dr. iur. Johannes Reich, LL.M (Yale), for his invaluable guidance and insightful feedback throughout my doctoral studies. I would also like to extend my heartfelt thanks to Prof. Dr. iur. Rolf H. Weber, the second reviewer of my dissertation, for his thoughtful critique and constructive suggestions. I am immensely grateful to the Republic of Turkey Ministry of National Education for their financial support, which made it possible for me to pursue my academic ambitions and complete my dissertation. I would also like to express my sincere gratitude to the Swiss National Science Foundation for its generous support through the open-access publication grant. Lastly, I would like to thank my family, whose unwavering belief in me has been my greatest source of strength throughout this journey.

Zurich, October 2024 Türkan Gülce Budak

Abstract

The landscape of international climate change law is evolving from a traditional consensus-based treaty model, characterized by comprehensive yet often slow-moving agreements, towards a more pragmatic approach known as minilateralism. In this emerging paradigm, smaller groups of countries negotiate and implement trade measures aimed at mitigating climate impacts. An exemplary case is the European Green Deal, which introduces climate-related trade measures as a key instrument for achieving sustainability goals within and beyond Europe. Additionally, countries are exploring minilateral cooperation platforms within the Paris Agreement framework to further their climate objectives. This book examines the implications of this shift towards minilateralism for international climate law, analysing how climate-related trade measures and Paris Agreement compatible platforms may enhance global climate governance. The central questions to be addressed in the book are twofold. First, how can the design of the minilateral schemes comply with the Paris Agreement's international cooperation, common but differentiated responsibilities and respective capacities, and market-based mechanisms principles? Second, to what extent does the climate-related trade measures conform with the WTO regime, particularly with the non-discrimination principles of the trade law, namely most favoured nation and national treatment?

Keywords Fragmentation in Climate Change Law, Climate Club Approach, Climate-related Market Mechanisms, Non-discrimination Principles of World Trade Organization Law

Contents

Abbreviations

AAUs	Assigned Amount Units
BAT	Best Available Technology
BCAs	Border Carbon Adjustments
CAs	Cooperative Approaches
CBAM	Carbon Border Adjustment Mechanism
CBDR	Common But Differentiated Responsibilities
CBDRRC	Common But Differentiated Responsibilities and Respective Capabilities
CDM	Clean Development Mechanism
CER	Certified Emission Reduction
CMA	Meeting of the Parties to the Paris Agreement
COP	Conference of Parties
CTG	Council for Trade in Goods
DSB	Dispute Settlement Body
DSU	Dispute Settlement Understanding
EFTA	European Free Trade Association
EGD	European Green Deal
ERUs	Emission Reduction Units
ETS	Emissions Trading System
EU	European Union
FIT	Feed-in Tariff
FTAs	Free Trade Agreements
FVA	Framework for Various Approaches
GATT	General Agreement on Tariffs and Trade
GHG	Greenhouse Gas
HS	Harmonized System
ICJ	International Court of Justice
IEA	International Energy Agency
IET	International Emissions Trading
IMF	International Monetary Fund
IPCC	Intergovernmental Panel on Climate Change

IRA	Inflation Reduction Act
ISO	International Organization for Standardization
ITMOs	internationally transferred mitigation outcomes
JI	Joint Implementation
JTF	Just Transition Fund
LCA	Life-Cycle Analysis
MEAs	Multilateral Environmental Agreements
MFN	Most Favoured Nation
MPIA	Multi-Party Interim Appeal Arbitration Arrangement
NDCs	Nationally Determined Contributions
NGOs	Non-Governmental Organizations
NMM	New Market Mechanism
NPR	Non-Product-Related
OECD	Organization for Economic Cooperation and Development
PPMs	Process and Production Methods
REDD+	Reducing Emissions from Deforestation and Forest Degradation
SCM	Subsidies and Countervailing Measures
SDM	Sustainable Development Mechanism
SDT	Special and Differentiated Treatment
TBT	Technical Barriers to Trade
UK	United Kingdom
UN	United Nations
UNCTAD	United Nations Trade and Development
UNEP	United Nations Environment Programme
UNFCCC	United Nations Framework Convention on Climate Change
US	United States
VCLT	Vienna Convention on the Law of Treaties
VCM	Voluntary Carbon Market
WMO	World Meteorological Organization
WTO	World Trade Organization

Chapter 1
Introduction

1 Setting the Stage

Climate change stands as the defining environmental challenge of the twenty-first century, distinguished by its extensive impact on ecosystems, economies, and societies. This phenomenon is primarily driven by human activities that release greenhouse gas (GHG) emissions into the atmosphere, leading to rising global temperatures, shifting weather patterns, and increasing sea levels.[1] Furthermore, rapid climate changes exacerbate other environmental issues, including air quality, water availability, biodiversity threats, and coastal zone vulnerabilities.[2] The severity and breadth of the harms caused by climate change highlight its position as the most critical environmental issue faced today, necessitating urgent and comprehensive responses to mitigate economic damages and human suffering.

The origins and impacts of climate change are rooted in international dynamics. Specifically, excessive GHG emissions affect the global climate system and are not produced in a particular place or time. The accumulation of emissions traps the heat in the atmosphere, which leads to temperature increases. The recent projections of the Intergovernmental Panel on Climate Change (IPCC) suggest that global warming is unequivocal, meaning it is beyond doubt, and human activities are its dominant source.[3] The report indicates that in case of not taking any preventive measures, global average temperatures will rise by 1.8–4.0 °C due to the increasing CO_2 emissions levels.[4] Most importantly, any warmer degrees than 2 °C will constitute

[1] Intergovernmental Panel on Climate Change (IPCC), *Climate Change 2023: Synthesis Report. Contribution of Working Groups I, II and III to the Sixth Assessment Report of the Intergovernmental Panel on Climate Change Summary for Policymakers* (2023) 35.

[2] Ibid 7.

[3] Andrew E Dessler and Edward A Parson, *The Science and Politics of Global Climate Change: A Guide to the Debate* (3rd edn, Cambridge University Press 2020), 85.

[4] Intergovernmental Panel on Climate Change, *Special Report: Global Warming of 1.5 °C Summary for Policymakers* (2018) 7. There is of course a need to consider all human induced emissions of

© The Author(s) 2025

T. G. Budak, *Beyond Treaties: Rethinking Legal Mechanisms for International Climate Governance*, https://doi.org/10.1007/978-3-031-86022-5_1

irrecoverable damage to the world's ecosystem.[5] As the global community confronts the undeniable realities of climate change's far-reaching consequences, the imperative to forge an international legal response becomes increasingly evident.

Climate change is tightly linked to global pressures, hence, it requires governance[6] at levels from the global to the local.[7] Its impacts not only create localised harms to individuals, societies, and economies but also extend to planetary systems, threatening our existence as civilizations.[8] Therefore, the transboundary nature and externality[9] of climate change can only be rationally addressed with an agreement involves multi-jurisdictions. The Paris Agreement under the United Nations Framework Convention on Climate Change (UNFCCC) scheme was the result of this understanding. It contemplates the countries' means and bridges the gap between developed and developing ones while addressing the externality of climate change. This stance is crucial for generating a commitment among countries with varying levels of economic development. Thus, it fosters a sense of shared responsibility that transcends mere rhetoric. Paris Agreement's goal is to prevent 1.5 °C degree heating of the atmosphere compared to the pre-industrial period.[10] In order to realise this goal, the world needs to achieve net-zero emissions by 2050.[11]

GHGs when deciding on a policy for mitigation. Nevertheless, the use of fossil fuels and the associated changes of the carbon turnover necessarily come in the forefront of discussions about preventive measures because of its dominating role as a GHG. Carbon emissions from fossil fuels represent approximately 75% of the current global emissions and understandably tend to get most of the attention. IPCC, *2023: Synthesis Report* (n 1) 4.

[5] Ibid 19.

[6] Governance refers to the multiple methods by which organized society directs, influences and coordinates public and private activities at local, national, regional and global levels of decision-making in order to supply goods and services. Ernst-Ulrich Petersmann, 'Multi-Level Governance and Public Goods' in Thomas Cottier and Krista Nadakavukaren Schefer (eds), *Elgar Encyclopedia of International Economic Law* (Edward Elgar 2017) 571.

[7] Thomas Dietz, Elinor Ostrom, and Paul C Stern, 'The Struggle to Govern the Commons' (2003) 302 Science 1907, 1908 https://doi.org/10.1126/science.1091015.

[8] Benoit Mayer, *The International Law on Climate Change* (Cambridge University Press 2018), 69.

[9] Typically, the parties of the exchange capture all the benefits and bear all the costs, thus having the best information about the desirability of the exchange. However, sometimes the costs of the exchange may also spill over other parties, which is defined as externality that can lead to market failure. This is because market prices do not accurately reflect true costs and benefits. A welfare-optimal allocation of resources can only be achieved if the external effects are internalized. The pollution of the environment is a form of negative externality since it creates external costs for other individuals or companies, beyond the borders of countries and into the future. Robert Cooter and Thomas Ulen, *Law and Economics* (6th edn, Berkeley Law Books 2016) 39.

[10] Conference of Parties 'Decision 1/CP.21 Adoption of the Paris Agreement' (12 December 2015) U.N. Doc. FCCC/CP/2015/L.9/Rev.1 (hereinafter Paris Agreement) art 2(1)(a).

[11] Intergovernmental Panel on Climate Change (IPCC), 'IPCC Sixth Assessment Report: Mitigation of Climate Change' (2022) <https://www.ipcc.ch/report/ar6/wg3/downloads/report/IPCC_AR6_WGIII_SPM.pdf> accessed 15 March 2024.

Accordingly, the Paris Agreement and IPCC draw a path toward reaching the long-term temperature goals.[12] Paris Agreement provides a platform for countries to pledge their nationally determined contributions (NDCs), which outline specific emission reduction targets and strategies.[13] Besides, it elevates public concern and awareness of the climate crisis around the world through negotiations and discussions under COP (Conference of Parties)[14] meetings. The agreement also has positive repercussions on the national level and leads to domestic movements supporting carbon abatement. It introduces tools for steering countries into global and national climate action.[15] However, the Paris Agreement cannot produce the desired results regarding pledged emissions reductions.[16] Even though more than 120 countries have proposed carbon neutrality targets, only a few have enacted corresponding regulations or policies to realise their goals.[17]

The shortcoming of the current climate regime is that it has only didactic and weak language, which establishes norms and frameworks but does not lead to stricter obligations and enforcement mechanisms.[18] Nevertheless, an effective agreement to address the problems associated with climate change should have three fundamental features.[19] First and foremost, it should catalyse immediate, urgent, and drastic emission reductions. Second, it must provide adequate support for transformation. Finally, it needs to deliver justice for impacted people. A climate agreement with these features can only be enforced under fairly strong restrictions in terms of targets and penalties.

However, countries with profound policy differences, natural resources and economic interests complicate the legal regime for climate change. They create disagreements regarding the climate policy instruments, their scope, stringency, and

[12] Lisa Benjamin, 'International and Transnational Climate Change Law and Policies' in *Companies and Climate Change: Theory and Law in the United Kingdom* (Cambridge University Press 2021) 81

[13] Paris Agreement art 4 (2).

[14] The COP serves as the supreme decision-making body of the UNFCCC. It is attended by all States that are Parties to the UNFCCC, where they review the implementation of the UNFCCC and any other legal instruments adopted by the COP. At these meetings, the Parties take decisions necessary to promote the effective implementation of the UNFCCC, including decisions related to institutional and administrative arrangements. United Nations Framework Convention on Climate Change, 1771 U.N.T.S. 107, 165; S. Treaty Doc No. 102-38 (1992); U.N. Doc. A/AC.237/18 (Part II)/Add.1; 31 I.L.M. 849, art 7.

[15] John Vogler, 'Energy, Climate Change, and Global Governance: The 2015 Paris Agreement in Perspective' in Debra J. Davidson and Matthias Gross (eds), *Oxford Handbook of Energy and Society* (Oxford University Press 2018), 28–29.

[16] Guri Bang, Jon Hovi, and Tora Skodvin, 'The Paris Agreement: Short-Term and Long-Term Effectiveness' (2016) 4 Politics and Governance 209, 213.

[17] Lixin Cui and others, 'How Policy Preferences Affect the Carbon Shadow Price in the OECD' (2022) 311 Applied Energy 1 <https://doi.org/10.1016/j.apenergy.2022.118686>.

[18] Benjamin (n 12) 82.

[19] Jon Hovi, Tora Skodvin and Stine Aakre, 'Can Climate Change Negotiations Succeed' (2013) 1 Politics and Governance 138 <https://doi.org/10.12924/PAG2013.01020138>.

timeline.[20] Consequently, these divergences block the negotiations from taking concrete measures.[21] Primarily, their concerns are directed toward economic growth.[22] As a result, the economic considerations become a stumbling block for reaching an effective carbon mitigation policy. Nonetheless, scientific research shows that the costs of combating climate change are considerably small when the long-term benefits are considered. As illustrated by the assessment conducted by Working Group III of the IPCC, the application of emission mitigation measures for constraining anticipated temperature rise to 2 °C potentially results in reductions to the global gross domestic product ranging between 1.3% and 2.7% by the year 2050.[23] Similarly, the pursuit of measures limiting the projected temperature increase to 1.5 °C will incur losses ranging from 2.6% to 4.2%.[24]

Additionally, the green transition can provide a competitive advantage for forward-thinking countries. Many climate policies have beneficial spillover effects such as energy-saving, resource efficiency, innovation, new employment opportunities in green industries, decreased import dependency on fossil fuels, increased energy security, and health conditions.[25] Consequently, in the long run, the climate action's social cost is lower than the consequences of unmitigated climate change.[26] However, non-harmonised climate policies result in free-riding, competition distortions and carbon leakage to countries with lax environmental standards. Given the interconnectedness of climate mitigation and economic development solutions, the climate change problem can be characterised as a development problem. Consequently, the focus of climate action should be on supporting environmental integrity[27] while minding economic growth. This understanding requires coupling

---

[20] Andrea Baranzini and others, 'Carbon Pricing in Climate Policy: Seven Reasons, Complementary Instruments, and Political Economy Considerations' (2017) 8 Wiley Interdisciplinary Reviews: Climate Change 462.

[21] Jonas J Monast, 'The Ends and Means of Decarbonization: The Green New Deal in Context' (2020) 50(1) Envtl L 21.

[22] David Victor and Robert Keohane, 'The Regime Complex for Climate Change' (2010) 9 Perspectives on Politics 7 <https://doi.org/10.1017/S1537592710004068>.

[23] Intergovernmental Panel on Climate Change (IPCC) 'Summary for Policymakers in Climate Change 2022: Mitigation of Climate Change. Contribution of Working Group III to the Sixth Assessment Report of the Intergovernmental Panel on Climate Change' (2022) para C.12.2,37 <https://www.ipcc.ch/report/ar6/wg3/downloads/report/IPCC_AR6_WGIII_SummaryForPolicymakers.pdf> accessed 24 March 2024.

[24] Ibid.

[25] Huaping Sun and others, 'Energy Efficiency: The Role of Technological Innovation and Knowledge Spillover' (2021) Technological Forecasting and Social Change <https://doi.org/10.1016/J.TECHFORE.2021.120659>

[26] Nicholas Stern, *The Economics of Climate Change: The Stern Review* (Cambridge University Press 2007), 191.

[27] Environmental integrity refers to the concept of conducting environmental management and mitigation activities in a manner that genuinely preserves or improves the natural environment. It implies ensuring that policies, actions, and interventions aimed at protecting the environment or reducing pollution and emissions are effective, sustainable, and do not lead to unintended negative consequences. Lambert Schneider and Stephanie La Hoz Theuer 'Environmental integrity of inter-

measurable and long-term emissions targets with other contributions that generate economic outputs.[28]

1.1 The Need for an Enforceable Climate Regime

The progressive international climate negotiations should centre around new regime formation and efficiency.[29] A more effective regime should be based on different dynamics. Most importantly, it must substantially reduce the emissions with an economic transformation. The significant implications of climate change regulations on economic activity[30] require the developed countries' economies to have a complete makeover with the green transition policy. For developing countries, a different way for economic growth is necessary compared to industrialised countries that used to adopt more depletory approaches to expand their economies.[31] In this connection, a new regime needs trade mechanisms that foster green industries. It should create incentives for the transition towards cleaner, more environmentally friendly economic activities. Also, it must be efficient by keeping costs down for climate action.[32] An effective regime would provide solutions based on incentive-compatible measures, meaning it enacts measures with attractive features beyond reducing climate risks.[33] In this way, it makes participation and compliance with the new regime attractive for countries.

Furthermore, in a new regime of deeper cooperation, the number of signatories must not be too large. Otherwise, they commit to relatively lax emission reduction targets.[34] It becomes increasingly challenging to reach a consensus and set

national carbon market mechanisms under the Paris Agreement' (2019) 19(3) Climate Policy 386, 387–389.

[28] Aviel Verbruggen, 'A Turbo Drive for the Global Reduction of Energy-related CO2 Emissions' (2011) 3 Sustainability 632.

[29] John S Dryzek, 'Global Environmental Governance' in Teena Gabrielson and others (eds), *The Oxford Handbook of Environmental Political Theory* (Oxford University Press 2016), 534.

[30] Michael Mehling, 'Implementing Climate Governance: Instrument Choice and Interaction' in Erkki J. Hollo, Kati Kulovesi, Michael Mehling (eds.) *Climate Change and the Law* (Springer 2013), 11.

[31] Wolfgang Sterk and others, *Submission to the Ad Hoc Working Group on the Durban Platform for Enhanced Action Workstream 1: The 2015 Agreement* (Wuppertal Institute for Climate, Environment, and Energy 2013).

[32] Nicholas Stern, 'Ethics, Equity and The Economics of Climate Change Paper 2: Economics and Politics' (2014) 30 Economics and Philosophy 445, 448.

[33] Nicholas Stern, 'The Economics of Climate Change' (2008) 98(2) The American Economic Review 1, 27.

[34] Michael Faure, 'Economics' in Lavanya Rajamani and Jacqueline Peel (eds), *The Oxford Handbook of International Environmental Law* (2nd edn, Oxford Handbooks 2021), 176.

ambitious targets when a multitude of diverse interests and priorities are involved.[35] On the flip side, the likelihood of compliance to agreement by any given country is directly proportional to two factors. These are; the number of countries that have ratified the agreement and the extent to which they have complied with agreements' rules.[36] In other words, there appears to be a trade-off between the stability of a climate agreement and its legal effectiveness. While a large number of signatories can contribute to agreement stability, it may also dilute the stringency of the targets and make enforcement challenging. This counterbalancing can be overcome by an appropriate treaty design, which combines incentive instruments, penalties, and precise goals.

Contemplating these concerns and as multilateral attempts to coordinate global action on climate change do not produce fruitful results that fill the emissions gap, alternative ways of achieving carbon abatement are envisioned. Among these alternatives, one prominent and extensively researched strategy is the climate club approach. Nordhaus, an economist and a Nobel laureate, proposed the climate club approach to encourage international cooperation on climate change.[37] Membership in this club would be contingent upon meeting specific emissions reduction targets and implementing certain climate policies. The club leverages climate-related market mechanisms to block free-riding in the efforts of climate-forerunner countries. Countries outside the club would face penalties, such as tariffs on their exports to club members, effectively creating a financial incentive to join the club and adhere to its policies.

This club model is increasingly being scrutinized within the realm of legal academia as a novel governance mechanism for climate mitigation. The approach offers a promising avenue for circumventing the shortcomings of traditional multilateral approaches. The climate club could tackle the challenges of consensus-driven decision-making processes in global climate negotiations.[38] At its core, this strategy involves the "coalitions of willing" among countries that are committed to take concrete measures for reducing carbon emissions. Through mechanisms for carbon pricing, participating countries can not only enhance their environmental stewardship but also harness economic advantages in the transition to a low-carbon future.[39]

[35] Naím Moisés, 'Minilateralsim: The Magic Number to Get Real International Action' (2009) Foreign Policy, 135.

[36] Faure (n 34) 175.

[37] William Nordhaus, 'The Climate Club: How to Fix a Failing Global Effort' (2020) 20 Journal of Environmental Economics and Policy 1. William Nordhaus, 'Climate Clubs: Overcoming Free-Riding in International Climate Policy' (2015) 105(4) American Economic Review 1339. William Nordhaus, 'Dynamic Climate Clubs: On the Effectiveness of Incentives in Global Climate Agreements', (2021) 118 (45) Proceedings of the National Academy of Sciences, <https://doi.org/10.1073/pnas.2109988118>.

[38] David G Victor, *Global Warming Gridlock: Creating More Effective Strategies for Protecting the Planet* (Cambridge University Press 2011). Stefano Carattini and Andreas Löschel, 'Managing Momentum in Climate Negotiations' (2021) 16 Environmental Research Letters 51001.

[39] Joseph Stiglitz and Nicholas Stern, 'Report of the High-Level Commission on Carbon Prices' (The World Bank 2017) <www.carbonpricingleadership.org/report-of-the-highlevel-commission--

However, by pursuing a non-comprehensive approach, the club creates considerations of equity, sovereignty, particularly with regard to the principle of common but differentiated responsibilities and respective capabilities (CBDRRC) enshrined in international climate agreements and non-discrimination principles under WTO Agreements. When certain countries form the climate club and impose carbon pricing or other environmental regulations, it can create trade barriers or disadvantages for non-club members. This discrimination may result in economic tensions and disputes, if not carefully managed.

2 Significance of Research

The global response to climate change requires a sophisticated legal structure that addresses the five essential themes. These are:

(i) "multiplication of the international fora,
(ii) strengthening of commitments,
(iii) innovative policy instruments,
(iv) increased emphasis on litigation and
(v) the mounting significance of non-state actors and transnational governance".[40]

The book focuses primarily on the first three themes and examines different governance approaches as global climate mitigation targets remain unmet. While it is imperative to address the international legal climate regime through these essential themes, the complex nature of climate change poses significant hurdles. This complexity stems from the need to modify or limit activities, businesses, and technologies that contribute to climate change, in particular through the implementation of sanctions and incentive mechanisms.[41] Such changes inevitably lead to political conflict as they involve managing trade-offs among various stakeholders and are often perceived as arbitrary or illegitimate, leading to resistance from the countries affected.[42]

Given the numerous political, economic, technological, and practical challenges, establishing an effective international legal regime for climate mitigation is neither easy nor direct. The nature of the climate change problem is unsuitable for a single-handed approach since it lies in the intersection of economic, environmental, and

on-carbon-prices/> accessed 22 April 2024.

[40] Haro van Asselt and others, 'The Changing Architecture of International Climate Change Law' in G Van Calster, W Vandenberghe and L Reins (eds), *Research Handbook on Climate Change Mitigation Law* (Edward Elgar 2015) 4.

[41] Henri Culot, 'Unilateral Sanctions in International Economic Law' in Thomas Cottier and Krista Nadakavukaren Schefer (eds), *Elgar Encyclopedia of International Economic Law* (Edward Elgar 2017), 345.

[42] Goran Dominioni and Daniel Esty, 'Designing Effective Border-Carbon Adjustment Mechanisms: Aligning the Global Trade and Climate Change Regimes' (2023) 65(1) Arizona Law Review, 16.

social policies.[43] Therefore, any effective response to climate change needs to consider the other relevant regimes and their interactions. Particularly, understanding the political and economic backdrop of climate change is essential. It illuminates the intricacies involved in tackling climate change within the legal domain, highlighting the multifaceted nature of formulating and implementing effective mitigation strategies. Ultimately, the eclectic and innovative selection of solutions can better fit the nature of the climate change problem.

With this in mind, the book analyses the strategy of the club approach to climate change regime, which brings together a small group of like-minded countries. The club combines various regulatory instruments that serve as a linkage among its members with the aspiration of achieving ambitious emission reduction. This goal requires identifying the most appropriate institutional arrangements to link members, build cooperation and, more importantly, mobilise critical actors.[44] The concept of the climate club presented in this book represents a proactive approach to climate change mitigation involving a broader scope and more comprehensive regulatory instruments. Therefore, it differs from the existing smaller groups of countries that act outside the UNFCCC regime. They are also generally referred to as climate clubs. However, they only facilitate dialogue or implement specific projects, not generate ambitious emission reductions.[45]

There is plenty of academic literature regarding climate change in economics, policy, and legal disciplines.[46] The economic discourse on climate change mitigation encompasses instruments that address competitive disadvantage and carbon

[43] Irene Musselli, Thomas Cottier, and Elisabeth Bürgi Bonanomi, *SECO Roundtable on Trade, Climate Change, and the SDGs* (CDE/WTI summary report, Bern, Switzerland, 23 June 2021), 2.

[44] Richard B Stewart, Michael Oppenheimer, and Bryce Rudyk, 'A New Strategy for Global Climate Protection' (2013) 120 Climatic Change 1, 9.

[45] Lutz Weischer, Jennifer Morgan, and Milap Patel, 'Climate Clubs: Can Small Groups of Countries Make a Big Difference in Addressing Climate Change?' (2012) 21(3) Review of European Community & International Environmental Law 177, 180. Ilaria Espa and Kateryna Holzer, 'From Unilateral Border Carbon Adjustments to Cooperation in Climate Clubs: Rethinking Exclusion in Light of Trade and Climate Law Constraints' in J. Bäumler and others (eds), *European Yearbook of International Economic Law 2022* (vol 13, Springer, 2023), 405 <https://doi.org/10.1007/8165_2022_101>.

[46] Nordhaus, 'Climate Clubs: Overcoming Free-Riding' (n 37). Robert Falkner, Naghmeh Nasiritousi and Gunilla Reischl 'Climate Clubs: Politically Feasible and Desirable?' (2021) Climate Policy https://doi.org/10.1080/14693062.2021.1967717, Robert Gampfer, 'Minilateralism or the UNFCCC? The Political Feasibility of Climate Clubs' (2016) 16(3) Global Environmental Politics. Kateryna Holzer, 'Proposals on Carbon-related Border Adjustment: Prospects for WTO Compliance' (2010) 4 Carbon and Climate Law Review 14 <https://doi.org/10.21552/CCLR/2010/1/127>. Christine Kaufmann and Rolf H Weber, 'Carbon-Related Border Tax Adjustments: Mitigating Climate Change or Restricting International Trade?' (2011) 10 World Trade Rev 497. Joel T Trachtman, 'WTO Law Constraints on Carbon Credit Mechanisms and Export Border Tax Adjustment' in Panagiotis Delimatsis (ed) *Research Handbook on Climate Change and Trade* (Edward Elgar 2016).

leakage effects with theoretical modelling exercises.[47] However, they leave many critical questions regarding legal feasibility unanswered. On the other hand, the international relations discipline researches climate clubs as a distinctive form of multilateral cooperation.[48] Nevertheless, there is a tendency to overlook the formulation of robust enforcement mechanisms, including trade instruments, or to perceive trade policy as an impediment to design effective climate regimes. Legal discussions frequently explore the compatibility of climate club linkages with World Trade Organization (WTO) law[49] and Multilateral Environmental Agreements (MEAs). However, they typically do not extend to proposing concrete legal and institutional frameworks that could guarantee the efficient operation of climate clubs.

As a result, the existing literature lacks a comprehensive analysis that integrates these disciplines and their interactions to achieve an effective legal solution to climate change. Mainly, in-depth analysis taking legal discipline at heart and benefiting from applicable knowledge is relatively scarce. However, the climate club would likely trigger retaliation from non-member countries, trade wars, counter-coalitions, and interactions between domestic and international political processes.[50] Hence, the failure to examine the legal feasibility of this initiative leaves the club members unprepared to deal with the political and diplomatic conflicts it could potentially provoke. In order to fill this gap, the book conducts a comprehensive analysis of the current body of literature pertaining to economics, international relations, and legal aspects of climate clubs. The book aims to find an alternative governance system that conforms with the Paris Agreement and WTO law while effectively resolving the competitive disadvantage and carbon leakage externalities of climate action.

---

[47] Mustafa H Babiker and Thomas F Rutherford, 'The Economic Effects of Border Measures in Subglobal Climate Agreements' (2005) 26 Energy J 99. Kun Zhang and others, 'Impacts of Mechanisms to Promote Participation in Climate Mitigation: Border Carbon Adjustments Versus Uniform Tariff Measures' (2020) 11 Clim. Change Econ. 2041007. Joost Pauwelyn, 'Trade Related Aspects of a Carbon Border Adjustment Mechanism. A Legal Assessment' in *Four Briefings on Trade-Related Aspects of Carbon Border Adjustment Mechanisms* (Directorate-General for External Policies of the Union, Strasbourg, France 2020) Micheal Jakob, 'Introduction' in Micheal Jakob (eds) *Handbook on Trade Policy and Climate Change* (Edward Elgar, 2022), 3.

[48] Gampfer (n 46) 62. Charlotte Unger, Mar Khan and K Gürtler, 'A Club's Contribution to Global Climate Governance: The Case of the Climate and Clean Air Coalition' (2020) 6 Palgrave Commun. 99. Keohane and Victor (n 22). Elinor Ostrom, 'A Polycentric Approach for Coping with Collective Action and Global Climate Change' (2010) 20(4) Global Environmental Change 550. Marcel J. Dorsch and Christian Flachsland, 'A Polycentric Approach to Global Climate Governance' (2017) 17 Global Environmental Politics 45 <https://doi.org/10.1162/GLEP_a_00400>.

[49] Holzer, 'Proposals on Carbon-related Border Adjustment' (n 46), Kaufmann and Weber (n 46), Trachtman (n 46), Ulrike Will, Climate *Border Adjustments and WTO Law Extending the EU Emissions Trading System to Imported Goods and Services* (Boston: Brill Nijhoff, 2019).

[50] Kimberly A Clausing and Catherine Wolfram. 'Carbon Border Adjustments, Climate Clubs, and Subsidy Races When Climate Policies Vary' (2023) 37(3) Journal of Economic Perspectives 137, 156. Simone Tagliapietra and Guntram B Wolff, 'Conditions are Ideal for a New Climate Club' (2021) 158 Energy Policy 112527, 2 <https://doi.org/10.1016/j.enpol.2021.112527>.

The book synthesises the principal findings on the slow pace of international climate policy and the potential of climate club to remedy this issue. Furthermore, it assesses what kind of incentive mechanisms can link the climate club members and the legality of these mechanisms under the Paris Agreement and the WTO law. The mechanisms analysed in this book are the following ones: import ban and quota for high carbon embedded products, an emissions trading system and carbon tax within climate club jurisdictions, carbon tariff or border carbon adjustment for the non-club members, and finally, technical regulations and standards to communicate the environmental performance of the products. The book extensively evaluates the climate-related market mechanisms under a club strategy. Throughout this evaluation, it takes the "economic analysis of law" approach as a lens to explore the effectiveness and feasibility of each distinctive policy option employed within the climate club.

3 Research Questions

While the climate club approach holds substantial theoretical promise and provides a better solution to competitiveness and carbon leakage than other existing mechanisms, its implementation is anticipated to be complicated by legal and political impediments. This study closely examines the climate club approach and its linkages from two perspectives. The first one is legality, which refers to full compatibility with the Paris Agreement and WTO law. The second perspective is non-discrimination, suggesting a transparent implementation of trade mechanisms and non-discriminatory treatment to trading partners.

On that note, the central research questions to be addressed are twofold. First, how can the design of the climate club align with the Paris Agreement's international voluntary cooperation, market-based mechanisms principles and common but differentiated responsibilities and respective capacities principle? Second, to what extent do the club linkages comply with the WTO legal regime, particularly with the non-discrimination principles of the trade law, namely the most favoured nation and national treatment?

Despite their persistent efforts, WTO members have encountered formidable challenges in reconciling trade and environmental law, particularly concerning the trade instruments employed to influence the production methods of foreign countries. While most countries rely on market-based instruments to implement their NDCs under the Paris Agreement,[51] the rules for their application are still unresolved in climate negotiations and WTO agreements and jurisprudence. Therefore, discussing the climate-related trade mechanisms is of paramount importance. Consequently, from a climate law perspective, the book aims to establish a

---

[51] Clara Brandi, *Trade Elements in Countries Climate Contributions under the Paris Agreement* (International Centre for Trade and Sustainable Development (ICTSD) 2017).

connection between the Paris Agreement and climate clubs via voluntary cooperation and market-based mechanisms regulated in Article 6. From a trade law perspective, it focuses on the legal challenges of climate club linkages under the WTO law.

Since the climate club idea is not yet put into practice, the book provides guidance on which climate-related trade instruments are legally possible to apply and which aspects of them need further legal assessment. Taken as a whole, the book provides a persuasive argument for using the club approach as a feasible form of governance that can adequately tackle the difficulties posed by climate change and an auspicious pathway toward achieving a sustainable future.

4 Structure of the Book

The following chapters of this book comprehensively explore critical legal themes that shape the landscape of climate governance. This exploration is guided by the "economic analysis of law" methodology, providing an analytical lens through which to assess the efficiency and effectiveness of regulatory approaches in achieving climate goals. Delving deeper, the methodology chapter uncovers the multifaceted factors that contribute to the often-perceived inadequacies of international climate cooperation, including challenges such as the collective action problem, free-riding, carbon leakage, competitiveness concerns, and the persistent asymmetry between developed and developing nations. Subsequently, the methodology section illustrates among various governance approaches, the climate club offers a more effective resolution to the identified problems from the standpoint of the economic analysis of law. Under Chap. 2, the book examines the existing framework of international climate law, with a focus on the pivotal roles of the UNFCCC and the landmark Paris Agreement. Thereby, it lays the groundwork for the successive arguments and discussions.

As a response to loopholes in the current regime, the Chap. 3 of the book probes into alternative governance structures that hold the potential to invigorate climate collaboration. Concepts such as minilateralism and climate club emerge as viable options, offering innovative pathways to enhance the effectiveness of collective climate action. Climate club is the primary focus, defined and explored in depth under the Chap. 4. It emphasises the climate club's reformative potential, advantages, and prospects in comparison to the existing climate regime. This strategy could encourage greater compliance and provide a fresh perspective on how global climate governance can evolve. However, the club approach has implications on the Paris Agreement's common but differentiated responsibilities and respective capacities principle since it foresees a uniform application of its linkages to all countries regardless of their development stage. Despite that, by exploring the prospects of this innovative approach, it becomes clear that the climate club model is a promising avenue for reinvigorating international efforts to combat climate change, making it a vital focus of this study's consideration.

The role of linkages in strengthening climate club forms another crucial segment and is analysed under Chap. 5. The study encompasses a thorough analysis of diverse climate-related mechanisms, including import bans and quotas, emissions trading systems, domestic carbon taxes and carbon tariffs, border carbon adjustments, and technical regulations and standards. These mechanisms serve as central tools to link climate club members and harmonise their climate goals. Additionally, the trade commitments made by climate club members are designed to support and advance environmentally friendly and sustainable practices on a global level.[52]

The intricate interplay between climate imperatives and international trade policies under the club approach forms another crucial dimension of the study. The book researches how these two realms intersect and potentially conflict. Under the legality of climate clubs, first, the Chap. 6 examines the relationship between climate-related market mechanisms and the Paris Agreement. Moreover, the book scrutinises them through the lens of WTO law. It aims to shed light on the compatibility and potential tensions between climate club linkages and the existing trade law framework. The book assesses the applicability of relevant WTO agreements provisions, including the schedule of commitments, tariff deconsolidation, and the general elimination of quantitative restrictions.

Within the framework for evaluating the non-discrimination aspect of the climate club approach, the Chap. 7 meticulously assesses the compatibility of climate club linkages with fundamental non-discrimination principles enshrined under the General Agreement on Tariffs and Trade (GATT) 1994. This examination delves into two principles: the Most Favoured Nation (MFN) principle and the National Treatment principle. Furthermore, the research explores these principles in the context of the Technical Barriers to Trade (TBT) Agreement concerning technical regulations and standards of the climate club. The examination extends to Article XX of the GATT 1994, which offers crucial flexibility for parties to address environmental concerns while mitigating trade conflicts. This analysis provides insight into how climate-related market mechanisms can harmonise with existing trade norms.

The study recognises the urgency of reconciling environmental protection and trade liberalization, which are often conflicting imperatives. Hence, this book undertakes a comprehensive exploration of climate-related market mechanisms within the contours of the Paris Agreement and the WTO law. By dissecting these mechanisms through the lenses of international climate law and trade law, the study aims to shed light on their potential under the climate club approach to facilitate effective climate action while ensuring compliance with international trade norms. Ultimately, this research contributes to the development of a nuanced understanding of how climate governance and trade governance can mutually reinforce global efforts to address the pressing challenges of climate change.

---

52 Thomas Cottier and Tetyana Payosova, 'Common Concern and Legitimacy of the WTO in Dealing with Climate Change' in Panagiotis Delimatsis (ed) *Research Handbook on Climate Change and Trade* (Edward Elgar 2016), 26.

5 Methodology

5.1 *Economic Analysis of Law*

Climate change stems from the activities that are at the core of our economies, such as consumption and energy production.[53] Parallel to this, the marketplace is exposed to climate change more than other global governance issues.[54] Hence, climate mitigation and economic development should be addressed simultaneously. As a result of this, how to distribute the costs of climate action among different countries and sectors turns out to be the key question of climate change law. In pursuit of a solution, policies rely on incorporating emissions' complete social and economic costs into current market prices of carbon-intensive goods.[55] This strategy requires the identification of climate-related market instruments and the assessment of their trade-offs. Hence, alternative international climate regimes can be examined through the lens of the economic analysis of law approach, which evaluates the costs and benefits of different policy options for balancing environmental goals with economic realities.

The "economic analysis of law" interests the application of economic theories and methods to the core institutions of the legal system,[56] such as taxation, market regulation, and competition law.[57] It seeks to understand how legal regulations affect economics or vice versa. Furthermore, it asks the question of how legal regimes can be designed to achieve more efficient and effective norms. In the similar vein, the book aims to contribute to the ongoing discourse on alternative climate change governance structure that adopts market-based regulatory instruments. The fundamental aim of the study is to enhance the efficiency and effectiveness of the current international climate regime. Hence, it adopts the "economic analysis of law approach" for analysing the effectiveness and feasibility of the climate club and its linkages as market-based instruments.

The "economic analysis of law" approach has two branches: the positive and the normative.[58] The positive economic analysis of law uses economic theory to explain or predict why the law developed in a specific way. It is descriptive and values the

---

[53] Roy Andrew Partain, 'Climate Change, Green Paradox Models and International Trade Rules' in Panagiotis Delimatsis (ed) *Research Handbook on Climate Change and Trade* (Edward Elgar Publishing 2016), 305.

[54] For example, the damages due to extreme weather event causes major losses and burden on the insurance industry. European Environmental Agency, *Economic Losses and Fatalities from Weather- and Climate-Related Events in Europe Briefing no. 21/2021* (TH-AM-21-018-EN-Q, 2021).

[55] Michael Faure and Roy Andrew Partain, *Environmental Law and Economics: Theory and Practice (*Cambridge University Press 2019) 28.

[56] Richard A. Posner, 'The Economic Approach to Law' (1975) 53 Texas Law Review 757.

[57] Niels Petersen and Emanuel V Towfigh, 'Economic Methods and Legal Reasoning' in Emanuel V Towfigh and Niels Petersen *Economic Methods for Lawyers* (Edward Elgar Publishing 2015) 6.

[58] Richard A. Posner, *Economic Analysis of Law* (Aspen Legal Education 2014), 31.

advantages and disadvantages of the legal norms on economics.[59] Hence, it explains legal rules and their outcomes as they are rather than changing them to make better. The primary function of this branch is to make people accountable for the consequences of their actions, even if they are not directly affected.[60] This accountability is achieved by addressing externalities, which are costs or benefits that spill over to third parties and are not accounted for in the original actions or decisions.[61] Therefore, positive economic analysis of law concerns the design of legal norms that will induce the internalization of public cost. Internalization can be realised with liability rules and taxation.[62] In the climate change context, addressing externalities can be better achieved with emission taxation and other pricing instruments rather than liability norms. This is because climate change distresses society as a whole and makes it challenging to establish individual liability for specific actors.

Normative economic analysis of law focuses on the economic efficiency of legal regulations as opposed to their normative legal value.[63] This methodology aims to reform legal norms to make them more efficient. It aims to diffuse wealth maximization in all spheres of public policy.[64] It asserts the adhered legal rules are those that most effectively promote social welfare.[65] This consideration is highly relevant in policymaking because public officials never advocate wasting money. In addition to effectiveness and efficiency, normative economic analysis of law deals with the distribution of costs and benefits among groups.[66] However, this approach is insufficient to prevent inequitable redistribution, where one group bears a disproportionate burden compared to another. This is due to the fact that the approach prioritises achieving the maximum benefit for society as a whole and ignores income inequality or disparities in wealth.[67] Nevertheless, policy decisions must also concern the challenges of distributional equity to secure public approval. Therefore, the legal analysis of regulations should focus on efficiency and equity objectives in a mutually reinforcing manner.

---

[59] Towfigh and Petersen (n 57) 2.

[60] Florian Faust, 'Comparative Law and Economic Analysis of Law' in Mathias Reimann and Reinhard Zimmermann (eds), *The Oxford Handbook of Comparative Law* (2nd edn, Oxford Handbooks 2019).

[61] Navraj Singh Ghaleigh 'Economics and International Climate Change Law' in Kevin R. Gray (ed), *The Oxford Handbook of International Climate Change Law* (Oxford University Press 2016), 80.

[62] Ibid 81.

[63] Towfigh and Petersen (n 57) 2.

[64] Richard A. Posner, 'The Ethical and Political Basis of the Efficiency Norm in Common Law Adjudication' (1981) 9 Hofstra L Rev 775, 780.

[65] Steven Shavell, 'Law and Economics' in *International Encyclopaedia of the Social & Behavioural Sciences* (2001), 8452.

[66] Towfigh and Petersen (n 57) 28. Cooter and Ulen (n 9) 4.

[67] Shavell (n 65) 8451.

5.1.1 Evaluating Climate Change Regulations Through the Lens of Economic Analysis of Law

The regulations and policymaking in the context of climate change indeed confront unique challenges that differentiate them from more traditional environmental management strategies. The three fundamental decision-making approaches in environmental regulation, prohibition of harmful activities or technologies, aiming for zero risk, and limiting risk to acceptable levels, do not seamlessly apply to climate change mitigation due to the complexity and global scale of the problem.[68] Prohibiting all activities contributing to climate change is impractical, if not impossible, because many of these activities are deeply embedded in the global economy and daily life.[69] Such an approach would likely face significant resistance from various sectors and could have profound economic repercussions. Similarly, the zero-risk policy, while idealistic, is unattainable. Climate change is a pervasive, long-term challenge that cannot be completely eradicated through immediate actions. It requires sustained efforts over time, including continuous innovation in green technologies, changes in consumption patterns, and adaptation strategies to mitigate the impacts of climate change that are already underway.[70] Limiting the risk of climate change to an acceptable level represents a more feasible approach but raises questions about what constitutes an "acceptable" level of risk. This involves complex considerations of economic costs, social equity, and ecological sustainability. Moreover, determining acceptable levels of risk and implementing measures to maintain risk within these levels necessitates global cooperation and coordination, given the transboundary nature of climate change.

Therefore, climate change policies must navigate these complexities by carefully balancing the costs and benefits of action or inaction across different sectors. It involves evaluating the economic implications of regulatory measures, their effectiveness in reducing GHG emissions, and their broader social and environmental impacts.[71] Policies should aim to achieve the best possible outcomes for society as a whole, considering both current and future generations. This necessitates a flexible, adaptive approach to policy-making that can respond to new information and technological advancements while fostering innovation and promoting sustainable development. As a result, addressing climate change requires a nuanced, multidimensional strategy that goes beyond the conventional frameworks of environmental regulation. It demands an integrated methodology that aligns economic, social, and

[68] Dessler and Parson (n 3) 160.

[69] Most significantly, energy production, transportation, agriculture, industrial processes, and residential and commercial buildings. International Energy Agency (IEA), 'CO2 Emissions from Fuel Combustion' (2020) <https://doi.org/10.1787/co2-data-en>.

[70] Ian Gough and James Meadowcroft, 'Decarbonizing the Welfare State' in John S Dryzek and others (eds), *The Oxford Handbook of Climate Change and Society* (Oxford University Press 2012), 495.

[71] Ibid 494–495.

environmental objectives to achieve sustainable, long-term solutions for mitigating climate change and its impacts.

In this regard, applying the economic analysis of law approach to climate change regulations can find solutions that effectively address environmental challenges while considering economic efficiency, individual incentives, and overall societal welfare.[72] It helps guide the design of policies that strike a balance between environmental protection and economic growth. Furthermore, this approach and climate change share inherently similar characteristics, which are made firm in the following paragraphs. These characteristics underscore the importance of adopting an economic analysis of law approach to address the complex challenges of climate change.

Primarily, economic analysis of law and climate change law examine the same two foundational research questions. The positive "economic analysis of law" enquires what kind of regulations can price externalities.[73] Climate change law similarly revolves around addressing the externality of emissions.[74] It aims to internalise the external costs associated with emissions through carbon pricing. By this way, it incentivises parties to consider the environmental impacts of their actions and encourages greener alternatives. While doing so, it refrains from harming the competitiveness of economies and reducing overall wealth. Whereas the normative "economic analysis of law" asks how legal regulations can ensure efficiency and collective welfare.[75] It is not just about understanding the existing rules but also about prescribing how they should be designed to achieve optimal outcomes. Climate change law seeks to optimise societal welfare by efficiently reducing emissions. It involves the design of legal frameworks that balance environmental goals with economic considerations. In this sense, it aligns with the normative economic analysis of law by aiming to achieve efficiency and collective welfare.

Secondly, the inherent problem that needs a solution is essentially the same in the "economic analysis of law" and climate law. The commonality lies in their shared recognition of the optimal allocation of finite resources.[76] Economics involves the rational selection of choices in a world where resources are finite, and individuals act to maximise their utility.[77] This very notion resonates strongly with the core issue of climate change. The root of the climate crisis can be traced back to the unsustainable use of the planet's limited resources, particularly regarding the unregulated GHG emissions. Hence, legal mechanisms regulating the market behaviour

---

[72] Ghaleigh, 'Economics and International Climate Change Law' (n 61) 77.

[73] Bruce Greenwald and Joseph Stiglitz, 'Externalities in Economies with Imperfect Information and Incomplete Markets' (1986) 101 Quarterly Journal of Economics 229 <https://doi.org/10.2307/1891114>.

[74] William Nordhaus, 'Climate Change: The Ultimate Challenge for Economics' (2019) 109(6) American Economic Review 1991, 1992 <https://doi.org/10.1257/aer.109.6.1991>.

[75] Nuno Garoupa and Tom Ginsburg, 'Economic Analysis and Comparative Law' in Mauro Bussani and Ugo Mattei (eds), *The Cambridge Companion to Comparative Law* (Cambridge University Press 2012) 57.

[76] Ghaleigh, 'Economics and International Climate Change Law' (n 61) 76.

[77] Posner, *Economic Analysis of Law* (n 58) 3.

of excessive use of the atmosphere can be implemented through "economic analysis of law". This approach recognises that harnessing the principles of economics, which are tied to "rational decision-making in resource-constrained environments",[78] can offer invaluable insights into crafting climate regulations.

Also, the "economic analysis of law" approach can help climate law to overcome the obstacle in achieving its goal, which is to prevent market failure due to uncontrolled emissions. Market failure occurs if the allocation of goods is inefficient in a given market. The four underlying reasons for it are (i) market power, (ii) externalities, (iii) asymmetric information, and (iv) common goods.[79] Each of these phenomena is observed in the climate change problem, and the following section analyses them as the reasons for the current hindrance of international climate law. Notably, inefficient allocation takes place in all industrial production since the real cost of emissions is not fully reflected in the products.[80] The legal remedy of the "economic analysis of law" approach against emissions-related market failure is the climate-related market mechanisms.

Therefore, the third similarity between "economic analysis of law" approach and climate law is that their outputs mutually reinforce each other. The significant aim of environmental economics research is to examine mechanisms that will find a balance between the costs and the benefits of emission abatement. These tools are referred to as climate-related market mechanisms and can be incorporated into the climate change legal regimes and legislations. They are considered as a feasible way to give a positive impetus to the existing stalemate in climate law.[81] They enable the assetization[82] of carbon emissions by putting a price on carbon.[83] In this way, these mechanisms equalise the real cost emissions across diverse countries and sectors to prevent market failure.[84] They ensure the most efficient allocation of economic resources while mitigating emissions. These mechanisms also entail identifying activities that pose a climate risk. Such practice complies with the precautionary principle of environmental law.[85] Hence, the collaboration between "economic

---

[78] Ibid 7.

[79] Ghaleigh, Economics and International Climate Change Law (n 61) 79–80.

[80] Ibid 81. Arthur C Pigou, *The Economics of Welfare* (Macmillan 1920).

[81] Hubertus Bardt and Galina V Kolev, *Trade Club for Climate: A Climate Approach to Revive Multilateralism*, IW-Policy Paper, No. 8/2021 (Institut der deutschen Wirtschaft (IW), Köln 2021).

[82] Assetization is a process of making things work in new ways in existing systems using a strong market logic, simply turning the things into an asset.

[83] Lionel Fontagné and Katheline Schubert, 'The Economics of Border Carbon Adjustment: Rationale and Impacts of Compensating for Carbon at the Border' (2023) 15 Annual Review of Economics 389, 390 <https://doi.org/10.1146/annurev-economics-082322-034040>.

[84] Rolf H Weber, 'Emission Trading Schemes: A Coasean Answer to Climate Change?' in Klaus Mathis and Bruce R. Huber (eds), *Environmental Law and Economics* (4th ed, Springer, 2017), 361.

[85] The precautionary principle posits that activities potentially harmful to the environment should be avoided and preventive actions implemented, notwithstanding any scientific uncertainty regarding the consequences of such environmentally sensitive activities. Meinhard Schröder, 'Precautionary Approach/Principle' in *Max Planck Encyclopaedia of Public International Law* (2014), para 2.

analysis of law" and climate law, through the use of climate-related market mechanisms, offers a powerful approach to addressing climate change.

Another significant benefit of using the "economic analysis of law" approach to assess climate law is that it aligns well with the different levels of the jurisdiction. According to the "economic analysis of law" approach, the primary objective of legal regulations in all jurisdictions is to promote economic growth. Hence, it offers similar solutions across different countries.[86] Similarly, the transboundary nature of climate externalities require an international legal regime for climate governance.[87] Herein, the "economic analysis of law" approach can provide a normative framework for global carbon pricing and international cooperation in reducing emissions. By this means, the research on an optimal legal system can be carried out on a principal level without discussing the current state of the law of each country in detail.[88] It can significantly expedite the process of assessing and implementing climate law measures. The outputs of a legal analysis at principal level prepare an agenda for the multilateral climate negotiations. Also, in this way individual countries do not necessarily develop entirely new legal systems, which saves cost and time. Additionally, countries can justify their national climate legislations based on the standards "economic analysis of law" provides. This approach provides a normative and economic rationale for adopting specific climate measures, which can enhance the legitimacy and acceptance of such policies at the domestic level.

The "economic analysis of law approach" has already taken a pivotal role in climate law, as it intersects with economic development concerns in several legal documents. For example, the UNFCCC Article 3(4) encourages parties to adopt policies and measures to protect the climate in their economic development plans. Moreover, the United Nations (UN) Sustainable Development Goals[89] focus on integrating environmental concerns into economic and other development programs.[90] Similarly, Paris Agreement Article 6 emphasised the importance of development while minding environmental integrity. The climate-related market instruments are the embodiment of this intersection. These instruments also have repercussions on the WTO Agreements, which are inherently economic contracts and govern a diverse range of economic relationships.[91] Therefore, the "economic analysis of law" approach better illustrates the regulatory aim of climate-related market

[86] Faust (n 60) 334.

[87] Margaret A Young, 'Trade Measures to Address Climate Change: Territory and Extraterritoriality' in Panagiotis Delimatsis (ed) *Research Handbook on Climate Change and Trade* (Edward Elgar Publishing 2016), 329.

[88] Faure and Partain (n 55) 7.

[89] Sustainability has been referred to as a key policy objective of the UN, EU, and other national governments for the past 20 years. The Brutland report defines sustainable development as 'development that meets the needs of the present without compromising the ability of future generations to meet their own needs'. In line with this definition the natural resources need to be protected for the benefit of the future generations and their utilization shall be conducted in a sustainable manner.

[90] Sands and Peel (n 90) 253.

[91] Posner, *Economic Analysis of Law* (n 58) 992.

instruments and becomes handy in balancing environmental concerns and economic effectiveness.

Ultimately, the legal reasoning with "economic analysis of law" perfectly guides the interpretation of climate change mitigation policies. It enables to dissect the intricate legal frameworks and policy mechanisms that underpin climate change mitigation efforts. "Economic analysis of law" can open a new pathway to interdisciplinary policy discussions by adopting tools from political science, public choice theory, game theory, and other social sciences schools.[92] Thuswise, climate change's complex and multifaceted challenges are better reflected. Through this lens, it is possible to comprehend the legal obligations, incentives, and disincentives that influence both individual and collective actions, along with their economic effects.

5.1.2 Addressing the Factors Behind Ineffective Global Climate Cooperation

5.1.2.1 Public Good Nature of the Climate and Collective Action Problem

Despite the long-term negotiations, the international legal regime cannot achieve a strictly binding agreement on climate change. The challenge here lies in the nature of the problem. Therefore, the most crucial step in analysing social problems is to identify the characteristics of the goods that underlie the problem.[93] This way, a suitable institutional mechanism can be structured to tackle them.[94] The international climate law deals with the public good, which is the atmosphere.[95] There are two standout characteristics of the public goods. The first is non-rivalrous consumption, where one person's consumption of a public good does not leave less for any other consumer.[96] The second feature is non-excludability, where the costs of dismissing non-contributing beneficiaries who consume public goods are so high that no profit-maximising firm is willing to supply the good.[97] Therefore, in theory, every individual can benefit from the public good for their private consumption or production without minding the cost.

The protected entity under climate change, the atmosphere, is a global public good subject to high exploitation and low excludability. It is regarded as depletable

[92] Faure and Partain (n 55) 4.

[93] Kelvin J Lancaster, 'A New Approach to Consumer Theory' (1966) 74 Journal of Political Economy 132.

[94] Matthew Potoski and Aseem Prakash, 'Green Clubs: Collective Action and Voluntary Environmental Programs' (2013) 16 Annual Review of Political Science 399, 402.

[95] William Nordhaus, 'Reflections on the Economics of Climate Change' (1993) 7(4) Journal of Economic Perspectives 11, 11.

[96] World Trade Organization-United Nations Environment Programme Report *Trade and Climate Change* (World Trade Organization, Geneva, 2009). Nordhaus, Climate Change: The Ultimate Challenge for Economics (n 74) 1992.

[97] Cooter and Ulen (n 9) 40.

and renewable simultaneously.[98] As a global public good, it is indivisibly spread worldwide.[99] Since the atmosphere is an open-access resource, the cost of extending the benefits to an additional person is zero. Also, it is almost impossible to exclude individuals from enjoying its benefits.[100] This common-pool ownership structure encourages over-utilization. Thus, the market cannot allocate the atmosphere efficiently.[101]

As a result, individual countries have no incentive to cooperate on globally beneficial plans for the atmosphere. Instead, they pursue their respective national interests.[102] The national cost-benefit analysis would lead many countries not to take any GHG abatement activity, even though it would be beneficial to contribute from a collective perspective.[103] This phenomenon was identified as a collective action problem.[104] The rationalist "economic analysis of law" perspective summarised the collective action problem as a tragedy of the commons.[105] Accordingly, rational individuals choose not to cooperate even if the cooperation maximises the total welfare.[106] Each individual increases their use of public goods without limit in a world where resources are limited. As a result, freedom in the commons brings ruin to all.[107] The solutions to the "tragedy of the commons" suggest privatising the ownership structure or keeping it as a public good but making the people pay the full costs of their use via regulation.[108]

The collective action problem is more pressing in climate law than in any other subject since the misalignment between private and public benefits leads to unrecoverable results.[109] In the context of climate change, addressing the tragedy of the commons requires treating GHG emissions as a matter of property law. However,

---

[98] Faure and Partain (n 55) 39.

[99] Thomas Cottier, 'The Principle of Common Concern of Humankind' in Thomas Cottier (ed) *The Prospects of Common Concern of Humankind in International Law* (Cambridge University Press, 2021) 45.

[100] Nordhaus, Climate Clubs: Overcoming Free-Riding (n 37) 1347.

[101] Morell (n 79) 57.

[102] Cottier and Payosova (n 52) 12.

[103] Emanuel V Towfigh and Niels Petersen, 'Public and Social Choice Theory' in Emanuel V Towfigh, and Niels Petersen *Economic Methods for Lawyers* (Edward Elgar Publishing 2015), 122.

[104] Garett Hardin, 'The Tragedy of the Commons' (1968) 162 Science 1243–1248. There are four key aspects of a commons problem as identified by Hardin. First one is that there needs to be a common pool resource. Second the use of that resource or an activity that depletes it needs to be legitimate and valuable for society in general. Third, the common resource should lead people to overuse or over-deplete the resource to a point which is non-optimal and exceeding sustainable limits. Fourth, there should be no technical solution, meaning that the use of technology to expand the resources should not be possible.

[105] Ronald H Coase, 'The Problem of Social Cost' (1960) 3 Journal of Law and Economics 1.

[106] Anne van Aaken, 'Behavioral Aspects of the International Law of Global Public Goods and Common Pool Resources' (2018) 112(1) The American Journal of International Law 67, 68.

[107] Hardin (n 104) 1242.

[108] Ibid.

[109] Potoski and Prakash (n 94) 399.

the atmosphere cannot be fenced or assigned to individuals. Therefore, the tragedy of the commons can only be prevented through regulation or tax, which make emissions costly for the polluters.[110] Consequently, the "economic analysis of law approach" provides a solid basis to favour market-based instruments, which allocate limited rights to deplete the public good or internalise consumption costs.

5.1.2.2 Free-Riding

The most fundamental reason for the reluctance to take concrete measures for GHG abatement is its additional costs for the state budgets. Hence, countries prefer to free-ride[111] on others' efforts instead of taking action by enjoining the benefits.[112] They contribute little or none to the global aim of emission abatement.[113] In this way, free-riders aim to keep prices low for carbon-intensive products in their domestic marketplace. Free-riding is a significant obstacle in addressing global externalities.[114] It lies at the heart of the failure to deal with climate change.[115] Free-riding can lead to an uneven distribution of the costs and burdens associated with reducing carbon emissions, making it more challenging for the international community to achieve meaningful progress in addressing the climate crisis.

Nordhaus identifies two main free-riding dimensions. The first one is geographical free-riding, which refers to countries enjoying the reduction of GHG emissions of other countries without implementing any policies.[116] In comparison, the temporal free-riding connotes that the present generation benefits from consuming high carbon emitted products, while future generations are paying the cost of those emissions as lower consumption or a degraded environment.[117] Nordhaus argues that the

[110] Coase (n 105) 2.

[111] Free-riding occurs, where a party benefits from a public good without contributing to its costs.

[112] Nordhaus, 'Climate Change: The Ultimate Challenge for Economics' (n 74) 2006.

[113] William Nordhaus, *The Climate Casino: Risk, Uncertainty, and Economics for a Warming World* (Yale University Press, 2013), 317.

[114] Nordhaus, 'Climate Change: The Ultimate Challenge for Economics' (n 74) 2007.

[115] Christoph Böhringer and others, 'Potential Impacts and Challenges of Border Carbon Adjustments' (2022) 12 Nat. Clim. Chang, 22, 22 <https://doi.org/10.1038/s41558-021-01250-z>.

[116] William Nordhaus, 'Geography and Macroeconomics: New Data and New Findings' (2006) 103(10) Proceedings of the National Academy of Sciences 3510.

[117] Nordhaus, 'Climate Clubs: Overcoming Free-Riding' (n 37) 1342. Fontagné and Schubert (n 83) 392.

free-riding phenomenon is the consequence of the Westphalian Dilemma[118] of exclusive national sovereignty versus global public goods.[119]

The classic solutions to opportunistic free-riding are twofold. At the individual level, incentives such as pricing the externality of the public good can be adopted. By imposing costs on those who contribute to environmental degradation, individuals can be encouraged to internalise their actions' adverse consequences.[120] More broadly, any market-driven activities threatening the public good need to be blocked or restricted with adequate enforcement power.[121] As such, the essential policies for realising this purpose could be emissions prices, limits, or other constraints on producer and consumer behaviour. These policies are designed to set clear boundaries on the level of pollution or resource consumption. Carbon price shines out among several alternatives because individuals tend to evade command-and-control regulation but respond positively to the pricing signals.[122] It offers a market-driven approach that empowers consumers and businesses to make environmentally responsible choices while promoting innovation and efficiency in emission reduction efforts.

Consequently, the crucial aspect for interrupting free-riding is to set a carbon price that has the supportable level to ensure the optimal abatement but, at the same time, does not distort market dynamics.[123] In addition to pricing regulations, international coordination has the utmost importance for properly implementing anti-free-riding policies because the actions causing climate change transgress national borders. The pricing instruments are regulated under international law with the consent of countries in joining and applying corresponding policies. However, few countries fully abide by these agreements. Climate governance, therefore, emphasises the need for international institutions with sanction power to overcome the problem of free-riding.[124]

---

[118] The Westphalian Dilemma is a concept in international relations that refers to the tension between the principles of state sovereignty and the need for international cooperation to address global challenges such as climate change. The dilemma arises in cases, where an effective cooperation and coordination among states is necessary to achieve global goals, but this can be difficult to achieve if it requires states to compromise their sovereignty or accept the authority of international institutions.

[119] William Nordhaus, *A Question of Balance: Weighing the Options on Global Warming Policies* (Yale University Press 2014). In this book, Nordhaus argues that the problem of climate change requires coordinated global action, but achieving such coordination is a daunting task. While this source does not specifically address the "Westphalian Dilemma", it provides a broad overview of the challenges of coordinating global action on climate change, which is a key issue related to the dilemma.

[120] Faure (n 34) 173.

[121] Faure (n 34) 179.

[122] Nordhaus, *The Climate Casino* (n 113) 7.

[123] Nordhaus, 'Dynamic Climate Clubs' (n 37) 2.

[124] Michaël Aklin and Matto Mildenberger, 'Prisoners of the Wrong Dilemma: Why Distributive Conflict, Not Collective Action, Characterizes the Politics of Climate Change' (2020) 20 (4) Global Environmental Politics 4, 5, <https://doi.org/10.1162/glep_a_00578>.

5.1.2.3 Carbon Leakage and Competitiveness Concerns

Climate mitigation commitments lead to "leakage", which refers to the movement of domestic industries to countries with less rigorous carbon legislation.[125] A transfer of emissions from one region to another due to changes in carbon control regulation is defined as "policy-induced carbon leakage".[126] The movement of industries can occur due to concerns about increased production costs resulting from measures like carbon pricing, emissions regulations, or renewable energy mandates.[127] As a result, the products manufactured in one region that has no carbon regulation but consumed in another with a carbon policy decrease the competitiveness of the regulated industries on a global and local scale.[128] Subsequently, leakage creates harmful competition among different jurisdictions, resulting in a race to the bottom.

Energy-intensive sectors, easily substitutable and internationally traded goods are more vulnerable to leakage and competitiveness problems.[129] These industries in carbon-regulated countries will lose profits, market share and related jobs. Thus, older and heavily polluting industries may find it more cost-effective to continue polluting and relocate their facilities to other countries than to install emission-reducing technologies. Relocation of industries leads to changes in trade patterns and increases the market share of countries with no emissions regulation.[130] Consequently, imports from countries with weak climate legislation will gain cost-of-production advantages over domestic products. As an increasing number of countries implement measures to reduce emissions and climate regulations cause a widening price disparity among products, carbon leakage becomes a more significant issue. This situation escalates the costs associated with climate mitigation efforts for pioneering countries and substantially undermines their motivation.

Leakage and international competitiveness concerns bring vague international\national climate regulations and policies.[131] Above all, they undermine the environmental effectiveness of carbon regulations such that the carbon price cannot achieve targeted emission reductions. Instead, emissions are just displaced in different countries. Only an agreement with broad coverage of countries and a strong emissions reduction commitment for all parties can overcome the leakage problem.

---

[125] Will (n 49) 33.

[126] There are also other reasons for the carbon leakage. For example, due to the lower labour costs or consumption.

[127] Organization for Economic Cooperation and Development (OECD), *Climate Policy Leadership in an Interconnected World: What Role for Border Carbon Adjustments?* (2020) 7–11.

[128] Felix Bierbrauer, and others, *A CO2-Border Adjustment Mechanism as a Building Block of a Climate Club* (Kiel Policy Brief No. 15, Kiel Institute for the World Economy (IfW), 2021), 6.

[129] Andrew Shoyer, Jung-ui Sul and Colette van der Ven, 'Carbon Leakage and the Migration of Private CO2 Emitters to other Jurisdictions' in Kevin R. Gray and others (eds), *The Oxford Handbook of International Climate Change Law* (Oxford University Press 2016), 287.

[130] Thomas Cottier, Olga Nartova and Anirudh Shingal, 'The Potential of Tariff Policy for Climate Change Mitigation: Legal and Economic Analysis' (2014) 48(5) Journal of World Trade 1007, 1015.

[131] Shoyer, Jung-ui Sul and van der Ven (n 129) 291.

5.1.2.4 Asymmetry Between the Developed and Developing Countries

The climate change negotiations are centred around the compromise between efficiency and equity. Most economists agree upon the definition of efficiency.[132] However, there are several approaches to the equity concept.[133] In developed countries, the ethics and equity discussions in climate change mainly focus on intergenerational issues and discounting.[134,135] Meanwhile, in developing countries, the primary emphasis is given to intra-generational equity and burden sharing, who cuts emissions by how much, when, and who will support finance and technology.[136] In essence, under climate mitigation, equity refers to how the benefits and burdens of climate change can be shared among countries, within societies, and over time.[137]

Equity is of utmost importance in inducing the participation of key developing countries in climate action. Therefore, the efforts related to equity will target redesigning the governance structure that harmoniously and fairly distributes the costs of climate change mitigation among countries with varying positions. For instance, developing countries are less responsible for the current climate crisis, but they will be affected earliest and most severely due to their geography, lack of adaptive capacity and poorly designed infrastructure.[138] Thus, they have a sense of injustice when the developed countries suggest them to find green and possibly costly routes for

[132] Efficiency involves the process of selecting a specific aim according to economic criteria. The term "efficiency" refers to the peak level of performance that uses the least amount of inputs to achieve the highest amount of output. Friedrich Soltau, *Fairness in International Climate Change Law and Policy* (Cambridge University Press 2009), 235.

[133] For example; vertical equity refers to reducing disparities between developed and developing nations, horizontal equity refers to treating all nations equally. Rawls maximin touches on favouring the least well-off nations, egalitarianism advocates treating all people equally regardless of location and market justice considers the exchange process itself to be able to lead to a fair outcome. T Tietenberg, 'Economic Analysis and Climate Change' (1998) 3(3) Environment and Development Economics 347, 393 <https://doi.org/10.1017/S1355770X98320197>.

[134] Discounting is the process of converting a value received in a future time period to an equivalent value received immediately.

[135] Tim Hayward, 'Climate Change and Ethics' (2012) 2(12) Nature Climate Change 843.

[136] Stern, 'Ethics, Equity and The Economics of Climate Change' (n 32) 476.

[137] Julia M Puaschunder, 'Mapping Climate in the Twenty-First Century' (2016) 59 Development 211, 215 <https://doi.org/10.1057/s41301-017-0110-0>

[138] Fran Sussman, Christopher P Weaver and Anne Grambsch, 'Challenges in Applying the Paradigm of Welfare Economics to Climate Change' (2014) 5(3) Journal of Benefit-Cost Analysis 347, 353 <https://doi.org/10.1515/jbca-2014-9001>. Tamma Carleton and others, 'Valuing the Global Mortality Consequences of Climate Change Accounting for Adaptation Costs and Benefits' (2022) 137(4) Quarterly Journal of Economics 2037. Among other things, the impacts of the climate change can be named as severity of droughts, land degradation, desertification, the intensity of floods, tropical cyclones, the incidences of malaria, decreasing crop yield and food security. Geographically and because of their dependence to nature, the developing countries are more prone to experience these impacts.

development, while developed countries first relied on cheaper alternatives in their growth, such as fossil fuels.[139]

Consequently, the most significant setbacks of climate cooperation are the member countries' diverging views and positions in economic competitiveness, energy policy, and aid flows,[140] which result in protracted and inconvenient negotiation fora.[141] The UNFCCC parties consist of large and small countries, importers and exporters of high-carbon embedded products, developed and developing countries, and fossil-rich and poor states, cumulatively representing an extensive range of interests.[142] A closer look shows the conflicting international interests of the stakeholders. For instance, the European Union (EU) seeks solid mitigation efforts, whereas developing countries point to developed countries for higher responsibilities. Conversely, oil-producing countries reject any substantial cut in fossil fuel consumption, but the small island developing countries are calling for more ambition.[143]

For this reason, legal research should examine alternative climate regimes, which provide a solution to the burden distribution of climate mitigation and are found rational by both developed and developing countries.[144] The ideal solution is an internationally consistent carbon price.[145] However, previous climate negotiations have demonstrated that segregating factors among countries also constitute a barrier to agreeing on the global carbon price, which leads countries to make their own arrangements.[146] In these arrangements, each country will attempt to maximise its individual welfare, which results in market failure. In order to prevent market failure, a neoliberal reform and a supranational forum regulating the pricing instruments need to be established.[147] Hence, successful negotiations on climate mitigation require balancing the interests of developing and developed countries and tariff and non-tariff measures, tackling trade barriers, establishing linkages with other regulatory areas and, most importantly, preventing carbon leakage.[148]

---

[139] Stern, 'The Economics of Climate Change' (n 33) 25.

[140] Richard B Stewart, Michael Oppenheimer, and Bryce Rudyk, 'Building Blocks for Global Climate Protection' (2013) 32(2) Stan Envti LJ, 351.

[141] Camilla Bausch and Micheal Mehling, 'Alternative Venues of Climate Cooperation: An Institutional Perspective' in Erkki J Hollo, Kati Kulovesi, Michael Mehling (eds.) *Climate Change and the Law* (Springer 2013), 114.

[142] Alan Boyle and Navraj Singh Ghaleigh, 'Climate Change and International Law beyond the UNFCCC' in Kevin R Gray (ed.), *The Oxford Handbook of International Climate Change Law* (Oxford University Press 2016), 37.

[143] Mayer, *The International Law on Climate Change* (n 8) 33.

[144] Puaschunder (n 137) 212.

[145] Carley Chavara and others, 'Continuity and Change in Carbon Market Politics' in Jeannie Sowers and others (eds), *The Oxford Handbook of Comparative Environmental Politics* (Oxford University Press 2021), 418.

[146] Jeroen Van den Bergh and others, 'A Dual-Track Transition to Global Carbon Pricing' (2020) Climate Policy, 3 <https://doi.org/10.1080/14693062.2020.1797618>.

[147] Cooter and Ulen (n 9) 41.

[148] Matthew Paterson, 'Who and What are Carbon Markets For? Politics and the Development of Climate Policy' (2012) 12(1) Climate Policy 82, 93 <https://doi.org/10.1080/14693062.201

5.1.3 Evaluating Alternative Climate Governance Schemes Through the Lens of Economic Analysis of Law

As rational actors,[149] countries focus on their self-interest rather than international cooperation for a common concern.[150] The pursuit of economic growth, energy security, and the protection of domestic industries often takes precedence, especially for nations that perceive themselves as having a lot to lose by reducing emissions.[151] The negotiations mainly deadlock on the issue of willingness to pay. Hence, the international community is facing difficulties in agreeing to adopt binding, long-term, comprehensive, and robust climate targets.[152]

Despite the hegemony of free-riding, some countries are eager to take action without a detailed international agreement and strengthen cooperation on climate change since they see its imminent threats. They are forward-thinking countries, often referred to as the "engine of international cooperation". In the economic analysis of law approach, it is commonly assumed that parties act with forward-looking rationality.[153] Also, in some situations, a rational actor decides how to act by considering the probable action of others, which is the domain of game theory.[154] Within a game-theoretic language, forward-thinking countries can be categorised as having bargaining power[155] and are highly committed to invest substantial resources and efforts into finding solutions.[156] In the context of climate change, forward-thinking countries are proactive in taking steps to reduce their GHG emissions, support renewable energy, and promote sustainable practices. They often serve as leaders and catalysts for positive change.[157] The commitment of some countries to

1.579259>.

[149] Rational actor is a term in rational choice theory, refers to the response of an individual to information and incentives. However, there is a plenty of evidence that individuals are also sensitive to the behaviour of others and not firmly self-interested. Elinor Ostrom, 'Collective Action and the Evolution of Social Norms' (2000) 14(3) Journal of Economic Perspectives 137.

[150] Ibid.

[151] Chavara and others (n 145) 422–423.

[152] Scott Barrett, *Environment and Statecraft: The Strategy of Environmental Treaty-Making* (Oxford University Press, 2003).

[153] Shavell (n 65) 8451.

[154] Posner, *Economic Analysis of Law* (n 58) 22.

[155] They are ready to carry some of the burden for collective climate action. This is because, they share an understanding of the need for international cooperation in some areas. Florian Kiesow Cortez, 'Enforcing International Deals: The System of International Organizations from a Politics-as-Exchange Perspective' in Florian Kiesow Cortez (ed), *The Political Economy of International Agreements* (Springer Nature 2021), 111.

[156] Nicholas Epley and Thomas Gilovich, 'The Mechanics of Motivated Reasoning' (2016) 30 Journal of Economic Perspectives 133, 135 <https://doi.org/10.1257/jep.30.3.133>. Roland Bénabou and Jean Tirole, 'Mindful Economics: The Production, Consumption, and Value of Beliefs' (2016) 30 Journal of Economic Perspectives 141.

[157] For example, in presenting its Fit-for-55 package, the European Commission stated that "what is good for the planet is good for people and the economy".

proactively tackle climate change, notwithstanding the absence of comprehensive international agreements, can be elucidated by a multifaceted array of factors.[158]

Firstly, the motivation derived from self-interest,[159] particularly for countries heavily reliant on the importation of fossil fuels or those constituting small island states, is profound. They stand at the frontline, facing the immediate and potentially catastrophic repercussions of climate change. For them, the investment in climate change mitigation is not merely a policy option but a survival strategy. The cost-benefit analysis directs them to make a strategic decision to take climate action.[160] These nations advocate for stringent global climate policies, not just to protect global commons but to safeguard their own territorial integrity and economic sustainability. The vulnerability of small island states to rising sea levels and the economic burden placed on fossil fuel importers by fluctuating oil prices exemplify the direct stimuli compelling these countries to adopt proactive climate policies.

Secondly, the aspiration for global leadership is another significant motivator for taking climate action without an international compromise.[161] Entities such as the EU, through initiatives like the Green Deal, aim not only to reduce its own carbon emissions drastically but also to set a benchmark for climate action worldwide.[162] Such leadership endeavours are underpinned by both moral obligation and strategic interests, including enhancing geopolitical influence and promoting their economic models as blueprints for sustainable development.[163] It can be seen as a commitment device for reform-oriented governments.[164] Also, having "power" to regulate specific issues, such as climate change, can mutually minimize externalities and make all countries better off.[165]

---

[158] Stefanie Bailer and Florian Weiler, 'A Political Economy of Positions in Climate Change Negotiations: Economic, Structural, Domestic, and Strategic Explanations' (2015) 10 Review of International Organization 43.

[159] States only enter treaties that serve to their interests. Eric A Posner and David Weisbach, *Climate Change Justice* (Princeton University Press 2015), 6.

[160] Axel Dreher and Valentin F Lang, 'The Political Economy of International Organizations' in Roger Congleton, Bernand Grofman and Stefan Voigt (eds), *The Oxford Handbook of Public Choice* (2nd edn, Oxford University Press 2019) 607.

[161] Sebastian Oberthür and Claire Dupont, 'The European Union's International Climate Leadership: Towards a Grand Climate Strategy?' (2021) 28 J Eur Public Policy 1095 <https://doi.org/10.1080/13501763.2021.1918218>.

[162] Communication from the Commission (COM) The European Green Deal 640 [2019], 3. It refers to the term 'global leader'.

[163] Ekaterina Domorenok and Paolo Graziano, 'Understanding the European Green Deal: A Narrative Policy Framework Approach' (2023) 9 Eur Policy Anal 9, 10-11, <https://doi.org/10.1002/epa2.1168>.

[164] Florian Kiesow Cortez, 'Domestic Institutions and the Political Economy of International Agreements: A Survey and Hypotheses', in Florian Kiesow Cortez (ed), *The Political Economy of International Agreements* (Springer Nature 2021), 16.

[165] Joel P Trachtman, 'The Theory of the Firm and the Theory of the International Economic Organization: Toward Comparative Institutional Analysis' (1996) 17 Northwestern Journal of International Law & Business 470.

Furthermore, the economic benefits of climate action with early adoption of renewable energy sources and technologies serve as a powerful incentive. Countries like China have recognized the economic growth potential inherent in renewable energy markets and technologies.[166] By investing heavily in these areas, they not only aim to meet their emissions abatement goals but also to establish themselves as leaders in the burgeoning global market for clean technologies. Lastly, the role of public sentiment in shaping climate policies cannot be understated. Governments are compelled to enact ambitious climate strategies in countries with significant public concern regarding climate change in response to the demand.[167] This democratic accountability acts as a crucial driver for the implementation of stringent climate measures, reflecting a collective will to address climate change proactively.

In summary, these diverse motivations collectively encourage countries to deviate from a free-riding stance towards a more engaged and proactive approach to climate change mitigation.[168] By aligning national interests with global environmental goals, these countries contribute significantly to the collective effort required to address the climate crisis. This shift from passive engagement is pivotal in galvanizing international momentum towards achieving substantial and meaningful progress in combating climate change.

In comparison, reluctant countries do not consider climate change mitigation as an essential national priority. [169] These countries generally hesitate to commit to ambitious targets, invest in emissions control measures, or participate actively in global initiatives.[170] Their reluctance can stem from various reasons, including economic concerns, political considerations, or a belief that other issues take precedence.[171] Forward-thinking countries recognise that traditional approaches to climate governance are insufficient to address the scale and complexity of the climate emergency.[172] Therefore, they shift their attention to alternative paths in climate mitigation.[173] The forerunners are willing to be exemplars in the abatement

[166] China leads the world in the total installed capacity of renewable energy, including solar, wind, and hydropower. International Energy Agency (IEA), *Renewable Energy Market Update: Outlook for 2023 and 2024*, (OECD Publishing Paris 2023) 37, <https://doi-org.ezproxy.uzh.ch/10.1787/89017c62-en>.

[167] Sijeong Lim and Andreas Duit, 'Partisan Politics, Welfare States, and Environmental Policy Outputs in the OECD Countries, 1975-2005', (2018) 12 Regulation and Governance, 220.

[168] Dieter Helm, Cameron Hepburn and Giovanni Ruta, 'Trade, Climate Change, and the Political Game Theory of Border Carbon Adjustments' 28 (2012) Oxf Rev Econ Policy 368.

[169] Lavanya Rajamani, 'Differentiation in the Emerging Climate Regime' (2013) 14 Theoretical Inquiries in Law 152 <https://doi.org/10.1515/til-2013-009>.

[170] Ostrom, A Polycentric Approach for Coping with Collective Action and Global Climate Change n (48).

[171] Anthony Giddens, *The Politics of Climate Change* (Polity Press, 2011).

[172] Carattini and Löschel (n 38).

[173] Michele Betsill and others 'Building Productive Links between the UNFCCC and the Broader Global Climate Governance Landscape' (2015) 15(2) Global Environmental Politics 1.

efforts that do not require deviation from economic stability and prosperity.[174] They understand that their actions can inspire other countries to adopt similar strategies and engage more actively in the fight against climate change.

Given that the top ten countries with the highest GHG emissions account for two-thirds of global emissions,[175] their leadership role and the equitable allocation of responsibilities and benefits must be central to any climate change initiative. Therefore, an approach that seeks common ground among the high-emitted smaller group of countries can better facilitate the pursuit of necessary climate action.[176] Success stories and collective efforts by this smaller group can serve as examples and inspiration for other nations, ultimately fostering a momentum for broader international action on climate change. Hence, forward-thinking countries are searching to improve the UNFCCC regime to live up to the pressing emissions accumulation problem or to design alternative fora that could provide more substantial compromises than the existing processes.[177]

In the context of climate change, minilateral approaches have gained attention for their ability to facilitate more focused and effective cooperation.[178] The concept of a minilateral design for addressing climate change is structured around four key pillars, each of which plays a crucial role in its effectiveness. First, it begins with a limited group of "forward-thinking" countries. They are the core participants in the minilateral scheme and are willing to take "ambitious steps to reduce GHG emissions".[179] These countries can act as leaders and set examples for others to follow, driving positive change and inspiring broader action. Subsequently, they agree on mechanisms that achieve greater global emissions coverage. With such mechanisms, minilateral design can expand its impact beyond its core group of forward-thinking countries Above all; a minilateral scheme imposes sanctions against

---

[174] Aaron McCright, and Dunlap Riley, 'The Politicization of Climate Change and Polarization in the American Public's Views of Global Warming, 2001–2010' (2011) 52(2) Sociological Quarterly 155.

[175] World Resources Institute, 'Interactive Chart Shows Changes in the World's Top 10 Emitters' <https://www.wri.org/insights/interactive-chart-shows-changes-worlds-top-10-emitters> accessed 17 March 2024.

[176] Anthony Brenton, 'Great Powers in Climate Politics' (2013) 13(5) Climate Policy 541.

[177] Countries taking unilateral actions against climate change are looking for cooperative approaches to strengthen their policies. From a neoliberal institutional perspective, the reasons are to decrease transaction costs for their policies, facilitate successful bargaining through the creation of forums for repeated interactions, and reduce information asymmetries that hinder successful implementation. Robert O Keohane, 'The Demand for International Regimes' (1982) 36(2) International Organization 325. Kenneth W Abbott and Duncan Snidal, 'Why States Act through Formal International Organizations' (1998) 42 Journal of Conflict Resolution 3. Furthermore, they can improve the credibility of their policies. A Dreher and S Voigt, 'Does Membership in International Organizations Increase Governments' Credibility? Testing the Effects of Delegating Powers' (2011) 39 Journal of Comparative Economics 326.

[178] Thomas Bernauer, 'Climate Change Politics' (2013) 16 Annual Review of Political Science 421.

[179] Lavanya Rajamani, 'Understanding the 2015 Paris Agreement' in Navroz K Dubash (ed), *India in a Warming World: Integrating Climate Change and Development* (Oxford University Press 2019) 215.

non-compliance to ensure that participating countries adhere to their commitments. At last, it should include measures that prevent carbon leakage from its members to countries with lax climate regulations.[180] By incorporating these four pillars, a minilateral approach to climate change leverages the commitment and leadership of forward-thinking countries to drive ambitious climate action. It encourages broader participation while ensuring accountability and minimising the risk of emissions leakage to less regulated regions.[181]

5.1.3.1 Climate Club as a Catalyst for Bridging the Gaps

In response to challenges behind global climate cooperation, this book explores how the concept of climate club addresses the inadequacies of the current climate change regime and promotes minilateral international cooperation in mitigating climate change. The climate club structure and its linkages are based on the variable geometry solution. The term "variable geometry" is a concept that recognises that not all countries in the international system have the same interests, capacities, or willingness to cooperate on every issue.[182] Therefore, the level and nature of involvement can vary depending on the participating countries' specific preferences.[183] Variable geometry, as a concept, is rooted in flexibility and adaptability.[184] It allows for a tailored approach to international cooperation, recognising that one size does not fit all in global governance.[185] This approach accommodates different countries' unique circumstances and priorities, which are crucial for fostering collaboration on complex global issues like climate change.[186] In smaller forum, each participant has a more significant impact on decision-making. Notably, key stakeholders may find it easier to come to an agreement within a small group. The absence of divergent

[180] Aklin and Mildenberger (n 124) 8.

[181] Trachtman (n 46) 109.

[182] Peter Lloyd, 'The Variable Geometry Approach to International Economic Integration' (2009) 1(1) International Journal of Business and Development Studies 51, 52.

[183] Robert Z Lawrence, 'Rulemaking Amidst Growing Diversity: A Club-of-Clubs Approach to WTO Reform and New Issue Selection' (2006) 9(4) Journal of International Economic Law 823.

[184] For instance, the European Union (EU) and the WTO are two international organizations that have successfully employed the variable geometry approach. David Victor, 'Toward Effective International Cooperation on Climate Change: Numbers, Interests, and Institutions' (2006) 6 Global Environmental Politics 90 <https://doi.org/10.1162/glep.2006.6.3.90>. Under the WTO all members are equal, however, the negotiations first started among the worlds' major trading nations and then extended to other countries. Experiments have also indicated that coordination in large groups is more easily developed if the group grows slowly and the new participants know the group history and norms. Roberto A Weber, 'Managing Growth to Achieve Efficient Coordination in Large Groups' (2006) 96(1) American Economic Review 114–126.

[185] Robyn Eckersley, 'Moving Forward in the Climate Negotiations: Multilateralism or Minilateralism?' (2012) 12(2) Global Environmental Politics 24 <https://doi.org/10.1162/GLEP_a_00107>. Petersmann (n 6) 574.

[186] Aklin and Mildenberger, (n 124) 4.

interests and viewpoints can streamline the decision-making process.[187] As a result, such a pronounced impact makes it more likely for the forum to generate the political will needed to drive change. Similarly, the climate club invites countries that prioritise emission abatement and are ready to commit seriously. By this means, the asymmetry between developed and developing countries does not hinder creating a regime with concrete obligations.

The climate club scheme responds to the "small cooperation paradox". According to this paradox, stable coalitions with many participants are open to free-riding due to fewer number of complying parties.[188] Thus, countries often hesitate to cooperate. However, the climate club only accepts countries genuinely committed to climate action and willing to meet their obligations. This selective approach helps ensure that participants are more likely to comply with the club's standards, reducing free-riding risk. Plus, the enforcement mechanisms within the club held countries accountable for their non-compliance. The club's uniform standards and climate-related market mechanisms eliminate discrepancies that could lead to free-riding.[189] In this way, the climate club addresses the collective action problem by providing a forum where countries commit to collective targets and actions. Consequently, the climate club is viewed as a supplementary approach to international cooperation, equipped with an enforcement mechanism to succeed the incremental and voluntary obligations of MEAs in addressing climate change.[190]

Membership in the climate club offers economic incentives and market access benefits. Access to markets with shared climate commitments can incentivise countries to participate and align their policies. Therefore, the climate club approach connects countries applying national carbon pricing policies and harmonises their schemes. In this way, it would address the competitiveness concerns of industries. With uniform carbon price and trade sanctions under the club, industries can plan and invest confidently, knowing that their competitive positions are not undermined when adopting low-carbon process and production methods. This certainty and transparency fosters trust among member nations and helps prevent free-riding or

[187] Jonas Meckling and Jonas Nahm, 'Strategic State Capacity: How States Counter Opposition to Climate Policy' (2022) 55(3) Comparative Political Studies 493.

[188] Scott Barrett, 'Self-enforcing International Environmental Agreements' (1994) 46 Oxford Economic Papers 878.

[189] Nordhaus, 'Climate Clubs: Overcoming Free-Riding' (n 37) found that modest trade penalties on non-club members can induce large stable coalition with high level of emission abatement. However, he did not consider the retaliation possibility from non-club members. Hagen and Schneider found that retaliation can reinforce the effects of trade sanctions and grow a stable coalition if the initial coalition is large. Achim Hagen and Jan Schneider, 'Boon or Bane? Trade Sanctions and the Stability of International Environmental Agreements' (2017) 5 Oldenburg Discussion Papers in Economics 403.

[190] Nordhaus, 'Climate Clubs: Overcoming Free-Riding' (n 37). Nordhaus, *The Climate Casino* (n 113). Robert Falkner, 'A Minilateral Solution for Global Climate Change? On Bargaining Efficiency, Club Benefits, and International Legitimacy' (2016) 14 Perspectives on Politics 87. Kenneth W Abbott, 'Strengthening the Transnational Regime Complex for Climate Change' (2014) 3(1) Transnational Environmental Law 57.

non-compliance, which can impact competitiveness. Furthermore, uniform pricing helps prevent carbon leakage by making it less attractive for industries to shift emissions to countries with lower carbon prices. Consequently, the club levels the playing field and encourages industries to adopt more environmentally responsible practices without the fear of being disadvantaged in global markets.[191]

In conclusion, the concept of the climate club presents a promising approach to addressing the complex and pressing challenges of climate change. It offers a range of advantages, including enhanced cooperation, tailored solutions, faster action, and stronger commitment.[192] However, it is crucial to acknowledge that the climate club must be thoughtfully designed and integrated within the broader international climate framework to ensure its effectiveness and to avoid disintegrating global efforts. As a dynamic and adaptable approach, the climate club has the potential to play a pivotal role in advancing climate action and achieving shared sustainability goals.

Bibliography

Legislation

Conference of Parties (COP), 'Decision 1/CP.21 Adoption of the Paris Agreement' (12 December 2015) U.N. Doc. FCCC/CP/2015/L.9/Rev.1

United Nations Framework Convention on Climate Change, 1771 U.N.T.S. 107, 165; S. Treaty Doc No. 102-38 (1992); U.N. Doc. A/AC.237/18 (Part II)/Add.1; 31 I.L.M. 849

Secondary Sources

Abbott KW, 'Strengthening the Transnational Regime Complex for Climate Change' (2014) 3(1) Transnational Environmental Law 57

— and Snidal D, 'Why States Act through Formal International Organizations' (1998) 42 Journal of Conflict Resolution 3

Aklin M and Mildenberger M, 'Prisoners of the Wrong Dilemma: Why Distributive Conflict, Not Collective Action, Characterizes the Politics of Climate Change' (2020) 20 (4) Global Environmental Politics 4 <https://doi.org/10.1162/glep_a_00578>

[191] David M McEvoy and John K Stranlund, ''Self-enforcing International Environmental Agreements with Costly Monitoring for Compliance' (2009) 42(4) Environmental and Resource Economics 491.

[192] Nicholas Stern and Hans Peter Lankes, *Collaborating and Delivering on Climate Action Through a Climate Club: An Independent Report to the G7* (London School of Economics and Political Science, 2022) 36.

Babiker MH and Rutherford TF, 'The Economic Effects of Border Measures in Subglobal Climate Agreements' (2005) 26 Energy J 99

Bailer S and Weiler F, 'A Political Economy of Positions in Climate Change Negotiations: Economic, Structural, Domestic, and Strategic Explanations' (2015) 10 Review of International Organization 43

Bang G, Hovi J, and Skodvin T, 'The Paris Agreement: Short-Term and Long-Term Effectiveness' (2016) 4 Politics and Governance 209

Baranzini A and others, 'Carbon Pricing in Climate Policy: Seven Reasons, Complementary Instruments, and Political Economy Considerations' (2017) 8 Wiley Interdisciplinary Reviews: Climate Change 462

Bardt H and Kolev GV, *Trade Club for Climate: A Climate Approach to Revive Multilateralism*, IW-Policy Paper, No. 8/2021 (Institut der deutschen Wirtschaft (IW), Köln 2021)

Barrett S, 'Self-enforcing International Environmental Agreements' (1994) 46 Oxford Economic Papers 878

—*Environment and Statecraft: The Strategy of Environmental Treaty-Making* (Oxford University Press, 2003)

Bausch C and Mehling M, 'Alternative Venues of Climate Cooperation: An Institutional Perspective' in E Hollo, K Kulovesi, M Mehling (eds), *Climate Change and the Law* (Springer, 2013)

Bénabou R and Tirole J, 'Mindful Economics: The Production, Consumption, and Value of Beliefs' (2016) 30 Journal of Economic Perspectives 141

Benjamin L, 'International and Transnational Climate Change Law and Policies' in *Companies and Climate Change: Theory and Law in the United Kingdom* (Cambridge University Press 2021)

Bernauer T, 'Climate Change Politics' (2013) 16 Annual Review of Political Science 421

Betsill M and others 'Building Productive Links between the UNFCCC and the Broader Global Climate Governance Landscape' (2015) 15(2) Global Environmental Politics 1

Bierbrauer F and others, *A CO2-Border Adjustment Mechanism as a Building Block of a Climate Club* (Kiel Policy Brief No. 15, Kiel Institute for the World Economy (IfW), 2021).

Böhringer C and others, 'Potential Impacts and Challenges of Border Carbon Adjustments' (2022) 12 Nat. Clim. Chang, 22, 22 <https://doi.org/10.1038/s41558-021-01250-z>

Boyle A and Ghaleigh NS, 'Climate Change and International Law beyond the UNFCCC' in KR Gray (ed), *The Oxford Handbook of International Climate Change Law* (Oxford University Press 2016)

Brandi C, *Trade Elements in Countries Climate Contributions under the Paris Agreement* (International Centre for Trade and Sustainable Development (ICTSD) 2017)

Brenton A, 'Great Powers in Climate Politics' (2013) 13(5) Climate Policy 541

Carattini S and Löschel A, 'Managing Momentum in Climate Negotiations' (2021) 16 Environmental Research Letters 51001

Carleton T and others, 'Valuing the Global Mortality Consequences of Climate Change Accounting for Adaptation Costs and Benefits' (2022) 137(4) Quarterly Journal of Economics 2037

Chavara C and others, 'Continuity and Change in Carbon Market Politics' in J Sowers and others (eds), *The Oxford Handbook of Comparative Environmental Politics* (Oxford University Press 2021)

Clausing KA and Wolfram C 'Carbon Border Adjustments, Climate Clubs, and Subsidy Races When Climate Policies Vary' (2023) 37(3) Journal of Economic Perspectives 137

Communication from the Commission (COM) The European Green Deal 640 [2019]

Coase RH, 'The Problem of Social Cost' (1960) 3 Journal of Law and Economics 1.

Cooter R and Ulen T, *Law and Economics* (6th edn, Berkeley Law Books 2016).

Cortez FK, 'Enforcing International Deals: The System of International Organizations from a Politics-as-Exchange Perspective' in FK Cortez (ed), *The Political Economy of International Agreements* (Springer Nature 2021)

— 'Domestic Institutions and the Political Economy of International Agreements: A Survey and Hypotheses', in FK Cortez (ed), *The Political Economy of International Agreements* (Springer Nature 2021)

Cottier T, 'The Principle of Common Concern of Humankind' in Thomas Cottier (ed) *The Prospects of Common Concern of Humankind in International Law* (Cambridge University Press, 2021)

—, Nartova O and Shingal A, 'The Potential of Tariff Policy for Climate Change Mitigation: Legal and Economic Analysis' (2014) 48(5) Journal of World Trade 1007

— and Payosova T, 'Common Concern and Legitimacy of the WTO in Dealing with Climate Change' in Panagiotis Delimatsis (ed) *Research Handbook on Climate Change and Trade* (Edward Elgar 2016)

Cui L and others, 'How Policy Preferences Affect the Carbon Shadow Price in the OECD' (2022) 311 Applied Energy 1 <https://doi.org/10.1016/j.apenergy.2022.118686>

Culot H, 'Unilateral Sanctions in International Economic Law' in T Cottier and K Nadakavukaren Schefer (eds), *Elgar Encyclopedia of International Economic Law* (Edward Elgar 2017)

Dessler AE and EA Parson, *The Science and Politics of Global Climate Change: A Guide to the Debate* (3rd edn, Cambridge University Press 2020)

Dietz T, Ostrom E and Stern PC, 'The Struggle to Govern the Commons' (2003) 302(5652) Science 1907 <https://doi.org/10.1126/science.1091015>

Dominioni G and Esty D, 'Designing Effective Border-Carbon Adjustment Mechanisms: Aligning the Global Trade and Climate Change Regimes' (2023) 65(1) Arizona Law Review

Domorenok E and Graziano P, 'Understanding the European Green Deal: A Narrative Policy Framework Approach' (2023) 9 Eur Policy Anal 9, <https://doi.org/10.1002/epa2.1168>

Dorsch MJ and Flachsland C, 'A Polycentric Approach to Global Climate Governance' (2017) 17 Global Environmental Politics 45 <https://doi.org/10.1162/GLEP_a_00400>

Dreher A and Lang VF, 'The Political Economy of International Organizations' in R Congleton, B Grofman and S Voigt (eds), *The Oxford Handbook of Public Choice* (2nd edn, Oxford University Press 2019

Dreher A and Voigt S, 'Does Membership in International Organizations Increase Governments' Credibility? Testing the Effects of Delegating Powers' (2011) 39 Journal of Comparative Economics 326

Dryzek JS, 'Global Environmental Governance' in Teena Gabrielson and others (eds), *The Oxford Handbook of Environmental Political Theory* (Oxford University Press 2016)

Eckersley R, 'Moving Forward in the Climate Negotiations: Multilateralism or Minilateralism?' (2012) 12(2) Global Environmental Politics 24 <https://doi.org/10.1162/GLEP_a_00107>

Epley N and Gilovich T, 'The Mechanics of Motivated Reasoning' (2016) 30 Journal of Economic Perspectives 133, <https://doi.org/10.1257/jep.30.3.133>

Espa I, and Holzer K, 'From Unilateral Border Carbon Adjustments to Cooperation in Climate Clubs: Rethinking Exclusion in Light of Trade and Climate Law Constraints' in J. Bäumler and others (eds), European Yearbook of International Economic Law 2022 (vol 13, Springer, 2023) <https://doi.org/10.1007/8165_2022_101>

European Environmental Agency, *Economic Losses and Fatalities from Weather- and Climate-Related Events in Europe Briefing no. 21/2021* (TH-AM-21-018-EN-Q, 2021)

Falkner R, 'A Minilateral Solution for Global Climate Change? On Bargaining Efficiency, Club Benefits, and International Legitimacy' (2016) 14 Perspectives on Politics 87.

—, Naghmeh Nasiritousi and Gunilla Reischl 'Climate Clubs: Politically Feasible and Desirable?' (2021) Climate Policy 1 <https://doi.org/10.1080/14693062.2021.1967717>

Faure M, 'Economics' in L Rajamani and J Peel (eds), *The Oxford Handbook of International Environmental Law* (2nd edn, Oxford Handbooks 2021)

— and Partain RA, *Environmental Law and Economics: Theory and Practice* (Cambridge University Press 2019)

Faust F, 'Comparative Law and Economic Analysis of Law' in Mathias Reimann and Reinhard Zimmermann (eds), *The Oxford Handbook of Comparative Law* (2nd edn, Oxford Handbooks 2019)

Fontagné L and Schubert K, 'The Economics of Border Carbon Adjustment: Rationale and Impacts of Compensating for Carbon at the Border' (2023) 15 Annual Review of Economics 389, <https://doi.org/10.1146/annurev-economics-082322-034040>

Gampfer R, 'Minilateralism or the UNFCCC? The Political Feasibility of Climate Clubs' (2016) 16(3) Global Environmental Politics

Garoupa N and Ginsburg T, 'Economic Analysis and Comparative Law' in M Bussani and U Mattei (eds), *The Cambridge Companion to Comparative Law* (Cambridge University Press 2012)

Ghaleigh NS 'Economics and International Climate Change Law' in KR Gray (ed), *The Oxford Handbook of International Climate Change Law* (Oxford University Press 2016)

Giddens A, *The Politics of Climate Change* (Polity Press, 2011)

Gough I and Meadowcroft J, 'Decarbonizing the Welfare State' in JS Dryzek and others (eds), *The Oxford Handbook of Climate Change and Society* (Oxford University Press 2012)

Greenwald B and Stiglitz J, 'Externalities in Economies with Imperfect Information and Incomplete Markets' (1986) 101 Quarterly Journal of Economics 229 <https://doi.org/10.2307/1891114>

Hagen A and Schneider J, 'Boon or Bane? Trade Sanctions and the Stability of International Environmental Agreements', (2017) 5 Oldenburg Discussion Papers in Economics 403

Hardin G, 'The Tragedy of the Commons' (1968) 162 Science 1243

Hayward T, 'Climate Change and Ethics' (2012) 2(12) Nature Climate Change 843

Helm D, Hepburn C and Ruta G, 'Trade, Climate Change, and the Political Game Theory of Border Carbon Adjustments' 28 (2012) Oxf Rev Econ Policy 368

Holzer K, 'Proposals on Carbon-related Border Adjustment: Prospects for WTO Compliance' (2010) 4 Carbon and Climate Law Review 14 <https://doi.org/10.21552/CCLR/2010/1/127>

Hovi J, Skodvin T and Aakre S, 'Can Climate Change Negotiations Succeed' (2013) 1 Politics and Governance 138 <https://doi.org/10.12924/PAG2013.01020138>

Intergovernmental Panel on Climate Change (IPCC), *Special Report: Global Warming of 1.5 °C Summary for Policymakers* (2018).

— 'Summary for Policymakers in Climate Change 2022: Mitigation of Climate Change. Contribution of Working Group III to the Sixth Assessment Report of the Intergovernmental Panel on Climate Change' (2022)<https://www.ipcc.ch/report/ar6/wg3/downloads/report/IPCC_AR6_WGIII_SummaryForPolicymakers.pdf> accessed 24 March 2024

— 'IPCC Sixth Assessment Report: Mitigation of Climate Change' (2022) <https://www.ipcc.ch/report/ar6/wg3/downloads/report/IPCC_AR6_WGIII_SPM.pdf> accessed 15 March 2024

— *Climate Change 2023: Synthesis Report. Contribution of Working Groups I, II and III to the Sixth Assessment Report of the Intergovernmental Panel on Climate Change Summary for Policymakers* (2023)

International Energy Agency (IEA), 'CO2 Emissions from Fuel Combustion' (2020) <https://doi.org/10.1787/co2-data-en>

— Renewable Energy Market Update: Outlook for 2023 and 2024, (OECD Publishing Paris 2023), <https://doi-org.ezproxy.uzh.ch/10.1787/89017c62-en>

Jakob M, 'Introduction' in Micheal Jakob (eds) *Handbook on Trade Policy and Climate Change* (Edward Elgar, 2022)

Kaufmann C and Weber RH, 'Carbon-Related Border Tax Adjustments: Mitigating Climate Change or Restricting International Trade?' (2011) 10 World Trade Rev 497

Keohane RO, 'The Demand for International Regimes' (1982) 36(2) International Organization 325

—and Victor DG, 'The Regime Complex for Climate Change' (2011) 9(1) Perspectives on Politics

Lancaster KJ, 'A New Approach to Consumer Theory' (1966) 74 Journal of Political Economy 132

Lawrence RZ, 'Rulemaking Amidst Growing Diversity: A Club-of-Clubs Approach to WTO Reform and New Issue Selection' (2006) 9(4) Journal of International Economic Law 823

Lim S and Duit A, 'Partisan Politics, Welfare States, and Environmental Policy Outputs in the OECD Countries, 1975-2005', (2018) 12 Regulation and Governance.

Lloyd P, 'The Variable Geometry Approach to International Economic Integration' (2009) 1(1) International Journal of Business and Development Studies 51

Mayer B, *The International Law on Climate Change* (Cambridge University Press 2018)

McCright A, and Riley D, 'The Politicization of Climate Change and Polarization in the American Public's Views of Global Warming, 2001–2010' (2011) 52(2) Sociological Quarterly 155

McEvoy DM and Stranlund JK, 'Self-enforcing International Environmental Agreements with Costly Monitoring for Compliance' (2009) 42(4) Environmental and Resource Economics 491

Meckling J and Nahm J, 'Strategic State Capacity: How States Counter Opposition to Climate Policy' (2022) 55(3) Comparative Political Studies 493

Mehling M, 'Implementing Climate Governance: Instrument Choice and Interaction' in EJ Hollo, K Kulovesi and M Mehling (eds), *Climate Change and the Law* (Springer 2013)

Moisés N, 'Minilateralism: The Magic Number to Get Real International Action' (2009) Foreign Policy 173

Monastj JJ, 'The Ends and Means of Decarbonization: The Green New Deal in Context' (2020) 50(1) Envtl L 21

Musselli I, Cottier T, and Bonanomi EB, *SECO Roundtable on Trade, Climate Change, and the SDGs* (CDE/WTI summary report, Bern, Switzerland, 23 June 2021) 06

Nordhaus W, 'Reflections on the Economics of Climate Change' (1993) 7(4) Journal of Economic Perspectives 11.

— 'Geography and Macroeconomics: New Data and New Findings' (2006) 103(10) Proceedings of the National Academy of Sciences 3510.

—*The Climate Casino: Risk, Uncertainty, and Economics for a Warming World* (Yale University Press, 2013).

— *A Question of Balance: Weighing the Options on Global Warming Policies* (Yale University Press 2014).

— 'Climate Clubs: Overcoming Free-Riding in International Climate Policy' (2015) 105(4) American Economic Review 1339.

— 'Climate Change: The Ultimate Challenge for Economics' (2019) 109(6) American Economic Review 1991 <https://doi.org/10.1257/aer.109.6.1991>.

— 'The Climate Club: How to Fix a Failing Global Effort' (2020) 20 Journal of Environmental Economics and Policy 1.

— 'Dynamic Climate Clubs: On the Effectiveness of Incentives in Global Climate Agreements', (2021) 118 (45) Proceedings of the National Academy of Sciences, <https://doi.org/10.1073/pnas.2109988118>

Oberthür S and Dupont C, 'The European Union's International Climate Leadership: Towards a Grand Climate Strategy?' (2021) 28 J Eur Public Policy 1095 <https://doi.org/10.1080/13501763.2021.1918218>

Organization for Economic Cooperation and Development (OECD), *Climate Policy Leadership in an Interconnected World: What Role for Border Carbon Adjustments?* (2020)

Ostrom E, 'Collective Action and the Evolution of Social Norms' (2000) 14(3) Journal of Economic Perspectives 137

— 'A Polycentric Approach for Coping with Collective Action and Global Climate Change' (2010) 20(4) Global Environmental Change 550

Partain RA, 'Climate Change, Green Paradox Models and International Trade Rules' in P Delimatsis (ed) *Research Handbook on Climate Change and Trade* (Edward Elgar Publishing 2016)

Paterson M 'Who and What are Carbon Markets for? Politics and the Development of Climate Policy' (2012) 12(1) Climate Policy 82, <https://doi.org/10.1080/14693062.2011.579259>

Pauwelyn J, 'Trade Related Aspects of a Carbon Border Adjustment Mechanism. A Legal Assessment' in *Four Briefings on Trade-Related Aspects of Carbon Border Adjustment Mechanisms* (Directorate-General for External Policies of the Union, Strasbourg, France 2020)

Petersen N and Towfigh EV, 'Economic Methods and Legal Reasoning' in EV Towfigh and N Petersen *Economic Methods for Lawyers* (Edward Elgar Publishing 2015)

Petersmann EU, 'Multi-Level Governance and Public Goods' in T Cottier and K Nadakavukaren Schefer (eds), *Elgar Encyclopedia of International Economic Law* (Edward Elgar 2017)

Pigou AC, *The Economics of Welfare* (Macmillan 1920)

Posner RA, 'The Economic Approach to Law' (1975) 53 Texas Law Review 757

— 'The Ethical and Political Basis of the Efficiency Norm in Common Law Adjudication' (1981) 9 Hofstra L Rev 775, 780

— *Economic Analysis of Law* (Aspen Legal Education 2014)

— and Weisbach D, *Climate Change Justice* (Princeton University Press 2015)

Potoski M and Prakash A, 'Green Clubs: Collective Action and Voluntary Environmental Programs' (2013) 16 Annual Review of Political Science 399

Puaschunder JM, 'Mapping Climate in the Twenty-First Century' (2016) 59 Development 211 <https://doi.org/10.1057/s41301-017-0110-0.>

Rajamani L, 'Differentiation in the Emerging Climate Regime' (2013) 14 Theoretical Inquiries in Law 152 <https://doi.org/10.1515/til-2013-009>

— 'Understanding the 2015 Paris Agreement' in NK Dubash (ed), *India in a Warming World: Integrating Climate Change and Development* (Oxford University Press 2019)

Schneider L and La Hoz Theuer S, 'Environmental Integrity of International Carbon Market Mechanisms Under the Paris Agreement' (2019) 19(3) Climate Policy 386

Schröder M, 'Precautionary Approach/Principle' in *Max Planck Encyclopaedia of Public International Law* (2014)

Shavell S, 'Law and Economics' in *International Encyclopaedia of the Social & Behavioural Sciences* (2001)

Shoyer A, Sul J, and van der Ven C, 'Carbon Leakage and the Migration of Private CO2 Emitters to other Jurisdictions' in KR Gray and others (eds), *The Oxford Handbook of International Climate Change Law* (Oxford University Press 2016)

Soltau F, *Fairness in International Climate Change Law and Policy* (Cambridge University Press 2009).

Sterk W and others, *Submission to the Ad Hoc Working Group on the Durban Platform for Enhanced Action Workstream 1: The 2015 Agreement* (Wuppertal Institute for Climate, Environment, and Energy 2013)

Stern N, *The Economics of Climate Change: The Stern Review* (Cambridge University Press 2007)

— 'The Economics of Climate Change' (2008) 98(2) The American Economic Review 1

— 'Ethics, Equity and The Economics of Climate Change Paper 2: Economics and Politics' (2014) 30 Economics and Philosophy 445

— and Lankes HP, *Collaborating and Delivering on Climate Action Through a Climate Club: An Independent Report to the G7* (London School of Economics and Political Science, 2022)

Stewart RB, Oppenheimer M, and Rudyk B, 'Building Blocks for Global Climate Protection' (2013) 32(2) Stan Envti LJ 351

—, 'A New Strategy for Global Climate Protection' (2013) 120 Climatic Change 1

Stiglitz J and Stern N, 'Report of the High-Level Commission on Carbon Prices' (The World Bank 2017) <www.carbonpricingleadership.org/report-of-the-highlevel-commission-on-carbon-prices/> accessed 22 April 2024

Sun H and others, 'Energy Efficiency: The Role of Rechnological Innovation and Knowledge Spillover' (2021) Technological Forecasting and Social Change <https://doi.org/10.1016/J.TECHFORE.2021.120659>

Sussman F, Weaver CP and Grambsch A, 'Challenges in Applying the Paradigm of Welfare Economics to Climate Change' (2014) 5(3) Journal of Benefit-Cost Analysis 347, <https://doi.org/10.1515/jbca-2014-9001>

Tagliapietra S and Wolff GB, 'Conditions are Ideal for a New Climate Club' (2021) 158 Energy Policy 112527 <https://doi.org/10.1016/j.enpol.2021.112527>

Tietenberg T, 'Economic Analysis and Climate Change' (1998) 3(3) Environment and Development Economics 347 <https://doi.org/10.1017/S1355770X98320197>

Towfigh EV and Petersen N, 'Public and Social Choice Theory' in EV Towfigh and N Petersen *Economic Methods for Lawyers* (Edward Elgar Publishing 2015)

Trachtman J, 'The Theory of the Firm and the Theory of the International Economic Organization: Toward Comparative Institutional Analysis' (1996) 17 Northwestern Journal of International Law & Business 470

— 'WTO Law Constraints on Carbon Credit Mechanisms and Export Border Tax Adjustment' in P Delimatsis (ed) *Research Handbook on Climate Change and Trade* (Edward Elgar 2016)

Unger C, Khan M and Gürtler K, 'A Club's Contribution to Global Climate Governance: The Case of the Climate and Clean Air Coalition' (2020) 6 Palgrave Commun. 99

Van Aaken A, 'Behavioral Aspects of the International Law of Global Public Goods and Common Pool Resources' (2018) 112(1) The American Journal of International Law 67

Van Asselt H and others, 'The Changing Architecture of International Climate Change Law' in G Van Calster, W Vandenberghe and L Reins (eds), *Research Handbook on Climate Change Mitigation Law* (Edward Elgar 2015)

Van den Bergh J and others, 'A Dual-Track Transition to Global Carbon Pricing' (2020) Climate Policy, <https://doi.org/10.1080/14693062.2020.1797618>

Verbruggen A, 'A Turbo Drive for the Global Reduction of Energy-related CO2 Emissions' (2011) 3 Sustainability 632

Victor DG, 'Toward Effective International Cooperation on Climate Change: Numbers, Interests and Institutions' (2006) 6(3) Global Environmental Politics 90 <https://doi.org/10.1162/glep.2006.6.3.90>

—, *Global Warming Gridlock: Creating More Effective Strategies for Protecting the Planet* (Cambridge University Press 2011)

Vogler J, 'Energy, Climate Change, and Global Governance: The 2015 Paris Agreement in Perspective' in Debra J. Davidson and Matthias Gross (eds), *Oxford Handbook of Energy and Society* (Oxford University Press 2018)

Weber RA, 'Managing Growth to Achieve Efficient Coordination in Large Groups' (2006) 96(1) American Economic Review

Weber RH 'Emission Trading Schemes: A Coasean Answer to Climate Change?' in K Mathis and BR Huber (eds), *Environmental Law and Economics* (4th edn Springer, 2017)

Weischer L, Morgan J, and Patel M, 'Climate Clubs: Can Small Groups of Countries Make a Big Difference in Addressing Climate Change?' (2012) 21(3) Review of European Community & International Environmental Law 177

Will U, Climate *Border Adjustments and WTO Law Extending the EU Emissions Trading System to Imported Goods and Services* (Boston: Brill Nijhoff, 2019)

World Resources Institute, 'Interactive Chart Shows Changes in the World's Top 10 Emitters' <https://www.wri.org/insights/interactive-chart-shows-changes-worlds-top-10-emitters> accessed 17 March 2024

World Trade Organization (WTO), and United Nations Environment Programme Report *Trade and Climate Change* (World Trade Organization, Geneva, 2009)

Young MA, 'Trade Measures to Address Climate Change: Territory and Extraterritoriality' in P Delimatsis (ed) *Research Handbook on Climate Change and Trade* (Edward Elgar Publishing 2016)
Zhang K and others, 'Impacts of Mechanisms to Promote Participation in Climate Mitigation: Border Carbon Adjustments Versus Uniform Tariff Measures' (2020) 11 Clim. Change Econ. 2041007.

Open Access This chapter is licensed under the terms of the Creative Commons Attribution 4.0 International License (http://creativecommons.org/licenses/by/4.0/), which permits use, sharing, adaptation, distribution and reproduction in any medium or format, as long as you give appropriate credit to the original author(s) and the source, provide a link to the Creative Commons license and indicate if changes were made.

The images or other third party material in this chapter are included in the chapter's Creative Commons license, unless indicated otherwise in a credit line to the material. If material is not included in the chapter's Creative Commons license and your intended use is not permitted by statutory regulation or exceeds the permitted use, you will need to obtain permission directly from the copyright holder.

Chapter 2
Existing Landscape of International Climate Law

1 Political and Economic Background of Climate Change

1.1 Introduction

Historically, the international community's response to climate change has evolved from initial scepticism to widespread recognition of its urgency.[1] Accordingly, the political and economic discourses on climate change are developed and deeply intertwined.[2] Politically, climate change is a contentious issue that requires global cooperation and commitment. By gaining importance in the global agenda,[3] climate change has moved from the periphery to the centre of international diplomacy. However, it is often challenged by national interests and geopolitical dynamics. Economically, climate change presents a significant threat to traditional industries but also constitutes an opportunity for innovation and growth of green economies.[4] Climate change is equally an economic and environmental issue, rendering various international economic institutions highly pertinent to international climate governance. Moreover, the costs of climate inaction have become increasingly apparent. The transition towards sustainable development models highlights the growing need for integrated approaches that do not compromise economic growth for environmental sustainability.[5]

---

[1] Lavanya Rajamani and Jacob Werksman, 'Climate Change' in Lavanya Rajamani and Jacqueline Peel (eds), *The Oxford Handbook of International Environmental Law* (2nd edn, Oxford University Press 2021) 495.

[2] William Nordhaus, 'Climate Change: The Ultimate Challenge for Economics' (2019) 109(6) American Economic Review 1991, 1994 <https://doi.org/10.1257/aer.109.6.1991>.

[3] Rajamani and Werksman (n 1) 492.

[4] Benoit Mayer, *The International Law on Climate Change* (Cambridge University Press 2018), 25.

[5] Lin Zhang and others, 'Globalization, Green Economy and Environmental Challenges: State of the Art Review for Practical Implications' (2022) Frontiers in Environmental Science.

© The Author(s) 2025

T. G. Budak, *Beyond Treaties: Rethinking Legal Mechanisms for International Climate Governance*, https://doi.org/10.1007/978-3-031-86022-5_2

Therefore, the importance of understanding the political and economic background of climate change cannot be overstated in analysing legal frameworks for climate governance.[6] Clearly, the governance landscape is in a state of flux, with more actors participating in a greater variety of activities across significantly more levels of governance.[7] The political and economic background provides a direction for analysing the feasibility of proposed climate policies, understanding the motivations behind political decisions, and evaluating the economic implications of climate action or inaction. Only then legal mechanisms can translate political agreements and economic incentives into actionable and accountable measures. By understanding the challenges inherent in politics and economics, legal frameworks can be designed to support climate governance effectively.

1.2 Evolution of Political and Economic Discourses

The journey of recognizing and responding to climate change has been a complex evolution of science, politics, and economics.[8] The recognition of climate change as a global issue has evolved significantly over the past few decades.[9] Initially considered a fringe scientific theory, the evidence of climate change and its potential impacts has gradually become undeniable.[10] Therefore, it prompts political and economic responses worldwide. However, it was not until the latter half of the 20th century that the broader scientific community began to acknowledge human activities, especially burning fossil fuels, as a significant driver of global warming.[11] Since then, climate change has transitioned from a purely scientific inquiry to an urgent political issue.

---

[6] Climate governance involves the creation of institutions – rules, organisations and policies – that seek to stabilise (or govern) behaviours associated with climate change. The term governance thus describes the patterns that emerge from the governing activities of social, political and administrative actors. Jan Kooiman, *Governing and Governance* (Sage 1993), 2.

[7] Michele Betsill and others 'Building Productive Links between the UNFCCC and the Broader Global Climate Governance Landscape' (2015) 15(2) Global Environmental Politics 1, 8.

[8] Mayer, *The International Law on Climate Change* (n 4) 19.

[9] Nordhaus, 'Climate Change: The Ultimate Challenge for Economics' (n 2) 1996.

[10] Spencer Weart, 'The Development of the Concept of Dangerous Anthropogenic Climate Change' in John S Dryzek and others (eds), *The Oxford Handbook of Climate Change and Society* (Oxford University Press 2011), 70.

[11] For example, CO_2 concentrations in the atmosphere were 280 parts per million (ppm) in 1750 and reached more than 413 ppm in 2018. Nordhaus, Climate Change: The Ultimate Challenge for Economics (n 2) 1996.

Nevertheless, decision-making in climate change is complex primarily due to three fundamental reasons.[12] The first one is its slow process.[13] Compared to other environmental challenges, the impacts of climate change are experienced later in time, and any action for combatting it brings fruitful results in the long term. Second, human activities resulting to climate change are at the core of world economies.[14] Like in other environmental challenges, simple technological corrections or mere incremental policy adjustments are not enough to address the issue. The most significant contributor to climate change is burning fossil fuels, which supply 82% of the world's energy needs.[15] Also, agriculture, deforestation and various other industrial processes contribute to climate change. The vast scale and societal importance of these activities require a substantial economic and technological revolution.[16] However, this change will create a significant economic burden on the sectors associated with high levels of GHG emissions.[17] Finally, there is still a biased attitude towards the certainty of climate change.[18] Some governments perceive it as an unserious problem. Therefore, climate change commands the widespread attention of the international community to bring an effective policy package.

The journey to recognize and address global warming traces back to the early 1980s when scientific organizations urged governments to consider the environmental implications of GHG emissions.[19] A landmark in this evolving recognition was the establishment of the IPCC by the UN in 1988. The IPCC is an intergovernmental body, carrying out a scientific assessment function; participation is open to all member countries of the United Nations Environment Programme (UNEP) and the World Meteorological Organization (WMO).[20] The IPCC has been instrumental in assessing scientific information related to climate change, evaluating its impacts,

[12] Andrew E Dessler and Edward A Parson, *The Science and Politics of Global Climate Change: A Guide to the Debate* (3rd edn, Cambridge University Press 2020), 3.

[13] Steinar Andresen, 'International Climate Negotiations: Top-Down, Bottom-Up or a Combination of Both?' (2015) 50(1) The International Spectator 15.

[14] Ian Gough and James Meadowcroft, 'Decarbonizing the Welfare State' in John S Dryzek and others (eds), *The Oxford Handbook of Climate Change and Society* (Oxford University Press 2012), 490.

[15] Energy Institute, 'Statistical Review of World Energy 2023' (2023), 3 <https://www.energyinst.org/statistical-review/resources-and-data-downloads> accessed 21 June 2024.

[16] Donald Huisingh and others, 'Recent Advances in Carbon Emissions Reduction: Policies, Technologies, Monitoring, Assessment and Modeling' (2015) 103 Journal of Cleaner Production 1 <https://doi.org/10.1016/J.JCLEPRO.2015.04.098>.

[17] Rajamani and Werksman (n 1) 495.

[18] Weart (n 10) 75.

[19] David Hirst, 'Negotiating Climates: The Politics of Climate Change and the Formation of the Intergovernmental Panel on Climate Change (IPCC), 1979-1992' (2014) <https://pure.manchester.ac.uk/ws/portalfiles/portal/54560421/FULL_TEXT.PDF> accessed 5 July 2024.

[20] World Meteorological Organization (WMO), *Thirty-Ninth Session of the Executive Council, General Summary 3.4 (1–5 June 1987)* (UNEP Governing Council, Decision 14/20, 17 June 1987).

and suggesting potential adaptation and mitigation strategies.[21] Comprising hundreds of scientists divided into three working groups, the IPCC's role encompasses a broad spectrum of climate change-related science.[22] Its work has culminated in the publication of six comprehensive assessment reports as of 2024, which are widely recognized as the most authoritative evaluations of scientific knowledge regarding climate change to date. These reports play a crucial role in informing the global climate change policy agenda, both at national and international levels.

The establishment of the IPCC marked a significant step towards acknowledging climate change as an issue that necessitates global cooperation and policy action. This recognition has led to the adopting of key international climate agreements such as the UNFCCC, the Kyoto Protocol, and the Paris Agreement. Each of these agreements seek and utilize information provided by the international organizations (e.g. IPCC)[23] and aims to unite countries in a global effort to mitigate climate change impacts and adapt to its unavoidable consequences. The IPCC's scientific assessments are vital for guiding climate policy, providing a clear understanding of the current state of scientific knowledge, potential future risks, and strategies for mitigation and adaptation.[24] The initiative underscores the global consensus on the need for an informed and coordinated approach to tackle climate change, highlighting the critical role of science in shaping effective climate policies and international cooperation.

Furthermore, the economic implications of climate change and its mitigation have been increasingly recognized over time. Early discussions focused primarily on the costs of reducing GHG emissions, often framed as a trade-off between environmental sustainability and economic growth.[25] However, as the impacts of climate change became more apparent, the economic discourse shifted towards the cost of inaction, highlighting the potential for severe economic consequences if climate change remained unaddressed.[26] This period also saw the emergence of the green

[21] Friedrich Soltau, *Fairness in International Climate Change Law and Policy* (Cambridge University Press 2009), 34.

[22] Dessler and Parson (n 12) 27.

[23] UNFCCC, art 7(2)(l). IPCC reports are referenced in several COP meetings as the best available scientific information. Although the COPs were not legally bound to adhere to the recommendations of the IPCC, in practice, UNFCCC decision-making processes treated the IPCC as unparalleled in its expertise, independence, and authority. Navraj Singh Ghaleigh, 'Science and Climate Change Law-The Role of the IPCC in International Decision-Making' in Kevin R Gray and others (eds), *The Oxford Handbook of International Climate Change Law* (Oxford University Press 2016) 61.

[24] ibid 67. John Vogler, 'Energy, Climate Change, and Global Governance: The 2015 Paris Agreement in Perspective' in Debra J. Davidson and Matthias Gross (eds), *Oxford Handbook of Energy and Society* (Oxford University Press 2018), 25.

[25] Kenneth Gillingham, 'The True Cost of Reducing Greenhouse Gas Emissions' (IMF Finance & Development 2019) <https://www.imf.org/external/chinese/pubs/ft/fandd/2019/12/pdf/the-true-cost-of-reducing-greenhouse-gas-emissions-gillingham.pdf> accessed 5 July 2024.

[26] HD Matthews and others, 'Assessing the Costs of Historical Inaction on Climate Change' (2018) 8(1) Scientific Reports 1. Mayer, *The International Law on Climate Change* (n 4) 7.

economy concept, which explores the compatibility of economic growth and environmental sustainability.[27] Accordingly, investments in renewable energy, energy efficiency, and other low-carbon technologies have been identified as drivers of economic development, job creation, and innovation.[28]

The evolution of political and economic discussions on climate change underscores a pivotal shift in global approaches to this pressing issue. The narrative has transitioned from the scientific acknowledgement of global warming to intricate debates on the necessity for urgent, collective action.[29] The new climate governance framework relies on national pledges, hence necessitates ongoing efforts and steadfast dedication from both developed and developing countries.[30] Central to these discussions is the concept of "action", which encapsulates the essence of the global climate governance. Defining "action" involves analysing the response to climate change, the effort's stringency, financial commitments, the type of measures and the distribution of the related cost among the members of the international community.[31] Overall, these facets of the action are at the forefront of shaping the political and legal frameworks for climate change mitigation and adaptation.

Consequently, the dialogue on climate governance is currently navigating these critical aspects, striving to formulate effective strategies for the future. The focus is on identifying actionable steps that can be taken within the constraints of political willingness and economic viability, ensuring that efforts are both impactful and sustainable.[32] The journey from recognition to action reflects the collective determination to confront climate change. It underscores the imperative for continued dialogue, innovation, and collaboration in the face of one of the world's most daunting challenges. Particularly, deepening the notion of climate governance involves understanding it as a complex, multi-level, and interdisciplinary framework. The legal instruments discussed below sections—such as the UNFCCC, the Paris Agreement, minilateral approaches like climate clubs, and national frameworks like the EU Green Deal—are integral to the operationalization of climate governance. They provide the legal foundation and mechanisms through which climate governance is implemented, ensuring that efforts to address climate change are both legally binding and globally coordinated. These instruments also illustrate how climate governance is evolving to meet the challenges of the 21st century,

[27] International Law Commission, *2018 Report of the Committee on Sustainable Development and the Green Economy in International Trade Law* paras 105-108.

[28] Shi Chen and Qingfei Yang, 'Renewable Energy Technology Innovation and Urban Green Economy Efficiency' (2024) Journal of Environmental Management 120130.

[29] Vogler (n 24) 17.

[30] Jale Tosun and Jonas J Schoenefeld, 'Collective Climate Action and Networked Climate Governance' (2017) 8 WIREs Clim Change, 1.

[31] Dessler and Parson (n 12) 35.

[32] Ifigenia Paliampelou, 'Chapter 5: Net Zero Targets and Governance: A Literature Review (2009-2021)' in *Handbook on Corporate Governance and Corporate Social Responsibility* (Edward Elgar Publishing 2024), 50.

emphasizing the need for innovative, flexible, and inclusive approaches to global environmental governance.

1.3 Regulatory Outcomes

The prevailing scientific consensus underscores an urgent need for transformative climate governance approaches that overhaul the entire economy.[33] The structure of international climate agreements is based on the principle of national consent,[34] which means that countries voluntarily commit to emission reduction targets and climate action plans. Hence, to ensure widespread participation and ambitious climate action, international climate regimes are designed to offer incentives for compliance[35] and set penalties at levels low enough to encourage the adoption of ambitious targets. This delicate balance aims to attract the maximum number of governments to commit to international climate efforts[36] without imposing overly burdensome obligations that might deter participation.

During international policy negotiations, countries work towards reaching a consensus on the specifics of national regulations designed to curb emissions.[37] These discussions also cover how to distribute the costs associated with climate action fairly, which is comprised of financial and responsibility aspects across different countries and over time.[38] Fairness in cost distribution is crucial for maintaining international cooperation and ensuring that countries with varying capacities and development levels can contribute effectively to global climate goals. Moreover, to remain responsive to evolving scientific knowledge and technological advancements, the international climate policy framework must include mechanisms for regular assessment and adjustment of national commitments and strategies.[39] Therefore, the legal instruments should not be static, instead they should continuously evolve to meet the ever-changing climate challenges. Climate governance must be innovative, adaptable, and inclusive, reflecting the diverse needs and

[33] Paul G. Harris, 'Reconceptualizing Global Governance' in John S. Dryzek and others (eds), *The Oxford Handbook of Climate Change and Society* (Oxford University Press 2011), 641.

[34] Jutta Brunnée, 'Consent' in *Max Planck Encyclopaedia of Public International Law* (2022), para 1.

[35] Scott Barrett, 'Climate Treaties and the Imperative of Enforcement' (2008) 24 Oxford Review of Economic Policy 239, 242 <https://doi.org/10.1093/oxrep/grn015>.

[36] Ibid.

[37] Delali Benjamin K Dovie and Shuaib Lwasa, 'Correlating Negotiation Hotspot Issues, Paris Climate Agreement and the International Climate Policy Regime' (2017) 77 Environmental Science & Policy 1.

[38] Dessler and Parson (n 12) 146.

[39] Giulia Claudia Leonelli, 'Carbon Border Measures, Environmental Effectiveness and WTO Compatibility: Is There a Way Forward for the Steel and Aluminium Carbon Club?' (2022) 21(5) World Trade Review, 630.

circumstances of different countries and regions. This evolution is evident in the growing emphasis on interdisciplinary approaches, which recognize the interconnectedness of environmental, economic, and social factors in addressing climate change.

In conclusion, the political and economic backgrounds of climate change not only inform our understanding of its complexities but also guide the strategies for its mitigation and adaptation. In light of these challenges, the design of climate governance frameworks should prioritize inclusivity and the capacity to drive higher levels of ambition in climate mitigation efforts. Emphasizing practical and effective linkages among jurisdictions will also be essential as they optimize the global response to climate change. Given that international regime will not fully achieve climate governance, currently the concept of polycentric governance is evident in practice,[40] as various international institutions, beyond the UNFCCC, govern climate change both directly and indirectly.[41] This allows for a more flexible and adaptive approach to climate action, enabling various stakeholders to address specific aspects of climate change in ways that align with their unique capabilities and interests. Still, UNFCCC has been the cornerstone for international climate efforts for over a quarter of a century, guiding global negotiations and setting the framework for concerted action against climate change. Therefore, alternative approaches can build upon the established momentum, filling gaps and addressing challenges within the current framework.

2 United Nations Framework Convention on Climate Change

2.1 *Foundation and Main Concepts*

The body of international environmental law, which encompasses customary international law as well as general principles, laid the groundwork for climate change law. Nonetheless, climate change law established its distinct identity following the conclusion of the UNFCCC.[42] The UN climate regime has high legitimacy and near-universal membership, which gives it a status of "having no alternative".[43] The UN

[40] Elinor Ostrom, 'A Polycentric Approach for Coping with Collective Action and Global Climate Change' (2010) 20(4) Global Environmental Change 550.

[41] Harro van Asselt and Fariborz Zelli, 'International Governance: Polycentric Governing by and beyond the UNFCCC' in Andrew Jordan and others (eds), *Governing Climate Change: Polycentricity in Action?* (Cambridge University Press 2018), 32.

[42] Cinnamon P Carlarne, Kevin R Gray and Richard Tarasofsky, 'International Climate Change Law: Mapping the Field' in Kevin R Gray and others (eds), *The Oxford Handbook of International Climate Change Law* (Oxford University Press, 2016) 7.

[43] Camilla Bausch and Micheal Mehling, 'Alternative Venues of Climate Cooperation: An Institutional Perspective' in Erkki J Hollo, Kati Kulovesi, Michael Mehling (eds.) *Climate Change*

operates classical multilateralism in climate change law with its framework convention, namely UNFCCC.[44] It was adopted in 1992 at the Rio Conference on Environment and Development and entered into force in 1994. The Convention is the product of a coordinated global effort against climate change. UNFCCC highlights that 'climate change is a common concern of mankind'[45] and frames climate change as a matter necessitating international collaboration. Consequently, the UNFCCC recognizes that "the global nature of climate change demands the broadest possible cooperation from all countries and their engagement in an effective and appropriate international response",[46] a statement that has been echoed extensively in customary obligation of cooperation.[47] With its 198 ratifiers, it is one of the most signed international treaties.[48] It creates an international scene for reporting the effects of climate change and scientific research in its annual meetings, known as COP. Therefore, UNFCCC provides a regular and institutionalised forum for discussion. This forum generates coordination among countries with diverse interests in the core aspects of climate mitigation measures[49] and groundwork for succeeding agreements. Concrete obligations are agreed in subsequent conferences and expressed through the adoption of an agreement or a protocol.

UNFCCC regime functions more as a collective attempt to promote compliance with the no-harm principle and state responsibility under general international law.[50] These principles underscore the shared responsibility of countries to prevent actions that harm the environment and, by extension, harm other states. In this regard, states are required to exercise due diligence to prevent actions that infringe upon the rights of other states, especially the activities leading to transboundary environmental damage.[51] Therefore, the duty to mitigate climate change can be seen as a component of the general customary obligations to prevent environmental damage and to collaborate in tackling global issues.[52] The ultimate objective of the UNFCCC is to stabilise GHG concentrations in the atmosphere at a level that prevents dangerous anthropogenic interference with the climate system.[53] The Convention seeks to

and the Law (Springer 2013), 138.

[44] Thomas Cottier and Tetyana Payosova, 'Common Concern and Legitimacy of the WTO in Dealing with Climate Change' in Panagiotis Delimatsis (ed) *Research Handbook on Climate Change and Trade* (Edward Elgar 2016), 15.

[45] UNFCCC Preamble para 2.

[46] UNFCCC Preamble para 7.

[47] Benoit Mayer, *International Law Obligations on Climate Change Mitigation* (Oxford University Press 2022), 112.

[48] United Nations Framework Convention on Climate Change, 'About the Secretariat' <https://unfccc.int/about-us/about-the-secretariat> accessed 22 March 2024.

[49] Soltau (n 21) 129.

[50] Mayer, *The International Law on Climate Change* (n 12) 17. This is affirmed under the Preamble of the UNFCCC paragraph 9.

[51] Mayer, *International Law Obligations on Climate Change Mitigation* (n 47) 96.

[52] Ibid 90.

[53] UNFCCC, art 2.

achieve this objective within a sufficient time frame to allow ecosystems to adapt naturally, ensure food production continues, and enable economic development to proceed with sustainability.[54] The core underpinning of the UNFCCC is its distinctly goal-oriented nature.[55] It sets out a vision and a time-bound target for mitigating climate change, emphasising the importance of not only reducing emissions but also providing countries with the opportunity to foster economic growth that is environmentally conscious.

Bodansky remarks that the UNFCCC has the characteristics of both the framework and substantive Convention.[56] In general, framework conventions are committed to considering scientific assessment results and monitoring their programs continuously for developing additional protocols as needed.[57] UNFCCC contains general undertakings as a framework convention, whereas its succeeding protocols regulate specific undertakings. Therefore, even though the UNFCCC has neither binding emission reduction targets nor offers mechanisms for abatement, it anticipates the conclusion of agreements and protocols with a quantifiable amount of emissions reductions by a specific date.[58] In comparison, substantive conventions set legally binding common standards and goals. Therefore, under its substantive part, UNFCCC includes fundamental principles and comprehensive obligations directly applicable to the members.[59] For instance, it requests relevant data from signatories to measure, verify and report the emissions.[60] In this way, it successfully legitimises policy decisions, fosters a better understanding of global emissions trends, and defines necessary actions. Ultimately, the UNFCCC creates a normative framework that underpins ethical considerations in decision-making processes.[61]

The provisions of the Convention can be grouped under four sections. These are introductory provisions, commitments and provisions, institutions, and finally, provisions relating to amendments, entry into force, etc. The Convention introduces several principles.[62] The most prominent ones are inter-generational[63] and

---

[54] Ibid.

[55] Mayer, *The International Law on Climate Change* (n 12) 36.

[56] Daniel M Bodansky, 'The United Nations Framework Convention on Climate Change: A Commentary' (1993) 18 Yale JIL 451, 496.

[57] Peter S Thacher, 'Alternative Legal and Institutional Approaches to Global Change' (1990) 1 Colo J Int'l Envtl L & Pol'y 101, 104.

[58] UNFCCC art 17.

[59] UNFCCC arts 3 and 4.

[60] UNFCCC art 10.

[61] Carlarne, Gray and Tarasofsky (n 42) 14.

[62] Bodansky, 'A Commentary' (n 56) 458-461.

[63] Intergenerational equity encompasses the preservation of the range of choices available to future generations to pursue their own conceptions. It is harmed when resources normatively belonging to the future generations are utilized ahead of their time by the previous generations, leading to the depletion of resources for the upcoming generations. The impacts of the climate change will exacerbate in the future and the generation who do not contribute to the excessive emission levels will be the ones who bear the cost of uncontrolled industrial growth. For example, use of non-renewable resources such as petroleum, coal, gas, etc. or the excessive use of renewable resources such as

intra-generational equity,[64] common but differentiated responsibilities and respective capabilities of developed and developing countries,[65] the specific needs and special circumstances of developing country Parties,[66] precautionary approach,[67] the right to sustainable development,[68] the principle of cooperation,[69] and the promotion of a supportive and open economic system.[70] These principles guide the interpretation and implementation of the legal norms. Therefore, the key aspect of international climate law involves the ongoing modification of these general principles, guided by the progression of scientific insights.[71] Ultimately, the principles serve as a theoretical basis for the practical and binding legal rules regarding climate.[72]

Among these principles common but differentiated responsibilities (CBDR) has been a defining feature and is at the source of the climate change law's complex

clean air. Gail E Henderson, 'Rawls & Sustainable Development' (2011) 7 McGill International Journal of Sustainable Development Law and Policy 1.

[64] Intra-generational equity aims to eliminate the existing inequalities in the present society such as economic, political and social differences. Common examples may include differences based on the economy like rich and poor or societal features such as different races, castes.

[65] UNFCCC art 3 (1). Pursuant to this article, "the Parties should protect the climate system for the benefit of present and future generations of humankind, on the basis of equity and in accordance with their common but differentiated responsibilities and respective capabilities. Accordingly, the developed country Parties should take the lead in combating climate change and the adverse effects thereof".

[66] UNFCCC article 3 (2).

[67] UNFCCC art 3 (3). This principle includes the considerations of risk prevention, cost-effectiveness, ethical responsibilities towards the climate. It requires that the actions need to be taken at an early stage before the damage, pollution or environmental loss has taken place. Minna Pyhälä, Anne Brusendorff and Hanna Paulomäki 'The Precautionary Principle', in Malgosia Fitmaurice, David Ong and Panis Merkouris (eds), *Research Handbook on International Environmental Law* (Edward Elgar Publishing 2010) 203. The principle of prevention, as a customary rule, has its origin in the due diligence. *Argentina v Uruguay (Pulp Mills on the River Uruguay)* (Judgment) [2010] ICJ Rep 14, para 101. However, the principle of due diligence has a broader scope. Pierre-Marie Dupuy, Ginevra Le Moli, and Jorge E Viñuales, 'Customary International Law and the Environment' in Lavanya Rajamani and Jacqueline Peel (eds), *The Oxford Handbook of International Environmental Law* (2nd edn, Oxford University Press 2021), 394.

[68] World Commission on Environment and Development, *Our Common Future* (Oxford University Press 1987) ch II, para 1. UNFCCC art 3 (4). This principle acknowledges that climate change policies should also be integrated with national development programmes and must not be used as a means for unjustified discrimination or restriction of international trade.

[69] UNFCCC art 4 creates binding and specific cooperation duties in the development, application, diffusion, and transfer of technologies and practices to decrease carbon emissions. Also, the Article promotes information exchange on socio-economic and legal information related to climate change. The principle of cooperation is particularly relevant as climate change is caused by the cumulative effect of emissions from activities taking place in multiple States. Hence, it could not be addressed by a State alone.

[70] UNFCCC, art 3 (5). This article suggest that mitigation measure should not impose disproportionate constraints on national development policies.

[71] Dupuy, Le Moli, and Viñuales (n 67) 389.

[72] *Gentini Case (Italy v Venezuela)* Mixed Claims Commission (1903) RIAA Volume X 477-692.

institutional and decision-making structure since the 1990s.[73] In the UNFCCC, the principle was initially articulated in the Preamble and Article 3(1). The emphasis was on acknowledging the lesser obligations of developing countries, mainly due to the more negligible historical contribution to climate problem.[74] Also, developed countries higher per capita emissions reflect the need for their leadership in climate mitigation.[75] The principle underscores the idea that, while nations collectively strive for a common goal of addressing climate change, they can undertake varied obligations based on their socio-economic conditions and historical contributions to the environmental challenges.[76] With this principle, UNFCCC has solidified equity and fairness into the burden sharing. Therefore, CBDR can guide all climate change legal frameworks and justify the degree of their legal obligations.[77] It reflects the political realities and interests.

The differentiation under the CBDR principle comprises two interconnected facets. First, it involves acknowledging responsibility in proportion to a country's historical contributions to environmental challenges. This facet recognizes that countries that have historically been significant contributors to environmental degradation should bear a proportionate share of the responsibility for these consequences. This understanding of the CBDR is to hold polluters responsible, which is a fundamental principle of environmental law.[78] Second, the CBDR principle considers the capability of each country to combat climate issues effectively.[79] This facet recognizes that developed countries, equipped with advanced technological and financial resources, possess a greater ability to undertake comprehensive and impactful measures in mitigating and adapting to climate change.[80] As a result, the

[73] Ellen Hey and Sophia Paulini, 'Common but Differentiated Responsibilities' in *Max Planck Encyclopaedia of Public International Law* (2021), para 19.

[74] The developed countries have been accountable for around half of the CO_2 emissions since the mid-19th century. Nicholas Stern, 'Ethics, Equity and The Economics of Climate Change Paper 2: Economics and Politics' (2014) 30 Economics and Philosophy 445, 476.

[75] For example, the per capita emissions of the India is 1.8 and 7.4 in China, whereas it is 15.2 in the United States and 15.5 in Canada. Climate Watch, 'GHG Emissions' (World Resources Institute, 2020) <climatewatchdata.org/ghg-emissions> accessed 3 April 2024.

[76] Hey and Paulini (n 73), para 1.

[77] Ibid para 19.

[78] The polluter-pays principle suggests that the person causing adverse environmental impact should bear the consequences. Assumedly, this would encourage polluters to reduce their pollution by any means available to them. It does not necessarily require the polluter to pay all the costs in every circumstance but supports the view that polluters should be charged some fee that would dissuade them from polluting. Allan Boyle, 'Polluter Pays' in *Max Planck Encyclopaedia of Public International Law* (2009), para 1.

[79] Angela Williams, 'Promoting Justice within the International Legal System: Prospects for Climate Refugees' in Benjamin J Richardson and others (eds), *Climate Law and Developing Countries: Legal and Policy Challenges for the World Economy* (Cheltenham: Edward Elgar, 2009), 90.

[80] Hey and Paulini (n 73) para 5.

differentiation in obligations reflects a pragmatic understanding of each country's unique circumstances and capacities.

2.2 Key Shortcomings

The UNFCCC has faced criticism for being perceived as not responsive enough to the urgent problem of climate change.[81] One of the primary reasons for this perception is the UNFCCC's decision-making process, which relies on unanimity among its signatories.[82] The comprehensiveness of the UNFCCC can become a double-edged sword. While consensus decision-making can promote inclusivity and encourage cooperation, it also helps reluctant countries to tie progress to the pace of the slowest marcher.[83] Consequently, UNFCCC cannot effectively address the underlying handicap of the climate problem, which is the collective action problem.[84]

UNFCCC also failed to provide stringent and binding targets on GHG emissions abatement. The targets often fall short of what some experts and environmental advocates consider necessary to prevent dangerous levels of global warming.[85] The Convention extends emissions reduction obligations over a long period of time.[86] This extended timeline can be seen as a limitation, as it may not respond adequately to the urgency of climate change, which requires more immediate and substantial action to curb emissions. Also, the UNFCCC aims to include all sources of emissions into a single universal agreement, which can be challenging to negotiate and implement.[87] The diversity of emissions sources, economic development levels, and priorities among countries make it difficult to reach a consensus on strict and

[81] David Bullock, 'Combating Climate Recalcitrance: Carbon-Related Border Tax Adjustments in a New Era of Global Climate Governance' (2018) 27 Washington International Law Journal 609, 612. Dessler and Parson (n 12) 219.

[82] UNFCCC art 15 (3).

[83] In this regard, customary norms are somewhat detached from the political bargaining process. They have the potential to enforce upon influential nations. However, given their current vested interests, these states might be hesitant to acknowledge customary principles in the realm of climate change discussions. Mayer, *International Law Obligations on Climate Change Mitigation* (n 47) 89.

[84] Alan Boyle and Navraj Singh Ghaleigh, 'Climate Change and International Law beyond the UNFCCC' in Kevin R Gray (ed.), *The Oxford Handbook of International Climate Change Law* (Oxford University Press 2016), 29.

[85] United Nations Environment Programme (UNEP), 'Emissions Gap Report 2022: The Closing Window-Climate Crisis Calls for Rapid Transformation of Societies' (2022) <https://www.unep.org/emissions-gap-report-2022> accessed 17 March 2024. This suggests that states have not agreed on a particularly high standard of due diligence, which is a customary law obligation of prevention. Mayer, *International Law Obligations on Climate Change Mitigation* (n 47) 103.

[86] UNFCCC art 2(1) "...Such a level should be achieved within a time-frame sufficient to allow ecosystems to adapt naturally to climate change..."

[87] Richard B Stewart, Michael Oppenheimer, and Bryce Rudyk, 'A New Strategy for Global Climate Protection' (2013) 120 Climatic Change 1. Six gases are covered by the emission reduc-

specific emission reduction targets for each source. Moreover, it does not employ deterrent mechanisms to expose uncooperative countries.[88] While reporting and review mechanisms are in place, there is limited capacity to enforce compliance with emission reduction commitments.

The international response to GHG emissions abatement is challenging due to its potential impacts on economic development, and this challenge has been a central issue in the negotiation process under the UNFCCC.[89] The Convention sought to strike a balance between the interests of developed and developing countries, leading to diplomatically formulated obligations which reflect this compromise. The need to accommodate the interests and concerns of all member states can dilute the effectiveness of the agreements. For example, Article 4(1) of the UNFCCC obliges all parties to implement national commitments.[90] However, it does so while taking into account the CBDRRC principle. This approach means that while all countries are expected to act, the nature and scale of their commitments can vary based on their development status and historical contributions to emissions. Meanwhile, Article 4(2) contains more concrete commitments applicable to developed countries listed in Annex I of the Convention. The developed countries are required to take the lead in reducing emissions. However, the language in subparagraph (a) is somewhat vague and obliges these developed countries to "limit their greenhouse gas emissions" rather than achieve quantified reductions.[91] There is no obligation to achieve specific reductions by a given date. This vagueness often results in resistance to implementing significant climate action measures.

Furthermore, the structure of COP meetings obstructs effective climate negotiations with the vast number of participants.[92] For instance, COP26 in Glasgow brought together 120 world leaders and over 40,000 registered participants, including 22,274 party delegates and 14,124 observers.[93] Hence, despite the intensive negotiations within the COP meetings, a profound gap exists between the enthusiasm and pledges made during these gatherings and their actual translation into tangible action. This divergence between intent and implementation is partly attributable to the sheer scale and complexity of the meetings. The vast number of participants

tion commitments in the UNFCCC; CO2, CH4, N2O, hydrofluorocarbons, perfluorocarbons and sulphur hexafluoride.

[88] Lukas Hermwille and others, 'UNFCCC Before and After Paris – What's Necessary For An Effective Climate Regime?' (2017) 17(2) Climate Policy 150, 151. Nordhaus, *The Climate Casino* (n 113) 8.

[89] Philippe J Sands and Ilona Millar, 'Climate, International Protection' in *Max Planck Encyclopaedias of International Law* (2011) para 1.

[90] UNFCCC art 4.1 (b) states an obligation for all States to "formulate, implement, publish and regularly update programmes containing measures to mitigate climate change".

[91] UNFCCC art 4.2 (a)

[92] Lavanya Rajamani and others, 'Re-invigorating the UN Climate Regime in the Wider Landscape of Climate Action' (*C2ES Discussion Paper*, 2023) <https://unfccc.int/documents/627184> accessed 6 April 2024.

[93] United Nations, 'COP26' <https://www.un.org/en/climatechange/cop26> accessed 17 March 2024.

can create logistical challenges, communication barriers, and divergent priorities. Moreover, the lack of robust follow-up mechanisms and the absence of clear timelines for executing commitments during these events further exacerbate the issue.[94]

Consequently, the consensus decision-making process, lack of political will, and concerns about international competitiveness and carbon leakage block the successful and timely response to climate change.[95] Therefore, even though UNFCCC has the expertise and infrastructure to monitor emissions and fulfil the transparency framework globally, its practical implementation lacks significant repercussions for the current and future of reaching climate goals.[96] The absence of penalties creates a system with very little deterrence value.[97] Signatories are reluctant to take specific actions. Consequently, a culture of accepted non-compliance appears to permeate the international community. These structural problems impede UNFCCC from creating momentous results in mitigation efforts.[98] Also, they could weaken the overall integrity of the UNFCCC as a regulatory tool and erode trust in the effectiveness of international climate agreements.

In sum, UNFCCC sets out the foundational elements of the envisioned climate change regime. The commitments under the UNFCCC are limited. It provides the overarching framework, principles, and broad objectives for addressing climate change at the global level.[99] Hence, the UN climate regime sets norms but does not deliver specific implementation targets. As already, in each meeting, countries pledged new targets but did not deliver them. This practice lowers the ambition among member states because climate action enthusiasm can grow with implementation. The pragmatic division of labour between norm-setting and detailed implementation emphasises international climate governance's flexible and adaptive nature. This approach also fulfils the international community's expectations because the UN works to set necessary international standards, such as what we can expect from states or what is the optimal conduct. Consequently, the UNFCCC represents a negotiation document. In comparison, the specifics are left to, the COPs, which have played a central role in shaping the global response to climate change by facilitating negotiations and adopting additional agreements that build upon the UNFCCC framework. Two key agreements that have emerged from this

94 UNFCCC, art 7.3. UNFCCC, Report of the Conference of the Parties on its First Session, UNFCCC document FCCC/CP/1995/7 (24 May 1995), para 14.

95 Luke Kemp, 'Framework for the Future? Exploring the Possibility of Majority Voting in the Climate Negotiations' (2016) 16 International Environmental Agreements: Politics, Law and Economics 757.

96 This was acknowledged at the UN climate summit in Durban, South Africa, in 2011. COP, 'Decision 1/CP.17 on the Establishment of an Ad Hoc Working Group on the Durban Platform for Enhanced Action' UN Doc FCCC/CP/2011/9/Add.1 (15 March 2012).

97 The non-compliance is conduct of states that deviates from treaty rules it is party to and not implement its actions treaty regime. Alexander Zahar, *International Climate Law and State Compliance* (1st ed Routledge, 2015) 26.

98 Steven Vanderheiden, 'Justice and Climate Finance: Differentiating Responsibility in the Green Climate Fund' (2015) 50(1) The International Spectator 31, 37.

99 Rajamani and Werksman (n 1) 498.

process are the Kyoto Protocol and the Paris Agreement. These agreements are complementary to the UNFCCC and contain more concrete and specific provisions, filling in some of the binding legal norms gaps left by the UNFCCC. It is important to note that even though these agreements are integral components of the UNFCCC, they apply only to the countries that have ratified them.

3 Kyoto Protocol

3.1 Foundation and Main Concepts

The Kyoto Protocol was adopted in 1997 and came into force in 2005.[100] The Protocol distinguishes between two groups of countries: Annex I Parties (developed countries) and non-Annex I Parties (developing countries). Annex I Parties are further divided into Annex B and non-Annex B. The quantified and legally binding emissions reduction commitments are assigned to parties under Annex B of the Protocol in line with the CBDR principle.[101] Therefore, the binding target applied only to 37 countries and the EU.[102] They were obliged to reduce their GHG emissions by an average of 5.2% compared to 1990 levels during the first commitment period from 2008 to 2012.[103] After the first commitment period ended, the Kyoto Protocol extended for a second commitment period from 2013 to 2020 through the Doha Amendment. It established new emission reduction targets for the Annex B countries, which were generally more ambitious than those in the first one.[104] Each Annex B Party had its own target, which varied based on the country's historical emissions and economic circumstances. There was no comparable commitment for developing countries. However, the Protocol called for the advancement of the commitments by all parties, including developing ones.

During the negotiations for the Kyoto Protocol, the primary concern for many countries was safeguarding their economies against the potential adverse effects of stringent emissions reduction commitments.[105] To address these concerns, the Kyoto Protocol introduced several market-based mechanisms. These mechanisms were designed to facilitate the flexible and cost-effective achievement of emissions reduction targets, allowing countries to pursue environmental objectives without

[100] Kyoto Protocol to the United Nations Framework Convention on Climate Change, 11 December 1997 37 I.L.M. 22 (1998); 2303 U.N.T.S. 162; U.N. Doc FCCC/CP/1997/7/Add.1, hereinafter Kyoto Protocol.

[101] Gracia Marín Durán, 'Securing Compatibility of Carbon Border Adjustments with the Multilateral Climate and Trade Regimes' (2023) 72(1) International and Comparative Law Quarterly 73, 85.

[102] Kyoto Protocol art 3.1 & Annex B.

[103] Kyoto Protocol art 3(1). Soltau (n 21) 6.

[104] Rajamani and Werksman (n 1) 497.

[105] Boyle and Singh Ghaleigh (n 84) 32.

compromising economic growth.[106] These flexibility mechanisms consist of Joint Implementation (JI),[107] Clean Development Mechanism (CDM)[108] and International Emissions Trading (IET).[109] They were the most innovative aspects of the Kyoto Protocol, since Annex I parties can meet their commitments by acquiring emissions credits from other countries. However, such trading must be supplemental to domestic actions taken to achieve emission reductions.[110] These market-based mechanisms recognised that environmental protection and economic growth need not be at odds. They harnessed market forces and international collaboration to incentivise emission reductions and provided countries with the tools to achieve their targets most cost-effectively.

The Kyoto Protocol took significant steps to enhance compliance and encourage signatories to meet their climate action commitments.[111] One key feature was the establishment of a Compliance Committee consisting of Facilitative and Enforcement Branches. Each branch had specific functions aimed at ensuring adherence to the Protocol's requirements. The Facilitative Branch played a proactive role in supporting parties to fulfil their obligations. Its primary functions included monitoring and verifying the climate action taken by each country. If potential non-compliance issues are identified, the Facilitative Branch can offer guidance and assistance to help the country come back into compliance. This support may include financial and technical assistance as well as opportunities for capacity building.[112] They are designed to act as preventive measures, helping parties meet their targets and obligations.[113]

While the Facilitative Branch focuses on providing support and assistance, the Enforcement Branch takes on a more punitive role in case of non-compliance.[114] If a country is found to be in significant non-compliance, the Enforcement Branch can

[106] Rajamani and Werksman (n 1) 501.

[107] Joint implementation was defined in Article 6 of the Kyoto Protocol, allows a developed country party of the Protocol to earn emission reduction units (ERUs) from an emission-reduction or emission removal project in another country having an emissions abatement target under the Kyoto Protocol.

[108] The Clean Development Mechanism was defined in Article 12 of the Protocol, allows a developed country party of the Protocol to implement an emission-reduction project in developing countries. Such projects can earn saleable certified emission reduction (CER) credits, which can be counted towards meeting Kyoto targets of developed countries.

[109] Emissions trading was set out in Article 16 of the Kyoto Protocol and was divided allowed emissions into assigned units. The developed countries can spare and sell its excess emissions units to countries that are over their targets.

[110] Kyoto Protocol, article 17.

[111] Rajamani and Werksman (n 1) 496.

[112] Anne van Aaken, 'Behavioral Aspects of the International Law of Global Public Goods and Common Pool Resources' (2018) 112(1) The American Journal of International Law 67, 77.

[113] Sebastian Oberthür, 'Compliance under the Evolving Climate Change Regime' in Kevin R Gray and others (eds), *The Oxford Handbook of International Climate Change Law* (Oxford University Press 2016), 122.

[114] Ibid 125.

recommend various measures to address the issue, depending on the Annex I countries' commitments.[115] These measures may include suspending the party's participation in flexibility mechanisms or providing a restoration plan, which specifies the steps the infringer must take to rectify its non-compliance. The severity of the sanctions is directly proportional to the responsibilities of the offender under the Agreement. In other words, the most severe sanctions will be imposed on Annex B countries, while the lightest sanctions will be imposed on Annex II countries. These enforcement and compliance mechanisms within the Kyoto Protocol served as a deterrent against non-compliance and added an element of accountability to the international efforts to combat climate change. By having both a supportive and enforcement approach, the Protocol aimed to encourage countries to fulfil their obligations and meet their emission reduction targets while providing assistance them do so.

3.2 *Key Shortcomings*

The Kyoto Protocol was a pioneering international agreement to address climate change, but it also faced several key shortcomings. One of the major restraints of the Kyoto Protocol was its limited global coverage. The binding emission reduction targets applied only to a specific group of developed countries known as Annex B Parties, leaving many other major emitters, such as China and India, without mandatory targets.[116] The developing countries were treated as a homogeneous group and the economic condition justified the distinction in emission abatement responsibilities. However, the economies of some developing countries experienced substantial growth, challenging the traditional categorization.[117] Consequently, developed countries became increasingly discontented with this static bipolar understanding of the CBDR concept. They argued for the reflection of actual current economic realities. Also, the emission reduction targets set for Annex B Parties were not always ambitious enough to address the magnitude of the climate challenge. The allocation of emission allowances in the first commitment period allowed some countries to possess excess emission allowances, often referred to as "hot air".[118] This inequity in the distribution of allowances undermined the Protocol's overall effectiveness.

---

[115] COP, Decision 27/CMP.1, 'Procedures and Mechanisms Relating to Compliance Under the Kyoto Protocol', (2005) UN Doc FCCC/KP/CMP/2005/8/Add.3.

[116] Boyle and Ghaleigh (n 84) 31.

[117] Axel Michaelowa and others 'Do Rapidly Developing Countries Take Up New Responsibilities for Climate Change Mitigation?' (2015) 133 Climatic Change 499 <https://doi.org/10.1007/s10584-015-1528-6>.

[118] Edwin Woerdman, 'Hot Air Trading under the Kyoto Protocol: An Environmental Problem or Not?' (2005) 14(3) European Environmental Law Review 71, 72.

Furthermore, the Kyoto Protocol's commitment periods were relatively short-term, and the mechanisms it introduced were seen as stopgap measures.[119] It did not provide a long-term solution to the climate problem, which requires sustained and substantial emission reductions over many decades.[120] While the Protocol had compliance mechanisms, including a Facilitative Branch and an Enforcement Branch, it lacked solid penalties for non-compliance. The absence of penalties limited the enforceability of the emission reduction commitments, and some countries failed to meet their targets without significant consequences.

The lack of universal participation restricted the Protocol's effectiveness in reducing global emissions. The rapid economic growth in China, along with its soaring GHG emissions, intensified US concerns. By the late 2000s, China had surpassed the US as the world's largest emitter of CO_2,[121] which intensified the debate over China's classification as a developing country and its lack of binding reduction targets under the Kyoto framework. Citing the exemption of developing countries from binding targets as a key reason, the US, under the administration of President George W. Bush, announced in 2001 that it would not ratify the Kyoto Protocol, arguing that it would harm the US economy.[122] Besides, the second commitment period of the Kyoto Protocol indeed presented a different dynamic compared to the first commitment period. During the second phase, the participation of Annex B countries was voluntary.[123] As a result, some countries chose to participate and set new targets, while others did not join the second commitment period or withdrew from the Kyoto Protocol entirely. Notably, the non-ratification of the US hindered the further mitigation outcomes, as it is one of the biggest emitter countries that also can influence regulatory politics worldwide. Several nations, mainly those aligned with the US,[124] withdrew from the treaty during the subsequent commitment period. These withdrawals reflected the influence of political and economic considerations on climate policy decisions. Also, they signalled the difficulties experienced by countries in maintaining their commitments. Despite the challenges faced under the Kyoto Protocol, many of the provisions and principles of it were integrated into the Paris Agreement, which serves as a successor framework. Consequently, the Paris Agreement built upon the lessons learned from the Kyoto Protocol.

---

[119] Amanda M Rosen, 'The Wrong Solution at the Right Time: The Failure of the Kyoto Protocol on Climate Change' (2015) 43(1) Politics & Policy 30 <https://doi.org/10.1111/polp.12105>.

[120] Boyle and Ghaleigh (n 84) 33.

[121] Zhen Wu and others, 'The United States and China on the Paths and Policies to Carbon Neutrality' (2022) 320 Journal of Environmental Management 115785, 4–5.

[122] Jon Hovi, Detlef F Sprinz and Guri Bang, 'Why the United States did not become a party to the Kyoto Protocol: German, Norwegian, and US perspectives' (2012) 18 European Journal of International Relations 129, 130.

[123] Boyle and Ghaleigh (n 84) 29.

[124] For example, Canada formally withdrew from the Protocol in 2012.

4 Paris Agreement

4.1 Foundation and Main Concepts

The Paris Agreement entered into force on 4 November 2016, representing a significant milestone in global climate action. As of now, it has 195 ratifiers, making it a nearly universal framework for addressing climate change. The central objective of the Paris Agreement is to limit global temperature increases to well below 2 °C above pre-industrial levels, with an aspirational goal of limiting the rise to 1.5 °C.[125] The temperature objective is a binding obligation for all parties. Article 4(1) of the Paris Agreement aims to materialise this goal by achieving net zero emissions by 2050. Herein, the key is to meet this target within a timeframe sufficient to allow ecosystems to adapt naturally to changing climatic conditions. Paris Agreement also aims to ensure economic development and financial flows consistent with a low emissions pathway.[126] Therefore, the regime tries to ensure that the economy grows sustainably while combatting climate change.[127] Incorporating economic and development considerations into the Paris Agreement is essential for gaining broad support and ensuring that climate action is seen as a driver of positive change rather than a constraint on growth.

The Paris Agreement is more ambitious than the Kyoto Protocol due to the temperature goal and the Meeting of the Parties to the Paris Agreement (CMA) that guide and influence parties' climate action.[128] It combines the Kyoto Protocol's top-down strategy and Copenhagen and Cancun's bottom-up structure.[129] In a top-down approach, targets are set by international agreements and then implemented by national governments.[130] This approach ensures a certain degree of uniformity and global consistency, as all countries work toward the same goals. However, a top-down approach may be perceived as overly prescriptive. It might not consider the specific circumstances and needs of different countries and regions. What works for one nation may not be suitable for another, and a one-size-fits-all approach may inadvertently hinder effective climate action. On the other hand, in a bottom-up approach, targets are set by individual countries based on their priorities and circumstances. This approach can generate a greater sense of ownership and commitment as nations set targets that align with their specific needs and development trajectories. However, the bottom-up approach is not without its challenges either. It may lead to inconsistencies and a lack of alignment among the climate targets of

---

[125] Paris Agreement art 2(1)(a).

[126] Paris Agreement art 2.

[127] Soltau (n 21) 55.

[128] Petra Minnerop, 'Climate Protection Agreements' in *Max Planck Encyclopaedia of Public International Law* (2018) para 19.

[129] 'History of UN Climate Talks' (Center for Climate and Energy Solutions, 2019) <https://www.c2es.org/content/history-of-un-climate-talks/> accessed 17 March 2024.

[130] Rajamani and Werksman (n 1) 496.

different countries. Thus, it makes the global assessment of progress in climate mitigation difficult.

Therefore, bottom-up and top-down approaches are not distinct alternatives to each other. Both have advantages and disadvantages. Specifically, the top-down approach is more successful in addressing collective action and free-riding problems. However, the bottom-up approach can more easily incentivise action to achieve domestic goals. Combining them will create a more robust response to climate change problem. The foundational obligations under the Paris Agreement apply universally to all parties, reflecting the top-down strategy.[131] For example, both developing and developed countries are voluntarily responsible for emissions reduction in line with their respective capacities.[132] In contrast, the Paris Agreement's core pledge and review mechanism presents a bottom-up approach, allowing nations to set their individual targets rather than impose them top-down. The pledge and review mechanism allows governments to autonomously set mitigation targets and submit them for periodic international review under their NDCs. It assesses both the policies implemented and the outcomes achieved.[133] The design of this mechanism aims to strike a balance between respecting national sovereignty and encouraging effective action against climate change. Also, it aims to install efficient climate mitigation measures while preserving equity between countries.

The equity concerns are reflected under the CBDRRC principle,[134] which underwent a significant revision with the advent of the Paris Agreement[135] by incorporating a more dynamic understanding that considers not only historical contributions but also current economic capabilities "in light of different national circumstances".[136] Hence, the developed countries take the lead in undertaking economy-wide absolute emission reduction targets. Conversely, developing countries are encouraged to progressively enhance their climate targets, taking into account their unique national circumstances and development stages.[137] Ultimately, they are urged to strive for economy-wide emission reductions over time.[138] This arrangement implies a normative expectation that as national circumstances improve, so too will the scope and ambition of contributions. Moreover, Article 9(1) of the Paris Agreement explicitly mandates developed countries to provide financial support to their developing counterparts, aiding them in both mitigation and adaptation efforts. Thereby, it reinforces

[131] Paris Agreement art 3.

[132] Paris Agreement art 4(3).

[133] Manjana Milkoreit and Kate Haapala, 'The Global Stocktake: Design Lessons for a New Review and Ambition Mechanism in the International Climate Regime' (2019) 19(1) International Environmental Agreements: Politics, Law and Economics 89.

[134] See Sect. 5.2.1 in Chap. 4.

[135] Jacqueline Peel, 'Re-evaluating the Principle of Common but Differentiated Responsibilities in Transnational Climate Change Law' (2016) 5(2) TEL 248–249.

[136] Christina Voigt and Felipe Ferreira, 'Dynamic Differentiation: The Principles of CBDR-RC, Progression and Highest Possible Ambition in the Paris Agreement' (2016) 5(2) TEL 294.

[137] Paris Agreement art 2(2).

[138] Paris Agreement art 4(4).

the Agreement's commitment to equity and creating a more inclusive framework for addressing climate change. This pragmatic approach reflects the ongoing efforts to find common ground among negotiating parties and foster a spirit of collaboration.

The Paris Agreement consists of three core pillars. These are mitigation, adaptation and compensation.[139] For mitigation, each country must plan and regularly report its climate action under the NDCs.[140] NDCs outline the intended contributions to mitigate climate change and cover not only emission reduction targets but also adaptation and finance aspects. Each State must submit their NDCs every five years.[141] This iterative process of pledge, review, and adjustment is referred as "ambitious cycle". It is envisioned to foster a self-reinforcing cycle of improvement in climate ambition. Through repeated cycles of commitment and review, countries are expected to learn from both their own experiences and those of others.[142]

NDCs are the reflection of goodwill and the bottom-up approach.[143] They enable countries to explore and implement different strategies that can help them meet their climate targets. Each successive NDC should enhance the previous one and reflect the highest possible ambition of the respective country, which is defined as the principle of progression.[144] It is designed to create a ratcheting-up mechanism for climate action, ensuring that collective efforts are enhanced over time to meet the Agreement's long-term temperature goals.[145] This mechanism is critical for addressing the dynamic nature of climate science and economic capabilities, allowing for adjustments in national efforts based on the latest scientific findings and technological advancements. In this way, NDCs gradually move towards more robust, tightly implemented, and potentially legally binding climate governance arrangements. Moreover, NDCs possess the benefit of offering greater motivation for less affluent nations. These nations can opt for mitigation measures that are more affordable for them compared to what might be agreed upon at a global level.[146] In other words, NDCs recognise the diverse economic situations of countries and allow them to choose measures that align with their financial capabilities. This structure can encourage greater participation and action in addressing climate change, as countries

[139] Minnerop (n 128) para 20. Ruo-Shui Sun and others, 'Is the Paris Rulebook Sufficient for Effective Implementation of Paris Agreement?' (2022) 13 Advances in Climate Change Research 600, 604.

[140] Paris Agreement art 4(2).

[141] Paris Agreement art 4(9).

[142] Steinar Andresen and others, 'Achieving the Ambitious Targets of the Paris Agreement: The Role of Key Actors' (2021) 21 Int Environ Agreements 1 <https://doi.org/10.1007/s10784-021-09527-6>.

[143] Durán, Securing Compatibility of Carbon Border Adjustments (n 101) 86.

[144] Paris Agreement, art 4(3). Lavanja Rajamani, 'Ambition and Differentiation in the 2015 Paris Agreement: Interpretative Possibilities and Underlying Politics' (2016) 65(2) ICLQ 493, 500–1. Voigt and Ferreira (n 136) 295–297.

[145] Rajamani and Werksman (n 1) 503.

[146] Rafeal Leal-Arcas and others 'Of International Trade, Climate Change, Investment and Prosperous Future' (2020) 12(2) Trade, Law and Development 405, 431.

are more likely to commit to actions that are feasible for their specific circumstances.

The second aspect is adaptation, which corresponds to a reaction in case of failing to mitigate climate change. Paris Agreement gives priority to successful mitigation and lowering the adaptation needs.[147] The final pillar is the Loss and Damage Fund.[148] It aims to provide financial support to countries most vulnerable to the devastating effects of climate change, particularly developing nations that have contributed least to global emissions yet face the brunt of climate-induced disasters. This initiative seeks to facilitate recovery and bolster resilience against future climate risks, embodying the principle of equity that underpins the Paris Agreement. By focusing on loss and damage, the agreement underscores the international community's commitment to not only mitigating climate change and adapting to its effects but also ensuring that countries facing disproportionate impacts receive the support needed to safeguard their communities and ecosystems.

The Paris Agreement Rulebook is a detailed set of procedures and requirements designed to operationalize the Agreement.[149] This Rulebook is critical for ensuring transparent, consistent, and comprehensive implementation of the Agreement across all signatory countries.[150] The Rulebook outlines how countries should report the specifics of NDCs, which consist of GHG emissions reductions and adaptation measures.[151] This includes detailed guidance on the information to be provided, how it should be updated, and the technical review processes to assess progress. Also, the Rulebook addresses the crucial aspect of financial support for climate action in developing countries. This includes the types and amounts of financial assistance, as well as guidelines for reporting on financial flows to ensure that developed countries fulfil their commitment to support developing nations in their climate action efforts.[152] Importantly, the Rulebook sets out the guidelines for countries that engage in international carbon markets as part of their strategy to meet their NDCs. These rules are designed to ensure environmental integrity and avoid double counting of emissions reductions.

[147] Paris Agreement, art 7(4).

[148] Tomoaki Nishimura, 'The Paris Agreement: Continuity and Change within the Climate Regime' in Neil Craikand others (eds), *Global Environmental Change and Innovation in International Law* (Cambridge University Press, 2018) 53.

[149] The full set of decisions agreed to at the 24th COP to the UNFCCC is characterized as the UNFCCC, 'Paris Rulebook' <https://unfccc.int/process-and-meetings/the-paris-agreement/paris-agreement-work-programme/katowice-climate-package> accessed 18 May 2024.

[150] Rajamani and Werksman (n 1) 502.

[151] COP, Decision 4/CMA.1, 'Further guidance in relation to the mitigation section of decision 1/CP. 21' (19 March 2019) UN Doc FCCC/PA/CMA/2018/3/Add.1, 6, para 7.

[152] COP, Decision 12/CMA.1, 'Identification of the information to be provided by Parties in accordance with Article 9, paragraph 5, of the Paris Agreement' (19 March 2019) UN Doc FCCC/PA/CMA/2018/3/Add.1, 35.

4.2 Key Shortcomings

Despite the adoption of the Paris Agreement Rulebook, the success of the Paris Agreement continues to rely heavily on the strong leadership of the participating countries. The differentiated climate mitigation obligations have been disputed from the beginning due to the challenges in striking a balance between equitable burden-sharing and the imperative to address the urgent and global nature of the climate crisis.[153] The Agreement's bottom-up approach, which allows countries significant flexibility in how they meet their commitments, underscores the importance of leadership.[154] This flexibility of NDCs is a crucial factor in securing a large number of signatories. However, it raises concerns about the effectiveness of commitments in achieving the Agreement's overarching goals. NDCs are binding in their procedural aspects, meaning that the agreement regulates the manner and timeline of their submission.[155] Nevertheless, they notably lack specific and content-based obligations. The absence of uniform content standards and benchmarks makes it inherently challenging to ascertain NDC's adequacy in addressing the climate crisis.[156] This dearth of specific content parameters raises questions about the accountability of member countries to fulfil the promises articulated within their NDCs. The wide-ranging flexibility of NDCs implies that they may differ significantly in their scope and ambition. These variations in commitment levels may have implications for the collective progress toward the Agreement's goals.[157]

Moreover, there is no compliance mechanism to review whether the NDCs are achieved. Under the Paris Agreement, the accounting is trusted on state parties. The expectation is that states will engage in transformative actions due to the collective understanding that all nations reshape their economies towards sustainability.[158] This perspective underscores the belief that inaction or failure by any state to implement its NDCs escalates the burden and costs for those committed to their climate pledges.[159] The Paris Agreement stands firmly for a facilitative and non-punitive process to ensure compliance.[160] While it establishes the transparency and review

[153] Paula Castro and Marlene Kammerer, 'The Institutionalization of a Cleavage: How Differential Treatment Affects State Behaviour in the Climate Negotiations' (2021) 65(3) International Studies Quarterly 683, <https://doi.org/10.1093/isq/sqab045>.

[154] The autonomy under NDCs necessitates proactive, visionary leadership to devise and implement effective strategies for meeting climate commitments and to foster international cooperation in combatting climate change.

[155] Rajamani and Werksman (n 1) 504.

[156] UNFCCC, *Nationally Determined Contributions under the Paris Agreement. Synthesis Report by the Secretariat* FCCC/PA/CMA/2021/2 (2021).

[157] Vogler (n 24) 26.

[158] Minnerop (n 128) para 26.

[159] Dessler and Parson (n 12) 149.

[160] Paris Agreement art 15.

process, no material sanctions exist for countries that do not meet their NDCs.[161] Article 15 of the Agreement established the Compliance Committee, which is only binding on procedural obligations. The committee plays an assisting role, helping Parties figure out how to comply with the Agreement.[162] For example, it checks whether NDCs are submitted, and transparency requirements of the Paris Agreement are fulfilled. However, it is not mandated to control whether the NDCs or other content-related substantial obligations are fulfilled. Article 14 of the Paris Agreement establishes the Global Stocktake procedure to check whether parties are collectively making progress towards meeting the Agreement's goals. It aims to identify barriers to implementation. In this collective assessment individual countries are not going to be examined. Hence, still, the Agreement lacks accountability, which undermines the regime's effectiveness.

Also, the majority of NDCs from developing countries are conditional upon financial support. In the Copenhagen Accord, developed nations pledged to establish a financial support fund amounting to 100 billion US Dollars annually.[163] This financial pledge was designed to aid developing countries in realising their NDCs.[164] However, this commitment has not been fully realised due to various factors, including domestic challenges in donor countries. Also, even though the financial support had been fully provided, the implementation of NDCs costs way higher than the promised fund. The resulting shortfall in financial resources has repercussions on developing countries' ability to fully realise their NDCs.

The nature of obligations embedded within the Paris Agreement are mostly procedural requirements.[165] They relate to the process, structure, and mechanisms that govern the implementation of climate action. For example, the submission of NDCs, transparency and reporting, and Global Stocktake fall into the category of procedural obligations. They ensure that countries are held accountable for their commitments and provide a basis for regular assessment.[166] However, their flexibility allows countries to interpret and implement procedural obligations differently. Diverse applications can result in a lack of uniformity and consistency in how countries report their emissions, set targets, or engage in the review process, making it challenging to compare and assess progress accurately. The regime is mainly based on accounting emissions data rather than accountability towards unfulfilled pledges.

---

[161] Susan Biniaz, 'Elaborating Article 15 of the Paris Agreement: Facilitating Implementation and Promoting Compliance' (Institut du Dévelоppement Durable et des Relations Internationales, 2017) 1-2, <https://www.iddri.org/sites/default/files/import/publications/pb1017_art-15-pa_sue-biniaz.pdf>, accessed 23 March 2024.

[162] Sandrine Maljean-Dubois, Imad Antoine Ibrahim and Jessica Owley, 'The Paris Agreement Compliance Mechanism: Beyond COP 26' (2021) The Wake Forest Law Review, 153.

[163] Jocelyn Timperley, 'The Broken $100-Billion Promise of Climate Finance-And How to Fix It' (2021) 598 Nature 400 <https://doi.org/10.1038/d41586-021-02846-3>.

[164] Paris Agreement, art 9(1).

[165] Sun and others (n 139) 605.

[166] Ibid 607.

Moreover, the NDCs submitted by countries are currently not in line with the Agreement's goals of limiting global warming. There is a radical gap between current commitments and the level of emissions reductions required to meet the temperature targets.[167] The predictions based on the current NDCs indicated that temperature increase can only be limited to 2.5–2.9 °C,[168] whereas it should be 1.5 °C to prevent catastrophic climate consequences. In order to fulfil the climate goals, the Paris Agreement has set net-zero emissions targets, but the time frame to reach this target is long distance.[169] Even though, there is expectation of progression in NDCs, it is difficult to establish that a country's capacity is enhanced enough to progress its ambition. Also, there is uncertainty regarding which emissions the Agreement covers, whether it applies solely to carbon emissions or all GHG. Consequently, net-zero targets by countries are generally presented as sole announcements since the Paris Agreement has loopholes, no accountability or transparency for the policy packages regarding to reach such targets and member countries do not enact corresponding binding domestic regulations.

The Paris Agreement acknowledges the crucial role of carbon markets as a tool for achieving the necessary emissions abatement.[170] These markets can facilitate the exchange of emissions reductions between countries. Thereby, they encourage more cost-effective and efficient ways to reduce GHG emissions. However, the Agreement leaves many essential details on how they will function open for negotiation and bilateral cooperation. This lack of clarity regarding the operation and governance of carbon markets presents several potential challenges. First, it can hinder the development of effective and robust carbon markets. Ambiguity about carbon trading rules and mechanisms can deter potential participants from engaging in these markets. The absence of clear guidelines can lead to inefficiencies and market disruptions, ultimately impeding the achievement of emissions abatement goals.[171] Furthermore, the lack of specific rules can cause variations in how different countries approach carbon markets. These discrepancies can create an uneven playing field for market participants, affecting the competitiveness of emissions reduction projects and trading practices. It can also raise questions about the environmental integrity of carbon credits generated through these markets.

Nevertheless, the Paris Agreement marked a critical step in climate cooperation. Its principles are referenced in some national and regional policies, such as in the EU.[172] Most importantly, the Agreement represents an exogenous international

[167] UNFCCC, (n 156) *Nationally Determined Contributions under the Paris Agreement*

[168] Climate Action Tracker '2100 Warming Projections: Emissions and Expected Warming Based on Pledges and Current Policies' (2024) <https://climateactiontracker.org/global/temperatures/> accessed 17 March 2024.

[169] Paris Agreement art 4(1) sets target to second half of the century.

[170] Paris Agreement art 6.

[171] Sun and others (n 139) 608.

[172] European Green Deal, and the EU's climate legislation, including the Effort Sharing Regulation, the Renewable Energy Directive, and the Energy Efficiency Directive, was aligned with the Paris Agreement's objectives to ensure a more integrated and coordinated approach. European

consensus[173] that can affect signatories' domestic climate policy development in at least two ways. First, it can institutionalise international commitments in domestic law. This legal pathway may affect the ambition of domestic policies. Second, it can help domestic actors to invoke international commitments for asserting their interests in internal policymaking. This political pathway may empower domestic institutions or non-state actors in climate action. Besides, the regime further facilitates the understanding of global emission trends. However, the soft commitments under the Agreement raise the question of how to guide and incentivise the member countries' domestic action.[174]

Also, the Paris Agreement is an achievement in terms of its scope and number of signatories. More than 70 countries, including the biggest polluters, China, the US, and the EU, have set a net-zero target, covering about 76% of global emissions.[175] However, the lack of a sanction mechanism results in less enthusiasm to combat climate change and free-ride on the efforts of high-ambition countries.[176] For this reason, the parties to the Agreement have invested considerable time and resources in substitute instruments. These efforts can act as a building block for alternative future climate fora. Without the internationally binding authority prescribing a strict abatement structure on its members, alternative coalitions among countries willing to reduce their emissions become more relevant.[177]

5 Concluding Remarks

The journey through the political and economic landscapes of climate change underscores the multifaceted challenges and opportunities that define most pressing global issue. As it has elucidated in this chapter, the path from recognizing climate change as a scientific curiosity to acknowledging it as a central diplomatic concern has been enlightening. Consequently, the climate change is regarded as a global problem that necessarily requires a global response. International cooperation is essential to limit the increase in temperature. The conclusion of the international

Commission, 'Report from the Commission to the European Parliament, the Council, the European Economic and Social Committee and the Committee of the Regions Accelerating the Transition to Climate Neutrality for Europe's Security and Prosperity: EU Climate Action Progress Report 2022' COM/2022/514 final (26 October 2022) <https://eur-lex.europa.eu/legal-content/EN/TXT/?uri=CELEX%3A52022DC0514>.

173 Nishimura (n 148) 42.

174 Xinyuan Dai, 'Global Regime and National Change' (2010), 10 Climate Policy 622.

175 United Nations, 'Net Zero Coalition' <https://www.un.org/en/climatechange/net-zero-coalition> accessed 17 March 2024.

176 Joeri Rogelj and others 'Paris Agreement climate proposals need a boost to keep warming well below 2°C' (2016) 536 Nature 631.

177 Matteo Roggero, Leonhard Kähler, and Achim Hagen, 'Strategic Cooperation for Transnational Adaptation: Lessons from the Economics of Climate Change Mitigation' (2019) 19 International Environmental Agreements 395, 399 <https://doi.org/10.1007/s10784-019-09442-x>.

climate law landscape examination highlights the pivotal roles of the UNFCCC, Kyoto Protocol, and Paris Agreement. It is evident that global climate governance architecture has been groundbreaking but also fraught with challenges. These agreements have collectively laid a foundation for addressing climate change through international collaboration. Moreover, they set the stage for an evolving regime that seeks to balance environmental urgency with equitable development needs. The UNFCCC established the framework for global climate efforts, emphasising the need for a collective response to climate change while recognising the differentiated responsibilities of countries based on their developmental stages and historical emissions. Despite its wide acceptance and legitimacy, the consensus-based decision-making process and lack of enforceable commitments limit its effectiveness in catalysing rapid and ambitious climate action.[178]

The Kyoto Protocol marked a significant step in operationalising the UNFCCC's goals by introducing quantifiable emissions reduction targets for developed countries. However, its impact was constrained by limited participation, notably the absence of major emitters and the challenge of addressing the dynamic nature of global emissions sources. The Paris Agreement represents a paradigm shift towards a more inclusive and flexible approach, allowing countries to set their own nationally determined contributions. This bottom-up mechanism has broadened participation and commitment but raises concerns about the sufficiency and comparability of national efforts towards the collective goal of limiting global warming. The gap exists between commitments made under the Paris Agreement and their actual implementation.[179] Moreover, the Paris Agreement is fragile and open to exploitation by its members due to a lack of sanctions and strict compliance mechanisms. A major deficiency within the regime is the insufficient availability of financial resources necessary to realise NDCs.

The current global stance on climate change is a testament to decades of scientific research, political negotiations, and economic recalibrations. Despite this consensus on the urgency of climate action, there remains a lack of uniform agreement on several critical aspects of climate governance. Looking ahead, the international climate regime must navigate several paths to enhance its efficacy and resilience. The main issue involves bridging the gap between developed and developing countries and ensuring adequate financial flows to support developing countries. Strengthening the linkages between climate commitments and tangible actions, and integrating more robust compliance mechanisms are also imperative. The emphasis on actionable steps, regardless of their initial scope, suggests a pragmatic approach to overcoming the inertia that has historically plagued climate action efforts.[180] This pragmatic approach suggests that climate action should leverage any available opportunity to take initial steps towards mitigation, no matter how small these may

[178] Boyle and Ghaleigh (n 84) 37.

[179] Climate Action Tracker 'CAT Emissions Gap' (Climate Analytics and New Climate Institute 2024) <https://climateactiontracker.org/global/cat-emissions-gaps/> accessed 17 March 2024.

[180] Dessler and Parson (n 12) 205.

be.[181] The emphasis here is on the importance of initiating action rather than the preliminary scope or perfection of the policies.[182] Such an approach allows for early policies to be less than optimal, with the understanding that these can be extended, strengthened, and improved over time based on experience, technological advancements, and changing political and economic contexts.[183]

Consequently, to bolster the efficacy of the UN climate regime, it becomes imperative to explore synergies with other relevant legal instruments. The climate norms can be strengthened with cross-fertilization from different areas, notably with the trade law.[184] The inherent limitations of the UN climate regime necessitate a complementary approach that leverages trade law mechanisms to fortify its objectives. The flexibility of trade instruments allows for a responsive approach to climate action, where measures can be calibrated to the evolving understanding of climate science, economic impacts, and societal needs. The alternative fora or collaboration with other realms of law do not suggest leaving the UN regime or consensus decision-making behind. It is essential to maintain respect and alignment with the principles established by UNFCCC. However, not all decisions require consensus. By fostering cooperation across borders and sectors and enabling the integration of diverse mitigation strategies, the structural deficiencies observed in the UNFCCC process can be minimized. Particularly, forums consist of a small number of parties can negotiate stricter obligations and have a signalling effect on its non-members.[185] If the forum is strengthened with the correct instruments, legitimacy follows later on.

Ultimately, the future of international climate governance will hinge on its ability to adapt to changing global dynamics, harness innovation, and foster an unwavering commitment among nations to safeguard the planet for future generations. Any delay in taking serious steps towards climate mitigation will result in increased severity of adverse impacts and further complicate the achievement of climate goals. The costs of inaction or delayed action are not only economic but also encompass environmental and social dimensions. As the world grapples with the escalating impacts of climate change, the collective resolution and actions taken under or outside the auspices of the UN climate regime will be a testament to the international community's capacity to confront and overcome its most daunting challenge.

[181] Fabrizio Ferraro and others, 'Tackling Grand Challenges Pragmatically: Robust Action Revisited' (2015) 36 Organization Studies 363 <https://doi.org/10.1177/0170840614563742>.

[182] Oscar Widerberg and others, 'The Expanding Field of Cooperative Initiatives for Decarbonization: A Review of Five Databases' (2016) 7 Wiley Interdisciplinary Reviews: Climate Change <https://doi.org/10.1002/wcc.396>.

[183] Marcel J. Dorsch and Christian Flachsland, 'A Polycentric Approach to Global Climate Governance' (2017) 17 Global Environmental Politics 45 < https://doi.org/10.1162/GLEP_a_00400>.

[184] Boyle and Ghaleigh (n 84) 49–50.

[185] Dorsch and Flachsland (n 183) 45.

Bibliography

Cases

Argentina v Uruguay (Pulp Mills on the River Uruguay) (Judgment) [2010] ICJ Rep 14.

Gentini Case (Italy v Venezuela) Mixed Claims Commission (1903) RIAA Volume X 477-692.

Legislation

Conference of Parties (COP), Decision 27/CMP.1, 'Procedures and Mechanisms Relating to Compliance Under the Kyoto Protocol', (2005) UN Doc FCCC/KP/CMP/2005/8/Add.3

— 'Decision 1/CP.17 on the Establishment of an Ad Hoc Working Group on the Durban Platform for Enhanced Action' UN Doc FCCC/CP/2011/9/Add.1 (15 March 2012)

— Decision 12/CMA.1, 'Identification of the information to be provided by Parties in accordance with Article 9, paragraph 5, of the Paris Agreement' (19 March 2019) UN Doc FCCC/PA/CMA/2018/3/Add.1

— Decision 4/CMA.1, 'Further guidance in relation to the mitigation section of decision 1/CP. 21' (19 March 2019) UN Doc FCCC/PA/CMA/2018/3/Add.1

Kyoto Protocol to the United Nations Framework Convention on Climate Change, 11 December 1997 37 I.L.M. 22 (1998); 2303 U.N.T.S. 162; U.N. Doc FCCC/CP/1997/7/Add.1.

Secondary Sources

'History of UN Climate Talks' (Center for Climate and Energy Solutions, 2019) <https://www.c2es.org/content/history-of-un-climate-talks/> accessed 17 March 2024

Andresen S, 'International Climate Negotiations: Top-Down, Bottom-Up or a Combination of Both?' (2015) 50(1) The International Spectator 15

— and others, 'Achieving the Ambitious Targets of the Paris Agreement: The Role of Key Actors' (2021) 21 Int Environ Agreements 1 <https://doi.org/10.1007/s10784-021-09527-6>

Barrett S, 'Climate Treaties and the Imperative of Enforcement' (2008) 24 Oxford Review of Economic Policy 239 https://doi.org/10.1093/oxrep/grn015

Bausch C and Mehling M, 'Alternative Venues of Climate Cooperation: An Institutional Perspective' in E Hollo, K Kulovesi, M Mehling (eds), *Climate Change and the Law* (Springer, 2013)

Benjamin DDK and Lwasa S, 'Correlating Negotiation Hotspot Issues, Paris Climate Agreement and the International Climate Policy Regime' (2017) 77 Environmental Science & Policy 1

Betsill M and others 'Building Productive Links between the UNFCCC and the Broader Global Climate Governance Landscape' (2015) 15(2) Global Environmental Politics 1

Biniaz S, 'Elaborating Article 15 of the Paris Agreement: Facilitating Implementation and Promoting Compliance' (Institut du Développement Durable et des Relations Internationales, 2017) 1-2, <https://www.iddri.org/sites/default/files/import/publications/pb1017_art-15-pa_sue-biniaz.pdf>, accessed 23 March 2024.

Bodansky D, 'The United Nations Framework Convention on Climate Change: A Commentary' (1993) 18 Yale JIL 451

Boyle A, 'Polluter Pays' in *Max Planck Encyclopaedia of Public International Law* (2009)

— and Ghaleigh NS, 'Climate Change and International Law beyond the UNFCCC' in KR Gray (ed), *The Oxford Handbook of International Climate Change Law* (Oxford University Press 2016)

Brunnée J, 'Consent' in *Max Planck Encyclopaedia of Public International Law* (2022)

Bullock D, 'Combating Climate Recalcitrance: Carbon-Related Border Tax Adjustments in a New Era of Global Climate Governance' (2018) 27 Washington International Law Journal 609

Carlarne C, Gray KR and Tarasofsky R, 'International Climate Change Law: Mapping The Field' in KR Gray and others (eds), *The Oxford Handbook of International Climate Change Law* (Oxford University Press, 2016)

Castro P and Kammerer M, 'The Institutionalization of a Cleavage: How Differential Treatment Affects State Behaviour in the Climate Negotiations' (2021) 65(3) International Studies Quarterly 683, <https://doi.org/10.1093/isq/sqab045>

Chen and Q Yang, 'Renewable Energy Technology Innovation and Urban Green Economy Efficiency' (2024) Journal of Environmental Management 120130

Climate Action Tracker, '2100 Warming Projections: Emissions and Expected Warming Based on Pledges and Current Policies' (2024) <https://climateactiontracker.org/global/temperatures/> accessed 17 March 2024

— 'CAT Emissions Gap' (Climate Analytics and New Climate Institute 2024) <https://climateactiontracker.org/global/cat-emissions-gaps/> accessed 17 March 2024

Climate Watch, 'GHG Emissions' (World Resources Institute, 2020) <climatewatchdata.org/ghg-emissions> accessed 3 April 2024

Cottier T and Payosova T, 'Common Concern and Legitimacy of the WTO in Dealing with Climate Change' in Panagiotis Delimatsis (ed) *Research Handbook on Climate Change and Trade* (Edward Elgar 2016)

Dai X, 'Global Regime and National Change' (2010), 10 Climate Policy 622

Dessler AE and EA Parson, *The Science and Politics of Global Climate Change: A Guide to the Debate* (3rd edn, Cambridge University Press 2020)

Dorsch MJ and Flachsland C, 'A Polycentric Approach to Global Climate Governance' (2017) 17 Global Environmental Politics 45 <https://doi.org/10.1162/GLEP_a_00400>

Dupuy PM, Le Moli G, and Viñuales JE, 'Customary International Law and the Environment' in L Rajamani and J Peel (eds), *The Oxford Handbook of International Environmental Law* (2nd edn, OUP 2021)

Durán GM, 'Securing Compatibility of Carbon Border Adjustments with the Multilateral Climate and Trade Regimes' (2023) 72 International & Comparative Law Quarterly 73

Energy Institute, 'Statistical Review of World Energy 2023' (2023) <https://www.energyinst.org/statistical-review/resources-and-data-downloads> accessed 21 June 2024

European Commission, 'Report from the Commission to the European Parliament, the Council, the European Economic and Social Committee and the Committee of the Regions Accelerating the Transition to Climate Neutrality for Europe's Security and Prosperity: EU Climate Action Progress Report 2022' COM/2022/514 final (26 October 2022) <https://eur-lex.europa.eu/legal-content/EN/TXT/?uri=CELEX%3A52022DC0514>

Ferraro F and others, 'Tackling Grand Challenges Pragmatically: Robust Action Revisited' (2015) 36 Organization Studies 363 <https://doi.org/10.1177/0170840614563742>

Ghaleigh NS 'Science and Climate Change Law-The Role of the IPCC in International Decision-Making' in KR Gray et al (eds), *The Oxford Handbook of International Climate Change Law* (Oxford University Press 2016)

Gillingham K, 'The True Cost of Reducing Greenhouse Gas Emissions' (IMF Finance & Development 2019) <https://www.imf.org/external/chinese/pubs/ft/fandd/2019/12/pdf/the-true-cost-of-reducing-greenhouse-gas-emissions-gillingham.pdf> accessed 5 July 2024

Gough I and Meadowcroft J, 'Decarbonizing the Welfare State' in JS Dryzek and others (eds), *The Oxford Handbook of Climate Change and Society* (Oxford University Press 2012)

Harris PG, 'Reconceptualizing Global Governance' in JS Dryzek and others (eds), *The Oxford Handbook of Climate Change and Society* (Oxford University Press 2011)

Henderson GE, 'Rawls & Sustainable Development' (2011) 7 McGill International Journal of Sustainable Development Law and Policy 1

Hermwille L and others, 'UNFCCC Before and After Paris – What's Necessary For An Effective Climate Regime?' (2017) 17(2) Climate Policy 150

Hey E and Paulini S, 'Common but Differentiated Responsibilities' in *Max Planck Encyclopaedia of Public International Law* (2021)

Hirst D, 'Negotiating Climates: The Politics of Climate Change and the Formation of the Intergovernmental Panel on Climate Change (IPCC), 1979-1992' (2014)

<https://pure.manchester.ac.uk/ws/portalfiles/portal/54560421/FULL_TEXT.PDF> accessed 5 July 2024

Hovi J, Sprinz DF and Bang G, 'Why the United States did not become a party to the Kyoto Protocol: German, Norwegian, and US perspectives' (2012) 18 European Journal of International Relations 129

Huisingh D and others, 'Recent Advances in Carbon Emissions Reduction: Policies, Technologies, Monitoring, Assessment and Modeling' (2015) 103 Journal of Cleaner Production 1 <https://doi.org/10.1016/J.JCLEPRO.2015.04.098>

— *2018 Report of the Committee on Sustainable Development and the Green Economy in International Trade Law*

Kemp L, 'Framework for the Future? Exploring the Possibility of Majority Voting in the Climate Negotiations' (2016) 16 International Environmental Agreements: Politics, Law and Economics 757

Kooiman J, *Governing and Governance* (Sage 1993)

Leal-Arcas R, and others 'Of International Trade, Climate Change, Investment and Prosperous Future' (2020) 12(2) Trade, Law and Development 405

Leonelli GC, 'Carbon Border Measures, Environmental Effectiveness and WTO Compatibility: Is There a Way Forward for the Steel and Aluminium Carbon Club?' (2022) 21(5) World Trade Review

Maljean-Dubois S, Ibrahim IA and Owley J, 'The Paris Agreement Compliance Mechanism: Beyond COP 26' (2021) The Wake Forest Law Review

Matthews HD and others, 'Assessing the Costs of Historical Inaction on Climate Change' (2018) 8(1) Scientific Reports 1

Mayer B, *The International Law on Climate Change* (Cambridge University Press 2018)

— *International Law Obligations on Climate Change Mitigation* (Oxford University Press 2022)

Michaelowa A and others 'Do Rapidly Developing Countries Take Up New Responsibilities for Climate Change Mitigation?' (2015) 133 Climatic Change 499 <https://doi.org/10.1007/s10584-015-1528-6>

Milkoreit M and Haapala K, 'The Global Stocktake: Design Lessons for a New Review and Ambition Mechanism in the International Climate Regime' (2019) 19(1) International Environmental Agreements: Politics, Law and Economics 89

Minnerop P, 'Climate Protection Agreements' in *Max Planck Encyclopaedia of Public International Law* (2018)

Nishimura T, 'The Paris Agreement: Continuity and Change within the Climate Regime' in N Craikand others (eds), *Global Environmental Change and Innovation in International Law* (Cambridge University Press, 2018)

Nordhaus W, 'Climate Change: The Ultimate Challenge for Economics' (2019) 109(6) American Economic Review 1991 <https://doi.org/10.1257/aer.109.6.1991>

Oberthür S, 'Compliance under the Evolving Climate Change Regime' in KR Gray and others (eds), *The Oxford Handbook of International Climate Change Law* (Oxford University Press 2016)

Paliampelou I, 'Chapter 5: Net Zero Targets and Governance: A Literature Review (2009-2021)' in *Handbook on Corporate Governance and Corporate Social Responsibility* (Edward Elgar Publishing 2024)

Peel J, 'Re-evaluating the Principle of Common but Differentiated Responsibilities in Transnational Climate Change Law' (2016) 5(2) TEL

Pyhälä M, Brusendorff A and Paulomäki H, 'The Precautionary Principle' in M Fitmaurice, D Ong and P Merkouris (eds), *Research Handbook on International Environmental Law* (Edward Elgar Publishing 2010)

Rajamani L, 'Ambition and Differentiation in the 2015 Paris Agreement: Interpretative Possibilities and Underlying Politics' (2016) 65(2) ICLQ 493

— and Werksman J, 'Climate Change' in L Rajamani and J Peel (eds), *The Oxford Handbook of International Environmental Law* (2nd edn, Oxford University Press 2021)

— and others, 'Re-invigorating the UN Climate Regime in the Wider Landscape of Climate Action' (C2ES Discussion Paper, 2023) <https://unfccc.int/documents/627184> accessed 6 April 2024.

Rogelj J and others 'Paris Agreement Climate Proposals Need a Boost to Keep Warming Well Below 2°C' (2016) 536 Nature 631

Roggero M, Kähler L, and Hagen A, 'Strategic Cooperation for Transnational Adaptation: Lessons from the Economics of Climate Change Mitigation' (2019) 19 International Environmental Agreements 395, <https://doi.org/10.1007/s10784-019-09442-x>

Rosen AM, 'The Wrong Solution at the Right Time: The Failure of the Kyoto Protocol on Climate Change' (2015) 43(1) Politics & Policy 30 <https://doi.org/10.1111/polp.12105>

Sands P, and Millar I, 'Climate, International Protection' in *Max Planck Encyclopaedias of International Law* (2011).

Soltau F, *Fairness in International Climate Change Law and Policy* (Cambridge University Press 2009).

Stern N, 'Ethics, Equity and The Economics of Climate Change Paper 2: Economics and Politics' (2014) 30 Economics and Philosophy 445

Stewart RB, Oppenheimer M, and Rudyk B, 'A New Strategy for Global Climate Protection' (2013) 120 Climatic Change 1

Stiglitz J and Stern N, 'Report of the High-Level Commission on Carbon Prices' (The World Bank 2017) <www.carbonpricingleadership.org/report-of-the-highlevel-commission-on-carbon-prices/> accessed 22 April 2024

Sun RS and others, 'Is the Paris Rulebook Sufficient for Effective Implementation of Paris Agreement?' (2022) 13 Advances in Climate Change Research 600

Ostrom E, 'A Polycentric Approach for Coping with Collective Action and Global Climate Change' (2010) 20(4) Global Environmental Change 550

Thacher PS, 'Alternative Legal and Institutional Approaches to Global Change' (1990) 1 Colo J Int'l Envtl L & Pol'y 101

Timperley J, 'The Broken $100-Billion Promise of Climate Finance-And How to Fix It' (2021) 598 Nature 400 <https://doi.org/10.1038/d41586-021-02846-3>

Tosun J and Schoenefeld JJ, 'Collective Climate Action and Networked Climate Governance' (2017) 8 WIREs Clim Change

United Nations (UN), 'COP26' <https://www.un.org/en/climatechange/cop26> accessed 17 March 2024.

— 'Net Zero Coalition' <https://www.un.org/en/climatechange/net-zero-coalition> accessed 17 March 2024

United Nations Environment Program (UNEP), 'Emissions Gap Report 2022: The Closing Window-Climate Crisis Calls for Rapid Transformation of Societies' (2022) <https://www.unep.org/emissions-gap-report-2022> accessed 17 March 2024

United Nations Framework Convention on Climate Change (UNFCCC), Report of the Conference of the Parties on its First Session, UNFCCC document FCCC/CP/1995/7 (24 May 1995)

— *Nationally Determined Contributions under the Paris Agreement. Synthesis Report by the Secretariat* FCCC/PA/CMA/2021/2 (2021)

— 'Paris Rulebook' <https://unfccc.int/process-and-meetings/the-paris-agreement/paris-agreement-work-programme/katowice-climate-package> accessed 18 May 2024

— 'About the Secretariat' <https://unfccc.int/about-us/about-the-secretariat> accessed 22 March 2024

Van Aaken A, 'Behavioral Aspects of the International Law of Global Public Goods and Common Pool Resources' (2018) 112(1) The American Journal of International Law 67

Van Asselt H and Zelli F, 'International Governance: Polycentric Governing by and beyond the UNFCCC' in A Jordan and others (eds), *Governing Climate Change: Polycentricity in Action?* (Cambridge University Press 2018)

Vanderheiden S, 'Justice and Climate Finance: Differentiating Responsibility in the Green Climate Fund' (2015) 50(1) The International Spectator 31

Vogler J, 'Energy, Climate Change, and Global Governance: The 2015 Paris Agreement in Perspective' in Debra J. Davidson and Matthias Gross (eds), *Oxford Handbook of Energy and Society* (Oxford University Press 2018)

Voigt C and Ferreira F, 'Dynamic Differentiation: The Principles of CBDR-RC, Progression and Highest Possible Ambition in the Paris Agreement' (2016) 5(2) TEL 294

Weart S, 'The Development of the Concept of Dangerous Anthropogenic Climate Change' in JS Dryzek and others (eds), *The Oxford Handbook of Climate Change and Society* (Oxford University Press 2011).

Widerberg O and others, 'The Expanding Field of Cooperative Initiatives for Decarbonization: A Review of Five Databases' (2016) 7 Wiley Interdisciplinary Reviews: Climate Change <https://doi.org/10.1002/wcc.396>

Williams A, 'Promoting Justice within the International Legal System: Prospects for Climate Refugees' in Benjamin J. Richardson and others (eds), *Climate Law and Developing Countries: Legal and Policy Challenges for the World Economy*, (Cheltenham: Edward Elgar, 2009)

Woerdman E, 'Hot Air Trading under the Kyoto Protocol: An Environmental Problem or Not?' (2005) 14(3) European Environmental Law Review 71
World Commission on Environment and Development, *Our Common Future* (Oxford University Press 1987)
World Meteorological Organization (WMO), *Thirty-Ninth Session of the Executive Council, General Summary 3.4 (1–5 June 1987)* (UNEP Governing Council, Decision 14/20, 17 June 1987)
Wu Z and others, 'The United States and China on the Paths and Policies to Carbon Neutrality' (2022) 320 Journal of Environmental Management 115785
Zahar A, *International Climate Law and State Compliance* (1st ed Routledge, 2015)
Zhang L and others, 'Globalization, Green Economy and Environmental Challenges: State of the Art Review for Practical Implications' (2022) Frontiers in Environmental Science

Open Access This chapter is licensed under the terms of the Creative Commons Attribution 4.0 International License (http://creativecommons.org/licenses/by/4.0/), which permits use, sharing, adaptation, distribution and reproduction in any medium or format, as long as you give appropriate credit to the original author(s) and the source, provide a link to the Creative Commons license and indicate if changes were made.

The images or other third party material in this chapter are included in the chapter's Creative Commons license, unless indicated otherwise in a credit line to the material. If material is not included in the chapter's Creative Commons license and your intended use is not permitted by statutory regulation or exceeds the permitted use, you will need to obtain permission directly from the copyright holder.

Chapter 3
Exploring Alternative Governance Structures for Climate Cooperation

1 Background

Climate change is a transboundary environmental threat and a "multifaceted and multi-layered issue",[1] which cannot be captured by a single overarching approach. Hence, the solution requires horizontal verein among jurisdictions, where multiple international, regional, national, local, and transnational[2] governance levels are involved. Also, it necessitates vertical administration that implements regulations and policies at these different governance levels.[3] In addition to effectively mobilising actors and administering regulations, which approach to adopt for target-setting presents a dilemma for climate regimes.[4] Consequently, the climate change problem is diluting the traditional categories of international law.[5]

---

[1] David Held and Angus Hervey, 'Democracy, Climate Change, and Global Governance. Democratic Agency and the Policy Menu Ahead' in David Held, Angus Hervey and Marika Theors (eds), *The Governance of Climate Change: Science, Economics, Politics & Ethics* (Cornwall: Polity Press, 2011), 89.

[2] The concept of transnational law is broader than international environmental law. Transnational environmental law applies to transboundary activities. It encompasses all the environmental law including the national environmental regulations, which have effects more than one jurisdiction and has a horizontal effect across jurisdictions by way of providing regulatory models to other countries or affecting the behaviour of foreign producers and consumers. It also entails the issuance of certification and labelling regimes for the private actors and influences the development of standards. Gregory Shaffer and Daniel Bodansky, 'Transnational Unilateralism and International Law' (2012) 1 Transnational Environmental Law 31, 32.

[3] Daniel H. Cole, 'Climate Change and Collective Action' (2008) 61 Current Legal Problems 229, 232.

[4] Jacqueline Peel, Lee Godden and Rodney Keenan, 'Climate Change Law in an Era of Multi-Level Governance' (2012) 1(2) Transnational Environmental Law 245, 249.

[5] Kelly Levin and others, 'Playing It Forward: Path Dependency, Progressive Incrementalism and the 'Super Wicked' Problem of Global Climate Change' (2009) IOP Conf. Ser.: Earth Environ. Sci. 6 502002, 9.

© The Author(s) 2025

T. G. Budak, *Beyond Treaties: Rethinking Legal Mechanisms for International Climate Governance*, https://doi.org/10.1007/978-3-031-86022-5_3

To this end, effective climate governance requires a high degree of cooperation to ensure that targets are ambitious, aligned, and equitable. Therefore, an ideal forum for climate change needs to encompass five fundamental characteristics.[6] First, it should include all the current and future high emitters as participants. Second, the governance scheme must provide sufficient resources and expertise to support abatement pledges. Third, an ideal climate forum needs to ensure procedural and substantive transparency for monitoring emissions abatement efforts. Procedural transparency involves making the decision-making process accessible and understandable. In comparison, substantive transparency means that the actions and progress of countries in reducing emissions are clear and verifiable. Most importantly, the forum should enable a climate agreement with binding commitments. This helps countries take their responsibilities seriously and are held accountable for meeting their targets. Finally, it should have a strong political will and vision on how to lower emission levels.[7] As a result, climate change requires ambitious and coordinated action and a forum which is committed to drive progress and inspire greater global cooperation.

Traditionally, climate change is addressed as a universal problem that demands all-inclusive participation. The current multilateral regimes and institutions establish principles, norms, and decision-making procedures for achieving mutually beneficial climate outcomes.[8] However, the UNFCCC and successive agreements cannot deliver an effective mandate for emissions abatement.[9] They envisage high aspirations towards long-term goals but accompany them with low ambition in short-term commitments and implementation. On the other hand, there are numerous examples of initiatives, policies, and projects around the world that have shown positive impacts in combatting climate change. For instance, the EU Emission Trading System (ETS) is the most extensive international system for trading GHG emission allowances. It covers 36% of the EU's total emissions, the European Free Trade Association (EFTA) countries, and power plants in Northern Ireland.[10]

In the face of the challenges associated with the current climate legal regime, it becomes increasingly evident that a single approach may not be sufficient to resolve the outstanding problems.[11] The countries' divergent economic, social, and political

[6] Camilla Bausch and Micheal Mehling, 'Alternative Venues of Climate Cooperation: An Institutional Perspective' in Erkki J Hollo, Kati Kulovesi, Michael Mehling (eds.) *Climate Change and the Law* (Springer 2013), 354–355.

[7] Bausch and Mehling (n 6) 132.

[8] Friedrich Soltau, *Fairness in International Climate Change Law and Policy* (Cambridge University Press 2009), 139.

[9] UNEP, *The Emissions Gap Report 2016: A UNEP Synthesis Report* (UNEP, 2016).

[10] European Commission, 'Report from the Commission to the European Parliament and the Council on the Functioning of the European Carbon Market in 2022 pursuant to Articles 10(5) and 21(2) of Directive 2003/87/EC' COM(2023) 654 final (31 October 2023), 5 <https://climate.ec.europa.eu/system/files/2023-10/COM_2023_654_1_EN_ACT_part1_CMR%2BSWD.pdf> accessed 23 March 2024.

[11] Naím Moisés, 'Minilateralsim: The Magic Number to Get Real International Action' (2009) Foreign Policy, 173.

priorities and positions create a solid resistance to top-down rules, which are found to be overly prescriptive. Consequently, compliance with them is low.[12] Similarly, the bottom-up approach cannot activate the international community to meet their climate commitments due to the absence of a binding legal framework. Also, it might lead to inconsistencies and a lack of alignment among the climate targets of different countries, making it difficult to assess the overall progress in combating climate change at a global level.

Currently, regional and sectoral initiatives with limited membership and smaller negotiating mandates gain greater support than multilateral ones in climate governance, hoping to create ambition in mitigation efforts.[13] Smaller fora allow a more focused and tailored approach for addressing unique climate challenges in a particular geographic area or sector.[14] These initiatives tend to attract forward-thinking countries that share similar conditions. Smaller groups can make decisions more efficiently and respond quickly to emerging problems.[15] They are often more agile in adapting to changing circumstances and can experiment with new approaches in a way that larger, more complex multilateral negotiations may not be capable of. Hence, the smaller foras would revitalise the willingness of the forerunner countries to act.

Several researchers have enlightened that the multiple coalitions of a few numbers of but willing countries or countries with comparable conditions and backgrounds tend to accomplish more than a single large alliance, where the interests are divergent, and the free-riding is prominent.[16] The parties to a smaller forum can more easily achieve a mutual understanding of the measures undertaken by each country. They can engage in discussions regarding critical factors for individual or

[12]Thomas Dietz, Elinor Ostrom, and Paul C Stern, 'The Struggle to Govern the Commons' (2003) 302 Science 1907, 1907 < https://doi.org/10.1126/science.1091015>

[13]Anthony Brenton, 'Great Powers in Climate Politics' (2013) 13(5) Climate Policy 541, 542. William Nordhaus, *The Climate Casino: Risk, Uncertainty, and Economics for a Warming World* (Yale University Press, 2013), 7. Richard B Stewart, Michael Oppenheimer, and Bryce Rudyk, 'Building Blocks for Global Climate Protection' (2013) 32(2) Stan Envti LJ, 356. Within the alternative fora discourse G7, G8+5, and the G20 came under scrutiny. These high-level fora, especially G7, are successful in bringing up the climate change issue to the agenda and allowed the discussions of this controversial topic among a small number of influential countries. However, these fora are lack of required expertise and focus on climate mitigation. Particularly, in the technical aspects such as the carbon market, specific guidance is required to govern the details in depth. On the other hand, specialized agencies like OECD or IEA have the technical expertise but they do not have an explicit mandate for climate change cooperation.

[14]Isatis Cintron-Rodriguez and others, 'Equitable and Empowering Participatory Policy Design Strategies to Accelerate Just Climate Action' (2021) 18 Journal of Science Policy & Governance <https://doi.org/10.38126/JSPG180203>.

[15]David Victor, 'Toward Effective International Cooperation on Climate Change: Numbers, Interests, and Institutions' (2006) 6 Global Environmental Politics, 90 <https://doi.org/10.1162/glep.2006.6.3.90>

[16]Matteo Roggero, Leonhard Kähler, and Achim Hagen, 'Strategic Cooperation for Transnational Adaptation: Lessons from the Economics of Climate Change Mitigation' (2019) 19 International Environmental Agreements 395, 404 <https://doi.org/10.1007/s10784-019-09442-x>.

joint action.[17] In smaller fora, it is easier to build consensus and agree on concrete measures, which can lead to more decisive action. This perspective in the climate negotiations provides a novel and sustainable approach, which can achieve the transformative change climate governance needs, compared to insisting on ineffective routines.

1.1 Minilateralism

The concept that involves small groups of countries is defined as minilateralism in the international relations discipline. Minilateral agreements are complementary to broader multilateral agreements and aim to bring together a select group of signatories to work on specific aspects of a complex issue.[18] Minilateralism recognises that not all countries have the same level of commitment or readiness to address complex global challenges.[19] A minilateral forum allows for incremental progress by involving nations that are ready to take action while remaining open to the engagement of reluctant countries over time. It creates specific benefits that can be limited to countries willing to join the institution and abide by its rules.[20] By focusing on smaller groups of countries with shared priorities and a common willingness to take action, minilateral approaches aim to achieve more tangible and immediate results. Understanding and recognising actors' heterogeneous preferences, competencies, and constraints can enhance ambitious climate cooperation.[21]

There are different minilateral climate cooperation proposals in the contemporary global climate governance literature. The coalition of the willing proposal refers to a group of countries voluntarily coming together to commit to ambitious climate targets and take joint action to achieve them.[22] Member countries within this coalition demonstrate their willingness to lead by example and go beyond existing commitments to address climate change. Bilateral cooperation involves two countries working together to develop and implement climate policies and projects.[23]

[17] Nicholas Stern, 'Ethics, Equity and The Economics of Climate Change Paper 2: Economics and Politics' (2014) 30 Economics and Philosophy 445, 478.

[18] William Nordhaus, 'Climate Clubs: Overcoming Free-Riding in International Climate Policy' (2015) 105(4) American Economic Review 1339, 1341.

[19] Marcel J. Dorsch and Christian Flachsland, 'A Polycentric Approach to Global Climate Governance' (2017) 17 Global Environmental Politics 45, 53 < https://doi.org/10.1162/GLEP_a_00400>.

[20] Robert Falkner, 'A Minilateral Solution for Global Climate Change? On Bargaining Efficiency, Club Benefits, and International Legitimacy' (2016) 14 Perspectives on Politics 87, 89.

[21] Dorsch and Flachsland (n 19) 53.

[22] Thomas Hale and Charles Roger, 'Orchestration and Transnational Climate Governance' (2014) 40(2) Review of International Studies 341. Daniel Bodansky, 'The Paris Climate Change Agreement: A New Hope?' (2016) 110(2) American Journal of International Law 288.

[23] J Park, 'Climate Change Cooperation between Korea and Vietnam: Bilateral Cooperation in Renewable Energy and the Global Climate Regime' (2019) 27(2) Asian Journal of Political

This approach allows for more direct and focused collaboration, where countries can tailor their efforts to specific circumstances and objectives. In the sectoral agreements approach, countries negotiate agreements on specific sectors, such as transportation or energy, to promote low-carbon development.[24] They recognise that addressing climate change often requires a sector-specific approach due to the unique challenges and opportunities within each area. Lastly, the climate club approach involves groups of countries forming regional or issue-specific coalitions to address particular aspects of the climate crisis, such as carbon pricing.[25] It is the fundamental focus of the book and meticulosity analysed under Chap. 4. Each of these approaches represents a distinct strategy for addressing climate change. The choice among them often depends on the specific priorities, capacities, and interests of the countries involved.

UN is a consensus-based regime where one country can block the development of new climate mitigation norms or agreements. The existence of alternative fora consisting of ambitious actors can avoid such a blockade. In this regard, Keohane and Victor have differentiated between a single climate regime and a regime complex, which 'emerged as a result of many choices … at different times and on different specific issues'.[26] Regime complexes consist of interlocking networks of international agreements and organizations. In this way, minilateralism bypasses some challenges and gridlock in large-scale, multilateral negotiations.[27] Furthermore, minilateralism complements and bolsters the larger, multilateral efforts undertaken within the UN framework. Smaller-scale initiatives can serve as laboratories for innovative policies and practices.[28] When successful, the progress made in minilateral fora can influence and inspire broader multilateral negotiations, potentially leading to the adoption of similar norms within the UN.

A minilateral governance design strengthens the pledges of its members and plays significant governance roles. It provides complementary norms and assistance for the existing multilateral schemes. Doing so can help fill gaps and enhance the effectiveness of these multilateral agreements.[29] Minilateral fora can plan and manage the carbon markets with ease.[30] Furthermore, minilateral approach can

---

Science 253.

[24] H Duan and Y Xu, 'Sectoral Cooperation on Climate Change: A Game Theoretic Analysis' (2018) 70 Energy Economics 114.

[25] David G Victor and D Cullenward 'The Strategic Logic of Organized Hypocrisy in Climate Change Policy' (2015) 6(2) Global Policy 190–200.

[26] David Victor and Robert Keohane, 'The Regime Complex for Climate Change' (2010) 9 Perspectives on Politics 7 <https://doi.org/10.1017/S1537592710004068>.

[27] Ibid 7.

[28] Johannes Reich, 'Federalism and Mitigating Climate Change: The Merits of Flexibility, Experimentalism, and Dissonance' (2021) TEL, 16.

[29] Kilian Raiser and others, 'Is the Paris Agreement Effective? A Systematic Map of the Evidence' (2020) 15 Environmental Research Letters 083006.

[30] Falkner (n 20) 100.

disseminate information and technology[31] for carbon mitigation and enable necessary funding.[32] In this way, it reduces the costs of mitigation, which can foster innovation and flexible adaptation in climate mitigation governance overall. As well as it can ensure the production and diffusion of knowledge and norms.[33] These aspects of the minilateral forum can increase bargaining efficiency for climate forerunner countries. Thereby, successful minilateral initiatives can influence and stimulate further climate negotiations at both the minilateral and multilateral levels.[34]

The proliferation of minilateral fora and voluntary climate cooperation outside the UNFCCC is a noteworthy trend in the global effort to address climate change.[35] These fora have gained prominence as they elevate the level of ambition for medium- and long-term emissions reduction targets at regional or global levels.[36] Most of them are based on voluntary protocol, where members assemble to present their climate commitments, learn from each other's experiences, provide mutual support, and spread their actions to non-committed countries. The primary goal of these fora is to disseminate climate norms to countries that have not yet made climate commitments through knowledge sharing and peer influence.[37] Consequently, they have attracted significant global participation. Over 100 countries are members of one form of climate cooperation, and 29 of them are members of at least five schemes.[38] Notably, two-thirds of them are high-income countries.[39] This trend reveals that the

[31] The development and deployment of wide range of low carbon technologies is essential to create GHG abatement. Greater cooperation in international arena will accelerate the technological innovation; and diffusion of innovation will reduce the cost of mitigation. Technology cooperation enables the sharing of risks, rewards, progress of development and coordination of priorities. Nicholas Stern, *The Economics of Climate Change: The Stern Review* (Cambridge University Press 2007), 23–24.

[32] David G Victor, *Global Warming Gridlock: Creating More Effective Strategies for Protecting the Planet* (Cambridge University Press 2011).

[33] Dorsch and Flachsland (n 19) 55.

[34] Robyn Eckersley, 'Moving Forward in the Climate Negotiations: Multilateralism or Minilateralism?' (2012) 12(2) Global Environmental Politics 24 <https://doi.org/10.1162/GLEP_a_00107>.

[35] Dorsch and Flachsland (n 19) 45.

[36] The Copenhagen Accord was also essentially produced in the minilateral setting of a confidential meeting between the USA and four large developing countries. It was then presented to a slightly larger group of 26 countries that had been earlier negotiating a text before finally being unsuccessfully presented to the full COP meeting (a further 160 states) for approval. Lavanya Rajamani, 'The Making and Unmaking of the Copenhagen Accord' (2010) 59 International & Comparative Law Quarterly 824. Furthermore, G-20 and G-7 are club schemes that are based on political dialogue.

[37] Slyvia I Karlsson-Vinkhuyzen and Jeffrey McGee 'Legitimacy in an Era of Fragmentation: The Case of Global Climate Governance' (2013) 13 Global Environmental Politics 56.

[38] Lutz Weischer, Jennifer Morgan, and Milap Patel, 'Climate Clubs: Can Small Groups of Countries Make a Big Difference in Addressing Climate Change?' (2012) 21(3) Review of European Community & International Environmental Law 177, 183.

[39] ibid.

climate change agenda can be advanced through bilateral or plurilateral arrangements, which allow participating countries to address their concerns separately.[40]

The minilateral approach in climate governance finds a parallel in the realm of trade governance through the mechanism of plurilateral agreements. Plurilateralism refers to agreeing on rules and market access commitments within a sizeable subgroup of WTO members. This approach closely mirrors the concept of minilateralism, where a select group of like-minded countries come together to deepen and broaden WTO rules and commitments on specific trade issues without requiring the participation of reluctant WTO members.[41] The roots of plurilateralism are not a novel concept in international trade. Since the inception of the GATT in 1947, the club approach has been employed as a strategic tool to achieve significant milestones, such as tariff liberalization and the reduction of non-tariff barriers.[42] In the broader context of economic diplomacy, plurilateralism represents one of the various tiers of international negotiations, wherein agreements forged at one level may have implications or exert influence at other levels of governance. This tiered approach allows for a more dynamic and responsive negotiation process, particularly in the face of evolving global trade challenges.

Plurilateralism is anticipated to be more efficient and effective in adapting the WTO to the evolving global trade challenges than multilateralism, which necessitates the consensus of all 164 WTO members for new rules and commitments. This is because modern trade policy requires states to find a finely tuned balance between trade and broader public policy objectives such as mitigating climate change.[43] Plurilateral agreements, per Article II.3 of the Agreement Establishing the WTO, are often better suited to finding mutually agreeable, legitimate, and welfare-maximizing agreements than multilateralism.[44] A key advantage of plurilateral agreements is their inherent flexibility and inclusivity. While they permit a degree of discrimination among participating countries by involving binding policy commitments, they also provide a safeguard against free-riding by non-participants.[45] This ensures that only those committed to the agreed-upon rules reap the benefits, thereby

[40] Ole Jacob Sending, Indra Øverland and Thomas Boe Hornburg, 'Climate Change and International Relations' (2020) 73(1) Journal of International Affairs 183, 188.

[41] Michel Dupuy, 'Plurilateralism: The Key to Saving the World Trade Organization and Boosting Global Trade Liberalization' (2015) 6(1) Journal of International Organizations Studies 47, 47.

[42] Olga Biryukova, "Shaken Not Stirred': WTO as a Ground for Plurilateral Initiatives' (2022) 17(3) Global Trade and Customs Journal 121, 129

[43] Robert Basedow, 'The WTO and the Rise of Plurilateralism—What Lessons can we Learn from the European Union's Experience with Differentiated Integration?' (2018) 21(2) Journal of International Economic Law 411, 415 <https://doi.org/10.1093/jiel/jgy020>.

[44] A notable plurilateral initiative, although unsuccessful, was the Environmental Goods Agreement. Between 2014 and 2016, approximately 46 WTO members representing nearly 90 percent of all world trade negotiated it within the WTO framework. The agreement ultimately failed when major negotiating parties introduced new demands shortly before its anticipated conclusion, causing the negotiations to collapse. Bernard M Hoekman and Petros C Mavroidis, 'Embracing Diversity: Plurilateral Agreements and the Trading System' (2015) 14(1) World Trade Review 101, 101.

[45] Ibid 104.

incentivizing participation and compliance. Moreover, plurilateral agreements are, in principle, open to any WTO member that wishes to join, thus maintaining an open-door policy that encourages broader inclusion over time. The ultimate goal is to gradually expand these plurilateral agreements into multilateral agreements encompassing all WTO members, thereby strengthening the global trade framework.[46]

In periods when the traditional, all-encompassing multilateral approach appears to falter, the plurilateral alternative emerges as a viable pathway for motivated members to tackle pressing challenges. By doing so, it not only addresses specific trade concerns but also contributes to restoring and reinforcing the WTO's central role in governing world trade. The parallels between minilateralism in climate governance and plurilateralism in trade governance underscore a shared imperative: the need for more agile, adaptable, and targeted forms of international cooperation. Both approaches recognize that the complexities of global challenges, whether in climate or trade, often require the flexibility to advance in smaller, more committed groups. This allows for more focused and timely action, which can later serve as a foundation for broader, more inclusive global agreements. In both arenas, these innovative governance models offer a promising route to achieving tangible progress in addressing some of the most pressing issues of our time.

The minilateral fora and critique of the UNFCCC process do not suggest abandoning the whole previous efforts. UNFCCC has made an essential contribution to climate law by providing fundamental principles and legitimising efforts undertaken at multiple levels. Therefore, the alternative approaches only aim to address the problems associated with the centralising and hyperbolic scheme of the multilateral process, not wholly disown it. The suggestion with minilateralism is an innovative and complementary scheme to fill the governance gaps left by the UNFCCC.[47] It seeks to expedite action and offer more flexible and focused strategies while recognising the importance of the UNFCCC's foundational principles and goals. As an umbrella political forum, UNFCCC would continue to serve the purposes of principle and methodology setting, information exchange, oversight, and funding mechanisms.[48] It continues to exert pressure on national governments to deliver their climate commitments.[49] The minilateral approach reimagines the UNFCCC as a coordinating hub within a diverse climate change initiative landscape rather than an authority attempting to govern climate change comprehensively.[50] Consequently, the evolution of climate governance is characterised by a dynamic interplay of

[46] See Agreements under Annex of the Agreement Establishing the WTO.

[47] Falkner (n 20) 90.

[48] Michele Betsill and others 'Building Productive Links between the UNFCCC and the Broader Global Climate Governance Landscape' (2015) 15(2) Global Environmental Politics 1, 3.

[49] Chiara Galiffa and Ignacio Garcia Bercero, 'How WTO-Consistent Tools Can Ensure the Decarbonization of Emission-Intensive Industrial Sectors' (2022) 116 AJIL Unbound 196 <https://doi.org/10.1017/aju.2022.32>.

[50] Matthew J Hoffman, *Climate Governance at the Crossroads: Experimenting with a Global Response after Kyoto* (Oxford University Press, 2011).

various initiatives and mechanisms, each contributing to the overarching goal of mitigating climate change and promoting sustainable practices.

2 The Advantages of Minilateralism

Particularly in regimes where the countries hold different beliefs and views on how to approach the problem, such as climate change, a less-than-global approach can create a more effective administration.[51] Similarly, Falkner highlights the theoretical advantages of climate negotiations with fewer parties.[52] Accordingly, specialised regimes can enable faster and more effective bargaining among like-minded and ambitious countries. Smaller groups may find it easier to reach agreements and make decisions, expediting the implementation of climate actions.[53] Whereas in larger, more diverse fora, negotiations can become complex and protracted. Therefore, minilateral fora can negotiate more quickly and with a greater focus on specific goals, leading to more decisive outcomes. Consequently, they can create incentive instruments for ensuring compliance and enabling broader participation.

Minilateral specialised regimes can simplify the enforcement of commitments since monitoring and enforcement mechanisms can be more straightforward and focused.[54] This opportunity can enhance accountability and abidance among members. Smaller regimes better serve the interests of countries. They allow countries to focus on specific aspects of climate change that align with their national priorities and capacities. Such flexibility can make climate action effective for individual nations. Also, by tailoring climate initiatives to the specific needs and interests of participating countries, the tendency to comply with a scheme will increase among the members. The accomplishments of these fora can serve as models for broader international cooperation, encouraging other countries to engage more actively in climate action.[55] Ultimately, minilateralism encourages "reluctant" countries and supports the ones with capacity constraints for successful climate action.

Smaller fora can help minimise opposition or obstruction from countries with differing interests. They can operate with a lower risk of encountering a single country's veto, allowing like-minded actors to move forward more swiftly. In some cases, minilateral fora can serve as a form of soft balancing against dominant global powers, which refers to a strategy employed by countries or groups to counterbalance the influence of dominant global powers without engaging in direct

[51] Charles F Sabel and David G Victor, 'Governing Global Problems Under Uncertainty: Making Bottom-Up Climate Policy Work' (2017) 144 Climatic Change 15 <https://doi.org/10.1007/s10584-015-1507-y>.

[52] Falkner (n 20) 91–92.

[53] Ibid 96.

[54] Ibid 104.

[55] Ibid 99.

confrontation.[56] Countries may utilise minilateral fora to balance the influence of more powerful nations by advancing their interests or countering potential hegemony. Consequently, minilateral strategy enhances smaller countries influence on the global stage, providing a counterweight to the dominance of major powers and promoting a more balanced international order.

Furthermore, minilateral approaches to climate governance can offer advantages over unilateral measures.[57] These advantages stem from the fact that individual national climate policies can create a patchwork of inconsistent regulations that are neither sustainable for the environment nor international trade. From an environmental perspective, varying national legislations result in different baselines in each jurisdiction, which can lead to higher levels of GHG emissions than what is sustainable. From a trade perspective, unilateral national policies potentially constitute trade barriers.[58] For instance, they might discriminate against foreign goods or services compared to domestic ones, be stricter than necessary and not based on internationally recognised standards. In contrast, by ensuring that markets in various jurisdictions are subject to similar emissions abatement regulations, minilateral approaches can help reduce the marginal cost of climate action. They seek to avoid unnecessary trade conflicts and barriers when designed and implemented collaboratively.[59]

3 Fragmentation

Minilateral cooperation will also result in the fragmentation of climate regulations and institutions. A significant feature of the contemporary international legal order is fragmentation, as evidenced by an increasing number of specialized regimes, rules, and institutions. It is argued that self-contained regimes,[60] which are the main

---

[56] TV Paul, *Restraining Great Powers: Soft Balancing from Empires to the Global Era* (Yale University Press 2018), 29–33.

[57] Joanne Scott, 'The Multi-Level Governance of Climate Change' (2011) 5 Carbon and Climate Law Review 25, 27-28. Kati Kulovesi, 'Addressing Sectoral Emissions outside the UNFCCC: What Roles for Multilateralism, Minilateralism and Unilateralism?' (2012) 21(3) Review of European Community and International Environmental Law 193.

[58] Henri Culot, 'Unilateral Sanctions in International Economic Law' in Thomas Cottier and Krista Nadakavukaren Schefer (eds), *Elgar Encyclopedia of International Economic Law* (Edward Elgar 2017), 343.

[59] Nicholas Stern and Hans Peter Lankes, *Collaborating and Delivering on Climate Action Through a Climate Club: An Independent Report to the G7* (London School of Economics and Political Science, 2022), 32.

[60] It refers to any interrelated cluster of rules addressing a specific issue, along with the administration of those rules. International Law Commission, 'Fragmentation of International Law: Difficulties Arising from the Diversification and Expansion of International Law' (A/CN.4/L.702, 2006), para 152.

sources of fragmentation, create coherence problems in international climate law.[61] In this regard, coherence is valued positively owing to its connection with predictability and legal security. Analysing the fragmentation of the global environmental governance architecture, one argument is that governments intentionally establish overlapping and even conflicting international organizations due to their fear of infringing upon national sovereignty.[62] Also, fragmentation appears to be advantageous for powerful countries, as exemplified by the rise of bilateral trade agreements where the interests of developed countries such as the US or EU are more predominant. They can selectively engage with a fragmented set of agreements, participating only in those decision-making processes that align with their individual interests. In comparison, developing countries may gain power relative to industrialized countries in multilateral agreements.[63] Furthermore, the diversity of obligations can hinder implementation in countries with limited international policy capacity.[64]

However, the fragmentation can also be seen as a positive indicator and an opportunity for strategic action. According to the economic analysis of law approach, the division of labour and specialization are essential for increasing productivity, ultimately leading to the betterment of society as a whole. In this regard, the neoliberal legal tradition has posited that fragmentation is not a problem but rather a component of a gradually evolving solution to the demands globalization imposes on the international system. It views fragmentation as a market-like response to pluralist diversity, which is vastly superior to more hierarchical alternatives.[65] Charney explains that alternative forums complement and strengthen the system of international law despite some loss of uniformity.[66] They demonstrate legal responsiveness to social change.[67] Mainly because they amplify diversity and expand legal norms to previously unregulated areas.[68] In this way, fragmentation creates specialization in various aspects of climate change law. It would lead to disseminating of the

---

[61] See for example, ibid para 14.

[62] Maria H Ivanova and Jennifer Roy, 'The Architecture of Global Environmental Governance: Pros and Cons of Multiplicity' in L Swart and E Perry (eds), *Global Environmental Governance: Perspectives on the Current Debate* (Center for UN Reform Education 2007) 48, 50.

[63] Silke Trommer, 'The WTO in an Era of Preferential Trade Agreements: Thick and Thin Institutions in Global Trade Governance' (2017) 16(3) World Trade Review 501.

[64] Jason Jabbour and others, 'Internationally Agreed Environmental Goals: A Critical Evaluation of Progress' (2012) 3 Environmental Development 5.

[65] Eyal Benvenisti and George W Downs, 'International Political Economy and the Fragmentation of International Law' in *Between Fragmentation and Democracy: The Role of National and International Courts* (Cambridge University Press 2017), 19.

[66] Jonathan Charney, 'International Law and Multiple International Tribunals' (1998) 271 RdC 145.

[67] Martti Koskenniemi and Päivi Leino, 'Fragmentation of International Law? Postmodern Anxieties' (2002) 15(3) Leiden Journal of International Law 553, 575.

[68] Daniel Bodansky, *The Art and Craft of International Environmental Law* (Harvard University Press, 2010) 17. Frank Biermann, *Earth System Governance: World Politics in the Anthropocene* (MIT Press, 2014) 222. JB Ruhl, 'Fragmentation and Environmental Regulation: Sacrifice Zones and the Problem of Regulatory Overlap' (2011) 22(1) Fordham Environmental Law Review 1.

regulatory schemes, which can develop a shared body of knowledge and best practices. Also, it promises to promote global economic integration and strengthen the rule of law beyond what could ever have been achieved through more formal, comprehensive institutions. Fragmentation creates competition among the various legal schemes, increasing the possibility of generic solutions. As countries experiment with different policies, the most effective and efficient ones can become models for others. Consequently, minilateral processes do not undermine the coherence of international law; instead, they can strengthen it.[69]

The positive impacts of fragmentation are increased if it is based on a cooperative architecture. Here, minilateral core institutions are loosely integrated with other institutions, and their core norms are not conflicting.[70] In this way, fragmentation enables more expeditious, innovative, and far-reaching decision-making among a highly collaborative yet smaller group of actors.[71] It facilitates tailor-made decisions with more specialized reporting frameworks and ensures that inaction in one decision-making process does not jeopardize others. Fragmentation may thus provide actors the flexibility to freely enter or exit non-confrontational negotiations where decisions are made through consensus.[72] Within this scope, scholars have advocated for a fragmented regime complex, wherein the climate convention serves as a central negotiating forum, providing substantial flexibility and diversity to accommodate a complex of sub-regimes.[73]

Fragmentation reflects the institutional expression of political pluralism internationally[74] or the increased demand for expertise within international institutions.[75] The competitive regulatory environment strives for different jurisdictions to demonstrate leadership in climate action and develop mechanisms to benefit from carbon regulation. This competition is not about rivalry but about demonstrating effective solutions and sharing successes that can inspire others.[76] Therefore, it is a competition among political interests for democracy.[77] Fragmentation also accommodates countries' conflicting interests. Hence, it can allow for more tailored approaches to

[69] Jonathan Charney, 'The Impact on the International Legal System of Growth of International Courts and Tribunals' (1999) 31 New York University Journal of International Law and Politics 697, 700.

[70] Frank Biermann and others, 'The Fragmentation of Global Governance Architectures: A Framework for Analysis' (2009) 9(4) Global Environmental Politics 14.

[71] Frank Biermann and others, 'Governance Fragmentation' in Frank Biermann and Rakhyun E Kim (eds), *Architectures of Earth System Governance: Institutional Complexity and Structural Transformation* (Cambridge University Press 2020), 168.

[72] Amitav Acharya, 'The Future of Global Governance: Fragmentation May Be Inevitable and Creative' (2016) 22 Global Governance 453.

[73] For example, Kevin W Abbott, 'The Transnational Regime Complex for Climate Change' (2012) 30(4) Government and Policy 571.

[74] Martti Koskenniemi, 'The Fate of Public International Law: Between Technique and Politics' (2007) 70 Mod L Rev 1, 4.

[75] Koskenniemi and Leino (n 67) 555.

[76] Reich (n 28) 16.

[77] Benvenisti and Downs (n 65) 15.

climate action, as policies can be designed to address specific regional circumstances. This flexibility enables countries to find solutions that align with their unique challenges and capacities. Multiple legal schemes and approaches allow for the cross-pollination of ideas and knowledge sharing. Different jurisdictions can learn from each other's experiences, adapt successful policies, and contribute to a shared pool of climate governance expertise.[78] Consequently, the most effective policy among them can take the lead and might be employed by the other systems.

In summary, the fragmentation of climate regulations can present significant advantages in promoting specialization, competition, and innovation.[79] When harnessed successfully, the diversity of legal norms and approaches can contribute to more effective and adaptive global responses to climate change. The specialization can lead to more efficient and operative climate policies, as countries can focus on areas where they can make the most significant contributions. Far from undermining the coherence of international law, the fragmentation can lead to the emergence of harmonised and enhanced global standards over time. For instance, if countries share their successful strategies, a body of common norms and practices can evolve. This shared knowledge can contribute to developing more comprehensive and effective international agreements, ultimately enhancing the overall coherence of the climate change framework. The goal of minilateral cooperation is to identify, refine, and disseminate the most effective and efficient policies for combating climate change. As these policies prove their worth on smaller scales, they can gain traction and potentially be adopted on a global scale, contributing to a more coherent international legal framework for climate action.

4 Challenges of Alternative Governance Structures

While minilateral fora can offer various advantages, they have also potential drawbacks and challenges that need to be addressed. In an increasingly interdependent world, global cooperation is not just a desirable option but a necessity to confront complex challenges. Therefore, successful global abatement can only be achieved if large numbers of participants are attracted to the climate alliance since the climate challenges are interconnected. However, minilateral fora, by their nature, involve a subset of countries rather than the entire international community. If the minilateral forum does not include at least some major emitter countries, it will not achieve

[78] Kurt Matzler and Julia Mueller, 'Antecedents of Knowledge Sharing – Examining the Influence of Learning and Performance Orientation' (2011) 32 Journal of Economic Psychology 317 <https://doi.org/10.1016/J.JOEP.2010.12.006>.

[79] In a similar vein, federalism demonstrates that, with its inherent features of flexibility, experimentalism, administrative coordination, participatory policymaking, and competition-driven efficiency, can offer a strategic example for the fragmentation in climate change governance approaches. Reich (n 28) 29.

substantial mitigation, potentially inducing low support.[80] In contrast, if the forum regulates a large share of global GHG emissions, it might receive higher international support despite procedural deficiencies. Therefore, including major emitters can garner legitimacy for the minilateral forum's initiatives.

Moreover, the critics claim that decision-making in a small group of countries will not be democratic.[81] Powerful or influential members' preferences might dominate the agenda, potentially side-line the interests and voices of smaller or less powerful countries. It can lead to concerns about representation and inclusivity, as smaller and less influential nations may be excluded from important discussions and decision-making processes.[82] Such implementation ignores the ethical principle of due process and creates a scheme that is self-serving to the interests of large-emitting countries.[83] Consequently, minilateralism inadequately deals with equity and distributional conflicts. This similar drawback is experienced under WTO plurilateralism and creates a risk of marginalizing opposition, particularly from developing and least developed countries.[84] Critics of plurilateralism caution that wealthy developed countries agree among themselves on sector-specific rules or controversial issues (e.g. trade and environment) tailored to their national interests.[85] While developing and least developed countries may not be legally bound by these rules, they may have to accept and follow them de facto if they wish to participate in relevant global value chains. Additionally, developing countries believe that plurilateral initiatives would divert the attention of WTO member countries from the issue of development, which can only be effectively addressed at a global level.[86]

Also, minilateral approaches might experience low legitimacy. In climate change, procedural and legal legitimacy are conveyed by the UNFCCC, which is considered the default venue for cooperating on global climate problems. Also, the UNFCCC has a robust institutional connection to scientific knowledge with IPCC. Even though this connection does not mean that knowledge has been the key driver for decisions made in the UNFCCC process, it has given the climate regime significant exposure to expertise. Therefore, the majority of countries prefer coercive foreign

[80] UNEP (n 9).

[81] At the international level, equal participation of states (i.e., universal multilateralism) can be viewed as a manifestation of one of the key principles of democracy. Maria Weimer, 'Reconciling Regulatory Space with External Accountability through WTO Adjudication – Trade, Environment and Development' (2017) 30(4) Leiden Journal of International Law 901, 905.

[82] Eckersley, 'Moving Forward in the Climate Negotiations' (n 34) Weischer, Morgan, and Patel (n 38).

[83] Jeffrey Mcgee, 'Exclusive Minilateralism: An Emerging Discourse within International Climate Change Governance?' (2011) 8 PORTAL Journal of Multidisciplinary International Studies, 12 <https://doi.org/10.5130/portal.v8i3.1873>.

[84] Dupuy (n 41) 57.

[85] Basedow (n 43) 419.

[86] Dupuy (n 42) 57.

policy measures to be in accordance with the UN regime.[87] However, minilateral fora often operate with less formal structure and oversight compared to larger, multilateral bodies like the UN. This organization can lead to a lack of procedural accountability in decision-making and implementation, which creates a greater risk of uncoordinated actions and policies. Likewise under the trade governance, the increased use of the plurilateral approach would shift WTO towards a two-track regime, with subsets of countries operating independently within their own frameworks. Many developing countries have argued that this approach contradicts the fundamental character of the WTO and conflicts with the consensus-based approach that has historically been the norm.[88]

The parties to a minilateral forum may indeed bear a significant economic burden due to their efforts to mitigate climate change. Implementing stringent climate policies, transitioning to cleaner energy sources, and investing in sustainable practices can be costly. This financial commitment can be a concern for governments, particularly if they fear that it might adversely impact their economies, industries, or fiscal stability. Their population might perceive the non-parties to the minilateral forum as free riders and thus oppose mitigation in the first place.[89] Subsequently, it becomes difficult for governments to sustain domestic support for these mitigation policies. Also, members of the forum might fear comparative disadvantages for their industries due to tighter domestic regulation and higher energy costs. They might worry that this could affect their global competitiveness, potentially leading to job losses and economic repercussions. In conclusion, the economic and political challenges associated with participation in minilateral fora might hinder some countries from being part of climate mitigation efforts.

Additionally, considering the duplication of efforts and forum shopping[90] under minilateralism is of utmost importance.[91] When multiple minilateral fora are formed to address similar or overlapping issues, there is a risk of duplicating efforts. It can lead to inefficiencies, fragmentation of resources, and confusion among stakeholders. The duplication of efforts can hinder the ability of these fora to achieve their intended goals. Moreover, it can lead to the misallocation of resources, which is a critical concern in a world where resources for addressing climate change are limited. Secondly, minilateral fora result in forum shopping, that occurs when countries

[87] Michael Tomz and Jessica Weeks 'Public Opinion and the Democratic Peace' (2013) 107(4) American Political Science Review 849.

[88] Hoekman and Mavroidis (n 44) 109.

[89] Thomas Bernauer, Robert Gampfer, and Florian Landis 'Burden Sharing in Global Climate Governance' in Todd Cherry, Jon Hovi, and David McEvoy (eds), *Toward a New Climate Agreement: Conflict, Resolution and Governance* (Routledge, 2014), 44–60.

[90] 'Forum shopping' is a corollary of multiple forum choices. Luiz Eduardo Salles, 'Forum Choice and Forum Shopping' in *Max Planck Encyclopedia of International Procedural Law*, in Hélène Ruiz Fabri (eds) (Max Planck Institute Luxembourg for Procedural Law 2020), para 2. Under minilateral context, it refers to engaging in forums where a state or group of states can exert more influence—either due to the forum's structure, the nature of the issues discussed, or the economic and political weight of the participants—can lead to more favourable outcomes.

[91] Betsill and others (n 48) 8.

strategically choose which forum to participate in based on their perceived interests or the regulatory environment that best suits them. It can lead to a situation where nations prioritise their agendas over collective global goals. Similarly, under plurilateral trade approach policymakers are concerned that overlapping and contradictory provisions and interpretations might impede free world trade.[92] Also, it could lower the legitimacy, which is critically needed for decisions made in the WTO. However, WTO consensus has become an unrestricted veto right. The increased heterogeneity of WTO membership and the failure of the Doha Development Round have reinforced the perception that minilateralism is necessary.[93]

Nonetheless, in climate negotiations, inevitably, the interests of some countries will prevail over others due to the discrepancy in expertise and capacity of each negotiating party. Even the UNFCCC negotiations are held by negotiating blocks of states, such as the EU and the G77.[94] The participation of developing countries is already limited, given their small delegations present at the negotiations.[95] The UNFCCC often empowers select small groups, known as "friends of the chair", to devise a final compromise for adoption under tight deadlines. For instance, during COP15 in Copenhagen, an alternative negotiation text was developed alongside the formal discussions, showcasing a strategic approach to overcoming negotiation impasses and facilitating consensus among parties. This method allows for more nimble and focused resolution efforts in the international climate negotiations. However, the lack of proper process raised criticism and prevented the Copenhagen Accord from being adopted as a COP decision.[96]

To address the risks of minilateralism, it is essential for countries participating in minilateral fora to establish clear communication channels, promote transparency, and actively seek to harmonise their policies and actions with broader international efforts.[97] Without a harmonised approach and a clear division of labour among minilateral initiatives, the effectiveness of climate mitigation actions may be compromised, potentially resulting in missed opportunities for making a meaningful

---

[92] Biryukova (n 42) 123.

[93] Basedown (n 43) 420.

[94] Maria Rubial, 'The Implementation Phase of the Paris Agreement: The Adaptation Provisions' in maria Rubial and Linda Siegele, (eds) *Negotiating Climate Change Adaptation* (Springer Cham. 2020), 112. Micheal A Mehling, Gilbert Metcalf and Robert Stavins, 'Linking Climate Policies to Advance Global Mitigation' (2018) 359 Science 997 <https://doi.org/10.1126/science.aar5988>.

[95] Espen Ronneberg, 'Small Islands and the Big Issue: Climate Change and the role of the Alliance of Small Island States' in Kevin R. Gray and others (eds), *The Oxford Handbook of International Climate Change Law* (Oxford University Press 2016), 766. Ayse Kaya and Lynne Steuerle Schofield, 'Which Countries Send More Delegates to Climate Change Conferences? Analysis of UNFCCC COPs, 1995–2015' (2020) 16(3) Foreign Policy Analysis 478 <https://doi.org/10.1093/fpa/orz031>.

[96] Per Meilstrup, 'The Runaway Summit: The Background Story of the Presidency of COP-15, the UN Climate Change Conference' in Nanna Hvidt and Hans Mouritzen (eds), *Danish Foreign Policy Yearbook 2010* (Danish Institute for International Studies, 2010) 112–136.

[97] Eckersley, 'Moving Forward in the Climate Negotiations' (n 34) 24.

impact. Minilateral fora should demonstrate that economic sacrifices lead to tangible environmental benefits. Moreover, countries should strive to engage in robust dialogue and coordination with other stakeholders, including non-participating nations, to ensure that their minilateral initiatives complement, rather than undermine, the larger goals of international cooperation.

Given the importance and urgency of mitigation efforts, any initiative, even among a minimal number of participants, has the potential to offer exploratory options and instruments. Small-scale cooperation can improve mutual trust between developed and developing countries and assist in enhancing the UNFCCC regime. They can contribute to the development of new ideas and strategies, which can be integrated into broader international agreements. Hence, minilateral approaches have great potential to accelerate subsequent action on climate change. The key lies in ensuring that these fora operate transparently and inclusively with a clear commitment to addressing the needs of climate change. By striking a balance between the advantages and challenges, minilateral approaches can be a valuable part of the global effort to combat climate change.

5 Concluding Remarks

The exploration of alternative governance structures for climate cooperation underscores the limitations of traditional, universal approaches in addressing the multifaceted challenges of climate change. The transition towards minilateralism represents a pragmatic evolution in global climate governance. It offers a platform for more focused, efficient, and effective climate action. This shift acknowledges the diversity of national priorities, capacities, and levels of commitment to climate mitigation; hence, it facilitates tailored strategies that align with specific regional needs. Minilateral fora have emerged as dynamic spaces for forward-thinking countries to lead by example, demonstrating the feasibility and benefits of ambitious climate action, and inspiring broader international cooperation.

The proliferation of minilateral initiatives outside the UNFCCC framework indicates a growing recognition of their potential to catalyse significant advancements in climate mitigation and adaptation. By enabling smaller groups of like-minded countries to spearhead innovative policies and practices, minilateralism complements existing multilateral efforts in enhancing the global response to climate change. These fora serve as laboratories for experimentation, allowing for the rapid development and dissemination of effective climate solutions that can be scaled up or integrated into larger international agreements. Therefore, minilateralism should not operate in isolation but rather complement and synergize with existing efforts. This requires a strategic approach to coordination, identifying gaps in global climate governance that minilateral initiatives can uniquely fill, and leveraging the strengths of various actors to maximize impact. By aligning closely with the objectives of the Paris Agreement and other international frameworks, minilateral efforts can contribute to a coherent and unified global response to climate change.

Despite the promise of minilateralism, its effectiveness is contingent upon addressing inherent challenges such as ensuring inclusivity, maintaining legitimacy, and avoiding the duplication of efforts. While minilateralism seeks to bring together key actors, there is a risk that smaller or less developed nations may be left out of the decision-making process. Ensuring that these voices are not only heard but also have influence in shaping outcomes is essential for the legitimacy and fairness of climate actions. The success of minilateral approaches will depend on their ability to integrate with broader global efforts, ensuring that they contribute constructively to the overarching goals of international climate cooperation. By fostering transparency, encouraging participation from all stakeholders, and harmonizing initiatives with existing climate agreements, minilateralism can offer a complementary pathway towards achieving global climate objectives.

In conclusion, as the global community seeks more effective ways to combat climate change, the evolution towards minilateralism offers a beacon of hope. The climate crisis is a multifaceted challenge that intersects with issues of economic development, social equity, and technological innovation. Minilateralism's flexible framework allows for these intersections to be addressed in a holistic manner, ensuring that climate action is integrated into broader goals of sustainable development. This approach's flexibility, innovative potential, and inclusivity make it a powerful tool in accelerating progress towards climate neutrality. It can accommodate the complex realities of the global climate crisis. In moving forward, it will be crucial to continue refining minilateral approach, ensuring it remains responsive to the ever-changing landscape of global climate governance.

Bibliography

Secondary Sources

Abbott KW, 'The Transnational Regime Complex for Climate Change' (2012) 30(4) Government and Policy 571

Acharya A, 'The Future of Global Governance: Fragmentation May Be Inevitable and Creative' (2016) 22 Global Governance 453

Basedow R, 'The WTO and the Rise of Plurilateralism—What Lessons can we Learn from the European Union's Experience with Differentiated Integration?' (2018) 21(2) Journal of International Economic Law 411 https://doi.org/10.1093/jiel/jgy020

Bausch C and Mehling M, 'Alternative Venues of Climate Cooperation: An Institutional Perspective' in E Hollo, K Kulovesi, M Mehling (eds), *Climate Change and the Law* (Springer, 2013)

Bernauer T, Gampfer R, and Landis F 'Burden Sharing in Global Climate Governance' in T Cherry, J Hovi, and D McEvoy (eds), *Toward a New Climate Agreement: Conflict, Resolution and Governance* (Routledge, 2014)

Betsill M and others 'Building Productive Links between the UNFCCC and the Broader Global Climate Governance Landscape' (2015) 15(2) Global Environmental Politics 1

Biermann F, *Earth System Governance: World Politics in the Anthropocene* (MIT Press, 2014)

— and others, 'The Fragmentation of Global Governance Architectures: A Framework for Analysis' (2009) 9(4) Global Environmental Politics 14

— and others, 'Governance Fragmentation' in F Biermann and RE Kim (eds), *Architectures of Earth System Governance: Institutional Complexity and Structural Transformation* (Cambridge University Press 2020)

Biryukova O, "Shaken Not Stirred': WTO as a Ground for Plurilateral Initiatives' (2022) 17(3) Global Trade and Customs Journal 121

Bodansky D, *The Art and Craft of International Environmental Law* (Harvard University Press, 2010)

— 'The Paris Climate Change Agreement: A New Hope?' (2016) 110(2) American Journal of International Law 288

Brenton A, 'Great Powers in Climate Politics' (2013) 13(5) Climate Policy 541

Charney J, 'International Law and Multiple International Tribunals' (1998) 271 RdC 145

— 'The Impact on the International Legal System of Growth of International Courts and Tribunals' (1999) 31 New York University Journal of International Law and Politics 697

Cintron-Rodriguez I and others, 'Equitable and Empowering Participatory Policy Design Strategies to Accelerate Just Climate Action' (2021) 18 Journal of Science Policy & Governance <https://doi.org/10.38126/JSPG180203>

Cole DH, 'Climate Change and Collective Action' (2008) 61 Current Legal Problems 229

Culot H, 'Unilateral Sanctions in International Economic Law' in T Cottier and K Nadakavukaren Schefer (eds), *Elgar Encyclopedia of International Economic Law* (Edward Elgar 2017)

Dietz T, Ostrom E and Stern PC, 'The Struggle to Govern the Commons' (2003) 302(5652) Science 1907 <https://doi.org/10.1126/science.1091015>

Duan H and Xu Y, 'Sectoral Cooperation on Climate Change: A Game Theoretic Analysis' (2018) 70 Energy Economics 114

Dupuy M, 'Plurilateralism: The Key to Saving the World Trade Organization and Boosting Global Trade Liberalization' (2015) 6(1) Journal of International Organizations Studies 47

Eckersley R, 'Moving Forward in the Climate Negotiations: Multilateralism or Minilateralism?' (2012) 12(2) Global Environmental Politics 24 <https://doi.org/10.1162/GLEP_a_00107>.

European Commission, 'Report from the Commission to the European Parliament and the Council on the Functioning of the European Carbon Market in 2022 pursuant to Articles 10(5) and 21(2) of Directive 2003/87/EC' COM (2023) 654 final (31 October 2023), 5 <https://climate.ec.europa.eu/system/files/202310/

COM_2023_654_1_EN_ACT_part1_CMR%2BSWD.pdf> accessed 23 March 2024

Falkner R, 'A Minilateral Solution for Global Climate Change? On Bargaining Efficiency, Club Benefits, and International Legitimacy' (2016) 14 Perspectives on Politics 87.

Galiffa C and Bercero IG, 'How WTO-Consistent Tools Can Ensure the Decarbonization of Emission-Intensive Industrial Sectors' (2022) 116 AJIL Unbound 196 <https://doi.org/10.1017/aju.2022.32>

Hale T and Roger C, 'Orchestration and Transnational Climate Governance' (2014) 40(2) Review of International Studies 341.

Held D and Hervey A, 'Democracy, Climate Change, and Global Governance: Democratic Agency and the Policy Menu Ahead' in David Held, Angus Hervey and Marika Theors (eds), *The Governance of Climate Change: Science, Economics, Politics & Ethics* (Cornwall: Polity Press, 2011)

Hoekman BM and Mavroidis PC, 'Embracing Diversity: Plurilateral Agreements and the Trading System' (2015) 14(1) World Trade Review 101, 101

Hoffman MJ, *Climate Governance at the Crossroads: Experimenting with a Global Response after Kyoto* (Oxford University Press, 2011)

International Law Commission, 'Fragmentation of International Law: Difficulties Arising from the Diversification and Expansion of International Law' (A/CN.4/L.702, 2006)

Ivanova MH and Roy J, 'The Architecture of Global Environmental Governance: Pros and Cons of Multiplicity' in L Swart and E Perry (eds), *Global Environmental Governance: Perspectives on the Current Debate* (Center for UN Reform Education 2007) 48.

Jabbour J and others, 'Internationally Agreed Environmental Goals: A Critical Evaluation of Progress' (2012) 3 Environmental Development 5

Karlsson-Vinkhuyzen SI and McGee J 'Legitimacy in an Era of Fragmentation: The Case of Global Climate Governance' (2013) 13 Global Environmental Politics 56

Kaya A and Schofield LS, 'Which Countries Send More Delegates to Climate Change Conferences? Analysis of UNFCCC COPs, 1995–2015' (2020) 16(3) Foreign Policy Analysis 478 <https://doi.org/10.1093/fpa/orz031>

Koskenniemi M, 'The Fate of Public International Law: Between Technique and Politics' (2007) 70 Mod L Rev 1

— and Leino P, 'Fragmentation of International Law? Postmodern Anxieties' (2002) 15(3) Leiden Journal of International Law 553

Kulovesi K, 'Addressing Sectoral Emissions outside the UNFCCC: What Roles for Multilateralism, Minilateralism and Unilateralism?' (2012) 21(3) Review of European Community and International Environmental Law 193

Levin K and others, 'Playing It Forward: Path Dependency, Progressive Incrementalism and the 'Super Wicked' Problem of Global Climate Change' (2009) IOP Conf. Ser.: Earth Environ. Sci. 6 502002

Matzler K and Mueller J, 'Antecedents of Knowledge Sharing – Examining the Influence of Learning and Performance Orientation' (2011) 32 Journal of Economic Psychology 317 <https://doi.org/10.1016/J.JOEP.2010.12.006>

Mcgee J, 'Exclusive Minilateralism: An Emerging Discourse within International Climate Change Governance?' (2011) 8 PORTAL Journal of Multidisciplinary International Studies <https://doi.org/10.5130/portal.v8i3.1873>

Mehling M, Metcalf GE, and Stavins RN 'Linking Climate Policies to Advance Global Mitigation' (2018) 359 Science 997 <https://doi.org/10.1126/science.aar5988>

Meilstrup P, 'The Runaway Summit: The Background Story of the Presidency of COP-15, the UN Climate Change Conference' in N Hvidt and H Mouritzen (eds), *Danish Foreign Policy Yearbook 2010* (Danish Institute for International Studies, 2010)

Moisés N, 'Minilateralism: The Magic Number to Get Real International Action' (2009) Foreign Policy 173

Nordhaus W, 'Climate Clubs: Overcoming Free-Riding in International Climate Policy' (2015) 105(4) American Economic Review 1339.

Park J, 'Climate Change Cooperation between Korea and Vietnam: Bilateral Cooperation in Renewable Energy and the Global Climate Regime' (2019) 27(2) Asian Journal of Political Science 253

Paul TV, *Restraining Great Powers: Soft Balancing from Empires to the Global Era* (Yale University Press 2018)

Peel J, Godden L and Keenan R, 'Climate Change Law in an Era of Multi-Level Governance' (2012) 1(2) Transnational Environmental Law 245

Raiser K and others, 'Is the Paris Agreement Effective? A Systematic Map of the Evidence' (2020) 15 Environmental Research Letters 083006

Rajamani L, 'The Making and Unmaking of the Copenhagen Accord' (2010) 59 International & Comparative Law Quarterly 824

Reich J, 'Federalism and Mitigating Climate Change: The Merits of Flexibility, Experimentalism, and Dissonance' (2021) Transnational Environmental Law

Roggero M, Kähler L, and Hagen A, 'Strategic Cooperation for Transnational Adaptation: Lessons from the Economics of Climate Change Mitigation' (2019) 19 International Environmental Agreements 395, <https://doi.org/10.1007/s10784-019-09442-x>

Ronneberg E, 'Small Islands and the Big Issue: Climate Change and the role of the Alliance of Small Island States' in KR Gray and others (eds), *The Oxford Handbook of International Climate Change Law* (Oxford University Press 2016)

Rubial M, 'The Implementation Phase of the Paris Agreement: The Adaptation Provisions' in M Bueno Rubial and L Siegele, (eds) *Negotiating Climate Change Adaptation* (Springer Cham. 2020)

Ruhl JB, 'Fragmentation and Environmental Regulation: Sacrifice Zones and the Problem of Regulatory Overlap' (2011) 22(1) Fordham Environmental Law Review 1

Sabel CF and Victor DG, 'Governing Global Problems Under Uncertainty: Making Bottom-Up Climate Policy Work' (2017) 144 Climatic Change 15 <https://doi.org/10.1007/s10584-015-1507-y>

Salles LE, 'Forum Choice and Forum Shopping' in *Max Planck Encyclopedia of International Procedural Law* [in Hélène Ruiz Fabri (eds) (Max Planck Institute Luxembourg for Procedural Law 2020)

Scott J, 'The Multi-Level Governance of Climate Change' (2011) 5 Carbon and Climate Law Review 25

Sending OJ, Øverland I and Hornburg TB, 'Climate Change and International Relations' (2020) 73(1) Journal of International Affairs 183

Shaffer G and Bodansky D, 'Transnational Unilateralism and International Law' (2012) 1 Transnational Environmental Law 31

Soltau F, *Fairness in International Climate Change Law and Policy* (Cambridge University Press 2009).

Stern N, *The Economics of Climate Change: The Stern Review* (Cambridge University Press 2007)

— 'Ethics, Equity and The Economics of Climate Change Paper 2: Economics and Politics' (2014) 30 Economics and Philosophy 445

— and Lankes HP, *Collaborating and Delivering on Climate Action Through a Climate Club: An Independent Report to the G7* (London School of Economics and Political Science, 2022)

Stewart RB, Oppenheimer M, and Rudyk B, 'Building Blocks for Global Climate Protection' (2013) 32(2) Stan Envti LJ 351

Tomz M and Weeks J 'Public Opinion and the Democratic Peace' (2013) 107(4) American Political Science Review 849

Trommer S, 'The WTO in an Era of Preferential Trade Agreements: Thick and Thin Institutions in Global Trade Governance' (2017) 16(3) World Trade Review 501

United Nations Environment Program (UNEP), *The Emissions Gap Report 2016: A UNEP Synthesis Report* (UNEP, 2016)

Victor DG, 'Toward Effective International Cooperation on Climate Change: Numbers, Interests and Institutions' (2006) 6(3) Global Environmental Politics 90 <https://doi.org/10.1162/glep.2006.6.3.90>

— and Keohane RO, 'The Regime Complex for Climate Change' (2011) 9(1) Perspectives on Politics

—, *Global Warming Gridlock: Creating More Effective Strategies for Protecting the Planet* (Cambridge University Press 2011)

— and Cullenward D 'The Strategic Logic of Organized Hypocrisy in Climate Change Policy' (2015) 6(2) Global Policy

Weimer M, 'Reconciling Regulatory Space with External Accountability through WTO Adjudication – Trade, Environment and Development' (2017) 30(4) Leiden Journal of International Law 901

Weischer L, Morgan J, and Patel M, 'Climate Clubs: Can Small Groups of Countries Make a Big Difference in Addressing Climate Change?' (2012) 21(3) Review of European Community & International Environmental Law 177

Open Access This chapter is licensed under the terms of the Creative Commons Attribution 4.0 International License (http://creativecommons.org/licenses/by/4.0/), which permits use, sharing, adaptation, distribution and reproduction in any medium or format, as long as you give appropriate credit to the original author(s) and the source, provide a link to the Creative Commons license and indicate if changes were made.

The images or other third party material in this chapter are included in the chapter's Creative Commons license, unless indicated otherwise in a credit line to the material. If material is not included in the chapter's Creative Commons license and your intended use is not permitted by statutory regulation or exceeds the permitted use, you will need to obtain permission directly from the copyright holder.

Chapter 4
Climate Club

1 Conceptualization

1.1 Definition

The climate club represents one of the categories within the broader framework of minilateral approaches to international climate governance. The club is a "voluntary group, which derives mutual interest from sharing production costs, regulatory scheme, and excludable benefits".[1] Club members share a common purpose and are governed by the same rules.[2] This arrangement allows for a more focused and coordinated effort on specific aspects of the climate problem. The rationale is to leverage the advantages of collective action while creating incentives for active participation in climate change mitigation. Therefore, the non-functioning model of current climate agreements can be reconceptualised with the climate club.[3]

The club creates club goods by excluding non-cooperatives from the membership and using its market.[4] The club goods are non-rival, meaning that their consumption by one member does not diminish their availability to others within the club. However, they are excludable; hence, their benefits are limited to club members

---

[1] Todd Sandler and John T Tschirhart, 'Club Theory: Thirty Years Later', (1997) 93 Public Choice 335. Todd Sandler and John T Tschirhart, 'The Economic Theory of Clubs: An Evaluative Survey' (1980) 18(4) Journal of Economic Literature 1481.

[2] Robert Falkner, Naghmeh Nasiritousi and Gunilla Reischl 'Climate Clubs: Politically Feasible and Desirable?' (2021) Climate Policy, 3 < https://doi.org/10.1080/14693062.2021.1967717>.

[3] William Nordhaus, 'Climate Clubs: Overcoming Free-Riding in International Climate Policy' (2015) 105(4) American Economic Review 1339. Charles F Sabel and David G Victor, 'Governing Global Problems Under Uncertainty: Making Bottom-Up Climate Policy Work' (2017) 144 Climatic Change 15 <https://doi.org/10.1007/s10584-015-1507-y>.

[4] Suzanne Scotchmer, 'Clubs' in Steven N Durlauf and Lawrence E. Blume (eds), *The New Palgrave Dictionary of Economics* (2nd edn, Palgrave Macmillan 2008), 1. Nordhaus, 'Climate Clubs: Overcoming Free-Riding' (n 3).

© The Author(s) 2025

T. G. Budak, *Beyond Treaties: Rethinking Legal Mechanisms for International Climate Governance*, https://doi.org/10.1007/978-3-031-86022-5_4

only.[5] Therefore, the club goods are financed through payments and fees. A real-world example for club good could be public park that charges an entry fee. The park itself is a non-rivalrous resource; one person's enjoyment of the park does not diminish the ability of others to enjoy it as well. However, by imposing an entry fee, the park becomes excludable, as only those who have paid the fee can legally enter and enjoy its amenities. The collected fees can be used to maintain the park, fund improvements, and ensure it remains a pleasant and safe environment for its visitors. This example shows how the club goods concept can apply to a wide range of services and amenities, providing a mechanism for funding and managing resources that are shared among a specific group of users. In the climate context, club goods are designed as benefits for encouraging member countries to adopt and adhere to stringent climate measures. Creating club goods motivates members to take climate action seriously and meet their commitments.

In order to create a successful club, three elements should be deliberated. These elements are pivotal in ensuring the club operates smoothly and delivers its objectives. First, the club's benefits must be significant and valuable, meaning their perceived gains outweigh the costs. In other words, joining the club should be an attractive proposition, where the benefits of membership serve as a strong incentive for participation. Second, the benefits must be exclusive to the club members. Otherwise, there will be an inclination to free-ride. Exclusivity creates a clear distinction between club members and non-members, motivating nations to join the club to access unique benefits. Finally, the benefits need to respect international law.[6] Adherence to international legal frameworks is essential to ensure the club's legitimacy and acceptance on the global stage. The harmony with existing international agreements prevents the risk of conflicting or competing priorities under different regimes. Also, collaboration is more likely when countries perceive that their climate actions are consistent with their broader international commitments.

1.2 Climate Club

In climate context, the club approach is a novel model that departs from the traditional global-scale approach under the UNFCCC.[7] Unlike ad-hoc coalitions in multilateral climate negotiations or one-off gatherings of state representatives, the club

[5] Stefan Magen, 'Game Theory and Collective Goods' in Emanuel V Towfigh and Niels Petersen (eds), *Economic Methods for Lawyers* (Edward Elgar Publishing, 2015), 79.

[6] Lutz Weischer, Jennifer Morgan, and Milap Patel, 'Climate Clubs: Can Small Groups of Countries Make a Big Difference in Addressing Climate Change?' (2012) 21(3) Review of European Community & International Environmental Law 177, 187–188.

[7] David Victor and Robert Keohane, 'The Regime Complex for Climate Change' (2010) 9 Perspectives on Politics 7, 10 <https://doi.org/10.1017/S1537592710004068>. Leonidas Paroussos and others 'Climate Clubs and the Macro-economic Benefits of International Cooperation on

would be a permanent conception.[8] It will represent a structured and ongoing commitment by a specific group of countries to address climate change collectively.[9] This permanence can provide a more stable and consistent platform for cooperation. Climate club typically has selective membership, with countries voluntarily joining based on shared interests and goals. This structure differs from the UNFCCC, which includes nearly all countries, resulting in complex and protracted negotiations. The selective nature of clubs can lead to more concrete efforts.

The primary goal of the climate club is to secure international emissions abatement discipline.[10] However, the asymmetries and different institutional landscapes of countries are stumbling blocks to homogenise emission-related regulatory practices.[11] In order to overcome these discrepancies, the climate club narrative can be tied to neoliberal climate politics by promoting market-based mechanisms, bolstering markets, and enabling capital accumulation.[12] Accordingly, the club benefits can include access to a shared carbon market, preferential trade, and financial incentives. In this way, they can encourage the participation of reluctant countries in climate action. Therefore, beyond its environmental aim, the climate club will protect its members' domestic industries from competitive disadvantages due to the carbon regulations.[13] Consequently, the climate club structure illuminates the problem of free-riding in the climate change problem.[14]

The concept of a "climate club" as a cooperative group is becoming increasingly recognized as an innovative mechanism to accelerate global climate action. This concept addresses two fundamental aspects of climate change mitigation and cooperation.[15] In the immediate term, the club can facilitate the linkage and coordination of market-based mitigation policies across member countries. This includes harmonizing approaches to carbon taxation, implementing border carbon adjustments, and synchronizing ETS.[16] Such coordination can lead to the establishment of larger, more liquid emissions markets, which mitigates the risk of carbon leakage,

---

Climate Policy' (2019) 9 Nature Climate Change 542. Simone Tagliapietra and Guntram Wolff 'Form a Climate Club: United States, European Union and China' (2021) 591 Nature 526.

[8] Falkner, Nasiritousi and Reischl (n 2), 3.

[9] Nicholas Stern and Hans Peter Lankes, *Collaborating and Delivering on Climate Action Through a Climate Club: An Independent Report to the G7* (London School of Economics and Political Science, 2022), 31. Nordhaus, 'Climate Change: The Ultimate Challenge for Economics' (n 74) 2011.

[10] William Nordhaus, 'Climate Change: The Ultimate Challenge for Economics' (2019) 109(6) American Economic Review 1991, 2011 <https://doi.org/10.1257/aer.109.6.1991>.

[11] Dale Jamieson, 'The Nature of the Problem' in John S Dryzek and others (eds), *The Oxford Handbook of Climate Change and Society* (Oxford University Press 2011), 47.

[12] David G Victor, *Global Warming Gridlock: Creating More Effective Strategies for Protecting the Planet* (Cambridge University Press 2011).

[13] Robert Gampfer, 'Minilateralism or the UNFCCC? The Political Feasibility of Climate Clubs' (2016) 16(3) Global Environmental Politics, 64–65.

[14] Nordhaus, 'Climate Change: The Ultimate Challenge for Economics' (n 10) 2010.

[15] Ibid 2010.

[16] Stern and Lankes (n 9) 26.

especially in high-emitting sectors that are heavily involved in international trade.[17] Over the longer term, the climate club can play a crucial role in laying the groundwork for more ambitious climate action and broader international cooperation. By serving as a platform for sharing best practices, demonstrating the viability of green technologies, and fostering market expansion for green products, climate club can reduce the costs associated with climate-friendly innovations.[18] Therefore, it can enhance the economic feasibility of transitioning to low-carbon technologies and encourage their adoption on a wider scale.

The dual function of climate club underscores the importance of alternative, smaller groups of cooperative attempts in advancing global climate action. While large-scale international agreements like the Paris Agreement are critical, the flexibility and focused approach of climate clubs can complement these broader efforts by addressing specific challenges and opportunities that arise in the process of implementing climate policies. Climate club exemplifies how targeted collaboration among willing countries can create momentum for change, showcasing successful policies and technologies that can then be scaled up or adopted by others. In essence, climate club represents a strategic and pragmatic approach to international climate cooperation, offering a pathway to more effective and inclusive action against one of the most pressing challenges of our time.[19]

2 Key Design Features

2.1 Emissions Abatement Target

The first key feature of the climate club is the agreement on harmonised emissions reduction goal.[20] It is the core objective that unites club members in pursuing significant climate mitigation. In order to achieve this goal, the club members need to adopt and administer the same regulatory emissions standards and climate policies in their jurisdictions.[21] Therefore, according to Nordhaus, the climate club relies on

---

[17] Aaron Cosbey and others, 'Developing Guidance for Implementing Border Carbon Adjustments: Lessons, Cautions, and Research Needs from the Literature' (2019) 13 Review of Environmental Economics and Policy 3.

[18] Håkan Pihl 'A Climate Club as a Complementary Design to the UN Paris Agreement' (2020) 3(1) Policy Design and Practice 45, 51.

[19] Karin Bäckstrand, 'The Democratic Legitimacy of Global Governance after Copenhagen' in John S. Dryzek and others (eds), *The Oxford Handbook of Climate Change and Society* (Oxford University Press, 2011), 676.

[20] Stern and Lankes (n 9) 23.

[21] Kimberly A Clausing and Catherine Wolfram. 'Carbon Border Adjustments, Climate Clubs, and Subsidy Races When Climate Policies Vary' (2023) 37(3) Journal of Economic Perspectives 137, 155.

a top-down structure despite its voluntary nature.[22] The top-down structure is characterised by the regime's design before countries decide whether to participate. This design entails the club's ability to establish and enforce common, ambitious standards to achieve substantial emissions abatement. Once agreed upon by the club members, these standards become binding commitments and serve as the backbone of the club's climate change mitigation efforts. In contrast, the Paris Agreement relies on a bottom-up approach where countries individually determine their climate pledges, often leading to a lack of uniformity in commitments.

The international carbon price is the most cost-effective way to reach a common emissions abatement policy.[23] More than 2500 economists, including 27 Nobel Laureates, have signed the "Economists' Statement" in support of carbon pricing.[24] Also, carbon pricing has been consistently backed by initiatives such as the International Carbon Action Partnership,[25] the World Bank Partnership for Market Implementation,[26] and the Carbon Pricing Leadership Coalition.[27] Therefore, it is widely accepted that carbon pricing can reduce carbon emissions at the necessary speed and scale.[28] Carbon price aims to internalise the harms born from emissions. As a result of the carbon price, the actors will face their preferences' total cost and benefit.[29] This mechanism ensures that the actual environmental and societal costs of carbon emissions are factored into decision-making processes, thus providing a powerful economic incentive to reduce emissions and transition to cleaner alternatives.[30]

---

[22] Nordhaus, 'Climate Clubs: Overcoming Free-Riding' (n 3) 1344.

[23] Gilbert E Metcalf, 'Carbon Taxes in Theory and Practice' (2021) 13 Annual Review of Resource Economics 245, 246. <https://doi.org/10.1146/annurev-resource-102519-113630>. Nordhaus, 'Climate Change: The Ultimate Challenge for Economics' (n 10) 2011. For example, Nordhaus suggests, countries agree that each one will implement policies that produce a minimum domestic carbon price of $25 per ton of CO_2. The choice of carbon price over quantities is the result of cost and benefit analysis. Weitzman has shown that it would be both less distortionary and easier to negotiate a single carbon price than to set multiple quantity limits. Martin L Weitzman, 'Voting on Prices vs. Voting on Quantities in a World Climate Assembly' (2017) 71 Research in Economics 199.

[24] 'Economists' Statement on Carbon Dividends' <https://www.econstatement.org> 25 April 2024. David G Tarr and others, 'Why Carbon Border Adjustment Mechanisms Will Not Save the Planet but a Climate Club and Subsidies for Transformative Green Technologies May' (2023) 122 Energy Economics 9.

[25] 'International Carbon Action Partnership' <https://icapcarbonaction.com/en/partnership/about> accessed 20 June 2024.

[26] 'World Bank Partnership for Market Implementation' <https://pmiclimate.org/> accessed 20 June 2024.

[27] 'Carbon Pricing Leadership Coalition' <https://www.carbonpricingleadership.org/> accessed 20 June 2024.

[28] Tarr and others (n 24) 9. Nordhaus, 'Climate Change: The Ultimate Challenge for Economics' (n 10) 2003.

[29] Samuel Kortum and David Weisbach, 'The Design of Border Adjustments for Carbon Prices' (2017) 70(2) National Tax Journal 421, 421.

[30] Olivier Blanchard, Christian Gollier and Jean Tirole, 'The Portfolio of Economic Policies Needed to Fight Climate Change' (2023) 15 Annual Review of Economics 689, 696 <https://doi.

An element that demands careful consideration is determining the carbon price level. A low price may fail to induce significant behavioural changes. Conversely, a price set too high might impose undue economic burdens on industries and individuals, potentially leading to social and economic upheaval. Hence, corporate or national interests should be eliminated to agree on economy-wide meaningful levels and targets.[31] In the short term, a sufficient carbon price level[32] incentivises households and industries to mitigate their emissions cost-effectively. In the long term, the prospect of continuing and rising carbon prices incentivises innovation in low-carbon technologies and eventually cuts carbon abatement costs.[33]

Currently, there is no binding global agreement regarding carbon price. The carbon pricing systems can only be found at regional (e.g. EU), national (e.g. China), or sub-national (e.g. California) levels, with some efforts to link them with each other.[34] Therefore, the social cost of carbon[35] is inherently relative and subjective from one jurisdiction to another. Herein, the club's legal scheme aims to grant carbon an asset status and reveal its value. In this way, the club's legal system can align carbon price in different jurisdictions and foster its efficient allocation. Climate club legal frameworks can provide a basis for linking different pricing systems, creating larger and more liquid carbon markets.[36] Consequently, the club creates a level playing field for carbon emissions regulation.[37]

Forming a carbon-pricing coalition as the climate club would put economic and moral pressure on non-members.[38] Economically, it demonstrates the benefits of

---

org/10.1146/annurev-economics-051520-015113>.

[31] Navraj Singh Ghaleigh 'Economics and International Climate Change Law' in Kevin R. Gray (ed), *The Oxford Handbook of International Climate Change Law* (Oxford University Press 2016), 88.

[32] The existing carbon prices are well below the levels recommended by climate policy analysts, either on the basis of the efficiency criterion or the safety criterion embodied in the Paris Agreement. James K. Boyce, 'Carbon Pricing: Effectiveness and Equity' (2018) 150 Ecological Economics 52, 54 <https://doi.org/10.1016/j.ecolecon.2018.03.030>.

[33] William Nordhaus, 'Climate Club Futures: On the Effectiveness of Future Climate Clubs' (Cowles Foundation Discussion Papers 2619, 2021), 5–6 <https://elischolar.library.yale.edu/cowles-discussion-paper-series/2619> accessed 18 May 2024.

[34] Martin Zapf, Hermann Pengg, and Christian Weindl, 'How to Comply with the Paris Agreement Temperature Goal: Global Carbon Pricing According to Carbon Budgets' (2019) 12(15) Energies 2983, 6 <https://doi.org/10.3390/en12152983> Clausing and Wolfram (n 21) 140.

[35] The social cost of carbon represents the economic damages associated with each additional metric ton of carbon dioxide emitted into the atmosphere. Rolf H Weber, 'Border Tax Adjustment-Legal Perspective' (2015) 133 Climatic Change 407, 409 <https://doi.org/10.1007/s10584-015-1414-2>.

[36] International Monetary Fund and OECD, 'Tax Policy and Climate Change: IMF/OECD Report for the G20 Finance Ministers and Central Bank Governors' (2021) <www.oecd.org/tax/tax-policy/imf-oecd-g20-report-tax-policy-and-climate-change.htm> accessed 20 June 2024.

[37] William Nordhaus, 'The Climate Club: How to Fix a Failing Global Effort' (2020) 20 Journal of Environmental Economics and Policy, 5. Pihl (n 18) 45.

[38] Pihl (n 18) 52.

internalising emissions costs.[39] Morally, it underscores the shared global responsibility for addressing climate change. Each club member adopts a shared policy package to create the same carbon price level in line with the club agreement.[40] It could simplify the emissions abatement negotiations. This is because country-specific quantitative emission limits would likely end up with no limits at all, as some nations desire low restrictions for themselves and high for others.[41] Ultimately, the carbon price encourages non-members to join the club or show a constructive attitude in ongoing climate change negotiations.[42]

2.2 *Common Policy Tools*

The tools to reach international carbon price represent another element of the climate club's top-down structure. Carbon pricing tools consist of market mechanisms. They act as an incentive and compel members to meet their climate obligations or face economic consequences.[43] The economic implications of market mechanisms make it more attractive for countries to meet climate obligations. They alter the nature of climate change from an expense-driven problem to a value-created opportunity.[44] Consequently, carbon pricing mechanisms help to align economic interests with climate objectives. They have a significant potential to incentivise the private sector to reduce emissions while promoting economic growth.

The second key feature of the climate club design is the agreement that includes "sticks" for outsiders and "carrots" for members.[45] The successful climate club will attract members if its' benefits go beyond the direct benefits of climate change mitigation and non-members are strictly restricted from enjoying them.[46] Otherwise, club members would tend to resist cooperation as climate mitigation advantages would accrue globally, but the economic burden of mitigation is born only on the members. Therefore, membership in the climate club depends on the members having an economy-wide carbon price, while non-members would be subject to tariff measures. This sanction and reward mechanism not only makes the club more

[39] Thomas Kuhn, Radomir Pestow and Anja Zenker, 'Building Climate Coalitions on Preferential Trade Agreements' (2019) 74(2) Environmental and Resource Economics 539.

[40] Ibid.

[41] Nordhaus, 'Climate Change: The Ultimate Challenge for Economics' (n 10) 2011.

[42] Stern and Lankes (n 9) 49.

[43] Andrew E Dessler and Edward A Parson, *The Science and Politics of Global Climate Change: A Guide to the Debate* (3rd edn, Cambridge University Press 2020), 139.

[44] Matthew Paterson 'Who and What are Carbon Markets for? Politics and the Development of Climate Policy' (2012) 12(1) Climate Policy 82, 89 <https://doi.org/10.1080/14693062.2011.579259>.

[45] Gampfer (n 13) 83.

[46] Stern and Lankes (n 9) 26.

politically feasible but also addresses concerns related to the equitable sharing of burdens and benefits among countries.[47]

The sanction and reward mechanism can be achieved with linkages among club members.[48] Linkages are the market-based mechanisms that set the carbon price. The negotiations on which measure to adopt are the core aspect of the club formation.[49] Within the limits of this book, pricing mechanisms of carbon taxes and tariffs, ETS, border carbon adjustments (BCAs), technical regulations and standards are analysed in Chap. 5. They equalise the costs of climate regulations across global sectors.[50] Market-based linkages play a significant role in minimising the perceived economic risks of participation in the climate club. They ensure that the costs of climate action are more evenly distributed among member nations, which is essential for political buy-in and continued cooperation.[51] Hence, linkages can convince club members that there are supplementary co-benefits derived from cooperation.[52] They demonstrate a commitment to both the environment and economic well-being, dispelling the myth that climate action is detrimental to national economies.

Linkages in the form of sanctions are the most critical aspect of incentivising membership to the club and penalising non-members or climate club members who do not meet their obligations.[53] These sanctions need to have two significant features, which are being external and incentive-compatible.[54] By making sanctions external to the member countries, the club encourages global engagement. Sanctions clearly convey that non-cooperative nations must be held accountable for their actions. The threat of external sanctions is a strong motivator for countries to comply with their climate commitments. In comparison, incentive-compatible sanctions are designed to align economic incentives and climate objectives. Their goal is not to be punitive but rather to promote climate objectives. Therefore, they leverage

---

47 Thomas Cottier, 'The Principle of Common Concern of Humankind' in Thomas Cottier (ed) *The Prospects of Common Concern of Humankind in International Law* (Cambridge University Press, 2021), 71.

48 William Nordhaus, 'Dynamic Climate Clubs: On the Effectiveness of Incentives in Global Climate Agreements', (2021) 118 (45) Proceedings of the National Academy of Sciences, 2-4 <https://doi.org/10.1073/pnas.2109988118>.

49 For example, the determination of quantity-based approach for the emissions quotas carries the risk of free-riding, since each country will negotiate for a higher cap for itself. Therefore, negotiating on one-fair price will be easier. Weitzman (n 23).

50 Phillip M Hannam and others, 'Incomplete Cooperation and Co-benefits: Deepening Climate Cooperation with a Proliferation of Small Agreements' (2017) 144 Climatic Change 65, 66 <https://doi.org/10.1007/s10584-015-1511-2>.

51 Elinor Ostrom, *Governing the Commons: The Evolution of Institutions for Collective Action* (Cambridge University Press, 1990) 59.

52 Kasturi Das, 'Climate Clubs: Carrots, Sticks and More' (2015) 50(34) Economic and Political Weekly 24.

53 It is argued that an effective climate deal could arise indirectly from the threat of unilateral trade policies. Dieter Helm, Cameron Hepburn and Giovanni Ruta, 'Trade, Climate Change, and the Political Game Theory of Border Carbon Adjustments' 28 (2012) Oxf Rev Econ Policy 368, 373.

54 Nordhaus, 'Climate Clubs: Overcoming Free-Riding' (n 3) 1351.

economic incentives to encourage the adoption of sustainable policies. Overall, linkages for sanctioning are carefully structured to ensure that the economic consequences of non-abidance to club scheme are unfavourable for the countries.[55]

Accordingly, two different sanction structures have been offered under the climate club scheme. The first one suggests that all club members impose uniform border measures on imports from non-club members, irrespective of the carbon content.[56] This measure would be a strong sanction with clear merits, which can increase the club's internal stability.[57] This framework is fully aligned with a policy-neutral stance towards decarbonization. Hence, it does not consider the commitments of the non-members or the rigor of the decarbonization targets set outside the club.[58] Also, uniform tariffs are not compatible with the WTO rules. Therefore, the second sanction structure targets the carbon content of the imports and applies individual tariffs and border adjustments to each product.[59] This approach is designed to be WTO-compliant and is, therefore, a more viable option from a legal standpoint.[60] No border carbon adjustment would be applied in trade between club members since all participating economies would commit to similarly strong measures to cut emissions. So that it would provide an incentive to remain committed to the agreement. Both types of sanctions create an economic and regulatory framework that fosters a collaborative approach to mitigate the impacts of climate change.[61]

---

[55] Antonio R Góis and others, 'Reward and Punishment in Climate Change Dilemmas' (2019) 9 Sci Rep 16193 <https://doi.org/10.1038/s41598-019-52524-8>.

[56] Nordhaus, Climate Clubs: Overcoming Free-Riding (n 3) 1357. Nordhaus calculated that a 5% tariff on all goods from non-participants would make it more advantageous for almost all countries to join the climate club. (ibid 1359). Zeynep B Irfanoglu, Juan P Sesmero and Alla Golub 'Potential of Border Tax Adjustments to Deter Free Riding in International Climate Agreements' (2015) 10 Environmental Research Letters 024009

[57] Internal stability refers to all club members are better-off complying, instead of deviating from club obligations. Juan Sesmero and Alecia Evans, 'The potential of Trade Sanctions to Overcome the Small Coalition Paradox: A Review of the Literature', in Micheal Jakob (eds) *Handbook on Trade Policy and Climate Change* (Edward Elgar, 2022), 125.

[58] Giulia Claudia Leonelli, 'The Long and Winding Road Towards the Creation of Climate Clubs: Transatlantic Negotiations, Potential Regulatory Models and Challenges Ahead' (2023) 32 RECIEL 453, 466.

[59] Jeroen C van den Bergh, 'Rebound Policy in the Paris Agreement: Instrument Comparison and Climate-Club Revenue Offsets' (2017) 17 Climate Policy 801. Michele Stua, *From the Paris Agreement to a Low-Carbon Bretton Woods: Rationale for the Establishment of a Mitigation Alliance* (Springer, 2017) 189–201.

[60] Geraldo Vidigal, 'Designing Climate Clubs: The Four Models, Trade Commitments and the Non-Discrimination Dilemma' (2023) Amsterdam Law School Research Paper No 2023-07, 7.

[61] Scott Barrett, 'The Strategy of Trade Sanctions in Environmental Agreements' (1997) 19(4) Resource and Energy Economics 345. However, this research assumed extreme climate-related trade instruments, such as import ban and did not consider the retaliatory measures from non-club members. Eyland and Zaccour demonstrate that BCAs can support participation in a climate agreement, even when retaliatory responses are considered. Terry Eyland and Georges Zaccour, 'Carbon Tariffs and Cooperative Outcomes' (2014) 65 Energy Policy 718.

3 Climate Club: Reforming International Climate Governance and Regulations

Given that the UNFCCC regime cannot produce quick results, the forerunner countries in climate mitigation are tempted to influence the behaviour of foreign countries and incentivise the actors beyond their borders.[62] Therefore, the underlying aim of the climate club is not restricted to simply having a border against non-members, but also seeks to shape their regulations. This mission is rooted in a proactive commitment to accelerate climate action and drive global development for a more sustainable future. By taking a hands-on approach, the climate club seeks to redefine the global narrative on climate change. The club members aim to be trendsetters and role models for other countries, lead by example and showcase innovative climate solutions. Under the climate club, dominant actors become standard-setters and bear the cost of being a first mover.[63] In exchange, they expect sufficient economic, strategic, or reputational benefits from their climate accomplishments.[64] Thereby, dominant actors present an example to non-club members and incentivise them to adopt similar measures and create a more sustainable global future.[65]

Due to its trade linkages, the climate club will act as an economic alliance and trade bloc, establishing a distinct boundary against non-member countries. However, it is essential to emphasise that the climate club will not be an exclusive forum. Instead, it will be designed not to isolate or exclude other nations but rather to provide a platform for those who actively wish to engage in ambitious climate change mitigation efforts. The primary aim of the climate club is to address the governance gaps within the current climate change law and introduce measures that hold governments accountable for inaction.[66] In essence, the climate club offers a dynamic and flexible approach to addressing climate change. By implementing a system of incentives and penalties, the club can drive meaningful reform and promote a culture of responsibility among its members.[67] As a result, it is possible for several climate clubs to be designed and coexist together, complementing the gaps of UNFCCC.[68]

---

[62] Cottier (n 47) 87. Giulia Claudia Leonelli, 'Carbon Border Measures, Environmental Effectiveness and WTO Compatibility: Is There a Way Forward for the Steel and Aluminium Carbon Club?' (2022) 21(5) World Trade Review, 626.

[63] Jon Hovi, Tora Skodvin and Stine Aakre, 'Can Climate Change Negotiations Succeed' (2013) 1 Politics and Governance 138, 140 <https://doi.org/10.12924/PAG2013.01020138>.

[64] Wolfgang Obergassel, Hanna Wang-Helmreich and Lukas Hermwill, 'A Sectoral Perspective on Climate Clubs' (2019), 9 <https://epub.wupperinst.org/frontdoor/deliver/index/docId/7547/file/7547_Climate_Clubs.pdf> accessed 28 March 2024.

[65] Falkner, Nasiritousi and Reischl (n 2) 4.

[66] Pihl (n 18) 45. Stern and Lankes (n 9) 27.

[67] Leon Martini and Benjamin Görlach, *What Role for a Climate Club under the German G7 Presidency? Options and Recommendations for a Climate Club* (Ecologic Institute, 2022), 4.

[68] Roggero, Kähler and Hagen (n 16) 399.

Correspondingly, the roadmap of the club scheme would be to adopt the migration of legal norms strategy, which refers to the extraterritorial application of national regulations by influential countries.[69] The climate club has an explicit international agenda, which is to foster reform in the behaviour of other countries. The genesis of the climate club can start among the countries that have already introduced carbon pricing instruments such as a carbon tax, emissions trading scheme, hybrid measures or are considering issuing one of these. Thereby, the key strength of this strategy is that the club begins as a small but determined entity.[70] In this way, the climate club creates a forum where like-minded countries can collaborate effectively and take the lead in climate action. It allows for more efficient decision-making and greater coordination among club members.[71] With the migration of legal norms strategy, the club uses market access as an element for attracting non-members. Consequently, it increases the proliferation of climate norms.[72] For instance, the EU tries to influence its trade partners' environmental regulations with its' far-reaching market.[73]

Reaching a critical mass has the utmost importance in the club approach[74] as the small club cannot have significant leverage on international trade and lower the cost of emission abatement.[75] Notably, without the participation of large emitters, the climate club lacks ambition, which in turn weakens the internal dynamic to achieve compliance with the club norms.[76] Therefore, the climate club needs a critical mass of members who collectively represent a significant portion of global emissions and trade. The critical mass gives the club more negotiating power when advocating for environmental standards in international agreements. Only in this way the club can positively impact international climate negotiations and promote transparent cooperation on technical and regulatory matters of climate action. Furthermore, the critical mass can work to recruit more members to its scheme. The larger the market

---

[69] Shaffer and Bodansky (n 2) 35.

[70] Robyn Eckersley, 'Moving Forward in the Climate Negotiations: Multilateralism or Minilateralism?' (2012) 12(2) Global Environmental Politics 24 <https://doi.org/10.1162/GLEP_a_00107>.

[71] Robert Falkner, 'A Minilateral Solution for Global Climate Change? On Bargaining Efficiency, Club Benefits, and International Legitimacy' (2016) 14 Perspectives on Politics 87.

[72] Slyvia I Karlsson-Vinkhuyzen and Jeffrey McGee 'Legitimacy in an Era of Fragmentation: The Case of Global Climate Governance' (2013) 13 Global Environmental Politics 56.

[73] Charles F Parker and Christer Karlsson, 'Climate Change and the European Union's Leadership Moment: An Inconvenient Truth?' (2010) 48 Journal of Common Market Studies 923, 928.

[74] Thomas L Brewer, Henry Derwent and Andrzej Błachowicz, *Carbon Market Clubs and the New Paris Regime* (Paper for the World Bank Group's Networked Carbon Markets Initiative 2016). Stern and Lankes (n 192) 22.

[75] Nordhaus, 'Dynamic Climate Clubs' (n 48) 6.

[76] Michele Stua, Colin Nolden and Michael Coulon, 'Climate Clubs Embedded in Article 6 of the Paris Agreement' (2022) 180 Resources, Conservation and Recycling 106178 <https://doi.org/10.1016/j.resconrec.2022.106178>.

power, the more likely the club will obtain a favourable response from non-members while the economic damage to club members minimises.[77]

Moreover, the club would address the issue of unilateral climate policies, which do not have the capacity to achieve intended emissions reductions due to increased global interactions.[78] The non-accountability in the current climate regime directs many countries to enforce unilateral climate measures, particularly against their trade partners. In the lack of coordination between the international structure and the domestic abatement activities, as in the unilateral attempts, the carbon market's strength, cohesiveness, and ultimate effectiveness are undermined. The carbon price signal is weakened. Lack of coordination may result in market fragmentation, with different jurisdictions operating under separate carbon market regulations. This multiplication may create confusion and make it challenging for participants to navigate in the market. Mainly, protective unilateral trade measures are much more likely to distress small countries' companies and consumers,[79] as they are more dependent on the supply of raw materials and components compared to large economies. The adverse consequences of these unilateral actions further emphasise the importance of coordinated efforts within the climate club framework to create a fair system for reducing carbon emissions.

In this regard, the club constitutes a step for cooperative attempts to implement climate policy on a common basis instead of an isolationist approach.[80] Members of the club collaborate on trade policies and collectively determine the foundational criteria for their application. As a result, the club mechanically links specific domestic abatement activities, which will increase the acceptance of these measures in the international market. In essence, the climate club offers a path toward international harmonization of climate policy, complementing the efforts of the UNFCCC. By uniting under the umbrella of the climate club, nations can bolster their collective impact on global emissions.[81] This cooperative approach streamlines the tracking and accounting of emission reductions, making monitoring and verifying progress easier. It not only enhances the effectiveness of climate policy but also aligns with the principles of public international law, which tends to favour consensual multilateral measures, such as state-to-state linkages, over arbitrary unilateral actions.[82] The proactive attitude of the climate club, seeking out new international partnership opportunities, has the potential to eliminate the need for unilateral policies. Instead of going alone, countries can find common ground within the club's framework,

[77] Nordhaus, 'Dynamic Climate Clubs' (n 48) 18.

[78] Zapf, Pengg and Weindl (n 34) 10.

[79] Charlotte Sieber-Gasser, 'Please, Reboot – Small Economies and the WTO Appellate Mechanism in Times of Trade War and COVID-19' (SIL International Economic Law Interest Group, Online Workshop 'International Economic Law between Emergencies and Reforms', 9 September 2020), 11.

[80] Stern and Lankes (n 9) 38.

[81] Ibid 48.

[82] Kateryna Holzer, 'The Possibility of Defense under General Exceptions of GATT Article XX' in *Carbon-Related Border Adjustment and WTO Law* (Edward Elgar Publishing 2014), 161.

fostering cooperation, trust, and shared responsibility. As a result, this approach not only makes climate action more effective but also contributes to the development of a more harmonious global response to the pressing issue of climate change.

4 Prospects of the Climate Club

The climate club is a form of cooperation in which climate measures and economic cooperation between the members are equally intensive. Therefore, club-based cooperation will be a new window to implement climate transition policies for the countries that are aware that economic development with traditional methods has reached its limits.[83] Particularly for smaller countries, the climate club helps them to gain more political support to realise their policy reforms thanks to the trade linkages.[84] These countries can strengthen their climate action only with the support of bigger markets and acting in an alliance. Accordingly, the club can support countries that do not have the market power to influence carbon-reducing activities. As a result, it contributes to the economic improvement of developing and least-developed countries and liberates the trade of green products among club members.

Moreover, forming the climate club represents a strategic move that promises significant advantages in the realm of international negotiations and diplomacy.[85] By acting as a bloc, the climate club members will have increased bargaining power and political influence in multilateral negotiations. The collective voice of the club can make a stronger case for specific policies and measures, potentially swaying the opinions of other nations and stakeholders. The ability to forge consensus within the club can serve as a model for broader international collaborations.[86] Consequently, the club structure has the potential to lay the groundwork for advancing to the next tier of multilateral trade and environmental agreements.[87] This collaborative approach can foster a spirit of collective responsibility and facilitate the development of effective international agreements aimed at advancing the cause of sustainability.

The climate club's commitment to upholding agreed climate standards is integral to its mission of advancing sustainable practices while preserving trade and

[83] Climate-related trade instruments of the club circumvent the reciprocal and voluntary climate measures. They provide trade gains, which can be translated into political support for ambitious climate action. Sesmero and Evans (n 57) 128.

[84] Trade linkages link cooperation in emission reduction to cooperation in trade liberalization. Therefore, there can be transfers of financial flows or R&D opportunities to smaller economies and enable them to enhance their climate action. ibid 127.

[85] Falkner (n 71).

[86] Stefano Carattini and Andreas Löschel, 'Managing Momentum in Climate Negotiations' (2021) 16 Environmental Research Letters 51001.

[87] Kateryna Holzer and Nashina Shariff, 'The Inclusion of Border Carbon Adjustments in Preferential Trade Agreements: Policy Implications' (2012) 3 Carbon & Climate L Rev 246, 246.

investment relationships.[88] This commitment extends beyond mere rhetoric, as the club employs climate-related market mechanisms and sanctions to enforce compliance with these standards. Thuswise, the club enables member countries and industries to clearly demonstrate their commitment to reducing emissions and adhering to environmentally responsible practices. Specifically, the club member's products signal that they comply with the emissions standards. More importantly, the club's coherent agenda will alleviate the uncertainty surrounding climate-related regulations.[89] This coherence, in turn, provides a stable and predictable environment where industries can operate and make informed decisions. Consequently, the establishment of new markets and export opportunities for eco-friendly products will emerge, enabling consumers to access less carbon-intensive goods at reduced prices.[90] Through this approach, the climate club aids in achieving sustainable development goals and ensures a fair competitive environment for producers who make environmental claims.[91]

The specific measures and actions the climate club takes can vary depending on the agreements and goals of the participating countries. There is not a single, established model for how they should operate. However, it is widely accepted that climate club should encompass promotional measures in addition to market instruments.[92] These measures include technology sharing for clean energy and climate mitigation, financial support to less-developed members, exchange of knowledge and best practices related to climate change mitigation and adaptation, research and development funding, and capacity building and technical assistance.[93] The climate club's promotional measures are less contentious than sanctions under international trade law. Hence, they are easier to implement globally.

For this reason, the climate club can offer significant advantages beyond trade linkages. The non-coercive nature of these promotional measures positions the climate club as a platform for fostering cooperation in various domains. It can open new technical and regulatory cooperation opportunities, create information and best-practice exchange channels, and promote scientific collaboration. Similar to the drugs and vaccines transnational partnerships, the clubs can manage access to

---

[88] Timothy Meyer and Todd N Tucker, 'A Pragmatic Approach to Carbon Border Measures' (2022) 21(1) World Trade Review 109, 114.

[89] Ibid.

[90] Hubertus Bardt and Galina V Kolev, *Trade Club for Climate: A Climate Approach to Revive Multilateralism*, IW-Policy Paper, No. 8/2021 (Institut der deutschen Wirtschaft (IW), Köln 2021) 12.

[91] Laurence Boisson de Chazournes and Makane Moise Mbengue, 'The Principles of Precaution and Sustainability' in Thomas Cottier and Krista Nadakavukaren Schefer (eds), *Elgar Encyclopaedia of International Economic Law* (Edward Elgar 2017), 622.

[92] Guri Bang, Jon Hovi, and Tora Skodvin, 'The Paris Agreement: Short-Term and Long-Term Effectiveness' (2016) 4 Politics and Governance 209.

[93] Stern and Lankes (n 9) 27.

intellectual property rights for green technologies.[94] With its supranational institutional and administrative authority, the club can prevent misuse of carbon tax revenue.[95] This revenue can be directed towards accelerating green goals, investing in clean technologies, and supporting projects that promote sustainability and environmental protection. In this way, the revenue channels towards the very goals of the club, reinforcing its commitment to addressing climate change.

Lastly, the climate club will create pro-environmental action to get green status and bring reputational advantages to its members.[96] Even though the reputation loss from having no carbon policies is hard to determine, the club can still play a role in the objective determination of reputational considerations.[97] The club establishes a consistent framework for evaluating a country's environmental commitment through its transparent reporting. Countries that actively engage in the club's climate plans can enhance their global image as environmentally responsible actors, thereby reaping the rewards associated with being at the forefront of sustainable practices. The influence of the climate club, thus, extends beyond climate protection, shaping the way nations are perceived in the international community and encouraging a race to the top in adopting environmentally friendly policies. This heightened reputation can, in turn, foster deeper diplomatic and economic partnerships with like-minded nations and organizations. Moreover, the positive image cultivated by climate club members can translate into tangible economic benefits.[98] Being recognised as environmentally responsible actors can attract green investments and businesses seeking reliable and sustainable partners.

To sum up, with the club collaboration, climate action accelerates, whereas the global cost of abatement decreases.[99] The uniform carbon price of the climate club will equalise the cost of carbon abatement among different countries. Hence, the club can also fulfil the national self-interest of its members and address their concerns about international burden distribution. Under the climate club, the differentiated responsibilities and capabilities of the countries will not be reflected in the application of carbon pricing instruments. Each member will be bound by the same scheme. This uniformity helps build trust and cooperation within the club by avoiding contentious negotiations about varying contributions and responsibilities. The

[94] Joshua D Sarnoff, 'Intellectual Property and Climate Change, with an Emphasis on Patents and Technology Transfer' in Kevin R Gray, Richard Tarasofsky, and Cinnamon P Carlarne (eds), *The Oxford Handbook of International Climate Change Law* (Oxford University Press 2016).

[95] Michael Faure and Roy Andrew Partain, *Environmental Law and Economics: Theory and Practice* (Cambridge University Press 2019)137.

[96] In the absence of strong supranational enforcement authority, reputation constitutes an important factor in honouring international agreements. George W Downs and Michael A Jones, 'Reputation, Compliance and International Law' (2002) 31 Journal of Legal Studies 95.

[97] Ole Jacob Sending, Indra Øverland and Thomas Boe Hornburg, 'Climate Change and International Relations' (2020) 73(1) Journal of International Affairs 183, 187.

[98] The cost and benefit analysis of compliance with the club measures results a positive outcome. Richard A. Posner, *Economic Analysis of Law* (Aspen Legal Education 2014), 996.

[99] Meyer and Tucker (n 88) 119.

climate club also mitigates the risk of free-riding and ensures that all members have a vested interest in achieving the club's ambitious goals. As a result, the underlying expectation of the climate club is to create a significant impact on emission abatement, which would be hard to achieve with multilateral fora. The club provides a more effective and pragmatic means of achieving emissions reduction targets,[100] making itself a compelling and dynamic framework for tackling the challenges of climate change.

5 Challenges and Limitations

5.1 Introduction

Climate club, while offering potential benefits in addressing climate change, also comes with its set of challenges and limitations. In the realm of international climate law, countries differ in terms of the economic resources at their disposal, priorities, capacity and impacts of climate change in their region.[101] Notably, the distribution of burdens and benefits under climate policy also impacts the opportunities for economic growth. Hence, the strict application of formal equality in the climate change context could have undesirable consequences, including levelling down efforts or cooperation.[102] In this regard, developing countries voice their demands regarding a more equitable international legal order and assistance from developed countries to resolve common concerns. They argue that the current legal structures may inadvertently perpetuate inequalities, hindering their capacity to fully participate and benefit from the international legal system. Their calls for reform are often grounded in the recognition that a one-size-fits-all approach may not adequately accommodate the diverse needs and capacities of countries at different stages of development.[103]

Therefore, the discourse surrounding the uniform application of international law[104] has evolved into balancing the sovereign equality of states with a recognition of the disparities in their capacities and vulnerabilities. International agreements both in the climate and trade have special provisions to reflect the asymmetry between developed and developing countries, in which treaty obligations are

[100] Gampfer (n 13).

[101] Clara Brandi, *Priorities for a Development-Friendly EU Carbon Border Adjustment (CBAM)* (Briefing Paper No 20/2021, Deutsches Institut für Entwicklungspolitik, 2021) 2 <https://doi.org/10.23661/bp20.2021>.

[102] Friedrich Soltau, *Fairness in International Climate Change Law and Policy* (Cambridge University Press 2009), 244.

[103] Christoph Böhringer, Jared C Carbone and Thomas F Rutherford, 'Embodied Carbon Tariffs' (2018) 120(1) Scandinavian Journal of Economics 183.

[104] Juliane Kokott, 'States, Sovereign Equality' in *Max Planck Encyclopaedia of Public International Law* (Oxford University Press 2011), para 1.

differentiated based on the signatories' varying capacities and economic resources. These are the CBDRRC under the UNFCCC regime and the SDT under the WTO regime. However, the climate the club regime is in conflict with these provisions, as explained below.

5.2 Common But Differentiated Responsibilities and Respective Capacities Principle under the UNFCCC

5.2.1 Overview

The CBDRRC principle fosters inclusivity by recognizing countries' varied capacities and responsibilities in addressing climate change. This acknowledgement is essential for building trust and ensuring that climate agreements are equitable and responsive to the diverse needs of countries at different stages of development. The CBDRRC principle has given developing countries a basis for claiming that their position is to be considered in formulating treaty regimes.[105] Essentially, the principle serves as a diplomatic tool for developing countries to advocate for a more inclusive approach in international climate negotiations.[106] In this way, they will not accept or will only accept minimal obligations unless developed countries transfer funds and technology to developing ones. Therefore, the CBDRRC principle becomes a key argument in negotiations, reinforcing that obligations should be commensurate with a country's capacity to address climate change effectively. This approach also aligns with the broader principle of climate justice, emphasizing the need for an equitable distribution of the burdens and benefits associated with climate action.[107]

Moreover, the perception of equity among states is highly subjective and can significantly influence the dynamics of international cooperation on climate change.

[105] According to Article 38(1)(b) of the Statute of the International Court of Justice for a legal norm to be recognized as a principle of customary international law, it must be supported by two key elements: state practice and opinio juris. This means there must be a consistent and broad pattern of state actions (as highlighted in the *North Sea Continental Shelf*, (Judgement), [1969] ICJ Rep 3, para 73) and a corresponding belief by states that such actions are mandated by an existing legal rule (as stated in the ibid para 44). Regarding the first requirement, the CBDR principle has been effectively implemented in several major environmental agreements, notably including the UNFCCC, the Kyoto Protocol and the Paris Agreement. Furthermore, the CBDR principle is featured in various non-legally binding instruments and documents of soft law, such as the Stockholm Declaration of 1972 and the Rio Declaration of 1992. There must also be evidence of opinio juris, indicating that states engage in these practices out of a belief that they are legally obligated to do so. It is evident that developed countries have acknowledged this obligation, particularly through their financial commitments under the Paris Agreement Article 9.

[106] Statute of the International Court of Justice (26 June 1945) 3 Bevans 1179, 59 Stat 1031, TS 993, 39 AJIL Supp 215, Cmd 7015, art 38(1)(c).

[107] Lukas H Meyer and Dominic Roser, 'Climate Justice and Historical Emissions' (2010) 13 Critical Review of Intl Social & Political Philosophy 229, 229.

Countries may have varying interpretations of what constitutes a fair and equitable distribution of responsibilities and resources.[108] The CBDRRC principle attempts to navigate these divergent perceptions by providing a structured framework comprising tailored commitments. It serves as a compass for negotiators and policymakers and provides a framework through which the global community can navigate the challenges of climate change mitigation, adaptation, and resilience.[109] It balances the need for global emission reductions with the right to develop economically and socially. The principle's focus on equity and responsiveness to the diverse needs of countries is not just a matter of ethical consideration but is also strategic in enhancing the legitimacy and effectiveness of international climate regimes.

While foundational to ensuring equity within international climate governance frameworks, the CBDRRC principle could present certain challenges in executing climate action. The principle prevents the effective implementation of the climate agreements. The CBDRRC principle could hinder the swift and collaborative efforts. Additionally, it necessitates a fundamental restructuring of economic and social relations on a global scale, attaching climate mitigation efforts to broader issues of economic equity and social justice. While this approach is crucial for addressing the root causes of climate change and ensuring a just transition, it complicates climate negotiations by intertwining them with larger debates on global inequality, trade, and development. This complexity can slow down the consensus-building process, making it more difficult to reach agreements that are ambitious enough to meet the scale of the climate crisis.

5.2.2 The Implications of the Principle on the Climate Club

International theories of justice seek to diffuse liberal egalitarian concerns into the international climate governance to protect the liberties of the least advantaged countries.[110] The distributive justice in the Paris Agreement is predicated on the principle of CBDRRC.[111] At a formal level, this principle ensures international justice, in the concern shown by developed countries to lead in reducing emissions and provide financial resources for developing countries in compliance, adaptation, and

[108] Gracia Marín Durán, 'Securing Compatibility of Carbon Border Adjustments with the Multilateral Climate and Trade Regimes' (2023) 72(1) International and Comparative Law Quarterly 73, 81.

[109] Anastasios Gourgourinis, 'Common but Differentiated Responsibilities in Transnational Climate Change Governance and the WTO: A Tale of Two 'Interconnected Worlds' or a Tale of Two 'Crossing Swords'?' in Panagiotis Delimatsis (eds) *Research Handbook on Climate Change and Trade* (Edward Elgar 2016), 33.

[110] Philippe Sands and Jacqueline Peel, *Principles of International Environmental Law* (4th ed, Cambridge University Press 2018), 244.

[111] Lavanja Rajamani, 'Ambition and Differentiation in the 2015 Paris Agreement: Interpretative Possibilities and Underlying Politics' (2016) 65(2) ICLQ 493, 500–1.

technology transfer.[112] However, despite these formal commitments, the practical actions of developed countries have often fallen short of their leadership responsibilities. There is a significant gap between the pledged contributions and the actual efforts made by these countries.[113] The emission reduction commitments made by developed countries under the Paris Agreement are frequently criticized for being insufficiently ambitious.[114] They fail to align with the scale of action required to limit global warming to well below 2 °C above pre-industrial levels, as stipulated by the Paris Agreement. Additionally, they neglect to provide adequate support for capacity building in developing nations, which is essential for complying with the CBDRRC principle.[115]

Therefore, the climate club approach, designed as a complementary regime to the UNFCCC, has shown less concern for equity. The climate club's growth-oriented and technology-based approach to climate change mitigation contributes to its source-based legitimacy. The core rationale behind the establishment of the climate club is a recognition that, under the voluntary and nationally determined framework of the Paris Agreement, some countries may not be contributing sufficiently to the global effort to combat climate change.[116] This unilateral non-compliance judgement aims to alter the dynamics in differentiated obligations. In this regard, the climate club aims to create a de facto elevation of global climate action standards and leverage its source-based legitimacy rooted in technological advancement and economic growth. However, this approach raises significant concerns regarding equity and international justice.[117] While potentially effective in reducing emissions, the emphasis on technology and growth may inadvertently sideline the needs and

---

[112] Sonja Klinsky and others, 'Operationalizing Equity and Supporting Ambition: Identifying a More Robust Approach to Respective Capabilities' (2017) 9 Climate and Development 287, 289.

[113] Romain Weikmans and J. Timmons Roberts, 'The International Climate Finance Accounting Muddle: Is There Hope on the Horizon?' (2019) 11(2) Climate and Development 97, 98.

[114] United Nations Trade and Development (UNCTAD), Joint Statement Issued at the Conclusion of the 30th BASIC Ministerial Meeting on Climate Change, 'A European Union Carbon Border Adjustment Mechanism: Implications for developing countries (8 April 2021) <https://unctad.org/system/files/official-document/osginf2021d2_en.pdf > accessed 2 April 2024. Simone Tagliapietra and Guntram Wolff 'Form a Climate Club: United States, European Union and China' (2021) 591 Nature 526, 529.

[115] WP Pauw and others 'Conditional Nationally Determined Contributions in The Paris Agreement: Foothold for Equity or Achilles Heel?' (2019) 20 Climate Policy 468, 470.

[116] The major source of emissions is deriving from several countries, which are the EU, the US, China, Brazil, Japan, Canada, Russia, and India. All these countries adopt different positions for climate change. The EU supports a sharp reduction in emissions, whereas the US and other developed countries are cautious to take strong action. On the other side, the developing countries defend the idea that the emissions reduction is primarily the developed countries' obligation considering their historical contribution to the current emissions levels.

[117] In April 2021, Brazil, South Africa, India, and China collectively voiced their 'grave concerns' regarding climate-related trade initiatives like the BCA, labelling them as discriminatory and contrary to the principles of equity and common but differentiated responsibilities and respective capabilities. This critique is based on the argument that BCAs effectively bypass the foundational principles of the Paris Agreement by making market access conditional upon adherence to emis-

capabilities of less developed countries.[118] Without adequately considering their specific constraints, the unilateral judgment of non-compliance or underperformance by these countries could exacerbate existing inequalities in the international system.

Therefore, the implementation of climate obligations within the club necessitates not just an equitable and just framework but also one that is perceived as such by the participating countries. This perception is crucial for ensuring broad-based support and commitment.[119] While innovative in its focus on efficiency and rapid implementation of climate-related trade measures, the climate club approach has sparked concerns due to its departure from the CBDRRC principle. Therefore, climate club linkages, which require all countries to adopt binding reduction commitments, affect the perceived procedural legitimacy of the climate club.[120] By diminishing the formal differentiation between developed and developing countries, the climate club potentially undermines "the foundational equity considerations of the global climate governance framework".[121] In this way, the club risks alienating a significant portion of the global community. Consequently, the primary focus of the club on efficiency will not guarantee a sufficient incentive for developing countries to take part in the climate club.[122]

The climate club is a collaborative and ambitious framework where every country assumes responsibility and sets targets based on the risks, the urgency for action, and the need for collaboration. Within the climate club, countries can collectively work towards meeting climate goals irrespective of their development status. This approach fosters a sense of shared responsibility without hiding behind the CBDRRC principle. This is because the climate club interprets the principle's focus on differentiated responsibilities as a loophole for some countries to delay their climate actions, under the guise of requiring more support or time to develop. The club approach critics the CBDRRC principle as it can lead to a collective action problem, where the sum of national commitments falls short of the global efforts needed to limit warming.

---

sion reduction standards that might surpass the commitments an exporting country has agreed to under the Paris Agreement. Joint Statement (n 114).

[118] Ibid 12.

[119] Eckersley, 'Moving Forward in the Climate Negotiations' (n 70) 24.

[120] The Paris Agreement preamble recognizes that "parties may be affected not only by climate change, but also measures taken in response to it." Climate-related trade measures has impacts on third countries, specifically developing ones. In the lack of just transition and support mechanisms, mitigation policies could have adverse impacts. Kimberley Botwright and Jeremy Stewart, 'Trade and Climate Change' in *The Elgar Companion to the World Trade Organization* (Edward Elgar Publishing 2022), 462.

[121] Chukwumerije Okereke, 'Equity and Justice in Polycentric Climate Governance' in Andrew Jordan and others (eds), *Governing Climate Change: Polycentricity in Action?* (Cambridge University Press 2018), 332.

[122] Cameron Hepburn and Nicholas Stern, 'A New Global Deal on Climate Change' (2008) 24(2) Oxford Review of Economic Policy 259, 261.

The climate club incorporates mechanisms such as border carbon adjustments to address competitiveness concerns and mitigate the risk of carbon leakage.[123] They seek to level the playing field by imposing a tariff on products from non-club countries based on their carbon content. This practice raises strong objections among non-club countries, arguing that such extra costs contradict the CBDRRC principle.[124] The non-club countries contend that BCAs disproportionately allocate the costs of climate action and disregard the economic disparities and developmental needs of different countries.[125] For instance, the costs for complying with the climate club linkages will be relatively higher in poorer countries than in industrialised ones, where governments and companies have better access to relevant data.

Therefore, the developing countries claim that they should be exempted from the key commitments of the climate club since the major contributors to climate change are the developed countries.[126] They believe the primary move shall come from developed countries as they have the wealth, scientific expertise, and technologies to pioneer green leadership.[127] Developing countries are concerned that making a substantial cut in their emissions will moderate their growth rate[128] and require a high level of additional investment, given that they have a less efficient industry, deficient adaption capacity, and dependence on fossil fuel consumption.[129] They assert that it would be unfair to abide by the climate club scheme in case of insufficient compensation for adverse effects, as these measures might weaken competitiveness, exacerbate income inequality and restrict market access.[130] These concerns mainly arise in countries that are greatly dependent on international trade of carbon-intensive products and whose populations are impoverished.[131]

[123] Jean-Charles Hourcade, Antonin Pottier and Etienne Espagne, 'Social Value of Mitigation Activities and Forms of Carbon Pricing' (2018) 155(C) International Economics, Elsevier 8, 9. World Bank High-Level Commission on Carbon Prices, *Report of the High-Level Commission on Carbon Prices* (2017) 18.

[124] Robyn Eckersley, 'The Politics of Carbon Leakage and the Fairness of Border Measures' (2010) 24(4) Ethics and International Affairs 363, 382.

[125] Joint Statement (n 114).

[126] Vanderheiden (n 290), 37.

[127] Gerold Vidigal and Ingo Venzke, 'Of False Conflicts and Real Challenges: Trade Agreements, Climate Clubs, and Border Adjustments' (2022) 116 AJIL Unbound 202, 206.

[128] World Bank, *Inclusive Green Growth: The Pathway to Sustainable Development* (Technical Report, World Bank, Washington DC 2012).

[129] However, the Environmental Kuznets Curve indicates that when income levels (growth of GDP) have increase to a level that the demand for higher environmental quality emerges, the economic development can lead to an enhancement in environmental protection. Moreover, the Porter hypothesis argues that both countries and firms can benefit from stringent environmental protection regulations. Faure and Partain (n 55) 293.

[130] Robyn Eckersley, 'The Big Chill: The WTO and Multilateral Environmental Agreements' (2004) 4 Global Environmental Politics 24, 43.

[131] Dominic Roser and Luke Tomlinson, 'Trade Policies and Climate Change – Border Carbon Adjustments as a Tool for a Just Global Climate Regime' (2014) Ancilla Iuris 223, 239.

Developing countries invite that capability and needs should be prioritized in the burden-sharing of the climate club in addition to the historically extensive involvement in emissions.[132] Being at the early stage of global trade competition, developing countries would incur a double disadvantage because they are inherently more fragile to the changes in the international trade system and climate. Hence, they are of the opinion that there should be minimum club linkages for countries with fewer economic and social resources.[133] The abatement cost of the club should be carried by countries with a greater ability to pay, so a correlation between mitigation efforts and GDP per capita needs to be established. According to developing countries, this nuanced allocation of responsibilities and costs is essential for fostering global cooperation on the climate club.

However, managing carbon regulations, especially those enacted to establish and maintain a carbon price, becomes challenging when adhering to the CBDRRC principle.[134] The competitive conditions faced by products from these club countries could be adversely impacted. Also, developed countries question their obligations due to the increasing emission levels of developing countries.[135] Developing countries grow rapidly, enhance their industries, and fight against poverty.[136] Therefore, they will likely be responsible for a significant amount of emissions in the future.[137] The fewer abatement obligations of developing countries create an opportunity for them to attract more investments with lax environmental standards, which leads to a race to the bottom in mitigation efforts.[138] Developed country governments are unwilling to take costly domestic actions for emission reduction when some major emitting countries do not show significant effort to reach their climate targets. Therefore, the CBDRRC principle could undermine the climate club's efforts by neglecting excess emissions in developing economies.

Additionally, there is only a small chance to form an effective climate club without the largest and fastest growing GHG emitters of China, Brazil, India and other

---

[132] Nicholas Stern, 'The Economics of Climate Change' (2008) 98(2) The American Economic Review 1, 27.

[133] Soltau (n 102) 164.

[134] Weber, 'Border Tax Adjustment-Legal Perspective' (n 35) 417.

[135] Developing countries have already exceeded the developed countries in total GHG emissions and will count more than 75% of GHG emissions growth in the next 25 years. European Commission Emissions Database for Global Atmospheric Research, 'GHG emissions of All World Countries' (2023) <https://edgar.jrc.ec.europa.eu/report_2023> accessed 3 April 2024. Rafael Leal-Arcas, 'Alternative Architecture for Climate Change - Major Economies' (2011) 4(1) European Journal of Legal Studies, 25, 27.

[136] World Bank, 'World Development Indicator' (2013), <https://databankfiles.worldbank.org/public/ddpext_download/WDI-2013-ebook.pdf> accessed 26 March 2024.

[137] Gampfer (n 13) 6.

[138] The differences in domestic climate change policy give rise to carbon leakage, which means the movement of domestic industries to countries with less rigorous carbon legislation, and a decrease in the competitiveness of domestic industries in global markets. Hourcade, Pottier and Espagne (n 123) 9.

major developing countries' participation.[139] To a great extent, the carbon emissions will only change location as industrial facilities divert their investments to no-carbon price locations and cause an ecological disaster in these regions. Therefore, while the CBDRRC principle is widely accepted, its interpretation and application should be questioned.[140] The CBDRRC principle leaves the GHG limitations of developing countries voluntary. This flexibility may lead to a lack of accountability and insufficient action from developing countries, potentially undermining global efforts to mitigate climate change. Even though the principle aims to address equity, its implementation must not become a barrier to the climate club.

The club forces all countries, including developing ones, to adopt climate measures through climate club linkages or to pay club's carbon price as higher tariffs or border adjustments, which are unilateral trade instruments.[141] Therefore, the strict imposition of club linkages can be considered as an "extraterritorial outreach" for attempting to regulate matters outside the club borders.[142] This outreach raises significant concerns about sovereignty and the equitable distribution of climate action costs. The developing countries do not want to extend their climate obligations beyond the NDCs under the Paris Agreement.[143] However, the climate club could unfairly shift the financial burden of carbon abatement costs onto non-club countries, effectively making them finance the environmental efforts of more developed countries within the climate club. This is because it imposes an indirect tax for the benefit of the climate club jurisdictions without corresponding membership benefits or decision-making power. Also, the club could lead to a form of environmental elitism, where only a select group of countries benefits from the trade measures or incentives, leaving behind those in most need of support and resources for sustainable development.

Consequently, the developing countries advocate that countries with better means of preserving climate should also have a greater responsibility to protect it.[144] In response to the challenges posed by climate club linkages, which could disproportionately affect developing countries, they propose an equity formula. This

---

[139] Kenneth W Abbott, 'Strengthening the Transnational Regime Complex for Climate Change' (2014) 3(1) Transnational Environmental Law 57, 59.

[140] Michael Mehling, 'Implementing Climate Governance: Instrument Choice and Interaction' in Erkki J. Hollo, Kati Kulovesi, Michael Mehling (eds.) *Climate Change and the Law* (Springer 2013), 12.

[141] Christoph Böhringer, Jared C Carbone, and Thomas F Rutherford, 'The Strategic Value of Carbon Tariffs' (2016) 8(1) American Economic Journal: Economic Policy 28 <https://doi.org/10.1257/pol.20130327>. Sarah Davidson Ladly, 'Border Carbon Adjustments, WTO-law and the Principle of Common but Differentiated Responsibilities' (2012) 12 International Environmental Agreements: Politics, Law and Economics 63, 67.

[142] Alice Pirlot, 'Carbon Border Adjustment Measures: A Straightforward Multi-Purpose Climate Change Instrument?' (2022) 34 Journal of Environmental Law 25, 34.

[143] Joachim Englisch and Tatiana Falcao, 'EU Carbon Border Adjustments for Imported Products and WTO Law' (9 June 2021), 74 <https://doi.org/10.2139/ssrn.3863038>.

[144] Julia M Puaschunder, 'Mapping Climate in the Twenty-First Century' (2016) 59 Development 211 <https://doi.org/10.1057/s41301-017-0110-0>.

formula involves allocating free emissions rights or employing payment incentives, which would facilitate a significant transfer of resources to them.[145] Such a scheme could help mitigate the adverse distributional effects of club's carbon pricing framework. The revenue generated from climate club linkages could be utilized to support developing countries, helping to offset the economic impacts of the club's carbon pricing.[146] It can be directed toward the needs of developing countries to transform their economy into a green one, such as investments, measures for adaptation, and compensation for the industries that collapsed during the fossil phase-out.[147] Alternatively, grants, loans and guarantees for green transition can be provided to developing countries.[148]

Efforts to assist developing countries can contribute to a more inclusive and equitable climate club. This approach, in turn, ensures compliance with the CBDRRC principle. By prioritizing inclusivity and equity, the climate club can evolve into a more effective tool for global climate governance, one that harmonizes the ambitious goals of environmental preservation with the imperative of equitable development. Enhanced support for capacity building in developing nations is vital for enabling these countries to contribute meaningfully to global climate efforts, ensuring that progress towards climate goals is both collective and balanced. It necessitates a deliberate focus on equitable resource distribution, technology transfer, and financial support tailored to developing countries' specific needs and circumstances.[149] Such a strategy ensures that the climate club leads by example, not only in terms of environmental action but also in fostering global equity and justice in climate action initiatives.

5.3 *Special and Differentiated Treatment*

The second principle that address asymmetries between developing and developed countries is the special and differentiated treatment (SDT) to developing and least-developed countries in their trade obligations.[150] SDT is enshrined into the Enabling Clause, which allows parties to "accord differential and more favourable treatment to developing countries as well as special treatment on the least developed

[145] Eckersley, 'The Politics of Carbon Leakage and the Fairness of Border Measures' (n 124) 382.

[146] Joint Statement (n 114).

[147] Zaker Ahmad, 'Trade-Related Measures to Spread Low-Carbon Technologies: A Common Concern–Based Approach' in Thomas Cottier (ed), *The Prospects of Common Concern of Humankind in International Law* (Cambridge University Press 2021), 119.

[148] Domien Vangenechten and Johannes Lehne, 'Can Climate Clubs Accelerate Industrial Decarbonisation?' (E3G, 2022) <https://www.e3g.org/publications/can-climate-clubs-accelerate-industrial-decarbonisation/> 21 June 2021.

[149] Martini and Görlach (n 67) 11.

[150] General Agreement on Tariffs and Trade (GATT 1994) (15 April 1994) LT/UR/A-1A/1/GATT/1 <https://docs.wto.org/dol2fe/Pages/SS/directdoc.aspx?filename=Q:/UR/FA/06-gatt.pdf&Open=True> hereinafter GATT art XXXVI:8.

countries".[151] The principle aims to create a "level of playing field" for the competition among countries with different development levels. It created a permanent legal basis for various measures that assist and protect developing countries, including tariff preferences[152] and various non-tariff preferences.[153]

The clause recognises that formal equal treatment could have materially different impacts on countries with varying development stages.[154] However, the climate club does not differentiate countries according to their development levels and obliges each of them to abide by its agreement architecture. It conveys the message that all nations have a crucial role in mitigating climate change, even though developing countries may face more significant economic challenges in transitioning to a low-carbon economy. Uniform club linkages may not adequately address these disparities. Hence, developing countries could argue that uniformity in the club hampers their economic growth. They could object to imposing a single, origin-neutral carbon price under the climate club. As a result, deriving from the Enabling Clause, they can desire an exemption or differential and more favourable treatment in the application of climate-related trade mechanisms to prevent disadvantages on their economies.

6 The EU Green Deal as a Climate Club Paradigm

6.1 Introduction

The UNFCCC regime and Paris Agreement reflect the positions of the least climate-concerned actors[155] since unanimity is required in decision-making. Therefore, the global climate objectives of the Paris Agreement cannot be met when international

[151] Contracting Parties to the GATT, 'Decision of 28 November 1979: Differential and More Favourable Treatment Reciprocity and Fuller Participation of Developing Countries' L/4903, para 2. The 1979 Decision on Differential and More Favourable Treatment, Reciprocity and Fuller Participation of Developing Countries, also known as the Enabling Clause, covers the Generalized System of Preferences, SDT provisions under GATT agreements, certain aspects of regional or global preferential agreements among developing countries, and special treatment for least-developed countries.

[152] Celine Tan, 'Development' in Thomas Cottier and Krista Nadakavukaren Schefer (eds), *Elgar Encyclopedia of International Economic Law* (Edward Elgar 2017), 257.

[153] Constantine Michalopoulos *The Role of Special Differential Treatment for Developing Countries in GATT and the World Trade Organization* (World Bank Policy Research Working Paper No. 2388, 2000). Such as rights, procedural advantages, exemptions, extended timelines for compliance, less strict inspections and formalities, technical assistance, capacity building, financing, measures to increase trading opportunities, safeguarding trade interests of developing countries, and flexibilities in the imposition of their obligations.

[154] Pananya Larbprasertporn, 'The Interaction between WTO Law and the Principle of Common But Differentiated Responsibilities in the Case of Climate-Related Border Tax Adjustment' (2014) 6(1) Goettingen Journal of International Law 145.

[155] Karen Mohlenkamp, Sabine Schulte-Beckhausen and Bertil Kapff, 'The European Green Deal' (2021) 32 Int'l Tax Rev 74, 75.

partners do not share the same ambitions. Given this context, the EU has observed a unique window of opportunity to show global leadership in climate mitigation efforts.[156] Since the early 1990s, it has strived to shape the global climate agenda, playing a pivotal role in the COP processes. It has been instrumental in influencing the structural design of these processes and fostering coalitions to advocate for stringent climate targets.[157] This proactive stance underscores its commitment to driving forward the global climate action agenda.[158] Notably, the EU has consciously positioned itself as a leading global actor for climate change mitigation to 2020 and beyond.[159]

Within this road, initially, the EU has relied predominantly on "directional leadership",[160] in which it adopted domestic emissions reduction measures and demonstrated their feasibility by being an example to the international community. Whereas recently, the EU shifted its approach to "structural leadership".[161] In this context, it has reinforced the use of economic power to promote sustainable practices and influence global norms and standards".[162] Accordingly, it has adopted significant changes in its foreign trade, international investment, and financing policies to fill the climate ambition gap,[163] which refers to EU raising its environmental standards but outsourcing products from countries with more carbon-intensive production.

In this regard, European Green Deal (EGD) is a pioneering initiative and represents a paradigm shift in climate regulations. Hence, assessing it through the lens of the climate club approach can elucidate EGD's potential impact on global climate initiatives. In the subsequent sections, the goals, conceptual framework, membership incentives and enforcement mechanisms of the EGD are analysed by

[156] Felix Bierbrauer, and others, *A CO2-Border Adjustment Mechanism as a Building Block of a Climate Club* (Kiel Policy Brief No. 15, Kiel Institute for the World Economy (IfW), 2021), 3.

[157] Christoff Peter and Robyn Eckersley, 'Comparing State Responses' in John S Dryzek, Richard B Norgaard and David Schlosberg (eds), *The Oxford Handbook of Climate Change and Society* (Oxford University Press, 2012), 440.

[158] Charles F Parker, Christer Karlsson and Matthias Hjerpe 'Assessing the European Union's Global Climate Change Leadership: From Copenhagen to the Paris Agreement' (2017) 39(2) Journal of European Integration 239.

[159] Miruna Butnaru-Troncota, 'European Green Deal and the New Policy Goals in Transport and Mobility - How Gamification Can Influence Pro-Environmental Behaviour for Cutting Carbon Emissions in the EU' (2020) 14(2) Europolity: Continuity & Change in European Governance 89, 91. Council Regulation (EC) 2021/1119 of 30 June 2021 establishing the framework for achieving climate neutrality and amending Regulations (EC) No 401/2009 and (EU) 2018/1999 ('European Climate Law') [2021] OJ L243/1, recital 17.

[160] Parker and Karlsson (n 73) 923.

[161] Ibid 926.

[162] European Climate Law, recital 10.

[163] Sebastian Oberthür and Ingmar von Homeyer, 'From Emissions Trading to The European Green Deal: The Evolution of The Climate Policy Mix and Climate Policy Integration in the EU' (2023) 30(3) Journal of European Public Policy 445, 452 < https://doi.org/10.1080/13501763.2022.2120528>.

highlighting how they align with the core principles of a climate club. Also, the examination extends to how the EGD serves as a catalyst for global climate action and influences other countries and regional blocs to intensify their efforts in combating climate change[164] in a similar vein to the climate club approach.

The choice of analysing the EGD as a climate club paradigm lies in the fact that the EU constitutes a club of countries, proliferated with development endowments to its members and a promise of improved governance levels. Therefore, the EU has achieved a high degree of policy integration among its member states. In contrast, most national frameworks operate in isolation, without the benefit of coordinated policy across multiple jurisdictions. Since the Kyoto Protocol, through its ETS, the EU represents the single largest and most developed climate club, with 31 national governments as participants. Further, with the EGD, the EU has a vital role in the global network, where its economic influence can catalyse for broader environmental change. EGD's instruments go beyond the EU's borders, reflecting an opportunistic value projection strategy.[165] The market size of the EU, which encompasses over 445 million people, gives it the leverage to use trade as a political tool.[166] Hence, the EGD constitutes a significant regulatory scheme not just for Europe but also for its trading partners.

Also, the EU is gradually adapting EGD into a major branch of its foreign policy.[167] In doing so, it is fostering cooperation with governments and industries in third countries and international organizations to form partnerships and alliances for climate protection, including G7, G20, and the COP 28 Climate Club.[168] Importantly, the EU would like to work with global partners to develop an international carbon market as a fundamental tool to create economic incentives for climate action.[169] These developments are designed to encourage partner countries to adopt rules that are at least as ambitious as those of the EU.[170] It aims to ensure that all products within the EU Single Market comply with the EGD requirements. The goal of EGD's green diplomacy chapter is to align all EU internal and external policies, encompassing trade policies and international climate agreements, to promote cohesive and sustainable policy frameworks across borders. This strategic alignment reinforces the EU's role in global environmental leadership and fosters international

[164] The European Green Deal, 20.

[165] Michael E Smith, 'A Liberal Grand Strategy in A Realist World? Power, Purpose and The EU's Changing Global Role' (2011) 18(2) Journal of European Public Policy 144, 153 <https://doi.org/10.1080/13501763.2011.544487>.

[166] Natalie Dobson, 'Chapter 25: Climate Protection versus Trade: Dilemmas for the EU' in *Handbook on European Union Climate Change Policy and Politics* (Edward Elgar Publishing, 2023), 378. Parker and Karlsson (n 547) 928.

[167] Ibid 4.

[168] Council Regulation (EC) 2023/956 of 10 May 2023 establishing a carbon border adjustment mechanism (Text with EEA relevance)' [2023] OJ L 130/1, (hereinafter CBAM Regulation), recital 72.

[169] The European Green Deal 20.

[170] Durán, 'Securing Compatibility of Carbon Border Adjustments' (n 108) 78.

climate action cooperation.[171] In essence, the EGD is chosen as the paradigm for the climate club in this book because it offers a comprehensive, legally binding, and globally influential model that aligns with the key principles and requirements of the club approach.

6.2 The Overview of the European Green Deal

The EU Commission unveiled EGD, the roadmap towards a new growth policy for Europe, in December 2019. The EGD aims for a climate-neutral, green, fair, and social Europe. It is founded on three fundamental pillars, which are (i) net-zero GHG emissions by 2050, (ii) economic growth decoupled from resource use, and (iii) no person and no place are left behind.[172] Per these pillars, the EGD essentially design three key areas. They are carbon pricing, sustainable investment and industrial policy, and finally, just transition.[173] Essentially, the EGD prepares the EU's economy for a green transition. First, it prices carbon-generating activities with trade instruments.[174] Subsequently, the EGD financially supports the transition with an investment plan, which mobilises public investment and helps unlock private funds through EU financial instruments, notably Invest EU.[175] Finally, recognising that the efforts to tackle climate change need to be socially legitimate, it created a Just Transition Fund (JTF) for the regions and sectors most affected by decarbonization.[176]

This transformative agenda of the EU transcends traditional sectoral approaches, as it systematically integrates sustainability considerations into a wide array of EU policies. By explicitly referencing the EU budget,[177] macroeconomics and fiscal policies,[178] taxation,[179] research and innovation,[180] trade policies,[181] and external

[171] Council Decision (EU) 2022/591 of 6 April 2022 on a General Union Environment Action Programme to 2030 [2022] OJ L114/22, 6.

[172] Ibid 2.

[173] Gregory Claeys, Simone Tagliapietra, and Georg Zachmann, *How to Make the European Green Deal Work (*Bruegel Policy Contribution No. 2019/13, 2019) 2.

[174] CBAM Regulation recital 12.

[175] Communication from the Commission (COM) Sustainable Europe Investment Plan European Green Deal Investment Plan 21 final [2020].

[176] Anna Kyriazi and Jordi Miró, 'Towards a Socially Fair Green Transition in the EU? An Analysis of the Just Transition Fund Using the Multiple Streams Framework' (2023) 21 Comparative European Politics 112 <https://doi.org/10.1057/s41295-022-00304-6>.

[177] The European Green Deal 15.

[178] Ibid 17.

[179] Ibid 5.

[180] Ibid 18.

[181] Ibid 21.

policies,[182] the EGD seeks to create a holistic and interconnected framework for achieving the green transition. As a result, EGD is supposed to serve as an "action plan", a "roadmap" or narrative for all existing and new EU regulations, policies and directives.[183] This approach ensures a cohesive effort across various policy domains and minimises potential conflicts to advance the green agenda. Crucially, the EGD recognizes the imperative to balance environmental sustainability with economic growth.[184] Thus, within the framework of the EGD, a noteworthy emphasis is placed on the economic instruments to enhance environmental standards. This choice signals a departure from conventional regulatory approaches and underscores the importance of climate-related trade measures, fiscal policies, and incentives to drive sustainable practices across industries.

Criticisms argue that implementing climate-related trade measures may be viewed as unilateralism, a stance that appears to penalize or discriminate against foreign countries.[185] These measures could strain international trade relations, as they might be perceived as imposing the EU's environmental standards on other countries without their consent. This perception could lead to accusations of economic protectionism or environmental imperialism,[186] where the EU uses its market power to enforce its environmental policies globally. However, the underlying motivation of the EGD is not punitive. Instead, it aims to motivate regulatory changes in jurisdictions beyond the EU's borders.[187] By setting stringent environmental standards, the EU hopes to create a ripple effect, prompting countries worldwide to adopt greener practices to maintain access to its lucrative market. Hence, the EU's ability to get support from neighbouring countries will be critical for its credibility as a global climate actor and the success of EGD.[188]

In its commitment to combat climate change, the EGD will ensure that the Paris Agreement remains an indispensable multilateral framework.[189] Accordingly, the EGD works towards strengthening the objectives and rules laid down in the Paris Agreement.[190] It supports third countries in doing the same, specifically to enhance

[182] Ibid 20.

[183] Thierry Portevin, 'The EU Green Deal – a roadmap to sustainable economies' (Switch 2 Green, 11 December 2019) <https://www.switchtogreen.eu/the-eu-green-deal-promoting-a-green-notable-circular-economy/> accessed 18 March 2024.

[184] The European Green Deal 23.

[185] UNFCCC, BASIC Ministerial, 'Joint Statement at the UNFCCC's Sharm el-Sheikh Climate Change Conference' (15 November 2022) COP27/CMP17/CMA4, para. 11.

[186] When the common concern becomes a justification for unilateral intervention and sanctions. Thomas Cottier and Sofya Matteotti-Berkutova 'International Environmental Law and the Evolving Concept of 'Common Concern of Mankind' in Thomas Cottier, Olga Nartova, and Sadeq Z Bigdeli *International Trade Regulation and the Mitigation of Climate Change: World Trade Forum* (Cambridge University Press, 2009), 45.

[187] The European Green Deal, 22.

[188] Ibid 20.

[189] Ibid 5.

[190] For example, the EGD's climate neutrality target by 2050 is in line with Article 4.4 of the Paris Agreement, which obliges developed country Parties to take lead in climate action with economy-

accountability regarding progress on the commitments made under the Paris Agreement.[191] So, it is possible to conclude that EGD aims to strengthen international environmental governance by closing ambition and compliance gaps.[192] Thus, the EGD would like to engage more intensely with all partners and help them to implement their NDCs. In essence, the EGD emerges not only as a domestic agenda but also as a tool for the EU to play a leadership role in strengthening international environmental governance.[193]

Correspondingly, the Commission unveiled in July 2021 its "Fit For 55" package, which consists of 13 policies promoting decarbonization. These policies extend the carbon emission scheme to new sectors for regulating carbon pricing, consumer and business behaviour, as well as sustainable public and private investment. Particularly, the regulation introduced carbon border adjustment mechanism (CBAM), expansion of the EU-ETS and the Free Trade Agreements (FTAs) with climate chapters.[194] Also, even though the package has not launched a specific budget for financial aid and technical assistance under its realm, it directs the available EU fundings towards initiatives aimed at promoting sustainable development and tackling climate change.[195]

In this context, the EU's main climate-related trade policy instrument is CBAM, which prices specific imports per their carbon content.[196] This mechanism serves a tripartite function that aligns with the objectives of the EGD.[197] Firstly, CBAM is designed to fulfil domestic climate policy objectives. By incorporating a carbon pricing mechanism for imports, the EU aims to ensure that its domestic industries experience a level of playing field. This approach not only helps in achieving the EU's climate targets but also prevents carbon leakage,[198] where industries might relocate to areas with less stringent environmental regulations. Secondly, CBAM contributes to shaping international climate governance.[199] Under the CBAM, importers of certain goods are required to purchase carbon certificates to offset the

---

wide absolute emission reduction targets.

[191] Pirlot, 'Carbon Border Adjustment Measures' (n 142) 45.

[192] Makane Moïse Mbengue and Elena Cima, '"Clubbing in the Club": Could Climate-Related Trade Arrangements Set the Pace for Future Climate Cooperation?' (2022) 116 American Journal of International Law Unbound 219.

[193] Diana Vela Almeida and others, 'The "Greening" of Empire: The European Green Deal as the EU first agenda' (2023) 105 Political Geography, 6.

[194] Communication from the Commission (COM) "Fit for 55": Delivering the EU's 2030 Climate Target on the Way to Climate Neutrality 550 [2021], 3.

[195] Ibid 11.

[196] CBAM Regulation art 1(1).

[197] European Parliament, Committee on the Environment, Public Health and Food Safety, Report Towards a WTO-Compatible EU Carbon Border Adjustment Mechanism Explanatory Statement [2021] A9-0019/2021.

[198] CBAM Regulation, recital 9.

[199] Pirlot, 'Carbon Border Adjustment Measures' (n 142) 33.

emissions associated with the production of their goods or lower their emissions levels if they wish to access the EU market.[200] Finally, the third function corresponds to becoming a tool for foreign trade policy. CBAM aims to influence the process and production methods (PPMs) of the EU's international trade partners.[201] As a result, the CBAM accelerates global efforts in climate mitigation while protecting the global competitiveness of the EU's domestic industries.

The cost of CBAM certificates will be based on the EU carbon price, which is the average price of carbon allowances auctioned within the EU ETS for each week.[202] With this CBAM revenue, the EU can finance its green transition while reducing the GHG levels globally.[203] The CBAM was introduced on 1 October 2023, initially as a pilot program for a limited number of industrial sectors with a high level of embedded carbon in their value chain, which are exposed to carbon leakage risk.[204] These sectors are iron and steel, cement, aluminium, fertilizers, hydrogen, and electricity generation.[205] This product-based focus is beneficial as a matter of regulatory design.[206] The permanent system will enter into force on 1 January 2026.

The second market instrument of the EGD is the EU ETS's expanded scope.[207] In this way, the ETS reinforces its role as a cornerstone in the EU's climate policy. Established in 2005, the EU ETS operates on the cap-and-trade principle, where a cap is set on the total amount of certain GHGs emitted by covered entities, such as power plants and industrial facilities.[208] Participants can buy or sell allowances, which provide economic incentives for industries to innovate and reduce their carbon footprint efficiently. The extension of the EU ETS under the EGD signifies a commitment to addressing a broader range of economic sectors and activities contributing to GHG emissions. Traditionally covering industries like energy production and heavy manufacturing, the EU ETS is now preparing to cover additional

---

200 CBAM Regulation, art 3(25).

201 Ibid recital 14.

202 Ibid article 21.

203 Lionel Fontagné and Katheline Schubert, 'The Economics of Border Carbon Adjustment: Rationale and Impacts of Compensating for Carbon at the Border' (2023) 15 Annual Review of Economics 389, 412 <https://doi.org/10.1146/annurev-economics-082322-034040.

204 European Commission, Commission Staff Working Document Impact Assessment Report Accompanying the document Proposal for a Regulation of the European Parliament and of the Council Establishing a Carbon Border Adjustment Mechanism SWD [2021] 643 final, 84. Pirlot, 'Carbon Border Adjustment Measures' (n 142) 44.

205 CBAM Regulation, art 4.

206 Leonelli, 'The Long and Winding Road Towards the Creation of Climate Clubs' (n 58) 456.

207 Communication from the Commission (COM) Stepping up Europe's 2030 Climate Ambition - Investing in a Climate-neutral Future for the Benefit of Our People 562 [2020].

208 Council Directive 2003/87/EC of 13 October 2003 establishing a system for greenhouse gas emission allowance trading within the Union and amending Council Directive 96/61/EC [2003] OJ L275/32.

sectors, such as transportation and buildings.[209] By widening the scope, the EGD aims to create a more comprehensive regulatory framework that reflects the interconnected nature of emissions across diverse sectors.

Finally, EGD's diplomatic trade instrument is the FTAs with climate chapters. FTAs are reciprocal trade agreements between two or more parties, which grant preferential and privileged access to each other's markets by removing tariff and non-tariff barriers to trade.[210] The distinguishing feature of FTAs from other climate-related trade instruments is their basis in reward mechanism. With the EGD, FTAs aim at a preferential free trade area open to countries ready to take on climate mitigation responsibilities and, in return, grant trade liberalization privileges to these countries.[211] This next-generation FTAs of the EGD adopt a holistic approach to trade relations and enhance deeper collaboration on trade-plus areas.[212] In this way, they set a standard for global climate change mitigation rules while deepening signatories' trade relations.

Given these trade instruments, the EGD's current state fits into the neoliberalist approach to adapting and mitigating climate change. One key criterion defining neoliberalism in the context of the EGD is the emphasis on policies that seek to address environmental concerns and foster economic competitiveness.[213] The EGD recognizes the potential for green economic growth as a driver for sustainability. Thereby, it intertwines environmental goals with economic objectives. Furthermore, the neoliberal nature of the EGD is evident in its focus on capital accumulation, technology, and innovation.[214] The EGD encourages investment in renewable technologies, sustainable infrastructure, and eco-friendly innovations. Additionally, allocating responsibility for action is another key criterion reflecting the neoliberal approach within the EGD. The EGD places a considerable emphasis on the individual responsibility of firms and consumers.[215] It entrusts businesses and consumers with the responsibility to make environmentally conscious choices. This decentralization of responsibility aligns with the neoliberal belief in the efficacy of individual actors within a free market.

---

[209] Fit for 55, 7. Council Regulation (EC) 957/2023 of 10 May 2023 amending Regulation (EU) 2015/757 in order to provide for the inclusion of maritime transport activities in the EU Emissions Trading System and for the monitoring, reporting and verification of emissions of additional greenhouse gases and emissions from additional ship types [2023] OJ L130/105, recital 8.

[210] Mostafa Beshkar and Eric Bond, 'Trade Agreements: Theoretical Foundations' in *Oxford Research Encyclopaedia of Economics and Finance* (Oxford University Press, 2019), 10.

[211] The European Green Deal, 21.

[212] [2017] ECR EU:C: 2017:376 Opinion 2/15 of the Court, para 17.

[213] Almeida and others (n 193) 8.

[214] The European Green Deal 2, 17.

[215] Ibid 2, 5.

6.3 European Green Deal Through the Lens of Club Approach

The EU's exercise of economic power through the market mechanisms of the EGD and its aim of triggering progressive climate legislation in partner countries with a diplomacy chapter corresponds to the main logic of the climate club approach. Acknowledging the challenges of global coordination, the EGD pivots towards forming a "coalition of the willing", a group of nations aligned in their environmental ambitions.[216] It seeks to foster a club of like-minded countries committed to shared climate goals, thereby reinforcing the EU's ambitious climate policies through collective action and partnership. Similar to the climate club, EGD constitutes an alternative way of achieving carbon abatement as multilateral attempts to coordinate global action for climate change do not produce fruitful results. It reinforces the EU's position as an aspirational actor that seeks to be a forerunner in the global climate mitigation agenda, mainly through its economic weight.[217]

The term "Brussels effect" is used to describe this phenomenon where unilateral regulatory policies are globally adopted due to the influence of policies and regulations set by the EU.[218] In the context of the EGD, the Brussels effect manifests as the externalization of environmental standards beyond the EU's jurisdiction through climate-related trade instruments and aid programs. Towards this end, EGD will work to facilitate the trade of environmental goods and services in bilateral or minilateral fora. Therefore, the EU's relations with trade partners gradually turn out to be conditional upon the values and the norms of the EGD. As a large single market, the EU has the capacity to realise climate goals and can set standards that apply across global value chains.[219] This ripple effect reflects the cooperative nature of the climate club, where shared norms and values drive collective action.

In a similar vein to the climate club, the EU aims to use its influence, expertise and financial resources to mobilise third countries to join its plan on a sustainable path.[220] The EU is committed to leading global efforts on climate change and seeks to form alliances with nations sharing similar environmental ambitions.[221] Recognizing the importance of securing its supply chains and maintaining competitiveness, the EU aims to pursue its climate objectives even in the face of inaction from other countries regarding emissions reduction. This strategic approach underscores the EU's dedication to both environmental leadership and economic resil-

[216] Goran Dominioni and Daniel Esty, 'Designing Effective Border-Carbon Adjustment Mechanisms: Aligning the Global Trade and Climate Change Regimes' (2023) 65(1) Arizona Law Review, 24.

[217] The European Green Deal 22.

[218] Anu Bradford, *The Brussels Effect: How the European Union Rules the World* (Oxford University Press 2020).

[219] Sebastian Oberthür and Claire Dupont, 'The European Union's International Climate Leadership: Towards a Grand Climate Strategy?' (2021) 28 J Eur Public Policy 1095 <https://doi.org/10.1080/13501763.2021.1918218>.

[220] The European Green Deal 21.

[221] Durán, 'Securing Compatibility of Carbon Border Adjustments' (n 108) 79.

ience. Such pragmatism aligns with the climate club's recognition of the necessity for dominant actors to take the lead in mitigation efforts, irrespective of the actions of other countries. Therefore, EGD adopts material incentives in the form of economic sanctions or trade preferences to ensure a coherent fusion of the EU's climate change acquis to external policy.[222]

Mainly, the new conditions set by the EGD for preferential trade liberalization with FTAs, sanctions on industries with CBAM and financial aid and technical assistance to neighbouring countries to realize the coherent fusion with the EU's climate change acquis represent club linkages that solidify cooperation and penalise non-members. These instruments create an exclusive benefit named as club good,[223] which is unrestricted access to the European market. Therefore, many exporting countries will progressively adopt these new measures to access the EU's Single Market without an additional cost or receive EU funding. This implication reflects the dynamics of the climate club exerting power on non-club members through market instruments, emphasizing the interplay between economic incentives and environmental goals. The linkages showcase how unilateral economic power can be harnessed to shape international behaviour and encourage sustainability practices beyond the EU's borders.[224] Thereby, the linkages are using trade as a political tool. For these reasons, it is possible to analyse EGD through the lens of the climate club paradigm.

The EGD and the climate club both strategically deploy environmental taxation, market-based instruments, green budgeting and financing tools as part of their comprehensive approaches to address climate change within a neoliberal framework.[225] At the national level, the EGD creates tax reforms for pollution.[226] This strategy aims to create economic incentives for industries and individuals to reduce their GHG emissions. In a similar vein, the climate club approach utilizes linkages that target emission levels of products. These linkages can take the form of carbon tax, tariffs or environmental standards imposed on traded goods.[227] By linking trade benefits or penalties to emission levels, the climate club incentivizes member and non-member countries to adopt and enforce measures that reduce their carbon footprint. Therefore, the EGD and the climate club also align in their neoliberal approach to use market-based instruments for the potential to drive sustainable practices and shape global environmental behaviour.

However, using economic power to pursue environmental objectives is still politically highly sensitive and potentially dangerous for international trade dynamics.[228]

---

[222] CBAM Regulation recital 72.

[223] See Sect. 1.1 in Chap. 4.

[224] Anatole Boute, 'Accounting for Carbon Pricing in Third Countries Under the EU Carbon Border Adjustment Mechanism' (2024) World Trade Review 1, 4.

[225] See Sects. 1.2 and 6.2 in Chap. 4.

[226] The European Green Deal 17.

[227] See Sect. 3 in Chap. 5.

[228] Dominioni and Esty (n 216) 19.

The political reception will depend on the narratives that the EU is able to impose on its partners but, at the same time, avoid a sense of *fait accompli*. Many developing countries specifically view the CBAM as a protectionist policy;[229] hence, they have an overall negative reception for the EGD.[230] However, the CBAM does not impose a value judgement on the carbon policies of the countries concerned.[231] Instead, it recognizes that the diversity of ambitions and policy instruments under the Paris Agreement introduces distortions in global competition and aims to rebalance these discrepancies.[232] Therefore, the EU must engage in transparent and inclusive dialogues, as in the climate club for inclusive cooperation. The criticisms can be partially neutralised by meticulous design, particularly compliance with the WTO rules, defining sectors to be covered, the counting rules, etc.[233] The emphasis on narratives, careful design, adherence to rules and proactive engagement within the EGD aligns with the climate club approach's collaborative and inclusive nature.

In the context of the EGD, the expansion of club membership becomes contingent upon countries meeting specific entry conditions. These conditions are linked to fulfilling the comprehensive requirements outlined in the EGD.[234] The entrance condition to the club based on the EGD is subjected to a carbon price equal to the EU ETS. The EU has already linked its ETS[235] with European Free Trade Association countries, Northern Ireland[236] and Switzerland[237] exemplifying its collaborative spirit. However, recognizing the diversity of global climate policy landscapes, the EGD acknowledges that not all countries may have established carbon pricing mechanisms comparable to the EU scheme. For these countries, the CBAM assumes the role of defining entry rules to the climate club. Acting as both a regulatory framework and a sanction mechanism,[238] the CBAM aims to address carbon leakage by imposing tariffs on imports with high carbon content. Also, it encourages non-member countries to adopt and implement carbon pricing measures.[239]

---

[229] Durán, 'Securing Compatibility of Carbon Border Adjustments' (n 108) 97.

[230] Boute (n 224) 2.

[231] CBAM Regulation recital 70–71.

[232] Ibid recital 10.

[233] Boute (n 224) 11–12.

[234] Indra Overland and M Sadaqat Huda, 'Climate Clubs and Carbon Border Adjustments: A Review' (2022) 17(9) Environ Res Lett, 17.

[235] Council Directive 2003/87/EC, art 25.

[236] European Commission, 'Scope of EU Emission Trading System' <https://climate.ec.europa.eu/eu-action/eu-emissions-trading-system-eu-ets/scope-eu-emissions-trading-system_en> accessed 6 July 2024.

[237] Federal Office for the Environment, 'Linking the Swiss and EU Emissions Trading Systems' <https://www.bafu.admin.ch/bafu/en/home/topics/climate/info-specialists/reduction-measures/ets/linking-swiss-eu.html> accessed 6 July 2024.

[238] Christoph Böhringer and others, 'Potential Impacts and Challenges of Border Carbon Adjustments' (2022) 12 Nat. Clim. Chang, 22, 27 <https://doi.org/10.1038/s41558-021-01250-z>.

[239] Boute (n 224) 6.

In addition to the EGD, there is a growing political willingness by important emitters to increase emissions abatement efforts. Under President Biden, the US re-joined the Paris Agreement and implemented a "whole-of-administration" approach to climate change.[240] It intends to scale up international climate finance significantly. In this context, the Inflation Reduction Act (IRA) was enacted as the most extensive federal legislation ever to address climate change.[241] It aims to mobilise investment in renewable energy and green technologies, including through subsidies and targeted state aid. While the IRA may help the US reduce emissions, achieve its climate goals and deliver economic benefits, concerns have been raised about its potential distorting effect on markets elsewhere.[242] Also, US have proposed similar measures to EU's CBAM.[243] Importantly, the Joint Statement of the EU and US on Global Steel and Aluminium Arrangement lays the foundations for the creation of a sectoral climate club.[244] Similar to the EU scheme, the United Kingdom (UK) government plans to introduce its own CBAM for carbon intensive products as of 1 January 2027.[245] On the other hand, China's ETS officially entered its operational phase in 2021,[246] and President Xi Jinping has pledged that the country aims to be carbon-neutral by 2060.[247]

Even though these international actors constitute more than half of global GHG emissions,[248] they cannot substantially solve the climate problem if they do not cooperate to close the emissions abatement gap globally. The idea of organising a climate club has arrived on the political agenda to build on the growing momentum in the world's three biggest economic blocs. A climate club can therefore become a

---

[240] 'Biden Administration Pushes for Multilateral Cooperation and Domestic Action to Combat Climate Change' (2022) 116(1) American Journal of International Law 171, <https://doi.org/10.1017/ajil.2021.70>.

[241] Leonelli, 'The Long and Winding Road Towards the Creation of Climate Clubs' (n 58) 458.

[242] Chad P Bown, *Industrial Policy for Electric Vehicle Supply Chains and the US-EU Fight Over the Inflation Reduction Act* (Peterson Institute for International Economics Working Paper No 23-1, 2023) <https://doi.org/10.2139/ssrn.4449020>.

[243] 'Market Choice Act 2023 House Bill 118th Congress 6665., Fair Transition and Competition Act 2021 117th Cong S. GAI21718 59G., Clean Competition Act 2022 117th Cong S. 4355.

[244] European Commission (EU) and US Trade Representative, 'Steel and Aluminium, EU-US Joint Statement of 31 October 2021' (2021). Although the specific design of this mechanism is yet to be finalized, the agreement anticipates that the EU and the US will establish a system to limit market access for countries failing to comply with low-carbon intensity standards and encourage participation from economies with similar outlooks in these arrangements.

[245] HM Revenue and Customs and HM Treasury, 'Introduction of a UK Carbon Border Adjustment Mechanism from January 2027: Consultation' (21 March 2024). <https://assets.publishing.service.gov.uk/media/65fc11fef1d3a0001132ac6f/Introduction_of_a_UK_carbon_border_adjustment_mechanism_from_January_2027.docx.pdf> accessed 5 April 2024.

[246] World Bank, 'State and Trends of Carbon Pricing 2023' (World Bank 2023) <https://openknowledge.worldbank.org/handle/10986/39796> accessed 25 March 2024.

[247] 'In-Depth Q&A: Will China's Emissions Trading Scheme Help Tackle Climate Change?' (Carbon Brief, 2023) <https://www.carbonbrief.org/in-depth-qa-will-chinas-emissions-trading-scheme-help-tackle-climate-change/> accessed 18 March 2024.

[248] Global Carbon Budget 'Annual CO_2 emissions – GCB' (2023) <https://ourworldindata.org/co2-emissions> accessed 19 May 2024.

useful forum for countries to coordinate their green industrial policies and avoid trade disputes. In this regard, the German government has expressed intentions to initiate a "cooperative and open climate club" that aims to start at the European level and successively bring on board more countries.[249] Its foundation was laid at COP 28.[250]

In conclusion, the global landscape is witnessing a remarkable surge in political commitment to address climate change, as exemplified by initiatives such as the EGD, the comprehensive measures taken in the US, and China's ambitious goals. However, while recognizing the interconnected nature of the climate challenge, it is evident that substantial progress cannot be achieved solely through the efforts of individual major emitters. The emerging concept of a climate club, championed by influential economic blocs, underscores the urgency for collaborative global action. To effectively close the emissions abatement gap and tackle climate change comprehensively, the international community must continue to build on this momentum, fostering a cooperative and inclusive approach that transcends national borders and unites countries in the shared pursuit of a sustainable and resilient future.

7 Concluding Remarks

The climate club concept, as explored in this book, offers a novel framework for enhancing global climate governance through focused collective action among willing countries. By adopting a minilateral approach, the club aims to sidestep the inefficiencies and gridlocks often encountered in broader multilateral climate negotiations. The climate club leverages mutual interests, shared goals, and market-based mechanisms to encourage stringent climate measures. Therefore, it demonstrates a pragmatic path towards significant emissions reductions. The club has a potential to serve as a catalyst for ambitious climate action. By creating exclusive benefits for members and imposing costs on non-cooperation, the club model can incentivize countries to adopt more ambitious emission reduction targets and policies. In this regard, the EGD serves as a compelling case study of the climate club paradigm.[251] The EGD illustrates how targeted policy instruments and economic incentives can drive substantial progress in climate governance at a regional and potentially global scale.

While the climate club approach presents a promising approach to catalysing global climate action, it is not without its challenges and limitations. Equity and inclusivity concerns stand at the forefront of these issues. It has been scrutinized for

---

249 German Federal Ministry of Finance, 'Steps Towards an Alliance for Climate, Competitiveness and Industry-Building Blocks of a Cooperative and Open Climate Club' (2021) <https://www.bundesfinanzministerium.de/Content/EN/Downloads/Climate-Action/key-issues-paper-international-climate-club.pdf> accessed 18 March 2024. Stern and Lankes (n 9) 8.

250 See Sect. 1.5.1 in Chap. 6.

251 Overland and Huda (n 234) 17.

its potential deviation from the CBDRRC principle. While aiming to fill the gaps left by the voluntary and nationally determined contributions of the Paris Agreement, the climate club risks sidelining the needs and capacities of less developed countries in its pursuit of technological and growth-oriented solutions. The risk of creating an exclusive club that marginalizes developing nations, due to their inability to meet stringent climate targets, cannot be overlooked. Such disparities could exacerbate global inequalities and hinder the cooperative spirit necessary for comprehensive climate action. Furthermore, practical challenges in implementing the climate club model pose significant hurdles. These include aligning diverse national interests, ensuring compliance without excessive punitive measures that could strain international trade, and managing the administrative complexities of coordinating policies and measures across different jurisdictions. The effectiveness of the climate club hinges on its ability to navigate these challenges while maintaining its appeal and momentum towards achieving its ambitious goals.

In conclusion, the climate club concept represents a strategic, pragmatic approach to international climate cooperation. It offers a pathway to more effective and inclusive action against one of the most pressing challenges of our time. The lessons learned from the climate club can inform and inspire collaborative efforts on an international scale, highlighting the importance of innovation, flexibility, and the strategic use of economic instruments in the fight against global warming. The future of global climate initiatives may depend on ability to embrace such targeted and cooperative approaches, balancing national interests with the imperative for collective action. Looking ahead, the climate club must focus on expanding its membership through inclusive strategies that accommodate the capacities and circumstances of a broader range of countries. This expansion is crucial for the club's effectiveness and legitimacy on the global stage. Additionally, enhancing the appeal of the climate club approach involves demonstrating tangible benefits of membership, not only in terms of climate mitigation but also economic and social gains. In this regard, strategies such as technology transfer, capacity building, and financial incentives could play pivotal roles. The club can provide free emissions allowances, and flexible timelines for developing countries. In this way, it can mitigate concerns of environmental elitism and unfair burdens on developing countries. The differentiation, grounded in the CBDRRC principle, enhances the legitimacy and attractiveness of the climate club as a complementary mechanism for accelerating global climate action under the Paris Agreement.

Bibliography

Cases

[2017] ECR EU:C:2017:376 Opinion 2/15 of the Court.
North Sea Continental Shelf, (Judgment) [1969] ICJ Rep 3.

Legislation

Clean Competition Act 2022 117th Cong S. 4355.

Contracting Parties to the GATT, 'Decision of 28 November 1979: Differential and More Favourable Treatment Reciprocity and Fuller Participation of Developing Countries' L/4903

Council Decision (EU) 2022/591 of 6 April 2022 on a General Union Environment Action Programme to 2030 [2022] OJ L114/22

Council Directive 2003/87/EC of 13 October 2003 establishing a scheme for greenhouse gas emission allowance trading within the Community and amending Council Directive 96/61/EC [2003] OJ L275/32.

Council Regulation (EC) 2021/1119 of 30 June 2021 establishing the framework for achieving climate neutrality and amending Regulations (EC) No 401/2009 and (EU) 2018/1999 ('European Climate Law') [2021] OJ L243/1

Council Regulation (EC) 2023/956 of 10 May 2023 establishing a carbon border adjustment mechanism (Text with EEA relevance)' [2023] OJ L 130/1

Council Regulation (EC) 957/2023 of 10 May 2023 amending Regulation (EU) 2015/757 in order to provide for the inclusion of maritime transport activities in the EU Emissions Trading System and for the monitoring, reporting and verification of emissions of additional greenhouse gases and emissions from additional ship types [2023] OJ L130/105.

Fair Transition and Competition Act 2021 117th Cong S. GAI21718 59G.

General Agreement on Tariffs and Trade (GATT 1994) (15 April 1994) LT/UR/A-1A/1/GATT/1 <https://docs.wto.org/dol2fe/Pages/SS/directdoc.aspx?filename=Q:/UR/FA/06-gatt.pdf&Open=True>

Market Choice Act 2023 House Bill 118th Congress 6665.

Statute of the International Court of Justice (26 June 1945) 3 Bevans 1179, 59 Stat 1031, TS 993, 39 AJIL Supp 215, Cmd 7015.

Secondary Sources

'Biden Administration Pushes for Multilateral Cooperation and Domestic Action to Combat Climate Change' (2022) 116(1) American Journal of International Law 171, <https://doi.org/10.1017/ajil.2021.70>

'Carbon Pricing Leadership Coalition' <https://www.carbonpricingleadership.org/> accessed 20 June 2024

'Economists' Statement on Carbon Dividends' <https://www.econstatement.org> 25 April 2024

'World Bank Partnership for Market Implementation' <https://pmiclimate.org/> accessed 20 June 2024

Abbott KW, 'The Transnational Regime Complex for Climate Change' (2012) 30(4) Government and Policy 571

Ahmad Z, 'Trade-Related Measures to Spread Low-Carbon Technologies: A Common Concern–Based Approach' in T Cottier (ed), *The Prospects of Common Concern of Humankind in International Law* (Cambridge University Press 2021)

Almeida DV and others, 'The "Greening" of Empire: The European Green Deal as the EU First Agenda' (2023) 105 Political Geography

Bäckstrand K, 'The Democratic Legitimacy of Global Governance after Copenhagen' in JS Dryzek and others (eds), *The Oxford Handbook of Climate Change and Society* (Oxford University Press, 2011)

Bang G, Hovi J, and Skodvin T, 'The Paris Agreement: Short-Term and Long-Term Effectiveness' (2016) 4 Politics and Governance 209

Bardt H and Kolev GV, *Trade Club for Climate: A Climate Approach to Revive Multilateralism*, IW-Policy Paper, No. 8/2021 (Institut der deutschen Wirtschaft (IW), Köln 2021)

Barrett S, The Strategy of Trade Sanctions in Environmental Agreements' (1997) 19(4) Resource and Energy Economics 345

Beshkar M and Bond E, 'Trade Agreements: Theoretical Foundations' in *Oxford Research Encyclopaedia of Economics and Finance* (Oxford University Press, 2019)

Bierbrauer F and others, *A CO2-Border Adjustment Mechanism as a Building Block of a Climate Club* (Kiel Policy Brief No. 15, Kiel Institute for the World Economy (IfW), 2021).

Blanchard O, Gollier C and Tirole J, 'The Portfolio of Economic Policies Needed to Fight Climate Change' (2023) 15 Annual Review of Economics 689 <https://doi.org/10.1146/annurev-economics-051520-015113>

Boyce JK, 'Carbon Pricing: Effectiveness and Equity' (2018) 150 Ecological Economics 52, <https://doi.org/10.1016/j.ecolecon.2018.03.030>

Böhringer C, Carbone JC, and Rutherford TF, 'The Strategic Value of Carbon Tariffs' (2016) 8(1) American Economic Journal: Economic Policy 28 <https://doi.org/10.1257/pol.20130327>

—, 'Embodied Carbon Tariffs' (2018) 120(1) Scandinavian Journal of Economics 183

and others, 'Potential Impacts and Challenges of Border Carbon Adjustments' (2022) 12 Nat. Clim. Chang, 22, 22 <https://doi.org/10.1038/s41558-021-01250-z>

Boisson de Chazournes L and Mbengue MM, 'The Principles of Precaution and Sustainability' in T Cottier and K Nadakavukaren Schefer (eds), *Elgar Encyclopaedia of International Economic Law* (Edward Elgar 2017)

Botwright K and Stewart J, 'Trade and Climate Change' in The Elgar Companion to the World Trade Organization (Edward Elgar Publishing 2022)

Boute A, 'Accounting for Carbon Pricing in Third Countries Under the EU Carbon Border Adjustment Mechanism' (2024) World Trade Review 1

Bown CP, *Industrial Policy for Electric Vehicle Supply Chains and the US-EU Fight Over the Inflation Reduction Act* (Peterson Institute for International Economics Working Paper No 23-1, 2023) <https://doi.org/10.2139/ssrn.4449020>

Bradford A, *The Brussels Effect: How the European Union Rules the World* (Oxford University Press 2020)

Brandi C, Priorities for a Development-Friendly EU Carbon Border Adjustment (CBAM) (Briefing Paper No 20/2021, Deutsches Institut für Entwicklungspolitik, 2021) <https://doi.org/10.23661/bp20.2021>

Brewer TL, Derwent H and Błachowicz A, *Carbon Market Clubs and the New Paris Regime* (Paper for the World Bank Group's Networked Carbon Markets Initiative 2016).

Butnaru-Troncota M, 'European Green Deal and the New Policy Goals in Transport and Mobility - How Gamification Can Influence Pro-Environmental Behaviour for Cutting Carbon Emissions in the EU' (2020) 14(2) Europolity: Continuity & Change in European Governance 89

Carattini S and Löschel A, 'Managing Momentum in Climate Negotiations' (2021) 16 Environmental Research Letters 51001

Claeys G, Tagliapietra S, and Zachmann G, *How to Make the European Green Deal Work (*Bruegel Policy Contribution No. 2019/13, 2019)

Clausing KA and Wolfram C 'Carbon Border Adjustments, Climate Clubs, and Subsidy Races When Climate Policies Vary' (2023) 37(3) Journal of Economic Perspectives 137

Communication from the Commission (COM) "Fit for 55": Delivering the EU's 2030 Climate Target on the Way to Climate Neutrality 550 [2021]

Communication from the Commission (COM) Stepping up Europe's 2030 Climate Ambition - Investing in a Climate-neutral Future for the Benefit of Our People 562 [2020]

Communication from the Commission (COM) Sustainable Europe Investment Plan European Green Deal Investment Plan 21 final [2020]

Cosbey A, and others, 'Developing Guidance for Implementing Border Carbon Adjustments: Lessons, Cautions, and Research Needs from the Literature' (2019) 13 Review of Environmental Economics and Policy 3

Cottier T, 'The Principle of Common Concern of Humankind' in Thomas Cottier (ed) *The Prospects of Common Concern of Humankind in International Law* (Cambridge University Press, 2021)

— and Matteotti-Berkutova S 'International Environmental Law and the Evolving Concept of 'Common Concern of Mankind' in T Cottier, O Nartova, and SZ Bigdeli *International Trade Regulation and the Mitigation of Climate Change: World Trade Forum* (Cambridge University Press, 2009)

Das K, 'Climate Clubs: Carrots, Sticks and More' (2015) 50(34) Economic and Political Weekly 24

Davidson-Ladly S, 'Border Carbon Adjustments, WTO-law and the Principle of Common but Differentiated Responsibilities' (2012) 12 International Environmental Agreements: Politics, Law and Economics 63

Dessler AE and EA Parson, *The Science and Politics of Global Climate Change: A Guide to the Debate* (3rd edn, Cambridge University Press 2020)

Dobson N, Chapter 25: Climate Protection versus Trade: Dilemmas for the EU' in *Handbook on European Union Climate Change Policy and Politics* (Edward Elgar Publishing, 2023)

Dominioni G and Esty D, 'Designing Effective Border-Carbon Adjustment Mechanisms: Aligning the Global Trade and Climate Change Regimes' (2023) 65(1) Arizona Law Review

Downs GW and Jones MA, 'Reputation, Compliance and International Law' (2002) 31 Journal of Legal Studies 95

Durán GM, 'Securing Compatibility of Carbon Border Adjustments with the Multilateral Climate and Trade Regimes' (2023) 72 International & Comparative Law Quarterly 73

Eckersley R, 'The Big Chill: The WTO and Multilateral Environmental Agreements' (2004) 4 Global Environmental Politics 24

'The Politics of Carbon Leakage and the Fairness of Border Measures' (2010) 24(4) Ethics and International Affairs 363.

'Moving Forward in the Climate Negotiations: Multilateralism or Minilateralism?' (2012) 12(2) Global Environmental Politics 24 <https://doi.org/10.1162/GLEP_a_00107>.

Englisch J and Falcao T, 'EU Carbon Border Adjustments for Imported Products and WTO Law' (9 June 2021) <https://doi.org/10.2139/ssrn.3863038>

European Commission, Commission Staff Working Document Impact Assessment Report Accompanying the document Proposal for a Regulation of the European Parliament and of the Council Establishing a Carbon Border Adjustment Mechanism SWD [2021] 643 final

and US Trade Representative, 'Steel and Aluminium, EU-US Joint Statement of 31 October 2021' (2021)

Emissions Database for Global Atmospheric Research, 'GHG emissions of All World Countries' (2023) <https://edgar.jrc.ec.europa.eu/report_2023> accessed 3 April 2024

'Scope of EU Emission Trading System' <https://climate.ec.europa.eu/eu-action/eu-emissions-trading-system-eu-ets/scope-eu-emissions-trading-system_en> accessed 6 July 2024

European Parliament, Committee on the Environment, Public Health and Food Safety, Report Towards a WTO-Compatible EU Carbon Border Adjustment Mechanism Explanatory Statement [2021] A9-0019/2021

Eyland T and Zaccour G, 'Carbon Tariffs and Cooperative Outcomes' (2014) 65 Energy Policy 718.

Falkner R, 'A Minilateral Solution for Global Climate Change? On Bargaining Efficiency, Club Benefits, and International Legitimacy' (2016) 14 Perspectives on Politics 87.

—, Naghmeh Nasiritousi and Gunilla Reischl 'Climate Clubs: Politically Feasible and Desirable?' (2021) Climate Policy 1 <https://doi.org/10.1080/14693062.2021.1967717>

Faure M and Partain RA, *Environmental Law and Economics: Theory and Practice* (Cambridge University Press 2019)

Federal Office for the Environment, 'Linking the Swiss and EU Emissions Trading Systems' <https://www.bafu.admin.ch/bafu/en/home/topics/climate/infospecialists/reductionmeasures/ets/linking-swiss-eu.html> accessed 6 July 2024

Fontagné L and Schubert K, 'The Economics of Border Carbon Adjustment: Rationale and Impacts of Compensating for Carbon at the Border' (2023) 15 Annual Review of Economics 389, <https://doi.org/10.1146/annurev-economics-082322-034040>

Gampfer R, 'Minilateralism or the UNFCCC? The Political Feasibility of Climate Clubs' (2016) 16(3) Global Environmental Politics

German Federal Ministry of Finance, 'Steps Towards an Alliance for Climate, Competitiveness and Industry-Building Blocks of a Cooperative and Open Climate Club' (2021) <https://www.bundesfinanzministerium.de/Content/EN/Downloads/Climate-Action/key-issues-paper-international-climate-club.pdf> accessed 18 March 2024

Ghaleigh NS 'Economics and International Climate Change Law' in KR Gray (ed), *The Oxford Handbook of International Climate Change Law* (Oxford University Press 2016)

Global Carbon Budget 'Annual CO_2 emissions – GCB' (2023) <https://ourworldindata.org/co2-emissions> accessed 19 May 2024

Góis AR and others, 'Reward and Punishment in Climate Change Dilemmas' (2019) 9 Sci Rep 16193 <https://doi.org/10.1038/s41598-019-52524-8>

Gourgourinis A, 'Common but Differentiated Responsibilities in Transnational Climate Change Governance and the WTO: A Tale of Two 'Interconnected Worlds' or a Tale of Two 'Crossing Swords'?' in P Delimatsis (eds) *Research Handbook on Climate Change and Trade* (Edward Elgar 2016)

Hannam PM and others, 'Incomplete Cooperation and Co-benefits: Deepening Climate Cooperation with a Proliferation of Small Agreements' (2017) 144 Climatic Change 65 <https://doi.org/10.1007/s10584-015-1511-2>

Helm D, Hepburn C and Ruta G, 'Trade, Climate Change, and the Political Game Theory of Border Carbon Adjustments' 28 (2012) Oxf Rev Econ Policy 368

Hepburn C and Stern N, 'A New Global Deal on Climate Change' (2008) 24(2) Oxford Review of Economic Policy 259

HM Revenue and Customs and HM Treasury, 'Introduction of a UK Carbon Border Adjustment Mechanism from January 2027: Consultation' (21 March 2024). <https://assets.publishing.service.gov.uk/media/65fc11fef1d3a0001132ac6f/Introduction_of_a_UK_carbon_border_adjustment_mechanism_from_January_2027.docx.pdf> accessed 5 April 2024

Holzer K, 'The Possibility of Defense under General Exceptions of GATT Article XX' in *Carbon-Related Border Adjustment and WTO Law* (Edward Elgar Publishing 2014).

and Shariff N, 'The Inclusion of Border Carbon Adjustments in Preferential Trade Agreements: Policy Implications' (2012) 3 Carbon & Climate L Rev 246

Hourcade JC, Antonin Pottier and Etienne Espagne, 'Social Value of Mitigation Activities and Forms of Carbon Pricing' (2018) 155(C) International Economics, Elsevier 8

Hovi J, Skodvin T and Aakre S, 'Can Climate Change Negotiations Succeed' (2013) 1 Politics and Governance 138 <https://doi.org/10.12924/PAG2013.01020138>

'In-Depth Q&A: Will China's Emissions Trading Scheme Help Tackle Climate Change?' (Carbon Brief, 2023) <https://www.carbonbrief.org/in-depth-qa-will-chinas-emissions-trading-scheme-help-tackle-climate-change/> accessed 18 March 2024.

International Carbon Action Partnership' <https://icapcarbonaction.com/en/partnership/about> accessed 20 June 2024.

International Monetary Fund and Organization for Economic Cooperation and Development, 'Tax Policy and Climate Change: IMF/OECD Report for the G20 Finance Ministers and Central Bank Governors' (2021) <www.oecd.org/tax/tax--policy/imf-oecd-g20-report-tax-policy-and-climate-change.htm> accessed 20 June 2024

Irfanoglu ZB, Sesmero JP and Golub A 'Potential of Border Tax Adjustments to Deter Free Riding in International Climate Agreements' (2015) 10 Environmental Research Letters 024009.

Jamieson D, 'The Nature of the Problem' in JS Dryzek and others (eds), *The Oxford Handbook of Climate Change and Society* (Oxford University Press 2011)

Karlsson-Vinkhuyzen SI and McGee J 'Legitimacy in an Era of Fragmentation: The Case of Global Climate Governance' (2013) 13 Global Environmental Politics 56

Klinsky S and others, 'Operationalizing Equity and Supporting Ambition: Identifying a More Robust Approach to Respective Capabilities' (2017) 9 Climate and Development 287

Kokott J, 'States, Sovereign Equality' in *Max Planck Encyclopaedia of Public International Law* (Oxford University Press 2011)

Kortum S and Weisbach D, 'The Design of Border Adjustments for Carbon Prices' (2017) 70(2) National Tax Journal 421

Kuhn T, Pestow R and Zenker A, 'Building Climate Coalitions on Preferential Trade Agreements' (2019) 74(2) Environmental and Resource Economics 539

Kyriazi A and Miró J, 'Towards a Socially Fair Green Transition in the EU? An Analysis of the Just Transition Fund Using the Multiple Streams Framework' (2023) 21 Comparative European Politics 112 <https://doi.org/10.1057/s41295-022-00304-6>

Larbprasertporn P, 'The Interaction between WTO Law and the Principle of Common But Differentiated Responsibilities in the Case of Climate-Related Border Tax Adjustment' (2014) 6(1) Goettingen Journal of International Law 145

Leal-Arcas R, 'Alternative Architecture for Climate Change - Major Economies' (2011) 4(1) European Journal of Legal Studies, 25

Leonelli GC, 'Carbon Border Measures, Environmental Effectiveness and WTO Compatibility: Is There a Way Forward for the Steel and Aluminium Carbon Club?' (2022) 21(5) World Trade Review

—, 'The Long and Winding Road Towards the Creation of Climate Clubs: Transatlantic Negotiations, Potential Regulatory Models and Challenges Ahead' (2023) 32 RECIEL 453

Magen S, 'Game Theory and Collective Goods' in Emanuel V Towfigh and Niels Petersen (eds), *Economic Methods for Lawyers* (Edward Elgar Publishing, 2015)

Martini L and Görlach B, *What Role for a Climate Club under the German G7 Presidency? Options and Recommendations for a Climate Club* (Ecologic Institute, 2022)

Mbengue MM and Cima E, '"Clubbing in the Club": Could Climate-Related Trade Arrangements Set the Pace for Future Climate Cooperation?' (2022) 116 American Journal of International Law Unbound 219

Mehling M, 'Implementing Climate Governance: Instrument Choice and Interaction' in EJ Hollo, K Kulovesi and M Mehling (eds), *Climate Change and the Law* (Springer 2013)

Metcalf GE, 'Carbon Taxes in Theory and Practice' (2021) 13 Annual Review of Resource Economics 245, <https://doi.org/10.1146/annurev-resource-102519-113630>

Meyer LH and Roser D, 'Climate Justice and Historical Emissions' (2010) 13 Critical Review of Intl Social & Political Philosophy 229.

Meyer T and Tucker TN, 'A Pragmatic Approach to Carbon Border Measures' (2022) 21(1) World Trade Review 109

Michalopoulos C *The Role of Special Differential Treatment for Developing Countries in GATT and the World Trade Organization* (World Bank Policy Research Working Paper No. 2388, 2000)

Mohlenkamp K, Sabine Schulte-Beckhausen and Bertil Kapff, 'The European Green Deal' (2021) 32 Int'l Tax Rev 74

Nordhaus W, 'Climate Clubs: Overcoming Free-Riding in International Climate Policy' (2015) 105(4) American Economic Review 1339.

'Climate Change: The Ultimate Challenge for Economics' (2019) 109(6) American Economic Review 1991 <https://doi.org/10.1257/aer.109.6.1991>.

'The Climate Club: How to Fix a Failing Global Effort' (2020) 20 Journal of Environmental Economics and Policy 1.

'Dynamic Climate Clubs: On the Effectiveness of Incentives in Global Climate Agreements', (2021) 118 (45) Proceedings of the National Academy of Sciences, <https://doi.org/10.1073/pnas.2109988118>

'Climate Club Futures: On the Effectiveness of Future Climate Clubs' (Cowles Foundation Discussion Papers 2619, 2021) <https://elischolar.library.yale.edu/cowles-discussion-paper-series/2619> accessed 18 May 2024.

Obergassel W, Wang-Helmreich H and Hermwill L, 'A Sectoral Perspective on Climate Clubs' (2019), <https://epub.wupperinst.org/frontdoor/deliver/index/docId/7547/file/7547_Climate_Clubs.pdf> accessed 28 March 2024.

Oberthür S and Dupont C, 'The European Union's International Climate Leadership: Towards a Grand Climate Strategy?' (2021) 28 J Eur Public Policy 1095 <https://doi.org/10.1080/13501763.2021.1918218>

Oberthür S and von Homeyer I, 'From Emissions Trading to The European Green Deal: The Evolution of The Climate Policy Mix and Climate Policy Integration in the EU' (2023) 30(3) Journal of European Public Policy 445 < https://doi.org/10.1080/13501763.2022.2120528>

Okereke C, 'Equity and Justice in Polycentric Climate Governance' in A Jordan and others (eds), *Governing Climate Change: Polycentricity in Action?* (Cambridge University Press 2018)

Ostrom E, *Governing the Commons: The Evolution of Institutions for Collective Action* (Cambridge University Press, 1990)

Overland I and Huda MS, 'Climate Clubs and Carbon Border Adjustments: A Review' (2022) 17(9) Environ Res Lett

Parker CF and Karlsson C, 'Climate Change and the European Union's Leadership Moment: An Inconvenient Truth?' (2010) 48 Journal of Common Market Studies 923

—, Karlsson C and Hjerpe M 'Assessing the European Union's Global Climate Change Leadership: From Copenhagen to the Paris Agreement' (2017) 39(2) Journal of European Integration 239

Paroussos L and others 'Climate Clubs and the Macro-economic Benefits of International Cooperation on Climate Policy' (2019) 9 Nature Climate Change 542.

Paterson M 'Who and What are Carbon Markets for? Politics and the Development of Climate Policy' (2012) 12(1) Climate Policy 82, <https://doi.org/10.1080/14693062.2011.579259>

Pauw WP and others 'Conditional Nationally Determined Contributions in The Paris Agreement: Foothold for Equity or Achilles Heel?' (2019) 20 Climate Policy 468

Peter C, and Eckersley R, 'Comparing State Responses' in JS Dryzek, RB Norgaard, and D Schlosberg (eds), *The Oxford Handbook of Climate Change and Society* (Oxford University Press, 2012)

Pihl H, 'A Climate Club as a Complementary Design to the UN Paris Agreement' (2020) 3(1) Policy Design and Practice 45, <https://doi.org/10.1080/25741292.2019.1710911>

Pirlot A, 'Carbon Border Adjustment Measures: A Straightforward Multi-Purpose Climate Change Instrument?' (2022) 34 Journal of Environmental Law 25

Portevin T, 'The EU Green Deal – a Roadmap to Sustainable Economies' (Switch 2 Green, 11 December 2019) <https://www.switchtogreen.eu/the-eu-green-deal-promoting-a-green-notable-circular-economy/> accessed 18 March 2024

Rajamani L, 'Ambition and Differentiation in the 2015 Paris Agreement: Interpretative Possibilities and Underlying Politics' (2016) 65(2) ICLQ 493

Roser D and Tomlinson L, 'Trade Policies and Climate Change – Border Carbon Adjustments as a Tool for a Just Global Climate Regime' (2014) Ancilla Iuris 223

Sabel CF and Victor DG, 'Governing Global Problems Under Uncertainty: Making Bottom-Up Climate Policy Work' (2017) 144 Climatic Change 15 <https://doi.org/10.1007/s10584-015-1507-y>

Sandler T, Tschirhart JT, 'The Economic Theory of Clubs: An Evaluative Survey' (1980) 18(4) Journal of Economic Literature 1481

Sands P and Peel J, *Principles of International Environmental Law* (4th edn Cambridge University Press, 2018)

Sarnoff JD, 'Intellectual Property and Climate Change, with an Emphasis on Patents and Technology Transfer' in KR Gray, R Tarasofsky, and CP Carlarne (eds), *The Oxford Handbook of International Climate Change Law* (Oxford University Press 2016)

Scotchmer S, 'Clubs' in SN Durlauf and LE Blume (eds), *The New Palgrave Dictionary of Economics* (2nd edn, Palgrave Macmillan 2008)

Sending OJ, Øverland I and Hornburg TB, 'Climate Change and International Relations' (2020) 73(1) Journal of International Affairs 183

Sesmero J and Evans A, 'The potential of Trade Sanctions to Overcome the Small Coalition Paradox: A Review of the Literature', in Micheal Jakob (eds) *Handbook on Trade Policy and Climate Change* (Edward Elgar, 2022)

Sieber-Gasser C, 'Please, Reboot – Small Economies and the WTO Appellate Mechanism in Times of Trade War and COVID-19' (SIL International Economic Law Interest Group, Online Workshop 'International Economic Law between Emergencies and Reforms', 9 September 2020)

Smith ME, 'A Liberal Grand Strategy in A Realist World? Power, Purpose and The EU's Changing Global Role' (2011) 18(2) Journal of European Public Policy 144 <https://doi.org/10.1080/13501763.2011.544487>

Stern N, 'The Economics of Climate Change' (2008) 98(2) The American Economic Review 1

and Lankes HP, *Collaborating and Delivering on Climate Action Through a Climate Club: An Independent Report to the G7* (London School of Economics and Political Science, 2022)

Soltau F, *Fairness in International Climate Change Law and Policy* (Cambridge University Press 2009).

Stua M, *From the Paris Agreement to a Low-Carbon Bretton Woods: Rationale for the Establishment of a Mitigation Alliance* (Springer, 2017)

Tagliapietra S and Wolff GB, 'Form a Climate Club: United States, European Union and China' (2021) 591 Nature 526

Tan C, 'Development' in T Cottier and K Nadakavukaren Schefer (eds), *Elgar Encyclopedia of International Economic Law* (Edward Elgar 2017)

Tarr DG and others, 'Why Carbon Border Adjustment Mechanisms Will Not Save the Planet but a Climate Club and Subsidies for Transformative Green Technologies May' (2023) 122 Energy Economics 9

United Nations Trade and Development (UNCTAD), Joint Statement Issued at the Conclusion of the 30th BASIC Ministerial Meeting on Climate Change, 'A European Union Carbon Border Adjustment Mechanism: Implications for developing countries (8 April 2021) <https://unctad.org/system/files/official-document/osginf2021d2_en.pdf > accessed 2 April 2024

United Nations Environment Program (UNEP), BASIC Ministerial, 'Joint Statement at the UNFCCC's Sharm el-Sheikh Climate Change Conference' (15 November 2022) COP27/CMP17/CMA4

Van den Bergh J, 'Rebound Policy in the Paris Agreement: Instrument Comparison and Climate-Club Revenue Offsets' (2017) 17 Climate Policy 801.

Vangenechten D and Lehne J, 'Can Climate Clubs Accelerate Industrial Decarbonisation?' (E3G, 2022) <https://www.e3g.org/publications/can-climate-clubs-accelerate-industrial-decarbonisation/> 21 June 2021.

Victor DG and Keohane RO, 'The Regime Complex for Climate Change' (2010) 9 Perspectives on Politics 7 <https://doi.org/10.1017/S1537592710004068>

—, *Global Warming Gridlock: Creating More Effective Strategies for Protecting the Planet* (Cambridge University Press 2011)

Vidigal G, 'Designing Climate Clubs: The Four Models, Trade Commitments and the Non-Discrimination Dilemma' (2023) Amsterdam Law School Research Paper No 2023-07

and Venzke I, 'Of False Conflicts and Real Challenges: Trade Agreements, Climate Clubs, and Border Adjustments' (2022) 116 AJIL Unbound 202, 206

Weber RH, 'Border Tax Adjustment-Legal Perspective' (2015) 133 Climatic Change 407, <https://doi.org/10.1007/s10584-015-1414-2>

Weikmans R and Roberts JT, 'The International Climate Finance Accounting Muddle: Is There Hope on the Horizon?' (2019) 11(2) Climate and Development 97

Weischer L, Morgan J, and Patel M, 'Climate Clubs: Can Small Groups of Countries Make a Big Difference in Addressing Climate Change?' (2012) 21(3) Review of European Community & International Environmental Law 177

Weitzman ML, 'Voting on Prices vs. Voting on Quantities in a World Climate Assembly' (2017) 71 Research in Economics 199

World Bank, *Inclusive Green Growth: The Pathway to Sustainable Development* (Technical Report, World Bank, Washington DC 2012)

'World Development Indicator' (2013), <https://databankfiles.worldbank.org/public/ddpext_download/WDI-2013-ebook.pdf> accessed 26 March 2024.

—, High-Level Commission on Carbon Prices, *Report of the High-Level Commission on Carbon Prices* (2017)

'State and Trends of Carbon Pricing 2023' (World Bank 2023) <https://openknowledge.worldbank.org/handle/10986/39796> accessed 25 March 2024

Zapf M, Pengg H, and Weindl C. 'How to Comply with the Paris Agreement Temperature Goal: Global Carbon Pricing According to Carbon Budgets' (2019) 12(15) Energies 2983 <https://doi.org/10.3390/en12152983>

Open Access This chapter is licensed under the terms of the Creative Commons Attribution 4.0 International License (http://creativecommons.org/licenses/by/4.0/), which permits use, sharing, adaptation, distribution and reproduction in any medium or format, as long as you give appropriate credit to the original author(s) and the source, provide a link to the Creative Commons license and indicate if changes were made.

The images or other third party material in this chapter are included in the chapter's Creative Commons license, unless indicated otherwise in a credit line to the material. If material is not included in the chapter's Creative Commons license and your intended use is not permitted by statutory regulation or exceeds the permitted use, you will need to obtain permission directly from the copyright holder.

Chapter 5
The Role of Linkages in Strengthening Climate Clubs

1 Background

The problematic aspects of the command-control mechanism have opened a pathway to the research for innovative instruments in climate regulation and policy.[1] Market-based instruments also referred to as incentive-based instruments, are advocated as an alternative to command-and-control regulation.[2] They are policy tools that use economic incentives to achieve environmental goals, including GHG emissions reduction.[3] They operate by creating a market for emissions, which allows the cost of environmental damage to be incorporated into the price of goods and services. Market-based regulation establishes the level of emissions deemed tolerable and under the penalty of fine or injunction compels polluters not to exceed this level but leave the choice of method to mitigate their pollution.[4] Alternatively, it can tax the emissions. Taxation distinguishes market-based regulation from

[1] Public regulation is often qualified as command-and-control system by the economists. This is an administrative system based on licenses, permitting and standard setting by administrative agencies. Under the command-and-control regulations, the regulator prescribes use of specific technology to avoid legal sanction. This approach requires that the regulator has significant amount of information about technologies and should try up-to date to avoid being obsolete. (Richard A. Posner, *Economic Analysis of Law* (Aspen Legal Education 2014), 505) After the specified command-and-control regulation is adopted, the industries have no incentive to develop better pollution control methods. Bettina Lange, 'Command and Control Standards and Cross-jurisdictional Harmonization' in Emma Lees and Jorge E Viñuales (eds), *The Oxford Handbook of Comparative Environmental Law* (Oxford University Press, 2019), 857.

[2] WTO Committee on Trade and Environment, 'Taxes and Charges for Environmental Purposes, Border Tax Adjustment, Note by Secretariat' WTO Doc WT/CTE/W/47 (2 May 1997) paras 3 and 16. Lange (n 1) 860.

[3] Lange (n 1) 859.

[4] Posner, *Economic Analysis of Law* (n 1) 506.

© The Author(s) 2025
T. G. Budak, *Beyond Treaties: Rethinking Legal Mechanisms for International Climate Governance*, https://doi.org/10.1007/978-3-031-86022-5_5

command-and-control as it target the social cost[5] of emissions instead of a fine intended to deter pollution in the usual manner of criminal sanctions.[6] Overall, market-based instruments aim to encourage cost-effective emissions reduction while providing flexibility for businesses and individuals to decide how best to meet their environmental obligations.

The concept of utilizing market instruments for environmental governance originated with North American economists in the late 1960s, as evidenced by the works of Coase (1960), Crocker (1966), and Dales (1968).[7] During the discussions leading up to the UNFCCC, the US advocated for the inclusion of carbon markets and adaptable approaches.[8] While the final text of the convention did not specifically incorporate provisions for carbon markets, the US managed to ensure the inclusion of three adaptable mechanisms in the Kyoto Protocol.[9] Especially after the Kyoto Protocol, market-based instruments became the keystone climate policy.[10] This shift is attributed to their characteristics, which better reflect the climate problem's features[11] than command-and-control regulation Furthermore, there is a political acknowledgment that the enactment of climate policies is unavoidable, and strategies rooted in market principles are anticipated to be more economically viable than command-and-control regulations.[12] Therefore, it is possible to adopt market-based instruments as linkages under the climate club to search for a new international climate regime. They substantiate the effective climate policy by internalising the social cost of carbon with the optimal price for emission-generating activities.[13] The economic cost-benefit considerations in these instruments positively influence the

[5] Social cost is the sum of all costs a certain activity imposes on all members of a certain economy. Ronald H Coase, 'The Problem of Social Cost' (1960) 3 Journal of Law and Economics 1.

[6] ibid.

[7] Coase (n 5), Thomas Crocker, 'The Structuring of Atmospheric Pollution Control System' in H Wolozin (ed), *The Economics of Air Pollution* (W. W. Norton 1966) 61. John H Dales, *Pollution, Property and Prices: An Essay in Policy-Making and Economics* (University of Toronto Press 1968).

[8] 'U.S. Positions in International Climate Change Negotiations' (2008) 102(1) American Journal of International Law 164 <https://doi.org/10.1017/S0002930000753012>.

[9] Katja Biedenkopf and Jørgen Wettestad, 'Harnessing the Market: Trading in Carbon Allowances' in Andrew Jordan and others (eds), *Governing Climate Change: Polycentricity in Action?* (Cambridge University Press 2018), 233.

[10] For example, motivated by the Kyoto Protocol, the EU embarked on creating an ETS to regulate large-scale industrial activities. ibid 234.

[11] The decision-making in climate policy is an intricate mixture of complexity, intangibility, cascading effects, interdependency, multi-generational impacts, and extended timeframes. Fran Sussman, Christopher P Weaver and Anne Grambsch, 'Challenges in Applying the Paradigm of Welfare Economics to Climate Change' (2014) 5(3) Journal of Benefit-Cost Analysis 347, 354 <https://doi.org/10.1515/jbca-2014-9001>.

[12] Lange (n 1) 858–859.

[13] OECD, *Climate, and Carbon: Aligning Prices and Policies* (2013), 9.

regulated party's reduction behaviour.[14] Thuswise, economic actors will take the opportunity to abate emissions if this is cheaper than the carbon price.[15]

Market-based instruments encompass various economic tools that governments can employ to address climate policy objectives. These instruments allow countries to choose and tailor their approach based on their unique economic, social, and environmental circumstances.[16] When implemented even-handedly on domestic and foreign entities, market-based instruments serve as a powerful tool in mitigating protectionist tendencies in global trade and level playing field for industries, regardless of origin.[17] This approach fosters fair competition and discourages carbon leakage that might otherwise arise from disparate regulations. Consequently, they enhance the effectiveness of environmental policies and contributes to developing a collaborative and cooperative framework for addressing global challenges.[18] Therefore, this chapter sheds light on market-based instruments' multifarious advantages in pursuing effective mitigation strategies under the club approach.

2 The Concept of Linkages

The most intricate characteristic of the climate club is to create incentives that motivate non-club member countries to adopt low-carbon PPMs and make them consider participating in a multilateral climate change mitigation scheme. Scholars have suggested linkages as an incentive mechanism for coalition formation.[19] In the context of climate change, a linkage refers to the instruments between different actors or initiatives working towards the common goal of mitigating GHG emissions

[14] Scott Barrett, 'Dikes versus Windmills: Climate Treaties and Adaptation' (2020) 11 Climate Change Economics 2040005.

[15] The marginal cost of abatement varies across techniques. Some options, like the installation of LED lighting or the conversion to wind power in favourable locations, are relatively low cost; others, like carbon capture and sequestration at coal-burning plants, would be very expensive. James K. Boyce, 'Carbon Pricing: Effectiveness and Equity' (2018) 150 Ecological Economics 52, 54 <https://doi.org/10.1016/j.ecolecon.2018.03.030>.

[16] Erin Rhodes, William A Scott, and Mark Jaccard, 'Designing Flexible Regulations to Mitigate Climate Change: A Cross-Country Comparative Policy Analysis' (2021) 156 Energy Policy 112419 <https://doi.org/10.1016/j.enpol.2021.112419>.

[17] Andrei Marcu, Micheal A Mehling and Aaron Cosbey, *Border Carbon Adjustments in the EU: Issues and Options*, (ERCTS Roundtable On Climate Change and Sustainable Transition, 2020), 3 <https://ercst.org/border-carbon-adjustments-in-the-eu-issues-and-options> accessed 3 April 2024.

[18] Zaker Ahmad, 'Trade-Related Measures to Spread Low-Carbon Technologies: A Common Concern–Based Approach' in Thomas Cottier (ed), *The Prospects of Common Concern of Humankind in International Law* (Cambridge University Press 2021), 120.

[19] Claudia Kemfert, 'Climate Coalitions and International Trade: Assessment of Cooperation Incentives by Issue Linkage' (2004) 32 Energy Policy 455 <https://doi.org/10.1016/S0301-4215(03)00148-4> Valentina Bosetti and others, 'Incentives and Stability of International Climate Coalitions: An Integrated Assessment' (2013) 55 Energy Policy 44–56 <https://doi.org/10.1016/j.enpol.2012.12.035>.

and adapting to the impacts of climate change. Linkages can facilitate the exchange of information, resources, and best practices, leading to greater efficiency and effectiveness in achieving climate goals. They represent the existence of multiple devices of governing within a broader landscape of climate governance. Linkages are essential aspects of climate club because linkages create networks that simplify collaboration among its members.[20]

The club goods or quasi-club goods can be created with linkages, which consist of market-based instruments, cooperation in research and development, or capacity building.[21] The essential feature of linkages is to provide exclusive benefits to climate club members that cannot be achieved with further means other than the linkage.[22] The insufficiency of global authority to manage environmental problems makes linkages politically more attractive, feasible, and effective.[23] Specifically, when political motivations prevent governments from taking meaningful action against climate change, market-based instruments could be the most effective resort to adopt as linkages.[24] Their benefits or punitive characteristics can offset the incentive to free-ride on environmental efforts. Hence, market-based instruments operate as linchpins within the climate club framework. They allow countries to set emissions reduction targets and allocate allowances, fostering a sense of shared responsibility.[25]

---

[20] Thomas Kuhn, Radomir Pestow and Anja Zenker, 'Building Climate Coalitions on Preferential Trade Agreements' (2019) 74(2) Environmental and Resource Economics 539, 540.

[21] ibid.

[22] Matthew Potoski, 'Green Clubs in Building Block Climate Change Regimes' (2017) 144 Climatic Change 53, 53 <https://doi.org/10.1007/s10584-015-1517-9>.

[23] Rachel Brewster, 'Stepping Stone of Stumbling Block: Incrementalism and National Climate Change Legislation' (2010) 28 Yale L & Pol Rev 245.

[24] For example, in the Montreal Protocol the combination of trade-based disincentives and incentives created a success story in international environmental law. Montreal Protocol on Substances that Deplete the Ozone Layer has a total of 196 Parties. It is generally considered as one of the most successful multilateral environmental agreements, in terms of the number of participant countries and its verified progress towards protecting ozone layer, cooperation among developed and developing countries and creating robust institutions. The Montreal Protocol governs the phase-out of production and consumption of several groups of ozone-depleting substances. Both developed and developing countries are subjected to same reduction and phase-out obligations, however, the time frames to complete phase-out procedure is longer for developing countries. Also, phase-out schedules can be revised on the basis of scientific and technological assessments.

[25] European Economic and Social Committee, 'Opinion of the European Economic and Social Committee on "The Impact of the Crisis on the Ability of European Firms to Undertake Pro-Climate Investments"' [2012] OJ C24/02.

3 Market-based Instruments as Club Linkages

The realization of a climate club involves a strategic combination of market-based instruments and the dominance of key actors. In this context, influential market players take the lead in climate governance by employing market-based instruments. The underlying rationales for the market-based linkages are twofold.[26] Foremost among these objectives is the commitment to ensure robust compliance with emissions abatement goals. By integrating market-based instruments, the climate club seeks to create a dynamic framework that incentivises and regulates emissions reductions across its member countries in the most cost-effective manner.[27] This approach not only fosters a collective commitment to environmental sustainability but also provides a structured mechanism for enforcing adherence to specified emission targets. The second pivotal rationale for adopting market-based linkages is safeguarding the competitive position[28] of climate club products compared to non-club counterparts. Recognising the interconnectedness of global markets, the climate club endeavours to shield its members from unfair competitive disadvantages that may arise due to divergent environmental standards. Through market-based instruments, the club aims to create a level playing field, thereby promoting the economic viability of environmentally responsible practices within the club.

Market-based linkages are crucial mechanisms for supporting the polluter pays principle due to the systematic collection of a carbon price. The carbon price, reflecting the environmental cost of emissions, becomes a tangible expression of this principle. Polluter pays principle is foundational to equitable environmental governance, emphasising the responsibility of those contributing to pollution to bear the associated costs.[29] It is operationalised through market-based linkages as industries and entities within the climate club are held accountable for their carbon footprint. In essence, the market-based linkages translate the abstract notion of the polluter pays principle into concrete action by creating an effective framework to

---

[26] Charles McLure, 'A Primer on the Legality of Border Adjustments for Carbon Prices: Through a GATT Darkly' (2011) 5(4) Carbon & Climate Law Review 456 <https://doi.org/10.21552/CCLR/2011/4/193>.

[27] Cinnamon Carlarne, 'Delinking International Environmental Law & Climate Change' (2014) 4(1) Michigan J of Environmental & Administrative L 1, 4 and 17.

[28] David Harrison and others, 'Economic Policy Instruments for Reducing Greenhouse Gas Emissions' in John S Dryzek, Richard B Norgaard, and David Schlosberg (eds), *The Oxford Handbook of Climate Change and Society* (Oxford University Press, 2011), 524.

[29] Rio Declaration on Environment and Development, principle 16 indicates that "National authorities should endeavor to promote the internalization of environmental costs and the use of economic instruments, taking into account the approach that the polluter should, in principle, bear the cost of pollution, with due regard to the public interest and without distorting international trade and investment." Deriving from this principle Arthur Pigou designed a model and advocated the use of environmental taxes against the polluting activity as the main instrument to internalize externalities. Nicolas de Sadeleer, 'The Polluter-Pays Principle' in *Environmental Principles: From Political Slogans to Legal Rules* (2nd ed Oxford University Press 2020), 31.

address climate change while simultaneously promoting economic responsibility among industry participants.

Moreover, the revenue generated from the collection of the carbon price can be strategically reinvested in furthering climate goals.[30] It may include funding sustainable initiatives, research and development of green technologies, and adaptation measures. Also, the capital raised from the pricing mechanisms can be used to pay for climate damages or remediation. Therefore, market-based linkages contribute to domestic and international climate finance resources[31] as well.[32] By leveraging economic incentives, the linkages create a sustainable financial ecosystem that encourages the adoption of cleaner technologies and facilitates proactive measures to address and mitigate the adverse effects of climate change. Therefore, the market-based linkages establish a self-sustaining mechanism that bolsters the financial resources available for ongoing initiatives within the climate club.

Also, the introduction of market-based linkages plays a transformative role in reshaping carbon pricing regulations from an origin-based perspective to a destination-based framework.[33] This shift signifies a fundamental change in how emissions are accounted for and regulated, leading to a more comprehensive and equitable approach.[34] The transition from origin-based to destination-based carbon prices and regulations captures the emissions generated within the territorial production of goods and considers the emissions associated with their consumption.[35] It represents a more holistic understanding of the product's carbon footprint, ensuring that the environmental impact is accounted for throughout the life cycle. Furthermore, this transition serves as a crucial medium-term strategy to prevent the exploitation of developing countries as environmental dumping areas. By capturing consumption-based emissions, market-based linkages discourage the practice of offshoring production to regions with lax environmental regulations.[36]

---

[30] Rolf H Weber, 'Innovative Taxation Strategies Supporting Climate Change Resilience', in Larry Kreiser and others (eds), *Environmental Taxation and Climate Change: Achieving Environmental Sustainability through Fiscal Policy* (Edward Elgar Publishing, 2011) 60.

[31] Climate finance refers to the use of financial resources in a way to contribute to climate change mitigation or adaptation. David Belis, 'Climate Finance in the European Union: Domestic and International Challenges' in Geert Van Calster, Wouter Vandenberghe, and Leonie Reins (eds), *Research Handbook on Climate Change Mitigation Law* (Edward Elgar Publishing 2015), 509.

[32] Kayla M Young, Kayla Gurganus, and Leigh Raymond, 'Framing Market-based Versus Regulatory Climate Policies: A Comparative Analysis' (2022) 39(6) Review of Policy Research 798, 801.

[33] Endre Tvinnereim and Michael A Mehling, 'Carbon Pricing and Deep Decarbonization' (2018) 121 Energy Policy 185.

[34] Michael P Devereux and others, *Taxing Profit in a Global Economy* (Oxford University Press 2020), 290–294.

[35] Alice Pirlot, 'Carbon Border Adjustment Measures: A Straightforward Multi-Purpose Climate Change Instrument?' (2022) 34 Journal of Environmental Law 25, 35.

[36] Christoph Böhringer and others, 'Potential Impacts and Challenges of Border Carbon Adjustments' (2022) 12 Nat. Clim. Chang, 22, 22 <https://doi.org/10.1038/s41558-021-01250-z>.

Given the climate change problem's features,[37] using multiple and consensus-based regulatory instruments would bring better and quicker results than single and unilateral tools. IPCC has identified several market-based instruments that are effective in climate change mitigation. These instruments can also be employed as a linkage in the club scheme. They are as follows;

- carbon taxes and charges,
- tradeable emissions allowances,
- unilateral additional tariffs for carbon-intensive products and polluting industries,
- technical regulations and standards that provide clarity about the emission levels,
- financial incentives in the form of subsidies and tax credits,
- voluntary agreements between the government and the industry for emission abatement,
- information instruments,
- research&development for green technological advances,
- voluntary actions by industry, local and regional authorities, and non-governmental organizations (NGOs).[38]

Due to these measures' inherent advantages and disadvantages, the critical consideration is determining which instruments are best suited to operate effectively for rapid climate mitigation. As Breyer's definition suggests, regulatory schemes fail when "instruments" are mismatched to the context in which they are applied".[39] Thus, it is essential to ensure coherence between the societal problem that necessitates a regulatory solution and the selection of regulatory tools employed to address that issue. Under the climate context, the objective is optimal carbon abatement, and it can be accomplished if various instruments are combined and function together.[40] Currently, regulators in varying countries have employed hybrid policy mixes and instruments that combine elements of price and quantity regulation.[41] Market tools of import restrictions, ETS, carbon taxes, carbon tariffs, BCAs, and technical

[37] See Sect. 5.1.2 in Chap. 1.

[38] IPCC, 'Summary for Policymakers' in Rajendra K. Pachauri and Andy Reisinger (eds), Climate Change 2007: Synthesis Report, Contribution to the Fourth Assessment Report of the Intergovernmental Panel on Climate Change (Cambridge University Press, 2007) 9 and 19. IPCC, *Climate Change 2022. Mitigation of Climate Change. Working Group III Contribution to the Sixth Assessment Report of the Intergovernmental Panel on Climate Change* (April 2022), chapter 14. Aaron Cosbey, 'Trade and Climate Change: Working Through the Conflicts and Synergies' in Micheal Jakob (eds) *Handbook on Trade Policy and Climate Change* (Edward Elgar, 2022), 14.

[39] Stephen Breyer, *Regulation and Its Reform* (Harvard University Press, Cambridge 1983).

[40] Michael Mehling, 'Implementing Climate Governance: Instrument Choice and Interaction' in Erkki J. Hollo, Kati Kulovesi, Michael Mehling (eds.) *Climate Change and the Law* (Springer 2013), 16.

[41] In 2020, WTO members submitted 827 environment-related notifications containing around 1391 separate environment-related trade measures. WTO. Most of these measures were technical regulations or specifications (46.9%), import licences (20.5%), import bans/prohibitions (14.9%), export licences (10.7%), nonmonetary support (9.8%) and grants and direct payments (7.8%). WTO, 'Environmental Database for 2020' (2022) Note by the Secretariat WT/CTE/ EDB/20, 5.

regulations and standards can individually distribute the burden of transition policies across different sectors.[42] Through this approach, more stable, predictable, and consistent outcomes can be attained.[43]

The empirical evidence underscores that selecting market mechanisms should be a nuanced process, considering their environmental effectiveness, cost-effectiveness, distributional implications, and institutional feasibility.[44] Moreover, market conformity, administrative and transaction costs, openness to innovation, and the level of flexibility affect the choice of instruments.[45] Therefore, identifying a suitable linkage under the climate club requires an engagement with interdisciplinary research of legal, economic, and international relations spheres.[46] Within the limits of this book, the focus is on the legal characteristics of climate club linkages and their possible breach of the WTO Agreements. It involves examining the legal implications and compliance requirements associated with different market-based linkages. The goal is to ensure that climate policies do not violate international trade rules and, conversely, to explore how trade rules can be conducive to environmentally sustainable practices. The book researches the instrumental coherence among the following market-based club linkages through the lens of economic analysis of law.[47] These are import restrictions or quotas, ETSs, carbon tax or tariffs, BCAs, and technical regulations and standards. The following sub-chapters systematically examine the legal definition of the linkages and their contribution towards ensuring a well-functioning regulatory system of climate club.

---

[42] Bruce Huber, 'Transition Policy in Environmental Law' (2011) 35 Harvard Environmental Law Review 91.

[43] Jonas Meckling and Steffen Jenner, 'Varieties of Market-Based Policy: Instrument Choice in Climate Policy' (2016) 25(5) Environmental Politics 853, 870.

[44] Jason E Bordoff and Andrew W Shoyer, *International Trade Law and the Economics of Climate Policy: Evaluating the Legality and Effectiveness of Proposals to Address Competitiveness and Leakage Concerns* (Brookings Trade Forum, Climate Change, Trade, and Competitiveness: Is a Collision Inevitable?, 2008/2009) 35–68.

[45] David M Konisky, 'The Politics of Climate Policy Instruments' (2024) 57(1) PS: Political Science & Politics 21, 23–24 <https://doi.org/10.1017/S1049096523000434>.

[46] Karen J Alter, 'Visions of International Law: An Interdisciplinary Retrospective' (2020) 33(4) Leiden Journal of International Law 837, 840. Dave Owen and Caroline Noblet, 'Interdisciplinary Research and Environmental Law' (2014) 41(4) Ecology Law Quarterly 887, 893–894.

[47] David Unterhalter, 'On Interpretation and Economic Analysis of Law' in Theresa Carpenter, Marion Jansen, and Joost Pauwelyn (eds), *The Use of Economics in International Trade and Investment Disputes* (Cambridge University Press 2017) 76.

3.1 *Import Ban and Quota*

3.1.1 Overview

Import bans and quotas are regulatory measures governments impose to control the flow of certain goods across borders.[48] In the framework of the climate club, an import ban restricts carbon-intensive products from entering the markets of member countries. Alternatively, the use of quotas limits the quantity of carbon-intensive imports allowed into the market.[49] The ban or restriction complies with the precautionary principle of environmental law, in which an activity that risks environmental integrity shall be prohibited or controlled in advance.[50] The rationale behind such bans or restrictions lies in their potential to contribute significantly towards global emissions reduction. By curbing the influx of carbon-intensive goods, these measures can prompt exporting countries to adjust their production methods or witness reduced demand for products manufactured through high-carbon-intensity processes. This approach aligns with the broader objectives of the climate club by fostering environmental responsibility and incentivising sustainable production practices on a global scale.

3.1.2 As a Club Linkage

Imposing import bans or quotas on carbon-intensive products as a linkage mechanism is part of broader efforts to address global climate goals by penalizing goods that contribute significantly to carbon emissions. In this way, it supports club industries that adhere to stricter environmental standards. Implementing an import ban or quota within the climate club is contingent on importers providing accurate information about the emissions content of the products in question. However, the current complexity of production chains and challenges associated with product traceability make obtaining such information a complex and costly endeavour. Also, the import ban is strictly regulated and hard to justify under the WTO law.[51] Any selective inclusion of products for a ban or quota could potentially lead to the claim of "disguised restriction on international trade". However, there might be an opportunity to justify quotas if the environmental objectives are achieved proportionately

---

[48] Henri Culot, 'Unilateral Sanctions in International Economic Law' in Thomas Cottier and Krista Nadakavukaren Schefer (eds), *Elgar Encyclopedia of International Economic Law* (Edward Elgar 2017), 344.

[49] Ilaria Espa, 'Quotas and Import Licensing' in Thomas Cottier and Krista Nadakavukaren Schefer (eds), *Elgar Encyclopaedia of International Economic Law* (Edward Elgar 2017), 363.

[50] Thomas Cottier and Sofya Matteotti-Berkutova 'International Environmental Law and the Evolving Concept of 'Common Concern of Mankind' in Thomas Cottier, Olga Nartova, and Sadeq Z Bigdeli *International Trade Regulation and the Mitigation of Climate Change: World Trade Forum* (Cambridge University Press, 2009), 40.

[51] See Sect. 3.3 in Chap. 6.

and fall within the exception clauses of regulation that allow for eliminating quantitative restrictions.[52]

3.2 *Emissions Trading System*

3.2.1 Overview

The most prevalent emissions pricing scheme is the ETS.[53] Under this system, the government establishes a framework in which facilities are granted a specific allowance for emissions, with the flexibility to buy or sell these allowances to align with an overall emissions budget.[54] This budget is commonly referred to as the cap.[55] Unlike more rigid regulatory approaches, such as prescriptive emissions limits, the ETS allows industries to explore a variety of strategies to meet their emissions targets.[56] Facilities that can reduce emissions more efficiently than their allocated allowances, can sell their surplus to those facing challenges in meeting their emission targets.[57] Conversely, industries struggling to adhere to their emissions cap can purchase additional allowances. This practice creates a market mechanism that encourages emissions reductions where they can be achieved most economically.[58]

Accurate emissions data are pivotal in establishing a meaningful cap within the ETS. The cap relies on precise data to ensure that it aligns with environmental goals and reflects the current state of carbon emissions. As technological advances continue to drive improvements in the carbon intensity of production methods and abatement targets become more ambitious, it becomes imperative to adjust the cap. This process, often referred to as cap tightening, is essential for maintaining the

[52] Article XI:2, Article XII (restrictions to safeguard the balance of payments), Article XVII (import or export restrictions made effective through state-trading operations), Article XVIII (governmental assistance for economic development through protective or other measures), Article XIX (safeguard actions), Article XX (general exceptions), and Article XXI (security exceptions). The Agreement on Agriculture, the Understanding on Balance of Payments, and the Agreement on Safeguards may allow a Member to introduce or maintain a quantitative restriction. Members have also adopted prohibitions or restrictions to trade as a result of international obligations undertaken outside the WTO framework.

[53] For example, EU ETS currently involves 10,000 installations and presents around 40% of the total GHG emissions of the EU. International Carbon Action Partnership, 'EU Emissions Trading System' <https://icapcarbonaction.com/en/ets/eu-emissions-trading-system-eu-ets> accessed 4 April 2024.

[54] Rolf H Weber, 'Emission Trading Schemes: A Coasean Answer to Climate Change?' in Klaus Mathis and Bruce R. Huber (eds), *Environmental Law and Economics* (4th ed, Springer, 2017), 359.

[55] James Munro, 'Carbon Units and Emissions Trading Schemes' in *Emissions Trading Schemes under International Economic Law* (Oxford University Press 2018), 31.

[56] Weber, 'Emission Trading Schemes' (n 54) 360.

[57] ibid 359.

[58] Harrison and others (n 28) 522.

integrity and effectiveness of the ETS.[59] In this way, the regulatory framework remains in sync with the evolving landscape of emissions reduction efforts. Tightening the cap helps minimise the rebound effects by ensuring that a subsequent increase does not negate emission reductions achieved through technological progress and abatement targets.

The ETS cap ensures certainty on the emission abatement levels and prevents the "green paradox", which refers to the acceleration of fossil fuel production due to the expected future abatement.[60] It would prevent the over-supply of fossil fuels with its cap.[61] Additionally, since the industries can sell their emission allowances to other facilities, the system offers motivation to decrease emissions beyond the levels permissible under the law. As long as the allowances can be sold in the market, using them would mean foregoing the opportunity of selling. Industries are incentivised to reduce emissions not only to comply with regulatory limits but also to capitalise on the opportunity to sell excess allowances in the market.[62] Hence, regulated industries have a stronger preference for emissions trading because the scheme creates tradable assets instead of revenue extraction. The ability to trade allowances allows industries to optimise their emission reduction strategies and adapt to changing market conditions.[63]

While the ETS offers a dynamic approach to managing carbon emissions, it is not without challenges, particularly concerning carbon price volatility.[64] The carbon price within the ETS can be subject to fluctuations influenced by economic and political circumstances.[65] The emission allowances market, politically driven and created by legislation, is highly susceptible to policy changes or expectations of future policy changes.[66] The allowance market responds to any changes or signals related to policy direction, which can significantly influence the value of emission allowances. The challenge for businesses operating within the ETS lies in managing this inherent volatility.[67] Uncertainties in carbon price can impact the emission reduction strategies and investment decisions in low-carbon technologies.

---

[59] Marc Gronwald and Beat Hintermann, 'Introduction' in Marc Gronwald and Beat Hintermann (eds), *Emissions Trading as a Policy Instrument: Evaluation and Prospects* (MIT Press Scholarship 2016).

[60] HW Sinn, 'Introductory Comment-The Green Paradox: A Supply-Side View of the Climate Problem' (2015) 9 Review of Environmental Economics and Policy 239.

[61] ibid.

[62] Robert N Stavins, 'The Problem of the Commons: Still Unsettled after 100 Years' (2011) 101 American Economic Review 81, 95.

[63] Olivier Blanchard, Christian Gollier and Jean Tirole, 'The Portfolio of Economic Policies Needed to Fight Climate Change' (2023) 15 Annual Review of Economics 689, 692 <https://doi.org/10.1146/annurev-economics-051520-015113>.

[64] Weber, 'Emission Trading Schemes' (n 54) 367.

[65] Weber, 'Innovative Taxation Strategies Supporting Climate Change Resilience' (n 30) 51.

[66] Tatu Hocksell, 'Legal Limitations in the Establishment of a Carbon Price Floor in the European Union', (2019), 25 <http://urn.fi/URN:NBN:fi:hulib-201903221516> accessed 4 April 2024.

[67] Shi-Ling Hsu, 'International Market Mechanisms' in Kevin R Gray, Richard Tarasofsky, and Cinnamon P Carlarne (eds), *The Oxford Handbook of International Climate Change Law* (Oxford

The allowances under the cap are either allocated freely or auctioned.[68] Each method has its advantages and problems, influencing the dynamics of the ETS and its broader implications. Allocating allowances initially for free can expedite industry acceptance of emissions reduction measures.[69] This approach may facilitate a smoother transition as industries adapt to the regulatory framework.[70] Further, the free allocation for developing countries can address equity considerations, since it acknowledges historical disparities in carbon emissions and economic development. Therefore, free allocation of allowances is a practical approach to operationalising the CBDRRC principle of the Paris Agreement and SDT under the Enabling Clause. However, the free allocation distributes wealth to covered entities and enables industries to extract revenue instead of contributing to government funds. Also, free allowance contradicts the non-discrimination principles of WTO as it distorts the competition among imported and domestic products or imports from different countries when free allowances are not provided to all countries to reflect equal opportunity.[71]

On the other hand, when the government auctions or sells the emissions allowances, ETS can generate revenue for the government. The funds obtained can be directed towards climate-related initiatives or other public goods. An auction system can enhance market efficiency by allocating allowances based on the principles of supply and demand.[72] However, the cost of allowances can impact domestic industries' competitiveness compared to regions with different allocation methods.[73] In navigating these trade-offs, policymakers must carefully weigh the benefits of industry acceptance, equity considerations, and market efficiency against wealth distribution, non-discrimination, and competitive disadvantage concerns. Striking a balance between these factors is essential to design an effective and fair ETS that aligns with both environmental goals and international trade principles.

3.2.2 As a Club Linkage

Theoretically, the ETS offers economic virtues. However, its legal and institutional design raises complexities,[74] particularly in linking multiple ETS jurisdictions. The challenge lies in fostering a collaborative approach that addresses all participants'

University Press, 2016), 243.

[68] Harrison and others (n 28) 522.

[69] Angelo Antoci and others, 'Free Allocation of Emissions Permits to Reduce Carbon Leakage' in Micheal Jakob (ed) *Handbook on Trade Policy and Climate Change* (Edward Elgar, 2022).

[70] Harrison and others (n 28) 529.

[71] See Sects. 1 and 2 in Chap. 7.

[72] Munro (n 55) 33.

[73] Angelica P Rutherford, 'Linking Emissions Trading Schemes: Lessons from the EU-Swiss ETSs' (2014) CCLR 282, 288.

[74] Gilbert E Metcalf, 'Carbon Taxes in Theory and Practice' (2021) 13 Annual Review of Resource Economics 245, 251. <https://doi.org/10.1146/annurev-resource-102519-113630>.

concerns while ensuring the ETS's overall effectiveness. In connecting different ETS, emissions allowances should be mutually interchangeable, accepted for compliance purposes among linked countries and have equal prices.[75] In order to realise this harmonization and prevent economic and equity concerns, the ETS design and comparability of different jurisdictions are crucial.[76] Disparities in allowance allocation and pricing mechanisms can lead to market distortions, affecting the linked system's overall integrity. Countries that allocate a large number of allowances or have a low-price ceiling will undermine the environmental effectiveness and efficiency of the ETS.[77] Equity concerns further come to the forefront as more influential countries in the negotiations may seek favourable terms, such as a smaller market coverage.[78] This practice could potentially create an imbalance in the distribution of environmental responsibilities and economic benefits among linked jurisdictions.

Due to the above reasons, linking different jurisdictions' ETSs can be more objectively realised under the club scheme, where the harmonization goes further than carbon price and covers the common climate target and administrative aspects. Within the climate club, all members are bound by absolute emissions caps and have the option to trade the emission units with each other. Crucially, burden-sharing is equally distributed among the club members, promoting a fair and collaborative approach to emissions reduction. The climate club can introduce strict regulations to minimise uncertainties and incentivise compliance, coupled with mechanisms to hold members accountable in case of non-compliance.[79] This robust regulatory framework enhances the ETS's credibility and encourages active participation from member countries. Reduced administrative costs can serve as a critical enticement, particularly for economically constrained countries, which foster their engagement in the global deal and promote a more inclusive approach to climate action. Also, the governance structure within the climate club is designed to be transparent and uncomplicated, offering advantages for companies operating within the ETS.[80] Consequently, the emissions markets can expand, making carbon prices more stable

[75] Thais Diniz Oliveira, Angelo Costa Gurgel, and Steve Tonry, 'International Market Mechanisms under the Paris Agreement: A Cooperation between Brazil and Europe' (2019) 129 Energy Policy 397, 399.

[76] Harrison and others (n 28) 531.

[77] Metcalf (n 74) 251.

[78] Håkan Pihl 'A Climate Club as a Complementary Design to the UN Paris Agreement' (2020) 3(1) Policy Design and Practice 45, 52.

[79] Robert N Stavins and Judson Jaffe, *Linking Tradable Permit Systems for Greenhouse Gas Emissions: Opportunities, Implications, and Challenges* (International Emissions Trading Association (IETA) and Electric Power Research Institute (EPRI), Geneva 2007).

[80] European Commission, 'EU ETS Handbook', 43 <https://climate.ec.europa.eu/system/files/2017-03/ets_handbook_en.pdf> accessed 4 April 2024.

than individualistic systems,[81] which contributes to the increased environmental effectiveness of the ETS.

On the other hand, the ETS will function as a barrier to non-club members accessing the climate club market. The club system creates a differentiated treatment among trade partners based on their climate club membership status. Such discrimination introduces a unique set of considerations related to trade dynamics and regulatory compliance.[82] The imports from the non-club member jurisdictions need to acquire carbon allowances from the club's ETS or be subject to appropriate border adjustments. Such measures can be categorised as regulatory compliance certificates at the border under the Agreement on Import Licensing Procedures. It is a multilateral trade agreement negotiated under the auspices of the GATT 1994. The Agreement aims to prevent the misuse of licensing requirements for protectionist purposes and to promote a more open and predictable trading system.[83]

Import licensing procedures are categorized into two types: automatic and non-automatic. Automatic import licensing is characterized by a non-restrictive approach, where applications are approved in all cases provided they meet certain conditions.[84] These conditions include eligibility based on legal requirements, the possibility to submit applications on any working day prior to customs clearance, and a mandate for immediate approval of properly completed applications within a maximum of ten working days.[85] On the other hand, non-automatic import licensing is used for implementing specific restrictions but must not impose additional trade-restrictive or distortive effects beyond the measure itself.[86] The Agreement mandates transparency and fairness in the administration of these procedures, including the publication of sufficient information for traders and other members to understand the basis for granting licenses.[87] It also outlines detailed requirements for the notification and review of members' licensing laws, to ensure compliance and address any issues related to import licensing procedures. The categorization of emissions allowances as licenses may suggest that they represent a non-tariff barrier to free trade, tantamount to a quantitative restriction, if they are imposed non-automatically.

Therefore, five fundamental principles should be observed per the Agreement on Import Licensing Procedures[88] to ensure fair and equitable emissions allowance

---

[81] Richard B Stewart, Michael Oppenheimer, and Bryce Rudyk, 'Building Blocks for Global Climate Protection' (2013) 32(2) Stan Envti LJ, 37.

[82] Emily Lydgate, 'Climate Equivalence and International Trade' (2023) 22(3–4) World Trade Review 484.

[83] Espa (n 49) 366.

[84] ibid 363.

[85] Agreement on Import Licensing Procedures (15 April 1994) LT/UR/A-1A/5 art 2 <https://docs.wto.org/dol2fe/Pages/SS/directdoc.aspx?filename=Q:/UR/FA/23-lic.pdf&Open=True?>.

[86] Espa (n 49) 363.

[87] Agreement on Import Licensing Procedures, art3.

[88] Autar K Koul, 'WTO Agreement on Import-Licensing Procedures' in *Guide to the WTO and GATT* (Springer, 2018).

trading.[89] Initially, the purchase of the allowances by the non-club members should be based on a fair and equitable manner.[90] This parity involves avoiding discriminatory practices and establishing a mechanism that considers the diverse circumstances of different regions or countries. Subsequently, the purchase procedure is published beforehand to give non-club members time for preparation.[91] It helps to create a level playing field. Third, the forms and procedures need to be as simple as possible.[92] Simplification makes it easier for non-club members to navigate the compliance process, reducing administrative burdens and fostering broader participation. Fourth, minor errors should not be a reason for restricting entry into a market.[93] Providing some level of tolerance ensures that inadvertent mistakes do not disproportionately impact trade. Finally, there should be no discrimination among different importers.

In essence, the Agreement on Import Licensing Procedures aims to streamline and demystify the import licensing process under the ETS. It promotes a more transparent, predictable, and equitable trading environment for emissions allowances. By establishing clear guidelines and oversight mechanisms,[94] the Agreement helps to prevent ETS for imports from becoming an undue obstacle to international trade. The climate club can strike a balance between environmental goals and fair-trade practices by adhering to Import Licensing Procedures principles. Otherwise, the general elimination of the quantitative restrictions clause of the GATT 1994 will be relevant for the ETS allowances purchased at the border.[95]

3.3 Domestic Carbon Tax

3.3.1 Overview

Tax is an essential instrument for achieving a wide variety of political objectives, including environmental protection.[96] The carbon tax is a straightforward approach, in which firms are not required to handle the complexities of managing and trading allowances, nor does the government need to monitor transactions and ownership of allowances.[97] Under the carbon tax, the government applies a tax on releasing

[89] Agreement on Import Licensing Procedures, art 1.

[90] ibid art 1.3.

[91] ibid art 1.4.

[92] ibid art 1.5.

[93] ibid art 1.7.

[94] Thomas Cottier and Matthias Oesch, 'Direct and Indirect Discrimination in WTO and EU Law' in Sanford E Gaines, Birgitte Egelund Olsen, and Karsten Engsig Sorensen (eds), *Liberalising Trade in the EU and the WTO: A Legal Comparison* (Cambridge University Press, 2012), 164.

[95] See Sect. 3.3 in Chap. 7.

[96] Weber, 'Innovative Taxation Strategies Supporting Climate Change Resilience' (n 30) 47.

[97] Stavins (n 62) 99.

emissions domestically.[98] If it costs less for a facility to decrease its emissions than to pay the tax, the facility will cut its emissions. If not, the facility will pay the tax. Therefore, tax enables facilities to control their emissions cost-effectively. The carbon tax does not aim for revenue extraction instead it is issued for regulatory purposes. The central concept of the carbon tax is to internalise the social cost of carbon in the final price of products to limit the use of carbon-intensive products.[99] However, a carbon tax, when implemented without any form of wealth redistribution, tends to disproportionately affect lower-income households.[100]

A carbon tax is a type of tax that is not applied directly to individuals or companies but rather to goods that create carbon emissions during their production, consumption, or disposal.[101] Hence, it falls under the category of indirect taxes.[102] Indirect taxes are applied to the production or sale of goods and services rather than directly to income or profits. Excise duties, sales taxes, cascade taxes, and value-added taxes constitutes different forms of indirect taxation.[103] In the case of indirect taxes like carbon tax, the tax burden is often passed on from the producer to the consumer, since the higher cost of production is reflected to consumers.[104] Such a method means that the producer collects the tax from the consumer at the point of sale and remits it to the government. Consumers bear the economic incidence of the tax, even though the producer is responsible for its collection.

Carbon taxes incentivise facilities to reduce their carbon discharges beyond levels allowed by law because they can reduce their tax burden towards zero with emissions abatement.[105] This financial motivation creates a dynamic where companies are not merely adhering to regulatory thresholds but actively seeking ways to minimize their carbon footprint.[106] Moreover, the prospect of reducing carbon taxes to near-zero levels through successful emissions abatement initiatives is a powerful catalyst for innovation. Facilities are incentivized not only to comply with existing

[98] Harrison and others (n 28) 522.

[99] Arthur C Pigou, *The Economics of Welfare* (Macmillan 1920).

[100] Metcalf (n 74) 256. For example, yellow vests demonstrations against the carbon tax in France. Blanchard, Gollier and Tirole (n 63) 691. Also, in Switzerland, Federal CO_2 Act represents administrative interlocking as the effective implementation of it depends on cantons. Johannes Reich, 'Federalism and Mitigating Climate Change: The Merits of Flexibility, Experimentalism, and Dissonance' (2021) TEL.

[101] Metcalf (n 74) 256.

[102] Joost Pauwelyn and David Kleimann, *Trade Related Aspects of a Carbon Border Adjustment Mechanism: Legal Assessment* (Study for the EU Parliament 2020) <https://www.europarl.europa.eu/RegData/etudes/BRIE/2020/603502/EXPO_BRI(2020)603502_EN.pdf> accessed 4 April 2024.

[103] Rolf H Weber, 'Border Tax Adjustment-Legal Perspective' (2015) 133 Climatic Change 407, 408. <https://doi.org/10.1007/s10584-015-1414-2>. Claudio Dordi, 'Taxation and Border Tax Adjustment' in Thomas Cottier and Krista Nadakavukaren Schefer (eds), *Elgar Encyclopaedia of International Economic Law* (Edward Elgar 2017), 360.

[104] Posner, *Economic Analysis of Law* (n 1) 508.

[105] Weber, 'Border Tax Adjustment-Legal Perspective' (n 103) 408.

[106] Blanchard, Gollier and Tirole (n 63) 692.

emission standards but also to explore and invest in cutting-edge technologies and processes that can lead to even greater reductions. However, it is crucial to recognize the inherent limitation of carbon taxes in controlling the price of emissions rather than directly regulating the quantity. While the tax is a powerful driver for emission reduction, it does not provide a fool proof mechanism for ensuring that overall emissions remain within the confines of the global carbon budget.[107]

The dynamic nature of technological advancements and the evolving landscape of environmental considerations underscore the necessity for regulators to adopt a forward-looking and adaptable approach when determining optimal carbon tax rates.[108] Over the coming years, new technologies may emerge that can contribute to more significant carbon reductions. The tax rate should be flexible enough to adapt to these changes and incentivise the adoption of cleaner technologies. Therefore, the calculation of tax rates is not a one-time task but rather an ongoing process that requires continuous assessment.

Fundamental design choice in carbon tax is the upstream, midstream, or downstream application, which corresponds to directly targeting emissions resources or indirectly pricing inputs or final products' carbon levels.[109] The carbon tax is most easily instituted upstream[110] at the ports, pipelines, terminals, or mining where traditional fossil fuels first enter the economy. This way, all the fossil fuels will be treated equally, regardless of where they are originated and burned. The upstream method indirectly taxes the entire supply chain using fossil fuel as the primary energy source. It enhances the accuracy of measuring emission levels. Moreover, administrative and monitoring costs are minimised.[111] Upstream pricing is advantageous in its ability to efficiently capture carbon content at the source, providing a more direct approach to carbon pricing.[112] It simplifies the implementation process and ensures uniform treatment of fossil fuels.

[107] Determining the optimal tax rate for pollution presents a significant challenge. To achieve social efficiency, this rate should match the marginal benefits of cleanup at the most effective level of pollution reduction. However, policymakers tend to conceptualize their goals in terms of a target cleanup level, without prior knowledge of how firms will react to specific tax levels. Robert N Stavins, 'The Problem of the Commons: Still Unsettled after 100 Years' (2011) 101 American Economic Review 81, 95.

[108] Martin Zapf, Hermann Pengg, and Christian Weindl, 'How to Comply with the Paris Agreement Temperature Goal: Global Carbon Pricing According to Carbon Budgets' (2019) 12(15) Energies 2983, 8 <https://doi.org/10.3390/en12152983>.

[109] Christina K Harper, 'Climate Change and Tax Policy' (2007) 30 Boston College International & Comparative Law Review 411, 429.

[110] Upstream pricing allocates emissions to specific input, such as an energy source. This approach minimizes efforts to measure the emissions of each product, instead smaller number of companies that bring input to the market will be under scrutiny (e.g. fossil fuel suppliers).

[111] Jennifer Winter, 'The Challenge of Border Carbon Adjustments as a Mechanism for Climate Clubs' (2023) 2(2) PLOS Climate, 3 <https://doi.org/10.1371/journal.pclm.0000135>.

[112] Joachim Englisch and Tatiana Falcao, 'EU Carbon Border Adjustments for Imported Products and WTO Law' (9 June 2021), 12 <https://doi.org/10.2139/ssrn.3863038>.

The existing carbon pricing systems often institute prices on midstream entities, such as power plants, or large industrial facilities, which are positioned between fossil fuel suppliers and the final consumer.[113] They represent key points of control in the carbon emission chain. The choice of midstream pricing lies in the reason that carbon pricing does not plan to cover all sectors.[114] This strategic focus allows for a more targeted and sector-specific approach to carbon mitigation. Midstream entities are often significant sources of carbon emissions due to their role in energy production, industrial processes, and fuel distribution. By targeting these entities, carbon pricing can address substantial portions of emissions without having to cover every individual source across all sectors. Also, midstream entities are relatively fewer in number compared to all potential emission sources in various sectors. Therefore, effectively monitoring, regulating, and administering midstream carbon pricing mechanisms is more feasible.

The downstream pricing of the carbon tax is more difficult given that final goods are assembled through a global value chain spanning many countries.[115] This complexity makes it challenging to accurately account for the carbon content at each production stage, particularly when goods incorporate components or services from various sources. Moreover, the definition of a final good is usually unclear as some goods can be intermediary products for a particular purpose, whereas in another context, they are directly consumed as a final product.[116] Therefore, achieving transparency across the entire global supply chain is a formidable challenge.[117] Ensuring that accurate information on the carbon content of each product is available and verifiable becomes increasingly difficult as the number of actors involved in production and distribution grows.

3.3.2 As a Club Linkage

Within the scope of the climate club, a uniform carbon tax becomes the club commitment among its members.[118]A uniform carbon tax refers to a consistent and standardised price on carbon emissions across all climate club members. Thus, the cost

[113] David A Weisbach, 'Carbon Taxation in the EU: Expanding the EU Carbon Price' (2012) 24(2) Journal of Environmental Law 183, 198, <https://doi.org/10.1093/jel/eqr033>.

[114] James K. Boyce, 'Carbon Pricing: Effectiveness and Equity' (2018) 150 Ecological Economics 52, 57 <https://doi.org/10.1016/j.ecolecon.2018.03.030> For instance, EU CBAM targets several emission intensive sectors to begin the implementation. These sectors are cement, iron and steel, aluminium, fertilizers and electricity.

[115] Winter (n 111) 3.

[116] Samuel Kortum and David Weisbach, 'The Design of Border Adjustments for Carbon Prices' (2017) 70(2) National Tax Journal 421, 431.

[117] Kimberly A Clausing and Catherine Wolfram. 'Carbon Border Adjustments, Climate Clubs, and Subsidy Races When Climate Policies Vary' (2023) 37(3) Journal of Economic Perspectives 137, 150.

[118] Pihl (n 78) 52.

of emission is equalised between domestic producers of each club jurisdiction.[119] This uniform approach helps mitigate concerns related to competitiveness, ensuring that businesses within the club jurisdiction face comparable costs for carbon emissions. The harmonization of carbon price levels the playing field and fosters a cooperative environment where the burden of addressing climate change is shared collectively. Also, such parity ensures that no member country becomes a pollution haven due to laxer standards, thus maintaining environmental integrity without sacrificing economic competitiveness.

Overall, the significance of a uniform carbon tax within a climate club extends beyond the mere equalization of costs. The commitment to a standardised carbon tax reflects a collective acknowledgement of the need for concerted action to combat climate change. This mutual understanding encourages collaborative efforts among member nations to innovate and implement sustainable practices, thereby advancing a low-carbon economy.[120] The reduced uncertainty regarding carbon costs fosters investment confidence, assists long-term planning for industries within the club, and contributes to the stability of both domestic and international markets. Moreover, by demonstrating the feasibility and benefits of coordinated carbon pricing, club countries can influence non-members to adopt similar measures, potentially leading to a broader international consensus on carbon pricing.

3.4 *Carbon Tariff*

3.4.1 Overview

Tariffs, in a general sense, are taxes levied on goods as they cross borders.[121] Traditionally, the primary objective of tariffs is to create a competitive disadvantage for foreign products. The use of tariffs is often viewed as a form of disguised protectionism, as high tariffs can protect domestic industries at the expense of foreign competition. Hence, it is crucial to consider the potential implications of imposing tariffs. Since the Uruguay Round,[122] bound or consolidated tariffs are the rule, and

[119] Alice Pirlot, 'Environmental Taxes' in Thomas Cottier and Krista Nadakavukaren Schefer (eds), *Elgar Encyclopaedia of International Economic Law* (Edward Elgar 2017), 629.

[120] Lionel Fontagné and Katheline Schubert, 'The Economics of Border Carbon Adjustment: Rationale and Impacts of Compensating for Carbon at the Border' (2023) 15 Annual Review of Economics 389, 391 <https://doi.org/10.1146/annurev-economics-082322-034040>.

[121] Thomas Cottier, Olga Nartova and Anirudh Shingal, 'The Potential of Tariff Policy for Climate Change Mitigation: Legal and Economic Analysis' (2014) 48(5) Journal of World Trade 1007, 1020.

[122] The Uruguay Round was the 8th round of multilateral trade negotiations conducted within the framework of the GATT, spanning from 1986 to 1993 and embracing 123 countries as 'contracting parties'. The Round led to the creation of the World Trade Organization, with GATT remaining as an integral part of the WTO agreements.

unbound tariffs[123] are the exception.[124] This rule signifies a broader effort to create a more transparent and predictable trading environment, by limiting the discretion of countries to impose arbitrary and unpredictable tariffs.

3.4.2 As a Club Linkage

In the context of the climate club, a carbon tariff is a measure that corresponds to a carbon tax on imports from non-club countries. The tariff serves as a market-based mechanism to internalise the environmental costs of carbon emissions. It ensures that imported products entering a club member country account for their carbon emissions. The tariff creates a market signal that encourages a shift towards lower-emission alternatives by making market access for products from non-club countries more costly. Therefore, carbon tariffs aim to address the potential competitiveness issues.[125] They are preferred to be applied when there are varying carbon pricing policies between club members and non-members. This is because, in the lack of a harmonised approach, businesses in countries with more stringent carbon regulations might face higher production costs, putting them at a disadvantage compared to counterparts in regions with laxer environmental standards.

Nordhaus argues that the simplest and most effective approach to apply carbon tariff linkage would be a uniform tariff on all imports from non-member countries.[126] It involves a consistent percentage tariff on all imports. According to Nordhaus's modelling, a regime with a carbon price of $25 per ton and a punitive tariff of 3 percent would provide a strong incentive for non-members to join the club.[127] This approach simplifies the tariff structure by applying a uniform rate across all goods.[128] Such convenience contributes to increased transparency and ease of implementation.[129] Despite their simplicity, uniform tariffs are often

[123] Unbound tariffs, by definition, are open to increases and thus do not offer legal security. They undermine the very purpose of tariff disciplines in the WTO and are detrimental to attracting foreign direct investment.

[124] Cottier, Nartova and Shingal (n 121) 1021.

[125] Juscelino F Colares and Ashwin Rode, 'The Opportunities and Limitations of Neutral Carbon Tariffs' (2017) 19(2) American Law and Economics Review 423, 424 <https://doi.org/10.1093/aler/ahx012>.

[126] William Nordhaus, 'Climate Clubs: Overcoming Free-Riding in International Climate Policy' (2015) 105(4) American Economic Review 1339, 1348.

[127] William Nordhaus, 'Dynamic Climate Clubs: On the Effectiveness of Incentives in Global Climate Agreements', (2021) 118 (45) Proceedings of the National Academy of Sciences, 1 <https://doi.org/10.1073/pnas.2109988118>.

[128] Minka Melin, 'The Climate Club Approach: The Key to Effective Climate Change Negotiations?' (2020) <https://urn.fi/URN:NBN:fi:aalto-202009275605> accessed 4 April 2024.

[129] William Nordhaus, 'The Climate Club: How to Fix a Failing Global Effort' (2020) 20 Journal of Environmental Economics and Policy 1, 16.

criticised for being highly trade-restrictive.[130] The justification for such tariffs lies in the argument that countries without strong climate regulations are causing damage to climate club countries through their total GHG emissions, not just those embodied in traded goods.[131] General and uniform tariffs are needed as a strong incentive for countries lacking robust climate regulations. The hope of this approach is to encourage non-member nations to adopt pricing instruments and strengthen their climate policies.

However, carbon tariffs create complexities since they are generally ad valorem duties, meaning applied as a percentage on the value of the product, not to capture the actual emissions. While the intent is to incentivise cleaner and more sustainable production practices by imposing a cost on carbon emissions, applying a percentage-based tariff may not necessarily align with the actual carbon footprint of a product. Products with different carbon intensities may end up facing similar tariff rates, potentially leading to an inadequate representation of their environmental impact. Similarly, implementing the same amount of carbon tariffs with domestic carbon tax might not cover the actual emissions of the imports. Therefore, determining carbon content in carbon tariff and tax measures proves its significance.[132] To address this issue, tariff deconsolidation emerges as a strategic solution, analysed under the Sect. 3.2 in Chap. 6 which discusses the meticulous legal considerations that accompany tariff adjustments within the international trade context.

3.5 Border Carbon Adjustment

3.5.1 Overview

The promising potential of climate club reducing emissions within the club jurisdictions comes with a complex set of challenges that can disproportionately impact non-club members. One critical concern is the phenomenon known as carbon leakage.[133] It occurs when stringent regulations within the climate club shift production and emissions to non-regulated jurisdictions. As a result, climate club measures may increase emissions in other areas and create toxic hot spots.[134] Moreover, the

[130] Matthew C. Porterfield, 'Carbon Import Fees and the WTO' (2023), 6 <https://clcouncil.org/summaries/Executive_Summary_Carbon_Import_Fees_and_the_WTO.pdf> accessed 4 April 2024.

[131] Nordhaus, 'Climate Clubs: Overcoming Free-Riding' (n 126) 1348–1349.

[132] Robert Howse and Antonia L Eliason, 'Domestic and International Strategies to Address Climate Change: An Overview of the WTO Legal Issues' in Thomas Cottier, Olga Nartova and Sadeq Z Bigdeli (eds.) *International Trade Regulation and the Mitigation of Climate Change: World Trade Forum* (Cambridge University Press, 2009), 62.

[133] See Sect. 5.1.2.3 in Chap. 1.

[134] Kateryna Holzer, 'The Role Environmental Processes and Production Methods' in Thomas Cottier and Krista Nadakavukaren Schefer (eds), *Elgar Encyclopedia of International Economic Law* (Edward Elgar 2017).

adverse effects of carbon leakage become more pronounced when goods produced in these non-regulated jurisdictions are exported to the climate club. Paradoxically, this means that the climate club's linkages may inadvertently result in the importation of carbon-intensive products, thus offsetting the progress made within the club. This scenario circumvents intended penalties for carbon-intensive consumption. Mitigating the negative impacts of carbon leakage requires not only effective climate policies within the club but also international cooperation to harmonise environmental regulations and prevent the displacement of emissions to non-regulated areas.[135] A holistic strategy should consider mechanisms to incentivise emission reductions globally, potentially incorporating incentives for non-club members to adopt environmentally friendly practices.[136]

A carefully designed border adjustment could avoid the increase of foreign and consumption-based emissions that would otherwise occur due to the climate club linkages.[137] In the legal literature, the border adjustment is defined as "any fiscal measures which enable imports charged or relieved with a tax of the importing country in respect of similar domestic products".[138] It is applied according to the destination principle, which means that goods will be taxed in a country where they are consumed.[139] In case of targeting carbon levels, it is named as border carbon adjustment or carbon border adjustment mechanisms.[140] They refer to the same unilateral tool under the climate club where the importing country imposes an extra tariff or other additional border measures on the imports from a country that does not have a comparably[141] stringent climate policy[142] or only partially complies with the regulatory regime at a comparable rate to like club products.[143] The adjustments aim to price the carbon content of traded products to reflect the emissions standards of the importing country.[144] Therefore, they induce non-club member countries to

[135] Fontagné and Schubert (n 120) 399–400.

[136] ibid 407. Susanne Droege and Maria Panezi, 'How to Design Border Carbon Adjustments' in Micheal Jakob (eds) *Handbook on Trade Policy and Climate Change* (Edward Elgar, 2022) 165.

[137] Tracy Epps and Andrew Green, *Reconciling Trade and Climate: How the WTO Can Help Address Climate Change* (Edward Elgar Publishing, 2010), 122.

[138] Report of the GATT Working Party on Border Tax Adjustment, adopted on 2 December 1970, L/3464, para. 4.

[139] Mitsuo Matsushita, Thomas J Schoenbaum, and Petros C Mavroidis, *The World Trade Organization: Law, Practice and Policy* (Oxford University Press 2006) 825.

[140] Porterfield (n 130) 3.

[141] The definition of 'comparable' is a GHG reduction program that leads to a percentage decrease in GHG emissions that is comparable to the percentage decrease achieved in the climate club jurisdictions.

[142] Krista Nadakavukaren Schefer and Pablo Arnaiz, 'Duty to Protect, Climate Change and Trade in Panagiotis Delimatsis (ed) *Research Handbook on Climate Change and Trade* (Edward Elgar 2016), 69.

[143] Laura Nielsen, 'Border Carbon Adjustments, the UNFCCC, and WTO Rules' (Proceedings of the Annual Meeting American Society of International Law, International Law as Law 2009) 369, 369.

[144] Metcalf (n 74) 259.

decrease their emissions so as to avoid the border charge. BCAs intend to create a level of playing field among the products from carbon pricing and non-pricing jurisdictions.[145] Hence, they offset the disadvantages of domestic production due to carbon taxation or ETS.[146]

BCAs also align with international ethics, addressing the disparity between the production-based and consumption-based emissions observed across various countries. Industrialised countries typically exhibit higher emissions consumption than production, while the picture is typically reversed in other countries.[147] The introduction of border adjustment corrects this problem and switches the burden of carbon regulations from producer to consumer.[148] In this way, the advantage of producing abroad and selling domestically due to the carbon price could be eliminated because the carbon price will be identical regardless of the country's club participation. Therefore, border adjustment can create an incentive for non-carbon taxing countries to adopt carbon pricing measures.

3.5.2 As a Club Linkage

BCAs apply to foreign products upon importation, constituting a corresponding linkage of the club's domestic carbon tax and ETS for non-club jurisdictions.[149] Thus, they incorporate a levy on imported goods corresponding to their carbon content or domestic carbon tax.[150] The purpose is to account for the carbon emissions associated with the production and transportation of imported products. Alternatively, under an ETS, BCAs can be applied either by obliging non-club member countries to purchase emissions allowances to cover the carbon content of their products or by paying BCAs equal to the allowance price.[151] Herein, the BCAs serve as a proxy for the emissions allowances.

The Report of the GATT Working Party on Border Tax Adjustments of 1970 is the primary guidance for the operation of BCAs. According to this Report, only

---

[145] Weber, Border Tax Adjustment-Legal Perspective (n 103) 410. Pirlot, 'Carbon Border Adjustment Measures' (n 35) 30.

[146] The developed countries' industries claim that the loss of profits due to the different regulatory scheme constitute unfairness. However, given the fact that the industrialised countries shall carry a greater burden in climate mitigation than developing countries, the uneven level of playing field between developed and developing countries reflects the fairness principle according to the developing countries. Robyn Eckersley, 'The Politics of Carbon Leakage and the Fairness of Border Measures' (2010) 24(4) Ethics and International Affairs 363, 380–383.

[147] Dominic Roser and Luke Tomlinson, 'Trade Policies and Climate Change – Border Carbon Adjustments as a Tool for a Just Global Climate Regime' (2014) Ancilla Iuris 223, 235.

[148] Erich Vranes, 'Carbon Taxes, PPMs and the GATT' in Panagiotis Delimatsis (ed) *Research Handbook on Climate Change and Trade* (Edward Elgar 2016), 87.

[149] Weber, 'Border Tax Adjustment-Legal Perspective' (n 103) 408.

[150] Vranes, 'Carbon Taxes, PPMs and the GATT' (n 148) 77.

[151] Bordoff and Shoyer (n 44) 36.

taxes imposed directly on the product can be adjusted at the border.[152] The carbon taxes imposed directly on products[153] signify their eligibility for border adjustments, presenting an avenue for countries to address potential trade imbalances arising from divergent carbon taxation policies. Furthermore, the Panel in the US-Superfund case affirmed that taxes or charges intended to curb pollution were no different from general revenue-generating taxes.[154] The Panel in this case solidifies the notion that the purpose behind a tax does not impede its eligibility for border tax adjustment. Hence, carbon taxes can be adjusted at the border to harmonise trade policies with environmental objectives.[155]

BCA measures should tailors tariff levels according to product's embedded carbon levels.[156] However, this approach introduces distinct challenges, chief among them being the accurate assessment of product-specific emissions.[157] Determining the precise carbon footprint of each import necessitates a rigorous and detailed examination. Due to the inherent challenges in accurately calculating emissions levels, a pragmatic approach for the application of BCAs involves targeting imports that are predominantly carbon-intensive products, exposed to international trade, and can be traced back to a single and discrete production facility.[158] By concentrating on specific sectors, particularly major emitting industries like electricity, steel, iron, aluminium and cement, BCAs cover a substantial portion of the economy with a comparatively lower administrative burden.[159] This focus facilitates a more manageable implementation of BCAs and aligns with the broader objective of addressing carbon leakage in sectors where the risk is most pronounced.

Furthermore, the effectiveness of BCAs targeting import emissions levels is contingent upon the capacity to address fluctuations in the carbon price within the climate club jurisdiction, particularly in the context of an ETS since the carbon tax has a fix rate.[160] The intricacies of carbon pricing dynamics may pose challenges in maintaining the stability of BCAs and achieving their intended environmental outcomes. When carbon prices are subject to market forces as well as external policy influences or policy changes, adapting BCA levels to these variable conditions becomes challenging. Primarily, the exporting country may face significant

[152] Working Party Report, 'Border Tax Adjustments' (n 138) para. 14.

[153] See Sect. 3.3 in Chap. 5.

[154] GATT Panel Report, *United States-Taxes on Petroleum and Certain Imported Substances, (US-Superfund)* (17 June 1987) L/6175, 34S/136, para 5.2.4. Porterfield (n 130) 24.

[155] Robert Lloyd Howse, 'Non-Tariff Barriers and Climate Policy: Border-Adjusted Taxes and Regulatory Measures as WTO-Compliant Climate Mitigation Strategies' in Christoph Hermann and others (eds), *European Yearbook of International Economic Law* 3 (2015) 8. Vranes, Carbon Taxes, PPMs and the GATT (n 148) 88.

[156] Josheph Stiglitz, 'Overcoming the Copenhagen Failure with Flexible Commitments' (2015) 4(2) Economics of Energy and Environmental Policy, 29.

[157] Roser and Tomlinson (n 147) 234.

[158] Howse and Eliason (n 155) 69. Fontagné and Schubert (n 120) 411.

[159] Kortum and Weisbach (n 116) 429.

[160] Droege and Panezi (n 136) 167.

challenges in monitoring and reporting the carbon content of products, leading to a substantial administrative burden under this particular design of BCAs.[161] Therefore, the call for a common approach to carbon measurement becomes imperative.[162]

Accordingly, the calculation of carbon levels under BCAs can adopt various methodologies. Firstly, it can base on the actual emissions of each product, which necessitates an assessment of the carbon footprint associated with the production of the goods.[163] This calculation involves conducting a comprehensive evaluation of the product's entire life cycle. While offering high accuracy, it requires detailed data collection, verification processes, and a nuanced understanding of the specific emission sources involved.[164] Hence, targeting actual carbon levels may pose challenges in terms of practical implementation.[165] From a legal standpoint, the complexities involved in this methodology highlight the importance of establishing clear and robust regulatory frameworks.[166] These frameworks would need to delineate precise protocols for data collection, verification standards, and a judicious allocation of responsibilities among stakeholders within the supply chain.[167]

Alternatively, using default values represents a simplified and standardised means of estimating carbon content. Default values provide a practical solution for industries where obtaining precise emission data is challenging or resource intensive.[168] However, the trade-off of this design lies in potential deviations from actual emission levels. The calculation of default values could be done with two different methods. The first one is the creation of an industry-wide average emissions baseline in the exporting country and applying it to all exports.[169] Clearly, this practice will discourage individual carbon abatement efforts in the exporting country.[170] The

[161] Madeline Condon and Agnieszka Ignaciuk, *Border Carbon Adjustment and International Trade: A Literature Review* (OECD Trade and Environment Working Papers, OECD Publishing 2013), 13 <https://doi.org/10.1787/5k3xn25b386c-en>.

[162] For getting verifiable information on the carbon content of products international standards such as ISO 14067 can be adopted, which was introduced in 2013 to measure the carbon footprint of products.

[163] Christoph Böhringer and others, 'Potential Impacts and Challenges of Border Carbon Adjustments' (2022) 12 Nat. Clim. Chang, 22, 24 <https://doi.org/10.1038/s41558-021-01250-z>.

[164] Goran Dominioni, 'Pricing Carbon Effectively: A Pathway for Higher Climate Change Ambition' (2022) 22 Climate Policy 897, 901.

[165] Michael A Mehling and others, 'Designing Border Carbon Adjustments for Enhanced Climate Action' (2019) 113(3) American Journal of International Law 433.

[166] Goran Dominioni and Daniel Esty, 'Designing Effective Border-Carbon Adjustment Mechanisms: Aligning the Global Trade and Climate Change Regimes' (2023) 65(1) Arizona Law Review, 25.

[167] Böhringer and others (n 163) 22–29.

[168] Carolyn Fischer and Alan K Fox, 'Comparing Policies to Combat Emissions Leakage: Border Carbon Adjustments versus Rebates' (2012) 64 Journal of Environmental Economics and Management 199.

[169] Stéphanie Monjon and Philippe Quirion, 'Addressing Leakage in the EU ETS: Border Adjustment or Output-Based Allocation?' (2011) 70(11) Ecological Economics 1957.

[170] Fontagné and Schubert (n 120) 410.

second one is to take the best available technology (BAT) as the basis for the benchmark.[171]The BAT proposal narrows the price gap between products with different carbon levels, as the tax will be determined according to the cleanest competitor. It aims to maintain trade policy consistency and simplify compliance, monitoring and enforcement. Nevertheless, under the climate club, BAT methodology may inadvertently create a scenario where non-members, even those with higher carbon level PPMs, face comparable tax burdens. This situation could diminish the motivation for non-member countries to adopt cleaner technologies, as the financial penalties imposed through border adjustments might not sufficiently differentiate between environmentally conscious and less sustainable production practices.[172]

A third option involves adopting a hybrid approach that combines actual emission data with default values.[173] This strategy seeks to strike a balance between accuracy and administrative feasibility. By integrating both sources of information, the hybrid approach retains a level of precision while moderating the data collection challenges associated with a purely actual-emission-based methodology. It allows for a more pragmatic implementation of BCAs,. Simultaneously, it emphasises a proactive role for importers, compelling them to integrate carbon auditing practices into their supply chains as a prerequisite for entering the climate club market. Adopting this hybrid model reflects consideration of the complex interplay between the precision required for robust carbon measurement and the need to streamline processes in the context of international trade regulation. It offers a sustainable approach by including disclosure of the embedded emissions of the imports.

In essence, irrespective of the chosen methodology for determining the import's emissions levels, BCAs serve as a formidable entry barrier into the climate club market. Consequently, the pricing structure should be crafted with a delicate balance, minimising adverse impacts on the international trade system while maximising global carbon emissions abatement.[174] This dual imperative reflects an approach, wherein BCAs become instrumental in driving a paradigm shift towards environmentally conscious practices on a global scale rather than solely serving as punitive measures. Such integration represents a forward-looking approach that recognises the interconnectedness of trade and climate goals.

[171] The BAT process entails evaluating different pollution control technologies, discarding those that are technically infeasible, calculating the GHG emissions linked to the use of the most efficient remaining technologies, and issuing permits contingent upon the facilities' adherence to established GHG emission limits. Giulia Claudia Leonelli, 'The Long and Winding Road Towards the Creation of Climate Clubs: Transatlantic Negotiations, Potential Regulatory Models and Challenges Ahead' (2023) 32 RECIEL 453, 461.

[172] Fontagné and Schubert (n 120) 409. Leonelli, 'The Long and Winding Road Towards the Creation of Climate Clubs' (n 171) 460.

[173] Droege and Panezi (n 136) 167.

[174] Fontagné and Schubert (n 120) 410.

3.6 *Technical Regulations and Standards*

3.6.1 Overview

Technical regulations and standards are commonly considered suitable and comparatively non-restrictive means for pursuing environmental goals.[175] They provide consumers with clear guidance on various product characteristics in a simplified manner. Given the delayed impact of product choices on the climate, the relationship between the choice and its eventual environmental consequences is often ambiguous. In this context, technical regulations and standards act as informative instruments that bridge the gap, offering consumers insights about the outcomes of their choices.[176] If the consumers do not have a specific inclination for a product, the technical regulations and standards can guide the preference formation.[177] They are steering to make a "greener" decision while not restricting the free market.[178] They are essential in holding unsustainable products liable regardless of where they are manufactured.

Technical regulations and standards differ significantly from establishing minimum product standards. The primary distinction lies in their aim to recognise environmental excellence. In comparison, minimum product standards aim to prevent the worst environmental practices and protect consumers from subpar products.[179] With technical regulations and standards, the environmental impacts of the chosen products are assessed throughout their life cycle. In 1997, International Organization for Standardization (ISO)[180] developed the life-cycle analysis (LCA) standard, which was adopted increasingly in practice.[181] LCA is "…the process of evaluating

[175] Jessica F Green, 'Climate Change, Regulatory Policy and the WTO. How Constraining are Trade Rules?' (2005) 8 Journal of International Economic Law 143, 186.

[176] If the consumers know the label and its meaning and purpose. John Thøgersen, 'Promoting Green Consumer Behavior with Eco-Labels' in Thomas Dietz and Paul C Stern (eds), *New Tools for Environmental Protection: Education, Information, and Voluntary Measures* (National Academy Press, 2002).

[177] WTO, Committee on Trade and Environment, note by the Secretariat, *Market Access Impact of Eco-Labelling Requirements*, Doc. No. 98-0962, WT/CTE/W/79, (9 March 1998), 1 <https://docs.wto.org/dol2fe/Pages/SS/directdoc.aspx?filename=Q:/WT/CTE/W79.pdf&Open=True> accessed 31 May 2024.

[178] For example, the EU energy label has created a clear and strong preference towards higher efficiency products since the introduction of the label. Folke Ölander and John Thøgersen, 'Informing Versus Nudging in Environmental Policy' (2014) 37 Journal of Consumer Policy 341, 343 <https://doi.org/10.1007/s10603-014-9256-2>.

[179] Thomas Cottier and Jonas Baumann, 'Minimum Standards' in Thomas Cottier and Krista Nadakavukaren Schefer (eds), *Elgar Encyclopedia of International Economic Law* (Edward Elgar 2017) 58.

[180] ISO is a global, non-governmental federation of national standardizing bodies responsible for the harmonization of international standards through the creation of voluntary measures.

[181] Particular ISO standards for environmental labels and declarations are ISO 14044(2006), Draft ISO/DIS 14067(2012), ISO 14025(2006) and ISO 14020(2000).

the effects of a product on the environment over the entire period of its life cycle such as extraction and processing, manufacture, transport and distribution, use, re-use, recycling, and final disposal".[182]

From a legal and regulatory perspective, the establishment and enforcement of standardised technical regulations and standards play a pivotal role in ensuring consistency and accuracy in information dissemination.[183] The life-cycle analysis of products acknowledges various stages of production and consumption that may occur in different countries. Therefore, different technical regulations and standards might conflict with one another in varying jurisdictions. For these reasons, harmonising technical regulations and standards under one scheme is born as a necessity.[184] Standardised schemes proliferate more easily in the international market and improve the global supply chain link. Subsequently, consumers become more conscious about the impacts of products on the environment and alter their purchasing decisions.[185] Harmonized technical regulations and standards serve as important tools for achieving multiple societal goals. They enhance consumer protection, foster fair competition among businesses, and contribute to broader environmental objectives by encouraging sustainable choices.[186]

3.6.2 As a Club Linkage

Therefore, within the scope of the climate club, technical regulations and standards can be employed as a linking instrument.[187] They differentiate products from high to low-carbon emitting.[188] These club linkages have the utmost importance in developing additional market opportunities for green products and lessening greenwashing. Furthermore, the technical regulations and standards as club linkages reduce the risk of unilateral measures. They prevent the proliferation of mediocre programs or

[182] Robin Clarke and others, 'Life Cycle Assessment: What It Is and How to Do It' (1996), 91, <http://digitallibrary.un.org/record/217945> accessed 4 April 2024.

[183] Panagiotis Delimatsis, 'Sustainable Standard Setting, Climate Change and the TBT Agreement' in Panagiotis Delimatsis (ed) *Research Handbook on Climate Change and Trade* (Edward Elgar 2016), 149.

[184] Katrin Kamin and others, 'Instruments of a Strategic Foreign Economic Policy' (2021) <https://www.ifw-kiel.de/experts/ifw/katrin-kamin/instruments-of-a-strategic-foreign-economic-policy-16764/> accessed 21 June 2024.

[185] Delimatsis, 'Sustainable Standard Setting, Climate Change and the TBT Agreement' (n 183) 149.

[186] Nicholas Stern and Hans Peter Lankes, *Collaborating and Delivering on Climate Action Through a Climate Club: An Independent Report to the G7* (London School of Economics and Political Science, 2022), 13.

[187] UNCTAD, *Making Trade Work for Climate Change Mitigation: The Case of Technical Regulations* UNCTAD/DITC/TAB/2022/7 (United Nations publication 2022).

[188] Most of the GHG programs rely on labelling regulations such as energy efficiency standards, energy labels, and standards for motor vehicles.

demanding standards set by environmental organizations or large corporations.[189] Consequently, the climate club enhances the legality and credibility of the technical regulations and standards.[190]

In the realm of emissions control, three distinct types of technical regulations and standards play crucial roles. They are quality and emission, target, and technology or production.[191] Each type serves a unique purpose in the regulatory landscape, addressing different aspects of emissions abatement. Quality and emission technical regulations and standards specify that certain product components must align with predefined criteria.[192] These non-market-based technical regulations and standards exclusively concentrate on the quantity and quality of emissions within each industry.[193] Hence, they serve as guidelines for individual emitters. Target technical regulations and standards encompass the reduction of emissions to meet certain levels by employing various tools.[194] Target schemes provide a framework where parties have the freedom to choose the most effective means to reach the desired emission reduction goals. Therefore, they introduce flexibility for parties in determining how to achieve the specified emission abatement level. They often guarantee that a specific amount of energy savings or emission reductions has been accomplished.

Technology or production technical regulations and standards dictate which abatement technology should be implemented.[195] The control mechanism in this type is straightforward, as it is limited to the installation and operation of the prescribed technology. However, a drawback is the possibility that technological standards become quickly obsolete, rendering them less effective in capturing emissions. As a result, technology technical regulations and standards may not always produce the intended effects due to rapid advancements in expertise. While each type of technical regulation and standard has advantages, careful consideration must be given to their potential limitations, ensuring that they remain effective and adaptable in the face of evolving technological and environmental challenges.

Under the climate club, both technical regulations and standards implicitly put a price on emissions by constraining specific actions or technologies that emit high carbon.[196] Their use as club linkage will make exporting labelled goods more

[189] Richard Bonsi, A Hammett and Robert Smith, 'Eco–Labels and International Trade: Problems and Solutions' (2008) 42 Journal of World Trade 407, 419.

[190] S. Case, 'Eco-labels: Making Environmental Purchasing Easier?' (2004) 12(3) Government Procurement Journal.

[191] Michael Faure and Roy Andrew Partain, *Environmental Law and Economics: Theory and Practice* (Cambridge University Press 2019), 64.

[192] ibid 65.

[193] UNCTAD and United Nations Economic and Social Commission for Asia and the Pacific, 'Trade Regulations for Climate Action? New Insights from the Global Non-Tariff Measures Database' (Geneva 2023) UNCTAD/DITC/TAB/2023/5, 7. Lange (n 1) 858.

[194] Faure and Partain (n 191) 64.

[195] ibid 68.

[196] Nicholas Stern, 'The Economics of Climate Change' (2008) 98(2) The American Economic Review 1, 25.

accessible and advantageous. Labelled products can have favourable access to the club market.[197] The prospect of easier access to the climate club market serves as a powerful motivator for producers to embrace and adhere to the prescribed technical regulations and standards. The club's endorsement becomes a valuable asset for labelled goods, potentially translating into increased market demand and competitiveness, expanding the economies of scale for green products.[198] Importers, in turn, are incentivised to align with the climate club's environmental objectives to leverage these advantages.

3.6.3 Categorization

Under the trade law, the TBT Agreement disciplines technical regulations and standards per their three fundamental characteristics.[199] These are government involvement, legal regime, and scope. The government involvement criterion considers whether public authorities or private organizations administer the programme. The second criterion, the legal regime, refers to whether labelling is mandatory or voluntary.[200] In the final criterion of scope, categorization is made according to whether the technical regulations and standards apply to product-related PPMs or non-product-related (npr) PPMs.[201] Understanding these distinctions is essential for evaluating the potential trade impacts of technical regulations and standards, ensuring they are appropriately tailored to address legitimate objectives without unnecessarily restricting trade.

Product-related PPMs pertain to the manufacturing or processing techniques that impact the ultimate characteristics of the product.[202] Hence, they address the impacts of a product's physical characteristics on the environment in importing and exporting countries. On the other hand, npr-PPMs do not impact the physical attributes of the end product. They are related to non-material characteristics, such as emissions levels.[203] Similarly, the climate club's technical regulations and standards for emissions prescribe specific quality and quantity of the emissions spread into the atmosphere. They are invisible product characteristics, hence, fall under the category of npr-PPM-based criterion. TBT Agreement does not explicitly mention on npr-PPMs

---

[197] Potoski (n 22) 54.

[198] Stern, 'The Economics of Climate Change' (n 196) 25.

[199] Erich Vranes, *Trade and the Environment: Fundamental Issues in International Law, WTO Law and Legal Theory* (Oxford University Press 2009), 343.

[200] Panel Report, *United States – Measures Concerning the Importation, Marketing and Sale of Tuna and Tuna Products*, (US–Tuna II (Mexico)), WT/DS381/R, adopted 13 June 2012, as modified by Appellate Body Report WT/DS381/AB/R, para. 7.142.

[201] Vranes, *Trade and the Environment* (n 199) 343.

[202] Christine Kaufmann and Rolf H Weber, 'Carbon-Related Border Tax Adjustments: Mitigating Climate Change or Restricting International Trade?' (2011) 10 World Trade Rev 497.

[203] Weber, 'Border Tax Adjustment-Legal Perspective' (n 103) 414.

criteria in the definition of technical regulations and standards.[204] Therefore, whether they are subjected to TBT Agreement is analysed under the Sect. 4 in Chap. 7. This chapter now examines how the TBT Agreement distinguishes between technical regulation and standards.

3.6.3.1 Technical Regulations

According to Paragraph 1 of Annex 1 to the TBT Agreement, a technical regulation is a document that specifies product characteristics or related PPMs. Such documents may also include administrative provisions, as well as requirements for terminology, symbols, packaging, marking, or labelling.[205] The identification of a technical regulation relies on three key criteria.[206] First, the regulation must apply to products that are identifiable and discernible.[207] In other words, the regulation should be targeted and specific in its application, addressing particular goods or categories of goods. Secondly, the technical regulation must articulate at least one product characteristic. It needs to provide clear and explicit features, whether they pertain to physical attributes, performance criteria, or other defining descriptions.[208] Lastly, and perhaps most crucially, compliance with the specified product characteristics within the technical regulation is mandatory.

The classification of a scheme as mandatory hinges on three key factors: legal enforceability, control over the claims reflected by the regulation, and the exclusivity of the standard embodied in the regulation.[209] First, the legal enforceability should go beyond the protection against abusive or misleading use under the general law since all schemes are protected against deceptive practices.[210] If the technical regulation imposes sanctions, it is classified as legally enforceable. In this context, market access can be restricted for non-labelled products.[211] This application

---

[204] Kateryna Holzer, 'Process and Production Methods (PPMs)' in Thomas Cottier and Krista Nadakavukaren Schefer (eds), *Elgar Encyclopedia of International Economic Law* (Edward Elgar 2017), 190.

[205] Agreement on Technical Barriers to Trade (15 April 1994) LT/UR/A-1A/10 art 1 <https://docs.wto.org/dol2fe/Pages/SS/directdoc.aspx?filename=Q:/UR/FA/17-tbt.pdf&Open=True>.

[206] Appellate Body Report, *United States – Measures Concerning the Importation, Marketing and Sale of Tuna and Tuna Products, (US – Tuna II (Mexico)),* WT/DS381/AB/R, adopted 13 June 2012, para. 183, referring to Appellate Body Report, *European Communities – Trade Description of Sardines*, (EC-Sardines), WT/DS231/AB/R, adopted 23 October 2002, para. 176.

[207] Appellate Body Reports, *European Communities – Measures Prohibiting the Importation and Marketing of Seal Products, (EC-Seal Products),* WT/DS400/AB/R / WT/DS401/AB/R, adopted 18 June 2014, para 5.10.

[208] Appellate Body Report, *European Communities – Measures Affecting Asbestos and Asbestos-Containing Products, (EC-Asbestos),* WT/DS135/AB/R, adopted 5 April 2001, para 67.

[209] Faisal Al-Nabhani, 'The TBT Agreement: Examining the Line Between Technical Regulations and Standards' (2012) 7(9) Global Trade and Customs Journal 355, 355.

[210] Panel Report, *US-Tuna II (Mexico),* para. 7.142.

[211] Al-Nabhani (n 209) 358.

constitutes market-oriented mandatory compliance, meaning that technical regulation is required to access the market. Alternatively, non-labelled imports can be subjected to BCAs. Secondly, the more control the technical regulation exercises over what it covers in that field, the more likely it will be considered mandatory. Therefore, the technical regulation should impose one or more physical or PPM-related product characteristics. Finally, the exclusivity of the procedure set by the technical regulation is another determining factor.[212] The measure would be considered mandatory if the technical regulation only accepts specific methods to obtain and comply with the scheme it created and excludes others.

Furthermore, determining the mandatory nature of a technical regulation can be influenced by the issuing body's status. According to Article 2 of the TBT Agreement, technical regulations are typically issued by the "central government". Therefore, the primary authority for creating and enforcing technical regulations lies with national governments. Article 3.1 extends this scope to cover "technical regulations by local government and non-governmental bodies". It is crucial to note that while non-governmental bodies are included in the ambit of Article 3.1, their role is circumscribed to involvement in preparing or applying technical regulations. These non-governmental bodies do not possess the authority to adopt such regulatory instruments independently. The exclusive function of adopting technical regulations remains within the purview of government bodies.

3.6.3.2 Standards

Paragraph 2 of Annex 1 to the TBT Agreement defines standards. According to this provision, a standard is a document approved by a recognised body. This document, intended for common and repeated use, delineates rules, guidelines, or characteristics applicable to products or related PPMs. Notably, compliance with standards is not mandatory. Therefore, they are voluntary schemes.[213] Manufacturers or importers employ the standards entirely at their own discretion. The non-possession of standards does not restrict de jure market access of the products. Despite its voluntary nature, many enterprises fulfil them for being responsive to consumer concerns[214] or due to practical considerations.

---

[212] Appellate Body Report, *US-Tuna II*, para. 188.

[213] Petros C Mavroidis, 'Last Mile for Tuna (to a Safe Harbour): What Is the TBT Agreement All About?' (2019) 30(1) European Journal of International Law 279, 283 <https://doi.org/10.1093/ejil/chz002>.

[214] For example, analyses show that consumers prefer and are even willing to pay more for products with a carbon label in advanced economies like Germany, France, the UK, and Norway. Yvonne Feucht and Katrin Zander, 'Consumers' Willingness to Pay for Climate-Friendly Food in European Countries' in Proceedings in System Dynamics and Innovation in Food Networks (2017) http://centmapress.ilb.uni-bonn.de/ojs/index.php/proceedings/article/view/1738, accessed 3 April 2024. Celine Michaud and others, 'Willingness to Pay for Environmental Attributes of Non-Food Agricultural Products: A Real Choice Experiment' (2013) 40 European Review of Agricultural Economics 313 <https://doi.org/10.1093/ERAE/JBS025>.

Under the TBT Agreement, standards are subject to Article 4 and Annex 3 Code of Good Practice for the Preparation, Adoption and Application of Standards. Article 4 imposes an obligation on members to ensure the acceptance and compliance with the Code of Good Practice by both governmental and non-governmental standardising bodies within their territories. Additionally, this obligation extends to regional standardising bodies in which WTO members participate. However, Article 4 does not explicitly define what constitutes a "standardizing body". The closest definition is found in paragraph B of Annex 3 to the TBT Agreement. This paragraph states, "any standardizing body within the territory of a member of the WTO". It encompasses a range of entities, including central government bodies, local government bodies, and non-governmental bodies involved in the development and establishment of standards. Furthermore, the definition extends to governmental and non-governmental regional standardising bodies, provided that one or more members of these regional bodies are also members of the WTO. This broad definition aims to encompass the diverse range of organizations that contribute to the development and implementation of standards within the territories of WTO member countries.

Given their voluntary nature, the effectiveness of standards is often contingent on their integration with other sophisticated pricing tools, including taxes and border measures. While standards are crucial in promoting environmental awareness and setting benchmarks, their impact can be significantly enhanced when coupled with complementary pricing mechanisms. Without them, the effectiveness of standards can be limited to raising awareness and fostering a sense of responsibility among climate club jurisdictions. However, integrating instruments such as taxes and border measures transform environmental standards into economically impactful tools. Consequently, this choice drives meaningful change in business practices and consumer choices.

The decision between implementing a technical regulation and a standard is contingent upon finding the appropriate balance between two critical considerations.[215] The primary factor influencing this choice is the significance of the policy objective in question. For example, in numerous jurisdictions, the lawful marketing of tobacco products hinges on the inclusion of specific labels.[216] It illustrates the crucial role of technical regulations in addressing health and safety concerns associated with such products. The second consideration entails the feasibility of achieving the policy

[215] Arwel Davies, 'Technical Regulations and Standards under the WTO Agreement on Technical Barriers to Trade' (2014) 41(1) Legal Issues of Economic Integration 37, 45.

[216] Elinor Devlin and others, 'Targeting Smokers via Tobacco Product Labelling: Opportunities and Challenges for Pan European Health Promotion' (2005) 20(1) Health Promotion International 41. David Hammond, 'Tobacco Packaging and Labeling Policies Under the U.S. Tobacco Control Act: Research Needs and Priorities' (2012) 14(1) Nicotine & Tobacco Research 62 <https://doi.org/10.1093/ntr/ntr182> Appellate Body Report, Appellate Body Reports, *Australia – Certain Measures concerning Trademarks, Geographical Indications and other Plain Packaging Requirements applicable to Tobacco Products and Packaging, (Australia-Tobacco Plain Packaging)* WT/DS435/AB/R and Add.1 *(Honduras)* / WT/DS441/AB/R and Add.1 *(Dominican Republic)*, adopted 29 June 2020.

objective through collaboration with the industry. Governments are inclined to employ voluntary standards, particularly when a high industry adoption rate is anticipated.[217] An illustrative example is the energy efficiency labelling for electrical appliances in different regions. In the US, there exists a preference for industry cooperation, allowing producers a degree of flexibility in determining energy efficiency labels for appliances.[218] In contrast, the EU adopts a more stringent stance, mandating energy efficiency labels for certain electrical appliances like fridge freezers and washing machines, without which lawful marketing is precluded.[219] As a result, the choice between technical regulations and standards is influenced by the nature and urgency of policy goals, the role of industry collaboration, and the level of compulsion deemed necessary to ensure uniformity and protect consumer interests.

4 Concluding Remarks

In conclusion, this chapter has demonstrated the pivotal role of market-based instruments as effective linkages within the framework of climate club. It highlights their capacity to mitigate global emissions without undermining economic effectives. Through a comprehensive analysis, it became evident that these instruments not only encourage a shared responsibility for environmental sustainability but also pave the way for a more cooperative global framework to combat climate change. The implications of market-based instruments are far-reaching, offering valuable insights for policymakers and international bodies. By embracing market-based linkages, such as carbon tax and tariff, ETS, BCAs and technical regulations and standards, climate club can serve as a powerful mechanism for achieving global emission reduction targets, promoting economic efficiency, and fostering a competitive yet sustainable market.

The chapter also acknowledges the challenges and limitations inherent in implementing such instruments, including the need to balance economic objectives with environmental imperatives and to ensure a fair distribution of mitigation responsibilities. The linkages are analysed through the WTO law lens, as their compatibility with the WTO Agreements will determine their long-term applicability. Looking ahead, this book underscores the necessity for enhanced international collaboration and inclusivity in climate club initiatives. By fostering an integrated approach that combines market-based mechanisms with robust legal support and international

---

[217] Davies (n 215) 46.

[218] Stephen Wiel and James E McMahon, *Energy-Efficiency Labels and Standards: A Guidebook for Appliances, Equipment, and Lighting* (2nd edn, U.S. Department of Energy Office of Scientific and Technical Information Technical Report, 2005) <https://doi.org/10.2172/877316>.

[219] Directive 2010/30/EU of the European Parliament and of the Council of 19 May 2010 on the indication by labelling and standard product information of the consumption of energy and other resources by energy-related products [2010] OJ L153/1.

cooperation, there lies a promising path toward a sustainable and resilient global economy.

Bibliography

Cases

GATT Panel Report, *United States-Taxes on Petroleum and Certain Imported Substances,* (17 June 1987) L/6175, 34S/136.

WTO Panel Report, *United States – Measures Concerning the Importation, Marketing and Sale of Tuna and Tuna Products,* WT/DS381/R, adopted 13 June 2012, as modified by Appellate Body Report WT/DS381/AB/R.

WTO Appellate Body Report *Australia – Certain Measures concerning Trademarks, Geographical Indications and other Plain Packaging Requirements applicable to Tobacco Products and Packaging*, WT/DS435/AB/R and Add.1 *(Honduras)* / WT/DS441/AB/R and Add.1 *(Dominican Republic)*, adopted 29 June 2020.

—*European Communities – Measures Affecting Asbestos and Asbestos-Containing Products,* WT/DS135/AB/R, adopted 5 April 2001,

—*European Communities – Measures Prohibiting the Importation and Marketing of Seal Products,* WT/DS400/AB/R / WT/DS401/AB/R, adopted 18 June 2014.

—*European Communities – Trade Description of Sardines,* WT/DS231/AB/R, adopted 23 October 2002.

—*United States – Measures Concerning the Importation, Marketing and Sale of Tuna and Tuna Products*, WT/DS381/AB/R, adopted 13 June 2012.

Legislation

Agreement on Import Licensing Procedures (15 April 1994) LT/UR/A-1A/5 <https://docs.wto.org/dol2fe/Pages/SS/directdoc.aspx?filename=Q:/UR/FA/23-lic.pdf&Open=True?>

Agreement on Technical Barriers to Trade (TBT) (15 April 1994) LT/UR/A-1A/10 <https://docs.wto.org/dol2fe/Pages/SS/directdoc.aspx?filename=Q:/UR/FA/17-tbt.pdf&Open=True>

Directive 2010/30/EU of the European Parliament and of the Council of 19 May 2010 on the indication by labelling and standard product information of the consumption of energy and other resources by energy-related products [2010] OJ L153/1.

Secondary Sources

'U.S. Positions in International Climate Change Negotiations' (2008) 102(1) American Journal of International Law 164 <https://doi.org/10.1017/S0002930000753012>

Ahmad Z, 'Trade-Related Measures to Spread Low-Carbon Technologies: A Common Concern–Based Approach' in T Cottier (ed), *The Prospects of Common Concern of Humankind in International Law* (Cambridge University Press 2021)

Al-Nabhani F, 'The TBT Agreement: Examining the Line Between Technical Regulations and Standards' (2012) 7(9) Global Trade and Customs Journal 355

Alter KJ, 'Visions of International Law: An Interdisciplinary Retrospective' (2020) 33(4) Leiden Journal of International Law 837

Antoci A and others, 'Free Allocation of Emissions Permits to Reduce Carbon Leakage' in M Jakob (ed) *Handbook on Trade Policy and Climate Change* (Edward Elgar, 2022).

Barrett S, 'Dikes versus Windmills: Climate Treaties and Adaptation' (2020) 11 Climate Change Economics 2040005

Belis D, 'Climate Finance in the European Union: Domestic and International Challenges' in G van Calster, W Vandenberghe, and L Reins (eds), *Research Handbook on Climate Change Mitigation Law* (Edward Elgar Publishing 2015)

Biedenkopf K and Wettestad J, 'Harnessing the Market: Trading in Carbon Allowances' in Andrew Jordan and others (eds), *Governing Climate Change: Polycentricity in Action?* (Cambridge University Press 2018)

Blanchard O, Gollier C and Tirole J, 'The Portfolio of Economic Policies Needed to Fight Climate Change' (2023) 15 Annual Review of Economics 689 <https://doi.org/10.1146/annurev-economics-051520-015113>

Bonsi R, Hammett A and Smith R, 'Eco–Labels and International Trade: Problems and Solutions' (2008) 42 Journal of World Trade 407

Bordoff JE and Shoyer AW, *International Trade Law and the Economics of Climate Policy: Evaluating the Legality and Effectiveness of Proposals to Address Competitiveness and Leakage Concerns* (Brookings Trade Forum, Climate Change, Trade, and Competitiveness: Is a Collision Inevitable?, 2008/2009)

Bosetti V and others, 'Incentives and Stability of International Climate Coalitions: An Integrated Assessment' (2013) 55 Energy Policy <https://doi.org/10.1016/j.enpol.2012.12.035>

Boyce JK, 'Carbon Pricing: Effectiveness and Equity' (2018) 150 Ecological Economics 52, <https://doi.org/10.1016/j.ecolecon.2018.03.030>

Böhringer C and others, 'Potential Impacts and Challenges of Border Carbon Adjustments' (2022) 12 Nat. Clim. Chang, 22, 22 <https://doi.org/10.1038/s41558-021-01250-z>

Brewster R, 'Stepping Stone of Stumbling Block: Incrementalism and National Climate Change Legislation' (2010) 28 Yale L & Pol Rev 245

Breyer S, *Regulation and Its Reform* (Harvard University Press, Cambridge 1983)

Carlarne C, 'Delinking International Environmental Law & Climate Change' (2014) 4(1) Michigan J of Environmental & Administrative L 1

Case S, 'Eco-labels: Making Environmental Purchasing Easier?' (2004) 12(3) Government Procurement Journal

Clarke R and others, 'Life Cycle Assessment: What It Is and How to Do It' (1996) <http://digitallibrary.un.org/record/217945> accessed 4 April 2024.

Clausing KA and Wolfram Ç 'Carbon Border Adjustments, Climate Clubs, and Subsidy Races When Climate Policies Vary' (2023) 37(3) Journal of Economic Perspectives 137

Coase RH, 'The Problem of Social Cost' (1960) 3 Journal of Law and Economics 1.

Colares JF and Rode A, 'The Opportunities and Limitations of Neutral Carbon Tariffs' (2017) 19(2) American Law and Economics Review 423 <https://doi.org/10.1093/aler/ahx012>

Condon M and Ignaciuk A, Border Carbon Adjustment and International Trade: A Literature Review (OECD Trade and Environment Working Papers, OECD Publishing 2013), <https://doi.org/10.1787/5k3xn25b386c-en>

Cosbey A, 'Trade and Climate Change: Working Through the Conflicts and Synergies' in M Jakob (ed) *Handbook on Trade Policy and Climate Change* (Edward Elgar, 2022).

Cottier T, and Matteotti-Berkutova S 'International Environmental Law and the Evolving Concept of 'Common Concern of Mankind' in T Cottier, O Nartova, and SZ Bigdeli *International Trade Regulation and the Mitigation of Climate Change: World Trade Forum* (Cambridge University Press, 2009)

— and Oesch M 'Direct and Indirect Discrimination in WTO and EU Law' in Sanford E Gaines, Birgitte Egelund Olsen, and Karsten Engsig Sorensen (eds), *Liberalising Trade in the EU and the WTO: A Legal Comparison* (Cambridge University Press, 2012)

—and Baumann J, 'Minimum Standards' in T Cottier and K Nadakavukaren Schefer (eds), *Elgar Encyclopedia of International Economic Law* (Edward Elgar 2017).

—, Nartova O and Shingal A, 'The Potential of Tariff Policy for Climate Change Mitigation: Legal and Economic Analysis' (2014) 48(5) Journal of World Trade 1007

Crocker T, 'The Structuring of Atmospheric Pollution Control System' in H Wolozin (ed), *The Economics of Air Pollution* (W. W. Norton 1966)

Culot H, 'Unilateral Sanctions in International Economic Law' in T Cottier and K Nadakavukaren Schefer (eds), *Elgar Encyclopedia of International Economic Law* (Edward Elgar 2017)

Dales JH, *Pollution, Property and Prices: An Essay in Policy-Making and Economics* (University of Toronto Press 1968)

Davies A, 'Technical Regulations and Standards under the WTO Agreement on Technical Barriers to Trade' (2014) 41(1) Legal Issues of Economic Integration 37

De Sadeleer N, 'The Polluter-Pays Principle' in *Environmental Principles: From Political Slogans to Legal Rules* (2nd eds Oxford University Press 2020)

Delimatsis P, 'Sustainable Standard Setting, Climate Change and the TBT Agreement' in T Cottier and K Nadakavukaren Schefer (eds), *Elgar Encyclopedia of International Economic Law* (Edward Elgar 2017)

Devereux MP and others, *Taxing Profit in a Global Economy* (Oxford University Press 2020)

Devlin E and others, 'Targeting Smokers via Tobacco Product Labelling: Opportunities and Challenges for Pan European Health Promotion' (2005) 20(1) Health Promotion International 41

Dominioni G, 'Pricing Carbon Effectively: A Pathway for Higher Climate Change Ambition' (2022) 22 Climate Policy 897

— and Esty D, 'Designing Effective Border-Carbon Adjustment Mechanisms: Aligning the Global Trade and Climate Change Regimes' (2023) 65(1) Arizona Law Review

Dordi C, 'Taxation and Border Tax Adjustment' in T Cottier and K Nadakavukaren Schefer (eds), *Elgar Encyclopaedia of International Economic Law* (Edward Elgar 2017)

Droege S and Panezi M, 'How to Design Border Carbon Adjustments' in Micheal Jakob (eds) *Handbook on Trade Policy and Climate Change* (Edward Elgar, 2022)

Eckersley R, 'The Politics of Carbon Leakage and the Fairness of Border Measures' (2010) 24(4) Ethics and International Affairs 363.

Englisch J and Falcao T, 'EU Carbon Border Adjustments for Imported Products and WTO Law' (9 June 2021) <https://doi.org/10.2139/ssrn.3863038>

Epps T and Green A, *Reconciling Trade and Climate: How the WTO Can Help Address Climate Change* (Edward Elgar Publishing, 2010)

Espa I, 'Quotas and Import Licensing' in T Cottier and K Nadakavukaren Schefer (eds), *Elgar Encyclopaedia of International Economic Law* (Edward Elgar 2017)

European Commission, 'EU ETS Handbook' <https://climate.ec.europa.eu/system/files/2017-03/ets_handbook_en.pdf> accessed 4 April 2024

European Economic and Social Committee, 'Opinion of the European Economic and Social Committee on "The Impact of the Crisis on the Ability of European Firms to Undertake Pro-Climate Investments"' [2012] OJ C24/02

Faure M and Partain RA, *Environmental Law and Economics: Theory and Practice* (Cambridge University Press 2019)

Feucht Y and Zander K, 'Consumers' Willingness to Pay for Climate-Friendly Food in European Countries' in Proceedings in System Dynamics and Innovation in Food Networks (2017) http://centmapress.ilb.uni-bonn.de/ojs/index.php/proceedings/article/view/1738, accessed 3 April 2024.

Fischer C and Fox AK, 'Comparing Policies to Combat Emissions Leakage: Border Carbon Adjustments versus Rebates' (2012) 64 Journal of Environmental Economics and Management 199

Fontagné L and Schubert K, 'The Economics of Border Carbon Adjustment: Rationale and Impacts of Compensating for Carbon at the Border' (2023) 15 Annual Review of Economics 389, <https://doi.org/10.1146/annurev-economics-082322-034040>

Green JF, 'Climate Change, Regulatory Policy and the WTO. How Constraining are Trade Rules?' (2005) 8 Journal of International Economic Law 143

Gronwald M and Hintermann B, 'Introduction' in M Gronwald and B Hintermann (eds), *Emissions Trading as a Policy Instrument: Evaluation and Prospects* (MIT Press Scholarship 2016)

Hammond D, 'Tobacco Packaging and Labeling Policies Under the U.S. Tobacco Control Act: Research Needs and Priorities' (2012) 14(1) Nicotine & Tobacco Research 62 <https://doi.org/10.1093/ntr/ntr182>

Harper CK, 'Climate Change and Tax Policy' (2007) 30 Boston College International & Comparative Law Review 411

Harrison D and others, 'Economic Policy Instruments for Reducing Greenhouse Gas Emissions' in JS Dryzek, RB Norgaard, and D Schlosberg (eds), *The Oxford Handbook of Climate Change and Society* (Oxford University Press, 2011)

Hocksell T, 'Legal Limitations in the Establishment of a Carbon Price Floor in the European Union', (2019) <http://urn.fi/URN:NBN:fi:hulib-201903221516> accessed 4 April 2024

Holzer K, 'Process and Production Methods (PPMs)' in T Cottier and K Nadakavukaren Schefer (eds), *Elgar Encyclopedia of International Economic Law* (Edward Elgar 2017)

— 'The Role Environmental Processes and Production Methods' in T Cottier and K Nadakavukaren Schefer (eds), *Elgar Encyclopedia of International Economic Law* (Edward Elgar 2017).

Howse R, 'Non-Tariff Barriers and Climate Policy: Border-Adjusted Taxes and Regulatory Measures as WTO-Compliant Climate Mitigation Strategies' in C Hermann and others (eds), *European Yearbook of International Economic Law* (2015)

— and Eliason AL, 'Domestic and International Strategies to Address Climate Change: An Overview of the WTO Legal Issues' in T Cottier, O Nartova, and SZ Bigdeli (eds.) *International Trade Regulation and the Mitigation of Climate Change: World Trade Forum* (Cambridge University Press, 2009)

Hsu SL, 'International Market Mechanisms' in KR Gray, R Tarasofsky and CP Carlarne (eds), *The Oxford Handbook of International Climate Change Law* (Oxford University Press, 2016)

Huber B, 'Transition Policy in Environmental Law' (2011) 35 Harvard Environmental Law Review 91

Intergovernmental Panel on Climate Change (IPCC), 'Summary for Policymakers' in RK Pachauri and A Reisinger (eds), Climate Change 2007: Synthesis Report, Contribution to the Fourth Assessment Report of the Intergovernmental Panel on Climate Change (Cambridge University Press, 2007).

— *Climate Change 2022. Mitigation of Climate Change. Working Group III Contribution to the Sixth Assessment Report of the Intergovernmental Panel on Climate Change* (April 2022)

International Carbon Action Partnership, 'EU Emissions Trading System' <https://icapcarbonaction.com/en/ets/eu-emissions-trading-system-eu-ets> accessed 4 April 2024.

Kamin K and others, 'Instruments of a Strategic Foreign Economic Policy' (2021) <https://www.ifw-kiel.de/experts/ifw/katrin-kamin/instruments-of-a-strategic-foreign-economic-policy-16764/> accessed 21 June 2024

Kaufmann C and Weber RH, 'Carbon-Related Border Tax Adjustments: Mitigating Climate Change or Restricting International Trade?' (2011) 10 World Trade Rev 497

Kemfert C, 'Climate Coalitions and International Trade: Assessment of Cooperation Incentives by Issue Linkage' (2004) 32 Energy Policy 455 <https://doi.org/10.1016/S0301-4215(03)00148-4>

Konisky DM, 'The Politics of Climate Policy Instruments' (2024) 57(1) PS: Political Science & Politics 21 <https://doi.org/10.1017/S1049096523000434>

Kortum S and Weisbach D, 'The Design of Border Adjustments for Carbon Prices' (2017) 70(2) National Tax Journal 421

Koul AK, 'WTO Agreement on Import-Licensing Procedures' in *Guide to the WTO and GATT* (Springer, 2018)

Kuhn T, Pestow R and Zenker A, 'Building Climate Coalitions on Preferential Trade Agreements' (2019) 74(2) Environmental and Resource Economics 539

Lange B, 'Command and Control Standards and Cross-jurisdictional Harmonization' in E Lees and JE Viñuales (eds), *The Oxford Handbook of Comparative Environmental Law* (Oxford University Press, 2019)

Leonelli GC, 'The Long and Winding Road Towards the Creation of Climate Clubs: Transatlantic Negotiations, Potential Regulatory Models and Challenges Ahead' (2023) 32 RECIEL 453

Lydgate E, 'Climate Equivalence and International Trade' (2023) 22(3–4) World Trade Review 484

Marcu A, Mehling M and Cosbey A, *Border Carbon Adjustments in the EU: Issues and Options*, (ERCTS Roundtable On Climate Change and Sustainable Transition, 2020) <https://ercst.org/border-carbon-adjustments-in-the-eu-issues-and-options> accessed 3 April 2024

Matsushita M, Schoenbaum TJ, and Mavroidis PC, *The World Trade Organization: Law, Practice and Policy* (Oxford University Press 2006)

Mavroidis PC, 'Last Mile for Tuna (to a Safe Harbour): What Is the TBT Agreement All About?' (2019) 30(1) European Journal of International Law 279 <https://doi.org/10.1093/ejil/chz002>

McLure C, 'A Primer on the Legality of Border Adjustments for Carbon Prices: Through a GATT Darkly' (2011) 5(4) Carbon & Climate Law Review 456 <https://doi.org/10.21552/CCLR/2011/4/193>

Meckling J and Jenner S, 'Varieties of Market-Based Policy: Instrument Choice in Climate Policy' (2016) 25(5) Environmental Politics 853

Mehling M, 'Implementing Climate Governance: Instrument Choice and Interaction' in EJ Hollo, K Kulovesi and M Mehling (eds), *Climate Change and the Law* (Springer 2013)

— and others, 'Designing Border Carbon Adjustments for Enhanced Climate Action' (2019) 113(3) American Journal of International Law 433

Melin M, 'The Climate Club Approach: The Key to Effective Climate Change Negotiations?' (2020) <https://urn.fi/URN:NBN:fi:aalto-202009275605> accessed 4 April 2024

Metcalf GE, 'Carbon Taxes in Theory and Practice' (2021) 13 Annual Review of Resource Economics 245, <https://doi.org/10.1146/annurev-resource-102519-113630>

Michaud C and others, 'Willingness to Pay for Environmental Attributes of Non-Food Agricultural Products: A Real Choice Experiment' (2013) 40 European Review of Agricultural Economics 313 <https://doi.org/10.1093/ERAE/JBS025>

Monjon S and Quirion P, 'Addressing Leakage in the EU ETS: Border Adjustment or Output-Based Allocation?' (2011) 70(11) Ecological Economics 1957

Munro J, 'Carbon Units and Emissions Trading Schemes' in *Emissions Trading Schemes under International Economic Law* (Oxford University Press 2018)

Nielsen L, 'Border Carbon Adjustments, the UNFCCC, and WTO Rules' (Proceedings of the Annual Meeting American Society of International Law, International Law As Law 2009)

Nordhaus W, 'Climate Clubs: Overcoming Free-Riding in International Climate Policy' (2015) 105(4) American Economic Review 1339.

— 'The Climate Club: How to Fix a Failing Global Effort' (2020) 20 Journal of Environmental Economics and Policy 1.

— 'Dynamic Climate Clubs: On the Effectiveness of Incentives in Global Climate Agreements', (2021) 118 (45) Proceedings of the National Academy of Sciences, <https://doi.org/10.1073/pnas.2109988118>

Organization for Economic Cooperation and Development (OECD), *Climate, and Carbon: Aligning Prices and Policies* (2013)

Oliveira TD, Gurgel AC, and Tonry S, 'International Market Mechanisms under the Paris Agreement: A Cooperation between Brazil and Europe' (2019) 129 Energy Policy 397

Owen D and Noblet C, 'Interdisciplinary Research and Environmental Law' (2014) 41(4) Ecology Law Quarterly 887

Ölander F and Thøgersen J, 'Informing Versus Nudging in Environmental Policy' (2014) 37 Journal of Consumer Policy 341 <https://doi.org/10.1007/s10603-014-9256-2>

Pauwelyn J and Kleimann D, *Trade Related Aspects of a Carbon Border Adjustment Mechanism: Legal Assessment* (Study for the EU Parliament 2020) <https://www.europarl.europa.eu/RegData/etudes/BRIE/2020/603502/EXPO_BRI(2020)603502_EN.pdf> accessed 4 April 2024.

Pigou AC, *The Economics of Welfare* (Macmillan 1920)

Pihl H, 'A Climate Club as a Complementary Design to the UN Paris Agreement' (2020) 3(1) Policy Design and Practice 45, <https://doi.org/10.1080/25741292.2019.1710911>

Pirlot A, 'Environmental Taxes' in T Cottier and K Nadakavukaren Schefer (eds), *Elgar Encyclopaedia of International Economic Law* (Edward Elgar 2017)

—, 'Carbon Border Adjustment Measures: A Straightforward Multi-Purpose Climate Change Instrument?' (2022) 34 Journal of Environmental Law 25

Porterfield MC, 'Carbon Import Fees and the WTO' (2023), <https://clcouncil.org/summaries/Executive_Summary_Carbon_Import_Fees_and_the_WTO.pdf> accessed 4 April 2024.

Posner RA, *Economic Analysis of Law* (Aspen Legal Education 2014)

Potoski M, 'Green Clubs in Building Block Climate Change Regimes' (2017) 144 Climatic Change 53 <https://doi.org/10.1007/s10584-015-1517-9>

Report of the GATT Working Party on Border Tax Adjustment, adopted on 2 December 1970, L/3464

Rhodes E, Scott WA, and Jaccard M, 'Designing Flexible Regulations to Mitigate Climate Change: A Cross-Country Comparative Policy Analysis' (2021) 156 Energy Policy 112419 <https://doi.org/10.1016/j.enpol.2021.112419>

Roser D and Tomlinson L, 'Trade Policies and Climate Change – Border Carbon Adjustments as a Tool for a Just Global Climate Regime' (2014) Ancilla Iuris 223

Rutherford AP, 'Linking Emissions Trading Schemes: Lessons from the EU-Swiss ETSs' (2014) CCLR 282

Schefer KN and Arnaiz P, 'Duty to Protect, Climate Change and Trade in P Delimatsis (ed) *Research Handbook on Climate Change and Trade* (Edward Elgar 2016)

Sinn HW, 'Introductory Comment-The Green Paradox: A Supply-Side View of the Climate Problem' (2015) 9 Review of Environmental Economics and Policy 239

Stavins RN, 'The Problem of the Commons: Still Unsettled after 100 Years' (2011) 101 American Economic Review 81

— and Jaffe J, *Linking Tradable Permit Systems for Greenhouse Gas Emissions: Opportunities, Implications, and Challenges* (International Emissions Trading Association (IETA) and Electric Power Research Institute (EPRI), Geneva 2007)

Stern N, 'The Economics of Climate Change' (2008) 98(2) The American Economic Review 1

— and Lankes HP, *Collaborating and Delivering on Climate Action Through a Climate Club: An Independent Report to the G7* (London School of Economics and Political Science, 2022)

Stewart RB and others, 'Building Blocks for Global Climate Protection' (2013) 32 Stanford Environmental Law Journal 34

Stiglitz J, 'Overcoming the Copenhagen Failure with Flexible Commitments' (2015) 4(2) Economics of Energy and Environmental Policy

Sussman F, Weaver CP and Grambsch A, 'Challenges in Applying the Paradigm of Welfare Economics to Climate Change' (2014) 5(3) Journal of Benefit-Cost Analysis 347, <https://doi.org/10.1515/jbca-2014-9001>

Thøgersen J, 'Promoting Green Consumer Behavior with Eco-Labels' in Thomas Dietz and Paul C. Stern (eds), *New Tools for Environmental Protection: Education, Information, and Voluntary Measures* (National Academy Press, 2002)

Tvinnereim E and Mehling M, 'Carbon Pricing and Deep Decarbonization' (2018) 121 Energy Policy 185

Unterhalter D, 'On Interpretation and Economic Analysis of Law' in T Carpenter, M Jansen, and J Pauwelyn (eds), *The Use of Economics in International Trade and Investment Disputes* (Cambridge University Press 2017)

United Nations Trade and Development (UNCTAD), Making Trade Work for Climate Change Mitigation: The Case of Technical Regulations UNCTAD/DITC/TAB/2022/7 (United Nations publication 2022)

— and United Nations Economic and Social Commission for Asia and the Pacific, 'Trade Regulations for Climate Action? New Insights from the Global Non-Tariff Measures Database' (Geneva 2023) UNCTAD/DITC/TAB/2023/5

Vranes E, *Trade and the Environment. Fundamental Issues in International Law, WTO Law and Legal Theory* (Oxford University Press 2009)

— 'Carbon Taxes, PPMs and the GATT' in P Delimatsis (eds) *Research Handbook on Climate Change and Trade* (Edward Elgar 2016)

Weber RH, 'Innovative Taxation Strategies Supporting Climate Change Resilience', in L Kreiser and others (eds), *Environmental Taxation and Climate Change: Achieving Environmental Sustainability through Fiscal Policy* (Edward Elgar Publishing, 2011)

—, 'Emission Trading Schemes: A Coasean Answer to Climate Change?' in K Mathis and BR Huber (eds), *Environmental Law and Economics* (4th edn Springer, 2017)

Weisbach DA, 'Carbon Taxation in the EU: Expanding the EU Carbon Price' (2012) 24(2) Journal of Environmental Law 183 <https://doi.org/10.1093/jel/eqr033>

Wiel S and McMahon JE, *Energy-Efficiency Labels and Standards: A Guidebook for Appliances, Equipment, and Lighting* (2nd edn, U.S. Department of Energy Office of Scientific and Technical Information Technical Report, 2005) <https://doi.org/10.2172/877316>

Winter J, 'The Challenge of Border Carbon Adjustments as a Mechanism for Climate Clubs' (2023) 2(2) PLOS Climate <https://doi.org/10.1371/journal.pclm.0000135>

World Trade Organization (WTO), Committee on Trade and Environment, 'Taxes and Charges for Environmental Purposes, Border Tax Adjustment, Note by Secretariat' WTO Doc WT/CTE/W/47 (2 May 1997)

— Committee on Trade and Environment, Note by the Secretariat, Market Access Impact of Eco-Labelling Requirements, Doc. No. 98-0962, WT/CTE/W/79, (9 March 1998) <https://docs.wto.org/dol2fe/Pages/SS/directdoc.aspx?filename=Q:/WT/CTE/W79.pdf&Open=True> accessed 31 May 2024

— 'Environmental Database for 2020' (2022) Note by the Secretariat WT/CTE/ EDB/20

Young KM, Gurganus K, and Raymond L, 'Framing Market-based Versus Regulatory Climate Policies: A Comparative Analysis' (2022) 39(6) Review of Policy Research 798

Zapf M, Pengg H, and Weindl C. 'How to Comply with the Paris Agreement Temperature Goal: Global Carbon Pricing According to Carbon Budgets' (2019) 12(15) Energies 2983 <https://doi.org/10.3390/en12152983>

Open Access This chapter is licensed under the terms of the Creative Commons Attribution 4.0 International License (http://creativecommons.org/licenses/by/4.0/), which permits use, sharing, adaptation, distribution and reproduction in any medium or format, as long as you give appropriate credit to the original author(s) and the source, provide a link to the Creative Commons license and indicate if changes were made.

The images or other third party material in this chapter are included in the chapter's Creative Commons license, unless indicated otherwise in a credit line to the material. If material is not included in the chapter's Creative Commons license and your intended use is not permitted by statutory regulation or exceeds the permitted use, you will need to obtain permission directly from the copyright holder.

Chapter 6
Legality of the Climate Club Scheme

1 Compatibility with the Paris Agreement

1.1 Background

The climate club should not lead to violation of obligations arising from other international agreements. In particular, adherence to the UNFCCC principles[1] and the Paris Agreement rules is paramount, given their central roles in shaping the international climate governance framework. Therefore, the Paris Agreement principles, such as the facilitation of global cooperation,[2] the encouragement of ambitious actions,[3] and the commitment to limit global temperature increase,[4] should guide the activities and objectives of the climate club. Compliance with these principles enhances the club's legitimacy and reinforces its contribution to the overarching climate goals set by the international community. Since climate-related market mechanisms constitute a central aspect of the climate club as linkages, it is required to analyse them through the provisions related to carbon trading and market mechanisms under the Paris Agreement.

The interest in carbon trading and mechanisms under the Paris Agreement builds on experiences gained with the CDM, the Voluntary Carbon Market (VCM) and Reducing Emissions from Deforestation and Forest Degradation (REDD+) under

[1] United Nations Framework Convention on Climate Change, 1771 U.N.T.S. 107, 165; S. Treaty Doc No. 102-38 (1992); U.N. Doc. A/AC.237/18 (Part II)/Add.1; 31 I.L.M. 849 (hereinafter UNFCCC,) arts 3(1), (2), (3), (4), (5), 4.

[2] Conference of Parties (COP), 'Decision 1/CP.21 Adoption of the Paris Agreement' (12 December 2015) U.N. Doc. FCCC/CP/2015/L.9/Rev.1 (hereinafter Paris Agreement), art 6 (1).

[3] ibid art 4(3).

[4] ibid art 2(1)(a).

© The Author(s) 2025

T. G. Budak, *Beyond Treaties: Rethinking Legal Mechanisms for International Climate Governance*, https://doi.org/10.1007/978-3-031-86022-5_6

the Kyoto Protocol.[5] Furthermore, this perspective is reinforced by the conviction that carbon finance, defined as the income generated from the sale of carbon credits, plays a crucial role in enabling countries to fulfil their international climate commitments, domestic sustainable development and green growth goals.[6] Therefore, the concept of carbon markets has proven resilient by fostering collaboration, incentivising emission reductions, and providing a flexible framework for countries to meet their climate goals.[7] While the success of these initiatives depends on subsequent negotiations and countries' active participation, their establishment demonstrated the evolving nature of international climate policy.

International carbon markets' continued development and refinement remain crucial as the world grapples with the urgent need to address climate change. The Sixth Assessment Report of the IPCC concluded that investment in low-carbon development must increase three to six times.[8] In this regard, international carbon trading under Article 6 of the Paris Agreement offers countries the opportunity to cooperate for reducing GHG emissions in a more cost-efficient manner. It offers a framework for governments, businesses, and civil society to work together with integrity towards achieving the transformative scale necessary to meet the objectives of the Paris Agreement. Within this framework, mitigation activities form the foundation of carbon trading, encompassing projects, programs, and policies aimed at reducing emissions and producing tangible benefits for the environment, economy, and social development. When designed effectively, these mitigation activities emerge as vital opportunities for green growth by creating a new revenue stream through the sale of carbon credits. Consequently, Article 6 of the Paris Agreement has the potential to reduce mitigation costs and significantly increase climate ambition, especially if the savings realized are reinvested into further mitigation efforts.

---

[5] Sebastian Lang, Mareike Blum and Sina Leipold, 'What Future for the Voluntary Carbon Offset Market after Paris? An Explorative Study Based on the Discursive Agency Approach' (2019) 19(4) Climate Policy 414. Rajamani and Werksman (n 193) 506.

[6] United Nations Framework Convention on Climate Change (UNFCCC), 'Achievements of the Clean Development Mechanism 2001–2018: Harnessing Incentive for Climate Action' (UNFCCC 2018), 3 <https://unfccc.int/sites/default/files/resource/UNFCCC_CDM_report_2018.pdf> accessed 20 May 2024.

[7] Michael A Mehling, Gilbert E Metcalf, and Robert N Stavins, *Linking Heterogeneous Climate Policies (Consistent with the Paris Agreement)* (Discussion Paper, ES 17-6 Harvard Project on Climate Agreements, October 2017).

[8] Intergovernmental Panel on Climate Change (IPCC) 'Summary for Policymakers in Climate Change 2022: Mitigation of Climate Change. Contribution of Working Group III to the Sixth Assessment Report of the Intergovernmental Panel on Climate Change' (2022), 51 <https://www.ipcc.ch/report/ar6/wg3/downloads/report/IPCC_AR6_WGIII_SummaryForPolicymakers.pdf> accessed 24 March 2024.

1.2 Article 6.1: A Catalyser of International Cooperation

The Paris Agreement in 2015 integrated international carbon markets into its realm with Article 6. Article 6 aims to provide a framework for voluntary international cooperation in achieving emission reduction targets. It replaces previous carbon trading schemes with cooperative approaches and sustainable development mechanisms.[9] Given the use of market approaches and bilateral cooperation, carbon market under Article 6 involves a delicate mix of commerce and diplomacy. Due to its complex nature, COP meetings have been focused on developing rules and guidance for implementing Article 6. A significant milestone in this ongoing process was reached at COP 26 in 2021, where the Article 6 Rulebook was adopted.[10] The negotiations have addressed critical issues, including the prevention of double counting, transparent accounting of emissions reductions, and mechanisms to uphold environmental integrity and economic safeguards. This development marks the completion of the Paris Agreement Rulebook, which allows parties to move forward with the implementation in all areas.[11]

Around half of the NDCs make reference to the use of cooperative approaches or international carbon trading.[12] Hence, Article 6 has the potential to be widely applied. However, its importance has not yet been fully demonstrated through action. Despite adopting the Rulebook, the specifics of how international carbon markets will function under the Paris Agreement are still being negotiated. As of now, Article 6 has not yet reached its full operational potential, and further discussions and negotiations are expected to continue in subsequent COP meetings. Nevertheless, there is an expectation that Article 6 will play a vital role in catalysing emission reductions, promoting sustainable development, and fostering a collective response to the pressing environmental issues outlined in the Paris Agreement. Therefore, future negotiations within the realm of Article 6 can enable the creation of the climate club and justify minilateral cooperation.

The opening paragraph of Article 6 in the Paris Agreement constitutes a cornerstone for the trajectory of global climate governance due to its explicit recognition of voluntary cooperation among Parties.[13] It states that "Parties recognise that some Parties choose to pursue voluntary cooperation in the implementation of their NDCs to allow for higher ambition in their mitigation and adaptation actions and to promote sustainable development and environmental integrity". This paragraph

---

[9] Shuai Gao and others, 'International Carbon Markets Under the Paris Agreement: Basic Form and Development Prospects' (2019) 10 Advances in Climate Change Research 21, 23.

[10] UNFCCC, Glasgow Climate Pact. UNFCCC Decision 1/CMA.3. (2021).

[11] Stephen Minas, 'Market Making for the Planet: The Paris Agreement Article 6 Decisions and Transnational Carbon Markets' (2022) 13 Transnational Legal Theory 287.

[12] World Bank Group and Ecofys, *State and Trends of Carbon Pricing 2018* (The World Bank, Washington, DC, May 2018).

[13] Carley Chavara and others, 'Continuity and Change in Carbon Market Politics' in Jeannie Sowers and others (eds), *The Oxford Handbook of Comparative Environmental Politics* (Oxford University Press 2021), 428.

establishes a normative framework that fosters diverse collaborative approaches within the Paris Agreement. Voluntary cooperation and the pursuit of higher ambition in climate action form a crucial link to the innovative concept of climate club within the realm of global climate governance. The recognition that "some Parties choose to pursue voluntary cooperation" catalyses the formation of alliances, where like-minded countries can collaborate under the climate club approach to amplify their collective impact.

The acknowledgement of voluntary cooperation suggests a departure from a strictly individualistic approach,[14] recognising that collective efforts may yield more significant outcomes. Thereby, it unlocks the potential for heightened ambition in mitigation and adaptation actions. Within this framework, the term "ambition raising" pertains to the enhancement of emissions reduction goals, both in the magnitude of deviation from usual business practices and in the broadening of the sectors covered by the NDCs.[15] Therefore, the potential for voluntary cooperation aligns seamlessly with the underlying logic of the climate club, which envisions groups of countries coming together to pursue shared climate goals. Similar to Article 6.1, climate club operates on the premise that collaboration can drive more ambitious and effective outcomes than sole individual efforts. As a result, climate clubs can emerge as dynamic entities within the Paris Agreement framework.

Besides, Article 6.1 implicitly underscores that cooperative approaches should not be isolated endeavours but should be connected to sustainable development objectives.[16] In doing so, it advocates for an integrated approach where climate policies are woven into national and global development agendas. This alignment ensures that efforts to combat climate change are not pursued at the expense of other critical development priorities but rather complement and reinforce broader socio-economic aspirations. These co-benefits could include better air quality, improved waste management, reduced electricity prices, less dependence on fossil fuels, green technology transfers, and green job creation. The integration of sustainable development and environmental integrity in the paragraph aligns with the broader objectives of the climate club. The club characterised the climate change problem as a development problem. Therefore, it is to be designed not only to advance climate goals but also to address broader sustainable development challenges.

In essence, the opening paragraph of Article 6 paves the way for the emergence of the climate club by recognising the value of voluntary cooperation among Parties to achieve higher ambition in climate action. It lays the groundwork for a new

---

[14] See nationally determined contributions (Paris Agreement Article 3 and 4) under Sect. 4.1 in Chap. 2.

[15] Andrew Howard, 'Incentivizing Mitigation: Using International Carbon Markets to Raise Ambition' (Federal Ministry for the Environment, Nature Conservation & Nuclear Safety of Germany 2018) 9–14, <https://www.carbonmechanisms.de/fileadmin/media/dokumente/Publikationen/Studie/Studie_2018_KoruClimate_Incentivizing.pdf> accessed 4 April 2024.

[16] Tomoaki Nishimura, 'The Paris Agreement: Continuity and Change within the Climate Regime' in Neil Craikand others (eds), *Global Environmental Change and Innovation in International Law* (Cambridge University Press, 2018), 52.

paradigm in global climate governance, where cooperative approaches are actively encouraged to amplify ambition. However, it remains to be seen if Article 6 will create a liquid carbon market and realise emission abatement beyond the level required for political statements. But indeed, Article 6 can become instrumental in shaping a collaborative and integrated approach to climate governance as the climate club approach gains prominence.

Article 6 of the Paris Agreement introduces three primary mechanisms in its following paragraphs. They are Cooperative Approaches (CAs) in Article 6.2, and Sustainable Development Mechanism (SDM) in Article 6.4 and Non-Market Approaches in Article 6.8. These mechanisms not only align with the overarching goals of the Paris Agreement but also provide a pragmatic framework for countries to navigate the intricacies of meeting their NDCs in an economically viable and environmentally impactful way.[17] Parties can also employ them to fulfil other international mitigation purposes. With market and non-market mechanisms, the Paris Agreement embraces the idea that countries can employ diverse strategies to achieve their climate goals while contributing to the broader objectives of sustainable development.[18]

1.3 Article 6.2 and 6.4: Carbon Market Instruments

Under Article 6.2,[19] the CAs bring a new basis for the common mitigation scheme with the internationally transferred mitigation outcomes (ITMOs) or the concept of carbon credits exchange.[20] The issuance of ITMOs can be agreed between the

[17] James Edmonds and others, 'How Much Could Article 6 Enhance Nationally Determined Contribution Ambition Toward Paris Agreement Goals Through Economic Efficiency?' (2021) 12 Climate Change Economics 7, <https://doi.org/10.1142/s201000782150007x> The World Bank has projected that the establishment of an international carbon market will lower the expenses associated with achieving NDCs by 32% from 2020 to 2030, translating to an annual cost reduction of USD 115 billion for countries worldwide. World Bank, Ecofys, and Vivid Economics, *State and Trends of Carbon Pricing: 2016* (IBRD/World Bank, October 2016).

[18] Karen Olsen and others, 'Sustainability Labelling as a Tool for Reporting the Sustainable Development Impacts of Climate Actions Relevant to Article 6 of the Paris Agreement' (2019) 19 International Environmental Agreements: Politics, Law and Economics 225, 227 <https://doi.org/10.1007/s10784-018-09428-1>.

[19] Article 6(2); Parties shall, where engaging on a voluntary basis in cooperative approaches that involve the use of internationally transferred mitigation outcomes towards nationally determined contributions, promote sustainable development and ensure environmental integrity and transparency, including in governance, and shall apply robust accounting to ensure, inter alia, the avoidance of double counting, consistent with guidance adopted by the Conference of the Parties serving as the meeting of the Parties to this Agreement.

[20] Sandra Greiner and Axel Michaelowa, *Cooperative Approaches under Art. 6.2 of the Paris Agreement: Status of Negotiations – Key Areas of Consensus and Contention* (Discussion Paper-January 2018) <https://climatefocus.com/publications/cooperative-approaches-under-art-62-paris-agreement/> accessed 4 April 2024.

Parties on a bilateral basis or through multilateral channels under any mitigation pathway. CAs cover all possible types of cooperation (sector-specific or activity-based) at all levels, local, national, regional, and global, as long as they involve engaging parties' authorization and use of ITMOs.[21] They allow the transfer of ITMOs between countries or even private actors or a combination thereof.[22] Under the auspices of a specific bilateral treaty, any signatory party is entitled to fulfil its NDCs through the procurement of "mitigation outcomes" achieved extraterritorially. In such arrangements, one party, the "receiver" finances "mitigation activities" that stimulate mitigation outcomes within the jurisdiction of the other party, the "transferor". These outcomes are subsequently accredited, in whole or in part, towards the NDCs of the receiver. The process through which these GHG emission reductions or removals are reallocated across national borders is designated as ITMOs. This concept at its very foundation enables an approach in which the NDCs can be fulfilled more flexible and cost-effective.

Article 6.2 mechanism recognises that the fight against climate change is a shared responsibility so that countries can complement each other's efforts through collaboration. It introduces a level of market-driven flexibility into the climate action landscape. The flexibility reflects itself in a variety of mechanisms such as direct governmental transfers, connections between emissions trading systems, or other collaborative mitigation efforts across multiple parties.[23] Also, the flexibility over prescriptiveness under Article 6.2 represent itself in the comparison with the wording of Article 6.4, which clearly states that its mechanism is "under the authority and guidance" of the CMA.[24] Whereas Articles 6.2 make no such reference and instead refer to the respective role of Parties.[25] This diversity in implementation is often driven by cost-effectiveness, as it may be more economical for one party to reduce emissions than for another party seeking to acquire ITMOs. The parties can capitalize on differences in mitigation costs for mutual benefit. The party acquiring ITMOs can do so at a lower cost than domestic reduction efforts would entail, while the transferring party benefits from financial compensation.[26] The main advantage of the exchange of ITMOs is the support among countries that face challenges in

[21] Andrei Marcu, 'Carbon Market Provisions in the Paris Agreement (Article 6)' (2016) <https://www.ceps.eu/ceps-publications/carbon-market-provisions-paris-agreement-article-6/> accessed 4 April 2024.

[22] Nicolas Kreibich and Wolfgang Obergassel, *New Paths to Policy Crediting? Challenges and Opportunities of Policy-Based Cooperation Under Article 6 of the Paris Agreement* (Wuppertal Inst. 2018) 4 <https://epub.wupperinst.org/frontdoor/deliver/index/docId/7205/file/7205_Policy_Crediting.pdf> accessed 4 April 2024.

[23] Nishimura (n 16) 51–52.

[24] Andrei Marcu, 'What is Standing in the Way of a Happy Ending Reflections on Art. 6 before SBSTA 48?' (2018) 1, 5 <https://ercst.org/what-is-standing-in-the-way-of-a-happy-ending-reflections-on-art-6-before-sbsta-48/> accessed 4 April 2024.

[25] ibid.

[26] Benito Müller, 'Article 6 Market Approaches under the Paris Agreement' (European Capacity Building Initiative 2018), 7 <https://ecbi.org/news/article-6-market-approaches-under-paris-agreement> accessed 4 April 2024.

delivering their climate goals.[27] This mechanism could significantly lower the global cost of achieving targets set in NDCs highlighting the economic and environmental potential of cross-border cooperation in climate mitigation efforts.[28]

The CAs in Article 6.2 align with the ethos of the climate club approach by fostering a collaborative spirit and enabling members to pool resources effectively. Both the climate club approach and CAs involve voluntary participation. Countries or entities choose to join the climate club or engage in cooperative measures according to their willingness to contribute to global climate efforts. Therefore, they both create a synergistic relationship and reinforce the collective mitigation efforts among their members. Climate club members can commit to ambitious climate actions beyond what they might have individually pledged under the Paris Agreement. Similarly, under Article 6.2, countries engaging in cooperative approaches aim to enhance their NDCs through trading ITMOs. By collectively contributing to and benefiting from emissions reductions, the club and CAs can achieve a more significant and sustainable impact than individual countries might attain on their own. Both approaches recognise the importance of overall efficiency and cost-effectiveness in achieving climate targets. Furthermore, they provide flexibility for countries to explore innovative solutions. The climate club allows tailored linkages to suit its members' specific needs and capabilities. Likewise, Article 6.2 enables countries to optimise their mitigation efforts by tapping into the strengths and capacities of their partners. Consequently, both the climate club and Article 6.2 share a common goal of promoting tailored mechanisms among their member countries. In summary, the CAs under Article 6.2 provide a tangible framework for the climate club to operationalise its collaborative efforts by facilitating the exchange of ITMOs. They embody the recognition that countries can optimise their resources and achieve more ambitious climate outcomes by working together within a club framework.

Second, Article 6.4[29] of the Paris Agreement establishes the SDM as a critical component for creating carbon market instruments under the framework of the Paris

[27] Kun Zhang and others, 'Recent Progress of Cooperation on Climate Mitigation: A Bibliometric Analysis' (2020) 277 Journal of Cleaner Production 123495 <https://doi.org/10.1016/j.jclepro.2020.123495>.

[28] Malin Ahlberg, 'Enhancing Ambition Carbon Pricing as a Tool to Step up Mitigation Efforts' (2018) 6 Carbon Mechanisms Review 22, 23–24.

[29] Article 6(4); A mechanism to contribute to the mitigation of greenhouse gas emissions and support sustainable development is hereby established under the authority and guidance of the Conference of the Parties serving as the meeting of the Parties to this Agreement for use by Parties on a voluntary basis. It shall be supervised by a body designated by the Conference of the Parties serving as the meeting of the Parties to this Agreement, and shall aim: (a) To promote the mitigation of greenhouse gas emissions while fostering sustainable development; (b) To incentivize and facilitate participation in the mitigation of greenhouse gas emissions by public and private entities authorized by a Party; (c) To contribute to the reduction of emission levels in the host Party, which will benefit from mitigation activities resulting in emission reductions that can also be used by another Party to fulfil its nationally determined contribution; and (d) To deliver an overall mitigation in global emissions.

Agreement.[30] This Article catalyses the integration of sustainability into carbon market activities, ensuring that climate action aligns with broader socio-economic objectives.[31] The Article encourages the use of ITMOs, provided they contribute to sustainable development objectives. One notable aspect of Article 6.4 is that it lays emphasis on the incentivizing and facilitating authorized public and private entities participation to SDM. Consequently, the SDM is opened up to various actors, which seek to credit the activities related to sustainable development. This inclusivity recognizes the efforts by different stakeholders and promotes a dynamic and cooperative forum towards the realization of the climate and development goals.

Furthermore, Article 6.4 stipulates that the global carbon market is overseen by the "Article 6.4 Supervisory Body". This Body is tasked with providing oversight and authorization for the exchange of carbon credits. It reviews the sustainable development co-benefits.[32] Parties will be able to specify certain elements, such as baseline approaches and methodologies, to be applied consistently with the guidelines of the Supervisory Body and under its supervision. Accordingly, it indicates that the Supervisory Body can override Parties' decisions if they are deemed not aligned with the guidelines. In sum, SDM allows for the efficient allocation of resources by trading emission reductions and fosters collaboration between countries under the control of the Supervisory Body.

The principles outlined in Article 6.4 and the climate club are grounded in the shared commitment to achieve climate objectives without compromising broader socio-economic concerns. Therefore, this Article provides a justifiable basis for the formation and activities of the climate club. The principles of the SDM recognise that climate action should go hand in hand with sustainable development,[33] echoing the collaborative spirit of climate club linkages, which ensure club members' economic competitiveness is not harmed. Therefore, by fostering a connection between sustainable development and emissions reduction activities, Article 6.4 substantiates the existence of climate clubs as platforms for collective action. In turn, climate clubs can leverage the SDM to operationalise. Consequently, establishing a global carbon market overseen by the "Article 6.4 Supervisory Body" can create a basis for the climate club to reinforce itself in line with the Paris Agreement's market-based mechanisms.

[30] Yves Steinebach and Julian Limberg, 'Implementing Market Mechanisms in the Paris Era: The Importance of Bureaucratic Capacity Building for International Climate Policy' (2021) 29 Journal of European Public Policy 1153.

[31] Gao and others (n 9) 22.

[32] Chaewoon Oh, 'Exploring the Way to Harmonize Sustainable Development Assessment Methods in Article 6.2 Cooperative Approaches of the Paris Agreement' (2023) 1(3) Green and Low-Carbon Economy 121, <https://doi.org/10.47852/bonviewGLCE32021065>.

[33] Laurence Boisson de Chazournes and Makane Moise Mbengue, 'The Principles of Precaution and Sustainability' in Thomas Cottier and Krista Nadakavukaren Schefer (eds), *Elgar Encyclopaedia of International Economic Law* (Edward Elgar 2017), 623.

1.4 Article 6.8: Non-Market Approaches

Article 6.8 of the Paris Agreement is pertinent to enhancing further climate action with the promotion of non-market approaches as an element GHG reductions.[34] Article 6.8 underscores the importance of balanced approach that goes beyond market mechanisms, while recognizing the essential role for carbon markets and emissions trading in facilitating cost-effective reductions in emissions. Therefore, it supports climate mitigation, through non-market approaches, which are meant to address climate change by strategies and actions that are not directly about emissions trading. Such approaches may include policy measures, technological deployment, capacity-building initiatives, and joint efforts.[35] As in the Article 6.4, the non-market approaches also address the issue of balancing emissions reduction with development objectives. Essentially, it supports the spirit of the Paris Agreement and mirrors an approach which has the concern to address the environmental challenges while also seeking the social and economic well-being in an integrated manner.

1.5 Climate Club as a Cooperative Approach Under Article 6

In essence, Article 6 is founded on the balanced application of market and non-market approaches due to the complexity of climate change, and the rather insufficiency of the sole market approach. It thus delivers an all-encompassing mechanism that combines carbon markets, cooperative mechanisms, and non-market approaches under a single framework governing the ITMOs.[36] This comprehensive structure is critically important in the transfer of the global mitigation results between the frameworks, mechanisms, and protocols under and beyond the UNFCCC scheme. This inclusivity of Article 6 fosters the ambition of cross-border cooperation ensuring benefits that accrue from carbon abatement policies are shared among countries.

[34] Article 6(8); Parties recognize the importance of integrated, holistic and balanced non-market approaches being available to Parties to assist in the implementation of their nationally determined contributions, in the context of sustainable development and poverty eradication, in a coordinated and effective manner, including through, inter alia, mitigation, adaptation, finance, technology transfer and capacity building, as appropriate. These approaches shall aim to: (a) Promote mitigation and adaptation ambition; (b) Enhance public and private sector participation in the implementation of nationally determined contributions; and (c) Enable opportunities for coordination across instruments and relevant institutional arrangements. Majid Asadnabizadeh, 'Development of UN Framework Convention on Climate Change Negotiations Under COP25: Article 6 of the Paris Agreement Perspective' (2019) 2 Open Political Science 113.

[35] Easwaran Narassimhan and others, 'Carbon Pricing in Practice: A Review of Existing Emissions Trading Systems' (2018) 18 Climate Policy 967.

[36] Michele Stua, Colin Nolden and Michael Coulon, 'Climate Clubs Embedded in Article 6 of the Paris Agreement' (2022) 180 Resources, Conservation and Recycling 106178, 2 <https://doi.org/10.1016/j.resconrec.2022.106178>.

Additionally, Article 6 enhances the possibility of market-based mechanisms' linkage in the national, regional, and international jurisdictions.

Therefore, even though the Paris Agreement has not set a global carbon price, with the international cooperation under Article 6, it has created a foundation for the proliferation of market-based mechanisms.[37] This Article has become a pivotal component for countries seeking to deploy market instruments in their efforts to address climate change. However, challenges persist in fully leveraging these mechanisms due to the lack of a robust accountability scheme and the voluntary nature of the Paris Agreement.[38] Therefore, the success of CAs and SDMs relies heavily on bilateral agreements or alternative forms of cooperation between countries. This situation introduces a level of uncertainty and variability in the implementation and enforcement of market-based mechanisms. Therefore, the operationalization of Article 6 hinges on the preparedness of participating countries, primarily because it requires these nations to establish institutional frameworks that are capable of authorizing and facilitating the transfer of ITMOs.

Consequently, political stability constitutes an essential prerequisite for Article 6 structure. Participation in the carbon market under CAs requires governments to make critical decisions on foundational aspects that are pivotal for the facilitation of carbon trading.[39] Firstly, governments must carefully select the activities, sectors, and technologies that will serve as sources for generating ITMOs. Equally crucial is the determination of the price of ITMOs. Establishing a clear and transparent pricing mechanism is essential for fostering confidence among market participants and encouraging sustained engagement in carbon trading.[40] The institution responsible for managing these transactions plays a crucial role in preventing over-selling risks and leveraging the potential of Article 6 to drive more ambitious climate action. Furthermore, the private sector, a vital player in the carbon market, has demonstrated an eagerness to engage; however, concerns such as regulatory, market, and capacity risks, along with a sense of inequity in the trading process, have tempered their enthusiasm, especially in the market's early phases.[41] Addressing these concerns is paramount for unlocking the full potential of CAs and ensuring that the benefits of carbon trading are equitably distributed within communities.

---

[37] Thais Diniz Oliveira, Angelo Costa Gurgel, and Steve Tonry, 'International Market Mechanisms under the Paris Agreement: A Cooperation between Brazil and Europe' (2019) 129 Energy Policy 397, 398.

[38] David Bullock, 'Combating Climate Recalcitrance: Carbon-Related Border Tax Adjustments in a New Era of Global Climate Governance' (2018) 27 Washington International Law Journal 609, 616.

[39] Christina Voigt, 'The Compliance and Implementation Mechanism of the Paris Agreement' (2016) 25(2) Review of European, Comparative & International Environmental Law 162–165.

[40] Bullock (n 38) 616.

[41] Justin D Macinante and others, 'Operationalizing Cooperative Approaches Under the Paris Agreement by Valuing Mitigation Outcomes' (2018) 12 Carbon and Climate Law Review 258, <https://doi.org/10.21552/cclr/2018/3/12>.

Since the adoption of the Article 6 rulebook, there has been a substantial increase in global efforts to harness CAs and market mechanisms for climate mitigation. However, decentralised CAs can create a patchwork of different standards and approaches. This inconsistency will highlight the need for further developments in creating a more standardised and accountable framework for market-based mechanisms. Additionally, there is a consensus among Parties and other relevant institutions that additional capacity building and technical support is required for many countries to be able to engage in carbon trade.[42] Consequently, to activate Article 6 mechanisms, political willpower needs to incline towards the opportunities and benefits of engaging in the carbon market. The Paris Agreement Parties should build institutions to regulate and establish governance frameworks and integrate a comprehensive "toolbox".[43]

Therefore, cooperation schemes under Article 6 can be clustered like climate clubs. The inherent flexibility, cooperation, and accountability design of Article 6 has already given rise to a membership pattern reminiscent of the climate club. The encouragement for collaboration across borders aligns with the cooperative spirit of the climate club, where like-minded countries voluntarily join forces to pursue shared climate goals. The climate club based on Article 6 can provide a platform for countries to navigate the complexities of international CAs. It can enable more tailored and flexible collaborations associated with participating countries' diverse needs and circumstances. Notably, the clubs may play a role in overcoming challenges related to accountability and enforcement by establishing shared standards and mechanisms for monitoring and reporting.

The recognition of climate clubs based on Article 6 of the Paris Agreement as a means of unlocking climate ambition and fostering broad participation is gaining traction among international organizations, including the World Bank.[44] This perspective reflects an understanding of the climate club's potential to trigger ambitious climate action and engage with a diverse range of actors to combat climate change. The efforts to operationalise Article 6 as a climate club can catalyse the spread of worldwide carbon markets and carbon pricing instruments. The international carbon market holds the potential to direct financial flows towards climate solutions, mobilize investments, and lower the costs for countries and companies engaged in the transition to low-carbon alternatives. Article 6 operationalization is currently dominated by early movers among the public sector in countries such as

[42] Michael A Mehling, 'Governing the Carbon Market' in Alastair Marke, Michael Mehling, and Fabiano de Andrade Correa (eds), *Governing Carbon Markets with Distributed Ledger Technology* (Cambridge University Press 2022), 25.

[43] Steinebach and Limberg (n 30) 1153.

[44] Sandhya Srinivasan and Florencia Sanchez Zunino, 'Unlocking Ambition Through a Climate Market Club' (World Bank Blogs, 2020) <https://blogs.worldbank.org/en/climatechange/unlocking-ambition-through-climate-market-club> accessed on 26 March 2024.

Switzerland.[45] The Swiss government proactively uses ITMOs to fulfil its NDC targets and has signed 13 bilateral agreements.[46]

In addition to the detailed framework provided by the Paris Agreement, the UNFCCC also emphasises cooperation in combating climate change under Article 3(5). The Article acknowledges the potential limitations of emissions abatement efforts. Thus, it leaves a window open for countries to consider unilateral measures in their climate strategies.[47] This provision underscores the flexibility inherent in the UNFCCC framework. Article 3(5) recognises that while global cooperation is crucial, individual nations may need to take independent actions to address climate change based on their unique circumstances, priorities, and capabilities. Therefore, it allows countries to implement climate-related trade policies that align with their national goals and circumstances. However, Article 3(5) states that "measures taken to combat climate change, including unilateral ones, should not constitute a means of arbitrary or unjustifiable discrimination or a disguised restriction on international trade". Thus, the legality of such measures will depend on analysing the WTO Agreements and how restrictive they are to free trade. This illustrates a 'cohesive polycentric legal structure that constitutes the backbone of the international environmental governance system'.[48] Consequently, Article 3(5) indirectly encourages countries to take ambitious actions even without comprehensive global agreements.[49] This encouragement aligns with the ambition-driven nature of the climate club, where members voluntarily commit to more ambitious climate goals.

Derived from these explanations, the best option to ensure the legitimacy of the climate club is to establish and host it under the aegis of the Paris Agreement, which is convenient to accommodate the alternative minilateral approaches.[50] The Paris Agreement is a universally accepted and legally binding treaty.[51] As a cornerstone

---

[45] Federal Office for the Environment, 'Bilateral Climate Agreements' <https://www.bafu.admin.ch/bafu/en/home/topics/climate/info-specialists/climate%2D%2Dinternational-affairs/staatsvertraege-umsetzung-klimauebereinkommen-von-paris-artikel6.html> accessed 4 April 2024.

[46] Johannes Reich and Nina Boss, 'E. Switzerland' (2022) 33 Yearbook of International Environmental Law 149, 151 <https://doi.org/10.1093/yiel/yvad032> Flora Hausammann and Johannes Reich, 'E. Switzerland' (2021) 32 Yearbook of International Environmental Law 145, 148–149 <https://doi.org/10.1093/yiel/yvac051>.

[47] UNFCCC, art 3(5). When the international cooperation is falling short on providing satisfying results, states tend to resort to unilateral action, frequently in the form of trade measures. Thomas Cottier and Tetyana Payosova, 'Common Concern and Legitimacy of the WTO in Dealing with Climate Change' in Panagiotis Delimatsis (ed) *Research Handbook on Climate Change and Trade* (Edward Elgar 2016), 22.

[48] Rakhyun Kim, 'The Emergent Network Structure of the Multilateral Environmental Agreement System' (2013) 23(5) Global Environmental Change 980, 988.

[49] Michael Hertel, 'Climate-Change-Related Trade Measures and Article XX: Defining Discrimination in Light of the Principle of Common but Differentiated Responsibilities' (2011) 45(3) JWT 653, 662.

[50] Daniel Bodansky, 'Legal Form of a New Climate Agreement: Avenues and Options' (Pew Center on Global Climate Change, Arlington, VA, 2009).

[51] See Sect. 4.1 in Chap. 2.

of international climate governance, it provides a legitimate and recognised platform for climate clubs to operate. Therefore, aligning the climate club with the Paris Agreement's goals and principles provides a strong foundation for the club's credibility and acceptance by the global community. This alignment ensures that the club's activities and commitments resonate with the broader international climate framework. It not only enhances the legitimacy of the climate club but also fosters coherence and synergy with global climate objectives.

In addition to conferring legitimacy, affiliating the climate club with the Paris Agreement offers the practical advantage of leveraging the administrative system and resources of the UNFCCC.[52] This access simplifies managing climate clubs' logistical and administrative requirements, including record-keeping, reporting, and coordination. Moreover, this affiliation allows the climate club to tap into the expertise and support mechanisms established by the UNFCCC. Access to the administrative resources of the UNFCCC streamlines operational aspects and minimises duplication of efforts. By utilising the present infrastructure, the climate club benefits from established processes and frameworks, facilitating smoother organization and oversight of its activities. In sum, aligning the climate club with the framework of the Paris Agreement ensures its legitimacy on the global stage and provides a pragmatic and efficient mechanism for administrative support.

1.5.1 The Climate Club Initiative at COP 28

1.5.1.1 Background

As a significant development, during their meetings in June 2022, the G7 countries agreed to establish a climate club.[53] This announcement serves as empirical evidence supporting the potential establishment of a climate club. In this regard, the G7 members demonstrated their commitment to leading by example in the global fight against climate change.[54] They envisaged a platform where countries, regardless of their economic status, could join forces in committing to higher environmental standards.[55] This initiative can facilitate a global shift towards renewable energy sources,

[52] For example, COP under Article 7, Subsidiary Body for Scientific and Technological Advice under Article 9, Subsidiary Body for Implementation under Article 10, Permanent Secretariat under Article 8 of the UNFCCC.

[53] G7 Germany, 'Statement on Climate Club Elmau' (28 June 2022) https://www.g7germany.de/resource/blob/974430/2057926/2a7cd9f10213a481924492942dd660a1/2022-06-28-g7-climate--club-data.pdf accessed 4 April 2024.

[54] Edward B Barbier, 'The G7 Needs to Boost Its Low-Carbon Strategy-Here's How' (2023) 617 Nature 459.

[55] Nicholas Stern and Hans Peter Lankes, *Collaborating and Delivering on Climate Action Through a Climate Club: An Independent Report to the G7* (London School of Economics and Political Science, 2022) 14.

green technologies, and sustainable development practices.[56] Therefore, the "Climate Club" is seen as a way to overcome the challenges posed by unilateral actions and the limitations of existing international agreements.[57] Moreover, it provides a more dynamic and flexible framework for achieving tangible progress in climate action.

Accordingly, the COP 28 marks a pivotal moment in the global efforts against climate change, officially introducing the "Climate Club" as an initiative to accelerate industrial decarbonization. The "Climate Club" represents an innovative cooperative forum aimed at bolstering the effective implementation of the Paris Agreement, with a particular emphasis on decarbonising the industrial sectors. The "Climate Club" is envisioned as an open, cooperative, and inclusive forum. This collective comprises 35 government members and the EU, each committed to driving forward climate ambitions to achieve global net-zero GHG emissions by mid-century in line with the Paris Agreement goal.[58] The members represent 55% of the global economy.[59] The initiative's governance arrangements provide a blueprint for operationalising CAs under Article 6 of the Paris Agreement. The "Climate Club" is also designed to coordinate challenges arising from other instruments and initiatives, such as the EGD industrial plan and the US IRA.

The Club members will engage in discussions and seek collaborative efforts aimed at enhancing the measurement and reporting of emissions for sectors covered under the agreed-upon framework of the "Climate Club".[60] Simultaneously, the Club emphasises the vital role of the industry sector in global economic growth, development, and job creation. This acknowledgement reflects a holistic understanding of the climate challenge; it is not merely an environmental issue but also an economic and social one. The Club's approach is to harmonise the imperatives of environmental sustainability with those of economic vitality, ensuring that the transition towards a greener future does not compromise the prosperity and well-being of communities worldwide.

The governance document of the "Climate Club" establishes the Body of Members as the principal body, steering the Club's direction, approving work programs, and discussing any relevant matters.[61] This body is expected to meet annually

---

[56] Edward B Barbier, 'Greening the G7 Economies' (2023) 39(4) Oxford Review of Economic Policy 731–751 <https://doi.org/10.1093/oxrep/grad039>.

[57] World Bank, 'State and Trends of Carbon Pricing 2020' (World Bank, 2020) <http://hdl.handle.net/10986/33809> accessed 4 April 2024.

[58] Press Release, '36 members launch Climate Club as a high-ambition forum to turbocharge decarbonization of key industry sectors' (01 December 2023) 1 <https://climate-club.org/wp-content/uploads/2023/12/Climate-Club-COP-28-Full-Launch-Press-Release-01.12.2023-1.pdf> accessed 4 April 2024.

[59] ibid.

[60] Geraldo Vidigal, 'Designing Climate Clubs: The Four Models, Trade Commitments and the Non-Discrimination Dilemma' (2023) Amsterdam Law School Research Paper No 2023-07, 10.

[61] Climate Club, 'Governance Arrangements' (13 October, 2023), 1 <https://climate-club.org/wp-content/uploads/2023/11/20231910_Climate-Club-Governance-Arrangements_Layout.pdf> accessed 4 April 2024.

at a senior official level, with thematic working groups formed as necessary to delve into specific issues. The introduction of Co-Chairs, elected for two-year terms, ensures geographical and developmental representation in leadership and strategic direction. A Steering Group supports the Body of Members in guiding the Club, with its formation contingent on the Club reaching forty members.[62] Meanwhile, a Secretariat, initially supported by the Organization for Economic Cooperation and Development (OECD) and International Energy Agency (IEA), is tasked with implementing the work program and facilitating dialogue and outreach, which underscores the Club's commitment to efficient and effective governance.[63]

The decision-making process within the Climate Club is designed to be inclusive and consensus-based, allowing for a broad agreement among members without necessitating unanimous approval. This method permits members to abstain or record non-blocking objections, fostering a cooperative atmosphere that respects diverse viewpoints.[64] It is essential for the "Climate Club" to effectively navigate the complex landscape of international climate policy. The Club welcomes voluntary financial contributions from members to support its activities.[65] This governance approach underscores the Club's reliance on collaborative and flexible operational mechanisms to achieve its objectives.

1.5.1.2 Pillars

The Climate Club's strategy is founded on three thematic pillars. They are advancing ambitious climate mitigation policies, transforming industries, and improving international cooperation and partnerships. Overall, the Climate Club Work Programme 2024 organised nine interconnected modules under the three pillars, constituting the Club's initial scope.[66] Under the first pillar, the Club emphasises the importance of sharing best practices, developing common standards, and enhancing cooperation among members to support climate action and mitigate carbon leakage while complying with international trade rules.[67] Therefore, the Club will engage in a strategic dialogue on risks to mitigation efforts and green growth opportunities. The cooperation will be based on market and non-market-based climate mitigation tools. The Climate Club will look for synergies in different national pathways while also making domestic policies more effective and preventing double counting.[68]

---

[62] ibid.

[63] ibid 2.

[64] ibid.

[65] ibid.

[66] Climate Club Work Programme 2024, 4 <https://climate-club.org/wp-content/uploads/2023/11/CC-Work-Programme-2024_bf_final.pdf> accessed 4 April 2024.

[67] Climate Club, 'Terms of Reference', 1 https://climate-club.org/wp-content/uploads/2023/11/TOR-CC-logo.pdf accessed 4 April 2024.

[68] Statement by the Climate Club, 'Accelerating the decarbonization of our industries' (1 December 2023) 1 <https://climate-club.org/wp-content/uploads/2023/11/231122_Statement-by-the-

Moreover, the Climate Club Programme emphasises the importance of mobilising public and private finance for decarbonization efforts. It aims to bridge the gap between current practices and the urgent need for increased ambition and action to achieve net-zero emissions by 2050. In this endeavour, a critical role is given to international collaboration and stakeholder engagement. Therefore, the Club develops an industry transition toolkit and facilitates a Global Matchmaking Platform for decarbonising industries in developing countries. This inclusive matchmaking platform connects member in need of technical and financial assistance from both public and private sources.

Accordingly, the second pillar is built on transforming industries.[69] The industrial sector is pivotal in the global emissions landscape, accounting for about a quarter of total energy-related carbon emissions.[70] Three major sectors, steel, cement, and chemicals, are the primary contributors that account for around 70% of CO_2 emissions from industry.[71] Moreover, the demand for these industrial materials is projected to grow, especially in developing countries, compounding the challenge of reducing emissions.[72] Global supply is rapidly expanding to meet this demand, though most of it relies on conventional, emissions-intensive processes. Therefore, there is an urgent need for targeted decarbonization strategies in hard-to-abate industrial sectors.[73] The Club focus on advancing decarbonization in the relevant sectors. Accordingly, the policies include coordinating globally recognised emission accounting methodologies and interoperable standards to make decarbonised industrial production the default business case.[74] Also, the Club highlights the role of research and development in decarbonising hard-to-abate sectors. Therefore, the Club Work Program promotes mutual learning and exchange of effective strategies and policies.[75]

In a move to broaden its impact, under the third pillar, the Climate Club invites governments and other non-state actors to join its efforts.[76] This inclusive approach aims to unite a wide range of stakeholders in the shared goal of industrial decarbonization, which features the collective effort required to address the climate crisis effectively. The members are expected to actively work together to advance the objectives of the Club and promote them in other fora. The promoted objectives

---

Climate-Club_FINAL_Layout.pdf> accessed 4 April 2024.

[69] Climate Club Work Programme 2024 (n 66) 10.

[70] ibid 4.

[71] Interim Secretariat of the Climate Club, 'Accelerating Global Industry Decarbonization Through Stronger International Collaboration Paper', 1 <https://climate-club.org/wp-content/uploads/2023/11/Climate-Club-COP-28-background-paper.pdf> accessed 4 April 2024.

[72] ibid.

[73] International Energy Agency (IEA), 'Achieving Net Zero Heavy Industry Sectors in G7 Members' (IEA, Paris 2022) <https://www.iea.org/reports/achieving-net-zero-heavy-industry--sectors-in-g7-members> accessed 4 April 2024.

[74] Stern and Lankes (n 55) 66.

[75] Climate Club Work Programme 2024 (n 66) 17.

[76] ibid 18.

include limiting the temperature increase to 1.5 °C in line with the Paris Agreement, pledging ambitious NDCs that align with the temperature target and accelerating sectoral decarbonization.[77] Notably, the Climate Club acknowledges the unique challenges developing economies face in industrial decarbonization. Accordingly, it aims to enhance multilateral and bilateral cooperation to attract greater number of participants.

In conclusion, the "Climate Club" initiative introduced at COP 28 represents a novel and ambitious approach to tackle the significant challenge of industrial decarbonization within the broader context of global climate change mitigation efforts. By focusing on collaboration, inclusivity, and practical strategies for hard-to-abate sectors, the Club sets a precedent for international climate action that is both ambitious and achievable.[78] This progress reinforces the feasibility of climate club theorization and underscores the evolving and dynamic nature of international climate governance.[79] The fact that the world's biggest economies are exploring the establishment of a climate club indicates the need for collaborative efforts in addressing the complex challenges of climate change. Overall, the recent development of the Climate Club of COP 28 as a multilateral cooperation under the Paris Agreement Article 6 provides tangible indications for climate clubs to become integral components of the international climate regime.

1.6 Navigating Obligations Derived from Climate Club

The climate club approach and the implementation of its linkages targeting non-signatories versus signatories of the Paris Agreement presents distinct considerations. When the climate club targets a country that is not a signatory to the Paris Agreement, the club linkages would not constitute a further obligation for that country.[80] In such cases, the targeted country is not subject to the specific commitments and obligations outlined in the Paris Agreement. Here, the effectiveness of these climate-related trade measures may depend on the willingness of non-signatory countries to engage in cooperative efforts and their perception of the benefits derived from such collaboration.[81] Furthermore, fostering international cooperation with non-signatory countries can contribute to building a more inclusive global response to climate change, recognising that collaborative efforts tran-

[77] Terms of Reference (n 67) 4.

[78] Stern and Lankes (n 55) 73.

[79] Stua, Nolden and Coulon (n 36) 7.

[80] Vienna Convention on the Law of Treaties (VCLT) (adopted on 23 May 1969, entered into force on 27 January 1980) 1155 UNTS 331., art 34. Mayer, *International Law Obligations on Climate Change Mitigation* (n 239) 51.

[81] Guilherme Magacho, Etienne Espagne and Antoine Godin, 'Impacts of the CBAM on EU Trade Partners: Consequences for Developing Countries' (2024) 24(2) Climate Policy 243 <https://doi.org/10.1080/14693062.2023.2200758>.

scend formal treaty obligations and may involve diverse actors on the international stage.

The situation becomes intricate when climate club measures are directed at a party to the Paris Agreement. The ratifiers of the Paris Agreement have already committed to specific obligations based on the principle of CBDRRC.[82] The Paris Agreement recognises different economic development levels among its parties and outlines differentiated responsibilities accordingly. In this context, if a climate club imposes additional measures on a Paris Agreement ratifier, it could be interpreted as extra climate change-related obligations beyond those outlined in the Agreement. This understanding raises questions about the compatibility of such measures with the principles and commitments established under the Paris Agreement. Therefore, Parties to the Agreement may scrutinise whether these additional measures align with the principles of equity and fairness embedded in CBDRRC.

However, the Paris Agreement acknowledges its limitations by explicitly identifying itself as not a complete and exhaustive solution to the complex challenges of climate change.[83] This recognition underscores the urgency of addressing climate issues and the need for a dynamic approach to supplement the Agreement's efforts. Therefore, Parties to the Agreement have the flexibility to adopt additional measures beyond the Agreement's specified obligations to meet their climate targets.[84] This allowance reflects the Agreement's pragmatic approach, recognising that the evolving nature of the climate crisis may require tailored and adaptive responses from individual countries. It empowers countries to take ambitious actions beyond the Agreement's baseline requirements to enhance their contributions to global climate mitigation and adaptation efforts.[85] Nevertheless, it is crucial to emphasise that these extra unilateral measures should align with the overarching goals and principles of the Paris Agreement, including the pursuit of limiting global temperature increase and promoting sustainable development. Since the Agreement sets the foundation for international cooperation, any additional actions should complement, rather than undermine, the collaborative spirit of the global climate governance framework.

---

[82] See Sect. 5.2 in Chap. 4.

[83] Benoit Mayer, *International Law Obligations on Climate Change Mitigation* (Oxford University Press 2022), 119–120 and 271–272. For example, Paris Agreement, recital 15 and arts 10.2, 11.3 and 12, encourage further cooperation among Parties outside its realm.

[84] Daniel Bodansky, 'The Legal Character of the Paris Agreement' (2016) 25 RECIEL 25.

[85] See Sect. 1.2 in Chap. 4.

2 Compatibility with the WTO Law

2.1 *Setting the Legal Landscape for the Climate Change and Trade Nexus*

The climate club linkages, constitute of climate-related market mechanisms, stand at the intersection of climate change and trade law.[86] In the previous section, their compatibility with the Paris Agreement Article 6 is analysed. This section shifts attention to examining their implications under the WTO law. Even though the WTO legal structure provides parameters for legitimate actions and aims to prevent the escalation of policy disagreements into trade conflicts, there is no clear understanding on the legal implications of the interaction between trade and climate policies.[87] Considering the transboundary impacts of the climate change problem, disputes concerning climate-related market measures present complexities unparalleled by any issues previously addressed through the WTO dispute settlement mechanism.[88]

2.1.1 A Complex Interplay

Despite the accepted close affiliation between trade and environmental protection,[89] no agreement under the auspices of the WTO or UN expands the regulatory scope of these institutions to deal with this connection.[90] The WTO was criticized for narrowly interpreting the conflicts between trade and the environment.[91] Decisions of the WTO Dispute Settlement Body (DSB) have attracted significant criticism from environmental organizations towards the international trade regime.[92] The DSB

[86] WTO, Committee on Trade and Environment, 'Matrix on Trade-Related Measures Pursuant to Selected Multilateral Environmental Agreements' (6–9 October 2017) WT/CTE/W/160/Rev.8 TN/TE/S/5/Rev.

[87] Beatriz Leycegui and Imanol Ramirez, *Addressing Climate Change: A WTO Exception to Incorporate Climate Clubs* (E15 Expert Group on Measures to Address Climate Change and the Trade System, May 2015).

[88] Rodrigo Polanco, 'Integrating Trade, Investment and Climate Change' in Thomas Cottier and Krista Nadakavukaren Schefer (eds), *Elgar Encyclopedia of International Economic Law* (Edward Elgar 2017), 634.

[89] Henok Asmelash, 'The WTO Dispute Settlement System as a Forum for Climate Litigation?' (2023) 32 RECIEL 321, 330. Nathalie Bernasconi-Osterwalder, Soledad Leal Campos, and Sofia Baliño, 'Trade and Environment' in *The Elgar Companion to the World Trade Organization* (Edward Elgar Publishing 2022), 453.

[90] Cottier and Payosova (n 47) 9.

[91] Damilola S Olawuyi, 'Environment' in Daniel Bethlehem and others (eds), *The Oxford Handbook of International Trade Law* (2nd edn, Oxford University Press 2022), 681.

[92] Kati Kulovesi, *The WTO Dispute Settlement System: Challenges of the Environment, Legitimacy and Fragmentation* (Kluwer 2011) 87.

showed reluctance to incorporate non-trade concerns into its deliberations. For instance, it was exemplified by the Panel's decision in EC-Biotech, where it did not consider relevant MEA.[93] Critics argue that the WTO's trade-centric approach may not adequately accommodate the nuances of environmental concerns.[94] Specifically, climate change has remained a peripheral issue.[95] It also produces a "regulatory chill" effect in interacting with other environmental regulatory venues.[96] The fear of potential challenges under WTO rules might influence countries to adopt less stringent environmental measures, hindering the pursuit of more ambitious climate and environmental goals.[97]

Nevertheless, the Appellate Body's practice indicates a growing tendency to accommodate environmental concerns.[98] Initially, in US-Gasoline, the Appellate Body emphasized that WTO law should not be interpreted in isolation,[99] moving further in US-Shrimp utilized MEAs for clarifying the term 'exhaustible natural resources.'[100] These cases demonstrate the Appellate Body's openness to integrating

---

[93] The Panel decided against integrating WTO law with other sources of treaty-based public international law, concluding that the obligation to consider these sources was limited to rules binding on all WTO members. Panel Reports, *European Communities – Measures Affecting the Approval and Marketing of Biotech Products*, (*EC- Biotech*) WT/DS291/R, Add.1 to Add.9 and Corr.1 / WT/DS292/R, Add.1 to Add.9 and Corr.1 / WT/DS293/R, Add.1 to Add.9 and Corr.1, adopted 21 November 2006, para 7.68. Furthermore, the Panel clarified that such sources were only relevant in determining or affirming the conventional meaning of treaty terms. Consequently, it deemed the Convention on Biological Diversity and the Cartagena Protocol on Biosafety to the Convention on Biological Diversity as not 'informative' and thus decided against considering them, due to their lack of utility in this context. ibid para 7.75.

[94] The function of the WTO's DSB has predominantly been confined to interpreting the environmental exceptions stipulated in WTO agreements. Such as, in US-Gasoline, US-Shrimp and Brazil- Retreaded Tyres disputes. Asmelash (n 89) 321.

[95] In the India-Solar Cells case, India attempted, without success, to defend its local content requirements (LCRs) for renewable energy on the grounds that these measures were essential for ensuring adherence to its obligations under both national and international laws, among which are those related to climate change. Appellate Body Report, *India – Certain Measures Relating to Solar Cells and Solar Modules*, *(India-Solar Cells)* WT/DS456/AB/R and Add.1, adopted 14 October 2016. However, the measures under scrutiny in this dispute were not solely focused on promoting the adoption of renewable energy; they were also intended to support the growth of domestic renewable energy industries.

[96] Robyn Eckersley, 'The Big Chill: The WTO and Multilateral Environmental Agreements' (2004) 4 Global Environmental Politics 24. The regulatory chill between trade and environment law refers to the adoption of modest trade measures and stalled negotiation under MEAs due to the fear of WTO challenge.

[97] James Bacchus, 'The Case for a WTO Climate Waiver' (CIGI, 2017) <https://www.cigionline.org/publications/case-wto-climate-waiver/> accessed 1 April 2024.

[98] Harro van Asselt, 'Trade and Climate Disputes before the WTO: Blocking or Driving Climate Action?' in I Alogna, C Bakker and JP Gauci (eds), *Climate Change Litigation: Global Perspectives* (Brill 2021), 457.

[99] Appellate Body Report, *United States – Standards for Reformulated and Conventional Gasoline*, *(US-Gasoline)*, WT/DS2/AB/R, adopted 20 May 1996, p. 17.

[100] The Appellate Body used MEAs only as interpretive guidance rather than applicable law. Asmelash (n 89) 332.

environmental considerations into the adjudication of trade disputes. Furthermore, in Canada-Renewable Energy, the Appellate Body notably endeavoured to exempt the Canadian Feed-in Tariff (FIT) program from being deemed inconsistent with the Subsidies and Countervailing Measures (SCM) Agreement, engaging in what some trade scholars have labelled as "legal gymnastics" and "legal fiction" to reconcile trade regulations with environmental objectives.[101] Nevertheless, it is critical to recognize the intrinsic limitations of the WTO DSB. Its primary role is "to preserve the rights and obligations of Members under the covered agreements, and to clarify the existing provisions of those agreements in conformity with the established rules of interpretation of public international law".[102] This mandate confines the scope within which the DSB can operate, emphasizing the need for its operations to remain within the bounds of existing trade agreements and international legal norms.

The absence of a comprehensive and integrated approach between the WTO and UNFCCC in addressing trade and environmental protection highlights the gap in the current global governance framework. It is identified as problem of fragmentation and "regime complex" in international law.[103] The need for enhanced collaboration between these regimes has been emphasized to ensure that trade policies and environmental goals can complement each other rather than create conflicts.[104] The coherence is particularly significant when considering the increasingly interconnected nature of climate change, which demands collaborative and synchronized efforts on a global scale. One noteworthy avenue for achieving this harmonization lies in the application of climate-related trade measures on a minilateral basis, such as the climate club. Such minilateral initiatives can be seen as proactive attempts to incorporate a multitude of perspectives and interests.

Despite the minilateral approaches, disputes regarding climate-related trade measures can arise and be resolved under WTO law, which is shaped by trade agreements. The WTO DSB has compulsory and exclusive jurisdiction for the purpose of these agreements.[105] In comparison, the UNFCCC has no formal dispute settlement mechanism to enforce climate-related trade instruments. Article 14(2) of the UNFCCC stipulates that member states shall consent to the resolution of disputes under the UNFCCC with other member states through the obligatory jurisdiction of either the International Court of Justice (ICJ) or arbitration, following procedures

---

[101] Luca Rubini, '"The Good, the Bad, and the Ugly:" Lessons on Methodology in Legal Analysis from the Recent WTO Litigation on Renewable Energy Subsidies' (2014) 48 Journal of World Trade 895, 916.

[102] Understanding on Rules and Procedures Governing the Settlement of Disputes (DSU) (15 April 1994) LT/UR/A-2/DS/U/1 art 3.2 <https://docs.wto.org/dol2fe/Pages/SS/directdoc.aspx?filename=Q:/UR/FA/28-dsu.pdf&Open=True>.

[103] David Victor and Robert Keohane, 'The Regime Complex for Climate Change' (2010) 9 Perspectives on Politics 7 <https://doi.org/10.1017/S1537592710004068>.

[104] Gracia Marín Durán, 'Securing Compatibility of Carbon Border Adjustments with the Multilateral Climate and Trade Regimes' (2023) 72(1) International and Comparative Law Quarterly 73, 75.

[105] DSU art 1(1), 6(1) and 23(1).

that the COP will establish promptly in an annex on arbitration. This provision is echoed in the Paris Agreement Article 24. Nonetheless, an annex on arbitration has not been formulated, and member states have avoided compulsory resolution mechanisms, instead favouring negotiation. Also, the WTO's dispute settlement system, with its binding enforcement capabilities, comprehensive legal framework, institutional structure, and importantly, experience of DSB in balancing trade and non-trade concerns, sets it apart from the non-compliance mechanisms of MEAs.[106] This enhanced authority grants the WTO DSB the ability to go beyond mere recommendations and authorize the application of retaliatory measures against members who are found to be non-compliant.[107] In contrast to other international fora where countries may primarily encounter reputational consequences for failing to fulfil their obligations under the respective agreements, the WTO's recourse to retaliatory trade measures injects a heightened sense of legally binding nature into international trade law.[108] This aspect distinguishes international trade law as one of the most robust and binding domains within the broader spectrum of international law. Therefore, the legitimacy of the climate club linkages strongly hinges on their compatibility with WTO law.

2.1.2 Interpreting WTO Agreements Through the Lens of Environmental Concerns

Before analysing the relevant WTO norms that govern climate club linkages, it is essential to examine the Preamble of the WTO, which is the fundamental resource for interpreting the provisions of WTO agreements.[109] The Appellate Body Report in US-Shrimp case underlined that, it is possible to obtain a comprehensive understanding of the trade and the environment intersection from the preambular statement.[110] The former WTO Director-General Pascal Lamy specified that "sustainable development is itself the end-goal of this institution, which is enshrined on page 1, paragraph 1, of the Agreement that establishes the WTO (the Preamble)."[111] This statement clarifies that one of the main WTO objectives is to oversee sustainable international trade or international trade based on the common policy of sustainable development. The Preamble implies that environmental goals should be a significant

[106] Durán, 'Securing Compatibility of Carbon Border Adjustments' (n 104) 75.

[107] Petros C Mavroidis, 'The Future of Dispute Resolution and Arbitration at WTO' in *The Elgar Companion to the World Trade Organization* (Edward Elgar Publishing 2020), 694.

[108] Thomas Cottier and Matthias Oesch, 'WTO Law, Precedents, and Legal Change' (2001) 3(1) JIEL 27, 38.

[109] VCLT art 31(1).

[110] Appellate Body Report, *United States – Import Prohibition of Certain Shrimp and Shrimp Products (US-Shrimp)*, WT/DS58/AB/R, adopted 6 November 1998, para 129–154.

[111] Pascal Lamy, 'Trade Can Be a Friend, not a Foe, of Conservation' (Speech, WTO Symposium on Trade and Sustainable Development within the Framework of Paragraph 51 of the Doha Ministerial Declaration, Geneva, 10 October 2005).

aspect of interpreting the WTO agreements in a manner consistent with economic development.[112] Therefore, environmental concerns could determine the substantive content and interpretation of WTO rules and, subsequently, the dispute settlement outcome.[113] This is because, measures that otherwise violate WTO Agreements could be justified as "necessary to ensure sustainable development". India cited this preamble statement in its defence of the India—Solar Cells case. However, both the Panel and the Appellate Body dismissed India's argument, stating that the preamble to the Marrakesh Agreement does not qualify as 'laws and regulations' under the definition provided by Article XX(d) of the GATT 1994.[114] Although the language of preamble can aid in interpreting WTO agreements and provisions, it alone provides an insufficient legal foundation for formally contesting the enactment of climate-related trade instruments. Therefore, WTO members indicate a growing willingness to explicitly reference and rely on sources of law particularly to those with trade-related components beyond the confines of WTO agreements into the dispute settlement process.[115]

The applicable substantive law for the WTO disputes is the covered agreements under the WTO.[116] Nonetheless, WTO agreements are born into the system of international law and, therefore, cannot be applied in isolation from other rules.[117] There arises a necessity to evaluate the scope and ramifications of legal provisions, general principles, and doctrines originating outside the WTO legal framework. In this regard, Article 3(2) of the Dispute Settlement Understanding (DSU) acknowledges that WTO Agreements should be interpreted in accordance with customary rules of interpretation of public international law. On this point, Articles 31 and 32 of the Vienna Convention on the Law of Treaties (VCLT) outline the principles for treaty interpretation and have achieved the status of customary international law. Both

---

[112] Marrakesh Agreement Establishing the World Trade Organization, (15 April 1994) LT/UR/A/2 Preamble <https://docs.wto.org/dol2fe/Pages/SS/directdoc.aspx?filename=Q:/UR/FA/04-wto.pdf&Open=True>.

[113] Christina Voigt, 'WTO Law and International Emissions Trading: Is There Potential for Conflict?' (2008) 2(1) Carbon & Climate Law Review 54, 66.

[114] Appellate Body Report, India-Solar Cells, para 5.149. Panel Report, *India – Certain Measures Relating to Solar Cells and Solar Modules (India-Solar Cells)*, WT/DS456/R and Add.1, adopted 14 October 2016, as modified by Appellate Body Report WT/DS456/AB/R, para 7.311. Neither the Panel nor the Appellate Body conducted a direct evaluation of the normative value of the Marrakesh Agreement's preamble. Their examination was confined to assessing whether the preamble justify India's measures that were inconsistent with GATT, had a direct effect in India.

[115] Peter van den Bossche, 'Non-WTO Dispute Settlement and WTO Law' in Geert Van Calster (eds) *Research Handbook on Environment, Health and the WTO* (Edward Elgar Publishing 2018) 239. Joost Pauwelyn, 'The Use of Non-WTO Agreements as a Basis for WTO Law' in Anne Peters and others (eds), *Non-State Actors as Standard Setters* (Cambridge University Press 2013) 393. R Adlung and M Molinuevo, 'The Role of Non-WTO Agreements in WTO Dispute Settlement: Issues and Challenges' (2019) 22(1) Journal of International Economic Law 75.

[116] DSU art 2.

[117] Joost Pauwelyn, 'How to Win a World Trade Organization Dispute Based on Non-World Trade Organization Law - Questions of Jurisdiction and Merits' (2003) 37 Journal of World Trade, 1001.

panels and the Appellate Body frequently cite the language of Articles 31 and 32.[118] Article 31, titled 'General Rule of Interpretation', and Article 32, titled 'Supplementary Means of Interpretation', primarily aim to delineate which materials, aside from the relevant agreement's text itself, are pertinent for interpretation. Essentially, these articles guide on the 'sources for treaty interpretation'.

Specific to our analysis here, Article 31 (3)(c) of the VCLT deals with the case where material sources external to the treaty are relevant in its interpretation. It dictates that together with the context "any relevant rules of international law that are applicable between parties shall be taken into account in interpretating a treaty". More comprehensively, an interpreter should be prepared to examine any material presented by a disputant that falls within the scope of Article 32 of the VCLT and holds potential relevance to the case.[119] Consequently, WTO panels may find themselves grappling with jurisdictional issues as the boundaries between WTO law and non-WTO law become increasingly intertwined. The rules of general international law, customs, principles, or standards binding on all states, can be referenced in WTO dispute settlements.[120]

However, in light of the previous scholarly debate and WTO jurisprudence, it is not possible to conclude that MEAs are directly applicable in the WTO dispute settlement process.[121] The ambiguity lies in determining the relevant law to the case. Even though the WTO Panels and the Appellate Body have jurisdiction only concerning WTO agreements, they must always interpret and apply relevant law according to the context of the case as discussed above in relation to Article 31(3)(c) of the VCLT. In addition to customary rules or general principles of international law, the relevant law might involve other international agreements.[122] The Article 31(3)(c)

[118] For instance, Appellate Body Report, *US- Gasoline*, p. 7, Appellate Body Report, *United States-Measures Affecting the Cross-Border Supply of Gambling and Betting Services (US-Gambling)* WT/DS285/AB/R, adopted 20 April 2005, para. 159.

[119] Donald H. Regan, 'Sources of International Trade Law: Understanding What the Vienna Convention Says About Identifying and Using 'Sources for Treaty Interpretation'' in Samantha Besson and Jean d'Aspremont (eds), *The Oxford Handbook of the Sources of International Law* (Oxford University Press 2017), 1055.

[120] Panel Report, *United States – Definitive Anti-Dumping and Countervailing Duties on Certain Products from China, (US – Anti-Dumping and Countervailing Duties (China))* WT/DS379/R, adopted 25 March 2011, as modified by Appellate Body Report WT/DS379/AB/R, para 308.

[121] The Appellate Body had considered environmental rationale in the Shrimp-Turtle case, but in the Biotech the Panel rejected the Cartagena Protocol as factual evidence. Therefore, the WTO DSB has broad discretionary power in using MEAs as factual evidence or interpretive sources. Panel Report, *EC- Biotech*, para. 7.71. Panel Report, *United States – Section 110(5) of the US Copyright Act (US-Copyright)* WT/DS160/R, adopted 27 July 2000, para 6.45. Gabrielle Marceau, 'Conflicts of Norms and Conflicts of Jurisdictions: The Relationship between the WTO Agreement and MEAs and other Treaties' (2001) Journal of World Trade, 1087. Panagiotis Delimatsis, 'Fragmentation of International Trade Law' (2011) 45 Journal of World Trade 87, 113–115. Panos Meerkouris, *Article 31(3)(c) VCLT and the Principle of Systemic Integration: Normative Shadows in Plato's Cave*, (Nijhoff/Brill 2015), 46–48.

[122] International Law Commission, 'Fragmentation of International Law: Difficulties Arising from the Diversification and Expansion of International Law' (A/CN.4/L.702, 2006), para 423.

articulates the goal of "systemic integration", asserting that treaties, irrespective of their specific content, are products of the international legal framework and their functionality is contingent upon this reality. The Appellate Body has yet to definitively specify the conditions under which WTO adjudicative bodies are required to consider other rules of international law. In EC - Computer Equipment and US-FSC case WTO adjudication bodies did look at a variety of bilateral and multilateral international agreements in order to interpret WTO law.[123] Similarly in EC-Bananas case, the Appellate Body explicitly held that "we have no alternative but to examine the provisions of the Lomé Convention ourselves in so far as it is necessary to interpret the Lomé waiver."[124] Article 7 of the DSU[125] provides guidance to WTO panels on how to approach the relevant law question. Accordingly, when a dispute arises, panels will look at the relevant agreements the parties involved have agreed to follow and use them to determine which law should apply to the case.[126] If the relevant law term is restricted to the law that all WTO parties are bound with,[127] then the applicability of the other legal norms will be severely limited. Therefore, the application of Article 31(3)(c) as a means to incorporate multilateral treaties not acceded to by all parties of the primary treaty is advocated.[128] This approach is seen as a

[123] Appellate Body Report, *European Communities – Customs Classification of Certain Computer Equipment*, (EC-Computer Equipment) WT/DS62/AB/R, WT/DS67/AB/R, WT/DS68/AB/R, adopted 22 June 1998 and Appellate Body Report, *United States – Tax Treatment for 'Foreign Sales Corporations' – Second Recourse to Article 21.5 of the DSU by the European Communities*, (*US – FSC (Article 21.5 – EC II)*) WT/DS108/AB/RW2, adopted 14 March 2006, DSR 2006:XI.

[124] Appellate Body Report, *European Communities – Regime for the Importation, Sale and Distribution of Bananas*, *(EC-Bananas III)* WT/DS27/AB/R, adopted 25 September 1997, para. 167.

[125] Article 7 of the DSU outlines the establishment and terms of reference for panels. The normative content under Article 7 requires panels to examine the matters referred to them in light of the relevant provisions in the covered agreements cited by the parties. In practice, Article 7 underlines the panels' role in interpreting the WTO agreements' provisions is in line with the principles of legal interpretation recognized in public international law, including the VCLT. Panels are expected to apply these principles to ensure that their findings are legally sound and consistent with the general international legal framework.

[126] DSU Annex 2, art 7.

[127] Panel Report, *EC-Biotech*, para 7.68, 7.71. VCLT Articles 31(2)(a) and 31(2)(b) both relate to agreements or instruments that have been accepted by all parties involved. Article 31(2)(a) directly mentions an agreement among 'all the parties'. Conversely, Article 31(2)(b) indirectly alludes to all parties involved, by describing the instrument as being made by 'one or more parties' and subsequently accepted by 'the other parties'. The wording of Article 31(3)(a) simply mentions a subsequent agreement between 'the parties'. The ILC Commentary regarding paragraph 31(3)(b) states that the phrase "the understanding of the parties" inherently signifies "the parties as a whole". International Law Commission, 'Draft Articles on the Law of Treaties, with Commentaries' (1966) II Yearbook of the International Law Commission, 222, para 15. There is no basis for questioning that this interpretation equally pertains to the interpretation of Article 31(3)(c). Regan (n 119) 1060.

[128] Philippe Sands, 'Treaty, Custom and the Cross-Fertilization of International Law' (1998) 1 Yale Human Rights and Development Law Journal 85. ILC, 'Fragmentation of International Law' (n 122) para 471.

method to achieve "systemic integration" of international law norms, facilitating a more cohesive and unified application of legal principles across various international agreements.[129] Enhanced coherence for the legal responsibilities can be achieved if the applicable law refers to ones binding on the parties to the dispute.[130] Hereby, the significant point is not amending the WTO Agreements by adding or diminishing its members' rights and obligations to solve the conflict between the WTO law and legal commitments arising from other international agreements.[131] Most importantly, third-party WTO members' rights should not be affected by applying other legal norms.[132]

However, even the "relevant law to the dispute" is strictly interpreted and the multilateral treaties that do not fall under the scope of Article 31(3)(c) unless adopted by all WTO members, they can still be considered pursuant to Article 32 of the VCLT.[133] The Article 32 of the VCLT reveals that, interpreters are both able and obligated to examine any form of evidence that may clarify the intentions of the parties involved. This evidence can be evaluated in all circumstances without the prerequisite that analysis under Article 31 of the VCLT must first result in an ambiguous or unreasonable interpretation.[134] Therefore, interpreters retain the autonomy to follow the directives of supplementary materials, even to the extent of revising an interpretation that might have appeared unequivocal without the consideration of these additional resources.[135] In this context, the non-WTO rules can constitute a source of interpretive material, factual evidence, or legal defence against claims of non-compliance to WTO law.[136]

A further challenge might arise when the rights and obligations of a WTO member under a WTO Agreement may conflict with its rights and obligations under

---

[129] ILC, 'Fragmentation of International Law' (n 122) 234.

[130] Appellate Body Report, *European Communities and Certain Member States – Measures Affecting Trade in Large Civil Aircraft*, (*EC and certain member States – Large Civil Aircraft*) WT/DS316/AB/R, adopted 1 June 2011, para 845.

[131] Marceau (n 121) 1130. Appellate Body Report, *EC and Certain Member States-Large Civil Aircraft*, para 845.

[132] ibid.

[133] Regan (n 119) 1060. Appellate Body Report, *Canada – Measures Affecting the Importation of Milk and the Exportation of Dairy Products, (Canada-Dairy),* WT/DS103/AB/R, WT/DS113/AB/R, and Corr.1, adopted 27 October 1999, para 82.

[134] Appellate Body Report, *EC – Computer Equipment*, para 86. Appellate Body Report, *Canada-Dairy*, para 138.

[135] Regan (n 119) 1064. Appellate Body Report, *European Communities – Customs Classification of Frozen Boneless Chicken Cuts, (EC-Chicken Cut)*, WT/DS269/AB/R, WT/DS286/AB/R, adopted 27 September 2005, para 283.

[136] Kati Kulovesi, 'Climate Change and Trade: At the Intersection of Two International Legal Regimes' in Erkki J Hollo, Kati Kulovesi and Michael Mehling (eds), *Climate Change and the Law* (Springer 2013), 441. Gabrielle Marceau, 'WTO Dispute Settlement and Human Rights' (2002) 14 European Journal of International Law 753. Joel Trachtman and Joost Pauwelyn, 'Conflict of Norms in Public International Law: How WTO Law Relates to Other Rules of International Law' (2004) 98 The American Journal of International Law, 476.

another international treaty regime. For example, an MEA might mandate quantitative restrictions for certain environmentally damaging products, whereas the GATT 1994 strictly prohibits this practice. In this context, Pascal Lamy stated, "The WTO, its treaty provisions, and their interpretation confirm the absence of any hierarchy between the WTO norms and the norms developed in other fora. WTO norms do not supersede or trump other international norms".[137] Further, Pauwelyn pointed out that the WTO obligations have a reciprocal nature, not integral ones".[138] Hence, they can be deviated from among a limited number of WTO members when the deviation does not infringe on third-party rights.[139] Notably, in case of a conflict between the substantive rules of environmental conventions and the reciprocal obligations under the WTO, the MEAs with integral obligations can prevail over the WTO obligations.[140] The primacy of non-WTO norms over WTO norms is subject to the principle of international law, which provides that non-WTO rules may supersede WTO ones if they are later in time (*lex posterior*) or more specific to the circumstances (*lex specialis*).[141] Therefore, WTO panels and the Appellate Body are required to adhere to the treaty interpretation principles established by the VCLT,[142] simultaneously, ensure that they neither expand nor reduce the rights and obligations stipulated in the WTO Agreement.[143]

The above explanations showcase the flexibility in interpreting WTO norms when a member is complying with another international treaty and has a justifiable basis to enact measures that violate WTO rules. This flexibility navigates the intricate intersection between trade law obligations and broader environmental concerns such as those addressed by the climate club. Also, based on the experience with existing MEAs, trade measures agreed under their auspices do not always lead to a dispute between WTO members.[144] In contrast, there is a much greater chance of

---

[137] Pascal Lamy, 'The Place of the WTO and Its Law in the International Legal Order' (2007) European Journal of International Law 978.

[138] Joost Pauwelyn, 'Conflict of Norms in WTO Dispute Settlement' in *Conflict of Norms in Public International Law: How WTO Law Relates to Other Rules of International Law* (Cambridge University Press 2003), 476.

[139] ibid 491.

[140] Appellate Body Report, *United States – Measures Affecting Trade in Large Civil Aircraft (Second Complaint)*, (*US – Large Civil Aircraft (2nd complaint)*) WT/DS353/AB/R, adopted 23 March 2012, para 845.

[141] Pauwelyn, 'How to Win a World Trade Organization Dispute' (n 117) 1005.

[142] ILC, 'Fragmentation of International Law' (n 122) para 423.

[143] Appellate Body Report, *India – Patent Protection for Pharmaceutical and Agricultural Chemical Products* (*India – Patents (US)*) WT/DS50/AB/R, adopted 16 January 1998, para 46. For example, in Peru -Agricultural Products the Appellate Body concluded that WTO members were not allowed to modify their obligations with FTAs between themselves. Appellate Body Report, *Peru – Additional Duty on Imports of Certain Agricultural Products, (Peru- Agricultural Products)*, WT/DS457/AB/R and Add.1, adopted 31 July 2015, para 5.111–5.112.

[144] Such as the Convention on International Trade in Endangered Species of Wild Fauna and Flora (CITES), the Basel Convention on the Control of Transboundary Movements of Hazardous Wastes and their Disposal, and the Montreal Protocol on Substances that Deplete the Ozone Layer.

disputes arising from unilateral climate-related measures. This experience suggests that it is possible to balance environmental protection and trade liberalization objectives through cooperation and dialogue between different international regimes, including the climate club.

In this context, the justification of climate club linkages under the WTO dispute settlement hinges on aligning the club approach with legal frameworks that supersede WTO norms. A crucial avenue for such justification lies in the compatibility of the climate club approach with other legal schemes, which can provide a robust defence. The Paris Agreement emerges as a pivotal non-WTO legal defence for climate club linkages. With its universal ratification, this landmark agreement signifies a collective commitment to addressing the urgent challenges posed by climate change. It is indisputably applicable to the relations among all WTO members.[145] The Paris Agreement's specific focus on climate-related issues (*lex specialis*) makes it an authoritative and comprehensive framework that can potentially supersede certain aspects of WTO norms in pursuing environmental objectives. This is because the WTO regime does not currently have a specific agreement on trade measures related to climate change. Other essential aspects bolstering the Paris Agreement's standing as a non-WTO legal defence is being later in time (*lex posterior*)[146] than WTO Agreements. The widespread ratification of the Paris Agreement by WTO Members, all members with the exception of Yemen, signifies its reflection of "contemporary concerns of the community of nations regarding environmental protection and conservation".[147] Also, this broad ratification indicates a "common intention" among WTO Members.[148] Thus, it can be argued that the Paris Agreement should be regarded as a pertinent source of international law for the parties involved, aimed at guiding the WTO DSB in interpreting disputes related to climate-related trade measures. Consequently, climate club's compliance with the Paris Agreement is crucial to justify climate club linkages that would otherwise be considered trade restrictive under WTO law. In this way, a WTO panel might accept the justification of any climate club linkage that complies with the Paris Agreement.

In brief, per the WTO Preamble, international trade law should aim to strike a balance between the need for trade liberalization and the need to address environmental concerns while considering the sovereign will of the parties involved. Moreover, due to international treaty interpretation principles the WTO dispute settlement needs to consider obligations under the relevant MEA and the WTO Agreements. Therefore, recent researches focus more on the mutual supportiveness of climate change and trade regimes. The climate club approach demonstrates this connection and facilitates the harmonization of environmental and trade objectives

---

145 Pananya Larbprasertporn, 'The Interaction between WTO Law and the Principle of Common But Differentiated Responsibilities in the Case of Climate-Related Border Tax Adjustment' (2014) 6(1) Goettingen Journal of International Law 145.

146 VCLT art 30.

147 Appellate Body Report, *US-Shrimp*, para 129.

148 Joost Pauwelyn, 'The Role of Public International Law in the WTO: How Far Can We Go?' (2001) 95 American Journal of International Law 535, 575–576.

through a network of like-minded countries committed to promote climate-related trade policies. Therefore, the climate club is an innovative and pragmatic way to navigate the legal landscape of the climate-trade nexus and achieve the goal of addressing climate change through the trade law regime.

3 Assessment of Climate-Related Market Mechanisms Under the WTO Law

The implementation of climate-related market instruments within the framework of a climate club introduces a spectrum of challenges that encompass practical, political, and legal dimensions. A leading one of them is the risk of trade retaliation.[149] It manifests as a tangible threat to the smooth flow of goods between climate club members and non-members. This is a valid concern, given that club linkages would potentially violate multiple WTO provisions.[150] Mainly, climate-related trade instruments raise concerns among the WTO members, whose development level is unsuitable to meet the environmental regulation requirements. Such countries are often characterized as export-oriented economies and have lax carbon regulations.[151] Thus, they face the prospect of being disproportionately impacted by the climate-related trade measures. As a result, climate club linkages could lead to escalating trade wars and protectionism.[152]

However, a WTO member may not unilaterally determine that a particular measure is illegal. The legal challenges regarding climate-related market tools can only be held at the WTO DSB. Even if other bilateral trade agreements might be relevant to the case, the WTO agreements and their pertinent case law still serve as a reference point. Also, as discussed in the previous section of this chapter, the WTO becomes a forum where public policy objectives like climate action can be adjudicated in addition to trade liberalization.[153] Therefore, upon the request of the complaining member, the WTO DSB convenes a panel of experts to assess the case's

[149] Achim Hagen and Jan Schneider, 'Trade Sanctions and the Stability of Climate Coalitions' (2021) 109 J Environ Econ Manag 102504.

[150] Ilaria Espa and Kateryna Holzer, 'From Unilateral Border Carbon Adjustments to Cooperation in Climate Clubs: Rethinking Exclusion in Light of Trade and Climate Law Constraints' in J. Bäumler and others (eds), *European Yearbook of International Economic Law 2022* (vol 13, Springer, 2023), 391 <https://doi.org/10.1007/8165_2022_101>.

[151] Magacho, Espagne and Godin (n 81) 245.

[152] Christoph Böhringer and others, 'Potential Impacts and Challenges of Border Carbon Adjustments' (2022) 12 Nat. Clim. Chang, 22, 23 <https://doi.org/10.1038/s41558-021-01250-z>.

[153] Ingo Venzke and Geraldo Vidigal, 'Are Trade Measures to Tackle the Climate Crisis the End of Differentiated Responsibilities? The Case of the EU Carbon Border Adjustment Mechanism (CBAM)' in M. den Heijer and H. van der Wilt (eds.) (2022) 51 Netherlands Yearbook of International Law, 187.

merits.[154] Should the Panel determine a trade measure contravenes WTO agreements and this verdict remains unchallenged or is upheld by the Appellate Body, the infringing member is then obligated to amend its legislation to align it with its WTO commitments. Failure to achieve compliance within an allotted reasonable timeframe permits the challenging party to pursue compensation, typically through tariff reductions or the removal of import quotas.[155] In instances where the involved Parties cannot agree on the extent of compensation, the complainant may request the DSB's permission to suspend trade concessions or other WTO obligations towards the violating member.[156]

Currently, the WTO Appellate Body is not functional due to the non-appointment of Appellate Body member by the US. The US's main argument for the blockade is that the Appellate Body has repeatedly overstepped its limits and created new rules never envisaged by the signatories.[157] This situation has significantly impacted the dispute resolution mechanism within the WTO. Nevertheless, the EU and 25 other WTO members have set up a formal Multi-Party Interim Appeal Arbitration Arrangement (MPIA) and appointed ten arbitrators who will hear appeals of WTO panel reports.[158] WTO membership as a whole commits itself to a truly rules-based system and finds common ground to revitalize the Appellate Body from the U.S.-induced blockage.[159] This body aims to fill the void left by the inoperable Appellate Body, providing WTO members with an alternative avenue for addressing appealed disputes and ensuring the continued effectiveness of the dispute settlement system.[160] All WTO members can resort to the MPIA under Article 25 of the of the WTO DSU.[161] Nonetheless, the MPIA serves as a temporary solution, thereby highlighting the ongoing need for a comprehensive and long-term reform of the WTO dispute settlement system.

The climate club linkages below can be challenged before the WTO DSB. In each case, the book engages in a nuanced examination of the legal landscape, drawing on relevant WTO agreements, case law, and established legal principles. The goal is to comprehensively understand how these climate club linkages interact with and potentially diverge from WTO agreements. These are:

- Import requirements leading to bans or quotas for carbon intensive products,

---

[154] DSU art 6(1).

[155] DSU art 3(7).

[156] DSU art 22.

[157] Office of the United States Trade Representative Ambassador Robert E. Lighthizer, 'Report on the Appellate Body of the World Trade Organization' (February 2020) Introduction, 14 <https://ustr.gov/sites/default/files/Report_on_the_Appellate_Body_of_the_World_Trade_Organization.pdf> accessed 4 April 2024.

[158] Joost Pauwelyn, 'The WTO's Multi-Party Interim Appeal Arbitration Arrangement (MPIA): What's New?' (2023) 22 World Trade Review 693, 694.

[159] Michael Hahn, 'Challenges for the Rule of Law in the WTO' (2019) 22 ZEuS 349, 360.

[160] WTO, 'Statement on a Mechanism for Developing, Documenting and Sharing Practices and Procedures in the Conduct of WTO Disputes' JOB/DSB/1/Add.12 (30 April 2020).

[161] ibid.

- Extra carbon tariffs, BCAs, or surrender of emission allowance certificates for certain imports, and
- Technical regulations and product standards regarding the GHG levels.[162]

The potential legal challenges arising from climate club linkages within the framework of international trade agreements are multifaceted and revolve around various aspects of trade commitments.[163] The climate-related market mechanisms could be disputed under the schedule of concessions, tariff deconsolidation and general elimination of quantitative restrictions. Also, the non-discrimination principles under the GATT 1994 and TBT Agreement are relevant since the club linkages have an inherently discriminatory nature. However, these legal challenges will be about optional and non-specific trade obligations rather than specific ones. In this context, the exception provisions of the GATT 1994, those articulated in Article XX, become crucial. The exceptions cover a range of policy objectives, including environmental protection, which could be invoked to justify climate club linkages.

Other than the exception clause, the relative eligibility of the climate-related market instruments under WTO depends on the design and the implementation of them.[164] For instance, this includes the design of border adjustment or how the products' characteristics will be determined (whether the npr-PPMs are relevant). Here, the risk is the abuse of these instruments for protectionist motives by the climate club members to lessen the global competitive pressure on their domestic industries. If these measures are designed with overly protective features, they may deviate from their intended purpose of addressing environmental concerns, instead serve as disguised protectionist tools and cannot be justified under the exception provisions. Another risk is that club measures regulating the carbon leakage can set a precedent for using border adjustments to compensate for other competitive disadvantages, such as minimum wage or health care regulations.[165] This expansion of the scope of border adjustments could lead to a broader application of trade measures beyond their original context. They potentially open the door to protectionist practices under the guise of addressing various economic or social issues.

Even though the design of club linkages is secured against formal objections, trade partners could still perceive them as extraterritorial overreach and an attempt to regulate matters outside the club's jurisdiction. The imposition of obligations related to environmental standards or trade practices, even to address global

[162] Micheal McKenzie 'Climate Change and the Generalized System of Preferences' (2008) 11 Journal of International Economic Law, 679.

[163] Krista Nadakavukaren Schefer and Pablo Arnaiz, 'Duty to Protect, Climate Change and Trade in Panagiotis Delimatsis (ed) *Research Handbook on Climate Change and Trade* (Edward Elgar 2016), 68.

[164] Kasturi Das, 'Can Border Carbon Adjustments Be WTO-Legal' (2011) 8 Manchester Journal of International Economic Law 65, 97.

[165] Alexandra Chapman, 'Walking the Talk? Examining the EU and China's Claims to Climate Leadership in the Negotiation and Implementation of the Paris Agreement' (University of British Columbia, 2020) <https://open.library.ubc.ca/soa/cIRcle/collections/ubctheses/24/items/1.0392041> accessed 4 April 2024.

challenges like climate change, may be seen as an undue burden on countries not party to the climate club. The danger of trade partners viewing them as intrusive can result in conflicts that may have far-reaching implications for international trade and climate cooperation. Therefore, the climate club may create trade disputes merely on its own, without violating specific obligations.[166] The non-club members could implement retaliatory measures as a response, as happened in the EU aviation emissions control.[167] Eventually, this friction with trading partners threatens international free trade.

Therefore, the book focuses on addressing a series of critical questions to establish the legality of climate club linkages within the international trade framework. The overarching goal is to navigate the complex interplay between climate-related trade measures and established international trade norms. The first question is, are the border adjustments in the form of import bans or quotas, emission allowance purchases, extra tariffs, or technical regulations consistent with WTO market access commitments? If so, are they also consistent with the non-discrimination obligations of WTO, namely MFN and national treatment? If not, are they permissible under one of the exceptions of GATT Article XX? This examination involves a detailed analysis of whether the climate club linkages can be justified as necessary measures for protecting the environment.

The precise legal interpretation and application of these provisions would be pivotal in determining the legality of climate club linkages within the international trade framework. This examination includes the relevant provisions, case law and evolving international trade jurisprudence for a comprehensive understanding of climate club linkages. The subsequent sections of the book delve into these issues in detail, presenting a thorough analysis of the legal landscape surrounding climate-related market instruments. By addressing these critical questions, the book aims to contribute to an informed discussion on the intersection of climate policies and global trade regulations, providing insights into the complex dynamics in the evolving landscape of the climate club approach.

---

[166] Susanne Droege, 'Using Border Measures to Address Carbon Flows' (2011) 11 Climate Policy 1191, 1194 <https://doi.org/10.1080/14693062.2011.592671>.

[167] In 2012 the EU tried to make intercontinental flights leaving from or arriving in the EU buying emission allowances for the whole emissions of each flight., WTO compliance of this scheme was challenged and fierce opposition from a group of 23 countries including US and China, threatened to retaliate by no longer buying Airbuses. Lorand Bartels, 'The WTO Legality of the Application of the EU's Emission Trading System to Aviation' (2012) 23 European Journal of International Law 429.

3.1 Schedule of Concessions

3.1.1 Overview

Upon accession to the WTO, each member established tariff concessions for individual products, defining the maximum permissible tariff rates, commonly referred to as customs duties.[168] This process is integral to the principles outlined in Article II:1 of the GATT 1994. According to Article II:1, existing tariff schedules are to be respected by each member, reflecting a commitment to maintaining a degree of continuity with pre-existing trade policies. Almost all the traded goods are now bound with the tariff rates, and each WTO member should apply them to the listed imported products upon importation.[169] The binding tariff rates provide predictability and stability in international trade. While WTO members have the flexibility to lower their tariff rates independently, any effort to increase these rates is subject to negotiation and agreement among the WTO members as examined in the following section of tariff deconsolidation.

In the EC – Chicken Cuts case, the Panel employed a comprehensive three-step analysis to ascertain whether there was a violation of Article II:1.[170] The first crucial step in this analytical process involves evaluating whether the products subjected to the regulatory measure were also regulated under the schedule of concessions. The classification of each product is made through the Harmonized System (HS) codes assigned to the products[171] when they are presented to customs authorities.[172] The codes clarify whether the product under the schedule is the same as the product subject to the border measure. Subsequently, the second facet of the analysis delves into examining whether the products in question were treated in accordance with the border measure. This facet ensures that the identified products received planned treatment upon entry into market. Finally, the third and conclusive step revolves around determining whether the measures implemented resulted in less favourable treatment for the imports in comparison to what was prescribed in the schedule of concessions.

---

[168] Davide Rovetta, 'Harmonized System and Schedules of Concession' in Thomas Cottier and Krista Nadakavukaren Schefer (eds), *Elgar Encyclopedia of International Economic Law* (Edward Elgar 2017), 350.

[169] General Agreement on Tariffs and Trade (GATT 1994) (15 April 1994) LT/UR/A-1A/1/GATT/1 <https://docs.wto.org/dol2fe/Pages/SS/directdoc.aspx?filename=Q:/UR/FA/06-gatt.pdf&Open=True> (hereinafter GATT 1994), art II:1(a).

[170] Panel Reports, European *Communities – Customs Classification of Frozen Boneless Chicken Cuts*, WT/DS269/R *(Brazil)* / WT/DS286/R *(Thailand)*, adopted 27 September 2005, as modified by Appellate Body Report WT/DS269/AB/R, WT/DS286/AB/R, para. 7.65.

[171] Appellate Body Report, *EC – Chicken Cuts*, para. 199.

[172] Panel Reports, *China – Measures Affecting Imports of Automobile Parts*, *(China-Autos Parts)*, WT/DS339/R, Add.1 and Add.2 / WT/DS340/R, Add.1 and Add.2 / WT/DS342/R, Add.1 and Add.2, adopted 12 January 2009, upheld (WT/DS339/R) and as modified (WT/DS340/R / WT/DS342/R) by Appellate Body Reports WT/DS339/AB/R / WT/DS340/AB/R / WT/DS342/AB/R, para. 7.415.

Article II:1(b) plays a crucial role in ensuring the effectiveness of tariff concessions by limiting all kinds of duties and charges as border measures that could create additional trade barriers. This provision encompasses various fiscal measures connected with the importation and import duties.[173] Under Article II:1(b), the barrier to trade corresponds to the application of ordinary customs duties in excess of those provided in the schedule.[174] The mere application of tariffs does not have an inherently discriminatory nature. Tariffs are accepted as legitimate trade instruments for a number of reasons, including revenue earning and environmental concerns. They are even preferred policy given that tariffs are not entirely prohibited as in quantitative restrictions but instead regulated to the extent they do not exceed the bound rates.[175]

The determination of an "excess" tariff is uniquely predicated on the presence of a numerical increase.[176] Hence, the Article II:1(b) bypasses the need for a trade effect test. This approach reflects the ethos of Article II, which is designed to safeguard the expectations of a competitive relationship among trading partners, not to preserve specific trade volume.[177] The provision thus prioritizes the protection of the competitive landscape, ensuring that trade practices adhere to a framework of predictability and fairness rather than being measured against quantitative trade outcomes. It acknowledges that the mere act of imposing tariffs beyond the agreed limits constitutes a breach of the mutual expectations inherent in trade agreements, irrespective of the immediate impact on trade flows.

3.1.2 Results on Carbon Tariffs

Under the climate club scheme, the critical point of carbon tariffs analysis is resolving the characteristics of this measures. The interpretation and application of the Article II:1hinge on determining whether a measure qualifies as a border measure, or an internal fiscal regulation. The Appellate Body concluded that the classificatory point of whether a measure is a border measure in the form of import tariff or an internal fiscal regulation as a tax lies in what triggers the obligation to pay.[178] The

[173] ibid para 4.100.

[174] Appellate Body Report, *Argentina – Measures Affecting Imports of Footwear, Textiles, Apparel and Other Items*, (*Argentina – Textiles and Apparel*) WT/DS56/AB/R and Corr.1, adopted 22 April 1998, para. 45.

[175] Appellate Body Report, *India – Additional and Extra-Additional Duties on Imports from the United States*, (*India – Additional Import Duties*), WT/DS360/AB/R, adopted 17 November 2008, para. 159.

[176] Appellate Body Report *Argentina – Textiles and Apparel*, para. 46.

[177] Panel Report, *Russia – Tariff Treatment of Certain Agricultural and Manufacturing Products*, (Russia – Tariff Treatment), WT/DS485/R, Add.1, Corr.1, and Corr.2, adopted 26 September 2016, paras. 7.18.

[178] Appellate Body Report, *China - Measures Affecting Imports of Automobile Parts (China – Auto Parts)*, WT/DS339/AB/R, WT/DS340/AB/R, WT/DS342/AB/R, adopted 12 January 2009, paras. 158, 159, 161.

moment when a charge is collected or paid is not determinative in this context.[179] Similarly, the policy objective attributed to the charge cannot catalogue the measure as import-related because it is challenging to objectively ascertain the policy intent behind charges. Often, charges can be interpreted as fulfilling both domestic objectives and those related to the importation of goods.[180] Only if the obligation to pay stems by virtue of the importation, it is possible to categorize regulation as a border measure.

In the context of climate club linkages, the carbon tariffs do not constitute typical border measures as they are not triggered solely by the importation itself. Instead, they are designed to be effective with comparable domestic measures.[181] They are implemented with the aim of targeting products that are subject to carbon price within the climate club jurisdiction. They aim to level the playing field between domestic and imported goods in terms of carbon costs. Carbon tariffs represent an effort to integrate environmental considerations into trade practices, ensuring that carbon pricing extends beyond club borders to influence global trade dynamics. This distinction becomes significant when considering that internal regulations cannot fall within Article II:1(b) scope. Article II:1(b) is primarily concerned with tariffs, which relate to the act of importation, but carbon tariff is implemented with respect to an internal fiscal regulation.[182] Consequently, the carbon tariff linkages are not necessarily examined under the schedule of concessions provision.

Nevertheless, to demonstrate how border measures and charges relating to internal regulation are differently regulated, this section is deemed to accept carbon tariff as within the scope of border measures.[183] This analytical stance allows for a direct comparison, highlight the regulatory nuances and the legal differentiation between the two types of measures within the framework of international trade law. In this case, the implications of Article II:1(b) analysis become significant. In the scenario where climate club linkage, as carbon tariffs, are considered a border measure, the potential inconsistency arises due to the imposition of charges on imports that exceed the maximum levels agreed upon in the WTO schedule of concessions. Such higher pricing typically manifests through the progressive increase in carbon prices over time and the application of carbon tariffs that surpass the limits stipulated in the schedule of concessions.

---

[179] ibid para 158.

[180] Thomas Cottier, Olga Nartova and Anirudh Shingal, 'The Potential of Tariff Policy for Climate Change Mitigation: Legal and Economic Analysis' (2014) 48(5) Journal of World Trade 1007, 1020.

[181] See Sect. 3.4 in Chap. 5.

[182] Natalie Dobson, 'Chapter 25: Climate Protection versus Trade: Dilemmas for the EU' in *Handbook on European Union Climate Change Policy and Politics* (Edward Elgar Publishing, 2023), 370.

[183] The term 'border measures' encompasses all measures governing or applicable upon importation, usually but not necessarily applied at the border. Venzke and Vidigal (n 153) 9.

If carbon tariffs apply equivalent to the burden imposed on domestic products, Article II:2 comes into play.[184] It suggests equal treatment for both imported and domestic goods. Therefore, under this scenario, the border measure does not consider the actual carbon content of the imports and is applied under the assumption that it is equal to the products manufactured in the club jurisdictions. The tariff only aims to level the playing field by addressing disparities in carbon prices. However, it undermines the environmental effectiveness as the actual carbon levels might far exceed the levels of club products. Hence, this provision allows the application of carbon tariffs only under particular conditions. Herein, it is essential to note that the analysis shifts to the national treatment principle, which prohibits any taxes or charges that afford protection to domestic production. In this regard, the Appellate Body held in the India-Additional Import Duties case that "border charge can merely be admissible under Article II:2(a) and be excluded from the limitations at Article II:1 only if it is consistent with the Article III:2 of the GATT1994".[185] This explanation outlines the conditions under which a border charge is permissible, explicitly pointing to Article II:2(a) as the relevant provision. It highlights that the border charge must be consistent with the requirements specified in Article III:2 of the GATT 1994 to be exempted from challenges under Article II.[186]

The interrelation between Articles II:1(b) and III:2 signifies a shared concern regarding the imposition of charges on products, albeit with distinct limitations. Article II:1(b) places restrictions on border measures, stipulating that they should not surpass the schedule of concessions the parties agreed upon. On the other hand, Article III:2 limits charges to those of a domestic nature, encapsulating the principle of national treatment. The substantive similarities between these articles are underscored by Article II:2(a), which explicitly mandates the harmonious interpretation of Articles II:1(b) and III: 2.Therefore, if a complainant brings its case in Article II, it is not required to file an independent claim for violation of the national treatment principle.[187] Due to the climate club linkage as a carbon tariff, a nuanced understanding of how charges are imposed and regulated under Articles II:1(b) and III:2 becomes pivotal. A holistic approach that considers the interconnectedness of these provisions will contribute to developing effective and equitable climate-related trade policies.

---

[184] GATT 1994 art II (2) "Nothing in this Article shall prevent any contracting party from imposing at any time on the importation of any product a charge equivalent to an internal tax imposed consistently with the provisions of paragraph 2 of Article III. in respect of the like domestic product or in respect of an article from which the imported product has been manufactured or produced in whole or in part; [...]"

[185] Appellate Body Report, *India-Additional Import Duties*, paras. 180–181.

[186] ibid para 159.

[187] ibid paras 170, 172 and 180. Panel Report, *Korea – Measures Affecting Imports of Fresh, Chilled and Frozen Beef, (Korea– Various Measures on Beef)*, WT/DS161/R, WT/DS169/R, adopted 10 January 2001, as modified by Appellate Body Report WT/DS161/AB/R, WT/DS169/AB/R, para. 780.

The determination of which aspects of imports are eligible for carbon tariff is indeed another crucial aspect in analysing the schedule concessions. Article II:2(a) permits levying taxes on any goods, which is the input of import. The US-Superfund case sheds light on the application of tariffs to inputs physically incorporated into the final product, thereby emphasising the relevance of product-related PPMs that leave a physical impact and traces on the end product.[188] However, in the case of carbon tariffs, the adjusted aspect is the carbon level, which does not leave a physical trace on the product. Carbon level constitutes npr-PPMs. The literal interpretation of the pertinent rules directs us to compare tariff rates between inputs concerning the physical effects on the final product. This explanation limits the tariffs for the embedded carbon levels of the imports. Therefore, a carbon tariff can be considered a violation of Article II:2 since the final product will be subjected to a higher charge than the domestic product due to a reason that does not alter the product's physical characteristics. However, the Panel Reports on Argentina-Hides and Leather and Mexico-Soft Drinks addressed the implications of tariffs on non-physical aspects of products and their alignment with the provisions of the GATT 1994.[189] These reports acknowledge that inputs need not to be physically present in the final product and npr-PPM related aspects of a product can be subjected to a tariff.

Consequently, the scope of application of Article II primarily hinges on the classification of carbon tariff as a border measure or internal regulation. Subsequently, the transparent calculation of the tax or tariff base and rate comes to the forefront.[190] This is because when border measures exceed the levels under the schedule of concessions or are deemed excessive compared to the domestic price, it raises concerns about compliance. Given the interconnected nature of Article II:1 with the national treatment principle and the possible discrepancy of foreign and domestic carbon prices, even if the aim is to reflect the actual carbon content of the imports, the carbon tariffs result in the infringement of Article II. This complexity highlights the ongoing challenge of balancing environmental considerations, such as reflecting the real carbon content of imports, with the need to abide by international trade obligations. As countries explore measures like carbon tariffs, finding solutions to this intricacy will be central to global trade discussions.

188 GATT Panel Report, *United States-Taxes on Petroleum and Certain Imported Substances, (US-Superfund)* (17 June 1987) L/6175, 34S/136, para 136.

189 Panel Report, *Argentina – Measures Affecting the Export of Bovine Hides and the Import of Finished Leather, (Argentina-Hides and Leather)*, WT/DS155/R and Corr.1, adopted 16 February 2001, para 11.183. The Report accepted the possibility of BTA that is related to non-physically incorporated inputs. Panel Report, *Mexico – Tax Measures on Soft Drinks and Other Beverages (Mexico-Soft Drinks)*, WT/DS308/R, adopted 24 March 2006, as modified by Appellate Body Report WT/DS308/AB/R, para 8.44. The Report understood that production inputs need not to be physically present in the final product.

190 Michael A Mehling and others, 'Designing Border Carbon Adjustments for Enhanced Climate Action' (2019) 113(3) American Journal of International Law 433.458.

3.2 *Tariff Deconsolidation*

3.2.1 Overview

The GATT 1994 allow for the modification or withdrawal of bound tariffs under certain conditions, reflecting the dynamic nature of international trade relations and the need for flexibility in trade policy. This process, often referred to as tariff deconsolidation, enables WTO members to adjust their commitments in light of changing economic circumstances or policy priorities.[191] Members can deconsolidate bound tariffs by offering compensation on different tariff lines to the substantially affected members due to this practice. In this way, they maintain the balance of concessions among WTO members, ensuring that the benefits of trade liberalization are preserved. However, it is essential to note that even though tariff deconsolidation is a legitimate instrument under WTO law, failure to reach a mutually agreeable arrangement may precipitate trade wars.[192]

The principles and procedures related to deconsolidation are explicitly addressed in Article XXVIII of the GATT 1994, supplemented by the corresponding note, the Understanding on the Interpretation of Article XXVIII of the GATT1994.[193] These legal instruments provide the foundation for WTO members to modify their tariff commitments. Mainly, the procedures for tariff deconsolidation are set out in Article XXVIII:1. In adherence to the established procedures, a WTO member interested in tariff deconsolidation is required to formally notify the Council for Trade in Goods (CTG) of its intent to initiate negotiations.[194] The notification should include the list of products and their tariff lines, which are intended to be modified.[195] It ensures transparency and facilitating the preparation for subsequent negotiations. The negotiations are held between the member who wishes tariff deconsolidation and other members with "principle supplying interest" or "substantial interest" in these concessions.[196] These negotiations aim to reach a mutually acceptable agreement on the proposed tariff modifications, balancing the interests of the initiating member with those of its trading partners.

---

[191] Cottier, Nartova and Shingal (n 180) 1024.

[192] Trade war is not firm legal definition, but it is described as an attempt by a state to gain economic advantages while harming other states through customs duties and quota restrictions. It corresponds to an unspecified, undefinable dissatisfaction with the rules/status quo, in which a country only asserts its own economic and political interest. Charlotte Sieber-Gasser, 'Please, Reboot – Small Economies and the WTO Appellate Mechanism in Times of Trade War and COVID-19' (SIL International Economic Law Interest Group, Online Workshop 'International Economic Law between Emergencies and Reforms', 9 September 2020), 2.

[193] WTO, The Understanding on the Interpretation of Article XXVIII of the GATT 1994, <http://www.wto.org/english/docs_e/legal_e/12-28_e.htm>.

[194] Cottier, Nartova and Shingal (n 180) 1023.

[195] Guidelines adopted on 10 November 1980, GATT documents C/113 and C/113/Corr.1, GATT BISD 27S/26-28, para 2.

[196] The Understanding on the Interpretation of Article XXVIII of the GATT 1994, (n 193) para 1.

The principle supplying interest is defined with quantitative measures of trade flows either per import or export shares.[197] In the former method, the import statistics are considered. A member with a large share of import capacity should be able to protect its contractual rights under the GATT 1994. Therefore, it becomes a principal negotiator in the tariff deconsolidation process. The export-based criterion is exceptionally regarded. This case considers a member as having a "supplying interest" if it has the highest ratio of exports affected by the schedule of concession.[198] Whereas there is no precise definition for "substantial interest". In practice, members with a 10% market share in the concession products are notified of the negotiations.[199] This threshold serves as a guideline for including members in the negotiation process, ensuring that those with significant trade interests are afforded an opportunity to participate and protect their trade interests.

Subsequently, the relevant parties seek to agree on compensation for the proposed changes. Crucially, should negotiations fail to yield a consensus and no agreement is reached, the requesting WTO member retains the freedom to increase its tariffs unilaterally.[200] However, this unilateral modification comes with potential consequences. The affected WTO members are granted the right to withdraw substantially equivalent tariff concessions, thereby resulting in trade retaliation.[201] The vast majority of Article XXVIII negotiations have concluded with an agreement between the interested parties, except for one single case.[202] Even under that case, no withdrawal of equivalent concessions had taken place. Nevertheless, the potential risks of retaliation serve as a deterrent and highlight the need for careful diplomacy and consensus-building to navigate the complexities of modifying tariff commitments.

The essence of tariff deconsolidation revolves around preserving reciprocal advantageous trade relations among WTO members. The objective is to allow countries the flexibility to adjust their schedule of concessions, reflecting changing economic circumstances, technological advancements, or shifts in global trade dynamics. Therefore, the increasing concern and need to act against climate change can be a justifiable reason for resorting to this method. In practice, tariff deconsolidation is not frequent. The report in 2020 indicated that there had been 46 negotiations within the scope of Article XXVIII since 1995.[203] Governments often choose to negotiate tariff bindings that are lower than existing levels but not to increase

[197] ibid.

[198] GATT 1994, Ad Note to paragraph 1 of Article XXVIII, para 5.

[199] Panel Report, *European Union – Measures Affecting Tariff Concessions on Certain Poultry Meat Products*, (*EU – Poultry Meat (China)*) WT/DS492/R and Add.1, adopted 19 April 2017 para. 7.407.

[200] Cottier, Nartova and Shingal (n 180) 1023.

[201] ibid.

[202] WTO, The Philippines, G/MA/W/123/Rev.6.

[203] WTO Secretariat, *Factual Report on the Status of Renegotiations under Article XXVIII of the GATT 1994* (G/MA/W/123/Rev.6) para 1.1.

them.[204] The delicate balance between the need for flexibility and the importance of maintaining predictable trade relations is reflected in the limited use of tariff deconsolidation in practice.

3.2.2 Results on Carbon Tariffs

The notion of tariff deconsolidation within the framework of the climate club represents a strategic manoeuvre instead of navigating the complex terrain of carbon tariffs. In essence, this approach entails the unravelling of tariffs established in the schedule of concession since it is not possible to exceed the agreed tariff rates with carbon tariffs. Therefore, to avoid Article II violation, the climate club can resort to tariff deconsolidation for high carbon embedded products and increase their formerly agreed rates instead of applying the carbon tariff. By doing so, member countries can mitigate potential economic repercussions and foster a cooperative atmosphere between the climate club members and non-members. The process of tariff deconsolidation, however, is contingent upon reaching an agreement among members who are affected by the proposed increase in tariffs. The agreement generally involves tariff decrease in other products.

Under the climate club, the compensation for tariff increase of carbon-intensive products can be lowering tariffs for certain environmental goods.[205] It represents a strategic and forward-thinking approach and aligns with the overarching goal of fostering sustainability and addressing environmental concerns while navigating the complexities of international trade. Lowering tariffs on environmental goods not only serves as a tangible way to offset the economic impact of increased tariffs but also encourages the adoption of environmentally responsible practices in international trade.[206] Countries can more effectively promote the use of environmentally friendly technologies. Such compensation contributes to the environmental objectives of the climate club and reinforces the notion that economic policies can be wielded as tools for positive environmental change.

However, the success of this compensation approach depends on identifying and classifying environmental goods to ensure clarity and fairness. It is worth noting that the definition and scope of environmental goods under WTO law are subject to negotiations among member countries.[207] The list of products considered as environmental goods can evolve over time as negotiations progress.[208] The WTO negotiations on environmental goods were held in the Doha Development Agenda,

[204] Thomas Cottier and Matthias Oesch, *International Trade Regulation: Law and Policy in the WTO, The European Union and Switzerland, Cases Materials and Comments* (Cameron May Ltd, London 2005) 606.

[205] As in the World Trade Organization, 'Ministerial Declaration' (14 November 2001) WT/MIN(01)/DEC/1, para 31(iii).

[206] Olawuyi (n 91) 687.

[207] ibid 687.

[208] Ministerial Declaration (n 205) para 31.

specifically focusing on the liberalization of trade in environmental goods and services.[209] However, progress in these negotiations has been challenging due to differing views among members on the coverage of the environmental goods category.[210] Therefore, there is no existing tariff line for environmental goods. Herein, the parties negotiating compensation can decide on environmental goods per their PPMs. Additionally, continuous evaluation and adaptation of the list of environmental goods may be necessary to keep pace with evolving technologies and environmental standards.

The extended employment of the tariff deconsolidation measure will adversely affect free trade. Hence, the use of tariff deconsolidation as a tool to address climate change, while potentially well-intentioned, must adhere to the overarching principles of non-discrimination[211] and the avoidance of unjustifiable trade restrictions. According to Article XX of the GATT 1994,[212] measures taken to combat climate change, including unilateral ones, should not constitute a means of arbitrary or unjustifiable discrimination or a disguised restriction on international trade. However, the practical application of tariff deconsolidation introduces a dilemma, particularly concerning the potential risk of trade retaliation. This inherent risk introduces complexities that may challenge the alignment of tariff deconsolidation with the principles outlined in Article XX. Striking a delicate balance that upholds the imperative of combating climate change and the principles of non-discrimination and trade liberalization is essential to ensure this climate-related trade instrument's long-term viability and effectiveness.

3.3 General Elimination of Quantitative Restrictions

3.3.1 Overview

Article XI of the GATT 1994 stands as a cornerstone in promoting free and fair international trade. A fundamental tenet of this Article is the limitation it places on quantitative restrictions or prohibitions. It places a strong emphasis on facilitating the flow of goods across borders.[213] Article XI restricts quantitative restrictions except for duties, taxes, or other charges. In essence, it encourages members to

[209] Bernard Hoekman and others, 'Conclude Doha: It Matters!' (2009) 9 World Trade Review 505 <https://doi.org/10.1017/S1474745610000297>.

[210] AJ Mathew and others 'The Green Dilemma about Liberalization of Trade in Environmental Goods' (2009) Journal of World Trade <https://doi.org/10.54648/trad2009016>.

[211] See Sects. 1 and 2 in Chap. 7.

[212] See Sect. 4 in Chap. 7.

[213] Petros C Mavroidis, 'Quantitative Restrictions and the GATT Framework' in *Understanding the Complexities of International Trade Law* (MIT Press 2020), 73.

refrain from adopting measures that limit the quantity or volume of traded goods.[214] This prohibition underscores the preference for tariffs over quotas as a means of regulating international trade. While tariffs involve imposing taxes or charges on imports, they do not outright restrict the quantity of goods that can be traded. This crucial distinction aligns with the broader objectives of GATT 1994, which seeks to dismantle trade barriers and ensure a level playing field for all members. Countries can generate revenue by favouring tariffs while allowing a more flexible trading environment. In contrast, quotas, which represent specific limits on the volume of imports, can potentially hinder the efficient allocation of resources across borders.[215]

Article XI:1 prohibits non-fiscal trade restricted measures. These measures encompass a spectrum of hindrances to free trade, including import bans, quotas, and the imposition of burdensome or arbitrarily accorded import licenses, among other similar restrictions.[216] A significant clarification of the scope and intent of Article XI:1 was provided by the Panel in the Japan-Semiconductors case. The Panel elucidated that the Article's focus extends beyond the mere existence of laws or regulations. It refers to a broader perspective that includes administrative requirements related to import and export transactions.[217] In this regard, the focus of Article XI:1 extends to ensuring not only the absence of explicit legal barriers but also the facilitation of market access by eliminating de facto regulatory requirements.[218] This perspective emphasises the commitment to creating a setting, where imports are not subject to hidden or indirect obstacles that could, in practice, limit the quantity of a product.[219] However, it is essential to emphasise that measures covered under the TBT Agreement, automatic import licencing procedures and tariff rate quotas are excluded from the quantitative restrictions clause.[220]

---

214 Appellate Body Reports, *Argentina – Measures Affecting the Importation of Goods (Argentina–Import Measures)* WT/DS438/AB/R / WT/DS444/AB/R / WT/DS445/AB/R, adopted 26 January 2015, para 5.217.

215 Mavroidis, 'Quantitative Restrictions and the GATT Framework' (n 213) 78.

216 Panel Report, *Argentina – Measures Relating to Trade in Goods and Services*, (*Argentina – Financial Services),* WT/DS453/R and Add.1, adopted 9 May 2016, as modified by Appellate Body Report WT/DS453/AB/R, para. 7.1067.

217 GATT Panel Report, *Japan - Trade in Semi-Conductors,* (4 May 1988) L/6309 - 35S/116, para 117.

218 Appellate Body Reports, *China – Measures Related to the Exportation of Various Raw Materials (China-Raw Materials)* WT/DS394/AB/R / WT/DS395/AB/R / WT/DS398/AB/R, adopted 22 February 2012, para. 320. Panel Report. *Argentina –Hides and Leather*, para 11.17. Panel Report, *India – Quantitative Restrictions on Imports of Agricultural, Textile and Industrial Products*, (India – Quantitative Restrictions), WT/DS90/R, adopted 22 September 1999, upheld by Appellate Body Report WT/DS90/AB/R, para 5.128.

219 Panel Report, *Dominican Republic – Measures Affecting the Importation and Internal Sale of Cigarettes, (Dominican Republic –Import and Sale of Cigarettes)*, WT/DS302/R, adopted 19 May 2005, as modified by Appellate Body Report WT/DS302/AB/R, paras. 7.261–7.262.

220 WTO, 'Quantitative Restrictions, Footnote 1 of the QR Decision' <https://www.wto.org/english/tratop_e/markacc_e/qr_e.htm> accessed 5 April 2024.

The most frequently employed restricted measure is the non-automatic licensing procedure and prohibition.[221] Quotas correspond to a small percentage of the quantitative restrictions.[222] Nevertheless, WTO members can adopt prohibitions or restrictions as a result of international obligations outside the WTO framework. For instance, the Montreal Protocol on Substances that Deplete the Ozone Layer[223] or the Basel Convention on the Control of Transboundary Movements of Hazardous Wastes and Their Disposal.[224] Even though the quantitative restrictions are born due to the commitments under another international agreement, the WTO members should justify them under the relevant WTO provisions. Such restrictions are generally accepted as necessary to protect the global environment.[225]

In essence, Article XI safeguards competitive opportunities and the continuity of existing trade relationships by fostering predictability for future trade endeavours.[226] It goes beyond merely preserving the number of trade flows. Instead, the Article is designed to protect the very spirit of competitive markets by ensuring that administrative hurdles or non-transparent licensing procedures do not unduly constrain market access.

3.3.2 Results on the Climate Club Linkages

The climate club linkages involve two distinct aspects, each with its own set of implications for international trade. The first aspect pertains to fiscal measures, particularly the imposition of charges on carbon emissions.[227] The primary goal of these charges is to establish a level playing field by ensuring neutral treatment between imports and the climate club products. This approach seeks to prevent unfair advantages for club products and encourages a globally coordinated effort to address climate change. Fiscal measures of the climate club are subjected to the schedule of concessions provision as explained in the above section[228] and MFN and national treatment principles,[229] which are analysed in the next chapter under the fairness of the climate club scheme.

[221] WTO, 'Import Licensing Notification Status' <https://importlicensing.wto.org/notification-status> accessed 21 May 2024.

[222] WTO, 'Quantitative Restrictions Notifications' <https://qr.wto.org/en#/notifications> accessed 21 May 2024.

[223] Montreal Protocol on Substances that Deplete the Ozone Layer (with Annex) (adopted 16 September 1987, entered into force 1 January 1989) 1522 UNTS 3, 26 ILM 1541, 1550 art 4.

[224] Basel Convention on the Control of Transboundary Movements of Hazardous Wastes and Their Disposal (adopted 22 March 1989, entered into force 5 May 1992), 1673 UNTS. 125, Preamble.

[225] See Sect. 4 in Chap. 7.

[226] Panel Report, *Argentina – Hides and Leather*, para 11.20. GATT Panel Report, *US-Superfund*, para. 5.2.2.

[227] See Sects. 3.3, 3.4 and 3.5 in Chap. 5.

[228] See Sect. 3.1 in Chap. 5.

[229] See Sects. 1 and 2 in Chap. 7.

The second aspect of climate club linkages involves internal regulations, including the purchase and surrender of emission allowance certificates due to the club's ETS by importers[230] and administrative requirements imposed to realise club linkages. While these measures are designed to enhance environmental cooperation and incentivize emissions reduction, they may inadvertently introduce new and potentially burdensome licensing, registration, and reporting requirements for trading partners outside the club. Critically, the climate club's ambition to "export its regulatory standards to third countries raises concerns about potential discrimination".[231] If imports need to obtain emissions allowance, in the form of licence, before they can legally bring products into the club jurisdiction, they would be subject to the general prohibition on trade-restrictive border measures outlined in Article XI:1.[232] In comparison, if these measures apply to both domestic and foreign products, they fall under the scrutiny of Article III:4 of the GATT. This article prohibits the application of internal regulations that afford less favourable treatment to imports compared to like domestic products and is examined under the national treatment chapter of this book.[233]

However, drawing a contour between measures subject to the national treatment obligation in Article III:4 and those falling under the prohibition on trade-restrictive measures in Article XI:1 is a problematic aspect of WTO law. The difficulty arises from the potential overlap of these articles, especially if Article XI:1 was interpreted broadly to encompass internal requirements. This broad interpretation could render Article III:4 partially superfluous, as both Articles aim to prevent discriminatory measures affecting imports.[234] Moreover, in the case of expansive interpretation, the exceptions outlined in Article XI:2 apply to internal measures as well. This implementation would be at odds with the fundamental aim of Article III, as the second paragraph of Article XI covers a wide range of exceptions.[235] Therefore, the interpretation of these Articles must consider the nature of the measure. Accordingly, the Appellate Body clarified the distinction between quantitative import restrictions and internal regulations applied at the time or point of importation.[236] It underscores that while Article XI:1 unequivocally prohibits restrictions on importation, Article III:4 and the Note Ad Article III, permit the imposition of internal regulations on products

---

[230] See Sect. 2 in Chap. 5.

[231] Joachim Englisch and Tatiana Falcao, 'EU Carbon Border Adjustments for Imported Products and WTO Law' (9 June 2021), 54 <https://doi.org/10.2139/ssrn.3863038>.

[232] GATT Panel Report, *Canada-Import, Distribution and Sale of Certain Alcoholic Drinks by Provincial Marketing Agencies*, (18 February 1992) DS17/R, 39S/27, 75, para. 5.4.

[233] See Sect. 2.4 in Chap. 7.

[234] Panel Report, *India – Measures Affecting the Automotive Sector (India-Autos),* WT/DS146/R, WT/DS175/R, and Corr.1, adopted 5 April 2002, para 7.220.

[235] Key exceptions under Article XI includes balance of payments, short supply, agricultural and fisheries protection and application of standards or regulations for the classification, grading, or marketing of commodities in international trade.

[236] Appellate Body Report, *Brazil – Measures Affecting Imports of Retreaded Tyres (Brazil-Retreaded Tyres),* WT/DS332/AB/R, adopted 17 December 2007, para 7.372.

imported from other contracting parties. However, this permission comes with a set of stringent conditions aimed at safeguarding the principles of non-discrimination.[237]

Furthermore, a measure might have restrictive effects on the competitive opportunities of imports in the domestic market and simultaneously produce restrictive effects on importation. The Panel in the India-Autos case clarifies this dichotomy.[238] Accordingly, Article III is implicated when competitive opportunities in the domestic market are affected. This includes situations where measures such as regulations or non-financial considerations favour domestic products over imports in the domestic market.[239] In contrast, Article XI is relevant when the opportunities for importation itself, i.e., entering the market, are affected. The significance of this distinction becomes particularly pronounced in the context of climate club linkages. Suppose regulatory and non-fiscal aspects of the club linkages create barriers that restrict the entry of imports into the club market. In that case, they will fall under the purview of the firmer requirement of Article XI:1.[240] This provision specifically addresses situations where measures act as barriers to the free flow of goods across borders. Therefore, it safeguards open international trade.

Nevertheless, Article XI does not impose a blanket prohibition on all requirements for importation. Instead, it scrutinizes measures that have a limiting effect on the entry of goods into a market. Therefore, this restrictive impact needs to be demonstrated through the nature, design, and architecture of the measure.[241] Specifically, the measure's structure and operational mechanism are scrutinized to ascertain whether they constitute a tangible barrier to importation, thereby influencing the market entry opportunities for foreign goods. In practice, a measure could be subject to scrutiny under Article XI if it is shown to have a discernible restrictive impact on the opportunities for importation, irrespective of its purported objectives or justifications. Therefore, a careful evaluation of the measure's impact on trade flows is needed and evidence that it not only possesses the potential but also actively curtails the importation process are required.

In order to illustrate the importance of measure's nature under Article XI analysis, the Panel in the Brazil-Retreaded Tyres case conducted a comprehensive examination. The Panel held that punitive measures aimed at circumventing an import ban were also considered a restriction on the importation of retreaded tyres, even though they were not applied at the border.[242] This interpretation implies that Article XI:1 covers measures beyond traditional border measures, extending to actions that may

237 See Sect. 2.4 in Chap. 7.

238 Panel Report, *India—Autos*, para 7.224.

239 See Sect. 2.4 in Chap. 7.

240 One could insist that Art. III applies even in this case; see Panel Report, *India – Autos*, para. 7.306.

241 Appellate Body Report, *Argentina—Import Measures*, para 5.217.

242 Panel Report, *Brazil – Measures Affecting Imports of Retreaded Tyres* (*Brazil- Retreaded Tyres*) WT/DS332/R, adopted 17 December 2007, as modified by Appellate Body Report WT/DS332/AB/R, paras. 7.360–7.368.

have a similar restrictive impact on imports. Likewise, the decisions of the Appellate Body and panels in previous cases have established that discretionary import licensing systems[243] and non-automatic import licensing systems[244] might result in substantive delays in the import or export of products. Such delays can be tantamount to restrictions on the free flow of goods across borders, contravening the principles under Article XI:1.[245] These cases highlight the importance of an all-inclusive analysis of the nature and impact of measures to determine their compatibility with Article XI:1. They reinforce the principle that restrictions on trade can take various forms, and the scrutiny extends beyond explicit border measures to encompass any measure that substantively impedes the importation or exportation of goods.

Consequently, under the climate club, the surrender of emissions allowances by importers to align with the club's carbon price or any other similar climate club requirements could potentially be viewed as measures that might hinder free international trade. While serving legitimate environmental goals, these types of regulations may have implications for the free flow of goods across borders. Therefore, the measures adopted by the climate club should aim to achieve environmental goals without unnecessarily restricting trade, ensuring that any trade-related measures are proportionate to the environmental benefits sought.[246] The key considerations to find violation with the climate linkages would be whether these requirements create practical obstacles, burdens, or disadvantages for foreign products by impeding their entry into the market and impose more onerous conditions than those applied to domestic products.

In the context of purchasing of club's emission allowances by the importers and its equivalent application to domestic products as part of a club ETS triggers the application of the first paragraph of Article III and the Additional Protocol to Article III (Ad Article III) of the GATT 1994. The first paragraph pertains to situations where internal taxes, charges, laws, regulations, or requirements are applied to imported and like domestic products at the time or point of importation. Therefore, while the allowances that imports must surrender at the border to enter the club's market are subject to Article XI, the national treatment rule becomes relevant because industries within the club's jurisdiction must also purchase the same amount of allowances under the ETS. Consequently, emissions allowances purchase by importers are regarded as internal regulation in nature due to their application to both imports and domestic products and are subject to the provisions of Article III. Thereby, the national treatment analysis, which is held in the following chapter, is relevant for the purpose of club linkage of allowance purchase at the border.[247]

---

[243] Panel Report, *India — Quantitative Restrictions*, para. 5.130.

[244] GATT Panel Report, *Japan - Trade in Semi-Conductors*, para. 118.

[245] Panel Reports, *Argentina – Measures Affecting the Importation of Goods, (Argentina—Import Measures),* WT/DS438/R and Add.1 / WT/DS444/R and Add.1 / WT/DS445/R and Add.1, adopted 26 January 2015, as modified (WT/DS438/R) and upheld (WT/DS444/R / WT/DS445/R) by Appellate Body Reports WT/DS438/AB/R / WT/DS444/AB/R / WT/DS445/AB/R, para 6.448.

[246] See Sect. 4.4 in Chap. 7.

[247] See Sect. 2.4 in Chap. 7.

4 Concluding Remarks

This chapter embarked on a legality examination of the climate club scheme, specifically focusing on its alignment with the Paris Agreement's principles and WTO norms. Section 1 assesses whether the climate club scheme, as a cooperative approach to addressing climate change, stands on legal ground within the ambit of the Paris Agreement and its broader objectives. Particularly, how the club scheme aligns with Article 6 of the Agreement is scrutinized. The role of club linkages in ensuring the scheme's effectiveness and contribution to achieving global climate targets is analysed concerning the carbon trading cooperation under Article 6 market and non-market approaches. Consequently, the examination has illuminated that the climate club scheme not only complements the Paris Agreement but also amplifies its call for heightened ambition and cooperation among countries. Notably, the Climate Club Initiative at COP 28, an innovative approach to industrial decarbonization and enhancing global climate governance, serves as empirical evidence supporting the climate club theory.

The implications of these findings are profound since the climate club's legality under the Paris Agreement enhances its capacity to drive international cooperation. The alignment with the Agreement's goals underscores the club's potential as a catalyst for innovative and ambitious climate solutions. Looking forward, the climate club scheme holds promise as a dynamic and effective tool for international climate governance. Its evolution and integration with the Paris Agreement's mechanisms will be critical in steering the global community towards achieving the ambitious targets set for climate action.

The alignment with the Paris Agreement also strengthens the legality of the climate club scheme under the framework of WTO law. Being more specific and later in time in the climate change realm, the Paris Agreement can be applied at the WTO dispute settlement for the reciprocal obligations of the WTO Agreements. In this context, one way to justify climate club linkages under the WTO dispute settlement hinges on aligning the club approach with Paris Agreement Article 6. However, still, the climate club linkages should balance ambitious climate action with fair and equitable treatment to all trading partners to comply with WTO regulations. They should not constitute unjustifiable trade barriers. This alignment is crucial for maintaining the club's legality and effectiveness in fostering global cooperation on climate change.

Under Sect. 3 of the Chap. 6, club linkages of extra carbon tariffs, import requirements leading to bans or quotas for high carbon emitted products, or surrender of emission allowance certificates for certain imports' with WTO norms are analysed. The examination of schedule of concessions, tariff deconsolidation, and the general elimination of quantitative restrictions has highlighted the intricate legal considerations involved in reconciling trade and climate policies. The club linkages are issued with respect to a domestic legislation. Hence, they do not qualify as a border measure subject to the restrictions of the schedule of concessions, which prohibits unilateral tariff increases unless the requirements of the tariff deconsolidation clause are met. Due to the reference given in the Article II:2(a) to the principle of national treatment, the additional carbon tariff for non-club members should not exceed the carbon tax on domestic products. With respect to tariff deconsolidation, although is not widely used by WTO members, it has the potential to expand international trade of environmental goods if compensation for tariff increases on carbon-intensive products is determined as a tariff decrease for climate-friendly products. Regarding the clause for the elimination of quantitative restrictions, the purchase of emission allowances from the club ETS is considered a domestic regulation measure. Therefore, its compatibility with the GATT 1994 is based on the national treatment analysis, which is evaluated under Sect. 2 in Chap. 7 of this book.

The potential conflicts between climate and trade policies highlight the need for innovative legal interpretations, policy coordination, and international cooperation. The climate club scheme exemplifies how such coordination can be achieved, proposing a model where member countries adopt shared standards for carbon emissions, implement carbon pricing mechanisms, and agree on mutual recognition of emissions allowances. By creating a common ground, the club can mitigate the risk of trade disputes and foster a global market for green goods. Through leveraging legal flexibilities and pursuing multilateral negotiations, it is possible to align climate actions with trade norms, thereby advancing the objectives of the Paris Agreement and promoting sustainable trade practices. The integration of environmental and trade policies will be paramount in realizing a sustainable future. With its dual legitimacy under the Paris Agreement and WTO law, the climate club scheme stands as a beacon of innovative and cooperative action in the face of climate change challenge. Moving forward, international climate governance must integrate innovative approaches and recognize club linkages' value in achieving the ambitious goals set forth in the Paris Agreement.

Bibliography

Cases

GATT Panel Report, *Canada-Import, Distribution and Sale of Certain Alcoholic Drinks by Provincial Marketing Agencies*, (18 February 1992) DS17/R, 39S/27, 75.

—*Japan - Trade in Semi-Conductors,* (4 May 1988) L/6309 - 35S/116.

—*United States-Taxes on Petroleum and Certain Imported Substances,* (17 June 1987) L/6175, 34S/136.

WTO Panel Report, *Argentina – Measures Affecting the Export of Bovine Hides and the Import of Finished Leather,* WT/DS155/R and Corr.1, adopted 16 February 2001.

—*Argentina – Measures Affecting the Importation of Goods*, WT/DS438/R and Add.1 / WT/DS444/R and Add.1 / WT/DS445/R and Add.1, adopted 26 January

2015, as modified (WT/DS438/R) and upheld (WT/DS444/R / WT/DS445/R) by Appellate Body Reports WT/DS438/AB/R / WT/DS444/AB/R / WT/DS445/AB/R.

—*Argentina – Measures Relating to Trade in Goods and Services*, WT/DS453/R and Add.1, adopted 9 May 2016, as modified by Appellate Body Report WT/DS453/AB/R.

—*Brazil – Measures Affecting Imports of Retreaded Tyres,* WT/DS332/R, adopted 17 December 2007, as modified by Appellate Body Report WT/DS332/AB/R.

—*China – Measures Affecting Imports of Automobile Parts*, WT/DS339/R, Add.1 and Add.2 / WT/DS340/R, Add.1 and Add.2 / WT/DS342/R, Add.1 and Add.2, adopted 12 January 2009, upheld (WT/DS339/R) and as modified (WT/DS340/R / WT/DS342/R) by Appellate Body Reports WT/DS339/AB/R / WT/DS340/AB/R / WT/DS342/AB/R.

—*Dominican Republic – Measures Affecting the Importation and Internal Sale of Cigarettes*, WT/DS302/R, adopted 19 May 2005, as modified by Appellate Body Report WT/DS302/AB/R.

—*European Communities – Regime for the Importation, Sale and Distribution of Bananas, (EC-Bananas III)* WT/DS27/AB/R, adopted 25 September 1997

—*European Communities – Customs Classification of Frozen Boneless Chicken Cuts*, WT/DS269/R (Brazil) / WT/DS286/R (Thailand), adopted 27 September 2005, as modified by Appellate Body Report WT/DS269/AB/R, WT/DS286/AB/R.

—*European Communities – Measures Affecting the Approval and Marketing of Biotech Products*, WT/DS291/R, Add.1 to Add.9 and Corr.1 / WT/DS292/R, Add.1 to Add.9 and Corr.1 / WT/DS293/R, Add.1 to Add.9 and Corr.1, adopted 21 November 2006.

—*European Union – Measures Affecting Tariff Concessions on Certain Poultry Meat Products*, WT/DS492/R and Add.1, adopted 19 April 2017.

—*India – Certain Measures Relating to Solar Cells and Solar Modules,* WT/DS456/R and Add.1, adopted 14 October 2016, as modified by Appellate Body Report WT/DS456/AB/R.

—*India – Measures Affecting the Automotive Sector*, WT/DS146/R, WT/DS175/R, and Corr.1, adopted 5 April 2002.

—*India – Quantitative Restrictions on Imports of Agricultural, Textile and Industrial Products*, WT/DS90/R, adopted 22 September 1999, upheld by Appellate Body Report WT/DS90/AB/R.

—*Korea – Measures Affecting Imports of Fresh, Chilled and Frozen Beef*, WT/DS161/R, WT/DS169/R, adopted 10 January 2001, as modified by Appellate Body Report WT/DS161/AB/R, WT/DS169/AB/R.

—*Mexico – Tax Measures on Soft Drinks and Other Beverages*, WT/DS308/R, adopted 24 March 2006, as modified by Appellate Body Report WT/DS308/AB/R.

—*Russia – Tariff Treatment of Certain Agricultural and Manufacturing Products,* WT/DS485/R, Add.1, Corr.1, and Corr.2, adopted 26 September 2016.

—*United States – Definitive Anti-Dumping and Countervailing Duties on Certain Products from China*, WT/DS379/R, adopted 25 March 2011, as modified by Appellate Body Report WT/DS379/AB/R

—*United States – Section 110(5) of the US Copyright Act,* WT/DS160/R, adopted 27 July 2000

WTO Appellate Body Report, *Argentina – Measures Affecting Imports of Footwear, Textiles, Apparel and Other Items,* WT/DS56/AB/R and Corr.1, adopted 22 April 1998

—*Argentina – Measures Affecting the Importation of Goods,* WT/DS438/AB/R / WT/DS444/AB/R / WT/DS445/AB/R, adopted 26 January 2015

—*Brazil – Measures Affecting Imports of Retreaded Tyres,* WT/DS332/AB/R, adopted 17 December 2007

—*Canada – Measures Affecting the Importation of Milk and the Exportation of Dairy Products*, WT/DS103/AB/R, WT/DS113/AB/R, and Corr.1, adopted 27 October 1999

—*China - Measures Affecting Imports of Automobile Parts,* WT/DS339/AB/R, WT/DS340/AB/R, WT/DS342/AB/R, adopted 12 January 2009.

—*China – Measures Related to the Exportation of Various Raw Materials (China-Raw Materials) WT/DS394/AB/R / WT/DS395/AB/R / WT/DS398/AB/R, adopted 22 February 2012*

—*European Communities and Certain Member States – Measures Affecting Trade in Large Civil Aircraft, (EC and certain member States – Large Civil Aircraft)* WT/DS316/AB/R, adopted 1 June 2011

—*European Communities – Customs Classification of Certain Computer Equipment*, WT/DS62/AB/R, WT/DS67/AB/R, WT/DS68/AB/R, adopted 22 June 1998

—*European Communities – Customs Classification of Frozen Boneless Chicken Cuts*, WT/DS269/AB/R, WT/DS286/AB/R, adopted 27 September 2005

—*India- Additional and Extra-Additional Duties on Imports from the United States*, WT/DS360/AB/R, adopted 17 November 2008

—*India – Certain Measures Relating to Solar Cells and Solar Modules*, WT/DS456/AB/R and Add.1, adopted 14 October 2016.

—*India – Patent Protection for Pharmaceutical and Agricultural Chemical Products*, WT/DS50/AB/R, adopted 16 January 1998

—*Peru – Additional Duty on Imports of Certain Agricultural Products,* WT/DS457/AB/R and Add.1, adopted 31 July 2015

—*United States – Import Prohibition of Certain Shrimp and Shrimp Products*, WT/DS58/AB/R, adopted 6 November 1998

—*United States – Measures Affecting the Cross-Border Supply of Gambling and Betting Services,* WT/DS285/AB/R, adopted 20 April 2005.

—*United States – Standards for Reformulated and Conventional Gasoline*, WT/DS2/AB/R, adopted 20 May 1996.

—*United States – Tax Treatment for 'Foreign Sales Corporations' – Second Recourse to Article 21.5 of the DSU by the European Communities*, WT/DS108/AB/RW2, adopted 14 March 2006.

Legislation

Basel Convention on the Control of Transboundary Movements of Hazardous Wastes and Their Disposal (adopted 22 March 1989, entered into force 5 May 1992) 1673 UNTS. 125

Conference of Parties (COP), 'Decision 1/CP.21 Adoption of the Paris Agreement' (12 December 2015) U.N. Doc. FCCC/CP/2015/L.9/Rev.1

General Agreement on Tariffs and Trade (GATT 1994) (15 April 1994) LT/UR/A-1A/1/GATT/1 <https://docs.wto.org/dol2fe/Pages/SS/directdoc.aspx?filename=Q:/UR/FA/06-gatt.pdf&Open=True>

Marrakesh Agreement Establishing the World Trade Organization (15 April 1994) LT/UR/A/2 <https://docs.wto.org/dol2fe/Pages/SS/directdoc.aspx?filename=Q:/UR/FA/04-wto.pdf&Open=True>

Montreal Protocol on Substances that Deplete the Ozone Layer (with Annex) (adopted 16 September 1987, entered into force 1 January 1989) 1522 UNTS 3, 26 ILM 1541, 1550.

Understanding on Rules and Procedures Governing the Settlement of Disputes (DSU) (15 April 1994) LT/UR/A-2/DS/U/1 https://docs.wto.org/dol2fe/Pages/SS/directdoc.aspx?filename=Q:/UR/FA/28-dsu.pdf&Open=True

United Nations Framework Convention on Climate Change, 1771 U.N.T.S. 107, 165; S. Treaty Doc No. 102-38 (1992); U.N. Doc. A/AC.237/18 (Part II)/Add.1; 31 I.L.M. 849

UNFCCC, Glasgow Climate Pact. UNFCCC Decision 1/CMA.3. (2021)

Vienna Convention on the Law of Treaties (VCLT) (adopted on 23 May 1969, entered into force on 27 January 1980) 1155 UNTS 331.

Secondary Sources

Guidelines adopted on 10 November 1980, GATT documents C/113 and C/113/Corr.1, GATT BISD 27S/26-28

Press Release, '36 members launch Climate Club as a high-ambition forum to turbocharge decarbonization of key industry sectors' (01 December 2023) 1 <https://climate-club.org/wp-content/uploads/2023/12/Climate-Club-COP-28-Full-Launch-Press-Release-01.12.2023-1.pdf> accessed 4 April 2024

Statement by the Climate Club, 'Accelerating the decarbonization of our industries' (1 December 2023) <https://climate-club.org/wp-content/uploads/2023/11/231122_Statement-by-the-Climate-Club_FINAL_Layout.pdf> accessed 4 April 2024

Adlung R and Molinuevo M, 'The Role of Non-WTO Agreements in WTO Dispute Settlement: Issues and Challenges' (2019) 22(1) Journal of International Economic Law 75

Ahlberg M, 'Enhancing Ambition Carbon Pricing as a Tool to Step up Mitigation Efforts' (2018) 6 Carbon Mechanisms Review 22

Asadnabizadeh M, 'Development of UN Framework Convention on Climate Change Negotiations Under COP25: Article 6 of the Paris Agreement Perspective' (2019) 2 Open Political Science 113

Asmelash H, 'The WTO Dispute Settlement System as a Forum for Climate Litigation?' (2023) 32 RECIEL 321

Bacchus J, 'The Case for a WTO Climate Waiver' (CIGI, 2017) <https://www.cigionline.org/publications/case-wto-climate-waiver/> accessed 1 April 2024.

Barbier EB, 'Greening the G7 Economies' (2023) 39(4) Oxford Review of Economic Policy 731<https://doi.org/10.1093/oxrep/grad039>

— 'The G7 Needs To Boost Its Low-Carbon Strategy-Here's How' (2023) 617 Nature 459

Bartels L, 'The WTO Legality of the Application of the EU's Emission Trading System to Aviation' (2012) 23 European Journal of International Law 429

Bernasconi-Osterwalder N, Campos SL, and Baliño S, 'Trade and Environment' in *The Elgar Companion to the World Trade Organization* (Edward Elgar Publishing 2022)

Bodansky D, 'Legal Form of a New Climate Agreement: Avenues and Options' (Pew Center on Global Climate Change, Arlington, VA, 2009)

— 'The Legal Character of the Paris Agreement' (2016) 25 RECIEL 25

Boisson de Chazournes L and Mbengue MM, 'The Principles of Precaution and Sustainability' in T Cottier and K Nadakavukaren Schefer (eds), *Elgar Encyclopaedia of International Economic Law* (Edward Elgar 2017)

Böhringer C and others, 'Potential Impacts and Challenges of Border Carbon Adjustments' (2022) 12 Nat. Clim. Chang, 22, 22 <https://doi.org/10.1038/s41558-021-01250-z>

Bullock D, 'Combating Climate Recalcitrance: Carbon-Related Border Tax Adjustments in a New Era of Global Climate Governance' (2018) 27 Washington International Law Journal 609

Chapman A, 'Walking the Talk? Examining the EU and China's Claims to Climate Leadership in the Negotiation and Implementation of the Paris Agreement' (University of British Columbia, 2020) <https://open.library.ubc.ca/soa/cIRcle/collections/ubctheses/24/items/1.0392041> accessed 4 April 2024

Chavara C and others, 'Continuity and Change in Carbon Market Politics' in J Sowers and others (eds), *The Oxford Handbook of Comparative Environmental Politics* (Oxford University Press 2021)

Climate Club, Work Programme 2024, <https://climate-club.org/wp-content/uploads/2023/11/CC-Work-Programme-2024_bf_final.pdf> accessed 4 April 2024

— 'Governance Arrangements' (13 October 2023), <https://climate-club.org/wp-content/uploads/2023/11/20231910_Climate-Club-Governance-Arrangements_Layout.pdf> accessed 4 April 2024

— 'Terms of Reference', https://climate-club.org/wp-content/uploads/2023/11/TOR-CC-logo.pdf accessed 4 April 2024

Cottier T and Oesch M, 'WTO Law, Precedents, and Legal Change' (2001) 3(1) JIEL 27

— *International Trade Regulation: Law and Policy in the WTO, The European Union and Switzerland, Cases Materials and Comments* (Cameron May Ltd, London 2005)

—, Nartova O and Shingal A, 'The Potential of Tariff Policy for Climate Change Mitigation: Legal and Economic Analysis' (2014) 48(5) Journal of World Trade 1007

— and Payosova T, 'Common Concern and Legitimacy of the WTO in Dealing with Climate Change' in Panagiotis Delimatsis (ed) *Research Handbook on Climate Change and Trade* (Edward Elgar 2016)

Das K, 'Can Border Carbon Adjustments Be WTO-Legal' (2011) 8 Manchester Journal of International Economic Law 65

Delimatsis P, 'Fragmentation of International Trade Law' (2011) 45 Journal of World Trade 87

Dobson N, Chapter 25: Climate Protection versus Trade: Dilemmas for the EU' in *Handbook on European Union Climate Change Policy and Politics* (Edward Elgar Publishing, 2023)

Droege S, 'Using Border Measures to Address Carbon Flows' (2011) 11 Climate Policy 1191 <https://doi.org/10.1080/14693062.2011.592671>

Durán GM, 'Securing Compatibility of Carbon Border Adjustments with the Multilateral Climate and Trade Regimes' (2023) 72 International & Comparative Law Quarterly 73

Eckersley R, 'The Big Chill: The WTO and Multilateral Environmental Agreements' (2004) 4 Global Environmental Politics 24

Edmonds J and others, 'How Much Could Article 6 Enhance Nationally Determined Contribution Ambition Toward Paris Agreement Goals Through Economic Efficiency?' (2021) 12 Climate Change Economics 7 <https://doi.org/10.1142/s201000782150007x>

Englisch J and Falcao T, 'EU Carbon Border Adjustments for Imported Products and WTO Law' (9 June 2021) <https://doi.org/10.2139/ssrn.3863038>

Espa I, and Holzer K, 'From Unilateral Border Carbon Adjustments to Cooperation in Climate Clubs: Rethinking Exclusion in Light of Trade and Climate Law Constraints' in J. Bäumler and others (eds), European Yearbook of International Economic Law 2022 (vol 13, Springer, 2023) <https://doi.org/10.1007/8165_2022_101>

Federal Office for the Environment, 'Bilateral Climate Agreements' <https://www.bafu.admin.ch/bafu/en/home/topics/climate/info-specialists/climate%2D%2Dinternational-affairs/staatsvertraege-umsetzung-klimauebereinkommen-von-paris-artikel6.html> accessed 4 April 2024

G7 Germany, 'Statement on Climate Club Elmau' (28 June 2022) https://www.g7germany.de/resource/blob/974430/2057926/2a7cd9f10213a481924492942dd660a1/2022-06-28-g7-climate-club-data.pdf accessed 4 April 2024

Gao S and others, 'International Carbon Markets Under the Paris Agreement: Basic Form and Development Prospects' (2019) 10 Advances in Climate Change Research 21

Greiner S and Michaelowa A, Cooperative Approaches under Art. 6.2 of the Paris Agreement: Status of Negotiations – Key Areas of Consensus and Contention (Discussion Paper-January 2018) <https://climatefocus.com/publications/cooperative-approaches-under-art-62-paris-agreement/> accessed 4 April 2024

Hagen A and Schneider J, 'Trade Sanctions and the Stability of Climate Coalitions' (2021) 109 J Environ Econ Manag 102504

Hahn M, 'Challenges for the Rule of Law in the WTO' (2019) 22 ZEuS 349

Hausammann F and Reich J, 'E. Switzerland' (2021) 32 Yearbook of International Environmental Law 145 <https://doi.org/10.1093/yiel/yvac051>

Hertel M, 'Climate-Change-Related Trade Measures and Article XX: Defining Discrimination in Light of the Principle of Common but Differentiated Responsibilities' (2011) 45(3) JWT 653

Hoekman B and others, 'Conclude Doha: It Matters!' (2009) 9 World Trade Review 505 <https://doi.org/10.1017/S1474745610000297>

Howard A, 'Incentivizing Mitigation: Using International Carbon Markets to Raise Ambition' (Federal Ministry for the Environment, Nature Conservation & Nuclear Safety of Germany 2018), <https://www.carbonmechanisms.de/fileadmin/media/dokumente/Publikationen/Studie/Studie_2018_KoruClimate_Incentivizing.pdf> accessed 4 April 2024

Interim Secretariat of the Climate Club, 'Accelerating Global Industry Decarbonization Through Stronger International Collaboration Paper' <https://climate-club.org/wp-content/uploads/2023/11/Climate-Club-COP-28-background-paper.pdf> accessed 4 April 2024

Intergovernmental Panel on Climate Change (IPCC), 'Summary for Policymakers in Climate Change 2022: Mitigation of Climate Change. Contribution of Working Group III to the Sixth Assessment Report of the Intergovernmental Panel on Climate Change' (2022) <https://www.ipcc.ch/report/ar6/wg3/downloads/report/IPCC_AR6_WGIII_SummaryForPolicymakers.pdf> accessed 24 March 2024

International Law Commission, 'Draft Articles on the Law of Treaties, with Commentaries' (1966) II Yearbook of the International Law Commission

— 'Fragmentation of International Law: Difficulties Arising from the Diversification and Expansion of International Law' (A/CN.4/L.702, 2006)

Kim R, 'The Emergent Network Structure of the Multilateral Environmental Agreement System' (2013) 23(5) Global Environmental Change 980

Kreibich N and Obergassel W, New Paths to Policy Crediting? Challenges and Opportunities of Policy-Based Cooperation Under Article 6 of the Paris Agreement (Wuppertal Inst. 2018) <https://epub.wupperinst.org/frontdoor/deliver/index/docId/7205/file/7205_Policy_Crediting.pdf> on 4 April 2024

Kulovesi K, *The WTO Dispute Settlement System: Challenges of the Environment, Legitimacy and Fragmentation* (Kluwer, 2011)

— 'Climate Change and Trade: At the Intersection of Two International Legal Regimes' in E J. Hollo, K Kulovesi and M Mehling (eds), *Climate Change and the Law* (Springer 2013)

Lamy P, 'Trade Can Be a Friend, Not a Foe, of Conservation' (Speech, WTO Symposium on Trade and Sustainable Development within the Framework of Paragraph 51 of the Doha Ministerial Declaration, Geneva, 10 October 2005)

— 'The Place of the WTO and Its Law in the International Legal Order' (2007) European Journal of International Law 978

Lang S, Blum M and Leipold S, 'What Future for the Voluntary Carbon Offset Market after Paris? An Explorative Study Based on the Discursive Agency Approach' (2019) 19(4) Climate Policy 414

Larbprasertporn P, 'The Interaction between WTO Law and the Principle of Common But Differentiated Responsibilities in the Case of Climate-Related Border Tax Adjustment' (2014) 6(1) Goettingen Journal of International Law 145

Leycegui B and Ramirez I, *Addressing Climate Change: A WTO Exception to Incorporate Climate Clubs* (E15 Expert Group on Measures to Address Climate Change and the Trade System, May 2015)

Macinante JD and others, 'Operationalizing Cooperative Approaches Under the Paris Agreement by Valuing Mitigation Outcomes' (2018) 12 Carbon and Climate Law Review 258, <https://doi.org/10.21552/cclr/2018/3/12>

Magacho G, Espagne E and Godin A, 'Impacts of the CBAM on EU Trade Partners: Consequences for Developing Countries' (2024) 24(2) Climate Policy 243 <https://doi.org/10.1080/14693062.2023.2200758>

Marceau G, 'Conflicts of Norms and Conflicts of Jurisdictions: The Relationship between the WTO Agreement and MEAs and other Treaties' (2001) Journal of World Trade

— 'WTO Dispute Settlement and Human Rights' (2002) 14 European Journal of International Law 753

Marcu A, 'Carbon Market Provisions in the Paris Agreement (Article 6)' (2016) <https://www.ceps.eu/ceps-publications/carbon-market-provisions-paris-agreement-article-6/> accessed 4 April 2024

— 'What is Standing in the Way of a Happy Ending Reflections on Art. 6 before SBSTA 48?' (2018) <https://ercst.org/what-is-standing-in-the-way-of-a-happy-ending-reflections-on-art-6-before-sbsta-48/> accessed 4 April 2024

Mathew AJ and others 'The Green Dilemma about Liberalization of Trade in Environmental Goods' (2009) Journal of World Trade <https://doi.org/10.54648/trad2009016>

Mavroidis PC, 'Quantitative Restrictions and the GATT Framework' in Understanding the Complexities of International Trade Law (MIT Press 2020)

— 'The Future of Dispute Resolution and Arbitration at WTO' in The Elgar Companion to the World Trade Organization (Edward Elgar Publishing 2020)

Mayer B, *International Law Obligations on Climate Change Mitigation* (Oxford University Press 2022)

McKenzie M 'Climate Change and the Generalized System of Preferences' (2008) 11 Journal of International Economic Law

Meerkouris P, *Article 31(3)(c) VCLT and the Principle of Systemic Integration: Normative Shadows in Plato's Cave*, (Nijhoff/Brill 2015)

Mehling M, 'Governing the Carbon Market' in A Marke, M Mehling, and F de Andrade Correa (eds), Governing Carbon Markets with Distributed Ledger Technology (Cambridge University Press 2022)

—, Metcalf GE, and Stavins RN, Linking Heterogeneous Climate Policies (Consistent with the Paris Agreement) (Discussion Paper, ES 17-6 Harvard Project on Climate Agreements, October 2017)

— and others, 'Designing Border Carbon Adjustments for Enhanced Climate Action' (2019) 113(3) American Journal of International Law 433

Minas S, 'Market Making for the Planet: The Paris Agreement Article 6 Decisions and Transnational Carbon Markets' (2022) 13 Transnational Legal Theory 287

Müller B, 'Article 6 Market Approaches under the Paris Agreement' (European Capacity Building Initiative 2018) <https://ecbi.org/news/article-6-market-approaches-under-paris-agreement> accessed 4 April 2024.

Narassimhan E and others, 'Carbon Pricing in Practice: A Review of Existing Emissions Trading Systems' (2018) 18 Climate Policy 967

Nishimura T, 'The Paris Agreement: Continuity and Change within the Climate Regime' in N Craikand others (eds), *Global Environmental Change and Innovation in International Law* (Cambridge University Press, 2018)

Office of the United States Trade Representative Ambassador Robert E. Lighthizer, 'Report on the Appellate Body of the World Trade Organization' (February 2020) <https://ustr.gov/sites/default/files/Report_on_the_Appellate_Body_of_the_World_Trade_Organization.pdf> accessed 4 April 2024

Oh C, 'Exploring the Way to Harmonize Sustainable Development Assessment Methods in Article 6.2 Cooperative Approaches of the Paris Agreement' (2023) 1(3) Green and Low-Carbon Economy 121 <https://doi.org/10.47852/bonviewGLCE32021065>

Olawuyi DS, 'Environment' in D Bethlehem and others (eds), *The Oxford Handbook of International Trade Law* (2nd edn, Oxford University Press 2022)

Olsen K and others, 'Sustainability Labelling as a Tool for Reporting the Sustainable Development Impacts of Climate Actions Relevant to Article 6 of the Paris Agreement' (2019) 19 International Environmental Agreements: Politics, Law and Economics 225 <https://doi.org/10.1007/s10784-018-09428-1>

Oliveira TD, Gurgel AC, and Tonry S, 'International Market Mechanisms under the Paris Agreement: A Cooperation between Brazil and Europe' (2019) 129 Energy Policy 397

Pauwelyn J, 'The Role of Public International Law in the WTO: How Far Can We Go?' (2001) 95 American Journal of International Law 535

— 'Conflict of Norms in WTO Dispute Settlement' in *Conflict of Norms in Public International Law: How WTO Law Relates to Other Rules of International Law* (Cambridge University Press 2003)

— 'How to Win a World Trade Organization Dispute Based on Non-World Trade Organization Law - Questions of Jurisdiction and Merits' (2003) 37 Journal of World Trade

— 'The Use of Non-WTO Agreements as a Basis for WTO Law' in A Peters and others (eds), *Non-State Actors as Standard Setters* (Cambridge University Press 2013)
— 'The WTO's Multi-Party Interim Appeal Arbitration Arrangement (MPIA): What's New?' (2023) 22 World Trade Review 693
Polanco R, 'Integrating Trade, Investment and Climate Change' in T Cottier and K Nadakavukaren Schefer (eds), *Elgar Encyclopedia of International Economic Law* (Edward Elgar 2017)
Regan DH, 'Sources of International Trade Law: Understanding What the Vienna Convention Says About Identifying and Using 'Sources for Treaty Interpretation'' in S Besson and J d'Aspremont (eds), *The Oxford Handbook of the Sources of International Law* (Oxford University Press 2017)
— and Boss N, 'E. Switzerland' (2022) 33 Yearbook of International Environmental Law 149 <https://doi.org/10.1093/yiel/yvad032>
Rovetta D, 'Harmonized System and Schedules of Concession' in T Cottier and K Nadakavukaren Schefer (eds), *Elgar Encyclopedia of International Economic Law* (Edward Elgar 2017)
Rubini L, '"The Good, the Bad, and the Ugly:" Lessons on Methodology in Legal Analysis from the Recent WTO Litigation on Renewable Energy Subsidies' (2014) 48 Journal of World Trade 895
Sands P, 'Treaty, Custom and the Cross-Fertilization of International Law' (1998) 1 Yale Human Rights and Development Law Journal 85
Schefer KN and Arnaiz P, 'Duty to Protect, Climate Change and Trade in P Delimatsis (ed) *Research Handbook on Climate Change and Trade* (Edward Elgar 2016)
Srinivasan S and Zunino FS, 'Unlocking Ambition Through a Climate Market Club' (World Bank Blogs, 2020) <https://blogs.worldbank.org/en/climatechange/unlocking-ambition-through-climate-market-club> accessed on 26 March 2024
Steinebach Y and Limberg J, 'Implementing Market Mechanisms in the Paris Era: The Importance of Bureaucratic Capacity Building for International Climate Policy' (2021) 29 Journal of European Public Policy 1153
Stern N and Lankes HP, *Collaborating and Delivering on Climate Action Through a Climate Club: An Independent Report to the G7* (London School of Economics and Political Science, 2022)
Trachtman J and Pauwelyn J, 'Conflict of Norms in Public International Law: How WTO Law Relates to Other Rules of International Law' (2004) 98 The American Journal of International Law
United Nations Framework Convention on Climate Change (UNFCCC), 'Achievements of the Clean Development Mechanism 2001–2018: Harnessing Incentive for Climate Action' (UNFCCC 2018), <https://unfccc.int/sites/default/files/resource/UNFCCC_CDM_report_2018.pdf> accessed 20 May 2024
Van Asselt H, 'Trade and Climate Disputes before the WTO: Blocking or Driving Climate Action?' in I Alogna, C Bakker and JP Gauci (eds), *Climate Change Litigation: Global Perspectives* (Brill 2021)

Van den Bossche P, 'Non-WTO Dispute Settlement and WTO Law' in G Van Calster (ed) *Research Handbook on Environment, Health and the WTO* (Edward Elgar Publishing 2018)
Venzke I and Vidigal G, 'Are Trade Measures to Tackle the Climate Crisis the End of Differentiated Responsibilities? The Case of the EU Carbon Border Adjustment Mechanism (CBAM)' in M den Heijer and H. van der Wilt (eds.) (2022) 51 Netherlands Yearbook of International Law
Vidigal G, 'Designing Climate Clubs: The Four Models, Trade Commitments and the Non-Discrimination Dilemma' (2023) Amsterdam Law School Research Paper No 2023-07
Voigt C, 'WTO Law and International Emissions Trading: Is There Potential for Conflict?' (2008) 2(1) Carbon & Climate Law Review 54
— 'The Compliance and Implementation Mechanism of the Paris Agreement' (2016) 25(2) Review of European, Comparative & International Environmental Law
World Bank, Ecofys, and Vivid Economics, *State and Trends of Carbon Pricing: 2016* (IBRD/World Bank, October 2016)
—Group and Ecofys, *State and Trends of Carbon Pricing 2018* (The World Bank, Washington, DC, May 2018)
— State and Trends of Carbon Pricing 2020 (World Bank, 2020) <http://hdl.handle.net/10986/33809> accessed 4 April 2024
World Trade Organization (WTO), 'Ministerial Declaration' (14 November 2001) WT/MIN(01)/DEC/1
— Committee on Trade and Environment, 'Matrix on Trade-Related Measures Pursuant to Selected Multilateral Environmental Agreements' (6-9 October 2017) WT/CTE/W/160/Rev.8 TN/TE/S/5/Rev
— *Factual Report on the Status of Renegotiations under Article XXVIII of the GATT 1994* (G/MA/W/123/Rev.6)
— The Philippines, G/MA/W/123/Rev.6
— Statement on a Mechanism for Developing, Documenting and Sharing Practices and Procedures in the Conduct of WTO Disputes' JOB/DSB/1/Add.12 (30 April 2020).
— The Understanding on the Interpretation of Article XXVIII of the GATT 1994, <http://www.wto.org/english/docs_e/legal_e/12-28_e.htm>
— 'Import Licensing Notification Status' <https://importlicensing.wto.org/notification-status> accessed 21 May 2024
— 'Quantitative Restrictions Notifications' https://qr.wto.org/en#/notifications accessed 21 May 2024
— 'Quantitative Restrictions, Footnote 1 of the QR Decision' <https://www.wto.org/english/tratop_e/markacc_e/qr_e.htm> accessed 5 April 2024
Zhang K and others, 'Recent Progress of Cooperation on Climate Mitigation: A Bibliometric Analysis' (2020) 277 Journal of Cleaner Production 123495 <https://doi.org/10.1016/j.jclepro.2020.12349>

Open Access This chapter is licensed under the terms of the Creative Commons Attribution 4.0 International License (http://creativecommons.org/licenses/by/4.0/), which permits use, sharing, adaptation, distribution and reproduction in any medium or format, as long as you give appropriate credit to the original author(s) and the source, provide a link to the Creative Commons license and indicate if changes were made.

The images or other third party material in this chapter are included in the chapter's Creative Commons license, unless indicated otherwise in a credit line to the material. If material is not included in the chapter's Creative Commons license and your intended use is not permitted by statutory regulation or exceeds the permitted use, you will need to obtain permission directly from the copyright holder.

Chapter 7
Navigating Non-discrimination in Climate Club Policies

1 Most Favoured Nation Principle

1.1 Introduction

According to the MFN clause found in Article I of the GATT 1994, a WTO member shall not discriminate between like products from different trading partners. In other words, member should give them equally most-favoured-nation status. The principle requires that "any advantage, favour, privilege or immunity granted … shall be accorded immediately and unconditionally to the like product of all contracting parties".[1] The fundamental objective of the MFN principle is to foster an environment of fair and competitive opportunities for imports characterised as "like" from every WTO member. It is a linchpin in promoting non-discrimination and preventing preferential treatment that could distort the level playing field among trading partners.[2] The principle does not "require a demonstration of the actual trade effects of a specific measure".[3] The mere fact of creating more favourable competitive opportunities for certain WTO members can trigger the inconsistency with the MFN treatment obligation.[4] Therefore, the MFN principle contributes to the overarching goal of creating a transparent, predictable, and non-discriminatory global trading

[1] Appellate Body Report, *Canada – Certain Measures Affecting the Automotive Industry (Canada-Autos)* WT/DS139/AB/R, WT/DS142/AB/R, adopted 19 June 2000, para. 79. Panel Report, *Indonesia — Safeguard on Certain Iron or Steel Products*, WT/DS490/R; WT/DS496/R, para. 7.44.

[2] Appellate Body Reports, *European Communities – Measures Prohibiting the Importation and Marketing of Seal Products (EC-Seal Products),* WT/DS400/AB/R / WT/DS401/AB/R, adopted 18 June 2014, para 5.87.

[3] ibid para 5.82.

[4] Panel Report, *European Communities – Regime for the Importation, Sale and Distribution of Bananas, Complaint by Mexico, (EC-Bananas III (Mexico))* WT/DS27/R/MEX, adopted 25 September 1997, as modified by Appellate Body Report WT/DS27/AB/R, para. 7.239.

© The Author(s) 2025

T. G. Budak, *Beyond Treaties: Rethinking Legal Mechanisms for International Climate Governance*, https://doi.org/10.1007/978-3-031-86022-5_7

system.[5] In essence, it underlines the importance of allowing economies to thrive based on their inherent competitive merits rather than undue favourable treatment.[6]

Article I not only addresses de jure discrimination but also encompasses de facto discrimination, thereby expanding the scope of the MFN principle.[7] De facto discrimination arises when a measure, on the surface, does not explicitly discriminate against a product based on its origin. However, upon closer examination of relevant facts, it becomes evident that the measure provides less favourable treatment to a like product from another WTO member.[8] In contemporary international trade, an increasing number of sophisticated trade measures are designed to achieve broader societal goals. While ostensibly neutral, these measures may be more likely categorised as de facto discrimination when scrutinised in light of their actual impact. One notable example involves instruments targeting specific countries based on their climate policies and membership in the climate club. These challenged instruments could give rise to allegations of de facto discrimination on the ground of national origin,[9] even though they seemingly target the emission levels of products.[10] Herein, the determinative aspect in finding MFN violation is the effect of club linkage in market reality. By considering the real-world consequences of seemingly neutral measures, the WTO seeks to ensure that the MFN principle remains a robust safeguard against any form of discrimination, whether explicit or hidden.

In principle, the climate club linkages of BCAs as carbon tariffs or emissions allowance purchase, and technical regulations uniformly and equally apply to non-club members. However, they can also be modified to target carbon leakage accurately and prioritise environmental leadership while being fair to countries active in combatting climate change.[11] To do so, they can be tailored per the individual exporting countries' economic development levels, climate regulation, and other unique features.[12] However, in this case, the issue of the MFN principle will come into the debate. Under the MFN rule, the BCAs of the climate club framework must be extended to similar imports from all WTO members, irrespective of whether they

[5]Appellate Body Report, *European Communities — Conditions for the Granting of Tariff Preferences to Developing Countries (EC – Tariff Preferences)*, WT/DS246/AB/R, adopted on 20 April 2004, para 101.

[6]Armand de Mestral, 'The Principle of Most-Favoured-Nation Treatment' in Thomas Cottier and Krista Nadakavukaren Schefer (eds), *Elgar Encyclopedia of International Economic Law* (Edward Elgar 2017), 166.

[7]Appellate Body Report, *Canada- Autos*, para. 178.

[8]Sakuya Sato, 'EU's Carbon Adjustment Mechanism: Will It Achieve Its Objective(s)?' (2022) 56(3) JWT 383, 393–399.

[9]Christine Kaufmann and Rolf H Weber, 'Carbon-Related Border Tax Adjustments: Mitigating Climate Change or Restricting International Trade?' (2011) 10 World Trade Rev 497, 503.

[10]Appellate Body Report, *Canada-Autos,* para 86.

[11]Alice Pirlot, 'Carbon Border Adjustment Measures: A Straightforward Multi-Purpose Climate Change Instrument?' (2022) 34 Journal of Environmental Law 25, 47.

[12]David Bullock, 'Combating Climate Recalcitrance: Carbon-Related Border Tax Adjustments in a New Era of Global Climate Governance' (2018) 27 Washington International Law Journal 609, 609.

are part of the climate club or have initiatives to reduce carbon emissions. Differentiated treatment to trade partners, meaning exempting certain countries from the climate club linkages, constitutes an advantage, thereby violates the MFN principle.[13]

Furthermore, the analysis of the MFN principle within the context of climate-related trade measures extends beyond mere differentiation among WTO members. It also covers whether the specific requirements to receive differential and favourable treatment are discriminatory. While WTO law might, in theory, allow for differential treatment based on the level of climate action, the practical implementation becomes intricate. Determining which countries possess comparably effective climate policies without giving rise to discrimination claims is a formidable challenge. The effectiveness of climate policies can vary significantly, and the evaluation process is not straightforward.[14] Countries may adopt diverse strategies and regulatory frameworks, making it challenging to establish a universal metric for evaluating their contributions to combating climate change. For instance, a country may implement non-market-based regulations to curb emissions. They showcase a commitment to carbon abatement efforts but do not establish carbon price. Hence, even if there is no comparable financial value, it could still be successful in the carbon abatement efforts. For the reasons stated above, the club linkages should be applied uniformly to all non-member countries without considering their equivalent climate action. This way, the climate club simplifies the implementation of trade mechanisms without the need to scrutinise each country's legislation. In this case, the MFN principle may still be violated but the climate club enables its members to act as a bloc and strengthens their position in WTO disputes.

In the following sections, the book delves into the details of the MFN principle examination. Accordingly, Article I:1 outlines the four criteria to determine whether the measure is inconsistent with the MFN principle. By delineating these four criteria, the book provides a comprehensive framework for evaluating the compatibility of climate-related trade measures with the MFN principle. The criteria are whether;

- The measure at issue is covered by Article I:1,
- The measure grants an advantage,
- The products concerned are like products and;
- The advantage at issue is not accorded immediately and unconditionally to all like products concerned, irrespective of their origin[15] or destination.[16]

---

[13] Gerold Vidigal and Ingo Venzke, 'Of False Conflicts and Real Challenges: Trade Agreements, Climate Clubs, and Border Adjustments' (2022) 116 AJIL Unbound 202, 207.

[14] Ingo Venzke and Geraldo Vidigal, 'Are Trade Measures to Tackle the Climate Crisis the End of Differentiated Responsibilities? The Case of the EU Carbon Border Adjustment Mechanism (CBAM)' in M. den Heijer and H. van der Wilt (eds.) (2022) 51 Netherlands Yearbook of International Law 19.

[15] Rules of origin are rules, which require proof of which country product was produced in, where the raw materials are collected.

[16] Appellate Body Report, *EC-Seal Products*, para 5.86, Appellate Body Report, *Canada-Autos*, paras. 76–77, 79 and 84.

1.2 The Characteristics of Measure

1.2.1 Definition

Article I:1 regulates the following measures: (i) customs duties, (ii) charges of any kind imposed on or in connection with importation or exportation, (iii) charges imposed on the international transfer of payments for imports or exports, (iv) the method of levying such duties and charges, such as the method of assessing the base value on which the duty or charge is levied, and (v) all rules and formalities in connection with importation and exportation.[17] Accordingly, the MFN principle guides the regulation of various aspects related to the movement of goods and services across borders. In essence, the multifaceted coverage of the MFN principle reflects its pivotal role in promoting fairness, transparency, and equal treatment among countries engaged in global trade. In order to clarify the application scope of the principle, it is necessary to explain these measures individually.

Firstly, Article I:1 encompasses the regulation of customs duties, ensuring that nations accord each other equal treatment by refraining from imposing discriminatory tariffs on imports.[18] Secondly, the MFN principle extends its purview to include charges of any kind imposed on or in connection with importation or exportation.[19] By standardizing the treatment in importation, countries maintain smoother trade relations and contribute to the overall stability of the international economic landscape.[20] Moreover, charges imposed on the international transfer of payments for imports or exports are addressed under this Article.[21] This facet of the principle ensures that financial transactions related to international trade are subject to fair and uniform regulations. It prevents any undue burdens or impediments that may hinder the flow of goods and capital between nations.

---

[17] General Agreement on Tariffs and Trade (hereinafter GATT 1994) (15 April 1994) LT/UR/A-1A/1/GATT/1 <https://docs.wto.org/dol2fe/Pages/SS/directdoc.aspx?filename=Q:/UR/FA/06-gatt.pdf&Open=True>, art I:1.

[18] GATT Panel Report, *Spain: Tariff Treatment of Unroasted Coffee* (11 June 1981) BISD 28S/102.

[19] For instance, consular fee (Cuba-Consular Taxes), tax rebates (India-Tax Rebates), customs user fees (US- Customs User Fee).

[20] Henrik Horn and Petros C Mavroidis, 'Economic and Legal Aspects of the Most-Favored-Nation Clause' (2001) 17 European Journal of Political Economy 233 <https://doi.org/10.1016/S0176-2680(01)00028-3>.

[21] Panel Reports, *European Communities – Regime for the Importation, Sale and Distribution of Bananas*, (EC–Bananas III), WT/DS27/R/ECU *(Ecuador)* / WT/DS27/R/GTM, WT/DS27/R/HND *(Guatemala and Honduras)* / WT/DS27/R/MEX *(Mexico)* / WT/DS27/R/USA *(US)*, adopted 25 September 1997, as modified by Appellate Body Report WT/DS27/AB/R, DSR 1997, para. 7.189. Panel Report, *Colombia – Indicative Prices and Restrictions on Ports of Entry, (Colombia–Ports of Entry)*, WT/DS366/R and Corr.1, adopted 20 May 2009, para. 7.342; Panel Report, *United States – Certain Measures Affecting Imports of Poultry from China, (US–Poultry (China))*, WT/DS392/R, adopted 25 October 2010, para. 7.410. Panel Report, *European Union – Anti-Dumping Measures on Certain Footwear from China, (EU–Footwear (China))*, WT/DS405/R, adopted 22 February 2012, para. 7.100.

In addition, the method of levying customs duties and charges is a crucial aspect covered by the MFN principle. This measure includes specifying the methodology for assessing the base value on which the duty or charge is levied.[22] The aim is to establish transparent and standardized procedures and providing a predictable framework for businesses engaged in cross-border trade. Lastly, the MFN principle extends its influence to encompass all rules and formalities associated with importation and exportation. They include procedural requirements, documentation standards, and other regulatory measures that may impact the movement of goods across borders.[23] By harmonizing and streamlining these rules, the MFN principle contributes to the efficiency and effectiveness of international trade processes.

1.2.2 Results on the BCAs

Within the framework of the climate club scheme, the following key climate club linkages fall under the scope of Article I as they are directly applicable to the importation of goods. They are BCAs as a carbon tariff and emissions allowance purchase from the club's ETS, and technical regulations. These measures collectively contribute to the overarching goal of integrating environmental considerations into international trade and aligning economic activities with climate objectives. Technical regulations, such as labels or certificates, are regulated separately and specifically by the TBT Agreement and analysed under Sect. 3 of this chapter.

Firstly, BCAs as carbon duties represent a critical linkage within the climate club scheme. These tariffs are designed to internalize the social costs of carbon emissions, by imposing an extra cost to non-club imports.[24] They are no different than ordinary customs tariffs, as explained in Sect. 3.4 in Chap. 5. By imposing carbon duties on imported products, the climate club aims to encourage countries to adopt cleaner production methods and reduce their carbon footprint. Thereby, it contributes to global efforts to combat climate change. Secondly, BCAs can take the form of emission allowances purchase from the club's ETS, which constitute another element that is covered in Article I. These BCAs are mechanisms designed to level the playing field by imposing additional requirements on products from countries that do not adhere to similar environmental standards.[25] As an emissions allowance

[22] Peter Van den Bossche and Werner Zdouc, *The Law and Policy of the World Trade Organization* (5th edn, Cambridge University Press 2022), 344.

[23] Panel Report, *Argentina – Measures Relating to Trade in Goods and Services* (*Argentina-Financial Services*) WT/DS453/R and Add.1, adopted 9 May 2016, as modified by Appellate Body Report WT/DS453/AB/R, para 7.984.

[24] Mark Sanctuary, 'Border Carbon Adjustments and Unilateral Incentives to Regulate the Climate' (2018) 26 Rev Int Econ 826 <https://doi.org/10.1111/roie.12344>.

[25] Olivier Blanchard, Christian Gollier and Jean Tirole, 'The Portfolio of Economic Policies Needed to Fight Climate Change' (2023) 15 Annual Review of Economics 689, 710 <https://doi.org/10.1146/annurev-economics-051520-015113>. Anatole Boute, 'Accounting for Carbon Pricing in Third Countries Under the EU Carbon Border Adjustment Mechanism' (2024) World Trade Review 11.

purchase, BCA requires importing goods to offset their carbon emissions by acquiring emission allowances from the climate club's ETS. Both types of BCAs constitute charges related to importation. Hence, the club linkages should be examined with respect to the MFN principle as they fall under the category of measures regulated under Article I:1.

1.3 Advantage

1.3.1 Definition

The term advantage under the MFN principle refers to any concession, privilege, or benefit granted to a specific imported product among like products from different WTO member countries. Accordingly, lower tariffs, reduced customs duties, more favourable terms of trade or other charges related to importation should be applied to all trading partners to ensure a level playing field and prevent discriminatory treatment.[26] The principle helps to eliminate trade barriers, reduce trading costs, and increase the predictability of international trade. In this way, the MFN clause fosters a more efficient allocation of resources across borders.

1.3.2 Results on the BCAs

In the context of the climate club scheme, the situation is nuanced. The climate club seeks to address environmental concerns, particularly those related to carbon emissions. Unlike traditional border measures that may be applied uniformly to all products, the climate club operates on the premise that club products internalize the social cost of carbon through mechanisms such as a club's ETS and domestic carbon tax. Hence, it does not apply charges to club members' imports. However, regulatory distinctions based solely on the membership status of countries within the climate club or countries' own carbon legislation are regarded as an "advantage" granted to products based on their origin, which would be considered discriminatory per MFN principle.[27]

The "advantage" can only be admissible if regulatory distinctions or favourable treatments are based on the individual characteristics of products, specifically their carbon content, rather than the overall climate mitigation policies of the countries.[28] Likewise, in the Indonesia-Autos case, the Panel underscores the fundamental principle that the MFN obligation focuses on the treatment of products, irrespective of

[26] Appellate Body Report, *EC – Seal Products*, paras 5.82 and 5.87.

[27] ibid para. 5.87.

[28] Panel Report, *Canada – Certain Measures Affecting the Automotive Industry, (Canada-Autos)* WT/DS139/R, WT/DS142/R, adopted 19 June 2000, as modified by Appellate Body Report WT/DS139/AB/R, WT/DS142/AB/R, para 10.25.

the diverse regulatory frameworks[29] or climate commitments of individual WTO members. In other words, if certain products demonstrate a lower carbon footprint, they can be granted an advantage based on their intrinsic features, not their country of origin.[30] By focusing on the carbon content of products, rather than the climate club membership, regulatory measures can be designed to encourage adopting environmentally friendly practices without violating the non-discrimination principle of the MFN clause. However, still the club linkage needs to be analysed with respect to other relevant WTO norms.

The exclusion from BCAs or providing favourable trade concessions to climate club members is defensible on environmental grounds and derives from the idea that these countries are already taking measures to address emissions abatement.[31] The rationale is that imposing additional border charges could potentially distort the competitive opportunities for these low-carbon embedded products without providing significant environmental benefits. In fact, applying BCAs towards club members' imports will constitute double pricing. Also, carbon leakage to club members will be a negligible concern because they have carbon legislation as well. Therefore, excluding club products from the charges related to importation, in essence, does not provide an advantage.

However, these environmental concerns can only be advocated under Article XX justification.[32] The MFN analysis does not have room for policy aim consideration. In the EC-Seal case, the Appellate Body held that Art. I:1 "permits regulatory distinctions to be drawn between like imported products, provided that such distinctions do not result in a detrimental impact on the competitive opportunities for like imported products from any member".[33] Consequently, the mere consideration in the MFN analysis is the distortion in the market circulation due to the imports from different WTO members and the prevention of protectionism among imported products of varying origins.[34] Thus, the selective application of BCAs under the club approach constitutes an advantage according to the MFN principle.[35]

---

[29] Panel Report, *Indonesia – Certain Measures Affecting the Automobile Industry, (Indonesia-Autos)*, WT/DS54/R, WT/DS55/R, WT/DS59/R, WT/DS64/R, Corr.1 and Corr.2, adopted 23 July 1998, and Corr.3 and Corr.4, para 14.143.

[30] Joachim Englisch and Tatiana Falcao, 'EU Carbon Border Adjustments for Imported Products and WTO Law' (9 June 2021), 71 <https://doi.org/10.2139/ssrn.3863038>.

[31] Rolf H Weber, 'Border Tax Adjustment-Legal Perspective' (2015) 133 Climatic Change 407, 412 <https://doi.org/10.1007/s10584-015-1414-2>.

[32] See Sect. 4 in Chap. 7.

[33] Appellate Body Report, *EC-Seal Products*, para 5.88.

[34] Panel Report, *Canada-Autos*, para 10.30.

[35] Ilaria Espa and Kateryna Holzer, 'From Unilateral Border Carbon Adjustments to Cooperation in Climate Clubs: Rethinking Exclusion in Light of Trade and Climate Law Constraints' in J. Bäumler and others (eds), *European Yearbook of International Economic Law 2022* (vol 13, Springer, 2023), 398 <https://doi.org/10.1007/8165_2022_101>.

1.4 Like Products

1.4.1 Definition

The MFN principle is applicable to like imported products of different WTO members. Nevertheless, a crucial challenge arises from the absence of a specific definition for "like products" in the GATT 1994 and other WTO Agreements. This ambiguity makes the application of Article I provision contingent upon the specific circumstances of each situation. The lack of a clear definition necessitates an examination of various factors, including physical characteristics, end-use, consumer preferences, and market conditions, among others, to ascertain the likeness of products.[36] Hence, the like products test under WTO law involves a complex and nuanced analysis that considers not only the immediate physical attributes of the products but also their broader economic and functional characteristics. This approach recognizes that products may be like in ways beyond mere visual or structural comparisons.

A broad interpretation of the like product's concept in Article I provision would expand the scope of application of MFN principle. On the other hand, it comes with the potential consequence of constraining the regulatory discretion of WTO member states. The expansive interpretation could limit the flexibility of member countries in designing and implementing trade regulations tailored to their specific economic and environmental circumstances. Conversely, a narrow understanding of like products might undermine the WTO's effectiveness in scrutinising its member states' trade regulations. A restrictive interpretation might overlook important product likeness factors, potentially allowing discriminatory practices to go unchecked. Striking the right balance in defining like products is, therefore, crucial to maintaining the delicate equilibrium between promoting fair trade practices and respecting the sovereign right of nations to regulate their economies.

1.4.2 Results on the BCAs

The critical step in the compatibility of the climate club linkages with the MFN principle is to understand whether differently treated products are like. This assessment is referred to as likeness test.[37] The likeness test is not exclusive to the MFN principle but equally applies to the national treatment principle. It serves as a common analytical tool by ensuring that products facing disparate trade measures are appropriately compared to ascertain whether they are indeed like. For a more in-depth exploration of the likeness test in the context of climate club linkages, it is

[36] See Sect. 2.2.3.1 in Chap. 7.

[37] See Sect. 2.2.3.1 in Chap. 7.

essential to delve into the detailed analysis. This analysis is located under the national treatment principle section[38] to avoid repetition of the same information.

1.5 Advantage Accorded Immediately and Unconditionally

1.5.1 Definition

According to the MFN principle, any advantage, favour, privilege, or immunity given to a product of one state must extend to like products of all WTO members. Notably, the application of possible benefits that affect competitiveness should be extended to other WTO members without delay or further requirements.[39] Therefore, if a product from a specific country receives trade-related benefits, such as exclusion from BCAs, the same benefit must be offered to like products from all other member states without delay or additional requirements. By ensuring that any advantage is promptly and automatically extended to others, the MFN principle contributes to the creation of a level playing field. It prevents countries from using trade policies to favour certain countries over others, thereby reducing the risk of trade wars and promoting a stable international economic environment. The principle also prevents the fragmentation in the global trading system and enhances the integration of global markets.

1.5.2 Results on the BCAs

Accordingly, the market access advantage for the climate club members should be extended to non-club members' exports immediately without any BCAs. This means that if a product from a climate club member is exempted from BCAs due to the environmental policies or commitments of its country of origin, similar products from all other WTO members must be granted the same exemption, irrespective of their climate club membership status or the environmental policies of their home countries.[40] If the extension of advantage to other countries is attached to the climate club membership, this constitutes a conditional extension. The WTO prohibits any conditions regarding the position or conduct of other countries.[41] Only conditions that are not essentially related to the origin of products are admissible under the MFN principle.[42] Whereas in the climate club, the condition of conferring

[38] See Sect. 2.2.3.1 in Chap. 7.

[39] Appellate Body Reports, *EC-Seal Products*, paras. 5.88–5.90, 5.93.

[40] Geraldo Vidigal, 'Designing Climate Clubs: The Four Models, Trade Commitments and the Non-Discrimination Dilemma' (2023) Amsterdam Law School Research Paper No 2023-07, 13.

[41] Panel Report, *Canada –Autos*, para. 10.23.

[42] ibid paras 10.24 and 10.25.

advantages is intrinsically linked with the club membership, meaning the origin country of the products.

This approach ensures that environmental measures and trade policies support global efforts to combat climate change without compromising the integrity of the multilateral trading system. It encourages countries to adopt and enhance environmentally friendly practices based on the intrinsic characteristics of products, such as their carbon content, rather than on geopolitical alignments or membership in specific international agreements. By upholding the MFN principle in the application of climate-related trade measures, the climate club can facilitate a more inclusive and equitable path toward sustainable development, where trade and environmental objectives are mutually supportive and universally beneficial.

1.6 Concluding Remarks

The MFN principle stands as a cornerstone of the WTO's efforts to foster an equitable and competitive global trading environment. By mandating that any favour granted to one member must be extended to all, the principle discourages discriminatory practices and promotes a uniform standard of treatment among trading partners. This section delves into the nuanced challenges posed by BCAs designed to serve the climate objectives of the club. Specifically, it scrutinizes whether climate-related trade instruments violate the MFN principle. The intricacy of this analysis is the delicate balance between advancing climate goals and adhering to established non-discrimination principle. Climate club linkage of BCAs as a carbon tariff or emissions allowance purchase potentially contravenes the MFN principle, which mandates equal treatment for like products from all WTO members. The tension arises when environmental measures, designed to favour products from countries with stronger environmental protections, inadvertently discriminate against products from countries with different regulatory regimes.

Under the climate club, the market access advantage or imposition of BCAs is contingent on climate club membership. This application could be seen as a violation of the MFN principle and lead to potential trade disputes. BCAs fall under the scope of the MFN clause by constituting a measure regulated under Article I and providing an advantage to club members' imports. An essential aspect of this analysis is understanding whether club and non-club products are like. This determination can be made only after examining the details of the likeness test, which is held under the following section. To sum up, if high and low-carbon-intensive products are found to be like, BCAs violate the MFN principle. This is because the BCAs discriminate products from different trading partners per their club membership. However, any discrimination based on factors other than the features of the product itself constitutes discrimination based on the origin and contradicts the MFN principle.

2 National Treatment Principle

2.1 Introduction

The WTO serves a purpose beyond merely overseeing the reduction of border measures. It also plays a pivotal role in discouraging the deployment of internal policy tools in a protectionist manner.[43] This commitment to fostering fair and non-discriminatory trade practices is exemplified through the national treatment principle enshrined in GATT 1994 and the TBT Agreement. The national treatment principle under Article III of the GATT 1994 stipulates that WTO member countries must refrain from discriminating between domestically produced goods and their foreign counterparts. The underlying rationale is to create a level playing field by ensuring that similar competition conditions are provided for domestic and foreign products. The Article covers de jure and de facto discrimination.[44] The former refers to a measure that discriminates on its face as to the origin of products. In comparison, de facto discrimination corresponds to a measure that, in its application, upsets the relative competitive position between domestic and imported products.[45]

Article III addresses the complex interplay between internal regulations, taxes, and other charges to ensure non-discriminatory treatment of domestic and foreign products within the purview of international trade. Paragraph 1 of Article III establishes a stringent prohibition. It stipulates that no internal regulation, whether of a fiscal or non-fiscal nature, should be adopted or applied in a manner that affords protection to domestic products.[46] This provision reflects the WTO's commitment to dismantling protectionist measures and fostering a competitive global trading system. Paragraph 2 of Article III specifically pertains to regulating internal taxes and other charges. In comparison, paragraph 4 of Article is related the national treatment principle for internal regulation. This nuanced distinction in the scope of application emphasizes the careful calibration required to address different aspects of internal policies.[47]

It is crucial to note that the narrower scope of Article III:4, compared to Article III:2, does not imply that internal taxes or charges are considered more significant barriers to trade than internal regulations. Instead, it reflects the recognition that the enactment of internal regulations should not unduly impede the sovereign choices

[43] Nicholas F Diebold, 'Different Functions in Goods and Services' in Thomas Cottier and Krista Nadakavukaren Schefer (eds), *Elgar Encyclopedia of International Economic Law* (Edward Elgar 2017), 184.

[44] Ruxton KDS McClure, 'Non-Discrimination Principle in WTO Law: Themes and Commonalities' (2023) 12(1) International Trade and Arbitration Law Journal 65, 83.

[45] Panel Report, *Japan – Measures Affecting Consumer Photographic Film and Paper*, (Japan-Film), WT/DS44/R, adopted 22 April 1998, para. 10.380.

[46] GATT 1994 art III:1.

[47] Appellate Body Report, *European Communities – Measures Affecting Asbestos and Asbestos-Containing Products (EC-Asbestos,)* WT/DS135/AB/R, adopted 5 April 2001, para 93.

of countries. Thereby, the Article allows countries the necessary flexibility in crafting domestic policies. Despite this, the Appellate Body has, in certain instances, expanded the scope of Article III:4 by incorporating a competitive relationship analysis within the relevant market.[48] This extension aims to prevent protectionist practices in internal regulations. The differentiated likeness test is analysed in the following sections of this book.

Cumulatively, the overarching purpose of the national treatment principle, as outlined in the different paragraphs of Article III, is to proactively prevent protectionist tendencies when implementing internal tax and internal regulatory measures.[49] This fundamental principle underscores the commitment of the WTO to foster a global trading environment that is characterized by the absence of discriminatory practices. Unlike some trade principles, the violation of national treatment is not contingent upon specific market outcomes. Instead, its primary concern lies in ensuring the impartiality of domestic regulations, irrespective of their impact on the market.[50] In essence, the focus is on the even-handed application of internal tax and regulatory measures to both domestic and foreign products.[51]

Within the context of climate club linkages, BCAs implemented as carbon tariffs assume a distinctive role as internal fiscal measures. The assessment of their conformity with the national treatment principle is rooted in Article III:2 of the GATT. Article III:2 imposes a dual obligation on the jurisdiction employing BCAs within a climate club framework. The initial obligation, encapsulated in the first sentence of Article III:2, directs countries not to impose a carbon tariff or any other charge on importation that exceeds the tax or charge applied to like domestic products. The second obligation, intricately woven into the second sentence of Article III:2 and Ad Note III, introduces a noteworthy nuance to the national treatment principle.[52] It emphasizes the continued applicability of national treatment even when the imported and domestic products are not deemed "like". This provision restraints the imposition of tariffs on "directly competitive or substitutable" products in a manner that would afford protection to domestic producers.

A critical note within Article III:2 is the narrowly construed "like products" concept in the first sentence. This deliberate limitation aligns with the interpretative principle of effectiveness, which aims to avoid redundancy or overlap with the broader considerations of the second sentence.[53] Consequently, a meticulous analysis is required. The initial step involves determining whether the imported and

---

[48] See Sect. 2.4.3 in Chap. 7.

[49] Erich Vranes, 'Carbon Taxes, PPMs and the GATT' in Panagiotis Delimatsis (ed) *Research Handbook on Climate Change and Trade* (Edward Elgar 2016), 89.

[50] Henrik Horn and Petros C Mavroidis, 'Still Hazy After All These Years: The Interpretation of National Treatment in the GATT/WTO Case-Law on Tax Discrimination' (2004) 15(1) European Journal of International Law 39, 50.

[51] Appellate Body Report, *Japan – Taxes on Alcoholic Beverages*, (*Japan–Alcoholic Beverages II*), WT/DS8/AB/R, WT/DS10/AB/R, WT/DS11/AB/R, adopted 1 November 1996, 16.

[52] ibid 19.

[53] ibid 18.

domestic products are like, and only if they are not considered "like" does the assessment of competitiveness or substitutability come into play. This sequential approach ensures a comprehensive yet focused application of the national treatment principle and streamlines the assessment process, especially in cases involving a broader product group.

The landscape of climate club linkages extends beyond fiscal considerations. It incorporates critical administrative aspects that shape the regulatory framework. These non-fiscal dimensions encompass BCAs as the acquisition and surrendering of emissions allowances by imported products. These administrative facets fall squarely within the realm of internal regulations and are subject to the scrutiny of Article III:4 and Article XI:1. Consequently, the application of these internal regulations should adhere to the national treatment principle, which ensures that they are no less favourable to imported products than their domestic counterparts.

Notably, the spectrum of likeness, a critical element in the national treatment analysis, varies across each paragraph of Article III.[54] By delving into the details of each paragraph within Article III, it is observable that the GATT 1994 provides a comprehensive and adaptable approach to ensure that internal fiscal and regulatory measures within climate club linkages align with the non-discrimination principles. Thereby, it fosters a balanced and equitable global trading system. The following sections separately analyse the application of the national treatment principle to internal taxation of like and competitive or substitutable products and its application to internal regulation.

2.2 Article III:2 (1); National Treatment for Internal Taxation on Like Products

2.2.1 Introduction

Article III:2 first sentence establishes a meticulous three-tier test to evaluate the consistency of internal taxation with the national treatment principle. Adhering to this three-tier test helps to ensure that international trade remains free from discriminatory fiscal practices. The conditions outlined in this test are as follows:

- The measure at issue corresponds to an internal tax or other internal charge on products,
- The imported and domestic products are like products, and
- The imported products are taxed "in excess of" the domestic products.[55]

---

[54] Appellate Body Report, *EC –Asbestos*, para 99.

[55] Appellate Body Reports, *Canada–Auto*, paras. 171 and 182–183; Appellate Body Report, *Canada – Certain Measures Concerning Periodicals*, (*Canada–Periodicals*), WT/DS31/AB/R, adopted 30 July 1997, 24.

2.2.2 Internal Taxes and Charges

2.2.2.1 Definition

A determination of whether a particular measure falls within Article III:2 of the GATT 1994 must be made in light of the measure's characteristics and the case's circumstances. Article III:2(1) is particularly concerned with internal taxes or charges on products[56] and serves to prevent discrimination against imported products compared to domestic ones with these charges. Various measures may be considered internal taxes or charges on products. Examples of such measures include value-added taxes, sales taxes, and excise duties.[57] When assessing compliance with Article III:2(1), it is crucial to analyse the specific features and implications of these taxes and charges to determine their impact on domestic and imported products.

2.2.2.2 Results on the BCAs

In the context of climate club, carbon tariffs and BCAs serve as strategic tools to address environmental concerns and level the playing field between domestic and imported goods.[58] They impose an additional charge on imported goods based on their carbon footprint. This approach signifies a paradigm shift towards a more sustainable and climate-conscious trade framework. Their primary objective is to incorporate the external cost of carbon emissions into imported products' prices. In this way, they seamlessly integrate imported goods into the domestic carbon pricing framework.

BCAs are collected at the time and point of importation.[59] Whether they are issued concerning internal tax or charges, or as a border measure necessitates a particular analysis. It is significant to make this distinction here because the GATT 1994 regulates ordinary customs duties, other import charges and internal taxes differently.[60] Consequently, the legal status of BCAs hinges on the "intricacies of their design and implementation".[61] Neither the mere description or categorization of a charge under the domestic law nor the regulatory intent of the member or the public policy purpose of the charge influence this classification.

---

[56] Van den Bossche and Zdouc (n 22) 352.

[57] Panel Report, Argentina – Measures Affecting the Export of Bovine Hides and the Import of Finished Leather (*Argentina-Hides and Leather*), WT/DS155/R and Corr.1, adopted 16 February 2001, para 11.143.

[58] See Sect. 3.4 and 3.5 in Chap. 5.

[59] Report of the GATT Working Party on Border Tax Adjustment, adopted on 2 December 1970, L/3464, para. 14.

[60] See Sect. 3.2 in Chap. 6.

[61] Appellate Body Report, *China - Measures Affecting Imports of Automobile Parts (China –Auto Parts),* WT/DS339/AB/R, WT/DS340/AB/R, WT/DS342/AB/R, adopted 12 January 2009, para. 171.

The imposition of ordinary customs duties as a border measure is allowed as long as it does not exceed tariff bindings. In this case, Article II will apply to BCAs for the WTO law compliance analysis.[62] All other duties and charges concerning importation are, in principle, prohibited for bound products due to Article II:1(b). However, internal taxes, which discriminate against imports, are prohibited for all products, either bound or not under Article III:2(1).[63] The national treatment principle will be relevant only if the charge is applied due to internal tax or regulation. The legal status of the BCAs, whether they are border measures or internal charges, is examined under schedule of concessions chapter of this book to elucidate the applicable GATT 1994 provision. That examination concluded that BCAs are imposed with regard to an internal event and, therefore, subject to the national treatment provision. Below, this analysis is summarized once again for the national treatment principle of internal taxes and charges section.

The Note Ad to Article III of the GATT 1994 provides essential clarifications regarding the distinction between internal and border measures. Typically, internal taxes and charges are applied domestically at the time of retail sale.[64] However, the Note Ad acknowledges an exception for internal excise taxes and explains that, due to administrative considerations, these taxes may be imposed at the time of importation.[65] Notably, the Note Ad specifies that an internal tax or charge and laws, regulations, or requirements should be examined under Article III of the GATT 1994 if it meets specific criteria. These criteria are: when the measure must apply to both the imported and like domestic product and be collected or enforced at the time or point of importation. These conditions ensure that measures affecting imported goods are scrutinised under the national treatment principle, which seeks to prevent discrimination against foreign products. The location or timing of the collection or enforcement does not absolve the measure from the requirement to treat imported and domestic products on an equal footing.

Correspondingly, carbon tariffs and BCAs under the climate club accrue "due to an internal event, and this internal factor arises after the importation of the products".[66] They are inseparable elements of an internal tax or charge because the imports are chargeable only after the pricing of domestic products. The rationale of the climate club linkages is to collect the internal tax or charge from the imports to compensate for the tax burden of the domestic products. This compensation mechanism aligns with the broader objectives of climate club linkages, which is to create a level playing field for domestic and imported goods. Even though they are collected upon importation, the "reason to pay tax or charge is pivotal instead of the

[62] See Sect. 3.2 in Chap. 6.

[63] GATT Panel Report, *EEC - Regulation on Imports of Parts and Components*, (16 May 1990), L/6657, 37S/132, 191–192, para. 5.4.

[64] Panel Report, *Argentina-Hides and Leather*, para 11.143.

[65] Summary Record of the Eleventh Meeting, E/CONF.2/C.3/SR.11, 1. Proposal E/CONF.2/C.3/1/Add.21. E/CONF.2/C.3/A/W.33, 1.

[66] Appellate Body Report, *China—Auto Parts*, para. 163. GATT Panel Report, *Canada-Administration of Foreign Investment Review Act,* (7 February 1984), L/5504 - 30S/140, para. 5.14.

timing of the payment".[67] Therefore, BCAs fall under the "measure covered by Article III:2(1)" and should be disciplined under the national treatment principle.

2.2.3 Like Products

The climate club linkages, whether manifesting as carbon tariffs, BCAs through allowance purchases or charges, or technical regulations, all undergo a meticulous analysis under the principles of MFN and national treatment. A crucial juncture in this assessment lies in determining the likeness of products because non-discrimination principles aim to prevent less favourable treatment between "like" domestic and foreign products. Recognizing the need for a nuanced approach to evaluate likeness, the Appellate Body has introduced the concept of an "accordion image".[68] This metaphor is instrumental in addressing the notion of likeness within distinct Articles of the GATT 1994 and the TBT Agreement. Since each of these Articles has a unique scope, the accordion image illustrates the flexible and adaptable nature of the likeness concept. It allows likeness to expand or tighten based on the specific context and provisions of the Agreements. First, the book examines the likeness test under Article III:2(1) since the competitiveness and substitutability analysis is only relevant if products are found to be not like per the test.[69]

2.2.3.1 Likeness Test

The term "like product" lacks a precise definition within the GATT 1994.[70] This ambiguity results in interpretative challenges that have led to significant cases within the WTO. The Japan-Alcoholic Beverages II case is noteworthy, as the Appellate Body endorsed the foundational approach to determine likeness, similar to the articulation in the Working Party Report in Border Tax Adjustments (1970). Consequently, the Appellate Body established four general criteria for the likeness test, which contributes to a comprehensive assessment. They are "(i) the physical features, nature, and quality of the products, (ii) the end-uses of the products in a given market, (iii) consumers' preferences, including how they perceive and use products as alternatives for performing certain functions or needs, can vary significantly across different countries,[71] and (iv) international tariff classification of the

[67] Appellate Body Report, *China—Auto Parts*, para 162. According to the Appellate Body, "the time at which a charge is collected or paid is not decisive" for the distinction between a "border charge"-type of adjustment and an "internal charge" adjustment for imported products.

[68] Appellate Body Report, *Japan–Alcoholic Beverages II*, p. 22.

[69] Appellate Body Report, *Canada-Periodicals*, p. 23.

[70] Van den Bossche and Zdouc (n 22) 392.

[71] Working Party Report, 'Border Tax Adjustments' (n 59) para 18.

products".[72,73] As a result, Article III:2(1) of the GATT tightly constrains the likeness accordion.[74]

An important point is that none of these criteria holds decisive weight in isolation. Instead, each of them needs to be considered in a holistic assessment and on a case-by-case basis.[75] The holistic approach recognizes the dynamic and multifaceted nature of products. Further, it acknowledges that products' likeness may be contingent on a combination of factors rather than a singular criterion. The established criteria for the likeness test provide a structured framework for assessing whether products are considered "like" under the GATT 1994. However, the complex nature of certain final products, especially those with different carbon content, introduces challenges in determining their likeness.[76] The PPMs, a contentious issue, might have a role in differentiating otherwise like products.[77] When high and low-carbon-emitted products share similar physical features, tariff classifications, and end-uses, an objective approach may categorize them as like products.[78] However, the nature and quality of the products or consumer preferences can differentiate products by assessing the environmental impact of their PPMs.[79]

The divergence in carbon content within apparently similar products raises questions about whether PPMs, representing the environmental footprint of production processes, should be recognized as decisive criteria for determining product likeness. The interpretation of the "like products" clause seems to have evolved to include environmental aspects increasingly.[80] However, recognising PPMs as a decisive criterion for determining likeness remains uncertain and subject to the evolving interpretative approach of the WTO Panels and the Appellate Body. As environmental considerations, including carbon emissions and PPMs, are gaining

---

72 The Appellate Body acknowledged that in Japan-Alcoholic Beverages II (1996) that classification under the same HS tariff heading or subheading can provide a useful basis for confirming likeness in products. Appellate Body Report, *Japan-Alcoholic Beverages II*, para 116.

73 Appellate Body Report, *EC –Asbestos*, para. 101. Van den Bossche and Zdouch (n 22) 316.

74 Appellate Body Reports, *Philippines – Taxes on Distilled Spirits, (Philippines–Distilled Spirits)*, WT/DS396/AB/R / WT/DS403/AB/R, adopted 20 January 2012, para. 205.

75 Panel Report, *United States - Certain Measures Relating to the Renewable Energy Sector (US-Renewable Energy)*, WT/DS510/R, adopted 27 June. 2019, para. 7.89.

76 Keith Kendall, 'Carbon Taxes and the WTO: A Carbon Charge without Trade Concerns' (2012) 29 Arizona Journal of International and Comparative Law 49.

77 Kateryna Holzer, 'The Role Environmental Processes and Production Methods' in Thomas Cottier and Krista Nadakavukaren Schefer (eds), *Elgar Encyclopedia of International Economic Law* (Edward Elgar 2017), 623.

78 ibid.

79 Panel Reports, *Philippines – Taxes on Distilled Spirits, (Philippines–Distilled Spirits)*, WT/DS396/R / WT/DS403/R, adopted 20 January 2012, as modified by Appellate Body Reports WT/DS396/AB/R / WT/DS403/AB/R, para. 7.37. The Panel held that when different production processes are used to create closely resembling final product, 'the difference in raw materials would only be relevant to the extent that it results in final products that are not similar'.

80 For example, in EC-Asbestos, US-Shrimp and US-Tuna II (Mexico), the Appellate Body acknowledged the importance of npr-PPMs in altering the product likeness.

prominence in trade disputes, the WTO's stance on their role in determining likeness remains dynamic. Under this book, instead of analysing PPMs as a criterion in the product likeness test, their impacts on the nature of products and consumer preferences are examined in the following subheadings.

In the early 1990s, the WTO DSB briefly employed the "aim and effect" test as part of the likeness analysis within Article III:2(1). This test involved scrutinizing the underlying motivation of the internal tax or charge to assess the likeness of products.[81] Accordingly, emissions levels could be considered a crucial factor in determining whether two products were "like" from a regulatory aim perspective. However, currently, the WTO strictly rejects the application of the aim and effects test in the context of the likeness test under Article III:2(1).[82] Regulatory aims are now only considered relevant under the specified exceptions provided in Article XX of the GATT 1994.[83] Moreover, the responsibilities arising from MEAs are not regarded as inherently relevant in the likeness context, as the WTO DSB structures the likeness analysis.[84] Therefore, the obligations derived from the climate club cannot differentiate otherwise like products.

While regulatory purposes may not directly play a role in determining likeness, they can indirectly influence the application of specific criteria within the likeness test, such as consumer preferences or end-uses. For instance, if a regulatory purpose aims to promote environmentally friendly practices, it may target to alter consumer preferences. In this indirect manner, regulatory objectives can influence the outcome of the likeness test.[85] Nevertheless, the emphasis on adhering to the WTO DSB's structured criteria for likeness analysis ensures a more precise and objective evaluation within the framework of international trade rules. The following sections of this Chapter assess the likeness test criteria individually and in detail.

---

[81] GATT Panel Report, *United States – Taxes on Automobiles*, (11 Oct. 1994) DS31/R, unadopted, para. 5.9 (see also para. 5.10)

[82] Kateryna Holzer, 'Comparability in International Economic Law: Goods' in Thomas Cottier and Krista Nadakavukaren Schefer (eds), *Elgar Encyclopedia of International Economic Law* (Edward Elgar 2017), 186.

[83] Appellate Body Reports, *Brazil – Certain Measures Concerning Taxation and Charges*, (Brazil-Taxation), WT/DS472/AB/R and Add.1 / WT/DS497/AB/R and Add.1, adopted 11 January 2019, para 5.27.

[84] Erich Vranes, 'Climate Labelling and the WTO: The 2010 EU Ecolabelling Programme as a Test Case Under WTO Law' in Christoph Herrmann and Jörg Philipp Terhechte (eds), *European Yearbook of International Economic Law* (Springer, 2011) 205–237.

[85] Appellate Body Report, *United States – Measures Affecting the Production and Sale of Clove Cigarettes, (US-Clove Cigarettes)* WT/DS406/AB/R, adopted 24 April 2012, para 117. In this ruling Appellate Body concerned the likeness analysis within the context of national treatment obligation of Article 2.1 of the TBT Agreement.

Product Characteristics

In the determination of product likeness under Article III:2(1), no single criterion holds an overarching role.[86] However, the logical starting point for analysis often begins with examining the product's physical features, nature, and quality. The assessment of physical similarity is informative, especially in cases where evidence on other factors might be limited. The physical characteristics of a product offer tangible and objective attributes that can be compared and evaluated. This initial step in the analysis provides a foundational understanding of the product's intrinsic qualities. It helps to ascertain whether products share similar physical features or composition. Such similarities can suggest a high probability that the products are perceived as close substitutes, particularly regarding their end-use and consumer preferences.

Nevertheless, under the likeness analysis, there should also be a distinct scrutinization of the product's physical characteristics and its nature or quality. While products may share similar physical features, it does not necessarily imply that they are "like" in terms of their nature or quality. The EC-Asbestos case serves as a notable example where the Appellate Body emphasized that factors such as carcinogenicity should be considered within a product's physical characteristics, as it can fundamentally alter the product's nature and quality.[87] This perspective recognizes that certain attributes, even if not immediately apparent in the physical characteristics, can significantly impact a product's overall nature and quality. In the case of carcinogenicity, despite not leaving a visible trace on the physical appearance, it was deemed pertinent to the product's nature and quality due to its profound health implications.[88] This conclusion is reaffirmed in EC- Biotech case.[89]

Applying a similar rationale to the context of released carbon emissions during the PPMs of products, products emitting high levels of carbon may differ in their nature and quality. Beyond the immediate physical characteristics, the environmental impact of high carbon emissions contributes to the nature of the product. This impact is particularly relevant in addressing climate change, as products with high carbon footprints play a more significant role in accumulating GHGs, posing risks to the global climate, human life, health, and the environment.[90] Therefore, the

---

[86] Appellate Body Report, *Philippines - Distilled Spirits*, para 119.

[87] The Appellate Body found that chrysotile asbestos fibres were not 'like' fibres made from other materials given the public health risks of asbestos.

[88] Appellate Body Report, *EC-Asbestos*, para 114.

[89] Panel Report, —*European Communities – Measures Affecting the Approval and Marketing of Biotech Products (EC –Biotech Products)*, WT/DS291/R, Add.1 to Add.9 and Corr.1 / WT/DS292/R, Add.1 to Add.9 and Corr.1 / WT/DS293/R, Add.1 to Add.9 and Corr.1, adopted 21 November 2006, para. 7.2514.

[90] Benoit Mayer, 'Obligations of Conduct in the International Law on Climate Change: A Defence' (2018) 27 Review of European, Comparative & International Environmental Law 130, 133 <https://doi.org/10.1111/reel.12237>.

consideration of the product's nature and quality extends beyond the visible attributes of it and encompass broader factors that can influence a product's overall impact.[91]

Correspondingly, in the context of climate club linkages, a central question arises: can two products be distinguished based on their carbon emissions, even when there is no discernible effect on the physical characteristics of the products?[92] Traditionally, the interpretation of "like" products in international trade does not allow differentiation based on the production method, whether it involves PPMs or npr-PPMs.[93] However, the concept of npr-PPMs introduces a nuanced dimension to this likeness analysis. Npr-PPMs are considerations that go beyond immediate physical characteristics and delve into life-cycle considerations.[94] These considerations may involve environmental impacts associated with the production methods, such as the amount or type of energy consumed during manufacturing. In a strict interpretation of the likeness test, products may appear identical regarding physical characteristics, end-uses, and tariff classifications, but npr-PPMs can provide a basis for distinguishing products based on their environmental impacts.[95]

In the climate club scenario, where the emphasis is on combatting climate change, distinguishing between products based on their npr-PPMs becomes critical. Countries implementing climate mitigation policies may produce goods with lower carbon emissions and reflect their commitment to environmental sustainability. It introduces a potential differentiation between a product from a country with no climate mitigation policies and a "like product" from a climate club country, solely based on their npr-PPMs. This dynamic raises questions about the evolving nature of the likeness test and its adaptability to address contemporary challenges such as climate change. Including npr-PPMs in the determination of likeness showcases the complex interplay between trade rules and environmental considerations within the context of climate club linkages. Accordingly, in Canada–Feed-In Tariff Program case the Appellate Body indicated that products with varying levels of GHG

---

[91] Appellate Body Report, *EC-Asbestos*, para 113.

[92] Richard G. Tarasofsky, 'Heating Up International Trade Law: Challenges and Opportunities Posed by Efforts to Combat Climate Change' (2008) 2 Carbon and Climate Law Review 7, 8–10.

[93] Jason E Bordoff and Andrew W Shoyer, *International Trade Law and the Economics of Climate Policy: Evaluating the Legality and Effectiveness of Proposals to Address Competitiveness and Leakage Concerns* (Brookings Trade Forum, Climate Change, Trade, and Competitiveness: Is a Collision Inevitable?, 2008/2009), 44. GATT Panel Report, *United States – Measures Affecting Alcoholic and Malt Beverages,* (19 June 1992) DS23/R - 39S/206, para 5.19.

[94] Amber Rose Maggio, 'Trade-Restrictive Environmental Measures and the GATT' in *Environmental Policy, Non-Product Related Process and Production Methods and the Law of the World Trade Organization* (European Yearbook of International Economic Law, vol 1, Springer, Cham 2017), 104.

[95] Zaker Ahmad, 'Trade-Related Measures to Spread Low-Carbon Technologies: A Common Concern–Based Approach' in Thomas Cottier (ed), *The Prospects of Common Concern of Humankind in International Law* (Cambridge University Press 2021), 124.

emissions embedded may not be considered like products.[96] According to the Appellate Body, determining whether products are like might necessitate an examination of the materials and production methods used to create them.[97]

By applying BCAs according to npr-PPMs that focus on carbon content, the climate club aims to ensure that carbon-intensive industries do not relocate to countries with lax environmental standards for undermining global efforts to address climate change.[98] Therefore, npr-PPMs on carbon content align with the broader goals of the WTO, as articulated in the WTO Agreement Preamble,[99] which is "the need for optimal use of the world resources in a sustainable manner".[100] Conversely, permitting differentiated treatment based on npr-PPMs can be considered as the legalization of unilateral measures and abuse of GATT 1994 non-discrimination principles.[101] Historically, exporting countries have contested the environmental requirements related to npr-PPMs set by importing countries, arguing that they represent protectionist measures and unacceptable forms of extraterritorial regulation.[102] The concerns raised by exporting countries often revolve around the potential imposition of financial and technological burdens on their industries, particularly those in developing countries. While there is a recognition of the importance of environmental sustainability, developing nations may hesitate to implement measures that could result in a competitive disadvantage for their economies.[103] They may argue that stringent environmental requirements tied to PPMs could place undue economic strain on industries that may not have the resources or technology to comply with such standards readily. The PPMs-based criteria could be perceived as a form of trade barrier or green protectionism,[104] hindering the ability of developing countries to participate fully in global trade.

---

[96] Appellate Body Reports, *Canada – Certain Measures Affecting the Renewable Energy Generation Sector / Canada – Measures Relating to the Feed-in Tariff Program,(Canada – Renewable Energy / Canada – Feed-in Tariff Program)* WT/DS412/AB/R / WT/DS426/AB/R, adopted 24 May 2013, para 5.63.

[97] The analysis focused on competitive products; however, the pertinent aspect here is the recognition of the inputs and production processes in determining product characteristics.

[98] Weber, 'Border Tax Adjustment-Legal Perspective' (n 31) 409.

[99] C Benoit, 'Picking Tariff Winners: Non-product-related PPMs and DSB Interpretations of Unconditionally within Article I:1' (2011) 42(2) Georgetown Journal of International Law 583, 601–602.

[100] Marrakesh Agreement Establishing the World Trade Organization, 15 April 1994, 1867 UNTS 154, 33 ILM 1144 (1994) (hereinafter WTO Agreement), Preamble, para 1.1.

[101] Van den Bossche and Zdouc, (n 22) 351.

[102] Thomas Cottier and Matthias Oesch, 'Direct and Indirect Discrimination in WTO and EU Law' in Sanford E Gaines, Birgitte Egelund Olsen, and Karsten Engsig Sorensen (eds), *Liberalising Trade in the EU and the WTO: A Legal Comparison* (Cambridge University Press, 2012), 166.

[103] WTO, 'Report on G20 Trade Measures' (28 Oct 2021), accessed 7 April 2024, <https://www.wto.org/english/news_e/news21_e/report_trdev_nov21_e.pdf>.

[104] International Monetary Fund and OECD, 'Tax Policy and Climate Change: IMF/OECD Report for the G20 Finance Ministers and Central Bank Governors' (2021), 22 <www.oecd.org/tax/tax-policy/imf-oecd-g20-report-tax-policy-and-climate-change.htm> accessed 20 June 2024.

However, the evolving dynamics of the global economy, mainly the prevalence of global value chains, have shifted the concept of likeness.[105] PPMs and npr-PPMs have become more relevant in the likeness analysis as a means to prevent a potential "race to the bottom" in regulations with societal concerns, particularly those related to environmental sustainability.[106] In the absence of clear guidelines in the relevant WTO agreements and jurisprudence regarding PPMs-based differentiation among like products,[107] countries have the flexibility to treat greener counterparts differently. However, it is crucial to strike a balance between environmental policy objectives and the principles of non-discrimination within the WTO framework.[108] Especially within the context of climate club, the use of measures related to PPMs and npr-PPMs should "not be employed as a punitive tool but rather as a means to incentivize and support the transition to more sustainable production methods".[109]

In summary, the differentiation of products based on npr-PPMs can be justified from a climate perspective, as processes emitting more carbon bear greater responsibility for climate change. However, from a trade perspective, this differentiation raises concerns about trade barriers and discrimination, primarily affecting exporters from developing countries. Additionally, if each country adopts different npr-PPMs, it may diminish economies of scale for those products, adding complexity to global trade. The npr-PPMs for climate-related concerns will open a way for further differentiation in other societal realms. Consequently, as the scope of market barriers and distortions arises due to governments implementing climate-related trade measures, panels and the Appellate Body may resort to a more conservative interpretation of the "like-product" clause.[110] They could exclude the relevance of npr-PPMs from the product characteristic criterion of the likeness test. In order to prevent this strict interpretation and application of different npr-PPMs in each country, cooperative solutions, such as the climate club, need to be sought. The climate club can minimize the market risks of npr-PPMs by harmonizing practices to a certain extent.

[105] Thomas Cottier, 'The Principle of Common Concern of Humankind' in Thomas Cottier (ed) *The Prospects of Common Concern of Humankind in International Law* (Cambridge University Press, 2021), 66.

[106] James A Haley, *Did Trade Liberalization Go Too Far? Trade, Inequality and Unravelling the Grand Bargain* (CIGI Papers No. 168, Centre for International Governance Innovation April 2018), <https://www.cigionline.org/publications/did-trade-liberalization-go-too-far-trade-inequality-and-unravelling-grand-bargain/> accessed 5 April 2024.

[107] Weber, 'Border Tax Adjustment-Legal Perspective' (n 31) 414.

[108] See Sect. 4.4 in Chap. 7.

[109] Robyn Eckersley, 'The Big Chill: The WTO and Multilateral Environmental Agreements' (2004) 4 Global Environmental Politics 24, 29.

[110] Matthias Buck and Roda Verheyen, *International Trade Law and Climate Change – A Positive Way Forward* (Friedrich-Ebert-Stiftung July 2001) <https://library.fes.de/pdf-files/stabsabteilung/01052.pdf> accessed 5 April 2024.

End-Uses

Another criterion to determine the products' likeness is whether two products serve the same end-use in the relevant market. The end-use adopts a market-based approach for concluding likeness.[111] So, how consumers perceive that product plays a significant role in analysing end-use in the market. The Appellate Body indicated that "consumer preferences may influence traditional usage of the products".[112] Whereas, consumer preferences and habits are dynamic and can evolve over time. Therefore, when applying the end-use criterion, it is essential to consider how the product is actually being used in the market at a given point in time.[113] If there has been a shift in consumer preferences, leading to the product being employed for different purposes than traditionally intended, the end-use test should reflect this real-market pattern. Therefore, the WTO DSB should conduct a comprehensive and specific analysis of the product's functions to provide meaningful guidance on likeness,[114] which considers the actual usage and market dynamics. The decisive factor in evaluating the product's likeness based on the end-use criterion is not only their current application but also the potential or future end-use in the market, as emphasized by the Panel in the Korea-Alcoholic Beverages case.[115] While considering potential or future end-use adds a forward-looking dimension to the analysis, it also introduces complexities. The subjective and evolving nature of consumer preferences and predicting future market dynamics can lead to interpretative challenges.

Within the framework of BCAs, the definition of end-use is contingent upon a comprehensive analysis conducted within the climate club market. This market dynamic is characterized by jurisdictions' active participation in addressing climate issues. Club members have a distinctive practice of publicly disseminating climate concerns and goals. This deliberate transparency serves as a mechanism through which these jurisdictions not only communicate their commitment to environmental sustainability but also actively shape consumer perspectives. In this context, the differential carbon levels of products become more than just an environmental metric. Instead, they transform into critical indicators influencing consumer perceptions regarding the end-use of these products. As the end-use analysis is substantially based on the market, where products are consumed, it is possible to conclude that products with different carbon levels are not "like" in the climate club market.

---

[111] Van den Boscche and Zdouc (n 22) 425. See Appellate Body Report, *EC-Asbestos* para 281.

[112] Appellate Body Report, *EC-Asbestos*, para 102.

[113] Appellate Body Report, *Philippines - Distilled Spirits*, para 118.

[114] Appellate Body Report, *US - Clove Cigarette*, para. 129. In the US - Clove Cigarette AB elucidates that all cigarettes do not share a common end-use unless panels prove otherwise in a comprehensive and specific manner, despite the multi-function of smoking cigarettes. No general classification is permitted.

[115] Panel Report, *Korea – Taxes on Alcoholic Beverages, (Korea-Alcoholic Beverages)*, WT/DS75/R, WT/DS84/R, adopted 17 February 1999, as modified by Appellate Body Report WT/DS75/AB/R, WT/DS84/AB/R, DSR 1999, para 10.78.

Consumer Preferences

Traditionally, consumer preferences have often been shaped by factors such as product availability and price rather than specific product characteristics.[116] However, this landscape is evolving, especially in the context of climate change policies. Consumers are increasingly becoming more ethically conscious, and their interests are shifting towards understanding the npr-PPMs of products, such as the source of electrical energy or emissions.[117] Consequently, this awareness can set the stage for the differentiation of high- and low-carbon emission products despite their likeness in other aspects. From a trade perspective, the shift in consumer preferences introduces a new dimension to the likeness test. Even if products share identical physical characteristics, the emphasis on npr-PPMs related to environmental impact could lead to differentiated treatment in the market.[118]

Notably, consumer behaviour is not solely driven by financial incentives or penalties. It is also significantly influenced by the ongoing discussions and policy choices surrounding climate change. The increased frequency and intensity of public discourse on climate change positively contribute to public understanding and promote responsible behaviour. For example, the Paris Agreement disseminates a significant amount of information on climate change and raises awareness of the seriousness of ecological problems, which increases individual responsiveness to climate change.[119] The EGD represents another impactful policy initiative that has successfully heightened awareness regarding sustainability within civil society. Research conducted within EU countries reveals that the citizens are highly aware of the seriousness of the climate change problems and take responsibility for that.[120] As public awareness continues to rise, there is a corresponding increase in support for differentiating products based on their PPMs or npr-PPMs.[121] Consumers, now better informed and conscious of the environmental impact of their choices, are more likely to endorse policies that promote sustainable practices.

While public awareness and policy discussions play a crucial role in shaping consumer behaviour towards environmentally friendly choices, the price level of products and the expendable income of the individuals still remain significant factors affecting their preferences for green products. For instance, this problem has

---

[116] Ahmad (n 95) 125.

[117] Public opinion backs strong climate action. A poll by the European Commission (2023) showed that 93% of citizens see global warming as a serious problem. European Commission, 'Citizen Support for Climate Action' <https://ec.europa.eu/clima/citizens/citizen-support-climate-action_en> accessed 5 April 2024.

[118] Meinhard Doelle 'Climate Change and the WTO: Opportunities to Motivate State Action on Climate Change through the World Trade Organization' (2004) 13 RECIEL 85, 92.

[119] Migle Jakučionytė-Skodienė and Genovaitė Liobikienė, 'The Changes in Climate Change Concern, Responsibility Assumption and Impact on Climate-friendly Behaviour in EU from the Paris Agreement Until 2019' (2022) 69 Environmental Management 1, 6 <https://doi.org/10.1007/s00267-021-01574-8>.

[120] ibid 11.

[121] Van den Bossche and Zdouc (n 22) 427.

been seen in the case of renewable energy preferences. Despite the increased public concern and awareness for climate change, individuals are less willing to switch to renewable energy suppliers due to the high costs or extra efforts.[122] Therefore, it is one thing to argue that an increasing number of consumers are interested in and sensitive to environmental concerns embodied in a product; it is quite another to demonstrate that such concerns truly shape consumer preferences and habits and guide consumer choices in the market.[123]

Under the WTO jurisprudence, the EC-Asbestos case provides an interesting perspective on the potential influence of product characteristics, specifically carcinogenicity, on consumer preferences. The Appellate Body's ruling suggests that even if consumers, at a particular moment, may not demonstrate differential treatment based on a specific feature, such as carcinogenicity, the availability of this information could potentially change their perception and behaviour.[124] In that particular case, the consumer behaviour did not show any differential treatment, but the Appellate Body still found that asbestos can change the consumer's perception if they were fully informed.[125] Hence, if imports carry environmental risks, it is possible to accept imports and domestic products as not like, even though consumers disregard the environmental effects in the first place.[126]

Applying this reasoning to the context of high and low-carbon emitted products suggests that non-likeness could be established based on the potential impact of carbon emissions, even if consumers currently do not treat them differently. This perspective recognizes the evolving nature of consumer awareness and suggests that policies and regulations may need to consider not only current preferences but also the potential influence of increased information and awareness on consumer behaviour in the future. However, given the contentiousness of npr-PPM-based distinctions, it remains yet to be seen whether panels or the Appellate Body will recognize consumer perceptions associated with the npr-PPMs as decisive criteria for determining the likeness.[127]

Tariff Classification

Tariff classification is a fundamental process in international trade that involves assigning the correct tariff code to imported and exported goods. This classification is typically carried out under the, World Customs Organization's Harmonized

[122] Jakučionytė-Skodienė and Liobikienė (n 119) 10.

[123] Vranes, Climate Labelling and the WTO (n 84)

[124] Appellate Body Report, *EC – Asbestos*, para 118.

[125] Herein, the problem is Appellate Body based its decision on the presumption that a rational consumer would not buy asbestos. However, rationality is a normative concept and how fully informed and rational consumer would behave is not an empirically observable fact. Donald H Regan, 'Regulatory Purpose and "Like Products" in Article III:4 of the GATT (With Additional Remarks on Article II:2)' (2002) 36(3) J World Trade 443, 466.

[126] Horn and Mavroidis, 'Still Hazy After All These Years' (n 50) 60.

[127] Cottier and Oesch, 'Direct and Indirect Discrimination in WTO and EU Law' (n 102) 150.

Commodity Description and Coding System,[128] which is an internationally standardized system for categorizing products.[129] The Appellate Body in the Japan-Alcoholic Beverages II case underscores the significance of tariff classification in determining the likeness of products. When goods fall under the exact HS tariff heading or subheading, it suggests that they share "like" characteristics.[130] This standard classification provides a helpful basis for confirming the likeness of products in the realm of national treatment principle. By using tariff classification as a criterion for determining likeness, dispute resolution bodies can establish a systematic and objective method to assess the similarities between different products.

However, the Appellate Body also remarked a fundamental distinction between tariff classification nomenclature and tariff bindings or concessions granted by WTO members.[131] While tariff classification provides a systematic method for categorizing products under standardized headings or subheadings of the HS, tariff bindings or concessions operate within the framework of trade negotiations among WTO members.[132] Tariff bindings, as specified in the schedules of concessions, represent commitments made by WTO members regarding the maximum import duties they will apply to goods. Several countries have imposed bindings in their schedule of concessions, which span across various HS tariff headings for a wide range of products. It is crucial to note that having the same binding across various HS tariff headings does not automatically imply that the products covered by that binding are "like".[133] Therefore, tariff classification serves a technical purpose in categorizing goods, while tariff bindings represent a negotiated aspect of trade agreements. The two elements, though related, have distinct roles in shaping the global trading system.

The detailed analysis of assigning tariff codes to products highlights the precision required in the international trade system.[134] While tariff lines provide a systematic method for categorizing goods, the very nature of this detailed analysis means that products deemed like based on other criteria in the likeness analysis may be assigned different codes.[135] On the other hand, the fact that two products share

[128] HS Code, a six-digit harmonized code, is used by customs authorities around the world to identify products when assessing duties and taxes, which are called tariffs for imports.

[129] Van den Bossche and Zdouc (n 22) 494.

[130] Appellate Body Report, *Japan-Alcoholic Beverages II*, para 116.

[131] ibid para 117.

[132] Rovetta (n 168) 350.

[133] WTO, 'General Rules for the Interpretation of the Harmonized System', para 4 <https://www.wcoomd.org/-/media/wco/public/global/pdf/topics/nomenclature/instruments-and-tools/hs-interpretation-general-rules/0001_2012e_gir.pdf?la=en>.

[134] Van den Bossche and Zdouc (n 22) 495.

[135] For example, the alloyed and non-alloyed iron have very similar physical characteristics, end-use, consumer preferences and they are likely to substitute each other. However, they have been assigned different tariff lines. Ulrike Will, Climate *Border Adjustments and WTO Law Extending the EU Emissions Trading System to Imported Goods and Services* (Boston: Brill Nijhoff, 2019) 140.

the same tariff classification does not automatically signify their likeness in all aspects. Tariff classification primarily serves administrative purposes and may not capture the full spectrum of product characteristics that could influence their overall likeness.[136] Even products with identical tariff codes can be considered not like if their nature, quality or consumer preferences differ significantly.[137] While tariff classification provides a standardized framework, the likeness analysis should extend beyond this technical categorization to consider the broader range of product characteristics. A comprehensive evaluation, considering factors such as physical features, end-use, and consumer preferences, ensures a more accurate determination.

However, in the MFN principle, tariff classification serves as a more helpful criterion if the tariff heading is sufficiently detailed.[138] In cases where WTO members have negotiated precise and different tariff bindings for certain products, these negotiated classifications carry significant weight in the likeness test despite their similarities in other various aspects for the purpose of MFN clause. The principle here is that such classifications should be respected in the determination of product likeness, meaning tariff bindings overrule the other criteria of the likeness test. Therefore, overall tariff classification can provide essential guidance in identifying likeness.[139]

Accordingly, the HS Code can play a pivotal role in justifying climate club linkages. The HS system can be modified to incorporate distinct codes for products based on their environmental effects and emissions levels. Modifying the HS system to reflect distinctions between high and low-carbon-emitted products allows the creation of differentiated tariff schedules for these products. This modification enables climate club members to implement climate-related trade instruments without reservations as low and high-carbon embedded products would not be found "like" due to the different HS codes. Moreover, the WTO members can even agree that tariffs on low-carbon intensive products are to be lowered, which represents a collaborative effort to incentivize and promote the trade of environmentally friendly goods.[140] This coordination aligns with the broader goals of climate clubs, which seek to encourage sustainable practices and mitigate the impact of carbon-intensive activities on the environment.

[136] Van den Bossche and Zdouc (n 22) 495.

[137] Will (n 135) 140. An example of it can be found in Appellate Body Reports, *Philippines-Distilled Spirits,* paras. 163–164.

[138] Appellate Body Report, *Philippines-Distilled Spirits*, para. 161.

[139] Appellate Body Report, *Japan-Alcoholic Beverages II*, paras 24.

[140] Discussions on the environmental goods and lowering tariffs barriers for these products were held at the Doha Rounds, but unfortunately did not able to reach a consensus. See Sect. 3.2 in Chap. 6.

2.2.4 Excess Taxes

2.2.4.1 Definition

Once the measures fall under the internal tax or charge category, the national treatment analysis starts with whether the domestic and imported products are "like". The subsequent step in the analysis focuses on whether the imported product is subjected to a tax or charge "in excess of" the domestic tax. The term "excess of" in this context denotes that an equivalent economic burden is not imposed similarly on domestic products and imports.[141] This nuanced understanding recognizes that regulatory distinctions may be justifiable among like products as long as the economic burden imposed on imports is not disproportionately higher than that on domestic products.[142]

The Appellate Body, establishes a stringent criterion for the "in excess of" requirement within the context of Article III:2. According to this benchmark, even the smallest amount above the domestic tax or charge is sufficient to classify it as "excess".[143] This interpretation underscores the precision and rigour with which the Appellate Body views the application of taxes or charges on imported products compared to their domestic counterparts. Furthermore, the Appellate Body's stance in the Canada-Periodicals case clarifies that Article III:2's first sentence does not necessitate demonstrating the actual trade effects of discriminatory taxes or charges.[144] Simply put, the mere existence of differentiated internal charges, where imported products face higher taxes than domestic ones, is considered adequate to identify violations of the national treatment principle.[145] Likewise, a member applying higher taxes on imported products, regardless of whether it balances this with lower taxes in other situations, is deemed inconsistent with Article III:2's first sentence.[146]

2.2.4.2 Results on the BCAs

To prevent what is considered "excessive tax" within the framework of Article III:2(1), applying carbon tariffs and BCAs as charges should adhere to a key principle: they should not exceed the lowest charge imposed on domestic products. Even if the carbon content embedded in imports exceeds the levels in the climate club, the taxation on these imports must be limited to the price within the club's jurisdiction to comply with Article III:2(1). Therefore, in practical terms,

[141] Appellate Body Reports, *Brazil-Taxation,* para 5.35.

[142] Appellate Body Report, *EC-Asbestos,* para. 100.

[143] Appellate Body Report, *Japan-Alcoholic Beverages II*, paras 27–28.

[144] Appellate Body Report, *Canada-Periodicals*, p. 18.

[145] Appellate Body Report, *Japan-Alcoholic Beverages II*, para 110.

[146] Panel Report, *Argentina-Hides and Leathers*, para 11.260.

calculating carbon charges on imports should be based on a benchmark derived from the best available production method.[147] This benchmark represents the most environmentally friendly and efficient production method currently attainable in the club jurisdictions. By using this benchmark, the emission levels of imported products are determined as if they adopt the best available production method, which emits less carbon into the atmosphere, even if this calculation does not reflect reality.

In summary, the "excess" criterion ensures that imports are not subjected to a disproportionately higher tax burden than domestic products to align with the national treatment obligation. Remarkably, the Appellate Body's strict interpretation in these cases underscores the importance of precision and equality in applying taxes or charges on imported products. Thereby, it provides a clear standard for determining violations of the national treatment obligation under Article III:2 of the GATT 1994. However, this limitation impedes the climate club from capturing the actual carbon content of imports, thereby restricting the environmental effectiveness of BCAs.

2.3 *Article III:2(2); National Treatment for Internal Taxation on Directly Competitive or Substitutable Products*

2.3.1 Introduction

Article III:2(2) of the GATT 1994 introduces a nuanced perspective by encompassing a broader category of products than the initial sentence of the same article.[148] In examining the implications of this provision, the extent to which market access is restricted and competitiveness is affected emerges as the central focal points. Therefore, the Appellate Body established distinct criteria for conducting an incompatibility analysis. These four-layered criteria include:

The measure is an internal tax or other internal charge on products,
The imported and domestic products are directly competitive or substitutable,
Directly competitive or substitutable imports and domestic products are not similarly taxed, and
The differentiated taxation among these products is applied so as to afford protection to domestic production.[149]

In sum, the combination of these criteria reflects the delicate considerations required to assess whether a measure violates the national treatment principle. The criteria address the nature of the measure and its impact on market dynamics, along with the potential for discriminatory practices that favour domestic production over imports. A thorough examination of these elements provides a comprehensive framework for evaluating the conformity of internal taxation measures with Article III:2(2) of the

[147] Englisch and Falcao (n 30) 70.

[148] Appellate Body Report, *Japan-Alcoholic Beverages II*, para 190.

[149] Appellate Body Report, *Japan-Alcoholic Beverages II*, para 116.

GATT 1994. The analysis of what constitutes an internal tax or other charge is the same under Article III:2 first sentence and second sentence. Hence, below, the distinguished aspects of these two sentences of Article III:2 are analysed.

2.3.2 Directly Competitive or Substitutable Products

2.3.2.1 Overview

In general, non-discrimination principles protect the potentiality to compete and set the basis for competition to grow.[150] In its competitiveness analysis, Article III:2 focuses on promoting economic opportunities for importers by eliminating discriminatory governmental fiscal measures that weaken fair international trade.[151] Hence, the Appellate Body emphasized that the quality and nature of the competition are more decisive than the quantitative overlap of it.[152] In other words, it is not adequate to just look at how much two products compete with each other. Also, the competition needs to be fair and equitable. A superficial assessment based solely on the degree of competition between two products may not capture the essence of fair competition. In this scope, the national treatment principle creates an environment conducive to fair competition by preventing discriminatory measures. It allows economic actors to operate on a meritocratic basis rather than facing artificial barriers based on their origin.

The term "substitutable" under Article III:2(2) encapsulates an economic concept that pertains to goods interchangeable in the eyes of consumers.[153] Products are substitutable when consumers remain indifferent to whether one product or another is chosen, given that both adequately fulfil their needs.[154] The notion of substitutability is crucial in Article III:2(2) since it extends the likeness analysis to directly competitive and substitutable products for internal taxation and charges. In practical terms, if two products are deemed substitutable, Article III:2(2) prevents discriminatory internal taxation or charges that could disadvantage imported products over domestic ones. The Article further commits to creating an equitable global trade environment where artificial barriers or discriminatory measures do not unduly influence consumer choices. Consequently, the broader implications of the national treatment principle under Article III:2(2) spread beyond the mere removal of discriminatory practices. It actively contributes to cultivating an economic landscape where fair competition thrives.

---

[150] Appellate Body Report, *Korea- Alcoholic Beverages*, para 114–120.

[151] Appellate Body Report, *Philippines -Distilled Spirits*, para 190.

[152] Appellate Body Report, *Korea –Alcoholic Beverages*, para 133.

[153] ibid para 11.

[154] Morell (n 79) 36.

2.3.2.2 Appellate Body Test

Similar to the likeness test, there is no specific definition for directly competitive or substitutable products under the GATT 1994.[155] Unlike a rigid and universal definition, the assessment of the competitive relationship and substitutability is a multifaceted process contingent on the unique characteristics of each case.[156] The absence of a singular and straightforward test implies a reliance on case-specific features to discern the nature of the products in question. A notable elucidation on this matter arises from the Korea-Alcoholic Beverages case, where the Appellate Body contributed crucial insights. It highlighted that "like products" represent a subset within the broader category of directly competitive or substitutable products.[157] This distinction is paramount as it underscores the precision required when identifying like products, a more narrowly construed category, versus directly competitive or substitutable products, which encompass a broader range. It is important to note that according to this recognition, imported and domestic products do not have to be fully substitutable to be considered directly competitive or substitutable. This is because full substitutability is a defining characteristic of like products.[158]

The significance of case law and reports from the WTO DSB cannot be overstated in providing clarity on the expression of directly competitive and substitutable products. Through a series of rulings and analyses, the WTO DSB has contributed to the parameters governing the determination of such products. They ensure a consistent and principled approach for resolving disputes related to discriminatory fiscal measures under Article III:2(2).[159] Accordingly, the Appellate Body developed comprehensive and non-exhaustive criteria to assess the directly competitive or substitutable products. These criteria consider various facets that collectively contribute to the assessment of the relationship between products in the relevant market. They ensure a holistic evaluation by considering not only economic factors but also legal and regulatory aspects that influence the competitive landscape. The following elements are considered in this evaluation:

- The competitive relationship between products in the relevant market,
- The cross-price elasticity of demand,
- The elasticity of substitution,
- Distribution channels of products,
- Products' physical characteristics,
- Products' end-uses and marketing,
- Products' tariff classification and

[155] Won-Mog Choi and Freya Baetens, 'Like Products' in Rüdiger Wolfrum (ed), Max *Planck Encyclopaedia of Public International Law* (2020).

[156] Holzer, 'Comparability in International Economic Law' (n 82) 186.

[157] Appellate Body Report, *Korea-Alcoholic Beverages*, para 118.

[158] Appellate Body Report, *Canada-Periodicals*, p. 28.

[159] Holzer, 'Comparability in International Economic Law' (n 82) 186.

- Internal regulation regarding imports and domestic products.[160]
- Product's inputs and process of production.[161]

Market Analysis

The first step and the most significant aspect in evaluating likeness for competitive or directly substitutable products is the market analysis.[162] In this context, the helpful method would be to look at the reference market to observe the competitive relationship.[163] Subsequently, it involves a meticulous exploration of substitutability, scrutinizing whether two products meet the same interchangeable consumer demand.[164] The insights derived from this step contribute to the nuanced understanding of the competitive dynamics between the products in question. The Appellate Body Report explained in the Philippines-Distilled Spirits case that even though some products have similar physical characteristics, they may not be "like" within the meaning of Article III:2 second sentence if their competitiveness or substitutability is low.[165] This insight emphasizes the need to prioritize economic realities over surface-level similarities. Therefore, the likeness analysis under Article III:2(2) will focus first on the competitive relationship and substitutability. The three other fundamental criteria of the likeness test, which are the product's physical characteristics, end-uses and tariff classification, will be considered in the later stage if they are found to be competitive and substitutable.

Cross-price Elasticity of Demand

The cross-price elasticity of demand emerges as a pivotal tool for determining the direct competitiveness and substitutability of imports and domestic products within the relevant market.[166] This economic metric sheds light on the responsiveness of demand for a product to changes in the price of another, offering valuable insights into the dynamics of market competition.[167] The substitute products compete for the same customers in the market. Therefore, price changes in one of them can influence the consumer's purchasing behaviour towards another. Specifically, within the scope of the national treatment principle, the cross-price elasticity calculates how much an increase in the import tax affects domestic product sales.[168] In essence, it assesses the sensitivity of consumers to price changes, thereby revealing the extent

---

[160] Appellate Body Report, *Philippines-Distilled Spirits*, para 198.
[161] Appellate Body Report, *Canada- Renewable Energy*, para 5.63.
[162] Appellate Body Report, *Japan–Alcoholic Beverages II*, p. 25.
[163] Appellate Body Report, *Korea- Alcoholic Beverages*, para 137.
[164] Appellate Body Report, *Korea- Alcoholic Beverages*, para 120.
[165] Appellate Body Report, *Philippines-Distilled Spirits*, para 242.
[166] Appellate Body Report, *Japan–Alcoholic Beverages II*, p. 25.
[167] Richard A. Posner, *Economic Analysis of Law* (Aspen Legal Education 2014), 664.
[168] Horn and Mavroidis, 'Still Hazy After All These Years' (n 50) 61.

to which imported and domestic products can be considered substitutes or direct competitors. Accordingly, a demand that reacts readily to alterations in taxes or charges is categorized as elastic, reflecting a higher degree of substitutability.[169]

However, conducting a thorough cross-price elasticity analysis necessitates high-quality data from the disputed market, a requirement that may pose challenges in terms of accessibility.[170] Recognizing this limitation, practitioners often resort to using data from comparable markets to carry out cross-price elasticity examinations. In such instances, it becomes imperative to validate the applicability of demand determinants, including income levels, consumer preferences, and other relevant factors, to ensure the robustness of the analysis.[171] In case of narrowing the scope and delineating the extent of substitutability, the analysis influences the perceived competitive relationships among products.[172] Therefore, the potential competition may be either bolstered or undermined based on the calculated cross-price elasticities, adding a layer of complexity to the overall assessment. Nevertheless, cross-price elasticity of demand offers a quantitative framework for understanding the intricacies of market dynamics and competition.

Elasticity of Substitution

The elasticity of substitution serves as another valuable approach for determining the direct competitiveness and substitutability of imports and domestic products.[173] This analytical method is mainly focused on assessing the impact of discriminatory measures on the competitive conditions "between interchangeable products, or products offering alternative ways of satisfying a particular need or taste".[174] The essence of this approach lies in understanding whether products are vying for the same market share and to what extent they can substitute each other.[175] In order to apply this method, a comparator product first needs to be selected by the WTO member. Then, the Panel will determine whether this comparator is legitimate to conduct an objective market-based test focusing on the competitive conditions

169 Morell (n 79) 42.

170 Horn and Mavroidis, 'Still Hazy After All These Years' (n 50) 62.

171 Horn and Mavroidis, 'Still Hazy After All These Years' (n 50) 64. Evidence from other market has been employed in Korea- Alcoholic Beverages case. However, the Appellate Body did not establish comparability between Japanese and Korean markets before using the evidence from the Japan on substitutability of alcoholic drinks in Korea.

172 Appellate Body Report, *Korea-Alcoholic Beverages*, para 134.

173 Panel Report, *Japan – Taxes on Alcoholic Beverages, (Japan- Alcoholic Beverages II)*, WT/DS8/R, WT/DS10/R, WT/DS11/R, adopted 1 November 1996, as modified by Appellate Body Report WT/DS8/AB/R, WT/DS10/AB/R, WT/DS11/AB/R, DSR 1996, para 6.22.

174 Appellate Body Report, *Korea-Alcoholic Beverages*, para 115.

175 Panel Report, *Japan- Alcoholic Beverages II*, para. 6.30. Holzer, 'Comparability in International Economic Law' (n 82) 187.

among the comparator and product subjected to the measure.[176] Crucially, the analysis focuses on the degree of proximity in the competitive relationship between domestic and imported products, which should be direct.[177] Therefore, the comparator should be meticulously chosen to prevent any overreaching interpretation.

However, this approach has a restricting scope as it may prevent Panels from considering latent demand.[178] The latent demand refers to a demand for a product or service that is not currently being met by the market.[179] By focusing solely on the competitive conditions between existing comparator products and the products subjected to the measure, the elasticity of substitution approach might overlook potential demand for new, innovative, or alternative products that are not yet present or prominent in the market. Static comparison can result in an incomplete understanding of the market dynamics. Meanwhile, the evaluation of competition in the market is an intricate and ever-evolving process that requires an understanding of the dynamics at play.[180]

In this context, the elasticity of substitution analysis extends beyond considering current consumer preferences.[181] The focus of the analysis also covers products with a high but imperfect degree of substitutability,[182] recognizing that the market is dynamic and consumer preferences may evolve over time. Hence, it is essential to emphasize that the existence of substitutability need not be confined to a given moment. Instead, the capability of products to substitute each other and potential competition among them are crucial parameters for applying the substitutability test.[183] This forward-looking perspective acknowledges that market conditions, consumer behaviours, and technological advancements can influence the potential for products to become substitutes in the future.[184] Consequently, the discriminatory effects of internal taxes or charges are adequately addressed, leading to prevent potential market inefficiencies and challenges in promoting fair competition.

[176] Won-Mog Choi, 'How More 'Likeness' in Addressing Technical Regulations?' (Society of International Economic Law (SIEL), 3rd Biennial Global Conference, 12 July 2012), 8 <https://doi.org/10.2139/ssrn.2104187>.

[177] Appellate Body Report, *Korea-Alcoholic Beverages*, para 116.

[178] Van den Bossche and Zdouc (n 22) 370. Appellate Body Report, *Korea– Alcoholic Beverages*, paras. 119–134.

[179] Van den Bossche and Zdouc (n 22) 407.

[180] Appellate Body Report, *Philippines-Distilled Spirits*, para 226.

[181] Appellate Body Report, *Korea-Alcoholic Beverages*, para 114.

[182] Appellate Body Report, *Philippines-Distilled Spirits*, para 205.

[183] Appellate Body Report, *Korea-Alcoholic Beverages*, para 114.

[184] Appellate Body Report, *Philippines-Distilled Spirits*, para 226.

2.3.2.3 Results on the BCAs

Consequently, the Appellate Body has adopted a market-based approach to delve into the competitiveness and substitutability of products under Article III:2(2).[185] In the climate club, the competition between club and non-club products is pronounced, as both vie for a share of the same market and demonstrate a significant degree of substitutability. The extent of this substitutability is contingent on how consumers perceive these products in terms of fulfilling their exact needs or demands. If consumers view club and non-club goods as satisfying similar needs, they are likely to be considered substitutes for each other, which leads to a robust competitive relationship in the market. Therefore, they will be considered "like" products and subject to national treatment scrutiny.

Notably, consumer preferences play a pivotal role in determining products' direct competitiveness and substitutability within the climate club framework.[186] Hence, consumer preferences influenced by factors such as environmental consciousness, sustainability, and carbon footprint become the primary criteria for evaluating the competitive dynamics between club and non-club products. If consumers do not regard these products as capable of meeting identical needs, the competitive relationship loses its intensity. Therefore, it cannot be established that club and non-club products are in direct competition.

In order to provide a quantitative and structured framework to assess the competitive relationships and substitutability of club and non-club products, WTO members and panels can employ the elasticity of substitution method. Precisely, the elasticity of substitution would measure the extent to which consumers are willing to switch between products with varying carbon levels. This approach recognizes the paramount importance of considering environmental factors, specifically carbon emissions, in determining the substitutability and competitiveness of products within the club market. As a result, the consumer-driven nature of the competition underscores the importance of aligning products with evolving preferences and values. Thus, the outcome of national treatment analysis for BCAs will be based on how consumers perceive high and low carbon content substitutable to each other.

---

[185] Appellate Body Report, *Korea-Alcoholic Beverages*, para 114.

[186] Holzer, 'Comparability in International Economic Law' (n 82) 111.

2.3.3 Dissimilar Taxation

2.3.3.1 Definition

In contrast to the first sentence of Article III:2, the *de minimis* tax differential is not sufficient to determine that products are not similarly taxed under Article III:2(2).[187] The Appellate Body has elaborated the difference in the first and second sentence of Article III:2 as follows; "there may be some amount of taxation on imported products that may well be 'in excess of' the tax on domestic like products but may not be so much as to compel a conclusion that directly competitive or substitutable imported and domestic products are 'not similarly taxed' for the purpose of the second sentence".[188] The Appellate Body's elucidation suggests that Article III:2(2) involves a more nuanced assessment, recognizing that some amount of taxation disparity may exist without automatically rendering the products dissimilarly taxed. Crucially, the Appellate Body indicated that dissimilar taxation is evaluated on a case-by-case basis.[189] This conclusion underscores the need for a contextual and detailed examination of each case's specific characteristics and dynamics. Such an approach ensures that the assessment is not overly reliant on a rigid threshold but considers the intricacies of the market and the competitive relationships between products.

2.3.3.2 Results on the BCAs

Consequently, under the climate club, determining whether there is dissimilar taxation to imports compared to "like" domestic products lies in calculating carbon tariffs and BCAs price levels. Ideally, these price levels should be contingent on each product's real embedded carbon content. However, the intricacies of global trade have given rise to challenges. Foreign manufacturers are asked to provide carbon levels of their product in detail may not be willing to do so or even be unable, given increasingly divided global supply chains for production.[190] This situation led many countries to adopt across-the-board approaches to streamline the administrative process, such as issuing baseline figures for imports.[191]The rationale behind these baseline figures is to alleviate the burdensome task of individually calculating

[187] Appellate Body Reports, *Japan–Alcoholic Beverages II*, pp. 29–31; *Canada– Periodicals*, p. 20; *Korea–Alcoholic Beverages*, paras. 119–134; and *EC–Seal Products*, para. 5.83.

[188] Appellate Body Report, *Japan-Alcoholic Beverages II*, para 118.

[189] ibid.

[190] Bordoff and Shoyer (n 93) 46.

[191] Michael A Mehling and Robert A Ritz, 'From Theory to Practice: Determining Emissions in Traded Goods under a Border Carbon Adjustment' (2023) 39(1) Oxford Review of Economic Policy 123, 130, <https://doi.org/10.1093/oxrep/grac043>.

the carbon content for each product.[192] Nevertheless, this approach has not been without controversy, as illustrated in the US-Gasoline case where the Appellate Body raised concerns that disparate baseline figures for domestic and foreign gasoline could potentially constitute dissimilar taxation.[193]

In response to such challenges, a more deliberate approach can be adopted under the climate club, which is the taxation according to the import's actual carbon content or the club's carbon price rather than being subjected to a predetermined baseline.[194] In this way, the club will create a level of playing field for the club members while abiding by its ambitious climate goals. The objective of these methods for calculating BCAs is not to distort trade between domestic and foreign products, meaning that the club has an even-handed approach.[195]

When considering the actual carbon content of imports in calculating BCA levels, challenges persist if the embedded carbon emissions of imports surpass those of domestic products. In such instances, a scenario emerges where imports necessitate a higher tax than their domestic counterparts, thereby constituting dissimilar taxation. However, within the scope of BCAs, dissimilar taxation is not applied "so as to afford protection" to domestic production. It only aims to enhance the environmental effectiveness of the BCAs. Moreover, the risk of dissimilar taxation persists when the carbon price for imports is based on the climate club jurisdiction's domestic carbon price. The non-club members could demonstrate that their imports have a lower carbon content than the club average. The consequence of such a scenario is, again, dissimilar taxation to imports. The very magnitude of the dissimilar taxation in a particular situation may be evidence of a protective application[196] and whether there is a violation of Article III:2(2).

---

192 Christoph Böhringer, Edward J Balistreri and Thomas F Rutherford, 'The Role of Border Carbon Adjustment in Unilateral Climate Policy: Overview of an Energy Modeling Forum Study (EMF 29)' (2012) 34(Supplement 2) Energy Economics S97.

193 Panel Report, *United States – Standards for Reformulated and Conventional Gasoline, (US-Gasoline),* WT/DS2/R, adopted 20 May 1996, as modified by Appellate Body Report WT/DS2/AB/R, paras 3.12–3.13.

194 Robert Howse, 'Distinguished Essay: Non-Tariff Barriers and Climate Policy: Border-Adjusted Taxes and Regulatory Measures as WTO-Compliant Climate Mitigation Strategies' in *European Yearbook of International Economic Law 2015* (6th edn, Springer 2015).

195 James Bacchus, 'Legal Issues with the European Carbon Border Adjustment Mechanism' (2021) <https://www.cato.org/briefing-paper/legal-issues-european-carbon-border-adjustment-mechanism> accessed 5 April 2024.

196 Appellate Body Report, *Japan - Alcoholic Beverages II,* 29.

2.3.4 So as to Afford Protection to Domestic Production

2.3.4.1 Definition

Within the framework of Article III:2(2), member countries have the latitude to impose dissimilar taxes on directly competitive or substitutable products, provided that they are not applied with the primary purpose of protecting domestic production. This allowance recognizes the sovereign right of members to formulate and implement internal taxation policies that suit their economic and environmental objectives. In essence, the WTO aims to ensure that internal taxation measures are not wielded as protectionism tools, distorting international trade to the detriment of foreign competitors.[197] Therefore, the critical consideration lies in scrutinizing the design, architecture, structure, and overall application of the tax measure to discern whether it is designed to afford protection to domestic industries.[198] Evaluating the intent behind a particular tax measure becomes paramount in making this determination, however, it is often a complex task.[199] The multifaceted nature of economic policies, coupled with varying national interests, makes it challenging to understand unequivocally whether a tax measure is protectionist in nature.

The introduction section of the national treatment analysis in this book explained that Article III does not incorporate an aim and effect test.[200] The regulatory purpose can only be discussed under the Article XX exception. Therefore, when like products are subjected to excessive taxation, it constitutes a breach of the national treatment principle, even if the regulation's intent is environmental rather than protectionist.[201] However, under Article III:2(2), the "so as to" term suggests that the intent and effect of the regulation become relevant in the national treatment analysis. In the same manner, the Appellate Body clarified that "a measure's purpose, objectively manifested in the design, architecture, and structure of it, are intensely pertinent to the task of evaluating whether or not that measure is applied so as to afford protection to domestic production".[202] This aim-and-effect approach provides regulatory autonomy to the members and an alternative pathway to protect domestic regulations based on legitimate purposes other than Article XX exceptions.[203]

The Panel in the US-Taxes on Automobiles decided that "a measure has an effect of affording protection to domestic production if it accorded greater competitive opportunities to domestic products than to imported products."[204] This interpretation

---

[197] ibid 27.

[198] ibid 29, Appellate Body Report, *Philippines–Distilled Spirits*, para. 250.

[199] Appellate Body Report, *Chile – Taxes on Alcoholic Beverages, (Chile-Alcoholic Beverages)* WT/DS87/AB/R, WT/DS110/AB/R, adopted 12 January 2000, para 71.

[200] Appellate Body Report, *Japan - Alcoholic Beverages II*, 27–28.

[201] Appellate Body Report, *Korea–Alcoholic Beverages*, para. 150.

[202] Appellate Body Report, *Chile- Alcoholic Beverages*, para. 71.

[203] Choi (n 176) 6.

[204] GATT Panel Report, *United States-Taxes on Automobiles*, para. 5.10.

emphasizes the significance of examining the practical effects of a measure as opposed to relying solely on the subjective intent of the regulator. In essence, the actual impact on competitive opportunities becomes a key determinant, rendering the regulator's intentions irrelevant if the measure's application lacks impartiality.[205] Hence, to provide clarity, the objective purpose of a regulation should be unequivocally expressed in the application statute.[206] This emphasis on objectivity aims to ensure that the implementation of a measure aligns with the stated goals and does not inadvertently discriminate against imported products. Furthermore, the decision highlights that, under Article III, the trade flows of the products in question are not considered relevant.[207] This is because changes in import flow can be influenced by various factors unrelated to internal taxation or charges.[208]

2.3.4.2 Results on the BCAs

Applying this reasoning to BCAs and regulatory differences related to the carbon footprint of products, the Appellate Body would likely interpret them in conformity with the national treatment principle only if the regulatory motivation of the climate club is clearly articulated in the BCA regulation. In other words, the regulatory framework should transparently communicate any distinctions between domestic and imported products stemming from their carbon content, not their geographical origin. Therefore, the internal taxes or charges ought to be framed to avoid undue favouritism towards domestic products, ensuring that carbon-related concerns are the primary determinants of differentiation.

Recognizing the growing global concern over climate change, trade policies incorporating BCAs are becoming integral tools for incentivizing environmentally sustainable practices. Therefore, in addition to protecting national treatment, the Appellate Body might consider the overall environmental impact of BCAs, recognizing them as measures designed not just for economic protectionism but also for addressing pressing global challenges. Consequently, even if "dissimilar taxation" between climate club and non-club products exists, it would not lead to the violation of "so as to afford protection to domestic products". Thereby, BCAs comply with national treatment for directly competitive or substitutable products.

---

[205] Appellate Body Report, *Japan–Alcoholic Beverages II*, 27. Appellate Body Report, *Chile–Alcoholic Beverages*, para. 55.

[206] Appellate Body Report, *Canada-Periodicals*, 30–31.

[207] Appellate Body Report, *Korea–Alcoholic Beverages*, para 153.

[208] ibid.

2.4 *Article III:4, National Treatment for Internal Regulation*

2.4.1 Introduction

Article III:4 of the GATT addresses concerns related to internal regulations that may result in discriminatory practices against imported products compared to their domestic counterparts. The climate club linkages necessitate a thorough examination of potential implications related to less favourable treatment towards importers in the context of Article III:4. This is because club linkages constitute "administrative requirements, which might be perceived as an additional burden on imported products, potentially creating disparities in treatment when compared to domestic goods".[209] These linkages are BCAs as surrendering emissions allowance certificates of the club's ETS, the obligation to verify and disclose the actual carbon content of their products to customs authorities and technical regulations and standards.[210]

Article III:4 establishes a three-tier test to evaluate the consistency of internal regulations with the national treatment principle. The criteria are:

- The measure at issue is a law, regulation, or requirement covered by Article III:4,
- Imports and domestic products are like, and
- Imports are accorded less favourable treatment.[211]

By applying the three criteria, a comprehensive analysis can be conducted to assess the consistency with Article III:4. There is no reference in Article III:4 to paragraph 1 of the same article. The absence of reference signifies that the national treatment analysis for internal regulations does not necessitate a direct inquiry into whether the measure is designed to protect domestic products. The departure from explicit protectionism scrutiny[212] broadens the scope of assessment, which can focus more on the substantive aspects of product likeness and less favourable treatment. Hence, the critical aspect of the national treatment analysis for internal regulations is to ask whether the high and low-carbon embedded products are like in the first place. Once the products are found to be like, differentiation among them, even due to an environmental aim, is inconsistent with national treatment rule.[213]

---

[209] Appellate Body Report, *Thailand – Customs and Fiscal Measures on Cigarettes from the Philippines, (Thailand – Cigarettes (Philippines))*, WT/DS371/AB/R, adopted 15 July 2011, para. 114. Appellate Body Report, *Brazil – Taxation*, paras. 5.51 and 5.53–54.

[210] See Sect. 3.5 in Chap. 5.

[211] Appellate Body Report, *Korea – Measures Affecting Imports of Fresh, Chilled and Frozen Beef, (Korea–Various Measures on Beef),* WT/DS161/AB/R, WT/DS169/AB/R, adopted 10 January 2001, para. 133.

[212] Appellate Body Report, *European Communities – Regime for the Importation, Sale and Distribution of Bananas, (EC-Bananas III)* WT/DS27/AB/R, adopted 25 September 1997, para 216.

[213] GATT Panel Report, *United States – Measures Affecting Alcoholic and Malt Beverages*, para. 5.72.

The regulatory aim of the internal regulation has no relevance under Article III:4.[214] The rationale of this approach is rooted in the challenges associated with identifying the purpose and political influences behind regulations. Tribunals may find it challenging to ascertain a regulatory measure's precise motivations or intent, making it difficult to apply a consistent and objective standard. The analysis of the regulatory aim is typically reserved for considerations under Article XX exceptions.[215] Notably, in Article III:4, the emphasis is placed on evaluating the practical effects of internal regulations on the competitive dynamics between imported and domestic "like" products.[216] Below, three criteria for national treatment compliance and their impact on climate club linkages are examined in detail.

2.4.2 Law, Regulation, or Requirement

2.4.2.1 Definition

The terms "laws, regulations, and requirements" in Article III:4 refer broadly to any measures or policies imposed by a country that can affect the treatment of imported products.[217] This definition includes legal statutes, administrative regulations and other government requirements that impact the sale, distribution, or use of products.[218] The broad scope indicates that the provision addresses situations where regulatory measures modify the competitive conditions between domestic and foreign products within the internal market.[219] The modification could result from various factors, such as differential treatment, additional burdens, or advantages conferred on one category of products over the other. Furthermore, the scope extends beyond substantive laws, regulations, and requirements to encompass procedural ones that affect the internal sale of imports.[220] This nuanced inclusion recognizes that both the substantive and the procedural elements of domestic regulations can significantly impact the competitive landscape by imposing burdensome tasks on importers or creating hurdles in the sales process. Therefore, they are considered within the purview of Article III:4.

[214] However, the Appellate Body in EC – Seal Products held that the regulatory objective is not taken into account in determining the existence of detrimental impacts that lead to Article III:4 inconsistency, rejecting the potential for previous Appellate Body decisions to be interpreted as having taken the opposite view. Appellate Body Report, *EC – Seal Products*, paras. 5.101–117.

[215] See Sect. 4 in Chap. 7.

[216] Appellate Body Report, *EC – Seal Products*, para 5.125.

[217] Van den Bossche and Zdouc (n 22) 378–379.

[218] Appellate Body Report, *EC–Bananas III*, para 220.

[219] ibid para 211.

[220] GATT Panel Report, *United States-Section 337 Tariff Act of 1930* (7 November 1989), L/6439 - 36S/345, para 5.10.

While what constitutes law and regulation is straightforward,[221] the concept of "requirement" introduces complexity. In the context of Article III:4, a requirement is not confined solely to legally binding and directly enforced measures by the government. The Canada-Autos case establishes that voluntary private actions can be categorized as "requirements" if there is a close link between private actions and government actions.[222] This recognition implies that even actions initiated by private entities, without direct governmental enforcement, may be considered relevant within the scope of Article III:4. The pivotal criterion for considering voluntary private actions as requirements is the existence of a close link between these actions and government actions. Such a close link may be established if the government grants advantages conditional upon certain private actions.[223] In this scenario, the government is held accountable for the private actions,[224] and these requirements are deemed integral to the regulatory landscape affecting international trade. Consequently, the interpretation provided in the Canada-Autos case expands the traditional understanding of "requirement" to encompass not only legally binding measures but also actions voluntarily undertaken to secure advantages from the government.

2.4.2.2 Results on the Climate Club Linkages

In the intricate framework of the climate club scheme, the surrender of emission allowances, the establishment of technical regulations or standards, and the imposition of administrative requirements mandating information on a product's carbon levels constitute a composite of laws, regulations or requirements falling squarely within the purview of Article III:4. The surrender of emission allowances encapsulates a pivotal regulatory mechanism wherein importers are obligated to cede a predetermined amount of emission allowances to align their practices with climate club objectives.[225] Concurrently, the technical regulations or standards broaden the regulatory spectrum. They encompass a diverse array of measures that span from defining product specifications to delineating manufacturing processes.[226] Technical regulations and standards are governed specifically by the TBT Agreement and examined separately under Sect. 3 of this chapter.

Moreover, the inclusion of administrative requirements, specifically mandating information on imported products' carbon levels, introduces an additional layer of regulatory complexity. Such administrative obligations not only underscore the

[221] See Appellate Body Report, *India – Certain Measures Relating to Solar Cells and Solar Modules, (India-Solar Cells)* WT/DS456/AB/R and Add.1, adopted 14 October 2016, para 5.150.

[222] Panel Report, *Canada-Autos*, para 10.107.

[223] Panel Report, *Canada-Autos*, para 10.106.

[224] Panel Report, *Turkey – Measures Affecting the Importation of Rice*, (Turkey-Rice), WT/DS334/R, adopted 22 October 2007, paras 7.217–7.226.

[225] See Sect. 3.5 in Chap. 5.

[226] See Sect. 3.6 in Chap. 5.

transparency and disclosure elements crucial for BCA-level calculation but also constitute a significant regulatory burden.[227] In the context of Article III:4, these administrative requirements become pivotal components as they illuminate the intersection between environmental considerations and international trade practices. Collectively, these climate club linkages constitute laws, regulations or requirements that are appropriate for national treatment analysis.

2.4.3 Like Products

2.4.3.1 Definition

The product scope of Article III:4 and Article III:2 first and second sentences are not significantly different from each other.[228] While these provisions separately address fiscal and non-fiscal measures, it is essential to recognize that the potential convergence of outcomes arising from both measures could lead to challenges in consistently applying the national treatment principle. The crucial aspect is that fiscal and regulatory measures, although distinct in nature, can achieve similar ends in shaping market conditions and influencing the competitiveness or substitutability of domestic and imported products.[229] Therefore, regulating fiscal and regulatory measures becomes paramount to avoid a scenario where the choice between them determines adherence to the national treatment principle. Even though Article III:4 does not refer to the direct competitiveness or substitutability as in Article III:2(2), the Appellate Body stated that Article III:4 has a broader scope than Article III:2 first sentence but not broader than the combined scope of two sentences of Article III:2.[230] Therefore, under Article III:4, both the likeness test and competitiveness or substitutability analysis are applicable to determine whether imports and domestic products are "like".[231]

The expansive definition of like products under Article III:4 reflects an acknowledgement of the contemporary realities of international trade. The WTO DSB recognizes that measures impacting the competitiveness of imported products and affecting their market access can take diverse forms, extending beyond explicit tariffs.[232] Therefore, a broader understanding of what constitutes "like products" becomes imperative to address the multifaceted challenges of non-tariff barriers effectively.[233] This interpretative shift is driven by the overarching goal of

[227] Mehling and Ritz (n 191) 128.

[228] Appellate Body Report, *EC-Asbestos*, para 98.

[229] ibid para 99.

[230] ibid.

[231] Holzer, 'Comparability in International Economic Law' (n 82) 187.

[232] Appellate Body Report, *Korea-Alcoholic Beverages*, para 130–131.

[233] Horn and Mavroidis, 'Still Hazy After All These Years' (n 50) 53.

circumventing protectionist measures.[234] By considering a wider range of factors, such as product characteristics, consumer preferences, and market dynamics, the DSB endeavours to ensure that internal regulations do not inadvertently discriminate against foreign products.[235]

As a result, whether two products are "like" under Article III:4 is determined by the four criteria of the likeness test and whether they are in a "competitive relationship". Accordingly, the Appellate Body stated that "the determination of likeness [...] is, fundamentally, a determination about the nature and extent of a competitive relationship between and among products".[236] Central to assessing substitutability and likeness, consumer preferences have a crucial role.[237] Products can only be considered in competition if consumers regard them as substitutes. Consequently, consumer preferences emerge as a paramount criterion in determining the extent to which two products are "like". Understanding how consumers perceive and choose between products becomes essential in discerning the competitive relationship in the marketplace.

However, the subjectivity inherent in consumer preferences poses a considerable challenge. Measuring and interpreting the perspectives of consumers can be inherently complex. Consumer behaviour is influenced by a myriad of factors, making it puzzling to obtain a precise and universally applicable understanding of preferences.[238] Also, the issue of consumer awareness adds another layer of complexity to likeness analysis.[239] The lack of awareness can impact consumer's ability to make informed choices and, consequently, influence the competitive relationship between products.[240] Therefore, the challenge lies in balancing the recognition of the importance of consumer preference in determining substitutability and likeness with acknowledging the inherent subjectivity and potential lack of awareness among consumers' choices. Striking this balance becomes crucial for a fair and comprehensive assessment of whether products are in a competitive relationship and "like" since consumer choices are pivotal in shaping market dynamics and influencing the competitive landscape.

2.4.3.2 Results on the Climate Club Linkages

Under Article III:4, the interpretation of likeness has shifted towards a broader perspective, driven by the goal of circumventing protectionist measures. Deriving from the above explanations, carbon-intensive and non-intensive products may be

234 Choi (n 176) 11.

235 Van den Bossche and Zdouc (n 22) 422.

236 Appellate Body Report, *EC –Asbestos*, para. 99.

237 ibid para 117.

238 Horn and Mavroidis, 'Still Hazy After All These Years' (n 50) 65.

239 ibid 66.

240 Van den Bossche and Zdouc (n 22) 427.

assessed for their likeness based on their characteristics, market dynamics, competitiveness and substitutability. Consumer preferences mainly shape these factors.[241] Therefore, they may play a crucial role in determining the likeness of products with different carbon levels, rendering otherwise similar products not "like" in terms of WTO law. Consumer preferences also constitute one of the criteria for conducting an objective analysis of "likeness".[242]

However, assessing likeness may be challenging due to subjective perceptions of environmental impact and potential disparities in consumer awareness. For example, consumers might not always be attentive to or informed about the carbon levels of intermediary goods. Working Party Report on Border Tax Adjustments emphasized an important point, which is that consumer preferences differ from country to country. Therefore, evidence from relevant markets is necessary to analyse consumer preferences in each case.[243] Further, the World Trade Report of 2005 indicated that consumer preferences constitute an elasticity value and are generally not precisely known.[244] Consumer choices mainly depend on bounded rationality,[245] willpower,[246] and self-interest.[247] Consumers frequently do not make deliberate choices but instead rely upon cognitive heuristics or established routines.[248] Hence, the errors or biases in consumer preferences assessment should not be underestimated.

Additionally, it is essential to distinguish that consumers exhibit sensitivity to the environmental ramifications of a product and whether such ramifications effectively shape their preferences. In most cases, environmental consciousness does not translate into action.[249] Therefore, the driving force of consumer preferences in the likeness analysis could be limited. However, evidence could prove the contrary of this in some instances. A notable example is the US-Tuna II case, where compelling evidence demonstrated that strong consumer preferences were fundamental in

[241] Appellate Body Report, *Philippines –Distilled Spirits*, para 119.

[242] See Sect. 2.2.3.1.3 in Chap. 7.

[243] Working Party Report, 'Border Tax Adjustments' (n 59) para 18.

[244] WTO, *World Trade Report 2005: Trade, Standards and the WTO* (2005), 177.

[245] Bounded rationality refers to consumers' limited ability to process information due to the behavioural heuristics that undermine rational purchasing decisions. Cass R Sunstein, 'Informational Regulation and Informational Standing: Akins and Beyond' (1999) 147 University of Pennsylvania Law Review 613, 626.

[246] Bounded willpower refers that people do things that are not in their own best interest, even when they are aware of this. Mark Kosters and Jeroen van der Heijden, 'From Mechanism to Virtue: Evaluating Nudge Theory' (2015) 21(3) Evaluation 276, 278 <https://doi.org/10.1177/1356389015590218>.

[247] Bounded self-interest refers that people act in a certain way because they consider benevolent behaviour fairer than selfish behaviour. ibid.

[248] Amos Tversky and Daniel Kahneman, 'Judgment Under Uncertainty: Heuristics and Biases' (1974) 185 Science 1124, 1130.

[249] Natalie Dobson, 'Chapter 25: Climate Protection versus Trade: Dilemmas for the EU' in *Handbook on European Union Climate Change Policy and Politics* (Edward Elgar Publishing, 2023), 373.

driving the industry to differentiate tuna products based on their catching method.[250] This case sets an example of how consumer preferences can significantly influence the outcome of the likeness analysis in products with different carbon levels.

With the increase in environmental awareness,[251] consumer tastes and habits shift in a way that differentiates products regarding their environmental impact.[252] Herein, climate club linkages can substantiate this shift by subjecting them to different internal regulations. For this reason, if products are identical in other criteria of the likeness test but divergent in consumer preferences, they are considered not "like or directly competitive and substitutable products". As a result, high and low-carbon content products can be subjected to differentiated treatment and are not disciplined with the national treatment principle.[253]

2.4.4 Less Favourable Treatment

2.4.4.1 Definition

The mere differentiation between like foreign and domestic products does not violate the national treatment principle under Article III:4. This differentiation also needs to result in a less favourable treatment to imports than domestic products.[254] Within the scope of WTO case law, a measure is considered a less favourable treatment if it modifies the conditions of competition in the relevant market to the detriment of the imports.[255] Specifically, in China-Publications and Audiovisual Products, the Panel ruled that a measure "is more than likely" or "may reasonably be expected" to adversely modify the conditions of competition to qualify as a less favourable treatment.[256] This standard acknowledges that assessing less favourable treatment involves a degree of anticipation and probability. It recognizes that even if the

[250] Panel Report, *United States – Measures Concerning the Importation, Marketing and Sale of Tuna and Tuna Products*, (US–Tuna II (Mexico)), WT/DS381/R, adopted 13 June 2012, as modified by Appellate Body Report WT/DS381/AB/R, para 7.289.

[251] A Dechezleprêtre and others, *Fighting Climate Change: International Attitudes toward Climate Policies* (OECD Economic Department Working Papers No 1714, Organisation for Economic Co-operation and Development, Paris 2022). This work shows that 70% of respondents from high-income countries and 81% of those from middle-income countries believe that climate change is happening and that it is anthropogenic.

[252] Erich Vranes, *Trade and the Environment: Fundamental Issues in International Law, WTO Law and Legal Theory* (Oxford University Press 2009), 323–324.

[253] Doelle (n 118) 92.

[254] Appellate Body Report, *EC-Asbestos*, para 100.

[255] Panel Report, *Japan-Film*, para 10.379. Appellate Body Report, *Korea-Various Measures on Beef*, para 135. Appellate Body Report, *Brazil-Taxation*, para 5.75.

[256] Panel Report, *China – Measures Affecting Trading Rights and Distribution Services for Certain Publications and Audiovisual Entertainment Products*, *(China-Publications and Audiovisual Products)*, WT/DS363/R and Corr.1, adopted 19 January 2010, as modified by Appellate Body Report WT/DS363/AB/R, para 7.1471.

adverse impact on competition is not immediate, a measure likely to have detrimental effects in the future can still be considered a violation of the national treatment principle. In essence, it reflects a forward-looking perspective by emphasizing the need to assess not only the immediate impact but also the potential future consequences of a measure on the conditions of competition for imported products.

Consequently, the analysis under Article III:4 begins with scrutiny of the internal regulation's design, structure, and expected operation.[257] This proactive approach recognizes that the potential for less favourable treatment may be inherent in the measure's design, irrespective of its immediate impact in the marketplace.[258] Even without concrete evidence of adverse effects, a measure can be deemed less favourable to imports if it imposes additional administrative burdens or modifies competitive conditions in a way that could potentially disadvantage foreign products.[259] By focusing on the measure's anticipated impact, WTO tribunals can identify and address potential obstacles to fair competition before they materialize. Notably, there should be a genuine relationship between the measure that modifies competition conditions and the detrimental effects on the imports in the relevant market.[260] This requirement ensures that the analysis is grounded in a clear connection between the measure's design and its potential impact on the competitive opportunities for foreign products.[261] In essence, this market-based approach underscores the preventive nature of the scrutiny under Article III:4 by aiming to identify and rectify potential trade distortions before they manifest in the market.

Critics of the market-based approach argue that the mere existence of a measure affecting the competitive relationship between two products is not adequate to decide on less favourable treatment.[262] According to critics, government policy should be protectionist and violate the WTO's rationale of prohibition of protectionist internal regulations.[263] By asserting that the government policy should be explicitly protectionist, critics seek to ensure that any finding of less favourable treatment is rooted in a clear and deliberate policy choice rather than unintended or incidental consequences of regulation. In essence, critics are advocating for a more stringent standard to ascertain less favourable treatment that considers not just the impact on competitive relationships but also the explicit protectionist intent behind the government's policy choices. However, Article III:4 does not directly refer to the same Article's first paragraph, which underlines the protectionist intent in favour of

---

[257] Appellate Body Report, *Thailand-Cigarettes (Philippines)*, para 134.

[258] Panel Report, *US-Renewable Energy*, para 7.247.

[259] Appellate Body Report, *EC-Seal Products*, para 5.116–5.117. Appellate Body Report, *Korea-Various Measures on Beef*, para.137.

[260] Appellate Body Report, *EC-Seal Products*, para 5.101.

[261] Appellate Body Report, *Thailand-Cigarettes (Philippines)*, para 134. Appellate Body Report, *Dominican Republic – Measures Affecting the Importation and Internal Sale of Cigarettes*, (*Dominican Republic-Import and Sale of Cigarettes*) WT/DS302/AB/R, adopted 19 May 2005, para 96.

[262] Appellate Body Report, *US-Clove Cigarettes*, para 179.

[263] Choi (n 176) 13.

domestic products. Even though Article III:1 is the introductory paragraph for anti-protectionism and non-discrimination in both fiscal and non-fiscal measures, the lack of specific reference, unlike Article III:2, signifies that the drafters of this Article aim to exclude the protectionism analysis from Article III:4.[264] Therefore, this critique will not be applicable for the less favourable treatment examination. The mere differentiated treatment is adequate to find national treatment principle violation for the internal regulations.

2.4.4.2 Results on the Climate Club Linkages

Within the context of a climate club, BCA as the requirement for importers to surrender emissions allowances and administrative requirements on disclosing carbon content are potential sources of less favourable treatment. Their primary consideration is the imports' carbon content compared to the like products of the club jurisdiction. The premise is that if the imports' embedded carbon levels are higher than the like products of the climate club, requiring importers to surrender emissions allowances can be considered a less favourable treatment. The underlying idea is that higher carbon content may result in more stringent requirements for imports compared to domestically produced low-carbon products. To mitigate the risk of less favourable treatment, allowance requirements between imports and the club member's industries can be equalised, irrespective of actual carbon content. However, this approach creates potential objections from low-carbon importers who may argue that their products are being treated less favourably.[265]

Due to the potential objections, the club BCAs need to avoid benchmarks and opt for individual analysis of each product's carbon levels.[266] While this method may provide a more tailored and nuanced assessment, it also introduces complexity and administrative burden.[267] The challenge lies in conducting detailed and accurate analyses for a diverse array of products, which may be resource-intensive and time-consuming.[268] The underlying tension in this scenario is the need to balance fairness in treatment with the overarching goal of reducing carbon emissions. The climate club aims to incentivize emission reductions, but the method chosen for implementing this goal should be crafted carefully to avoid unintended consequences and objections from stakeholders. In summary, the proposal to adopt individual analysis for each product's carbon levels reflects an attempt to navigate the challenges of potential less favourable treatment within the climate club.

---

[264] Appellate Body Report, *EC-Bananas III*, para 216.

[265] Mehling and Ritz (n 191) 124.

[266] ibid 129.

[267] ibid 126.

[268] ibid.

2.5 Concluding Remarks

The national treatment principle embodies the essence of equity in international trade law. It alleviates protectionism and promotes a level playing field among trading nations. As global trade dynamics converge with environmental goals, the significance of this principle extends far beyond the legal text of the GATT 1994. This section has traversed the conceptual underpinnings, practical applications, and the pivotal role of the national treatment principle for the climate club approach's BCA linkage. The application of the national treatment principle is fraught with complexities due to the diverse regulatory landscapes and economic priorities of club and non-club member countries. The principle demands a delicate balance between respecting national regulatory autonomy and ensuring that such regulations do not discriminate against or disadvantage imported goods. Since international trade expands to include more climate-related trade instruments, the challenges of applying the national treatment principle grow more intricate.

The national treatment principle has a distinct set of criteria for internal charges and regulations. Notably, the difference lies in the determination of like products. Internal taxes and charges apply likeness test, whereas in internal regulations the national treatment principle is applicable for directly competitive or substitutable products. The significant point in both analyses is the inclusion of environmental considerations, such as npr-PPMs and the carbon content of products. This consideration in the likeness debate reflects the growing importance of sustainability and environmental protection in the global trade agenda. However, this evolution also presents challenges, particularly in reconciling the principles of non-discrimination with the urgent need to address climate change. Ultimately, the definition of like products will be based on the specifics of each case and the Appellate Body's determination. Due to the increase in environmental consciousness, the evolving landscape of climate governance, and the Paris Agreement's temperature increase limit target, the Appellate Body might consider the climate impacts of products as a differentiating factor in product likeness.

Furthermore, the effectiveness of internal charges or regulations is contingent upon the intensity of border intervention. The level of border intervention, intense or moderate, shapes the trajectory of market dynamics. Accordingly, the relevance of the national treatment rule becomes less pronounced when governments refrain from strictly restricting imports of high-carbon emitted products or imposing heavy taxes on them. If the interventions are subtle and aim to provide information rather than imposing restrictive measures, the likelihood of running afoul of the national treatment rule diminishes. In low-impact restrictions, high and low-carbon products coexist in the market, and the treatment towards them depends mainly on consumer choices. The climate club linkages, which aim to equalize conditions between carbon-intensive and non-intensive products, provide information for consumers to make informed choices. If they merely ensure equal conditions without impinging on the market dynamics, they may not be considered to be violating the national treatment rule. The focus here is on the degree to which government interventions alter the competitive landscape and influence consumer preferences.

It is crucial to recognize that club linkages are essential in steering consumer preferences toward a specific regulatory aim. Through their legislation, governments promote distinct regulatory objectives, and the success of these measures hinges on their ability to alter market conditions to realize the intended regulatory outcomes effectively. In navigating this complex terrain, policymakers need to carefully assess the impact of their interventions on market conditions and consumer choices to avoid violation of national treatment principle. In this way, they ensure compliance with international trade law and demonstrate the potential for trade policy to serve as a catalyst for environmental sustainability.

3 Non-Discrimination Principles Under the TBT Agreement

3.1 Introduction

The climate club linkages can consist of labels, standards, and certifications, which are crucial facets in distinguishing products with varying carbon emissions levels. They foster environmental consciousness and facilitate informed consumer choices. Under international trade law, providing information about a product through labelling is permissible as long as the provided information is accurate and meaningful.[269] Therefore, labelling schemes are recognised as a legitimate marketing tool to boost sales and the product image[270] if they do not impact the importation of products nor impose any burden on goods at the border.[271] In a contrary situation, the legal implications and challenges posed by labelling schemes need to be analysed.

Under WTO law, labels, standards, and certifications are categorised as technical regulations and standards defined in Chap. 5 of this book. They are guided by the principles and obligations under the TBT Agreement and the GATT 1994. The TBT Agreement assumes a distinguished role in addressing technical regulations and standards, with a specific focus on non-discrimination principles to pre-empt the emergence of non-tariff barriers to trade.[272] Its overarching objective is to ensure that such measures do not unduly impede international trade. Within the TBT

---

[269] Panel Reports, *United States – Certain Country of Origin Labelling (COOL) Requirements*, (*US – COOL*) WT/DS384/R / WT/DS386/R, adopted 23 July 2012, as modified by Appellate Body Reports WT/DS384/AB/R / WT/DS386/AB/R, para 7.641.

[270] Van den Bossche and Zdouc (n 22) 965.

[271] Aik Hoe Lim and Kateryna Holzer, 'Trading in the Era of Carbon Standards: How Can Trade, Standard Setting, and Climate Regimes Cooperate?' (2023) 39(1) Oxford Review of Economic Policy 110, 111 <https://doi.org/10.1093/oxrep/grac039>.

[272] Panagiotis Delimatsis, 'Sustainable Standard Setting, Climate Change and the TBT Agreement' in Panagiotis Delimatsis (ed) *Research Handbook on Climate Change and Trade* (Edward Elgar 2016), 161.

Agreement, six general principles guide the formulation and application of technical regulations and standards. These principles encompass a comprehensive framework aimed at fostering fair and equitable trade practices. The principles include (i) no discrimination unless justified by legitimate regulatory motivations,[273] (ii) no more trade restrictive than necessary,[274] (iii) minimization of the number of standards and regulations,[275] (iv) the use of performance over design requirements, (v) transparency,[276] and (vi) risk and conformity assessment.[277] The subsequent sections of this book scrutinise relevant principles to provide a comprehensive understanding of their implications on the non-discrimination obligations.

Examining the legal compatibility of technical regulations and standards is a nuanced process involving dual scrutiny under the TBT Agreement and GATT 1994. The hierarchy of legal norms within the WTO framework is guided by the Marrakesh Agreement Establishing the WTO, stipulating that in the event of a conflict between a provision of the GATT 1994 and another agreement under Annex IA, such as the TBT Agreement, the articles of the latter Agreement shall take precedence.[278] A pivotal precedent in this context is the EC-Asbestos case, wherein the Panel emphasised that if a measure falls within the categories of technical regulation, standard, or conformity assessment procedures, it must be initially analysed under the TBT Agreement.[279] The TBT Agreement, a specialised instrument dealing "specifically and in detail" with such measures,[280] is considered the primary reference for evaluating the legality of regulatory actions in these domains. Meanwhile, the GATT 1994 practice can still guide the scope of the TBT Agreement in interpreting the relevant articles. The obligations under the TBT Agreement and GATT 1994 are cumulative, and WTO members must comply with both agreements simultaneously.[281] Therefore, compliance with the TBT Agreement would not *ipso facto* result in consistency with the GATT 1994.[282]

---

[273] Agreement on Technical Barriers to Trade (TBT) (15 April 1994) LT/UR/A-1A/10 <https://docs.wto.org/dol2fe/Pages/SS/directdoc.aspx?filename=Q:/UR/FA/17-tbt.pdf&Open=True> (hereinafter TBT Agreement), arts 2(4), 2(5), 2(6), 5(4), 5(5).

[274] ibid arts 2(2), 2(3)

[275] ibid arts 2(7), 5(5), 6, 9.

[276] ibid arts 2(9), 2(11).

[277] ibid arts 5(4), 5(5).

[278] Interpretative Note to Annex 1A to the WTO Agreements.

[279] Panel Report, *European Communities – Measures Affecting Asbestos and Asbestos-Containing Products*, (EC-Asbestos) WT/DS135/R and Add.1, adopted 5 April 2001, as modified by Appellate Body Report WT/DS135/AB/R, paras 8.15–8.17.

[280] Panel Report, *European Communities – Trade Description of Sardines, (EC-Sardines)* WT/DS231/R and Corr.1, adopted 23 October 2002, as modified by Appellate Body Report WT/DS231/AB/R, paras 7.14 7.19.

[281] Appellate Body Report, *Korea – Definitive Safeguard Measure on Imports of Certain Dairy Products, (Korea-Dairy)*, WT/DS98/AB/R, adopted 12 January 2000, para 81.

[282] Appellate Body Report, *United States – Measures Concerning the Importation, Marketing and Sale of Tuna and Tuna Products, (US – Tuna II (Mexico))*, WT/DS381/AB/R, adopted 13 June 2012. para 405.

Technical regulations and standards as labels regarding the emissions levels fall under the category of internal regulations per GATT 1994 Article III:4. Therefore, the explanations under the national treatment principles for internal regulations are also valid in this analysis. The TBT Agreement and the GATT 1994 provisions support each other regarding the discrimination in non-tariff barriers of technical regulations.[283] Consequently, the legal analysis of the climate club's labelling requirements starts with the TBT Agreement and, in case of consistency, continues under Article III:4 of the GATT 1994. It is crucial to highlight that the impact of technical regulations and standards of the climate club manifests after the importation of products. Hence, the focus is on the treatment of goods once they have successfully cleared customs within the climate club market. These measures may exert influence on the market participation opportunities for products lacking the stipulated label, potentially creating disparities in the treatment of labelled and non-labelled goods.

Since the climate club's labels and standards do not impose any direct burden on the entry of goods at the border, the legal compatibility analysis excludes Article XI of the GATT 1994. Article XI pertains specifically to measures that affect the importation of products, regulating the entry of goods into a market.[284] In the case of the climate club's labelling requirements, the focus shifts to the post-customs phase, where the treatment of goods within the market becomes the focal point. If Article XI:1 were interpreted broadly to cover also internal requirements, the TBT Agreement and Article III:4 of the GATT 1994 would be partly superfluous.[285]

The technical regulations and standards are adopted to identify the environmentally preferred products.[286] However, the differentiation generally reaches beyond the product's environmental performance and evolves into a de facto discrimination between domestic and foreign products.[287] Therefore, technical regulations and standards need to be scrutinised regarding whether they constitute protectionism for the internal market[288] and violate non-discrimination principles under the TBT Agreement, namely MFN and national treatment.[289] The non-discrimination principles are regulated under Article 2 of the TBT Agreement for technical regulations

[283] Appellate Body Report, *US-Clove Cigarettes*, para 91.

[284] See Sect. 3.3 in Chap. 6.

[285] GATT Panel Report, *Canada- Administration of Foreign Investment Review Act*, para. 5.14.

[286] Lim and Holzer (n 271) 111.

[287] Panel Report, *Japan –Film*, para. 10.85. This paragraph defined de facto discrimination as "measures which have a disparate impact on imports" and clarified that "the complaining party is called upon to make a detailed showing of any claimed disproportionate impact on imports resulting from the origin-neutral measure". Similarly, the Appellate Body in the US-Tuna II case reaffirmed that any adverse impact on competitive opportunities for imported products vis-à-vis like domestic products might potentially be relevant for de facto discrimination analysis. Appellate Body Report, *US – Tuna II*, para 225.

[288] Appellate Body Report, *US – Clove Cigarettes*, paras 54, 166.

[289] Thomas Cottier and Jonas Baumann, 'Minimum Standards' in Thomas Cottier and Krista Nadakavukaren Schefer (eds), *Elgar Encyclopedia of International Economic Law* (Edward Elgar 2017), 57.

and TBT Agreement Article 4 and Annex 3 Articles D and E for standards. The provisions for standards have identical wording to those for technical regulations under the TBT Agreement. As a result, interpretations and case law developed for one set of provisions are equally applicable to the other.[290] Since the standards are voluntarily adopted, they are less likely to be challenged under the WTO DSB. Hence, this chapter focuses on the technical regulations disciplined with Article 2 of the TBT Agreement.

Within the framework of the TBT Agreement, the principles of MFN and national treatment converge under the same clause, namely Article 2(1). This provision establishes a comprehensive framework for analysing potential violations of non-discrimination principles in the context of technical regulations. To constitute a breach of non-discrimination, Article 2(1) stipulates that three essential conditions must be met. These are:

- the measure in question qualifies as a technical regulation,
- the imported and domestic products are like, and
- the treatment extended to imported products is less favourable than that accorded to like domestic products or products originating from another country.[291]

Given that the definition of technical regulations is expounded upon in Chap. 5 of this book, the focus here shifts to the examination of the potentially less favourable treatment accorded to imports relative to like domestic or other foreign imports. Subsequently, the exception clause of TBT Agreement Article 2(2) is examined to find whether there is a legitimate public policy objective justifying the enactment of the technical regulation. These aspects of non-discrimination compliance involve a meticulous and context-specific analysis. By delving into these intricacies, this book contributes to a comprehensive understanding of the legal implications surrounding the non-discrimination principles under the TBT Agreement, shedding light on how these principles operate in practice.

---

[290] Arthur E Appleton, 'Regulatory Barriers to Trade: Regulations and Standards' in Thomas Cottier and Krista Nadakavukaren Schefer (eds), *Elgar Encyclopedia of International Economic Law* (Edward Elgar 2017), 412.

[291] Appellate Body Report, *US – Clove Cigarettes*, para 87. Appellate Body Reports, *United States – Certain Country of Origin Labelling (COOL) Requirements (US–COOL)*, WT/DS384/AB/R / WT/DS386/AB/R, adopted 23 July 2012, para. 267.

3.2 *Like Products*

3.2.1 Overview

"Like product" is a crucial concept for the MFN and national treatment principles analysis. It answers the complex question of which products are comparable and should be treated equally.[292] While the TBT Agreement provides a more detailed regulatory scope than the GATT 1994, it does not explicitly define "like product". In the absence of a specific definition, insights can be drawn from GATT 1994 Articles and case law to delineate the contours of this crucial concept. Under Article III:2(1), the like product analysis is based on the objective likeness test developed by the Appellate Body.[293] In this clause, the violation parameter of the national treatment principle is any internal charge "in excess of" domestic ones. This threshold constitutes a strict standard, as mere *de minimis* excess tax is deemed sufficient to violate national treatment.[294]

In comparison, Article III:2(2) reviews like products through a market-based approach and focuses on the direct competitiveness and substitutability of imports and domestic products.[295] In this scope, internal charges violate national treatment if they are "not similarly taxed" the imports, which is a less stringent parameter than the first sentence of the Article. Likewise, Article III:4 has adopted the "no less favourable treatment" standard, which is flexible compared to "in excess of" in Article III:2(1). Hence, the likeness determination under it is based on the combination of the like products test and market-based analysis.[296] Under the MFN provision, the likeness is based on the objective test, and the threshold to violate the principle is *de minimis*, meaning any advantage should be provided to all WTO member's imports.[297]

Coming to the TBT Agreement, Article 2.1 establishes the "no less favourable treatment" standard as the parameter for examining potential violations of non-discrimination principles. This standard provides flexibility that can allow for a broader interpretation of the like product definition under the TBT Agreement. Therefore, it is possible to conclude that the like product definition is not necessarily restricted by the objective likeness test. Instead, similar to Article III:2(2) and Article III:4 of the GATT 1994, the TBT Agreement allows for an analysis based on the market-based approach of direct competitiveness or substitutability.[298] The

[292] Van den Bossche and Zdouc (n 22) 981.

[293] See Sect. 2.2.3.1 in Chap. 7.

[294] Petros C Mavroidis 'Standard of Review' in Thomas Cottier and Krista Nadakavukaren Schefer, *Elgar Encyclopedia of International Economic Law* (Edward Elgar 2017), 194.

[295] See Sect. 3.3.2 in Chap. 7.

[296] See Sect. 2.3.2 in Chap. 7.

[297] See Sect. 1 in Chap. 7.

[298] Appellate Body Report, *US-Clove Cigarette*, para.100. The national treatment obligation of TBT Agreement Article 2(1) and GATT 1994 Article III:4 are built around the same core terms, namely, "like products" and "treatment no less favourable".

Appellate Body also confirmed this understanding and clarified that "the less favourable treatment to imports relates to the design, structure, and application of the technical regulation to modify competition between domestic and foreign products or among imports of different origins".[299] This acknowledgement underscores the need for a context-specific analysis to ensure that non-discrimination principles are effectively upheld within the framework of the TBT Agreement.

3.2.2 Direct Competitiveness and Substitutability

Contextual and teleological interpretations emphasise the importance of preventing protectionism in favour of domestic products and ensuring international competition as a relevant background to understand the term "like products".[300] WTO DSB confirmed this market-based approach for the likeness. Hence, in addition to the objective likeness test compromised of four established criteria,[301] it indicated that under the TBT Agreement,[302] "the determination of likeness is, fundamentally, a determination about the nature and extent of a competitive relationship among products".[303] This interpretation acknowledges that the essence of determining likeness lies in understanding how products interact in the marketplace, influencing competition between domestic and foreign products, as well as among imports of different origins.[304]

The evaluation of the competition in the market is a dynamic and evolving process.[305] In this regard, the competitive relationship analysis acknowledges the complexity of market interactions and recognises that products may exhibit a high but imperfect degree of substitutability.[306] Imperfect substitutability reflects the idea that products may not be identical or fully interchangeable, yet they possess characteristics that make them sufficiently competitive in the market.[307] This recognition aligns with the evolving nature of consumer preferences, technological advancements, and changes in production methods that continually shape the dynamics of

[299] Appellate Body Report, *US-Tuna II*, para. 225.

[300] Vranes, 'Climate Labelling and the WTO' (n 84) 218.

[301] See Sect. 3.2.3.1 in Chap. 7.

[302] The Panel in the TBT dispute US–Tuna II directly quoted the Appellate Body's precedent in EC– Asbestos, concluding: "Although this statement was made in the context of Article III:4 of the GATT 1994, we find it pertinent also to an interpretation of the terms "like products" in Article 2.1 of the TBT Agreement" Panel Report, *US–Tuna II*, para. 7.224.

[303] Appellate Body Report, *EC-Asbestos*, para. 99.

[304] Appellate Body Report, *US—Clove Cigarettes*, para 111.

[305] ibid para 192.

[306] Appellate Body Report, *Philippines-Distilled Spirits*, para 205.

[307] Robert E Hudec, '"Like Product": The Differences in Meaning in GATT Articles I and III' in Thomas Cottier and Petros C Mavroidis (eds), *Regulatory Barriers and the Principle of Non-Discrimination in World Trade Law* (University of Michigan Press 2000) 101, 108.

the marketplace.[308] Moreover, the analysis focuses not only on the current circumstances but also on the potential competition between imports and domestic products.[309] Anticipating future market dynamics is crucial in ensuring trade regulations effectively respond to evolving economic landscapes.

The determination of likeness involves a nuanced and context-related value judgment, acknowledging that certain products may be considered "like" under WTO law but might not be included in the same product group under a specific labelling scheme or vice versa. This complexity introduces the possibility that products deemed "like" from a WTO legal perspective may be denied the opportunity to bear a label under certain technical regulation schemes. As a result, the inquiry into competitive relationships and substitutability is not subject to a single simple test but instead relies on specific features of each case and may involve quantitative and qualitative market analysis.[310] The methodologies for assessing direct competitiveness and substitutability are explained in the national treatment analysis under Article III:2(2) of the GATT 1994.[311] While not repeated here, it is worth noting that these methodologies guide the evaluation of the competitive relationships among products, considering factors such as the product's nature, cross-price elasticity of demand, and elasticity of substitution.

Labels are generally developed based on life-cycle assessments and differentiate products per environmental impacts attributed to npr-PPMs.[312] The npr-PPMs do not impact the physical characteristics of the final product, such as the energy source during the production phase.[313] They communicate the invisible characteristics of the products; thereby, they can differentiate products per their nature and quality. Furthermore, npr-PPM-based technical regulations can alter consumer preferences due to their influence on informed decision-making.[314] Consequently, the impacts of npr-PPMs on competitive relationship and substitutability of labelled and non-labelled products necessitate a detailed section in the likeness analysis.

---

[308] Marios C Iacovides, 'Marginal Consumers, Marginalized Economics: Whose Tastes and Habits Should the WTO Panels and Appellate Body Consider When Assessing "Likeness"?' (2014) 48(2) Journal of World Trade 323, 325.

[309] Panel Report, *Philippines– Distilled Spirits*, para. 7.100.

[310] Appellate Body Report, *Philippines– Distilled Spirits*, para 207.

[311] See Sect. 2.3.2 in Chap. 7.

[312] Tania Voon, Andrew Mitchell and Catherine Gascoigne, 'Consumer Information, Consumer Preferences and Product Labels under the TBT Agreement' in Tracey Epps and Michael J Trebilcock (eds), *Research Handbook on the WTO and Technical Barriers to Trade* (Edward Elgar Publishing 2013) 454, 465.

[313] Van den Bossche and Zdouc (n 22) 967.

[314] WTO (n 911) para 4.

3.2.2.1 Non-Product Related Process and Production Methods

The debated issue under the TBT Agreement is whether the Agreement disciplines the npr-PPMs-based technical regulations.[315] The definition of technical regulations and standards under the TBT Agreement suggests that their scope is limited to covering the product itself and product-related PPMs.[316] The Explanatory Note of Annex 1 reinforces this interpretation by explicitly stating that "this agreement deals with the technical regulations, standards, and conformity assessment procedures related to the products or PPMs".[317] In negotiations within the WTO Committee on Trade and the Environment, developing countries have put forth the argument that, given the lack of explicit reference to npr-PPMs in the relevant definitions, the introduction of npr-PPM-based technical regulations by other members would be prohibited under the TBT Agreement.[318]

However, the notification requirement for all labelling schemes, regardless of the information provided on the label, by member States to the TBT Committee underscores the inclusive nature of the TBT Agreement.[319] Similarly, Article 2(9)(2) of the TBT Agreement mandates the notification of technical regulations, irrespective of the information contained within those regulations. This broad notification requirement implies including npr-PPMs in the Agreement if they take the form of technical regulations.[320] In essence, these notification provisions suggest that the TBT Agreement does not per se exclude npr-PPMs. The Agreement's inclusive approach recognises that various aspects of technical regulations and labelling requirements, including those related to npr-PPMs, can impact international trade.

Even if one takes the view that npr-PPM-based technical regulations are exempted from the scope of the TBT Agreement, then GATT 1994 provisions of Article III:4 (national treatment principle for internal regulations) or XXIII:1 (b) (nullification or impairment) will find a field of application. The coexistence of the TBT Agreement and GATT 1994 implies that measures not explicitly covered by the former may be scrutinized under the latter.[321] The TBT Agreement imposes additional obligations beyond those established by the GATT 1994. Therefore, even if the TBT Agreement

---

[315] ibid.

[316] TBT Agreement, art 1.3.

[317] The explanatory note to Annex 1, para 2 to the TBT Agreement.

[318] Committee on Trade and Environment, Report (1996) of the Committee on Trade and Environment, WT/CTE/1, dated 12 November 1996, paras 55–81.

[319] WTO Committee on Technical Barriers to Trade, 'Decisions and Recommendations Adopted by the Committee since Jan. 1, 1995 – Note by the Secretariat' G/TBT/1/Rev.7 (28 November 2000) sec III:10.

[320] NJ Schrijver, Peter van den Bossche, and G Faber, *Unilateral Measures Addressing Non-Trade Concerns: A Study on WTO Consistency, Relevance of other International Agreements, Economic Effectiveness and Impact on Developing Countries of Measures concerning Non-Product-Related Processes and Production Methods* (OBT, Den Haag 2007) <https://hdl.handle.net/1887/12563> accessed 5 April 2024.

[321] Appellate Body Report, *US-Tuna II (Mexico)*, para 405.

were deemed inapplicable, this does not automatically mean that requirements based on npr-PPMs are outright banned. Instead, such measures can still be regulated under the scope of the GATT 1994. This suggests a layered and interlinked regulatory approach within WTO law, where different agreements work in tandem to cover a comprehensive spectrum of trade-related measures.

Furthermore, the WTO case law has confirmed that labelling requirements should be scrutinised under the TBT Agreement, regardless of the information contained.[322] This approach ensures the consistent application of the TBT Agreement to labelling measures and reinforces the Agreement's significance in controlling diverse aspects of trade-related regulations. Also, in the EC-Seal Products case, the Appellate Body interpreted the "related PPMs" term as a "sufficient nexus to the characteristics of a product in order to be considered related to those characteristics".[323] This interpretation affirms that the TBT Agreement covers technical regulations based on npr-PPMs. Having established that npr-PPMs fall under the purview of the TBT Agreement, the subsequent analysis of the effects of npr-PPM-based technical regulations on product characteristics and consumer preferences becomes a crucial step in understanding the likeness test of the non-discrimination principle.

Product Characteristics

The substitutability of products within a market is a complex interplay of various factors, each playing a crucial role in determining consumer choices and shaping the competitive landscape.[324] One pivotal aspect influencing substitutability is the product's characteristics. Products that possess similar physical attributes and functionalities are often deemed more interchangeable, leading consumers to view them as substitutes for one another.[325] This product similarity can stem from shared features, specifications, or even materials used in the manufacturing process. According to the Appellate Body, a product's characteristics encompass "any objectively definable features, qualities, attributes, or other distinguishing marks of a product".[326] The list of examples further clarifies the breadth of what can be considered as characteristics. These examples range from intrinsic features, such as composition, size, shape, colour, texture, hardness, strength, flammability, conductivity, density, or

[322] Panel Report, *European Communities – Protection of Trademarks and Geographical Indications for Agricultural Products and Foodstuffs, Complaint by Australia, (EC – Trademarks and Geographical Indications (Australia)),* WT/DS290/R, adopted 20 April 2005, para 7.451. Appellate Body Report, US – Tuna II para 199. Panel Report, US – COOL, para 7.212. Appellate Body Report, *United States – Measures Concerning the Importation, Marketing and Sale of Tuna and Tuna Products – Recourse to Article 21.5 of the DSU by Mexico,(US – Tuna II (Mexico) (Article 21.5 – Mexico))* WT/DS381/AB/RW and Add.1, adopted 3 December 2015. The panels and Appellate Body in principle endorsed the possibility to regulate production methods through non-mandatory labels.

[323] Appellate Body Report, *EC-Seal Products*, para 5.12.

[324] Voon, Mitchell and Gascoigne, (n 312) 465.

[325] ibid.

[326] Appellate Body Report, *EC-Asbestos*, para 64.

viscosity, to extrinsic features, such as means of identification, presentation, and product appearance.[327] Intrinsic features pertain to the inherent properties of the product itself, such as its physical or chemical properties. On the other hand, extrinsic features involve aspects that may be external but still contribute to defining and distinguishing the product.

This comprehensive understanding of product characteristics is crucial in the context of the TBT Agreement. It ensures that technical regulations affecting these characteristics are appropriately scrutinised to uphold the non-discrimination principles and prevent unnecessary obstacles to trade. The interpretation of the Appellate Body's statement that "product characteristics may be intrinsic, or they may be related to the product" indeed opens the door to a broad understanding of what falls within the scope of the TBT Agreement.[328] Some experts argue that this broad interpretation implies that npr-PPM-based technical regulations differentiate like products to the extent that they impact the characteristics of a product.[329] However, the absence of specific WTO DSB examinations on applying npr-PPMs under the TBT Agreement leaves room for interpretation and further exploration.[330] As a result, the broad interpretation of the Appellate Body's statement on product characteristics offers a theoretical basis for considering product differentiating features of npr-PPMs under the TBT Agreement.[331]

Consumer Preferences

Consumer perceptions also play a significant role in the substitutability equation. How consumers perceive and interpret product information greatly influences their preferences and choices.[332] Consumers differentiate between products based on a deeper understanding of their features. Technical regulations, which provide information on npr-PPMs, such as product specifications, safety standards, and compliance requirements, can significantly impact these perceptions.[333] If technical regulations highlight certain attributes or qualities as essential, consumers may

---

[327] ibid para 67.

[328] Appellate Body Report, *European Communities – Trade Description of Sardines, (EC-Sardines)*, WT/DS231/AB/R, adopted 23 October 2002, para 176.

[329] Charles Verill, 'Maximum Carbon Intensity Limitations and the Agreement on Technical Barriers to Trade; (2008) 1 Carbon and Climate Law Review, 46–47.

[330] The Tuna-Dolphin case was regarding the npr-PPM application for voluntary environmental labelling, but the claim was based on Article I:1 of the GATT. In the US-COOL case again the labelling requirement was about npr-PPMs, but the US, the respondent, did not argue that the measure fell outside the scope of application of the TBT Agreement.

[331] Appellate Body Report, *EC-Asbestos*, para 117–118.

[332] Voon, Mitchell and Gascoigne (n 312) 465.

[333] Vranes, 'Carbon Taxes, PPMs and the GATT' (n 49) 92.

adjust their preferences accordingly.[334] Thereby, they affect the perceived substitutability of products.

Furthermore, the influence of technical regulations extends beyond individual consumer choices to impact market dynamics as a whole. Npr-PPM-based technical regulations can create entry barriers for certain products, shaping the competitive landscape by favouring those that adhere to its standards.[335] Moreover, the alteration of consumer usage patterns is a noteworthy consequence of changing preferences driven by technical regulations.[336] As consumers become more aware of specific product features, technical regulations may modify how they traditionally use products. This shift in usage patterns can have a cascading effect on the competitiveness and substitutability of products in the market. In a similar vein, the Appellate Body indicated that "consumer preferences may influence traditional usage of the products" as well.[337] Thus, any technical regulation aiming to create an informed choice and alter consumer preferences can shape direct competitiveness and substitutability analysis by altering multiple dimensions of the likeness analysis, including consumer perception and usage patterns associated with specific goods.

3.2.2.2 Results on Climate Club's Technical Regulations

The club's technical regulations are not just about compliance with the club goals; they embody a collective commitment to shaping a marketplace that reflects societal values. Consequently, they prioritise products and practices aligning with environmental consciousness, ecological integrity, and sustainability. Technical regulations based on npr-PPMs, which include life cycle analysis covering emission levels, serve as reliable indicators that provide information on product characteristics and guide consumers towards environmentally friendly choices.[338] Thereby, they create a landscape, where adherence to societal preferences becomes a key driver of competitiveness and substitutability of products.[339] This distinction acknowledges that consumer choices are increasingly influenced by values beyond mere physical attributes of products.[340] Products that align with specific environmental, social, or sustainability standards may be perceived as distinct in the eyes of consumers, leading to differentiated treatment. When products are identical in other aspects of the

[334] Appellate Body Report, *EC – Asbestos*, paras. 67–70. Appellate Body Report, *EC – Sardines*, para. 191.

[335] Cottier and Baumann (n 289) 56.

[336] Voon, Mitchell and Gascoigne (n 312) 456.

[337] Appellate Body Report, *EC-Asbestos*, para 102. According to Horn and Mavroidis, consumers perspective was central in panel decisions before this case. Horn and Mavroidis, 'Still Hazy After All These Years' (n 50) 61.

[338] Holzer (n 77) 190.

[339] Appellate Body Report, *US - Clove Cigarettes*, para 116–119.

[340] Panel Report, *US – Tuna II (Mexico)*, para 7.287.

likeness test but differ in terms of consumer preferences influenced by technical regulations, they may be considered not "like products" in terms of WTO law.[341]

3.3 *Less Favourable Treatment*

3.3.1 Overview

Labelling schemes, particularly those focused on environmental considerations, are typically designed to identify and promote environmentally preferred products.[342] The differentiation they introduce is not driven by a discriminatory intent but rather by the need to provide consumers with the information that guides them toward making environmentally conscious choices. By highlighting products that meet specific environmental standards or criteria, labelling serves as a tool to promote goods with lower environmental impacts. Consequently, even though the intention of labelling schemes is not to discriminate between products *per se*, they necessarily differentiate between products because only in this way they can identify the environmentally preferred products.

Therefore, the differentiation introduced by labelling schemes is a mean to achieve positive environmental outcomes rather than a form of discrimination against certain products.[343] It is essential for achieving the scheme's objectives. Accordingly, adopting a labelling scheme does not constitute discrimination against foreign firms as long as a country applies these regulations uniformly to all goods, domestically produced or imported.[344] When the same requirements are applied consistently, both domestic and foreign producers have an equal opportunity to meet the specified criteria and provide information to consumers in a standardised manner.

Nevertheless, even if regulations based on npr-PPMs are drafted in origin-neutral terms, there is a risk that they could be found *de facto* discriminatory non-tariff trade barriers if they alter competitive conditions.[345] For instance, the implementation of labelling schemes may pose financial challenges for economically less developed countries. This situation may hinder their ability to participate fully in international trade and raises concerns about the equitable impact of such technical regulations. Moreover, if large retailers or consumers heavily favour labelled products, non-labelled goods might face reduced market access, creating an effective trade barrier.[346] Labelling schemes might also discriminate against imported products if local industry influences the selection of the products subjected to technical

---

[341] Vranes, 'Climate Labelling and the WTO' (n 84) 219.

[342] Maggio (n 94) 208.

[343] Appellate Body Report, *US - Clove Cigarettes*, para 110.

[344] ibid para 180.

[345] ibid para 175. Appellate Body Report, *US - COOL* para 269.

[346] Appellate Body Report, *US - Tuna II (Mexico)* para. 225.

regulations.[347] This possibility underscores the need for careful consideration of the practical impact of regulations beyond their formal wording.

Problems could arise if technical regulations were designed to penalise foreign firms effectively in favour of domestic ones. Therefore, the distinctions based on a product's origin, ownership, manufacturer, or importer should be avoided.[348] Technical regulations should uphold fair competition, ensuring that foreign firms face a level playing field compared to their domestic counterparts. Addressing these challenges requires a thoughtful and inclusive approach to the design and implementation of labelling schemes. Striking a balance between promoting sustainability and preventing discrimination is crucial for ensuring the abidance of technical regulations with the TBT Agreement.

However, the Appellate Body sets a high threshold for demonstrating a violation of non-discrimination principles.[349] A mere detrimental effect on competition is not, in itself, sufficient to establish a less favourable treatment. This differentiating impact must be intentionally imposed on imported products to make them less competitive in the relevant market.[350] The intentional element introduces an additional layer of complexity to the less favourable treatment analysis. It acts as a safeguard, ensuring that technical regulations with unintentional or incidental impacts on competition do not automatically fall afoul of the TBT Agreement.

The requirement for intentional discrimination to detect less favourable treatment underscores the need for a thorough examination of the regulatory framework's purpose and application.[351] This is because the TBT Agreement does not contain a general exceptions clause similar to Article XX GATT 1994.[352] Determining intent often involves scrutinising legislative or administrative records, statements by regulatory authorities, or other relevant evidence to establish a deliberate effort to disadvantage imports.[353] Consequently, the intentional discrimination element distinguishes between legitimate regulatory measures, such as those designed to address environmental concerns, and those with unjustifiable protectionist intent.[354]

In this context, in the Canada–Autos case, the Panel clarifies that, in the absence of discriminatory intent between like products, the mere fact that conditions are related to npr-PPMs does not automatically render a measure inconsistent with the non-discrimination principles of the GATT 1994.[355] Applying this conclusion to the technical regulations, the decision suggests that the presence of npr-PPMs in a

---

[347] Bradly J Condon and Tapen Sinha, 'Unresolved Issues in WTO Law' in *The Role of Climate Change in Global Economic Governance* (Oxford University Press, 2013), 83.

[348] Appellate Body Report, *US—COOL* paras. 287–8.

[349] Appellate Body Report, *US-Tuna II (Mexico)*, para 286.

[350] Panel Report, *Japan- Alcoholic Beverages II*, paras 174, 175.

[351] Appellate Body Report, *US-Tuna II (Mexico)*, para 286.

[352] Appellate Body Report, *US-Clove Cigarettes*, paras 94, 96 and 101.

[353] Appellate Body Report, *US-COOL*, para 271.

[354] Appellate Body Report, *US-Clove Cigarettes*, para 175.

[355] Panel Report, *Canada-Autos*, para 10.30.

labelling scheme, by itself, does not necessarily violate the non-discrimination principles under the TBT Agreement. Instead, the focus should be on whether the labelling scheme, with its specific conditions related to npr-PPMs, results in disparate impacts between foreign and domestic like products. In essence, for a labelling scheme to be considered inconsistent with the WTO legal framework, there must be evidence of discriminatory treatment that unfavourably distinguishes between like products based on their origin. This nuanced approach ensures that regulatory measures, including those related to npr-PPMs, are evaluated based on their impact on fair competition rather than their form alone.

3.3.2 Results on Climate Club's Technical Regulations

The nexus between technical regulations as club linkage and the market is critical when assessing whether there is less favourable treatment.[356] Governments within a climate club may play a central role in shaping market conditions by promoting the procurement of labelled products.[357] This influence could inadvertently create a market that disadvantages non-labelled products, raising questions about fair competition and adherence to non-discrimination principles.[358] The concern also arises from the possibility of negative attributions to non-labelled products by both consumers and retailers. If the presence of a label is linked to market advantages, non-labelled products may face challenges in the marketplace, potentially resulting in discriminatory effects.[359]

Moreover, the risk of club industries influencing the selection of products subjected to technical regulations within a climate club introduces concerns about potential discrimination against imported products. The influence may result in a regulatory environment that unintentionally disadvantages imported products. It could be exerted through various means, such as shaping the criteria for product eligibility, drafting technical regulations, or advocating for specific standards that align more closely with domestic production practices.[360] Consequently, the potential less favourable treatment raises concerns about imposing domestic values and standards on exporting countries, an issue commonly referred to as "extraterritoriality".[361] In this context, "extraterritoriality" refers to applying domestic regulations or standards to products and processes outside the climate club's borders. If the climate club defines its eligibility criteria for technical regulations based on domestic environmental standards, the club may inadvertently extend its

[356] See Appellate Body Report, *US-Clove Cigarettes*, para 182 and 215.

[357] Leon J Martini, Benjamin Görlach, and Camilla Bausch, 'Accelerating the Global Transformation of Industry at the G7' (2022) <https://www.ecologic.eu/18490> accessed 21 June 2024.

[358] Appellate Body Report, *US-Clove Cigarettes*, para 180.

[359] ibid para 182.

[360] Appellate Body Report, *US - COOL* para. 270.

[361] Ming Du, 'Voluntary Eco-Labels in International Trade Law: A Case Study of the EU Eco-Label' (2021) 33(1) Journal of Environmental Law 167.

regulatory reach. This overreach can lead to less favourable treatment, as exporting countries may find it difficult to comply with standards that are influenced by the domestic values and priorities of the importing country.

To address these concerns, ensuring transparency in the decision-making process becomes paramount. Transparency involves clearly defining the criteria for product selection, openly communicating the rationale behind technical regulations, and providing opportunities for input from diverse stakeholders.[362] In this way, the environmental intent of the club's technical regulations is clearly communicated. Notably, the products originating outside the club jurisdiction can also be awarded labels under the same conditions is significant. It suggests that the eligibility criteria for receiving labels are applied uniformly, irrespective of the product's origin. In this way, the climate club's labelling regime can be consistent with the non-discrimination principles of the TBT Agreement.

3.4 Legitimate Public Policy Objectives

3.4.1 Overview

The absence of a specific exception clause or reference to Article XX of the GATT in the TBT Agreement does not preclude recognising legitimate public objectives or members' right to regulate.[363] The TBT Agreement emphasises a delicate balance between pursuing trade liberalization and acknowledging members' regulatory autonomy.[364] The Sixth Recital of the TBT Agreement Preamble explicitly affirms that no country should be prevented from taking measures necessary to protect human, animal, plant life, health, or the environment. However, it adds the condition that such measures should not be arbitrary or unjustifiable among WTO members. Consequently, it allows for the justification of otherwise trade-distortive discriminatory technical regulations if they are undertaken for environmental protection and are not deemed arbitrary or unjustifiable.[365] Also, the principle of WTO provisions being applicable cumulatively suggests that the provisions of the GATT 1994, including Article XX, can be considered part of the broader legal framework.[366] For this reason, the general principles and exceptions under the GATT 1994 can play a

---

[362] TBT Agreement, art 2.11.

[363] Appellate Body Report, *US - Clove Cigarettes*, para 96. Cottier and Baumann (n 289) 57.

[364] Appellate Body Report *US - Clove Cigarettes*, para 91.

[365] ibid para 182.

[366] Gabrielle Marceau and Joel Trachtman, 'The Technical Barriers to Trade Agreement, the Sanitary and Phytosanitary Measures Agreement, and the General Agreement on Tariffs and Trade' (2002) 36 Journal of World Trade 811, 874–875.

role in interpreting the TBT Agreement, especially when issues related to the pursuit of legitimate public objectives arise.[367]

Accepting the role of regulatory purpose under Article 2(2) of the TBT Agreement marks an essential aspect in interpreting and applying the Agreement.[368] To determine the regulatory justifiability of technical regulations, the Appellate Body employs a weighing and balancing test, analysing the following factors: (i) the extent to which the measure contributes to the legitimate objective in question,[369] (ii) the trade restrictiveness and necessity of the measure,[370] and (iii) the severity of consequences resulting from the implementation of the measure.[371] This test emphasises that if a technical regulation is even-handedly applied[372] and the competition-distorting impact results from a legitimate regulatory distinction,[373] it may not be considered a violation of Article 2(1) of the TBT Agreement. This approach reflects a commitment to ensuring that the TBT Agreement accommodates legitimate regulatory measures while maintaining a balance with the principles of non-discrimination and avoiding unnecessary trade barriers.[374]

Consequently, the first and third criteria of the above test can be resolved with the aim and the effect of a technical regulation.[375] The aim and effect are also crucial in analysing whether a "less favourable treatment" exists under the Agreement. The aim and effect approach involves evaluating not only the explicit purpose or objective stated by a country when implementing a technical regulation but also considering the practical impact or consequences of the regulation on imported products.[376] This approach recognises that the design, structure, and application of technical regulations can have significant implications for competition between domestic and foreign products, as well as among imports from different origins.[377]

By adopting the aim-and-effect approach, the Appellate Body enhances the depth of analysis when assessing the compliance of technical regulations with the non-discrimination principles under the TBT Agreement. It also acknowledges the

---

[367] Gracia Marin Durán, 'Measures with Multiple Competing Purposes after EC - Seal Products: Avoiding a Conflict between GATT Article XX-Chapeau and Article 2.1 TBT Agreement' (2016) 19 J Int'l Econ L 467, 486.

[368] Appellate Body Report, *Canada- Autos*, paras 180–182.

[369] Appellate Body Report, *US- COOL*, paras 347–349.

[370] Appellate Body Report, *US-Tuna II (Article 21.5),* paras 7.153 and 7.160.

[371] Appellate Body Report, *US-Tuna II (Mexico),* para. 322.

[372] Appellate Body Report, *US-COOL*, para 5.93.

[373] Panel Report, *Japan–Alcoholic Beverages II*, paras 174, 175. Appellate Body Report, *US-Tuna II* (Mexico), para, 225.

[374] Appellate Body Report, *US-Clove Cigarettes*, para 175.

[375] Appellate Body Report, *US-Tuna II (Mexico),* para 313 and 315.

[376] Appellate Body Report, *US-Tuna II (Article 21.5)* paras 7.85 and 7.97.

[377] Appellate Body Report, *US-COOL*, para 271. Appellate Body Report, *US-Clove Cigarettes*, para 182.

legitimate public policy objectives that regulations aim to achieve.[378] This recognition is significant, particularly for regulations designed to address broader societal concerns such as public health, safety, environmental protection, or other social objectives.[379] The aim and effect approach ensures that regulations intended to serve legitimate public policy objectives are not unduly weakened solely based on their impact on competition.[380] Simultaneously, they do not create results that go beyond the regulatory intent.[381] Hence, the aim and effect analysis strikes a balance between facilitating trade and respecting the right of WTO members to regulate for the public concerns.

The second criterion entails the analysis of trade restrictiveness and how necessary the technical regulation is in order to contribute to the legitimate objective at issue.[382] This examination ensures that the regulation is not imposed arbitrarily or without a clear rationale tied to its intended purpose.[383] Article 2(2) of the TBT Agreement clarified that technical regulation should not be adopted or applied in a way that creates unnecessary obstacles to international trade. Therefore, they should not be more trade-restrictive than necessary to fulfil a legitimate objective. The proportionality of the technical regulations requires consideration of whether there are alternative and less trade-restrictive measures that could still effectively contribute to the intended goal.[384] It does not restrict the members from deciding the level and strictness of regulation.[385]The aim is to make members think about how effective the technical regulation is and whether there are creative alternatives that could improve the efficiency of the technical regulation and reduce the trade restrictiveness.[386]

The assessment of necessity often requires a robust understanding of scientific and technical information relevant to the regulated products.[387] Relying on sound scientific evidence helps ensure the technical regulation is grounded in objective and verifiable information.[388] Also, related processing technology or intended

[378] Appellate Body Report, *US-Tuna II (Mexico)*, para 317. Appellate Body Reports, *Australia – Certain Measures concerning Trademarks, Geographical Indications and other Plain Packaging Requirements applicable to Tobacco Products and Packaging*, (*Australia-Tobacco Plain Packaging*), WT/DS435/AB/R and Add.1 (Honduras) / WT/DS441/AB/R and Add.1 (Dominican Republic), adopted 29 June 2020, para 6.373.

[379] Rolf H Weber, 'Designing Trade Rules to Promote Climate Sustainability' (2014) 8 J Energy Power Eng 612.

[380] Panel Report, *US-Clove Cigarettes*, paras 7.247, 7.248.

[381] Appellate Body Report, *US-COOL*, paras 347, 349.

[382] Appellate Body Report, *US-Tuna II (Mexico)*, para 297.

[383] ibid para 317.

[384] ibid para 322.

[385] Appellate Body Report, *US-COOL*, para 373.

[386] Appellate Body Report, *United States- Measures Affecting the Cross-Border Supply of Gambling and Betting Services (US-Gambling)* WT/DS285/AB/R, adopted 20 April 2005, para 309.

[387] Van den Bossche and Zdouc (n 22) 1004.

[388] Condon and Sinha (n 347) 86.

end-uses of products can guide us in determining the necessity factor.[389] In sum, the necessity analysis for legitimate purposes prevents the misuse of technical regulations for protectionist purposes and fosters a balance between regulatory objectives and trade facilitation.

3.4.2 Results on Climate Club's Technical Regulations

The TBT Agreement recognises that technical regulations may be necessary to protect human, animal, and plant life, health, or the environment. In the climate club's case, limiting emissions levels aligns with the broader goal of environmental protection. By regulating the emission content of products, the club's technical regulations directly contribute to the climate goals and justify the necessity of labelling requirements to achieve this legitimate aim.

The climate club's technical regulations fall under the category of npr-PPMs-based labels.[390] Even though they are adopted for a legitimate objective, such regulations also influence other countries' policies, which raises questions about the less favourable treatment.[391] The concern is that attempting to enforce specific environmental standards extraterritorially could force other countries to change their policies.[392] However, a strict prohibition on extraterritorial regulation also poses risks, as it may encourage a race to the bottom in environmental legislation. If technical regulations do not apply to foreign competitors, there may be lobbying efforts within the climate club jurisdictions to repeal or weaken these laws.[393] The relaxation of extraterritorial restrictions is contingent upon establishing a sufficient nexus between the aim of the regulation and the regulated entity.[394]

In the face of the urgent global challenge posed by climate change, the technical regulations established by the climate club can be seen as beneficial and a necessary and legitimate means to address and mitigate the environmental impacts of economic activities. These regulations respond proactively to the pressing need for sustainable practices and environmental stewardship. They also align with broader efforts to combat climate change and its associated consequences. Moreover, the technical regulations of the climate club can be perceived as necessary tools for creating a level playing field. By establishing common standards, the technical regulations ensure that all participants adhere to guidelines that prioritise environmental responsibility. This implementation fosters fair competition among businesses and industries, preventing a race to the bottom regarding environmental impact and

[389] ibid 85.

[390] See Sect. 3.6 in Chap. 5.

[391] See Sect. 3.3 in Chap. 7.

[392] GATT Panel Report, *United States – Restrictions on Imports of Tuna (Tuna II)*, DS29/R, 16 June 1994, unadopted, para. 5.25.

[393] Appellate Body Report, *US-Tuna II (Mexico)*, para 297.

[394] Appellate Body Report, *United States – Import Prohibition of Certain Shrimp and Shrimp Products (US-Shrimp)*, WT/DS58/AB/R, adopted 6 November 1998, para 133.

promoting innovation in sustainable practices. In summary, the urgency of responding to climate change lends legitimacy to the technical regulations implemented by the climate club.

3.5 Concluding Remarks

This section of the book has delved into the intricate dynamics of climate club linkages composed of labels, standards, and certifications and their compatibility with the principles of non-discrimination under the TBT Agreement. These tools are defined as technical regulations or standards within the ambit of the TBT Agreement. Due to the mandatory nature of the technical regulations, they are more likely to be challenged in the WTO DSB. Therefore, this section examines the TBT Agreement's provisions on technical regulations. Technical regulations constitute bridges between environmental sustainability and market mechanisms. Also, they serve as vital instruments for consumers to make informed choices regarding the carbon footprint of the products they purchase.

Labelling through technical regulations is commonly seen as a suitable and comparatively rather non-restrictive means for pursuing environmental goals. Nevertheless, the critical examination of the club's technical regulations under the TBT Agreement highlights the delicate balance that must be maintained between promoting climate-friendly practices and ensuring that such measures do not constitute disguised restrictions on international trade. Under the climate club scheme, the criteria-setting process is restricted to the groups in member states, which can turn into de facto discrimination based on origin. Therefore, the examinations under this section emphasised the significance of ensuring that technical regulations as club linkages are grounded in scientific evidence and transparent, avoiding unnecessary obstacles to trade while fostering an international market that is conducive to sustainable development. Otherwise, the club's labelling schemes might violate the non-discrimination principles by establishing environmental criteria that can be met only by countries with financial and technological resources, basically the developed countries and climate club members.

However, abolishing labelling programmes under considerations of free trade principles seems disproportionally restrictive. Instead, the mechanism of international standardization under the aegis of the climate club could be more appropriate. The TBT Agreement also requires that international standards be used as the basis for national regulations.[395] In this regard, the negotiation process of international standards on club labels can enable more countries to present their concerns on specific requirements or environmental criteria. Harmonization of technical regulations under the club scheme reduces the risk of unilateral measures, which is one of the significant threats to the trading system and international efforts to protect the

[395] TBT Agreement art 2.4.

environment. However, if the international standards are used in a protectionist way even after the harmonization, they are still subject to a potentially successful challenge under the WTO legal system.

The harmonization under the club also aligns with the Appellate Body's definition of non-discrimination, which is "not only when countries in which the same conditions prevail are differently treated, but also when the application of the measure at issue does not allow for any inquiry into the appropriateness of the regulatory program for the conditions prevailing in those exporting countries."[396] In simpler terms, non-discrimination implies that countries facing similar conditions should be treated similarly, without arbitrary or unjustified distinctions. So, the broader aspect of non-discrimination considers the appropriateness of technical regulations for exporting countries. Therefore, the technical regulations should not be rigid or insensitive to the specific circumstances and conditions in the exporting countries. The club scheme should also incorporate the non-club members' particular apprehensions.

As a result, the section on technical regulations as club linkage concludes with a call for continued collaboration among nations, industries, and other stakeholders to refine and implement environmental standards that respect the non-discrimination principles of the TBT Agreement. Such efforts are crucial in fostering an international trading system that supports both economic growth and environmental sustainability. By fostering a dialogue that is inclusive, transparent, and evidence-based, the climate club can ensure that technical regulations serve as tools for positive change rather than as barriers to trade. Moreover, the process of refining and implementing technical regulations must have a spirit of fairness. Hence, they should acknowledge the diverse capabilities and resources among countries, particularly the distinction between club and non-club members. Finally, continued collaboration emphasizes the importance of monitoring, review, and adaptation of technical regulations. As scientific understanding and technological advances emerge, environmental standards must be periodically adjusted to remain relevant and effective. This dynamic process ensures that the framework for technical regulations remains responsive to the changing landscape of global trade and climate challenges.

[396] Appellate Body Report, *US – Shrimp*, para 165.

4 Article XX Exception

4.1 Introduction

The provisions of the GATT 1994 have been strategically crafted to serve as a barrier against unilateral trade measures that may be deemed abusive or discriminatory.[397] Meanwhile, the general structure of the WTO law exhibits a more inclusive approach, enabling the consideration and balancing of external and non-trade interests alongside the imperative of facilitating international trade.[398] This broader perspective acknowledges that trade policies often intersect with various societal concerns beyond purely economic considerations. Article XX of the GATT 1994 stands out as a crucial provision, offering a legal basis for measures that may deviate from WTO consistency under Articles I, III, and XI of the GATT 1994. This deviation is permitted if these measures are implemented to address legitimate public policy concerns.[399] In essence, Article XX serves as a safeguard, allowing WTO members to enact measures that may otherwise be inconsistent with trade rules, provided they are grounded in justifiable and bona fide public policy objectives. In navigating the complex interplay between trade imperatives and non-trade interests, Article XX thus acts as a legal mechanism that strikes a delicate balance.[400]

Although a comprehensive list of all legitimate societal goals is not practically feasible,[401] the Article provides a closed list of legitimate goals for government intervention. In order to justify its measure under the Article XX exception, a WTO member must pass a two-tier test.[402] The first tier of the test involves establishing that the measure falls within one of the exemptions outlined in paragraphs (a) to (j) of Article XX. These exemptions encompass a range of legitimate public policy objectives, including but not limited to public health, environmental protection, and the conservation of exhaustible natural resources. The member must demonstrate that its measure is taken to achieve one or more of these specified goals and provide a direct link between the policy objective and the trade-restrictive action.

---

397 WTO, *Report on the Future of the WTO: Addressing Institutional Challenges in the New Millenium* (World Trade Organization, 2014), para 39.

398 Christina Voigt, 'WTO Law and International Emissions Trading: Is There Potential for Conflict?' (2008) 2(1) Carbon & Climate Law Review 54, 61.

399 Lorand Bartels, 'The Chapeau of the General Exceptions in the WTO GATT and GATS Agreements' (2015) 109 American Journal of International Law 95.

400 Peter van den Bossche, 'Article XX GATT, Article XIV GATS' in Thomas Cottier and Krista Nadakavukaren Schefer (eds), *Elgar Encyclopedia of International Economic Law* (Edward Elgar 2017), 260.

401 Horn and Mavroidis, 'Still Hazy After All These Years' (n 50) 55.

402 Appellate Body Report, *United States – Standards for Reformulated and Conventional Gasoline, (US – Gasoline)*, WT/DS2/AB/R, adopted 20 May 1996. p. 22. Appellate Body Report, *US–Shrimp*, paras. 119–21. Appellate Body Report, *Brazil – Measures Affecting Imports of Retreaded Tyres, (Brazil- Retreaded Tyres)*, WT/DS332/AB/R, adopted 17 December 2007, para 139. Van den Bossche (n 400) 260.

The second tier, commonly referred to as the "Chapeau" of Article XX, ensures that the measure complies with the general terms and conditions outlined in the first paragraph of the Article. It includes requirements such as non-discrimination, avoiding arbitrary or unjustifiable discrimination between countries, and not constituting a disguised restriction on international trade. In essence, Chapeau sets the broader framework within which the specific exemptions in paragraphs (a) to (j) must operate, ensuring that the measures are applied consistently with the overarching principles of the WTO.[403] In practice, the two-tier test provides a structured framework for evaluating trade measures, promoting transparency and accountability in applying trade-related policies.

As established in the US-Gambling case, where a WTO member invokes an exception under Article XX, the burden of proof initially lies with the defending party, the one invoking the defence.[404] This party must demonstrate that the measure in question falls within the scope of one of the specific exemptions outlined in paragraphs (a) to (j) of Article XX. Subsequently, it must establish that the measure is necessary to achieve a legitimate public policy goal. Once the defending party successfully establishes the measure's necessity, the burden of proof then shifts to the complaining party.[405] The complaining party must show that an alternative, less-trade-restrictive measure is available to achieve the same legitimate policy goal. This requirement ensures that, even when exceptions are invoked for legitimate reasons, the WTO trade restrictions are not more broad than necessary to address the specified public policy concern. The burden-shifting mechanism encourages parties to thoroughly and transparently examine the trade measures at hand.

Article XX plays a pivotal role in potentially integrating concerted climate-related trade measures and establishing the climate club within the framework of WTO law. This article creates a legal avenue for club members to adopt measures necessary to address climate change concerns. Specifically, paragraphs (b) and (g) of Article XX emerge as relevant provisions that may serve as legal foundations for implementing the climate club and its linkages.[406] Subsequently, the possible justification of climate club linkages largely hinges on conformity with the Chapeau. The below sections examine the subparagraphs (b) and (g), then the Chapeau of Article XX.

---

[403] Appellate Body Report, *Indonesia - Importation of Horticultural Products, Animals and Animal Products, (Indonesia – Import Licensing Regimes),* WT/DS477/AB/R, adopted 22 November 2017, paras 5.94–5.97.

[404] Appellate Body Report, *US-Gambling*, paras 309–311.

[405] Appellate Body Report, *Brazil- Retreaded Tyres*, para 156.

[406] Dobson (n 249) 375.

4.2 Article XX (b)

4.2.1 Overview

Article XX (b) allows for trade measures that are deemed "necessary to protect human, animal, or plant life or health". To qualify a measure under this exception, the invoking party must satisfy three-fold requirements. Accordingly,

- the policy objective of the measure is designed to protect human, animal, or plant life or health,
- the inconsistent measure is necessary to fulfil the policy objective, and
- the conditions under the Article XX Chapeau are met.[407]

There is no single exhaustive test for determining what constitutes necessary under this Article.[408] Several distinct aspects must be evaluated with a weighing and balancing approach.[409] Therefore, the "necessity" concept involves evaluating numerous distinct facets, focusing on the effectiveness and proportionality of the trade measure.[410] Effectiveness assesses the extent to which the policy contributes to achieving the intended objective.[411] In comparison, proportionality involves balancing the trade restrictiveness of the measure against the importance of the interests or values at stake.[412] Hence, there should be a direct relationship between the measure and the intended policy objective under Article XX(b).[413] In this way, the trade restriction is targeted and proportionate to the specific risks.

The interpretation provided by the Appellate Body in the Korea-Various Measures in Beef case further refines the understanding of necessity. The first key aspect identified is "the relative importance of the common interest or values that the law (…) is intended to protect". The decision underlines that "the more vital or important those common interests or values are, the easier it would be to accept that measure as "necessary" to enforce particular aim."[414] Second consideration is the measure's contribution to the realization of the end pursued.[415] The measure needs to be

---

[407] Panel Report, *US- Gasoline*, para. 6.20.

[408] Van den Bossche and Zdouc (n 22) 608.

[409] Appellate Body Report, *EC—Asbestos*, para 172. Van den Bossche (n 400) 262.

[410] Cottier and Oesch, 'Direct and Indirect Discrimination in WTO and EU Law' (n 102) 164.

[411] Van den Bossche and Zdouc (n 22) 607. Appellate Body Report, *Colombia – Measures Relating to the Importation of Textiles, Apparel and Footwear, (Colombia-Textiles),* WT/DS461/AB/R and Add.1, adopted 22 June 2016, para 5.68. (with regard to the Article XX(a) and (d)).

[412] Appellate Body Report, *Brazil—Retreaded Tyres*, para. 156.

[413] Panel Report, *Indonesia – Importation of Horticultural Products, Animals and Animal Products*, (Indonesia-Import Licensing Regimes), WT/DS477/R, WT/DS478/R, Add.1 and Corr.1, adopted 22 November 2017, as modified by Appellate Body Report WT/DS477/AB/R, WT/DS478/AB/R, para 7.632.

[414] Appellate Body Report *Korea – Various Measures on Beef*, para. 162. Appellate Body Report, *EC-Asbestos*, para 172.

[415] Appellate Body Report, *Brazil—Retreaded Tyres*, para 145.

indispensable and bring a material contribution to achieving relevant objectives.[416] Hence, the chosen trade measure should not only be necessary but also suitable for achieving the specified policy objective. Consequently, the second aspect involves carefully examining the appropriateness of the trade measure in relation to the identified concerns and the effectiveness of achieving the intended outcome.[417]

Finally, the measure's impact on trade is a paramount factor in understanding the necessity.[418] In this regard, any alternative measures appropriate to achieve the intended policy objective should be evaluated to accept that the invoked measure is indeed "necessary".[419] Therefore, the party invoking the exception is expected to demonstrate that no reasonably available alternatives could achieve the same contribution to the policy objective in a less trade-restrictive manner.[420] This balance ensures that pursuing legitimate goals does not automatically override the principles of non-discrimination and market access.[421]

4.2.2 Results on Climate Club Linkages

The overarching goal of the climate club linkages, which is the carbon abatement, aligns with the protection of human, animal, or plant life or health.[422] Even though Article XX (b) does not explicitly mention the environment, the Appellate Body extended the scope of this subparagraph to the general protection of the environment and measures for the reduction of carbon emissions.[423] The rationale for broadening the scope of regulation is tied to the intricate nature of environmental issues and the necessity for holistic policies that incorporate a range of measures across various levels.[424] Climate change represents one of these intricate environmental problems and, hence, falls under the scope of Article XX (b).

However, the crucial requirement for justification under this provision is the necessity of the measure to fulfil that particular objective. In other words, the

---

[416] Venzke and Vidigal (n 14) 20. This could be demonstrated for example with the empirical data.

[417] Weber, 'Border Tax Adjustment-Legal Perspective' (n 31) 416.

[418] Appellate Body Report, *EC-Seal Products*, para 5.214.

[419] Appellate Body Report, *China – Measures Affecting Trading Rights and Distribution Services for Certain Publications and Audiovisual Entertainment Products, (China – Publications and Audiovisual Products)* WT/DS363/AB/R, adopted 19 January 2010, paras 239 and 242.

[420] Appellate Body Report, *Brazil—Retreaded Tyres*, para 174.

[421] ibid para 154. The Appellate Body specified that the ban is a necessary regulatory scheme … apt to induce sustainable changes in the practices and behaviour of the domestic retreaders, as well as other actors.

[422] Intergovernmental Panel on Climate Change, *Special Report: Global Warming of 1.5 °C Summary for Policymakers* (2018).

[423] Panel Reports, *Brazil – Certain Measures Concerning Taxation and Charges, (Brazil-Taxation)* WT/DS472/R, Add.1 and Corr.1 / WT/DS497/R, Add.1 and Corr.1, adopted 11 January 2019, as modified by Appellate Body Reports WT/DS472/AB/R / WT/DS497/AB/R.

[424] Appellate Body Report, *Brazil-Retreaded Tyres*, para 182.

invoking party needs to demonstrate not only that the measure is designed to protect the environment but also that it is the least trade-restrictive means available to achieve the intended objective. This necessity requirement implies a duty to explore and consider alternative, less restrictive options that could still effectively address environmental concerns without unduly hindering international trade.[425]

Under the climate club linkages, the necessity can be proven with the Paris Agreement, or the scientific reports presented by the party invoking the exception. The Paris Agreement leaves the parties free to determine the appropriate means of mitigation, while leaving open the opportunity to develop cooperation-based market measures for the purposes of mitigation.[426] Also, given that measures adopted for climate change mitigation can only be evaluated with time,[427] the defendant could bring future quantitative projections into the necessity analysis.[428] Herein, the WTO DSB does not make judgments on the substance of scientific evidence, instead it assesses whether the disputed party conducted a genuine scientific assessment.[429] Therefore, the DSB's examination focuses on whether climate club linkages are consistent with limiting temperature increase to 2 °C.

Furthermore, the evaluation of less-trade-restrictive alternatives goes beyond the mere availability of another instrument.[430] The alternative measure should also align with the comprehensive strategy of the WTO member invoking the defence.[431] The challenges associated with combatting climate change require innovative approaches to address the interplay between environmental objectives and international trade.[432] In this context, unlike other potentially less trade-restrictive alternatives, climate club linkages offer a collaborative framework that brings together like-minded countries committed to ambitious climate goals. This distinct nature of the climate club allows for coordinated efforts to address climate change, fostering a collective commitment that may not be easily replicated by other means.[433] Also, the club linkages are part of a larger strategy that considers various factors, including economic and social considerations. Given the urgency and global nature of climate change, introducing climate-related trade restrictions becomes a strategic imperative to mitigate the risk of carbon leakage and ensure the effectiveness of climate policies. As

---

[425] Panel Report, *US-Gasoline*, paras. 6.24, 6.25 and 6.28. WTO Committee on Trade and Environment, 'Note by the Secretariat: GATT/WTO Dispute Settlement Practice Relating to GATT Article XX, Paragraphs (b), (d) and (g)' para 36, 38, WTO Doc WT/CTE/W/203 (adopted 8 March 2002).

[426] Conference of Parties (COP), 'Decision 1/CP.21 Adoption of the Paris Agreement' (12 December 2015) U.N. Doc. FCCC/CP/2015/L.9/Rev.1 (hereinafter Paris Agreement), art 4 and 6.

[427] Dobson (n 249) 376.

[428] Appellate Body Report, *Brazil- Retreaded Tyres*, para. 146.

[429] Appellate Body Report, *EC – Seal Products*, paras 5.223–5.224.

[430] Appellate Body Report, *US – Shrimp*, para 129.

[431] Appellate Body Report, *Brazil- Retreaded Tyres*, para 156.

[432] ibid para 151.

[433] Timothy Meyer and Todd N Tucker, 'A Pragmatic Approach to Carbon Border Measures' (2022) 21(1) World Trade Review 109, 119.

a result, the introduction of climate club linkages becomes not only necessary but also indispensable for achieving the overarching goal of environmental stewardship on a global scale. Therefore, they are justifiable under the Article XX (b).

4.3 Article XX (g)

4.3.1 Overview

Article XX (g) covers trade measures related to the conservation of "exhaustible natural resources if such measures have been taken in conjunction with restrictions on domestic production or consumption." Breaking down the requirements under Article XX(g) can provide a clear understanding of the conditions that must be met for a measure to qualify under this exception. These conditions require a trade measure to be:

- concerned with the conservation of exhaustible natural resources,[434]
- related to the conservation of this exhaustible resource,[435] and
- applied in conjunction with restrictions on domestic production or consumption, meaning even-handed application.[436]

Accordingly, The WTO DSB first needs to define what is an exhaustible natural resource. The definition of exhaustible natural resources, as interpreted by the Appellate Body in various cases, encompasses both living and non-living resources.[437] This broad categorization acknowledges the diverse range of resources that may be subject to conservation measures.[438] Such as non-living resources, including petroleum and gasoline, reflect the importance of addressing the depletion of non-renewable resources.[439] Meanwhile, including living species in the definition recognizes the significance of biodiversity conservation as part of the exhaustible natural resource framework.[440] The renewability of the resource does not exclude it from being exhaustible. This perspective recognizes that even renewable resources, such as clean air,[441] can be depleted or degraded if not managed sustainably. Consequently, it emphasizes the need for conservation measures that consider both the renewability and vulnerability of different resources.

---

[434] Appellate Body Report, *US - Shrimp*, para 127.

[435] ibid para 135.

[436] Appellate Body Report, *US - Gasoline*, p. 21.

[437] Appellate Body Report, *US-Shrimp*, paras 128 and 131.

[438] Gracia Marín Durán, 'Exhaustible Natural Resources and Article XX(g)' in Panagiotis Delimatsis and L Reins (eds), *Trade and Environmental Law* (Edward Elgar 2021) 223–226.

[439] Appellate Body Report, *US-Shrimp*, para 128.

[440] Appellate Body Report, *US-Shrimp*, paras. 128 and 134.

[441] Panel Report, *US- Gasoline*, para. 6.37. Appellate Body Report, *US – Gasoline*, p. 19.

Article XX (g) imposes lesser requirements than subparagraph (b) since proving the relationship between the trade measure and goal is "related to" is easier than showing that it is "necessary".[442] Importantly, the general structure and design of the trade measure should be narrowly focused on the conservation of exhaustible natural resources.[443] This principle emphasizes that the measure should have a clear and direct connection to the conservation objective, avoiding broad or ambiguous provisions that may go beyond the scope of resource preservation.[444] The trade measure should not be disproportionately broad in its scope. Blanket prohibitions or measures that extend far beyond what is required for resource conservation may face scrutiny.[445] It ensures that the trade measure is tailored to address the specific challenges posed by the depletion of natural resources without unnecessarily restricting trade.

Also, the trade measure should have the capacity to reach the policy objective of conserving exhaustible natural resources.[446] This principle underscores the need for a rational and effective connection between the measure and the intended goal.[447] It ensures that the measure is not only related to the conservation objective in theory but also capable of contributing meaningfully to its realization. Therefore, the means of the measure should be closely and genuinely related to the aim of conserving an exhaustible natural resource.[448] This genuine relationship focuses on the design of the measure. The natural resources at stake, the market structure, the geographical scope of the market, and the interactions between foreign and domestic market players cumulatively determine the relationship.[449] In sum, the less strict requirement of proving that the challenged measure is primarily "related to" conserving natural resources recognizes the flexibility needed to address environmental challenges.[450] This approach acknowledges that conservation measures may take various forms, and a rational connection to the conservation goal, coupled with the three principles above, is sufficient to meet the "related to" standard under Article XX(g).

---

[442] Van den Bossche (n 22) 262.

[443] Appellate Body Reports, *China – Measures Related to the Exportation of Rare Earths, Tungsten, and Molybdenum, (China-Rare Earths),* WT/DS431/AB/R / WT/DS432/AB/R / WT/DS433/AB/R, adopted 29 August 2014, para 5.111.

[444] Appellate Body Report, *China – Measures Related to the Exportation of Various Raw Materials, (China-Raw Materials)* WT/DS394/AB/R / WT/DS395/AB/R / WT/DS398/AB/R, adopted 22 February 2012, para 355.

[445] Panel Reports, *China – Measures Related to the Exportation of Various Raw Materials*, (China-Raw Materials) WT/DS394/R, Add.1 and Corr.1 / WT/DS395/R, Add.1 and Corr.1 / WT/DS398/R, Add.1 and Corr.1, adopted 22 February 2012, as modified by Appellate Body Reports WT/DS394/AB/R / WT/DS395/AB/R / WT/DS398/AB/R, para 7.435.

[446] Appellate Body Report, *US - Shrimp*, para 136.

[447] ibid para 133.

[448] Appellate Body Report, *China-Rare Earths*, para. 5.90. Appellate Body Report, *Brazil-Retreaded Tyres*, paras 145, 210.

[449] Appellate Body Report, *China-Rare Earths*, para 5.96.

[450] Appellate Body Report, *US—Gasoline*, 16–18.

Overall, the Appellate Body takes a holistic approach to analyse the suitability of the standard imposed by the trade measure. A trade-restrictive measure must not be based on unpredictable conditions and must be applied equally to domestic and foreign industries to qualify under Article XX(g) GATT.[451] Otherwise, it could potentially hinder fair competition and the ability of countries to plan and adapt their policies accordingly. The trade measure should not unduly force other countries to alter their policies by employing trade restrictions as a means of coercion.[452] Hence, trade limitations imposed by the measure should be lifted once other countries have achieved the policy objectives. This conditionality emphasizes the temporary and targeted nature of the trade restrictions, reinforcing that the measure is designed to encourage policy adjustments rather than perpetuating unjustified trade barriers. Consequently, Article XX(g) exception entails an even-handed application of a trade-restrictive measure, which refers to the non-distortion of competitive relationships between foreign and domestic products.[453]

4.3.2 Results on Climate Club Linkages

In the US-Gasoline case, clean air qualifies as an exhaustible natural resource due to the potential depletion caused by pollutants from gasoline consumption.[454] This conclusion provides a foundation for recognizing the climate as an exhaustible natural resource. The extension of the concept enables the understanding that the atmosphere, a key component of the climate, can be depleted through the accumulation of high levels of GHG emissions. The Appellate Body's guidance to read Article XX(g) in light of contemporary environmental concerns, particularly the universal apprehension about climate change,[455] further solidifies the applicability of this provision to the conservation of the climate as an exhaustible resource.

The climate club linkages involve trade-restrictive measures to control carbon emissions. They exemplify a collective strategy to address the depletion of the climate resource. Therefore, the climate club linkages can be justified under Article XX(g) if they stress their goal of contributing to the carbon abatement efforts rather than focusing on the competitiveness concerns of the domestic industry. In this way, they express a clear and genuine relationship[456] to the conservation of climate. Consequently, the climate club measures prioritising environmental objectives over

[451] Appellate Report, *China-Rare Earths*, para 5.124.

[452] Panel Report, US – Tuna II (Mexico), paras 5.24 to 5.27. Here the Panel referred to an embargo on the imported any tuna products, without investigating the environmental damage caused by their harvesting practice and police, as long as their regulations was not comparable to the US ones.

[453] Appellate Body Report, *US- Gasoline*, 20–21.

[454] ibid 14.

[455] Michael A Mehling and others, 'Designing Border Carbon Adjustments for Enhanced Climate Action' (2019) 113(3) American Journal of International Law 433 467.

[456] Appellate Body Report, *US – Shrimp*, paras 136 and 141.

narrow domestic interests are more likely to be viewed as legitimate contributions to global efforts rather than disguised protectionist measures.

In the China-Rare Earths case, the Appellate Body decided that a trade-restrictive measure cannot be justified if it does not consider the similar regulations of the origin country.[457] Since this practice may be seen as discriminatory. Therefore, in the climate club, if non-club members are *a priori* subjected to club linkages regardless of their corresponding domestic carbon pricing instruments, the club linkage might be found to be excessively trade restrictive and cannot be justified under Article XX(g).[458] While climate clubs aim to foster collective action on climate change, a balanced approach is essential to avoid unintended negative consequences on international trade. Hence, carefully examining the trade measures' design and impact ensures that they genuinely contribute to conserving the exhaustible natural resource, the climate, without unduly hindering fair trade.[459]

On the other hand, the climate club is based on solid standards and rules towards climate action. These standards could include specific carbon pricing mechanisms, emission reduction targets, or other quantifiable metrics that provide a clear framework for assessing and addressing climate-related concerns. In this way, the climate club enhances the predictability of trade-restrictive measures. Non-club members can reasonably anticipate the effects of the club linkages based on these established criteria. In summary, the climate club's adherence to solid standards and rules towards climate action strengthens the argument that the trade measures meet the "predictable effects" condition under Article XX(g).[460]

The final requirement of Article XX(g) justification is the even-handed application of climate club linkages. In order to fulfil this condition, the club's jurisdiction must impose a domestic tax or regulation similar to the trade measure applicable to non-club members. But they do not necessarily be identical.[461] Also, such requirements should be significantly similar for imports and domestic goods.[462] This condition ensures that foreign and domestic products are subject to comparable regulatory standards, preventing discrimination and distortion of competitive relationships.[463] The similarity of the taxes or regulations for climate mitigation establishes a level playing field for all market participants. Therefore, by requiring similar domestic taxes or regulations to club and non-club members, the climate club demonstrate its commitment to address climate change in a manner consistent with Article XX (g).[464]

[457] Appellate Report, *China - Rare Earths*, para 5.124.

[458] Gracia Marín Durán, 'Securing Compatibility of Carbon Border Adjustments with the Multilateral Climate and Trade Regimes' (2023) 72(1) International and Comparative Law Quarterly 73, 97.

[459] Appellate Report, *China - Rare Earths*, para 5.96.

[460] ibid para 5.113.

[461] Appellate Body Report, *US-Gasoline*, para 20–21.

[462] Tatiana Falcao, 'Ensuring an EU Carbon Tax Complies with WTO Rules (2021) 101(1) Tax Notes International, 41.

[463] Appellate Report, *China - Rare Earths*, para 5.132.

[464] Vidigal (n 40) 16.

4.4 *Article XX Chapeau*

4.4.1 Overview

GATT 1994 Article XX Chapeau plays a pivotal role in preventing the abusive application of the exceptions outlined in Article XX subparagraphs.[465] Its overarching objective is to strike a delicate balance between a member's right to invoke an Article XX exception and the rights of other members to ensure non-discriminatory trade practices.[466] The analysis under the Chapeau unfolds in two distinct yet interconnected segments, each addressing specific dimensions of the measure's impact on international trade. Firstly, the Chapeau requires an examination of the measure's discriminatory nature in other countries where the same conditions prevail.[467] This scrutiny ensures that the measure does not result in arbitrary or unjustifiable discrimination with a rigid implementation.[468] It emphasises the importance of treating all trade partners fairly and equally.[469] The aim is to uphold the non-discrimination principles inherent in the GATT 1994 and foster an environment where countries with similar circumstances are not subject to unwarranted trade disadvantages.

Secondly, the Chapeau assesses whether the measure constitutes a disguised restriction on international trade, particularly by favouring certain products over others based on their production methods.[470] This facet of the analysis delves into the potential adverse effects on trade flows, ensuring that the measure does not unduly impede the access of certain products to markets or unfairly advantage products adopted different production methods.[471] The goal is to prevent the creation of trade barriers that could distort competition and hinder the free flow of goods. The dual nature of the Chapeau analysis underscores its comprehensive approach in safeguarding the integrity of international trade. By evaluating the discriminatory aspects vis-à-vis other countries and the potential disguised restrictions on specific products, the Chapeau seeks to maintain equilibrium between a member's legitimate public policy goals and the principles of fair and open trade.[472] This nuanced examination ensures that the invocation of Article XX exceptions remains in line

[465] Ahmad (n 95) 131. For example, in the US–Gasoline, US–Shrimp, US–Gambling, Brazil–Tyres and lately the EC–Seals disputes, the measure in question failed to pass the chapeau test.

[466] Appellate Body Report, *US-Shrimp*, para 156. Van den Bossche (n 400) 262.

[467] Panel Report, *—Brazil – Measures Affecting Imports of Retreaded Tyres, (Brazil- Retreaded Tyres)* WT/DS332/R, adopted 17 December 2007, as modified by Appellate Body Report WT/DS332/AB/R., paras 7.226–7.251.

[468] Appellate Body Report, *US-Shrimp*, para 164.

[469] Appellate Body Report, *United States – Import Prohibition of Certain Shrimp and Shrimp Products – Recourse to Article 21.5 of the DSU by Malaysia, (US-Shrimp (Article 21.5 Malaysia))* WT/DS58/AB/RW, adopted 21 November 2001, para 149.

[470] Van den Bossche and Zdouc (n 22) 648.

[471] Panel Report, *EC-Asbestos*, para 8.236.

[472] Appellate Body Report *Brazil –Retreaded Tyres*, para. 232.

with the fundamental tenets of the GATT 1994, promoting a harmonious and equitable global trading system.

Consequently, the Appellate Body allowed discrimination results from a rational and legitimate aim but still looked for a relationship between the goal of the provisionally justified measure under the Article XX subparagraphs and the rationale for the discrimination. Otherwise, the measure could still be "arbitrary and unjustifiable" discrimination. Under the US-Shrimp case, the Appellate Body defined an arbitrary measure as capricious, unpredictable, or inconsistent.[473] This definition emphasizes the importance of coherence, predictability, and consistency in the design and application of trade measures,[474] even when they involve elements of discrimination. Subsequently, "arbitrary or unjustifiable discrimination" is interpreted as requiring essentially the same program as the measure-imposing country to address a legitimate problem.[475] Consequently, Article XX Chapeau ensures that discriminatory measures are attentive to prevailing conditions in foreign countries.[476] The mere focus on a legitimate and specific purpose in pursuing public policy goals is insufficient to justify a measure under Article XX of the GATT 1994.

4.4.2 Results on Climate Club Linkages

Under Article XX Chapeau analysis, the critical point is to pay attention to whether the club linkages are employed to achieve legitimate environmental goals or as market policies with some environmental concerns interspersed into it. The club linkages might be a form of secret protectionism, given the significant impact on protecting local industries' competitive advantage. However, to be justified under the Chapeau, the club linkages and emission abatement goal should have a "close and genuine relationship".[477] The Appellate Body confirmed that the mere consideration of the measure's rationale is insufficient to justify it under the general exception clause. The examination should extend to the actual effects of the trade-restrictive measures, emphasizing a results-oriented analysis that considers the broader

---

473 Panel Report, *United States – Import Prohibition of Certain Shrimp and Shrimp Products – Recourse to Article 21.5 of the DSU by Malaysia*, (*US – Shrimp (Article 21.5 – Malaysia)*) WT/DS58/RW, adopted 21 November 2001, upheld by Appellate Body Report WT/DS58/AB/RW, para. 5.124.

474 Panel Report, *EC – Asbestos*, para. 8.236.

475 Appellate Body Report, *US-Shrimp*, para 144. "it is not acceptable, in international trade relations, for one WTO Member to use an economic embargo to require other Members to adopt essentially the same comprehensive regulatory program, to achieve a certain policy goal, as that in force within that Member's territory, without taking into consideration different conditions which may occur in the territories of those other Members. …"

476 Appellate Body Report, *Brazil –Retreaded Tyres*, paras 225–227. Appellate Body Report, *EC – Seal Products*, para 5.318.

477 Appellate Body Report, *US–Shrimp*, para. 136. Appellate Body Report *Brazil –Retreaded Tyres*, para. 210.

implications on trade flows, competitiveness and market dynamics.[478] Therefore, even though the club linkages aims for carbon abatement, they cannot be qualified under the Chapeau if they provide protectionism for domestic products.

Consequently, climate club linkages should clearly distinguish between climate-related aims and competitiveness concerns for ensuring legitimacy under Article XX Chapeau. While vigilance is necessary to prevent protectionism, there is also a need to balance the risks of protectionism against the urgent and devastating effects of climate change.[479] The climate club's "design, architecture, and nature should not reveal any protectionism",[480] and trade restrictive objectives should not be disguised behind the climate mitigation goal.[481] This clarity avoids potential disputes within the WTO framework. Therefore, the analysis of disguised restriction to trade will involve a serious purpose inquiry and consider a range of evidence during the climate-related trade measure's enactment process. For example, in the Australia-Salmon case, the Appellate Body held that lack of risk assessment is a strong indication of a disguised restriction.[482] Therefore, the climate club should be diligent and clearly articulate the environmental purposes behind their trade measures with evidence-based decision-making.

Furthermore, the imposition of climate club linkages on trading partners whose climate regulations may not be "comparable in effectiveness" carries the risk of being perceived as arbitrary or unjustifiable discrimination.[483] Determining what refers to sufficient and comparable effectiveness of climate regulations among different countries is a blurring aspect.[484] The extent to which non-club members' climate regulations or carbon pricing mechanisms align with global goals and international agreements, such as the Paris Agreement, becomes critical in determining their comparable effectiveness. Also, multiple mechanisms beyond club linkages can effectively curb emissions.[485] Hence, comparable effectiveness analysis should encompass a broader view of how each country contributes to global

---

478 Appellate Body Report, *Brazil- Retreaded Tyres*, para. 230. Appellate Body Report, *US–Shrimp*, para. 160.

479 Diether Helm, *The Carbon Crunch: How We're Getting Climate Change Wrong – and How to Fix It* (Yale University Press, 2012). Robert S Pindyck, 'Climate Change Policy: What Do the Models Tell Us?' (2013) 51(3) Journal of Economic Literature 860.

480 Appellate Body Report, *US - Shrimp*, para 140.

481 Panel Report, *EC- Asbestos*, para. 8.236.

482 Appellate Body Report, *Australia – Measures Affecting Importation of Salmon, (Australia-Salmon)* WT/DS18/AB/R, adopted 6 November 1998 para.3.12. Even though this case was decided under the SPS Agreement, it is relevant to understand the Appellate Body's position to what entails a disguised restriction to trade.

483 Andrei Marcu and others, *Methods of Crediting Carbon Prices under the CBAM* (European Roundtable on Climate Change and Sustainable Transition 2023) 5–8 <https://ercst.org/crediting-carbon-prices-under-the-cbam/> accessed 5 April 2024.

484 Venzke and Vidigal (n 14) 213.

485 Such as filters or carbon sink activity. Espa and Holzer (n 45) 400.

emission reduction goals. It should recognise that different approaches can be equally valid and impactful.[486]

The key concern within the climate club linkages lies in the potential lack of flexibility, where a uniform application of specific production methods or standards may be imposed without due consideration for the varying circumstances across countries.[487] The essence of trade-restrictive measures within the climate club should achieve specific environmental goals rather than mandating a uniform application of production methods or standards. Therefore, in the case of climate club measures, the critical aspect is to provide flexibility[488] and negotiate the measure with as many countries as possible prior to their imposition.[489] In conclusion, the success and defensibility of climate club linkages hinge on a nuanced and flexible approach that considers the varying climate regulations among trade partners.

In this regard, Article XX Chapeau requires contemplating countries where the same conditions prevail.[490] The requirement to consider prevailing conditions is tied to countries, emphasizing a country-centric approach rather than product or service-specific considerations.[491] Therefore, the economic and institutional capacity of the country subjected to the trade-restrictive measure needs to be considered.[492] This consideration helps avoid imposing disproportionate burdens on countries facing challenges in meeting specific climate targets. Accordingly, the climate club members must consider special conditions in different countries.[493] Failure to do so may constitute arbitrary discrimination.[494] However, the club imposes climate-related trade instruments uniformly on all countries. In order to comply with the Chapeau, the club can differentiate the application of its linkages according to developed countries' greater historical responsibility for cumulative carbon emissions and higher current emissions per capita. Considering each country's unique carbon reduction initiatives and acknowledging differences in their circumstances enhances

---

[486] ibid 401.

[487] Englisch and Falcao (n 30) 71. For example, in US – Shrimp case, the US ban on shrimp caught without using a special turtle excluder device failed the GATT 1994 Article XX Chapeau test because of its rigidity and its imposition of identical treatment on countries with different environmental considerations.

[488] Appellate Body Report, *Brazil- Retreaded Tyres*, para 227. Appellate Body Report, *EC – Seal Products*, para 5.306.

[489] Appellate Body Report, *US-Shrimp,* para 166.

[490] Bartels, 'The Chapeau of the General Exceptions in the WTO GATT and GATS Agreements' (n 399) 123–125.

[491] Ahmad (n 95) 132 in Chap. 7.

[492] Appellate Body Report, *US-Shrimp*, para 164.

[493] Appellate Body Report, *EC – Seal Products*, para 5.303.

[494] Appellate Body Report, *US-Shrimp*, para 164, 165, 177.

the flexibility of the club linkages.[495] This flexibility is crucial to avoid arbitrariness.[496]

Also, the club linkages must be even-handedly applied to comply with the Chapeau.[497] Transparency in the design and consistent application of linkages to both imports and domestic goods contribute to minimizing the risk of being found arbitrary or discriminatory.[498] Also, the emissions levels of industrial goods vary dramatically depending on the energy source and the production process. Therefore, applying a single baseline for carbon content to all import or domestic products, irrespective of their actual emissions, could be perceived as discriminatory. Furthermore, the fixed club linkages disregard individual less-emitting countries and create no incentive to decrease the carbon content of imported goods since doing so would not change how goods are treated at the border.[499] The US-Gasoline case illustrates the potential challenges associated with baseline establishment methods that are found to be arbitrary.[500] Therefore, carefully considering and adapting baseline methodologies is necessary to avoid unjustifiable and discriminatory outcomes.

Similarly, if the import has already paid a carbon tax or was subject to an emissions control requirement in the origin country, that amount must be deducted from the club's border adjustment.[501] In this way, the imposition of additional burdens on those already engaged in climate change regulation is prevented. Treating those imports the same way as imports from a country without any climate change regulation would treat different situations the same and, hence, arbitrary and unjustifiable discrimination.[502] However, comparing different emission reduction policies would obviously lead to substantial technical difficulties, especially when comparing price-based and non-price-based climate measures.[503]

495 Giulia Claudia Leonelli, 'Carbon Border Measures, Environmental Effectiveness and WTO Compatibility: Is There a Way Forward for the Steel and Aluminium Carbon Club?' (2022) 21(5) World Trade Review, 622–624 and 626–628.

496 Appellate Body *Report Brazil – Retreaded Tyres*, paras 232 and 234.

497 Panel Report, *US - Tuna II (Mexico) (Article 21.5—Mexico),* para 7.554.

498 Appellate Body Report, *US - Shrimp*, para. 136. Appellate Body Report, *US-Gasoline*, para. 20.

499 Bordoff and Shoyer (n 93) 53.

500 In the US-Gasoline case the domestic refiners were permitted to establish an individual baseline while foreign refiners had to accept the Environmental Protection Agency's statutory baseline. Developing countries protested this particular act as discriminatory. The Appellate Body rejected the US defence that data from foreign gasoline producers was unverifiable, though it agreed with the Panel's suggestion that using a statutory baseline might be permissible when "the source of imported gasoline could not be determined or a baseline could not be established because of an absence of data". Appellate Body Report, *US-Gasoline*, para 27.

501 Kateryna Holzer, 'The Possibility of Defense under General Exceptions of GATT Article XX' in *Carbon-Related Border Adjustment and WTO Law* (Edward Elgar Publishing 2014), 170.

502 Appellate Body Report, *US–Shrimp*, paras. 165, 177. Voigt (n 1069) 64.

503 Vidigal (n 40) 19. Leonelli, 'Carbon Border Measures, Environmental Effectiveness and WTO Compatibility' (n 495) 629.

Finally, the Appellate Body's interpretation of the Chapeau requires that the climate club members engage in "serious, across-the-border negotiations" before imposing a club linkage.[504] This prerequisite underscores the imperative for inclusive dialogues[505] between the climate club and other countries that could potentially become targets of climate-related trade measures. Therefore, the climate club should engage in due process of dialogue with all its trade partners before setting and applying its club linkages. Failure to meet the threshold of "serious" negotiations could carry significant consequences. The WTO's assessment of the adequacy and sincerity of these efforts holds the potential to influence the legal standing of the imposed club linkage. If the WTO deems the negotiations insufficiently serious, it may determine that the climate-related trade measure is arbitrary and discriminatory and cannot be justified under Article XX Chapeau.

Consequently, the prospect of mutual recognition of trade measures within the framework of the climate club constitutes a preventive function for the occurrence of trade disputes. By aligning trade measures with environmental objectives within the climate club, the members may find it easier to argue that the measures are essential for achieving legitimate policy goals, such as the protection of the environment.[506] As a result, there will be fewer contentious trade cases before the WTO, or the challenged measures will be easier to justify under the Article XX exception.

4.5 Concluding Remarks

This section has delved into the relationship between climate-related trade measures and their legal justification with the GATT 1994 Article XX. The compatibility of climate club linkages with overarching climate goals becomes crucial in evaluating their justification under Article XX (b), (g), and Chapeau. The analysis has revealed that Article XX offers a viable legal basis for adopting climate-related trade measures if they follow a legitimate public policy concern. This integration is also contingent upon the club linkages being neither arbitrary nor unjustifiably discriminatory. Moreover, the Chapeau of Article XX requires the climate club to engage in serious and inclusive negotiations before imposing trade measures, which refers to the need for a collaborative approach to global climate governance. Consequently, the journey towards integrating climate action with international trade is fraught with legal, technical, and diplomatic challenges.

The exceptions under Article XX highlight the significant challenge of aligning international trade policies with global climate action goals. This alignment must be achieved in a manner that is both legally sound and effective in fostering sustainable

---

[504] Appellate Body Report, *US-Shrimp*, para 166–71.

[505] Appellate Body Report, *US- Gasoline*, p. 28.

[506] Nathalie Dobson, 'The EU's Conditioning of the "Extraterritorial" Carbon Footprint: A Call for an Integrated Approach in the Trade Law Discourse' (2018) 27(1) RECIEL 78–88.

development. Therefore, the application of Article XX is not conducted in isolation. Instead, it is intricately linked to the broader landscape of public international law. In essence, exploring climate-related trade measures within the framework of Article XX necessitates a holistic examination, considering not only the specific GATT 1994 provisions but also their alignment with the Paris Agreement. This approach highlights the importance of coherence across legal regimes, emphasizing that the objectives of international trade and climate action should not be pursued at the expense of one another. Only then may the climate club find a legal basis in GATT 1994 Article XX.

In conclusion, the legal landscape of Article XX reveals a path forward for integrating climate action with international trade. This book advocates for a balanced approach that does not compromise environmental integrity for economic gain or economic development for environmental protection. By navigating the legal, technical, and diplomatic challenges inherent in this endeavour, the climate club can move closer to a more sustainable and equitable international trade model that fully embraces the urgent need for comprehensive climate action. This vision for the future underscores the importance of legal frameworks, such as Article XX, in facilitating a transition towards climate-friendly trade practices.

Bibliography

Cases

GATT Panel Report, *Canada- Administration of Foreign Investment Review Act* (7 February 1984), L/5504 - 30S/140

—*EEC - Regulation on Imports of Parts and Components*, (16 May 1990), L/6657, 37S/132, 191-192

—*Spain: Tariff Treatment of Unroasted Coffee* (11 June 1981) BISD 28S/102.

—*United States – Measures Affecting Alcoholic and Malt Beverages*, (19 June 1992) DS23/R - 39S/206

—*United States – Measures Affecting Alcoholic and Malt Beverages*, (19 June 1992) DS23/R.

—*United States – Taxes on Automobiles*, (11 Oct. 1994) DS31/R, unadopted.

—*United States – Restrictions on Imports of Tuna (Tuna II)*, (16 June 1994) DS29/R, unadopted.

—*United States-Section 337 Tariff Act of 1930* (7 November 1989), L/6439 - 36S/345

WTO Panel Report, —*Argentina – Measures Relating to Trade in Goods and Services*, WT/DS453/R and Add.1, adopted 9 May 2016, as modified by Appellate Body Report WT/DS453/AB/R.

—*Argentina – Measures Affecting the Export of Bovine Hides and the Import of Finished Leather*, WT/DS155/R and Corr.1, adopted 16 February 2001.

—*Brazil – Certain Measures Concerning Taxation and Charges*, WT/DS472/R, Add.1 and Corr.1 / WT/DS497/R, Add.1 and Corr.1, adopted 11 January 2019, as modified by Appellate Body Reports WT/DS472/AB/R / WT/DS497/AB/R.
—*Brazil – Measures Affecting Imports of Retreaded Tyres,* WT/DS332/R, adopted 17 December 2007, as modified by Appellate Body Report WT/DS332/AB/R.
—*Canada – Certain Measures Affecting the Automotive Industry*, WT/DS139/R, WT/DS142/R, adopted 19 June 2000, as modified by Appellate Body Report WT/DS139/AB/R, WT/DS142/AB/R.
—*China – Measures Affecting Trading Rights and Distribution Services for Certain Publications and Audiovisual Entertainment Products,* WT/DS363/R and Corr.1, adopted 19 January 2010, as modified by Appellate Body Report WT/DS363/AB/R.
—*China – Measures Related to the Exportation of Various Raw Materials,* WT/DS394/R, Add.1 and Corr.1 / WT/DS395/R, Add.1 and Corr.1 / WT/DS398/R, Add.1 and Corr.1, adopted 22 February 2012, as modified by Appellate Body Reports WT/DS394/AB/R / WT/DS395/AB/R / WT/DS398/AB/R.
—*Colombia – Indicative Prices and Restrictions on Ports of Entry,* WT/DS366/R and Corr.1, adopted 20 May 2009.
—*European Communities – Measures Affecting the Approval and Marketing of Biotech Products*, WT/DS291/R, Add.1 to Add.9 and Corr.1 / WT/DS292/R, Add.1 to Add.9 and Corr.1 / WT/DS293/R, Add.1 to Add.9 and Corr.1, adopted 21 November 2006.
—*European Communities – Measures Affecting Asbestos and Asbestos-Containing Products*, WT/DS135/R and Add.1, adopted 5 April 2001, as modified by Appellate Body Report WT/DS135/AB/R.
—*European Communities – Protection of Trademarks and Geographical Indications for Agricultural Products and Foodstuffs,* Complaint by Australia, WT/DS290/R, adopted 20 April 2005.
—*European Communities – Regime for the Importation, Sale and Distribution of Bananas,* Complaint by Mexico, WT/DS27/R/MEX, adopted 25 September 1997, as modified by Appellate Body Report WT/DS27/AB/R.
—*European Communities – Regime for the Importation, Sale and Distribution of Bananas*, WT/DS27/R/ECU (Ecuador) / WT/DS27/R/GTM, WT/DS27/R/HND (Guatemala and Honduras) / WT/DS27/R/MEX (Mexico) / WT/DS27/R/USA (US), adopted 25 September 1997, as modified by Appellate Body Report WT/DS27/AB/R, DSR 1997
—*European Communities – Trade Description of Sardines*, WT/DS231/R and Corr.1, adopted 23 October 2002, as modified by Appellate Body Report WT/DS231/AB/R.
—*European Union – Anti Dumping Measures on Certain Footwear from China*, WT/DS405/R, adopted 22 February 2012.
—*Indonesia – Certain Measures Affecting the Automobile Industry*, WT/DS54/R, WT/DS55/R, WT/DS59/R, WT/DS64/R, Corr.1 and Corr.2, adopted 23 July 1998, and Corr.3 and Corr.4.

—*Indonesia – Importation of Horticultural Products, Animals and Animal Products*, WT/DS477/R, WT/DS478/R, Add.1 and Corr.1, adopted 22 November 2017, as modified by Appellate Body Report WT/DS477/AB/R, WT/DS478/AB/R.

—*Indonesia — Safeguard on Certain Iron or Steel Products*, WT/DS490/R ; WT/DS496/R.

Japan–Measures Affecting Consumer Photographic Film and Paper, WT/DS44/R, adopted 22 April 1998.

—*Japan – Taxes on Alcoholic Beverages*, WT/DS8/R, WT/DS10/R, WT/DS11/R, adopted 1 November 1996, as modified by Appellate Body Report WT/DS8/AB/R, WT/DS10/AB/R, WT/DS11/AB/R, DSR 1996.

—*Korea – Taxes on Alcoholic Beverages*, WT/DS75/R, WT/DS84/R, adopted 17 February 1999, as modified by Appellate Body Report WT/DS75/AB/R, WT/DS84/AB/R, DSR 1999.

—*Philippines – Taxes on Distilled Spirits,* WT/DS396/R / WT/DS403/R, adopted 20 January 2012, as modified by Appellate Body Reports WT/DS396/AB/R / WT/DS403/AB/R.

—*Turkey – Measures Affecting the Importation of Rice*, WT/DS334/R, adopted 22 October 2007,

—*United States - Certain Measures Relating to the Renewable Energy Sector*, WT/DS510/R, adopted 27 June. 2019.

—*United States – Certain Country of Origin Labelling (COOL) Requirements*, WT/DS384/R / WT/DS386/R, adopted 23 July 2012, as modified by Appellate Body Reports WT/DS384/AB/R / WT/DS386/AB/R.

—*United States – Certain Measures Affecting Imports of Poultry from China*, WT/DS392/R, adopted 25 October 2010.

—*United States – Import Prohibition of Certain Shrimp and Shrimp Products – Recourse to Article 21.5 of the DSU by Malaysia,* WT/DS58/RW, adopted 21 November 2001, upheld by Appellate Body Report WT/DS58/AB/RW.

—*United States – Measures Concerning the Importation, Marketing and Sale of Tuna and Tuna Products*, WT/DS381/R, adopted 13 June 2012, as modified by Appellate Body Report WT/DS381/AB/R.

—*United States – Standards for Reformulated and Conventional Gasoline,* WT/DS2/R, adopted 20 May 1996, as modified by Appellate Body Report WT/DS2/AB/R.

WTO Appellate Body Report, *Australia – Certain Measures concerning Trademarks, Geographical Indications and other Plain Packaging Requirements applicable to Tobacco Products and Packaging*, WT/DS435/AB/R and Add.1 *(Honduras)* / WT/DS441/AB/R and Add.1 *(Dominican Republic)*, adopted 29 June 2020.

—*Australia – Measures Affecting Importation of Salmon*, WT/DS18/AB/R, adopted 6 November 1998.

—*Brazil – Certain Measures Concerning Taxation and Charges*, WT/DS472/AB/R and Add.1 / WT/DS497/AB/R and Add.1, adopted 11 January 2019

—*Brazil – Measures Affecting Imports of Retreaded Tyres,* WT/DS332/AB/R, adopted 17 December 2007

—*Canada – Certain Measures Affecting the Automotive Industry,* WT/DS139/AB/R, WT/DS142/AB/R, adopted 19 June 2000.
—*Canada – Certain Measures Affecting the Renewable Energy Generation Sector / Canada – Measures Relating to the Feed-in Tariff Program*, WT/DS412/AB/R / WT/DS426/AB/R, adopted 24 May 2013.
—*Canada – Certain Measures Concerning Periodicals,* WT/DS31/AB/R, adopted 30 July 1997.
—*Chile – Taxes on Alcoholic Beverages*, WT/DS87/AB/R, WT/DS110/AB/R, adopted 12 January 2000.
—*China - Measures Affecting Imports of Automobile Parts,* WT/DS339/AB/R, WT/DS340/AB/R, WT/DS342/AB/R, adopted 12 January 2009.
—*China – Measures Affecting Trading Rights and Distribution Services for Certain Publications and Audiovisual Entertainment Products*, WT/DS363/AB/R, adopted 19 January 2010.
—*China – Measures Related to the Exportation of Rare Earths, Tungsten, and Molybdenum*, WT/DS431/AB/R / WT/DS432/AB/R / WT/DS433/AB/R, adopted 29 August 2014.
—*China – Measures Related to the Exportation of Various Raw Materials,* WT/DS394/AB/R / WT/DS395/AB/R / WT/DS398/AB/R, adopted 22 February 2012.
—*Colombia – Measures Relating to the Importation of Textiles, Apparel and Footwear*, WT/DS461/AB/R and Add.1, adopted 22 June 2016.
—*European Communities- Conditions for the Granting of Tariff Preferences to Developing Countries,* WT/DS246/AB/R, adopted on 20 April 2004.
—*European Communities – Measures Affecting Asbestos and Asbestos-Containing Products,* WT/DS135/AB/R, adopted 5 April 2001
—*European Communities and Certain Member States – Measures Affecting Trade in Large Civil Aircraft,* WT/DS316/AB/R, adopted 1 June 2011
—*European Communities – Measures Prohibiting the Importation and Marketing of Seal Products,* WT/DS400/AB/R / WT/DS401/AB/R, adopted 18 June 2014
—*European Communities – Regime for the Importation, Sale and Distribution of Bananas,* WT/DS27/AB/R, adopted 25 September 1997
—*European Communities – Trade Description of Sardines*, WT/DS231/AB/R, adopted 23 October 2002
—*India – Certain Measures Relating to Solar Cells and Solar Modules*, WT/DS456/AB/R and Add.1, adopted 14 October 2016
—*Indonesia - Importation of Horticultural Products, Animals and Animal Products,* WT/DS477/AB/R, adopted 22 November 2017.
—*Japan – Taxes on Alcoholic Beverages,* WT/DS8/AB/R, WT/DS10/AB/R, WT/DS11/AB/R, adopted 1 November 1996.
—*Korea – Definitive Safeguard Measure on Imports of Certain Dairy Products,* WT/DS98/AB/R, adopted 12 January 2000
—*Korea – Measures Affecting Imports of Fresh, Chilled and Frozen Beef,* WT/DS161/AB/R, WT/DS169/AB/R, adopted 10 January 2001
—*Philippines – Taxes on Distilled Spirits,* WT/DS396/AB/R / WT/DS403/AB/R, adopted 20 January 2012

—*Thailand – Customs and Fiscal Measures on Cigarettes from the Philippines*, WT/DS371/AB/R, adopted 15 July 2011
—*United States- Measures Affecting the Cross-Border Supply of Gambling and Betting Services*, WT/DS285/AB/R, adopted 20 April 2005
—*United States – Certain Country of Origin Labelling (COOL) Requirements*, WT/DS384/AB/R / WT/DS386/AB/R, adopted 23 July 2012.
—*United States – Import Prohibition of Certain Shrimp and Shrimp Products*, WT/DS58/AB/R, adopted 6 November 1998.
—*United States – Import Prohibition of Certain Shrimp and Shrimp Products – Recourse to Article 21.5 of the DSU by Malaysia*, WT/DS58/AB/RW, adopted 21 November 2001.
—*United States – Measures Affecting the Production and Sale of Clove Cigarettes*, WT/DS406/AB/R, adopted 24 April 2012.
—*United States – Measures Concerning the Importation, Marketing and Sale of Tuna and Tuna Products*, WT/DS381/AB/R, adopted 13 June 2012.
—*United States – Measures Concerning the Importation, Marketing and Sale of Tuna and Tuna Products –Recourse to Article 21.5 of the DSU by Mexico*, WT/DS381/AB/RW and Add.1, adopted 3 December 2015
—*United States – Standards for Reformulated and Conventional Gasoline*, WT/DS2/AB/R, adopted 20 May 1996

Legislation

Agreement on Technical Barriers to Trade (TBT) (15 April 1994) LT/UR/A-1A/10 <https://docs.wto.org/dol2fe/Pages/SS/directdoc.aspx?filename=Q:/UR/FA/17-tbt.pdf&Open=True>
Conference of Parties (COP), 'Decision 1/CP.21 Adoption of the Paris Agreement' (12 December 2015) U.N. Doc. FCCC/CP/2015/L.9/Rev.1
General Agreement on Tariffs and Trade (GATT 1994) (15 April 1994) LT/UR/A-1A/1/GATT/1 <https://docs.wto.org/dol2fe/Pages/SS/directdoc.aspx?filename=Q:/UR/FA/06-gatt.pdf&Open=True>
Marrakesh Agreement Establishing the World Trade Organization, 15 April 1994, 1867 UNTS 154, 33 ILM 1144 (1994)

Secondary Sources

Ahmad Z, 'Trade-Related Measures to Spread Low-Carbon Technologies: A Common Concern–Based Approach' in T Cottier (ed), *The Prospects of Common Concern of Humankind in International Law* (Cambridge University Press 2021)

Aman AC, ‘The Limits of Globalization and the Future of Administrative Law: From Government to Governance’ (2001) 8 Indianan Journal of Global Legal Studies 379

Appleton AE, ‘Regulatory Barriers to Trade: Regulations and Standards’ in T Cottier and K Nadakavukaren Schefer (eds), *Elgar Encyclopedia of International Economic Law* (Edward Elgar 2017)

Bacchus J, ‘Legal Issues with the European Carbon Border Adjustment Mechanism’ (2021) <https://www.cato.org/briefing-paper/legal-issues-european-carbon-border-adjustment-mechanism> accessed 5 April 2024.

Bartels L, ‘The Chapeau of the General Exceptions in the WTO GATT and GATS Agreements’ (2015) 109 American Journal of International Law 95

Benoit C, ‘Picking Tariff Winners: Non-product-related PPMs and DSB Interpretations of Unconditionally within Article I:1’ (2011) 42(2) Georgetown Journal of International Law 583

Blanchard O, Gollier C and Tirole J, ‘The Portfolio of Economic Policies Needed to Fight Climate Change’ (2023) 15 Annual Review of Economics 689 <https://doi.org/10.1146/annurev-economics-051520-015113>

Bordoff JE and Shoyer AW, *International Trade Law and the Economics of Climate Policy: Evaluating the Legality and Effectiveness of Proposals to Address Competitiveness and Leakage Concerns* (Brookings Trade Forum, Climate Change, Trade, and Competitiveness: Is a Collision Inevitable?, 2008/2009)

Boute A, ‘Accounting for Carbon Pricing in Third Countries Under the EU Carbon Border Adjustment Mechanism’ (2024) World Trade Review 1

Böhringer C, Balistreri EJ and Rutherford TF, ‘The Role of Border Carbon Adjustment in Unilateral Climate Policy: Overview of an Energy Modeling Forum Study (EMF 29)’ (2012) 34(Supplement 2) Energy Economics S97

Buck M and Verheyen R, *International Trade Law and Climate Change – A Positive Way Forward* (Friedrich-Ebert-Stiftung July 2001) <https://library.fes.de/pdf--files/stabsabteilung/01052.pdf> accessed 5 April 2024

Bullock D, ‘Combating Climate Recalcitrance: Carbon-Related Border Tax Adjustments in a New Era of Global Climate Governance’ (2018) 27 Washington International Law Journal 609

Burniaux JM, Chateau J, and Duval R, ‘Is There a Case for Carbon-Based Border Tax Adjustment? An Applied General Equilibrium Analysis’ (2013) 45 Appl. Econ. 2231.

Choi WM, ‘How More ‘Likeness’ in Addressing Technical Regulations?’ (Society of International Economic Law (SIEL), 3rd Biennial Global Conference, 12 July 2012) <https://doi.org/10.2139/ssrn.2104187>

— and Baetens F, ‘Like Products’ in R Wolfrum (ed*), Max Planck Encyclopaedia of Public International Law* (2020)

Condon BJ and Sinha T, ‘Unresolved Issues in WTO Law’ in *The Role of Climate Change in Global Economic Governance* (Oxford University Press, 2013)

Cottier T, ‘The Principle of Common Concern of Humankind’ in Thomas Cottier (ed) *The Prospects of Common Concern of Humankind in International Law* (Cambridge University Press, 2021)

— and Oesch M 'Direct and Indirect Discrimination in WTO and EU Law' in Sanford E Gaines, Birgitte Egelund Olsen, and Karsten Engsig Sorensen (eds), *Liberalising Trade in the EU and the WTO: A Legal Comparison* (Cambridge University Press, 2012)

De Mestral A, 'The Principle of Most-Favoured-Nation Treatment' in T Cottier and K Nadakavukaren Schefer (eds), *Elgar Encyclopedia of International Economic Law* (Edward Elgar 2017)

Dechezleprêtre A and others, *Fighting Climate Change: International Attitudes toward Climate Policies* (OECD Economic Department Working Papers No 1714, Organisation for Economic Co-operation and Development, Paris 2022)

Diebold NF, 'Different Functions in Goods and Services' in T Cottier and K Nadakavukaren Schefer (eds), *Elgar Encyclopedia of International Economic Law* (Edward Elgar 2017)

Dobson N, 'The EU's Conditioning of the "Extraterritorial" Carbon Footprint: A Call for an Integrated Approach in the Trade Law Discourse' (2018) 27(1) RECIEL 78

— Chapter 25: Climate Protection versus Trade: Dilemmas for the EU' in *Handbook on European Union Climate Change Policy and Politics* (Edward Elgar Publishing, 2023)

Doelle M 'Climate Change and the WTO: Opportunities to Motivate State Action on Climate Change through the World Trade Organization' (2004) 13 RECIEL 85

Dreyfus R and S Frankel, 'From Incentive to Commodity to Asset: How International Law is Reconceptualising Intellectual Property' (2015) 36(4) Mich J Int Law 557

Du M, 'Voluntary Eco-Labels in International Trade Law: A Case Study of the EU Eco-Label' (2021) 33(1) Journal of Environmental Law 167

Durán GM, 'Measures with Multiple Competing Purposes after EC - Seal Products: Avoiding a Conflict between GATT Article XX-Chapeau and Article 2.1 TBT Agreement' (2016) 19 J Int'l Econ L 467

— 'Exhaustible Natural Resources and Article XX(g)' in P Delimatsis and L Reins (eds), *Trade and Environmental Law* (Edward Elgar 2021)

— 'Securing Compatibility of Carbon Border Adjustments with the Multilateral Climate and Trade Regimes' (2023) 72 International & Comparative Law Quarterly 73

Eckersley R, 'The Big Chill: The WTO and Multilateral Environmental Agreements' (2004) 4 Global Environmental Politics 24

Englisch J and Falcao T, 'EU Carbon Border Adjustments for Imported Products and WTO Law' (9 June 2021) <https://doi.org/10.2139/ssrn.3863038>

Espa I, and Holzer K, 'From Unilateral Border Carbon Adjustments to Cooperation in Climate Clubs: Rethinking Exclusion in Light of Trade and Climate Law Constraints' in J. Bäumler and others (eds), European Yearbook of International Economic Law 2022 (vol 13, Springer, 2023) <https://doi.org/10.1007/8165_2022_101>

European Commission, 'Citizen Support for Climate Action' <https://ec.europa.eu/clima/citizens/citizen-support-climate-action_en> accessed 5 April 2024

Falcao T, 'Ensuring an EU Carbon Tax Complies with WTO Rules (2021) 101(1) Tax Notes International

Haley JA, Did Trade Liberalization Go Too Far? Trade, Inequality and Unravelling the Grand Bargain (CIGI Papers No. 168, Centre for International Governance Innovation April 2018), <https://www.cigionline.org/publications/did-trade-liberalization-go-too-far-trade-inequality-and-unravelling-grand-bargain/> accessed 5 April 2024

Holzer K, 'The Possibility of Defense under General Exceptions of GATT Article XX' in *Carbon-Related Border Adjustment and WTO Law* (Edward Elgar Publishing 2014).

— 'Comparability in International Economic Law: Goods' in T Cottier and K Nadakavukaren Schefer (eds), *Elgar Encyclopedia of International Economic Law* (Edward Elgar 2017)

— 'The Role Environmental Processes and Production Methods' in T Cottier and K Nadakavukaren Schefer (eds), *Elgar Encyclopedia of International Economic Law* (Edward Elgar 2017)

Horn H and Mavroidis PC, 'Economic and Legal Aspects of the Most-Favored-Nation Clause' (2001) 17 European Journal of Political Economy 233 <https://doi.org/10.1016/S0176-2680(01)00028-3>

— 'Still Hazy After All These Years: The Interpretation of National Treatment in the GATT/WTO Case-Law on Tax Discrimination' (2004) 15(1) European Journal of International Law 39

Howse R, 'Distinguished Essay: Non-Tariff Barriers and Climate Policy: Border-Adjusted Taxes and Regulatory Measures as WTO-Compliant Climate Mitigation Strategies' in *European Yearbook of International Economic Law 2015* (6th edn, Springer 2015)

Hudec RE, '"Like Product": The Differences in Meaning in GATT Articles I and III' in T Cottier and PC Mavroidis (eds), *Regulatory Barriers and the Principle of Non-Discrimination in World Trade Law* (University of Michigan Press 2000)

Iacovides MC, 'Marginal Consumers, Marginalized Economics: Whose Tastes and Habits Should the WTO Panels and Appellate Body Consider When Assessing "Likeness"?' (2014) 48(2) Journal of World Trade 323

Intergovernmental Panel on Climate Change (IPCC), *Special Report: Global Warming of 1.5 °C Summary for Policymakers* (2018)

International Monetary Fund and Organization for Economic Cooperation and Development, 'Tax Policy and Climate Change: IMF/OECD Report for the G20 Finance Ministers and Central Bank Governors' (2021) <www.oecd.org/tax/tax--policy/imf-oecd-g20-report-tax-policy-and-climate-change.htm> accessed 20 June 2024

Jakučionytė-Skodienė M and Liobikienė G, 'The Changes in Climate Change Concern, Responsibility Assumption and Impact on Climate-friendly Behaviour in EU from the Paris Agreement Until 2019' (2022) 69 Environmental Management 1 <https://doi.org/10.1007/s00267-021-01574-8>

Kendall K, 'Carbon Taxes and the WTO: A Carbon Charge without Trade Concerns' (2012) 29 Arizona Journal of International and Comparative Law 49

Kosters M and van der Heijden J, 'From Mechanism to Virtue: Evaluating Nudge Theory' (2015) 21(3) Evaluation 276 <https://doi.org/10.1177/1356389015590218>

Leonelli GC, 'Carbon Border Measures, Environmental Effectiveness and WTO Compatibility: Is There a Way Forward for the Steel and Aluminium Carbon Club?' (2022) 21(5) World Trade Review

Lim AH and Holzer K, 'Trading in the Era of Carbon Standards: How Can Trade, Standard Setting, and Climate Regimes Cooperate?' (2023) 39(1) Oxford Review of Economic Policy 110 <https://doi.org/10.1093/oxrep/grac039>

Maggio AR, 'Trade-Restrictive Environmental Measures and the GATT' in *Environmental Policy, Non-Product Related Process and Production Methods and the Law of the World Trade Organization* (European Yearbook of International Economic Law, vol 1, Springer, Cham 2017).

Marceau G and Trachtman J, 'The Technical Barriers to Trade Agreement, the Sanitary and Phytosanitary Measures Agreement, and the General Agreement on Tariffs and Trade' (2002) 36 Journal of World Trade 811

Marcu A and others, Methods of Crediting Carbon Prices under the CBAM (European Roundtable on Climate Change and Sustainable Transition 2023) <https://ercst.org/crediting-carbon-prices-under-the-cbam/> accessed 5 April 2024

Martini L, Görlach B, and Bausch C, 'Accelerating the Global Transformation of Industry at the G7' (2022) <https://www.ecologic.eu/18490> accessed 21 June 2024.

Mavroidis PC, 'Standard of Review' in T Cottier and K Nadakavukaren Schefer, *Elgar Encyclopedia of International Economic Law* (Edward Elgar 2017)

Mayer B, 'Obligations of Conduct in the International Law on Climate Change: A Defence' (2018) 27 Review of European, Comparative & International Environmental Law 130 <https://doi.org/10.1111/reel.12237>

Mehling M and others, 'Designing Border Carbon Adjustments for Enhanced Climate Action' (2019) 113(3) American Journal of International Law 433

Meyer T and Tucker TN, 'A Pragmatic Approach to Carbon Border Measures' (2022) 21(1) World Trade Review 109

Pindyck RS, 'Climate Change Policy: What Do the Models Tell Us?' (2013) 51(3) Journal of Economic Literature 860

Pirlot A, 'Carbon Border Adjustment Measures: A Straightforward Multi-Purpose Climate Change Instrument?' (2022) 34 Journal of Environmental Law 25

Posner RA, *Economic Analysis of Law* (Aspen Legal Education 2014)

Ruxton KDS McClure, 'Non-Discrimination Principle in WTO Law: Themes and Commonalities' (2023) 12(1) International Trade and Arbitration Law Journal 65

Regan DH, 'Regulatory Purpose and "Like Products" in Article III:4 of the GATT (With Additional Remarks on Article II:2)' (2002) 36(3) J World Trade 443

Report of the GATT Working Party on Border Tax Adjustment, adopted on 2 December 1970, L/3464

Sanctuary M, 'Border Carbon Adjustments and Unilateral Incentives to Regulate the Climate' (2018) 26 Rev Int Econ 826 <https://doi.org/10.1111/roie.12344>

Sandler T and Tschirhart JT, 'Club Theory: Thirty Years Later', (1997) 93 Public Choice 335

Sato S, 'EU's Carbon Adjustment Mechanism: Will It Achieve Its Objective(s)?' (2022) 56(3) JWT 383

Schrijver NJ, van den Bossche P, and Faber G, Unilateral Measures Addressing Non-Trade Concerns: A Study on WTO Consistency, Relevance of other International Agreements, Economic Effectiveness and Impact on Developing Countries of Measures concerning Non-Product-Related Processes and Production Methods (OBT, Den Haag 2007) <https://hdl.handle.net/1887/12563> accessed 5 April 2024

Skjærseth JB, 'Towards a European Green Deal: The Evolution of EU Climate and Energy Policy Mixes' (2021) 21 International Environmental Agreements 25 <https://doi.org/10.1007/s10784-021-09529-4>

Stewart RB and others, 'Building Blocks for Global Climate Protection' (2013) 32 Stanford Environmental Law Journal 34

Stua M, Nolden C and Coulon M, 'Climate Clubs Embedded in Article 6 of the Paris Agreement' (2022) 180 Resources, Conservation and Recycling <https://doi.org/10.1016/j.resconrec.2022.106178>

Summary Record of the Eleventh Meeting, E/CONF.2/C.3/SR.11, 1. Proposal E/CONF.2/C.3/1/Add.21. E/CONF.2/C.3/A/W.33

Sunstein CR, 'Informational Regulation and Informational Standing: Akins and Beyond' (1999) 147 University of Pennsylvania Law Review 613

Tarasofsky RG, 'Heating Up International Trade Law: Challenges and Opportunities Posed by Efforts to Combat Climate Change' (2008) 2 Carbon and Climate Law Review 7

Tversky A and Kahneman D, 'Judgment Under Uncertainty: Heuristics and Biases' (1974) 185 Science 1124

Van den Bossche P, 'Article XX GATT, Article XIV GATS' in T Cottier and K Nadakavukaren Schefer (eds), *Elgar Encyclopedia of International Economic Law* (Edward Elgar 2017)

— and Zdouc W, *The Law and Policy of the World Trade Organization* (5th edn, Cambridge University Press 2022)

Venzke I and Vidigal G, 'Are Trade Measures to Tackle the Climate Crisis the End of Differentiated Responsibilities? The Case of the EU Carbon Border Adjustment Mechanism (CBAM)' in M den Heijer and H. van der Wilt (eds.) (2022) 51 Netherlands Yearbook of International Law

Verill C, 'Maximum Carbon Intensity Limitations and the Agreement on Technical Barriers to Trade; (2008) 1 Carbon and Climate Law Review

Victor DG and Keohane RO, 'The Regime Complex for Climate Change' (2010) 9 Perspectives on Politics 7 <https://doi.org/10.1017/S1537592710004068>

Vidigal G, 'Designing Climate Clubs: The Four Models, Trade Commitments and the Non-Discrimination Dilemma' (2023) Amsterdam Law School Research Paper No 2023-07

— and Venzke I, 'Of False Conflicts and Real Challenges: Trade Agreements, Climate Clubs, and Border Adjustments' (2022) 116 AJIL Unbound 202, 206

Voigt C, 'WTO Law and International Emissions Trading: Is There Potential for Conflict?' (2008) 2(1) Carbon & Climate Law Review 54

Voon T, Mitchell A and Gascoigne C, 'Consumer Information, Consumer Preferences and Product Labels under the TBT Agreement' in Tracey Epps and Michael J Trebilcock (eds), *Research Handbook on the WTO and Technical Barriers to Trade* (Edward Elgar Publishing 2013)

Vranes E, *Trade and the Environment. Fundamental Issues in International Law, WTO Law and Legal Theory* (Oxford University Press 2009)

— 'Climate Labelling and the WTO: The 2010 EU Ecolabelling Programme as a Test Case Under WTO Law' in C Herrmann and JP Terhechte (eds), *European Yearbook of International Economic Law* (Springer, 2011)

— 'Carbon Taxes, PPMs and the GATT' in P Delimatsis (eds) *Research Handbook on Climate Change and Trade* (Edward Elgar 2016)

Weber RH, 'Designing Trade Rules to Promote Climate Sustainability' (2014) 8 J Energy Power Eng 612

— 'Border Tax Adjustment-Legal Perspective' (2015) 133 Climatic Change 407, <https://doi.org/10.1007/s10584-015-1414-2>

Will U, Climate *Border Adjustments and WTO Law Extending the EU Emissions Trading System to Imported Goods and Services* (Boston: Brill Nijhoff, 2019)

World Trade Organization (WTO), Committee on Trade and Environment, *Report (1996) of the Committee on Trade and Environment*, (WT/CTE/1, 12 November 1996)

— Committee on Technical Barriers to Trade, 'Decisions and Recommendations Adopted by the Committee since Jan. 1, 1995 – Note by the Secretariat' G/TBT/1/Rev.7 (28 November 2000)

—, Committee on Trade and Environment, 'Note by the Secretariat: GATT/WTO Dispute Settlement Practice Relating to GATT Article XX, Paragraphs (b), (d) and (g)' WTO Doc WT/CTE/W/203 (adopted 8 March 2002)

— *World Trade Report 2005: Trade, Standards and the WTO* (2005)

— *Report on the Future of the WTO: Addressing Institutional Challenges in the New Millenium* (World Trade Organization, 2014)

— 'General Rules for the Interpretation of the Harmonized System' <https://www.wcoomd.org/-/media/wco/public/global/pdf/topics/nomenclature/instruments-and-tools/hs-interpretation-general-rules/0001_2012e_gir.pdf?la=en>

Open Access This chapter is licensed under the terms of the Creative Commons Attribution 4.0 International License (http://creativecommons.org/licenses/by/4.0/), which permits use, sharing, adaptation, distribution and reproduction in any medium or format, as long as you give appropriate credit to the original author(s) and the source, provide a link to the Creative Commons license and indicate if changes were made.

The images or other third party material in this chapter are included in the chapter's Creative Commons license, unless indicated otherwise in a credit line to the material. If material is not included in the chapter's Creative Commons license and your intended use is not permitted by statutory regulation or exceeds the permitted use, you will need to obtain permission directly from the copyright holder.

Chapter 8
Epilogue

1 Summary of Findings

The core objective of the book is to propose a shift beyond traditional treaty-based approaches to more dynamic, club-based strategies that address the challenges of climate governance and emphases the integration of climate and trade laws. Initially, the book provides an extensive introduction to the complexities of climate change by highlighting its far-reaching impacts on ecosystems, economies, and societies. It discusses the origins and effects of climate change and highlights the role of human activities in exacerbating the adverse impacts. Mainly, the global responses to climate change evolved from scepticism to widespread acknowledgement of its urgency. Accordingly, the UN regime shapes international climate policy and law with the UNFCCC.

While acknowledging the necessity of an international legal response to global warming, the book critiques the current climate regime's shortcomings, particularly under the Paris Agreement. The main problem is the lack of effectiveness under this framework. Therefore, the book represents the need for more enforceable approaches and explores alternative strategies like the climate club approach. The previous scholarly research substantiates the significance of integrating economics, policy, and legal disciplines to address climate change comprehensively. These analyses suggest a transition towards approaches that better link climate commitments to tangible economic benefits. This connection necessitates the exploration of synergies with legal instruments from other realms, such as trade law. Therefore, the book adopted the economic analysis of law approach to evaluate and enhance climate regulations with market mechanisms. It highlights the importance of developing a comprehensive legal framework that balances environmental protection with economic growth by leveraging market-based instruments. In this way, international cooperation can achieve sustainable climate solutions.

The analysis under the book contrasts two approaches to climate change mitigation: international agreements, exemplified by the Paris Agreement, and minilateral

© The Author(s) 2025

T. G. Budak, *Beyond Treaties: Rethinking Legal Mechanisms for International Climate Governance*, https://doi.org/10.1007/978-3-031-86022-5_8

approaches, like the climate club approach. International agreements aim for global participation and commitments. They focus on shared responsibilities and collective targets, like the Paris Agreement's goal to limit global warming to 2 °C. These agreements rely on voluntary national contributions and aim for broad consensus, which can lead to challenges in enforcement and ambition due to differing national interests. Furthermore, the book identifies key challenges, such as consensus-based decision-making and the need for greater financial resources to realise NDCs, as additional reasons for the current climate action hindrance. On the other hand, the club approach is based on smaller and willing coalitions that are more ambitious. They leverage market mechanisms and aim for deeper cooperation among members, potentially leading to more significant emission reductions. However, this approach bears the risk of creating trade barriers and excluding non-members, which could lead to trade retaliation. Both strategies have their merits and challenges. The international agreements provide a universal framework for action, while climate clubs may offer a pathway to more effective and immediate outcomes for their members. Due to its growing importance in the scholarship, the book analysed the club approach in detail.

The club approach is one form of a minilateral cooperation regime. Currently, climate policy negotiations focus on the transition towards minilateralism as a pragmatic evolution in global climate governance. The book highlights the emergence of minilateral fora as dynamic spaces for enthusiastic countries to lead by example. They can demonstrate the feasibility and benefits of ambitious climate action and complement broader international cooperation. Minilateral initiatives can catalyse significant advancements in climate mitigation and adaptation by enabling smaller groups of like-minded countries to spearhead innovative policies. They act as laboratories for stronger policies, which can be extended to multilateral regimes. However, they also carry challenges, such as non-inclusivity and duplication of efforts. Importantly, the legitimacy of the minilateral fora could be questionable. Therefore, ensuring strategic coordination and integration of minilateral approaches with broader global efforts is paramount.

Minilateralism can be conceptualised and practically implemented with the club approach to international climate governance. The climate club is a voluntary group that shares regulatory costs and benefits to motivate members towards stringent climate measures. The book discusses the necessity for such clubs. This is because they provide exclusive benefits that comply with climate and trade law and, in this way, ensure active participation and legitimacy. The operational dynamics of climate clubs include harmonised emission reduction goals, carbon pricing, and using common policy tools to achieve emissions abatement. The book evaluates the potential of climate clubs to overcome the challenges faced by current climate agreements. It advocates for targeted collaboration among willing countries to create momentum for global climate action. On the other hand, the challenges and limitations associated with the climate club approach, such as equity and the possibility for economic and informational asymmetries between developed and developing countries, are emphasised.

The research on environmental regulations revealed that market-based approaches have economic advantages in achieving environmental goals compared to traditional command-control mechanisms. Based on this, the club approach adopted market-based instruments as linkages to unite its members and draw a boundary against non-member countries. Market-based tools price the carbon emissions, thereby internalising the social cost of carbon. In this way, the club linkages can cost-effectively promote emissions reduction. Importantly, they are adopted to ensure a level playing field in international trade. The book elaborates on the following market mechanisms as a club linkage. They are carbon taxes and ETS for the club members, carbon tariffs and BCAs for non-members, and lastly, technical regulations and standards. Each of these instruments uniquely tackles one aspect of the climate necessity. They are assessed for their potential to encourage shared environmental responsibility, enhance economic efficiency, and promote membership in the club scheme.

Initially, the book evaluates the climate club's role in enhancing the effectiveness of international climate governance. The club can tackle the collective action problem, free-riding, carbon leakage, and asymmetry between developed and developing countries problems that are inherent in the current regime. Uniform carbon pricing instruments within the climate club framework can mitigate these challenges by incentivising member countries to reduce emissions while imposing sanctions on non-compliant countries. This approach aims to promote sustainability and reduce global emissions through shared responsibility. The exploration of the climate club scheme presents uniform carbon pricing instruments as a promising avenue for reforming international climate governance and propelling impactful action. However, the success of the club approach is contingent upon its integration within the broader international climate framework and securing a substantial membership base to exert meaningful influence over international trade and emission reduction costs.

Particularly, the book researched the CBDRRC principle, which is a reflection of climate justice under the Paris Agreement. The principle ensures that climate action is equitable and considers the varied capacities of countries. Therefore, it acknowledges countries' common yet varied responsibilities in combating climate change. Specifically, the principle factors the countries' historical GHG contributions, economic capacities, and developmental stages. The climate club approach deviates from this principle since it applies the same linkages to every country regardless of their development levels or capacity. This is because the club would like to strive for more ambitious climate action without locking in the CBDRRC principle. Also, the CBDRRC principle has challenges in defining and operationalising due to its flexible nature. This vagueness can lead to varied interpretations and potentially hinder ambitious climate action. Even though, the book suggests providing free emissions allowances and financial mechanisms for developing countries in the initial stage of the climate club by considering the CBDRRC principle.

Following this, the book examines the legality of the climate club approach within the framework of the Paris Agreement and the WTO law. First, it explores the compatibility of climate club mechanisms with the rules of the Paris Agreement. It emphasises the role of such mechanisms in promoting global cooperation and ambitious climate action. The book delves into the operational aspects of international carbon markets under Article 6 of the Paris Agreement. Notably, it considers the challenges and potential of these markets to facilitate cost-efficient GHG emissions reduction.

Mainly, the book addressed the intricate relationship between trade and environmental policies. It explored how climate-related market mechanisms can be aligned with WTO law to avoid potential legal disputes. Furthermore, the book accentuates the necessity of integrating sustainable development goals in interpreting trade norms under the WTO. It criticises the WTO's narrow interpretation of environmental conflicts and its potential to create a regulatory chill effect. This analysis presents an in-depth examination of the legal frameworks necessary to balance ambitious climate goals with international trade obligations. Importantly, the book advocates for a harmonised approach of these two realms to provide a stronger governance structure for climate change. Therefore, the analysis suggests initiatives like the climate club could institute innovative solutions for harmonising climate and trade objectives.

The chapter on the legality of the climate club focuses on the trade measures implemented as the club linkages. The linkages are import requirements leading to bans or quotas for high carbon emitted products, extra carbon tariffs, BCAs, or surrender of emission allowance certificates, and technical regulations and product standards regarding the emissions levels. The analysis illuminates that carbon tariffs do not constitute a border measure; hence, they are immune from the schedule of concessions norm under the GATT 1994 Article II. Subsequently, tariff deconsolidation was examined for increasing the carbon-intensive products tariff lines while decreasing the environmental goods tariffs. However, there is no exact definition of what constitutes environmental goods. Therefore, in order to resort to this option, the WTO members first need to agree on the conditions to determine the merits of being an environmental product. Under the legality analysis, the final aspect is the general elimination of quantitative restrictions clause regulated by Article XI of the GATT 1994. The purchase and surrender of emission allowance certificates due to the club's ETS by importers and administrative requirements of the climate club can potentially be effective as a quantitative restriction for imports of non-club members. However, this norm can only be applied if the restrictions are imposed concerning importation. If the club and non-club products are required to submit the same number of allowances or are regulated with similarly stringent administrative requirements, Article XI is not going to be applied. Instead, compliance with the WTO regime hinges on fair treatment between club and non-club members' products.

Therefore, the book's final chapter pivoted towards the climate club's discriminatory aspect and examines club linkages with respect to the non-discrimination principles of the WTO law. This is because the most critical aspect of the climate club's operationalization is to comply with these principles. The club linkages can create trade disputes from non-member countries, and the foundation of these challenges is the violation of non-discrimination in international trade. Accordingly, the examination first focuses on the MFN principle. It explores how climate club BCAs, as carbon tariffs and emissions allowance purchases, align with or challenge the MFN principle, which mandates non-discriminatory treatment among WTO members. The analysis covers the potential for de facto discrimination through climate policies. It stressed the need for club measures to be applied uniformly across all WTO members regardless of the club membership. Furthermore, it considers the complexities of determining “like” products and the potential for differential treatment based on environmental standards. This consideration must balance fostering environmental goals and adhering to MFN commitments under international trade law.

Following that, another non-discrimination principle, national treatment under Article III of the GATT 1994, was analysed. It aims to prevent discrimination against foreign products through internal taxes and regulations. The book explores the challenges and nuances of applying this principle to BCAs. The analysis suggests that while BCAs are designed to align with WTO principles by not discriminating against imports per their origin, their implementation must carefully navigate creating less favourable conditions for imported goods due to their club membership and embedded carbon levels. The solution to this intricacy lies in the definitions of “like products”. The likeness is interpreted differently for internal charges and regulations and in different sentences of paragraph 2 of Article III. The likeness is based on the objective approach for the internal charges of Article III:2(1). The analysis reveals that the carbon content of products constitutes a npr-PPM and has a differentiating effect on imported and domestic products’ likeness to the extent that it affects their nature, end-use and consumer preferences. The book concluded that npr-PPMs do not discriminate by reference to nationality but instead by process-based impacts. Therefore, they are origin-neutral and imposing different charges on imports due to their emissions levels does not amount to discrimination under national treatment principle.

Under Article III:2(2) and internal regulations, the likeness analysis is based on the market-based approach, which corresponds to directly competitive and substitutable products. The competition between club and non-club products exists in the climate club, as both vie for a share of the same market. The extent of low and high-carbon embedded product substitutability is contingent on how consumers perceive these products in terms of fulfilling their needs or demands. If consumers view them as satisfying similar needs, they are likely to be considered substitutes for each other. The WTO Panels can employ the elasticity of substitution method to measure the extent to which consumers are willing to switch between products with varying carbon levels. Consequently, club and non-club products can be considered not “like” products and immune from national treatment scrutiny. However, the final determination will rest on the empirical evidence that suggest consumers do not perceive carbon-intensive and non-intensive products as substitutable to each other in the relevant market.

The club’s technical regulations and standards’ compliance with the WTO law was examined under the TBT Agreement as it specifically governs them. The section on technical regulations emphasises the importance of non-discrimination, the necessity of measures, and their impact on trade and environmental objectives. Under the climate club scheme, the criteria-setting process is restricted to the member states, which can turn into de facto discrimination based on origin. Therefore, the examinations under this section emphasised the significance of ensuring that technical regulations as club linkages are grounded in scientific evidence and are transparent, avoiding unnecessary obstacles to trade while fostering an international market conducive to sustainable development. The section delves into how emissions-related technical regulations based on npr-PPMs navigate the fine line between promoting environmental objectives and adhering to fair trade. The npr-PPMs can alter consumer preferences due to their influence on informed decision-making. Also, npr-PPM-based technical regulations can create entry barriers for certain products, shaping the competitive landscape by favouring those that adhere to its standards. Consequently, they impact the likeness analysis. This is because the likeness of products subject to technical regulation is based on the market-based approach, which constitutes direct competitiveness or substitutability. The extent to which they alter the consumer preferences, technical regulations can be immune from violation of non-discrimination principles of the TBT Agreement. One other way to justify technical regulations is to outline their necessity, which is parallel to the analysis under Article XX of the GATT 1994 explained in the following paragraph.

Finally, the book provides an in-depth examination of the GATT 1994 Article XX, the exception clause for non-discrimination principles. The club linkages can be justified due to their contribution to mitigate climate change under this provision. However, it is also vital to balance trade restrictions and public policy objectives; hence, club linkages should be non-discriminatory and not constitute a disguised restriction on international trade. The necessity of club linkages can be proved with the well-established research output that exhibits the need to impose trade sanctions on non-cooperative countries to accelerate climate action and reach international climate targets. Also, club measures should not be implemented unilaterally in case other countries take the climate mitigation efforts as well. Instead, a group of countries needs to come together and follow an open membership policy. It indicates that club linkages do not target products due to origin but pursue a societal goal. The club applies similar domestic taxes or regulations to its members, thereby demonstrating its even-handed approach. Therefore, climate-related trade instruments can be justified under Article XX if they are found to be violating substantive WTO norms.

2 Contributions and Implications

A growing number of countries are exploring alternative legal regimes outside the UN to combat climate change. Their priority is to use trade law mechanisms to penalise countries that do not support climate action. In this way, they can raise revenue to support economic development while meeting climate targets. For instance, the EU enacted the European Green Deal industrial plan, and the US aims to accelerate climate action with the US Inflation Reduction Act. They showcase a proactive stance towards accelerating climate action through domestic policy instruments. These efforts can create a patchwork of different standards and approaches. It could potentially hamper global trade relations and climate target's unity. Therefore, bringing forerunner countries into a climate club umbrella can eliminate the concerns of disguised restrictions to trade. Since the club aspires to unify pioneering countries under a collective banner and offer a cohesive platform to standardise climate actions.

In a similar vein, the "Climate Club" was formed at COP28 to coordinate challenges arising from unilateral instruments and initiatives. The Climate Club creates a structured and dynamic environment where countries can work together to achieve their climate objectives. The very essence of the Club lies in its ability to harness the flexibility and cooperation embedded within the Paris Agreement. However, the Climate Club announced at COP 28 has not yet fully corresponded to the club approach analysed in this book. This is because it is designed to complement the cooperative approaches under Article 6 of the Paris Agreement. Third countries are not sanctioned through climate-related trade mechanisms. Nevertheless, as the negotiations continue, there is a potential that the Climate Club will operationalise beyond being an innovative cooperative forum. It can incorporate trade instruments to strengthen its strategic objectives. This progress reinforces the feasibility of climate club theorization and underscores the evolving and dynamic nature of international climate governance. The fact that the world's biggest economies are exploring the establishment of a climate club indicates the need for collaborative efforts in addressing the complex challenges of climate change. Therefore, the recent development of the Climate Club of COP 28 provides tangible indications for the club approach to become an integral component of the international climate regime.

Establishing the climate club approach under the Paris Agreement, as in COP 28, represents a strategic pathway to achieving global legitimacy and operational effectiveness. With its cooperative approaches, market and non-market instruments of Article 6, the Paris Agreement can provide a recognised platform for climate clubs to operate. Additionally, affiliating the climate club with the Paris Agreement offers the practical advantage of leveraging the administrative system and resources of the UNFCCC. The climate club can tap into the expertise and support mechanisms established by the UNFCCC. Significantly, this affiliation minimises duplication of efforts. Through this synergy, climate clubs can significantly contribute to the overarching goals of the Paris Agreement and drive ambitious climate action while fostering global solidarity.

The climate club is criticised for being indifferent to CBDRRC and imposing uniform club linkages to all trade members regardless of their specific capacities. However, the CBDRRC principle's flexibility creates lack of accountability and insufficient action from developing countries. Their voluntary contribution to emissions abatement undermines global climate change mitigation efforts. Currently, the largest and fastest-growing GHG emitters are major developing countries. In case they are exempted from uniform carbon pricing instruments, the emissions will be displaced to their jurisdiction, and the global temperature increase will continue. Consequently, the inherent subjectivity in the formulation of the CBDRRC principle can be exploited by political interests and undermine ambitious climate action. The climate club aims to offer solutions to eliminate slow climate action and directs developing countries to adopt binding mitigation targets with its trade instruments. It functions with the rationale that, even though the CBDRRC principle aims to address equity, its implementation must not become a barrier to tackling climate change effectively.

The book claims that it is possible to create a fair and non-discriminatory climate club which operates with climate-related trade linkages. The WTO's exception clause under Article XX and like product interpretation adequately address the complex interplay between trade and environmental objectives. Given the urgency of climate mitigation and the necessity of more robust instruments to lessen the devastating impacts of climate change, the club linkages can be justified under Article XX. Applying Article XX is intricately linked to the broader landscape of public international law. Therefore, exploring climate-related trade measures within the framework of Article XX necessitates considering not only the specific GATT 1994 provisions but also their alignment with the Paris Agreement. This approach highlights the importance of coherence across legal regimes, emphasising that the objectives of international trade and climate action should not be pursued at the expense of one another. Only then may the climate club find a legal basis in GATT 1994 Article XX.

Second, the environmental concerns can diffuse into "like products" interpretation without constituting discriminatory bias. In the absence of clear guidelines of the relevant WTO agreements and jurisprudence regarding npr-PPMs-based differentiation among like products, such as their carbon footprint, countries have the flexibility to treat greener counterparts differently. Club countries can produce goods with lower carbon emissions and reflect their commitment to environmental sustainability. Therefore, they can differentiate between a product from a country with no climate mitigation policies and a "like product" from a climate club country, solely based on their npr-PPMs. Consequently, it can be possible to reconcile environmental policies with existing fair-trade norms. The differentiation among products per their npr-PPMs reflects the evolving nature of the likeness test and its adaptability to address contemporary challenges such as climate change. Consequently, the climate club can be established without concern of trade retaliation, thus fostering an innovative approach to integrating climate considerations into global trade practices.

Furthermore, while the effectiveness of club linkages is contingent upon the intensity of border intervention, the high level of border intervention shapes the market dynamics and draws the attention of non-club countries. Hence, they might resort to the WTO DSB to challenge club linkages for MFN or national treatment principles. If the climate-related trade instruments are subtle, the likelihood of running afoul of the non-discrimination rules diminishes. In low-impact restrictions, the club measures cannot reflect the actual emission levels of the imports. Nonetheless, they will create an environment, where the climate club can extend its coverage by being an example to non-members. Therefore, club regulations should only aim to equalise conditions between carbon-intensive and non-intensive products and these products coexist in the club market. Ultimately, the purchasing decision should be left to consumers in order to integrate into the non-discriminatory trade practices seemly.

Even though club regulations are adopted for a legitimate objective, they enforce specific environmental standards and extraterritorially influence non-club countries' policies. However, a strict prohibition on extraterritorial regulation poses risks, as it may encourage a race to the bottom in environmental legislation. If climate-related trade instruments do not apply to foreign competitors, they might be repealed or weakened due to lobbying efforts within the climate club jurisdictions. Consequently, the urgency of responding to climate change lends legitimacy to the climate club linkages that influence the regulatory landscape of non-club member countries. The club not only directs ambitious environmental policies but also influences the global regulatory landscape, encouraging non-member countries to elevate their environmental commitments to avoid economic disadvantages. As a result, it fosters a broader coalition of climate action.

Therefore, in the face of the global challenge posed by climate change, the trade instruments established by the climate club can be seen as beneficial, necessary and legitimate means to address and mitigate the environmental impacts of economic activities. These regulations respond proactively to the pressing need for sustainable practices and environmental stewardship. They also align with the broader international climate regime as the Paris Agreement encourages any cooperative approach, even a unilateral one. Moreover, the climate club linkages are required tools for creating a level playing field. By establishing common standards, they ensure that all trading partners adhere to guidelines that prioritise environmental responsibility. This implementation fosters fair competition among industries, prevents a race to the bottom in environmental regulations and promotes innovation in sustainable practices.

As a result, the book evaluates the climate club approach's legality, questioning its compliance with the Paris Agreement and WTO regulations. It explores the potential of climate clubs to address climate change challenges effectively and sustainably. The book reaches the conclusion that the club can be integrated into voluntary cooperation principles and market-based mechanisms outlined in the Paris Agreement. As well as, the club can navigate the legal intricacies within the WTO legal framework. Its successful operation is fundamentally based on design features. If the climate club does not opt for decisive punitive intervention to non-club members, it has a growing potential to include many countries into its jurisdiction. This is because the current political developments reflect how the international community's perception and response to climate change have evolved. Instead of waiting for all countries to agree on climate measures, the forerunner countries are ready to step outside the climate agreements and leverage tools from other legal disciplines to mitigate climate change. By building on the foundation laid under the UNFCCC and addressing its limitations, the climate club can enhance the global response to climate change, ensuring that strategies are not only practical but also aligned with the overarching principles of international climate and trade agreements.

3 Future Research Directions

This book has shed light on the legal viability of the climate club and climate-related trade measures under the Paris Agreement and WTO law. Meanwhile, it acknowledges the complexity of navigating the diverse interests of WTO member states. The climate club implements trade mechanisms to all countries regardless of their development levels or capacities. The neoliberal policies and market-based instruments adopted in the climate club support economic growth. However, they exacerbate social and environmental injustices, especially in developing and least-developed countries. Countries that "lose" due to climate-related trade mechanisms or countries that have difficulty adapting to green transition for socio-economic reasons do not constitute one of the central concerns of the club scheme. The concept of climate justice in the club scheme instead focuses on the countries that attract investments to themselves by not having carbon regulations, distorting the competitiveness of club members in global trade, and refraining from taking action based on the club's efforts. Consequently, the club scheme does not comply with international climate justice. Therefore, future research can focus on the just transition framework for climate club to answer concerns towards its uniform carbon pricing instruments.

Internationally, just transition can be evaluated in terms of access to financing opportunities necessary for the continuation of inclusive and sustainable development to address the impacts of the climate crisis. The developing and least developed countries can enact legal regulations that will direct their industries and economies to adopt production methods with low environmental impact only if pioneer countries support them with just transition mechanisms. Under the climate club, the revenue generated from climate club linkages can be directed to support developing countries, mainly to offset the economic impacts of the club's carbon pricing. This revenue can support just green transition activities, such as investments, adaptation measures, and compensation for the industries that collapsed during the fossil phase-out. Alternatively, additional grants, loans and guarantees for green transition can be provided to developing countries. The climate club will only be feasible and sustainable if climate justice concerns are comprehensively taken into account.

By prioritising inclusivity and equity, the climate club can evolve into a more effective tool for global climate governance that harmonises the ambitious goals of environmental preservation with the imperative of equitable development. This approach, in turn, ensures compliance with the CBDRRC principle of the Paris Agreement. Therefore, the club needs a deliberate focus on equitable resource distribution, technology transfer, and financial support tailored to developing countries' specific needs and circumstances. Such a strategy ensures that the climate club leads by example, not only in terms of environmental action but also in fostering global justice in climate action initiatives. Addressing equity concerns in the transition to a low-carbon emission economy will accelerate the global acceptance of the club and politically legitimise its policies. Therefore, for the club approach to compensate for the adverse effects and increase the positive ones it generates for climate action, it is necessary to include the principles of just transition in its relations with third countries. Further legal research on this subject matter has the utmost importance.

Another subject in the future research agenda could entail the impacts of consumer choices on the definition of like products and, thereby, the non-discrimination principles of the WTO. The trend of consumer behaviour placing a greater emphasis on climate change considerations is expected to become increasingly relevant in the future. As the effects of climate change become more noticeable and widespread, there are clear indications that consumers will continue to prioritise products and services that align with their environmental values and contribute to sustainability. Consumer preferences shape the likeness of carbon-intensive and non-intensive products, market dynamics, competitiveness and substitutability. Therefore, they are determinative in the outcome of MFN and national treatment analysis for club linkages.

Notably, consumer behaviour is not solely driven by financial incentives or penalties. It is also significantly influenced by the ongoing discussions and policy choices surrounding climate change. The increased frequency and intensity of public discourse on climate change positively contribute to public understanding and promote responsible behaviour. Furthermore, consumer choice mainly depends on bounded rationality, willpower, and self-interest. Consumers frequently do not make deliberate choices but instead rely upon cognitive heuristics or established routines. Also, the errors or biases in consumer preferences assessment should not be underestimated. Due to these reasons, the driving force of consumer preferences in the likeness analysis can be researched by benefiting from behavioural economic analysis of law methodology in further research endeavours.

Open Access This chapter is licensed under the terms of the Creative Commons Attribution 4.0 International License (http://creativecommons.org/licenses/by/4.0/), which permits use, sharing, adaptation, distribution and reproduction in any medium or format, as long as you give appropriate credit to the original author(s) and the source, provide a link to the Creative Commons license and indicate if changes were made.

The images or other third party material in this chapter are included in the chapter's Creative Commons license, unless indicated otherwise in a credit line to the material. If material is not included in the chapter's Creative Commons license and your intended use is not permitted by statutory regulation or exceeds the permitted use, you will need to obtain permission directly from the copyright holder.

The manufacturer's authorised representative in the EU is Springer Nature Customer Service Centre GmbH, Europaplatz 3, 69115 Heidelberg, Germany. If you have any concerns regarding our products, please contact ProductSafety@springernature.com

Printed and bound by CPI Group (UK) Ltd, Croydon, CR0 4YY
05/10/2026
02227652-0003